VOLUME 2A

# Handbook of
# ECONOMIC GROWTH

# INTRODUCTION TO THE SERIES

The aim of the Handbooks in Economics series is to produce Handbooks for various branches of economics, each of which is a definitive source, reference, and teaching supplement for use by professional researchers and advanced graduate students. Each Handbook provides self-contained surveys of the current state of a branch of economics in the form of chapters prepared by leading specialists on various aspects of this branch. These surveys summarize not only received results but also newer developments, from recent journal articles and discussion papers. Some original material is also included, but the main goal is to provide comprehensive and accessible surveys. The Handbooks are intended to provide not only useful reference volumes for professional collections but also possible supplementary readings for advanced courses for graduate students in economics.

KENNETH J. ARROW and MICHAEL D. INTRILIGATOR

VOLUME 2A

# Handbook of
# ECONOMIC GROWTH

Edited by

**PHILIPPE AGHION**
*Harvard University*

and

**STEVEN N. DURLAUF**
*University of Wisconsin at Madison*

Amsterdam • Boston • Heidelberg • London • New York • Oxford
Paris • San Diego • San Francisco • Singapore • Sydney • Tokyo
North Holland is an imprint of Elsevier

North Holland is an imprint of Elsevier
The Boulevard, Langford Lane, Kidlington, Oxford, OX5 1GB
525 B Street, Suite 1800, San Diego, CA 92101-4495, USA

First published 2014

**Notices**
Knowledge and best practice in this field are constantly changing. As new research and experience broaden our understanding, changes in research methods, professional practices, or medical treatment may become necessary.

Practitioners and researchers must always rely on their own experience and knowledge in evaluating and using any information, methods, compounds, or experiments described herein. In using such information or methods they should be mindful of their own safety and the safety of others, including parties for whom they have a professional responsibility.

To the fullest extent of the law, neither the Publisher nor the authors, contributors, or editors, assume any liability for any injury and/or damage to persons or property as a matter of products liability, negligence or otherwise, or from any use or operation of any methods, products, instructions, or ideas contained in the material herein.

**British Library Cataloguing in Publication Data**
A catalogue record for this book is available from the British Library

**Library of Congress Cataloging-in-Publication Data**
A catalog record for this book is available from the Library of Congress

ISBN: 978-0-444-53546-7 (SET)
ISBN: 978-0-444-53538-2 (Vol. 2A)
ISBN: 978-0-444-53540-5 (Vol. 2B)

For information on all North Holland publications
visit our website at **store.elsevier.com**

Printed and bound by CPI Group (UK) Ltd, Croydon, CR0 4YY

14 15 16 17   10 9 8 7 6 5 4 3 2 1

# CONTENTS OF VOLUME 2A

# CONTENTS OF VOLUME 2B

# CONTRIBUTORS

**Philippe Aghion**
Harvard University, NBER, and CIFAR, USA.

**Ufuk Akcigit**
University of Pennsylvania and NBER, USA.

**Alberto Alesina**
Harvard University, USA.
IGIER Bocconi, Italy.

**Yann Algan**
Sciences Po, France.

**Holger Breinlich**
University of Essex, CEP and CEPR.

**Pierre Cahuc**
ENSAE-CREST, Ecole Polytechnique, France.

**A.W. Carus**
Faculty of Economics, University of Cambridge, United Kingdom.

**Gregory Clark**
University of California, Davis, CA 95616, USA.

**Diego Comin**
Harvard University, NBER and CEPR, USA.

**Nicholas Crafts**
Warwick University.

**Matthias Doepke**
Department of Economics, Northwestern University and NBER, 2001 Sheridan Road, Evanston, IL 60208, USA.

**Gilles Duranton**
Wharton School, University of Pennsylvania, 3620 Locust Walk, Philadelphia, PA 19104, USA. CEPR.

**Paola Giuliano**
UCLA Anderson School of Management, NBER and CEPR.

**Berthold Herrendorf**
Department of Economics, Arizona State University, Tempe, AZ 85287, USA.

**Peter Howitt**
Brown University and NBER, USA.

**Christopher M. Meissner**
Department of Economics, University of California, Davis and NBER, Davis, CA 95616, USA.

**Martí Mestieri**
Toulouse School of Economics, France.

**Nathan Nunn**
Department of Economics, Harvard University, NBER, and BREAD, 1805 Cambridge Street, Room M25, Cambridge, MA 02138, USA.

**Sheilagh Ogilvie**
Faculty of Economics, University of Cambridge, United Kingdom.

**Kevin Hjortshøj O'Rourke**
All Souls College, Oxford, United Kingdom.

**Gianmarco I.P. Ottaviano**
London School of Economics, CEP and CEPR, United Kingdom

**Diego Puga**
Centro de Estudios Monetarios y Financieros (CEMFI), Casado del Alisal 5, 28014 Madrid, Spain.

**Richard Rogerson**
Princeton University & NBER, Princeton, United States.

**Enrico Spolaore**
Department of Economics, Tufts University, NBER, CESIfo and CAGE, Medford, MA 02155-6722, USA.

**Jonathan R.W. Temple**
University of Bristol and CEPR.

**Ákos Valentinyi**
Cardiff Business School, IE-CERSHAS & CEPR, United Kingdom.

**Romain Wacziarg**
UCLA Anderson School of Management, NBER and CEPR, 110 Westwood Plaza, Los Angeles, CA 90095, USA.

**David N. Weil**
Brown University and NBER, USA.

**Yang Yao**
China Center for Economic Research, National School of Development, Peking University, China.

**Fabrizio Zilibotti**
Department of Economics, University of Zurich, Muehlebachstrasse 86, Zurich, CH 8008, Switzerland.

CHAPTER ONE

# Culture, Entrepreneurship, and Growth

## Matthias Doepke[*] and Fabrizio Zilibotti[†]

[*]Department of Economics, Northwestern University and NBER, 2001 Sheridan Road, Evanston, IL 60208, USA
[†]Department of Economics, University of Zurich, Muehlebachstrasse 86, Zurich, CH 8008, Switzerland

## Abstract

We discuss the two-way link between culture and economic growth. We present a model of endogenous technical change where growth is driven by the innovative activity of entrepreneurs. Entrepreneurship is risky and requires investments that affect the steepness of the lifetime consumption profile. As a consequence, the occupational choice of entrepreneurship hinges on risk tolerance and patience. Parents expecting their children to become entrepreneurs have an incentive to instill these two values in their children. Cultural transmission is Beckerian, i.e. parents are driven by the desire to maximize their children's happiness. We also consider, in an extension, a paternalistic motive for preference transmission. The growth rate of the economy depends on the fraction of the population choosing an entrepreneurial career. How many entrepreneurs there are in a society hinges, in turn, on parental investments in children's patience and risk tolerance. There can be multiple balanced growth paths, where in faster-growing countries more people exhibit an "entrepreneurial spirit." We discuss applications of models of endogenous preferences to the analysis of socio-economic transformations, such as the British Industrial Revolution. We also discuss empirical studies documenting the importance of culture and preference heterogeneity for economic growth.

## Keywords

Culture, Entrepreneurship, Innovation, Economic growth, Endogenous preferences, Intergenerational preference transmission

## JEL Classification Codes

J24, L26, N30, O10, O32, O33, O43, Z10

## 1.1. INTRODUCTION

The relationship between economic development and culture—broadly defined as the set of preferences, values, and beliefs that are at least partially learned—has attracted increasing attention in the economic literature over the last decade.

The notion that accounting for cultural heterogeneity is important for explaining individual behavior and economic success was a familiar one to classical economists. For instance, Smith (1776) described members of different social classes of his time as distinct types of human beings driven by different motives: *"A merchant is accustomed to employ his money chiefly in profitable projects; whereas a mere country gentleman is accustomed to employ it*

*Handbook of Economic Growth*, Volume 2A
ISSN 1574-0684, http://dx.doi.org/10.1016/B978-0-444-53538-2.00001-0

*chiefly in expense. The one often sees his money go from him and return to him again with a profit: the other, when once he parts with it, very seldom expects to see any more of it"* (p. 432).

A century later, Karl Marx postulated that culture is the effect, rather than the cause, of the structure of production relations. In his view, culture, religion, and ideology (the "superstructure") are mere reflections of the material interests of the class that controls the means of production. Marx' materialism was disputed by Max Weber, who argued, that cultural and spiritual factors are independent drivers of socio-economic transformations. For Weber, the emergence of a "spirit of capitalism" with the ensuing emphasis on the virtue of entrepreneurial success was a major engine of the industrial revolution, not just a mere reflection of it. Weber did not fully reverse Marx' perspective, but rather acknowledged that the causation can run both ways.[1] For instance, he held the view that Protestant Asceticism had been an engine of economic transformation, but "was in turn influenced in its development and its character by the totality of social conditions, especially economic" (Weber, 1905, p. 183).

In contrast to the thinking of Smith, Marx, and Weber, the marginalist revolution in economics in the late 19th century sidelined cultural factors. According to the neoclassical paradigm, economics should focus on optimal individual choice and efficient resource allocation, while treating preferences and technology as exogenous primitives. Consistent with this paradigm, until recently economists have regarded preference formation, and culture more broadly, as issues lying outside the realm of economics. Over time, however, as economic imperialism has broken into new territories, exogenous preferences and technology have become straitjackets. The erosion of the neoclassical tenets began from technology. It is by now widely recognized, following the intuition of Schumpeter (1942), that technology cannot be viewed as exogenous if one wants to understand the mechanics of the growth process of industrial as well as developing economies. Rather, the efforts and risk-taking behavior of a particular group of individuals that aims to change the set of technological constraints, namely inventors and entrepreneurs, are the engines of economic growth. This observation motivated the development of the neo-Schumpeterian endogenous technical change paradigm throughout the 1990s (see, e.g. Aghion and Howitt, 1992).

Recently, the paradigm shift has extended to the realm of preferences. The availability of large data sets such as the World Value Survey has revealed that there is a great deal of heterogeneity in values and preferences across both individuals (see, e.g. Guiso and Paiella, 2008; Beauchamp et al. 2011), and world regions (see, e.g. Inglehart et al. 2000). Preference heterogeneity has also become a salient issue in mainstream macroeconomics. For instance, Krusell and Smith (1998), Coen-Pirani (2004), De Nardi (2004), Guvenen (2006), Hendricks (2007), and Cozzi (2011) have argued that individual variation in

---

[1] "It is, of course, not my aim to substitute for a one-sided materialistic an equally one-sided spiritualistic causal interpretation of culture and of history" (Weber, 1905, p. 183).

preferences is necessary for calibrated macroeconomic models with incomplete markets to reproduce the large wealth inequality observed in the data.

Preference heterogeneity as such is not in conflict with the neoclassical paradigm. Traditionally, extra-economic factors have served as the motivations for error terms in regressions and individual or regional fixed effects. However, treating preferences and culture as exogenous factors in growth and development theory is problematic if, on the one hand, cultural factors respond to changes in the economic and institutional environment (see Alesina and Glaeser, 2004; Alesina and Giuliano, 2009), and, on the other hand, culture and preferences have an important feedback on institutions and economic performance (see Greif, 1994; Grosjean, 2013; Guiso et al. 2006; Gorodnichenko and Gerard, 2010; Tabellini, 2010).

Motivated by these observations, a growing number of studies incorporate endogenous cultural change into economic models.[2] A particularly important link is the one connecting preferences, culture, and innovation (see Mokyr, 2011). In many recent models of endogenous technical change, innovation and economic growth ultimately are determined by policy and preference parameters, such as the time discount rate and risk aversion. Yet, there is a lack of studies of the joint determination of preferences and technology. A key issue is the extent to which different societies differ in terms of the average propensity of their citizens to carry out entrepreneurial or innovative activities. This is the focus of the investigation of this chapter.

To this aim, we present a model of endogenous technical change where growth is driven by the innovative activity of entrepreneurs. The focal point of the analysis is the occupational choice between being a worker and being an entrepreneur in an economy with capital market imperfections. Entrepreneurs face more risk and make investments that force them to defer consumption. As a consequence, the occupational choice hinges on patience and risk tolerance. These preference traits are distributed heterogeneously in the population and subject to the influence of family upbringing. Cultural transmission is driven by the desire of parents to maximize their children's happiness, conditional on the expectations they hold about the children's future occupation. Parents expecting their children to become entrepreneurs have stronger incentives to raise them to be patient and risk tolerant.

At the aggregate level, the growth rate of the economy depends on the fraction of entrepreneurs in the population, since this determines the rate of technological innovation. The theory identifies a self-reinforcing mechanism linking preferences and growth. In a highly entrepreneurial society, a large proportion of the population is patient and risk tolerant. These preferences sustain high human capital investment and risky innovation, leading to a high growth rate and incentives for entrepreneurial preferences to develop

---

[2] The recent literature in behavioral economics has proposed a psychological foundation for endogenous preferences. Fehr and Hoff (2011) argue that individual preferences are susceptible to institutional, familiar, and social influences due to their intrinsic psychological properties.

in the next generation, too. Societies with identical primitives may end up in different balanced growth paths characterized by different degrees of entrepreneurial culture, innovativeness, and growth. In addition, changes in institutions or policies can feed back into the evolution of culture and preferences, giving rise to potentially long-lasting effects on economic growth and development.

This chapter is organized as follows. Section 1.2 presents a model of endogenous technical change with an occupational choice, where entrepreneurship is the driver of innovation. Sections 1.3 and 1.4 endogenize culture and preference transmission analyzing, respectively, the endogenous accumulation of patience and risk tolerance. While in Sections 1.3 and 1.4 the cultural transmission of preferences hinges on an altruistic Beckerian motive, Section 1.5 considers an alternative model incorporating parental paternalism. Section 1.6 reviews the existing theoretical and empirical literature. Section 1.7 concludes. Proofs of propositions and lemmas are deferred to the mathematical appendix.

## 1.2. A FRAMEWORK FOR ANALYZING THE INTERACTION OF CULTURAL PREFERENCES, ENTREPRENEURSHIP, AND GROWTH

In this section, we develop a dynamic model where culture and economic growth are jointly determined in equilibrium. The underlying process of technical change is related to the model of Romer (1990), where growth takes the form of an expanding variety of inputs. However, unlike Romer we assume that innovation is driven by a specific group of people, namely entrepreneurs, whose economic lives (for example, in terms of risk and lifetime consumption profiles) are distinct from those of ordinary workers. Cultural preferences determine people's propensity to entrepreneurship, and conversely the return to entrepreneurship affects parents' incentives for forming their children's preferences. In other words, there is a two-way interaction between culture and growth. In this section, we develop the general setup, turning to specific dimensions of endogenous preferences further below.

### 1.2.1 A Model of Endogenous Innovation

Consider an endogenous growth model where innovation takes the form of an increasing variety of intermediate inputs. New inputs are created by people in a specific occupation, namely entrepreneurs (as in Klasing, 2012). Innovative activity has two key features: it involves investments and deferred rewards (as in Doepke and Zilibotti, 2008), and it may also involve risk (as in Doepke and Zilibotti, 2012 and Klasing, 2012). In addition, financial markets are incomplete: agents can neither borrow to smooth consumption over the life cycle, nor hedge the entrepreneurial risk.[3] Since entrepreneurs and regular workers face

---

[3] While these assumptions are stark, models with moral hazard typically imply imperfect consumption smoothing or risk sharing. Empirically, we observe that entrepreneurs can neither borrow without

different consumption profiles (across both time and states of nature), the choice between these two occupations hinges on heterogeneous cultural preferences.

The measure of the intermediate input varieties invented before the start of period $t$ is denoted by $N_t$. Time is discrete. Final output at time $t$ is produced using the production function:

$$Y_t = \frac{1}{\alpha} \left( \int_0^{N_t} \bar{x}_t(i)^\alpha \, di + \int_{N_t}^{N_{t+1}} x_t(i)^\alpha \, di \right) Q^{1-\alpha},$$

where $Q$ is a fixed factor (e.g. land or unskilled labor) that will be normalized to unity; $\bar{x}_t(i)$ is the supply of intermediates $i$ that were invented up until time $t$; and $x_t(i)$ is the supply of new varieties $i$ invented during period $t$. Following Matsuyama (1999), we assume that old varieties with $i \in [0, N_t]$ are sold in competitive markets, whereas new varieties $i \in (N_t, N_{t+1}]$ are supplied monopolistically by their inventors. Put differently, inventors enjoy patent protection for only one period.

Innovation (i.e. the introduction of $N_{t+1} - N_t$ new varieties) is carried out by entrepreneurs. The return to entrepreneurial effort is assumed to be stochastic. In particular, entrepreneurs do not know in advance how successful they will be at inventing new varieties. With probability $\kappa > 0$ an entrepreneur will be able to run $(1 + \nu) N_t$ projects, whereas with probability $1 - \kappa$ he or she will manage only $\left(1 - \nu \frac{\kappa}{1-\kappa}\right) N_t$ projects, where $\nu \geq 0$. In the aggregate, $\kappa$ is the fraction of successful entrepreneurs. Intermediate-good production is instead carried out by workers using a linear technology that is not subject to uncertainty.

In order for the equilibrium to feature balanced growth, we assume that a knowledge spillover increases the productivity of both workers and entrepreneurs as knowledge accumulates. More precisely, productivity is indexed by $N_t$, and thus grows at the equilibrium rate of innovation. Given these assumptions, the labor market-clearing condition at time $t$ is given by:

$$N_t X_t^W = N_t \bar{x}_t + (N_{t+1} - N_t) x_t,$$

where the left-hand side is the labor supply by workers in efficiency units, and the right-hand side is the labor demand given the production of intermediates $\bar{x}_t$ and $x_t$.[4] The corresponding market-clearing condition for entrepreneurs is:

$$N_t X_t^E = \left( \frac{N_{t+1} - N_t}{\xi} \right),$$

where $X_t^E$ is the number of entrepreneurs, and the parameter $\xi$ captures the average productivity per efficiency unit of entrepreneurial input in innovation. Hence, an efficiency unit of the entrepreneurial input produces measure $\xi$ of new varieties. Denoting

---

constraints to finance their investments, nor separate their personal economic success from the fate of their enterprises. Thus, our stylized model captures some important features of the real world that are well-understood outcomes of models of imperfect information.

[4]  Note that the market-clearing expression is written under the assumption that all old varieties $i \in [0, N_t]$ are supplied at the same level, $\bar{x}_t$, and that all new varieties $i \in (N_t, N_{t+1}]$ are supplied at the same level, $x_t$. We show later that this the case in equilibrium.

the growth rate of technology by $g_t \equiv (N_{t+1} - N_t)/N_t$ allows us to simplify the two market-clearing conditions as follows:

$$X_t^W = \bar{x}_t + g_t x_t, \tag{1.1}$$

$$X_t^E = \frac{g_t}{\xi}. \tag{1.2}$$

We now turn to the goods-market equilibrium. The representative competitive final-good producer maximizes profits by solving:

$$\max_{\bar{x}(i), x(i)} \left\{ \frac{1}{\alpha} \left( \int_0^{N_t} [\bar{x}_t(i)^\alpha - \alpha \bar{p}_t(i) \bar{x}_t(i)] di + \int_{N_t}^{N_{t+1}} [x_t(i)^\alpha - \alpha p_t(i) x_t(i)] di \right) \right\},$$

where $\bar{p}_t(i)$ and $p_t(i)$ are the prices of old and new intermediates, respectively.[5] The first-order conditions for the maximization problem imply:

$$\bar{x}_t(i) = \bar{p}_t(i)^{\frac{1}{\alpha-1}} \quad \text{and} \quad x_t(i) = p_t(i)^{\frac{1}{\alpha-1}}. \tag{1.3}$$

Next, we consider the intermediate-goods producers. Let $w_t^W$ denote the market wage of workers, and let $\omega_t^W = w_t^W / N_t$ denote the wage per efficiency unit of labor. The maximization problem for the competitive producers of old intermediates with $i \in [0, N_t]$ can then be written as:

$$\max_{\bar{x}_t(i)} \left\{ \left( \bar{p}_t(i) - \omega_t^W \right) \bar{x}_t(i) \right\},$$

so that we have $\bar{p}_t(i) = \omega_t^W$ and, hence:

$$\bar{x}_t(i) = \left( \omega_t^W \right)^{\frac{1}{\alpha-1}}. \tag{1.4}$$

The producers of new goods (i.e. the firms run by entrepreneurs) are monopolists that maximize profits subject to the demand function (1.3). More formally, they solve:

$$\max_{x_t(i), p_t(i)} \left\{ \left( p_t(i) - \omega_t^W \right) x_t(i) \right\}$$

subject to (1.3). The solution to this problem yields:

$$p_t(i) = \frac{\omega_t^W}{\alpha} \equiv p_t, \tag{1.5}$$

$$x_t(i) = \left( \frac{\omega_t^W}{\alpha} \right)^{\frac{1}{\alpha-1}} \equiv x_t, \tag{1.6}$$

[5] The fixed factor $Q = 1$ is owned by firms, so that profits correspond to the return to the fixed factor. For simplicity, we assume that firms are held by "capitalist" dynasties that are distinct from the workers and entrepreneurs, although allowing for trade in firm shares would not change our results.

and the realized profit per variety is:

$$\Pi_t = \left(p_t - \omega_t^W\right) x_t = (1 - \alpha) \left(\frac{\alpha}{\omega_t^W}\right)^{\frac{\alpha}{1-\alpha}}.$$

We can now solve for the equilibrium return to labor and entrepreneurship as functions of the aggregate supply of regular and entrepreneurial labor. First, combining (1.1), (1.4), and (1.6) yields:

$$X_t^W = \left(\omega_t^W\right)^{\frac{1}{\alpha-1}} + g_t \left(\frac{\omega_t^W}{\alpha}\right)^{\frac{1}{\alpha-1}}.$$

Using (1.2) to eliminate $g_t$, and rearranging terms, yields the following expression for the workers' normalized wage:

$$\omega_t^W = \left(\frac{1 + g_t \alpha^{\frac{1}{1-\alpha}}}{X_t^W}\right)^{1-\alpha} = \left(\frac{1 + \alpha^{\frac{1}{1-\alpha}} \xi X_t^E}{X_t^W}\right)^{1-\alpha}.$$

Next, denote by $w_t^E$ the expected profit of entrepreneurs, and let $\omega_t^E = w_t^E / N_t$.[6] Then, the following expression for the return to entrepreneurship obtains:

$$\omega_t^E = \xi \Pi_t = \xi^{1-\alpha} (1 - \alpha) \left(\frac{\alpha^{\frac{1}{1-\alpha}} \xi X_t^W}{1 + \alpha^{\frac{1}{1-\alpha}} \xi X_t^E}\right)^{\alpha}.$$

Finally, let $\eta_t \equiv w_t^E / w_t^W$ denote the expected entrepreneurial premium. Taking the ratio between the expressions of the two returns obtained above yields:

$$\eta_t = \frac{(1 - \alpha) \alpha^{\frac{\alpha}{1-\alpha}} \xi X_t^W}{1 + \alpha^{\frac{1}{1-\alpha}} \xi X_t^E}. \tag{1.7}$$

Innovation and growth are ultimately pinned down by the share of the population choosing entrepreneurship. The occupational choice, in turn, hinges on both technological variables and the endogenous distribution of individual preferences. We therefore turn, next, to the structure of preferences in the economy.

## 1.2.2 Demographics and Structure of Preferences

The model economy is populated by overlapping generations of altruistic people who live for two periods. Every person has one child, and a measure one of people is born each period. The lifetime utility $V_t$ of a person born at time $t$ is given by:

$$V_t = \chi U(c_{1,t}) + \beta U(c_{2,t}) + z V_{t+1}, \tag{1.8}$$

---

[6] Recall that the entrepreneurial return is stochastic. Each entrepreneur earns $(1 + v) w_t^E$ with probability $\kappa$ and $\left(1 - v\frac{\kappa}{1-\kappa}\right) w_t^E$ with probability $1 - \kappa$.

where $c_{1,t}$ is consumption when young, $c_{2,t}$ is consumption when old, and $V_{t+1}$ is the lifetime utility of the person's child. Preferences are pinned down by the shape of the period utility function $U(\cdot)$ and by the weights $\chi, \beta$, and $z$ attached to young-age consumption, old-age consumption, and the utility of the child, respectively. Below, we endogenize the determination (via intergenerational transmission) of specific preference parameters. More specifically, we assume that people can shape certain aspects of their children's preferences, but cannot change their own preferences. Economic decisions within a generation are taken therefore for fixed preference parameters. This feature allows us to discuss economic choices and preference transmission separately.

People have one unit of time in each period. When young, they make a career choice between being workers or being entrepreneurs. Workers supply one unit of labor to the labor market in each period. Entrepreneurs supply a fraction $\psi$ of their time to the labor market when young, and use the remainder $1 - \psi$ for human capital investment.[7] When old, entrepreneurs use all their time for innovating, with a return to innovation as described in Section 1.2.1.

As generations overlap, at time $t$ labor is supplied by the people born in periods $t - 1$ and $t$. Let $\lambda_t$ denote the fraction of entrepreneurs in the generation born at time $t$. Then, aggregate labor supply at time $t$ is given by:

$$X_t^W = 1 - \lambda_t + \lambda_t \psi + 1 - \lambda_{t-1}, \tag{1.9}$$

namely, it is the sum of labor supply by young workers, young entrepreneurs, and old workers. The supply of entrepreneurial input is given by the labor supply of old entrepreneurs:

$$X_t^E = \lambda_{t-1}. \tag{1.10}$$

Equations (1.2) and (1.10) imply that the growth rate of the economy is given by $g_t = \lambda_{t-1} \xi$.

### 1.2.3 Balanced Growth Path for Fixed Preferences

To establish a benchmark, we first analyze balanced growth paths for the case of fixed preferences. That is, parents do not affect their children's preferences, and the preference parameters $\chi, \beta$, and $z$, as well as the $U(\cdot)$ function are fixed. For simplicity, we focus initially on the case where entrepreneurship is not risky, $\nu = 0$. In a balanced growth path, the growth rates of output and consumption are constant, as is the fraction of the population comprised of entrepreneurs. This balanced growth path requires that preferences feature a constant intertemporal elasticity of substitution, so that period utility

---

[7] Other ways of modeling the cost of becoming an entrepreneur would yield similar results as long as the cost results in lower utility at young age, and therefore has the characteristic of an investment.

is given by:

$$U(c) = \frac{c^{1-\sigma}}{1-\sigma}.$$

We restrict attention to the case $0 \leq \sigma < 1$, because the analysis of the economy with endogenous preferences will require utility to be positive (although this can be generalized, see Doepke and Zilibotti, 2008). We also impose the following restriction:

$$(1+\xi)^{1-\sigma} z < 1,$$

which guarantees that discounted utility is well defined.

Given that with fixed preferences everyone's preferences are the same, the key condition for a balanced growth path with a positive growth rate is that the entrepreneurial premium, $\eta$, makes people just indifferent between being workers and being entrepreneurs.[8] The indifference condition for people born at time $t$ can be written as:

$$\chi u\left(w_t^W\right) + \beta u\left(w_{t+1}^W\right) + z V_{t+1} = \chi u\left(\psi w_t^W\right) + \beta u\left(w_{t+1}^E\right) + z V_{t+1},$$

where the left-hand side is the utility of workers and the right-hand side is the utility of entrepreneurs. Note that the utility derived from children is identical for both occupations, and therefore does not feature in the indifference condition. In a balanced growth path, wages and entrepreneurial returns are given by $w_t^W = N_t \omega^W$ and $w_t^E = N_t \omega^E$, respectively, where $\omega^W$ and $\omega^E$ are constants and $N_t$ grows at the constant rate $g$. Canceling common terms allows us to rewrite the indifference condition in this form involving only variables that are constant in the balanced growth path:

$$\chi \frac{\left(\omega^W\right)^{1-\sigma}}{1-\sigma} + \beta \frac{((1+g)\omega^W)^{1-\sigma}}{1-\sigma} = \chi \frac{(\psi\omega^W)^{1-\sigma}}{1-\sigma} + \beta \frac{((1+g)\omega^E)^{1-\sigma}}{1-\sigma}. \qquad (1.11)$$

Condition (1.11) can be further simplified by dividing both sides of the equality by $(\omega^W)^{1-\sigma}$, and rewriting it in terms of the entrepreneurial premium $\eta = \omega^E/\omega^W$:

$$\chi + \beta(1+g)^{1-\sigma} = \chi(\psi)^{1-\sigma} + \beta((1+g)\eta)^{1-\sigma}. \qquad (1.12)$$

Next, consider the expression for the entrepreneurial premium, (1.7). Plugging in the balanced growth levels of $X^W$ and $X^E$ from (1.9) and (1.10), we can express the premium as a function of the fraction of entrepreneurs, $\lambda$:

$$\eta = (1-\alpha)\,\alpha^{\frac{\alpha}{1-\alpha}}\xi\,\frac{2-(2-\psi)\lambda}{1+\alpha^{\frac{1}{1-\alpha}}\xi\lambda}. \qquad (1.13)$$

[8] The analysis here applies to interior balanced growth paths where positive proportions of agents choose either occupation, worker, or entrepreneur. More discussion is provided below.

Combining (1.12) and (1.13), recalling that $g = \lambda \xi$, and rearranging terms yields:

$$\chi \left(1 - (\psi)^{1-\sigma}\right) = \beta(1 + \lambda\xi)^{1-\sigma} \left(\left((1 - \alpha)\, \alpha^{\frac{\alpha}{1-\alpha}} \xi \frac{2 - (2 - \psi)\lambda}{1 + \alpha^{\frac{1}{1-\alpha}} \xi \lambda}\right)^{1-\sigma} - 1\right). \quad (1.14)$$

Here the left-hand side is the (normalized) cost of becoming an entrepreneur in terms of forgone utility when young, and the right-hand side is the (normalized) benefit in terms of higher utility when old. Equation (1.14) pins down the equilibrium fraction of entrepreneurs, $\lambda$, which in turn determines the entrepreneurial premium and the rate of economic growth.

Depending on parameters, there can be corner solutions with $\lambda = 0$ or $\lambda = 1$, i.e. there aren't any entrepreneurs or all old agents are entrepreneurs. In addition, the balanced growth path need not be unique. The reason is that on the one hand an increase in the fraction of entrepreneurs lowers the entrepreneurial premium (making entrepreneurship less attractive), but on the other hand it also increases the growth rate (making entrepreneurship, where higher rewards occur later in life, relatively more attractive). To provide a sharp contrast with the case of endogenous preferences, we will focus on parameter configurations where the balanced growth path for fixed preferences is both interior and unique.

**Assumption 1.** The parameters $\alpha, \xi$, and $\psi$ satisfy:

$$2\,(1 - \alpha)\, \alpha^{\frac{\alpha}{1-\alpha}} \xi > 1 > \frac{(1 - \alpha)\, \alpha^{\frac{\alpha}{1-\alpha}} \xi \psi}{1 + \alpha^{\frac{1}{1-\alpha}} \xi}.$$

**Proposition 1.** *Under Assumption 1, there exists a $\bar{\chi}(\alpha, \xi, \psi) > 0$ such that for all $\chi < \bar{\chi}(\alpha, \xi, \psi)$ a unique interior balanced growth equilibrium exists, i.e. there is a unique $\lambda \in (0, 1)$ that satisfies Equation (1.14).*

## 1.3. ENDOGENOUS CULTURE I: WEBER AND THE TRANSMISSION OF PATIENCE

The balanced growth analysis in the previous section shows that the growth rate in our economy is determined by both technology parameters (such as the efficiency of the innovation technology $\xi$) and preference parameters (such as the time discount factor $\beta$). Despite this fact, when using similar growth models to address variations in economic growth across time and space, the literature has typically focused on variations in technology as the driving force. Unlike technology, preferences usually are assumed to be exogenous. Deviating from this practice, we now endogenize preferences, and analyze the interaction of preference formation with technology, occupational choice, and ultimately, economic growth.

### 1.3.1 Endogenizing Patience

We start by focusing on patience, parameterized by the time discount factor $\beta$. Since risk is not important for the analysis in this section, we abstract from uncertainty and assume that $\nu = 0$. Adult agents in period $t$ are endowed with a predetermined discount factor, $\beta_t$, but they can affect the discount factor of their children, $\beta_{t+1}$. For example, in their children's upbringing parents can emphasize the appreciation of future rewards. Given that we assume $\sigma < 1$, a higher $\beta$ always yields higher utility. However, investing in children's patience is costly, so parents face a tradeoff. More precisely, denoting by $l_t$ the effort a parent of generation $t$ spends on raising her child's patience, the parent's discounted utility is:

$$\chi(l_t) \frac{c_{t,1}^{1-\sigma}}{1-\sigma} + \beta_t \frac{c_{t,2}^{1-\sigma}}{1-\sigma} + z V_{t+1}(\beta_{t+1}(l_t)),$$

where $\chi$ is a strictly decreasing, strictly concave, and differentiable function, and effort is bounded by $0 \leq l_t \leq 1$. The structure of preferences is still of the form given in (1.8), although $\chi$ and $\beta$ are now endogenous variables rather than given parameters. The child's patience is given by:

$$\beta_{t+1}(l_t) = (1-\delta)\beta_t + f(l_t), \tag{1.15}$$

where $f$ is an increasing, non-negative, and strictly concave function, and $\delta$ satisfies $0 < \delta \leq 1$. Notice that if $\delta < 1$ there is some direct persistence in preferences across generations, which captures children's imitation of their parents and other transmission channels that do not require direct parental effort. In addition to this direct transmission, the function $f(l_t)$ captures the return to parental effort in terms of increasing the child's patience.

### 1.3.2 Transmission of Patience in the Balanced Growth Path

We now characterize balanced growth paths with endogenous patience. People face a twofold decision problem. First, when young they choose whether to be workers or become entrepreneurs. This decision hinges only on returns within the person's lifetime, and much of the previous analysis for fixed preferences still applies. Second, people choose the investment $l_t$ in instilling patience in their children.

We proceed by analyzing the individual decision problem under the assumption that a balanced growth path has already been reached, so that the entrepreneurial premium is constant, and wages and profits grow at the constant rate $g$. The decision problem can be analyzed recursively, with the discount factor $\beta$ serving as the state variable of a dynasty. In principle, the state of technology $N_t$ is a second state variable, because growth in $N_t$ scales up all wages and returns. However, due to the homothetic utility function, in a balanced growth path utility at time $t$ can be expressed as:

$$V_t(\beta_t, N_t) = \left( \frac{N_t w_0^W}{N_0} \right)^{1-\sigma} v(\beta_t),$$

where $v$ is a value function that does not depend on $N_t$ and is scaled so that it gives utility conditional on the worker's wage being equal to one. This value function, in turn, satisfies the following set of Bellman equations:

$$v(\beta) = \max \left\{ v^W(\beta), v^E(\beta) \right\},  \tag{1.16}$$

where:

$$v^W(\beta) = \max_{0 \le l \le 1} \left\{ \chi(l) + \beta (1+g)^{1-\sigma} + z (1+g)^{1-\sigma} v(\beta') \right\},  \tag{1.17}$$

$$v^E(\beta) = \max_{0 \le l \le 1} \left\{ \chi(l)\psi^{1-\sigma} + \beta ((1+g)\eta)^{1-\sigma} + z (1+g)^{1-\sigma} v(\beta') \right\}.  \tag{1.18}$$

The maximization in (1.17) and (1.18) is subject to the law of motion for patience across generations:

$$\beta' = (1-\delta)\beta + f(l).  \tag{1.19}$$

The Bellman equations (1.17) and (1.18) represent the utilities conditional on choosing to be a worker or an entrepreneur, respectively, and (1.16) captures the optimal choice between these two careers.

Given our assumptions on $f$ and $l$, there is a maximum level of patience, $\beta_{max}$, that can be attained. The decision problem is therefore a dynamic programming problem with a single state variable in the interval $[0, \beta_{max}]$, and can be analyzed using standard techniques. The following proposition summarizes the properties of the value function and the associated policy functions for investing in patience and for choosing an occupation.

**Proposition 2.** *The system of Bellman equations* (1.16)–(1.18) *has a unique solution. The value function $v$ is increasing and convex in $\beta$. The optimal occupational choice is either to be a worker for any $\beta$, or there exists a $\bar{\beta}$ such that impatient people with $\beta < \bar{\beta}$ strictly prefer to be workers, patient people with $\beta > \bar{\beta}$ strictly prefer to be entrepreneurs, and people with $\beta = \bar{\beta}$ are indifferent. The optimal investment in patience $l = l(\beta)$ is non-decreasing in $\beta$.*

The proof of the proposition is contained in the mathematical appendix. The convexity of the value function follows from two features of the decision problem: the discount factor enters utility linearly, and there is a complementarity between being patient and being an entrepreneur.

To gain intuition, consider the decision problem without the occupational choice, i.e. assume that all members of a dynasty are forced to be either workers or entrepreneurs regardless of their patience. If we vary the discount factor $\beta$ of the initial generation, while holding constant the investment choices $l$ of all generations, the utility of the initial generation is a linear increasing function of $\beta$. This is because initial utility is a linear function of present and future discount factors, and the initial discount factor, in turn, has a linear effect on future discount factors through the term $1 - \delta$ in the law of motion (1.19). In addition, if the occupation of all generations is held constant, it is in fact optimal to choose a constant $l$ for all $\beta$, because the marginal return to investing in patience depends only on the choice of occupation, and not on $\beta$.

Now consider the full model with a choice between the two occupations. The career with the steeper income profile, namely entrepreneurship, is more attractive when $\beta$ is high. As we increase $\beta$, each time either a current or future member of the dynasty switches from being a worker to being an entrepreneur, the value function also becomes steeper in $\beta$. The optimal $l$ increases at each step, because the cost of providing patience declines with the steepness of the income profile, while the marginal benefit increases. Since there are only two possible occupations, the value function is piecewise linear, where the linear segments correspond to ranges of $\beta$ for which the optimally chosen present and future occupations are constant. At each kink of the value function, some member of the dynasty is indifferent between being a worker and an entrepreneur. Since the choice of $l$ depends on the chosen occupation, there may be multiple optimal choices $l$ at a $\beta$ where the value function has a kink, whereas in between kinks the optimal choice of $l$ is unique. The following proposition summarizes our results regarding the optimal choice of income profiles and investment in patience.

**Proposition 3.** *The state space $[0, \beta_{\max}]$ can be subdivided into (at most) countably many closed intervals $[\underline{\beta}, \overline{\beta}]$ such that over the interior of any range $[\underline{\beta}, \overline{\beta}]$, the occupational choice of each member of the dynasty (i.e. parent, child, grandchild, and so on) is constant and unique (though possibly different across generations), and $l(\beta)$ is constant and single-valued. The value function $v(\beta)$ is piecewise linear, where each interval $[\underline{\beta}, \overline{\beta}]$ corresponds to a linear segment. Each kink in the value function corresponds to a switch, from being a worker to being an entrepreneur, by a present or future member of the dynasty. At a kink, the optimal choices of occupation and $l$ corresponding to both adjoining intervals are optimal (thus, the optimal policy functions are not single-valued at a kink).*

The proposition implies that the optimal policy correspondence $l(\beta)$ is a non-decreasing step-function, which takes multiple values only at a step. Proposition 3 allows us to characterize the equilibrium law of motion for patience. Since the policy correspondence $l(\beta)$ is monotone, the dynamics of $\beta$ are monotone as well and converge to a steady state from any initial condition.

**Proposition 4.** *The law of motion of $\beta$ is described by the following difference equation:*

$$\beta' = g(\beta) = (1 - \delta)\,\beta + f\,(l\,(\beta))\,,$$

*where $l(\beta)$ is a non-decreasing step-function (as described in Proposition 3). Given an initial condition $\beta_0$, patience in the dynasty converges to a constant $\beta$ where parents and children choose the same profession.*

Notice that while the discount factor of a dynasty always converges, the steady state does not have to be unique even for a given $\beta_0$. For example, if the initial generation is indifferent between the two occupations, the steady state can depend on which one is chosen.

Given the optimal occupational choices of parents and children, the optimal choice of $l$ has to satisfy first-order conditions. This allows us to characterize more sharply the decisions on patience and their interaction with occupational choices. We have already established that both patience $\beta$ and occupation converge within a dynasty. Thus, the population ultimately divides into worker dynasties and entrepreneur dynasties, and these two types face different incentives for investing in patience. Consider the case in which the solutions for $l$ are interior. For workers, the first-order condition characterizing the optimal effort $l^W$ for investing in patience is given by:

$$- \chi'(l^W) = \frac{z(1+g)^{2(1-\sigma)} f'(l^W)}{1 - z(1+g)^{1-\sigma}(1-\delta)}. \tag{1.20}$$

The corresponding condition for entrepreneurial dynasties is given by:

$$- \chi'(l^E)\psi^{1-\sigma} = \frac{z(1+g)^{2(1-\sigma)}\eta^{1-\sigma} f'(l^E)}{1 - z(1+g)^{1-\sigma}(1-\delta)}. \tag{1.21}$$

In both equations, the left-hand side is strictly increasing in $l$, and the right-hand side is strictly decreasing. Moreover, for a given $l$ the left-hand side is smaller for entrepreneurial dynasties, and the right-hand side is larger. Therefore, in the balanced growth path we must have $l^E > l^W$: The returns to being patient are higher for entrepreneurs because of their steeper income profile, inducing them to invest more in patience. In the balanced growth path, we therefore also have $\beta^E > \beta^W$, where:

$$\beta^W = \frac{f(l^W)}{\delta},$$

$$\beta^E = \frac{f(l^E)}{\delta}.$$

These findings line up with Max Weber's (1905) view of entrepreneurs as future-oriented individuals who possess a "spirit of capitalism". However, in our theory, differences in patience are not just a determinant of occupational choice (as in Weber), but also a consequence of it. Entrepreneurial dynasties develop patience because of the complementarity between this preference trait and their occupation. In contrast, Weber focused on religion as a key determinant of values and preferences across social groups.

Figure 1.1 provides an example of the characteristics of the value and policy functions analyzed in Propositions 2 and 3.[9] In the example, the value function has two linear segments. Below the threshold of $\beta = 0.65$, the optimal choice is to become a worker, and investment in patience in this range is such that all subsequent generations are workers too. Thus, investment in patience is constant over this range, as displayed in the lower panel. Above the threshold, the optimal choice for both the current and future generations

---

[9] The parametrization is as in the balanced growth computations in Section 1.3.3 with the equilibrium fraction of entrepreneurs given by $\lambda = 0.35$.

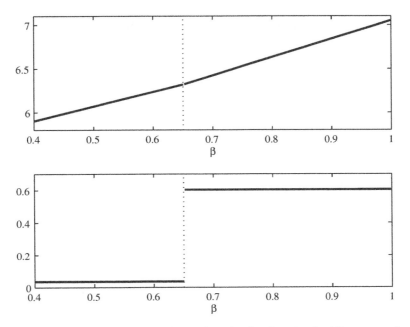

**Figure 1.1** Example of value function (upper panel) and policy function for $I$ (lower panel).

is to become entrepreneurs. Consequently, investment in patience is constant over this range as well, but considerably higher compared to worker dynasties. The value function has a kink at $\beta = 0.65$ and becomes steeper, because the return to patience is higher for entrepreneurs given their steeper lifetime income profiles. The differential investment results in a substantial gap in patience across occupations in the balanced growth path, with a discount factor $\beta^W = 0.55$ for workers, and $\beta^E = 0.95$ for entrepreneurs.

### 1.3.3 Multiplicity of Balanced Growth Paths with Endogenous Patience

Given the preceding analysis, it is clear that there is no balanced growth path in which all dynasties have identical preferences, and in which there are positive fractions of both entrepreneurs and workers. The reason is that the entrepreneurs have a steeper income profile, given the need to acquire skills when young and the entrepreneurial return that is received when old. This steeper income profile implies that parents of entrepreneurs have a higher incentive to invest in patience compared to parents of workers. Moreover, in any given period the population will sort such that the more patient individuals become entrepreneurs and the less patient become workers. Finally, because of persistence of patience within dynasties, occupations also will be persistent within dynasties.

Hence, a balanced growth path has the property that the two groups are characterized by different preferences, patient entrepreneurs and impatient workers. Given the patience gap between these groups, at least one of them will strictly prefer their own occupation over the alternative, both for themselves and for their children. In fact, generically there exists a continuum of balanced growth path where both workers and entrepreneurs strictly prefer their own occupation, and where the fraction of entrepreneurs, the entrepreneurial premium, and the equilibrium growth rate vary across growth paths. For given parameters, the balanced growth path that is reached depends on initial conditions. More generally, the multiplicity of balanced growth paths opens up the possibility of history dependence and a persistent impact of policies or institutions on the performance of an economy.

To illustrate these results, we focus on the case where preferences are not persistent, $\delta = 1$. We would like to characterize the set of balanced growth paths in terms of the growth rate $g$, the entrepreneurial premium $\eta$, and the patience levels $\beta^W$ and $\beta^E$ of workers and entrepreneurs. From (1.20) and (1.21), we know that the investments in patience $l^W$ and $l^E$ by workers and entrepreneurs have to satisfy:

$$-\chi'(l^W) = z(1+g)^{2(1-\sigma)} f'(l^W),$$
$$-\chi'(l^E)\psi^{1-\sigma} = z(1+g)^{2(1-\sigma)}\eta^{1-\sigma} f'(l^E),$$

and we have $\beta^W = f(l^W)$ and $\beta^E = f(l^E)$. Here, focusing on the $\delta = 1$ case implies that the choice of future patience depends only on today's occupational choice, but not directly on the current patience.

The balanced growth values of the value functions (1.17) and (1.18) are:

$$v^W = \frac{\chi(l^W) + \beta(1+g)^{1-\sigma}}{1 - z(1+g)^{1-\sigma}},$$
$$v^E = \frac{\chi(l^E)\psi^{1-\sigma} + \beta((1+g)\eta)^{1-\sigma}}{1 - z(1+g)^{1-\sigma}}.$$

In the balanced growth path, each group has to prefer their own occupation over the alternative, for the present generation and future descendants. In particular, there are four constraints to consider. The first is that a person with patience $\beta^E$ prefers entrepreneurship for all members of the dynasty over everyone being a worker:

$$v^E \geq \chi(l^W) + \beta^E(1+g)^{1-\sigma} + z(1+g)^{1-\sigma} v^W. \tag{1.22}$$

The right-hand side has two components, because the first generation still has patience $\beta^E$, with all following generations in the deviation would have patience $\beta^W$. The second constraint is that entrepreneurship for all generations is preferred to the first generation being an entrepreneur, but all following generations switching to being workers. This constraint can be written as:

$$v^E \geq \chi(l^{EW})\psi^{1-\sigma} + \beta^E((1+g)\eta)^{1-\sigma} + z(1+g)^{1-\sigma}\left(\chi(l^W) + \beta^{EW}(1+g)^{1-\sigma}\right)$$
$$+ z^2(1+g)^{2(1-\sigma)} v^W. \tag{1.23}$$

Here $l^{EW}$ and $\beta^{EW}$ are the investment and patience level that are optimal given that path of occupational choices, characterized by:

$$-\chi'(l^{EW})\psi^{1-\sigma} = z(1+g)^{2(1-\sigma)}f'(l^{EW}).$$

and $\beta^{EW} = f(l^{EW})$. The parallel constraints for worker dynasties with patience $\beta^W$ are given by:

$$\chi(l^E)\psi^{1-\sigma} + \beta^W((1+g)\eta)^{1-\sigma} + z(1+g)^{1-\sigma}v^E \leq v^w. \qquad (1.24)$$

and:

$$\chi(l^{WE}) + \beta^W(1+g)^{1-\sigma} + z(1+g)^{1-\sigma}\left(\chi(l^E)\psi^{1-\sigma} + \beta^{WE}((1+g)\eta)^{1-\sigma}\right)$$
$$+z^2(1+g)^{2(1-\sigma)}v^E \leq v^W, \qquad (1.25)$$

where $l^{WE}$ and $\beta^{WE}$ are characterized by:

$$-\chi'(l^{WE}) = z(1+g)^{2(1-\sigma)}\eta^{1-\sigma}f'(l^{WE}),$$

and $\beta^{WE} = f(l^{WE})$. It can now be shown that a continuum of balanced growth paths exists. Because of the gap in balanced growth preferences, when one occupational group is just indifferent between their occupation and the alternative, the other group strictly prefers their own occupation. It is therefore possible to raise the return of the indifferent group in some range so that both groups strictly prefer to stay in their own occupation. The potentially binding constraints are given by (1.23) and (1.25). The following lemma contains the main result underlying the multiplicity of balanced growth paths.

**Lemma 1.** *When the entrepreneurial premium $\eta$ in the balanced growth path is such that (1.23) holds as an equality, then (1.22), (1.24), and (1.25) hold as strict inequalities.*

Building on this lemma, we can now establish the main result:

**Proposition 5.** *If there exists a balanced growth with path a fraction of entrepreneurs $\lambda$ such that $0 < \lambda < 1$, there exists a continuum of additional balanced growth paths with different fractions of entrepreneurs and thus different growth rates.*

That is, there are multiple balanced growth paths unless the only feasible balanced growth path features a corner solution with all agents choosing the same profession.

We have focused on the $\delta = 1$ case for analytical convenience. When there is direct persistence in patience across generations ($\delta < 1$), the forces generating multiple balanced growth paths are strengthened even more, and generally a wider range of rates of entrepreneurship and economic growth can be long-run outcomes. Figure 1.2 illustrates this with a computed example. The parameter values used are as follows: $z = 0.5, \sigma = 0.5, \xi = 3, \alpha = 0.3, \psi = 0.5$. The cost function for investing in patience is given by $\chi(l) = 1 - l$, and the law of motion for patience is parameterized as:

$$\beta' = (1-\delta)\beta + \delta\tilde{\beta} + \theta_1 l^{\theta_2},$$

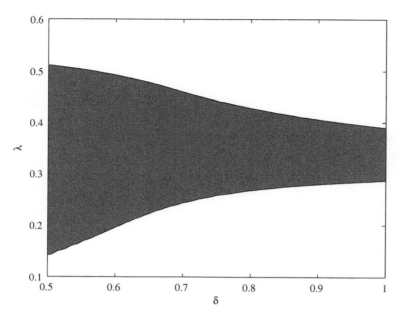

**Figure 1.2** Range of balanced growth paths for different $\delta$.

where we set $\tilde{\beta} = 0.5$ and $\theta_2 = 0.8$. We computed outcomes for a variety of values of the persistence parameter $\delta$. For $\delta = 1$, we set $\theta_1 = 1$, and for lower $\delta$ the value of $\theta_1$ is adjusted, to hold the impact of investing in patience on utility constant in the balanced growth path (so that changing $\delta$ does not lead to a level shift in patience).

For these parameters, Figure 1.2 plots the range for $\lambda$ (the fraction of entrepreneurs in the population) that can be supported as a balanced growth path. At $\delta = 1$ (no direct persistence in patience across generations), the balanced growth level of $\lambda$ varies between 0.29 and 0.39, which corresponds to growth rates (per generation) between $g = 0.87$ and $g = 1.27$, or, if a generation is interpreted to last 25 years, between 2.5 and 3.3% per year. As we lower $\delta$ and make patience more persistent, the range of balanced growth paths widens. At $\delta = 0.5$, $\lambda$ can vary between 0.15 and 0.51 in the balanced growth path, which corresponds to annual growth rates between 1.5 and 3.8% per year.

Figure 1.3 demonstrates what the law of motion for patience looks like in the balanced growth path for different values of $\lambda$. In all panels, the persistence of patience is set to $\delta = 0.8$. In the top panel, we set $\lambda = 0.26$, which is close to the lowest fraction of entrepreneurs that can be sustained in a balanced growth path. In this growth path, the return to entrepreneurship is high. The law of motion for patience intersects the 45-degree line twice, where the lower intersection corresponds to the long-run patience of workers, and the higher intersection corresponds to entrepreneurs. Given high returns to entrepreneurship, dynasties that start out with patience that is only a little higher

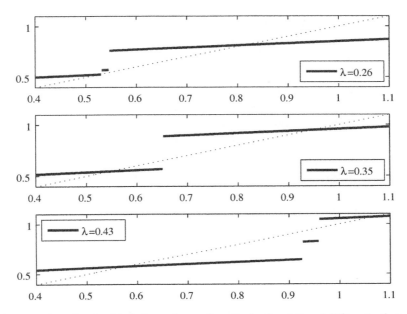

**Figure 1.3** Laws of motion for $\beta$ in balanced growth paths for $\delta = 0.8$ and different values of $\lambda$.

than the long-run patience of workers, ultimately converge to entrepreneurship. The law of motion has three linear segments, where the bottom one corresponds to worker dynasties and the top one to entrepreneur dynasties. The (small) middle segment pertains to dynasties where the current generation consists of workers who invest sufficiently in patience for all following generations to switch to entrepreneurship. In the middle panel, we set $\lambda = 0.35$. Here the law of motion has only two segments. All dynasties are either workers or entrepreneurs forever; there are no transitions between the occupations. The bottom panel for $\lambda = 0.43$ corresponds to a low return to entrepreneurship. The law of motion is a mirror image of the top panel. There are three segments, where the middle segment now corresponds to dynasties where the current generation consists of entrepreneurs, but all subsequent ones will be workers. Comparing across the levels of $\lambda$, it is apparent that as we move to higher levels of $\lambda$ the long-run levels of patience (i.e. the intersections with the 45-degree line) increase both for workers and for entrepreneurs. This is because a higher $\lambda$ implies a higher growth rate, which results in steeper income profiles for both professions, and thus more investment in patience.

### 1.3.4 Implications of Multiplicity of Balanced Growth Paths

Taken at face value, our finding of multiplicity of balanced growth paths implies that different economies, although characterized by identical technological parameters, can experience permanently different growth rates, driven by cultural differences across their populations. Of course, cultural differences themselves are endogenous in our theory. From this perspective, the theory suggests the possibility of path dependence, that is, a country's success at entrepreneurship and innovation may depend on the cultural and economic makeup of the country at the onset of modern economic growth. This theme is explored in more detail in Doepke and Zilibotti (2008), where we explicitly model the transition of an economy with endogenous preferences from a stagnant, pre-industrial economy to capital-driven growth. In that paper, the distribution of preferences at the onset of modern growth depends on the nature of pre-industrial occupations in terms of lifetime income profiles and the distribution of land ownership. Combining the approach of Doepke and Zilibotti (2008) with the theory outlined here would lead to the prediction that the nature of the pre-industrial economy can have long-term repercussions for economic development.

Another implication of multiplicity of balanced growth paths is that policies or institutions that affect preferences can have a long-term impact on economic growth. Consider a country that imposes high taxes on entrepreneurs or discourages entrepreneurship through other means, as in the centrally planned economies of Eastern Europe during the 20th century. Over time, such policies would shift the culture of the population toward being less future-oriented with a lower propensity for entrepreneurship. Consider now the transition of the economy when the political constraints on entrepreneurship are removed. We would expect to observe a small class of entrepreneurs gaining high returns, but lower rates of entrepreneurship and a lower rate of economic growth compared to a country undergoing a similar transition from more favorable initial cultural conditions.

The model can also be extended to allow for open economies. The simplest case is that of a world economy in which trade across borders is frictionless, so that all goods are traded at the same price, and workers and entrepreneurs get the same returns regardless of where they live. In such an environment, initial cross-country differences would manifest themselves in permanent differences in rates of entrepreneurship and innovation across countries, even though ultimately all countries would benefit from innovation (and experience the same growth rates) because of integrated markets.

### 1.3.5 The Model with Financial Markets

In the sections above, we showed that workers and entrepreneurs face different incentives for investing in patience, because entrepreneurs face a steeper income profile. However, the difference in the income profile would not matter if people could use financial markets to smooth consumption. A steep income profile directly translates into a steep utility profile only if financial markets are absent or incomplete.

To illustrate this point, consider the opposite extreme of perfect financial markets, i.e. people can borrow and lend at a fixed interest rate $R$ subject to a lifetime budget constraint. For simplicity, we abstract from financial bequests. The only occupations that are chosen in equilibrium are now those that maximize the present value of income,

$\gamma_1 + \gamma_2/R$. Therefore, the lifetime returns of being a worker and being an entrepreneur have to be equalized:

$$\omega^W + \frac{(1+g)\omega^W}{R} = \psi\omega^W + \frac{(1+g)\omega^E}{R},$$

which implies that:

$$\eta = 1 + \frac{(1-\psi)R}{1+g} = 1 + \frac{(1-\psi)R}{1+\lambda\xi}.$$

The equilibrium condition (1.13) continues to hold, hence:

$$\eta = (1-\alpha)\alpha^{\frac{\alpha}{1-\alpha}}\xi \frac{2-(2-\psi)\lambda}{1+\alpha^{\frac{1}{1-\alpha}}\xi\lambda}.$$

Combining these equations yields a relationship between the proportion of entrepreneurs, $\lambda$ (or, alternatively, the growth rate), and the market interest rate:

$$1 + \frac{(1-\psi)R}{1+g} = (1-\alpha)\alpha^{\frac{\alpha}{1-\alpha}} \frac{2\xi-(2-\psi)g}{1+\alpha^{\frac{1}{1-\alpha}}g}. \qquad (1.26)$$

Since workers and entrepreneurs have the same lifetime income, it is sufficient to consider the individual saving decision of one group, e.g. the workers:

$$\max_s \frac{(\omega^W - s)^{1-\sigma}}{1-\sigma} + \frac{\beta}{\chi}\frac{(Rs + \omega^W(1+g))^{1-\sigma}}{1-\sigma}.$$

The solution yields a standard Euler equation:

$$\frac{Rs + \omega^W(1+g)}{\omega^W - s} = \left(\frac{\beta}{\chi}R\right)^{\frac{1}{\sigma}}.$$

Hence, denoting by $c^Y$ and $c^O$ the consumption of the young and the old, respectively,

$$c^Y = \omega^W \frac{1+g+R}{R + \left(R\frac{\beta}{\chi}\right)^{\frac{1}{\sigma}}},$$

$$c^O = \left(R\frac{\beta}{\chi}\right)^{\frac{1}{\sigma}} \omega^W \frac{1+g+R}{R + \left(R\frac{\beta}{\chi}\right)^{\frac{1}{\sigma}}}.$$

Given this solution to the saving problem, the optimal investment in patience is given by:

$$l(\beta, g) = \underset{0 \le l \le 1}{\operatorname{argmax}} \left\{ \left(\omega^W\right)^{1-\sigma} \left( \frac{1+g+R}{R + \left(R\frac{\beta}{\chi(l)}\right)^{\frac{1}{\sigma}}} \right)^{1-\sigma} \right.$$

$$\left. \left( \chi(l) + \beta \left(\frac{\beta}{\chi(l)}R\right)^{\frac{1-\sigma}{\sigma}} \right) + z(1+g)^{1-\sigma} v(\beta') \right\}.$$

The policy function, $l(\beta, g)$ determines the equilibrium law of motion of $\beta$, and hence the steady-state value of $\beta$. This is a function of $g$ and $R$.

So far we have found two equilibrium conditions for three endogenous variables, $g$, $\beta$, and $R$. The model is closed by an asset market-clearing condition that pins down the interest rate. We assume that the young cannot borrow from the old, since the latter cannot obtain repayment within their lifetime. Hence, all borrowing and lending takes place between workers and entrepreneurs of a given cohort. The market-clearing condition then yields $s^W + s^E = 0$, or:

$$\left(R\frac{\beta}{\chi}\right)^{\frac{1}{\sigma}} - (1+g) + \psi \left(R\frac{\beta}{\chi}\right)^{\frac{1}{\sigma}} - \eta(1+g) = 0$$

$$\left(R\frac{\beta}{\chi}\right)^{\frac{1}{\sigma}} (1+\psi) = (1+g)(1+\eta).$$

This is the third of the conditions that jointly pin down $g$, $\beta$, and $R$ in the balanced growth path.

The next proposition summarizes our main findings for the model with a perfect market for borrowing and lending.

**Proposition 6.** *When a perfect market exists for borrowing and lending within generations, the only occupations that are chosen in equilibrium are those that maximize the present value of income. The set of optimal occupations is independent of patience $\beta$. If both occupations yield the same present value of income, investment in patience $l$ is independent of which occupation is chosen.*

The intuition for this result is simple: with perfect borrowing and lending, every adult will choose the income profile that yields the highest present value of income, regardless of patience.[10] The proposition shows that at least some degree of financial market imperfection is necessary for occupational choice and investments in patience to be interlinked.

---

[10] In the model of the previous section, general equilibrium forces ensure that there exist equilibria with positive growth where both occupations yield the same present value of income.

A positive implication of this finding is that the degree of discount-factor heterogeneity in a population depends on the development of financial markets. In an economy where financial markets are absent, workers and entrepreneurs face very different incentives for investing in patience, and consequently the gap in patience across occupations is large in the balanced growth path. In contrast, in a modern economy with deeper financial markets we would expect to observe smaller cultural differences across occupations.

## 1.4. ENDOGENOUS CULTURE II: KNIGHT AND THE TRANSMISSION OF RISK TOLERANCE

In our economic environment, entrepreneurs face not only a steeper income profile than workers; they also face risk, provided that $v > 0$. As a result, risk preferences too should be relevant for explaining entrepreneurship, in line with Frank Knight's characterization of risk-taking entrepreneurs (see Knight, 1921, and more recently Kihlstrom and Laffont, 1979; Vereshchagina and Hopenhayn, 2009). In this section, we provide a formal analysis of this possibility.

### 1.4.1 Endogenizing Risk Preferences

To facilitate our analysis of endogenous risk preferences, we focus on a period utility function with mean-variance preferences. That is, the period utility function evaluating (potentially stochastic) consumption $c$ is given by:

$$U(c) = E(c) - \sigma\sqrt{Var(c)}, \tag{1.27}$$

where $E(c)$ is expected consumption and $Var(c)$ is the variance of consumption, and $\sigma$ is a measure of risk aversion. The specific functional form is chosen to be consistent with balanced growth.[11] The utility function implies that people are always better off with a lower risk aversion, i.e. a higher risk tolerance. However, as in our analysis of patience, there is a cost of investing in children's preferences. The effort that a parent of generation $t$ spends on raising the child's risk tolerance is denoted by $l_t$. Total utility is then given by:

$$\chi(l_t)\left(E(c_{t,1}) - \sigma_t\sqrt{Var(c_{t,1})}\right) + \beta\left(E(c_{t,2}) - \sigma_t\sqrt{Var(c_{t,2})}\right) + zV_{t+1}(\sigma_{t+1}(l_t)),$$

where $\chi$ is a strictly decreasing, strictly concave, and differentiable function, and effort is bounded by $0 \le l_t \le 1$. The child's risk preferences are given by:

$$\sigma_{t+1}(l_t) = (1 - \delta)\sigma_t + \delta\sigma_{max} - f(l_t), \tag{1.28}$$

where $f$ is an increasing and strictly concave function with $f(0) = 0$, and $\delta$ satisfies $0 < \delta \le 1$. Here, $\sigma_{max}$ denotes the level of risk aversion exhibited by a dynasty that never

---

[11] While this utility function is not of the expected-utility form, the main results carry over to expected utility as well. For an analysis of the usual CRRA case see Doepke and Zilibotti (2012).

invests in risk tolerance. If $\delta < 1$ there is some direct persistence in preferences across generations.

Let $w^W$ denote the workers' wage, and $\eta$ the ratio of the expected return of entrepreneurs to this wage. To simplify the analysis, we assume that the risk of entrepreneurship takes the form that with probability $\kappa$, the entrepreneur is successful and earns a positive return, whereas with probability $1 - \kappa$ the entrepreneur fails and earns zero. That is, in the notation of Section 1.2.1 we have:

$$\nu = \frac{1 - \kappa}{\kappa},$$

so that if successful, the earnings are:

$$(1 + \nu)\eta w^W = \frac{\eta w^W}{\kappa},$$

whereas with probability $1 - \kappa$ entrepreneurial output is zero. The mean return is then $\eta w^W$, and the variance of the return is given by:

$$Var(c^E) = \kappa \left( \frac{\eta w^W}{\kappa} - \eta w^W \right)^2 + (1 - \kappa) \left( \eta w^W \right)^2$$

$$= \frac{1 - \kappa}{\kappa} \left( \eta w^W \right)^2.$$

Thus, the old-age felicity of an entrepreneur is given by:

$$E(c^E) - \sigma \sqrt{Var(c^E)} = \eta w^W \left( 1 - \sigma \sqrt{\frac{1 - \kappa}{\kappa}} \right).$$

## 1.4.2 Transmission of Risk Preferences in the Balanced Growth Path

We now consider balanced growth paths. People choose both a career, and whether and how much to invest in their child's risk tolerance. We analyze the individual decision problem under the assumption that the economy is in a balanced growth path, so the entrepreneurial premium is constant, and wages and profits grow at the constant rate $g$. The decision problem admits a recursive representation with the risk aversion parameter, $\sigma$, serving as the state variable of the dynasty. As in our analysis of endogenous patience, the state of technology $N_t$ is in principle a second state variable. However, the linear homogeneity of utility in expected consumption allows us to express the value function at time $t$ in a multiplicatively separable form:

$$V_t(\sigma_t, N_t) = \frac{N_t w_0^W}{N_0} v(\sigma_t),$$

where $v(\sigma_t) = V_t(\sigma_t, 1)$ satisfies the following set of Bellman equations:

$$v(\sigma) = \max \left\{ v^W(\sigma), v^E(\sigma) \right\}, \tag{1.29}$$

$$v^W(\sigma) = \max_{0 \leq l \leq 1} \left\{ \chi(l) + \beta(1+g) + z(1+g)v(\sigma') \right\}, \qquad (1.30)$$

$$v^E(\sigma) = \max_{0 \leq l \leq 1} \left\{ \chi(l)\psi + \beta(1+g)\eta\left(1 - \sigma\sqrt{\frac{1-\kappa}{\kappa}}\right) + z(1+g)v(\sigma') \right\}, \qquad (1.31)$$

the maximizations in (1.30) and (1.31) being subject to:

$$\sigma' = (1-\delta)\sigma + \delta\sigma_{\max} - f(l). \qquad (1.32)$$

Here, $v^W$ and $v^E$ are the present-value utilities conditional on choosing to be a worker or an entrepreneur, respectively, and $v$ yields the optimal occupational choice.

Since $l$ is bounded and $\delta > 0$, there is a lower bound $\sigma_{\min}$ for feasible levels of risk aversion. Note that, depending on $f$ and $\delta$, $\sigma_{\min}$ could be negative, corresponding to risk-loving individuals who would choose a risky lottery over a safe one with the same expected return. For a given growth rate $g$ and average return to entrepreneurship $\eta$, the decision problem is a standard dynamic programming problem with a single state variable in the interval $[\sigma_{\min}, \sigma_{\max}]$. The following propositions summarize the properties of the value function and the associated optimal policy functions.

**Proposition 7.** *The system of Bellman equations (1.29)–(1.31) has a unique solution. The value function $v$ is decreasing and convex in $\sigma$. The optimal occupational choice is either to be a worker for any $\sigma$, or to be an entrepreneur for any $\sigma$, or there exists a $\bar{\sigma}$ such that people with high risk aversion, $\sigma > \bar{\sigma}$, strictly prefer to be workers; people with low risk aversion, $\sigma < \bar{\sigma}$, strictly prefer to be entrepreneurs; and people with $\sigma = \bar{\sigma}$ are indifferent. The optimal investment in risk tolerance $l = l(\sigma)$ is non-increasing in $\sigma$.*

**Proposition 8.** *The state space $[\sigma_{\min}, \sigma_{\max}]$ can be subdivided into (at most) countably many closed intervals $[\underline{\sigma}, \overline{\sigma}]$ such that over the interior of any range $[\underline{\sigma}, \overline{\sigma}]$ the occupational choice of each member of the dynasty (i.e. parent, child, grandchild, and so on) is constant and unique (though possibly different across generations), and $l(\sigma)$ is constant and single-valued. The value function $v(\sigma)$ is piecewise linear, where each interval $[\underline{\sigma}, \overline{\sigma}]$ corresponds to a linear segment. Each kink in the value function corresponds to a switch from being a worker to being an entrepreneur by a present or future member of the dynasty. At a kink, the optimal choices of occupation and $l$ corresponding to both adjoining intervals are optimal (thus, the optimal policy functions are not single-valued at a kink). If there is an interval $[\underline{\sigma}, \overline{\sigma}]$ such that over this interval all present and future members of the dynasty are workers, the value function $v(\sigma)$ is constant over this interval, and there is no investment in risk tolerance: $l(\sigma) = 0$.*

The proofs of the propositions (omitted) are analogous to the proofs of Propositions 2 and 3. The final part of Proposition 8 arises because workers do not face any risk, so that in all-worker dynasties utility is independent of risk preferences, and the return on investing in risk tolerance is zero.

The next proposition characterizes the dynamics of risk aversion within dynasties.

**Proposition 9.** *The law of motion of σ is described by the following difference equation:*

$$\sigma' = g(\sigma) = (1 - \delta)\,\sigma + \delta\sigma_{\max} - f\left(l\left(\sigma\right)\right),$$

*where* $l\left(\sigma\right)$ *is a non-increasing step-function (as described in Proposition 8). Given an initial condition* $\sigma_0$, *risk aversion in the dynasty converges to a constant* σ *where parents and children choose the same profession. If the dynasty ends up as a worker dynasty, the limit for risk aversion is given by* $\sigma = \sigma_{\max}$.

The proof (omitted) is analogous to the proof of Proposition 4.

We have already established that in worker dynasties the return to investing in risk tolerance is zero, so that these dynasties do not invest in risk tolerance and hence we have $l^W = 0$ and $\sigma^W = \sigma_{\max}$. For entrepreneurs, in contrast, the return to investing in risk tolerance is positive. If their choice of investment is interior, the investment $l^E$ is characterized by a first-order condition:

$$-\chi'(l^E)\psi = \frac{z(1+g)^2\beta\eta\sqrt{\frac{1-\kappa}{\kappa}}f'(l^E)}{1 - z(1+g)(1-\delta)}. \tag{1.33}$$

Here, the left-hand side is strictly increasing in $l$, and the right-hand side is strictly decreasing. The optimal parental investment in risk tolerance is increasing in the entrepreneurial premium $\eta$, the growth rate $g$, and the entrepreneurial risk $1 - \kappa$.

Parallel to our analysis of endogenous patience, the gap in risk preferences between workers and entrepreneurs leads to a multiplicity of balanced growth paths. There can be long-run differences in growth rates across countries, where faster-growing countries are characterized by a larger group of entrepreneurial individuals with low risk aversion. As in the discussion of Section 1.3.4, the multiplicity of balanced growth paths can give rise to path dependence, to persistent effects of institutions and policies that affect risk-taking, and (in an open-economy context) to specialization of certain groups or countries in innovative and risk-taking activities. Also, the development of financial markets once again interacts with endogenous culture and growth, as discussed in Section 1.3.5 for the patience case. For example, for a given distribution of preferences, better risk-sharing institutions (e.g. through insurance markets or tax and transfer policies) can make entrepreneurship more attractive to individuals with high risk aversion, and thereby lead to faster economic growth. However, there is also a downside to the provision of more insurance. In the limit with perfect risk sharing there would be no incentive to invest in risk tolerance, and consequently over time the population would end up more risk averse compared to a country where less insurance is available. Consider now the arrival of a new technology that involves some uninsurable idiosyncratic risk. The population in the well-insured country would be less likely to pick up such new opportunities, and thus might fall back over time compared to a less well-insured, but more risk tolerant and innovative country.

## 1.5. PATERNALISTIC MOTIVES FOR PREFERENCE TRANSMISSION

Up to this point, in our model of preference transmission parents are motivated solely by altruism, i.e. they evaluate the welfare of the children using the same utility function that drives the children's choices. However, preference transmission could be driven also by paternalistic motives. This is the case when there are potential disagreements between parents and children about optimal choices, and parents use preference transmission as a tool to influence their children's choices.

The paternalistic motive is especially salient in the relationship between parents and adolescent children. It is common for parents to desire to control the tendency of adolescents to take risks parents disapprove of, such as reckless driving, the use of drugs or alcohol, or risky sexual behavior.[12]

### 1.5.1 Allowing for Conflict Between Parents and Children

To analyze how paternalistic motives affect preference transmission, we extend the model by allowing children to make an additional choice at a young age, denoted by $x$, that depends on risk preferences. For simplicity, we assume this choice to be orthogonal to the adult occupational choice, i.e. $x$ does not affect the relative return of the adult occupations or the child's ability to enter either occupation. The environment is a simplified version of Doepke and Zilibotti (2012), where we propose a general theory of parenting style related to paternalism.

Children choose from a set of feasible lotteries so as to maximize the felicity function $U_y(x, \sigma)$, whereas their parents evaluate the choice with a different felicity function, $U(x, \sigma)$, where $\sigma$ denotes the adult's risk aversion parameter. As a concrete example, let the choice of the lottery $x$ result in a random consumption process $c(x)$, and consider parental preferences given by:

$$U(x, \sigma) = E(c(x)) - \sigma \sqrt{Var(c(x))},$$

as in (1.27), whereas the child's preferences are given by:

$$U_y(x, \sigma) = E(c(x)) - (\sigma - \xi)\sqrt{Var(c(x))}.$$

That is, children have intrinsically lower risk aversion (which is consistent with empirical evidence), where $\xi > 0$ captures the gap in risk aversion between the young and the old. For a given $\sigma$, children would choose riskier lotteries $x$ than what their parents would prefer.

---

[12] There is well-documented evidence that children are especially prone to risk-taking. For instance, in a series of laboratory experiments carried out in New Mexico, Harbaugh et al. (2002) it was found that 70–75% of children in the 5–8 year age group chose fair gambles with varying odds over a certain outcome, while only 43–53% of the adults did.

We denote by $x(\sigma)$ optimal choice from the children's standpoint. This choice is given by:

$$x(\sigma) = \underset{x}{\operatorname{argmax}} \left\{ U_y(x, \sigma) \right\}.$$

This choice is static, because the choice of $x$ does not have dynamic consequences. Assuming the choice set to be continuous and differentiable implies:

$$\partial U_y(x(\sigma), \sigma) / \partial x = 0.$$

We now turn to the parents' decision problem. The utility of adult workers and entrepreneurs can be written as:

$$v^W(\sigma) = \max_{0 \le l \le 1} \left\{ \chi(l) + \beta(1+g) + z(1+g) W(\sigma', \sigma) \right\},$$

$$v^E(\sigma) = \max_{0 \le l \le 1} \left\{ \chi(l)\psi + \beta(1+g)\eta \left( 1 - \sigma\sqrt{\frac{1-\kappa}{\kappa}} \right) + z(1+g) W(\sigma', \sigma) \right\},$$

where $W(\sigma', \sigma)$ captures the utility that the parents derive from their children. This function is given by[13]:

$$W(\sigma', \sigma) = U(x(\sigma'), \sigma) + \beta \max \left\{ v^W(\sigma'), v^E(\sigma') \right\}.$$

Notice that $x(\sigma')$ is written as a function of $\sigma'$. This is because the parent cannot control $x$ directly, but must take as given the child's decision based on the child's preference parameter $\sigma'$. The choice $\sigma'$ is constrained by the law of motion:

$$\sigma' = (1 - \delta)\sigma + \delta\sigma_{\max} - f(l).$$

## 1.5.2 Optimal Preference Transmission with Paternalistic Motives

Consider a parent who anticipates her child to become an entrepreneur, and assume, for simplicity, $\delta = 1$. If the optimal $l$ is interior, the following first-order condition obtains:

$$\chi'(l^E)\psi = z(1+g) \left( \underbrace{\frac{\partial U(x(\sigma'), \sigma)}{\partial x} \frac{\partial x}{\partial \sigma'} + \beta \frac{\partial v^E}{\partial \sigma}}_{\text{paternalistic motive}} \right) f'(l^E).$$

Relative to the model of Section 1.4, a new term appears in the first-order condition which captures the paternalistic motive. This terms vanishes whenever there is no disagreement between parents and children, i.e. when $U = U_y$ and $\sigma = \sigma'$, because in

---

[13] In Doepke and Zilibotti (2012), we consider a formulation with partial paternalism, where the $W$ function takes the form:

$$W(\sigma', \sigma) = qU_y(x(\sigma'), \sigma') + (1-q)U(x(\sigma'), \sigma) + \beta \max \{v^W(\sigma'), v^E(\sigma')\}.$$

this case we have:

$$\frac{\partial U\left(x(\sigma'), \sigma\right)}{\partial x} = 0,$$

i.e. the envelope theorem applies. Likewise, the paternalistic motive would also be mute if a fixed choice of $x$ were imposed on the child, because this would imply $\partial x / \partial \sigma' = 0$. In contrast, paternalism does affect the parent's decision problem whenever three conditions are all satisfied: There is disagreement between parent and child regarding the choice of $x$; the child is free to choose $x$; and the child's choice depends on the endogenous preference parameter $\sigma'$. In this case, it is valuable for the parent to distort the child's preferences in order to induce the child to choose an $x$ that is more to the parent's liking. Alternatively, if the option were available, the parent would impose restrictions on the ability of the child to choose freely. When forming a child's preferences, parents realize that reducing the child's risk tolerance comes at the expense of the child's future utility, implying a tradeoff for the altruistic parents. Thus, in general the parent will strike a compromise, and accept that the child chooses an $x$ that is different from the parents' most preferred option.

The discussion above assumes that the parental choice of $\sigma'$ (via $l$) does not affect the child's occupational choice. However, if the paternalistic motive is sufficiently strong, the occupational choice of the child may be affected. More formally, if $\hat{\sigma}$ denotes the risk aversion parameter such that $v^W(\hat{\sigma}) = v^E(\hat{\sigma})$, it is possible that absent the paternalistic motive the parent would choose $\sigma' < \hat{\sigma}$, inducing the child to become an entrepreneur, whereas the paternalistic motive induces a choice $\sigma' > \hat{\sigma}$, implying that the child will choose to be a worker. This scenario is more likely if $\xi$ (i.e. the child's intrinsic risk-loving bias) is large, and if the set of feasible lotteries $x$ among which the child can choose includes choices the parent would strongly disapprove of. In practice, this choice set would depend on various features of the environment in which the adolescent grows up. For instance, adolescents living in areas infested by juvenile gangs are more exposed to risky choices than are children in safe middle-class neighborhoods, where risky choices are limited to more innocuous transgressions. An implication of this analysis, which we explore in more detail in Doepke and Zilibotti (2012), is that families living in areas exposed to acute juvenile risk will emphasize values that are less conducive to an entrepreneurial spirit. When integrated into the general equilibrium model of Section 1.2.1, the theory bears the prediction that countries where juvenile risk is more severe will have a smaller equilibrium proportion of entrepreneurs as well as larger risk premia.

## 1.6. LITERATURE REVIEW

### 1.6.1 Cultural Transmission, Human Capital, and Non-cognitive Skills

The theory presented in the previous sections provides a two-way link between the economic environment and preferences. A pioneering contribution to this literature is Becker and Mulligan (1997), which formalizes a model where people choose their own preferences rather than those of their children. In Mulligan (1997), parents choose their own level of altruism toward their children. Along similar lines, in Haaparanta and Puhakka (2004), agents invest in their own patience and in health. Doepke and Zilibotti (2008) (discussed in more detail below) provide the first theory where altruistic parents shape their children's preferences in order to "best prepare" them for the economic environment in which they will operate.

In these studies, as in our model above (except in the extension of Section 1.5), parents evaluate their children's wellbeing using their children's preferences. Namely, parents choose their investments in preference optimally by maximizing their children's utility. There is no explicit desire of parents to preserve their own culture or to instill values that they regard as intrinsically good or moral. In particular, parents may choose to teach their children preferences that differ from their own. In contrast, a number of recent studies postulate that cultural transmission hinges on a form of "imperfect empathy" (see Bisin and Verdier, 2001; Hauk and Saez-Marti, 2002; Gradstein, 2007; Klasing, 2012; Saez-Marti and Sjoegren, 2008; Tabellini, 2008; and Saez-Marti and Zenou, 2011). According to this approach, parents use their own preferences to evaluate the children's utility and are driven by a desire to make the children's values similar to their own. The two approaches and their differences are reviewed in more detail by Saez-Marti and Zilibotti (2008).[14]

In the Beckerian approach, parents transmit traits to their children that are supposed to make them fit for success. Thus, investment in preference transmission resembles a standard human capital investment. From this perspective, preferences are closely related to what the recent labor literature has labeled "non-cognitive skills." These skills determine how well people can focus on long-term tasks, behave in social interactions, and exert self-restraint, and include patience, perseverance, and self-discipline, among others. Recent empirical studies emphasize the importance of such human assets for economic success (see Heckman et al. 2006; Segal, 2013).

Within the realm of non-cognitive skills, we emphasize the role of patience and of the propensity to take risks. The importance of patience for economic success has been documented by experimental studies. A longitudinal study by Mischel et al. (1992) finds that individuals who were more patient as children were subsequently more likely to acquire formal education, to choose market-oriented occupations, and to earn higher income. More recently, Sutter et al. (2013) found that measures of time preferences of young people aged 10–18 elicited through experiments predict saving behavior, smoking and alcohol abuse, BMI, and conduct at school. Reyes-Garcia et al. (2007) study the effect of patience on economic outcomes among the Tsimanes, an Amazonian tribal society that only recently transitioned from self-sufficiency to a market economy. They found

---

[14] Our analysis in Section 1.5.2 and in Doepke and Zilibotti (2012) provides a bridge between these two approaches. Our analysis proposes an explicit microfoundation of the child-adult preference conflict, whereas in the existing literature imperfect empathy is postulated as a primitive.

that individuals who were already more patient in the pre-market environment (when patience was a latent attribute with no effect on individual success) acquired on average more education and engaged more often in entrepreneurial activity when the society introduced markets.[15]

The importance of the propensity to take risk for entrepreneurship has been emphasized, among others, by Kihlstrom and Laffont (1979). Several studies point to robust evidence that risk tolerant people are more likely to become entrepreneurs; see, e.g. Van Praag and Cramer (2001), Cramer et al. (2002), and Kan and Tsai (2006).

The evidence discussed above leaves open the extent to which patience and risk tolerance hinge on parental effort or on the influence of the environment, as opposed to being genetically inherited. The long-standing debate among anthropologists and population geneticists on the role of nature versus nurture has reached no clear conclusion.[16] Both genes and culture appear to be important, likely in a non-linear interactive fashion. The recent economic literature has explored, in different contexts, both the evolutionary selection and the cultural transmission mechanisms. For instance, recent studies focusing on economic development from a very long-run perspective have emphasized the importance of Darwinian evolution of preferences and of genetic diversity for the process of development (see, e.g. Galor and Michalopoulos, 2012; Ashraf and Galor, 2013). We view the selection and investment in preference approaches to endogenous preference formation as complementary, because they operate on different time horizons.[17]

There is direct evidence that non-cognitive skills are influenced by social factors and family upbringing at a shorter time horizon. Heckman (2000) and Carneiro and Heckman (2003) review the evidence from a large number of programs targeting disadvantaged children. They show that most programs were successful in permanently raising the treated children's non-cognitive skills. These children were more motivated to learn, less likely to engage in crime, and altogether more future-oriented than children of non-treated families. Similar conclusions are reached by studies in child development psychology such as Shonkoff and Philips (2000) and Taylor et al. (2000).

Some studies focus explicitly on preference parameters of economic models. For example, Knowles and Postlewaite (2004) provide evidence of cultural transmission of patience. Using the PSID, they find that parental savings behavior is highly correlated with the education and savings choices of their children's households, after controlling for standard individual characteristics. Moreover, the correlation is stronger between mothers and children than between fathers and children. Since mothers tend to be more actively involved than fathers in the child-rearing process, this observation suggests that there is

---

[15] These results are consistent with other studies on developing countries.

[16] See, e.g. Cavalli-Sforza and Feldman (1981), Bowles and Gintis (2002), and Richerson and Boyd (2005).

[17] Earlier articles emphasizing the evolutionary selection of preferences include Galor and Moav (2002) and Clark and Hamilton (2006). A recent paper by Baudin (2010) incorporates the interaction of evolutionary forces and cultural transmission in a Beckerian model of endogenous fertility. The interplay between cultural diversity and economic growth is analyzed in Ashraf and Galor (2012).

cultural transmission in patience and propensities to save. In the same vein, Dohmen et al. (2012) document that trust and risk attitudes are strongly correlated between parents and children in the German Socio-Economic Panel. Using the same data set, Zumbuehl et al. (2013) find that parents who invest more in child-rearing efforts are more similar to their children in terms of attitudes toward risk. All these studies concur on the importance of the transmission of non-cognitive skills within families.

## 1.6.2 Investments in Patience and the Spirit of Capitalism

Doepke and Zilibotti (2008) are closely related to the model discussed in this chapter. The authors propose a dynamic dynastic model rooted in the Beckerian tradition where parents invest in their children's patience and work ethic (modeled as the inverse of the marginal utility of leisure).[18] Preferences are treated as a human-capital-like state variable: parents take their own preferences as given, but can invest in those of their children. The focus of the theory is on the interaction of this accumulation process with the choice of an occupation and savings.

The authors show that the endogenous accumulation of "patience capital" can lead to the stratification of a society into social classes, characterized by different preferences and occupational choices. This occurs even if all individuals initially are identical. In the presence of such endogenous differences in preferences, episodes of technological change can trigger drastic changes in the income distribution, including the leapfrogging of a lower class over the existing elite. The theory is applied to the changes in the distribution of income and wealth that occurred during and after the Industrial Revolution in Britain. Before the onset of industrialization, wealth and political power were associated with the possession of land. Over the 19th century, a new class of entrepreneurs and businessmen and women emerged as the economic elite, replacing the landed elite.

From a theoretical standpoint, the focal point of Doepke and Zilibotti (2008) is an association between occupations and consumption profiles, similar to the model presented in this chapter. In some professions, lifetime earnings are relatively flat, while in others, in particular those requiring the acquisition of skills, high returns are achieved only late in life. These differences affect the incentive of altruistic parents for investing in their children's patience capital: the steeper the consumption profile faced by their children, the stronger the incentive for parents to teach them to be patient. The converse is also true: patient agents have a higher propensity to choose professions entailing steep earnings and consumption profiles.

In the historical application they consider, the pre-industrial middle class had accumulated patience capital, and consequently was better prepared to exploit the new economic opportunities than was the existing elite. The differences in patience, in turn, had their roots in the nature of pre-industrial professions. For centuries, artisans, craftsmen, and

---

[18] Doepke and Zilibotti (2005) developed a simplified model that focuses only on patience.

merchants were used to sacrificing consumption and leisure in their youth to acquire skills. Consequently, middle-class parents had the strongest incentive to instill into their children a patience and work ethic, that is, a "spirit of capitalism" in Weberian terms. In contrast, the landed elite had accumulated little patience, but a strong appreciation for leisure. The preference profile of the elite arises because the traditional aristocratic sources of income were mostly rents, which neither grew steeply over time, nor hinged on labor effort.

Doepke and Zilibotti (2008) differ from the model presented in this chapter insofar as it abstracts from innovation. In that model, cultural differences that were formed in pre-industrial times explain why different classes responded differently to the new technological opportunities arising at the outset of the Industrial Revolution. However, technology is exogenous, whereas in this chapter cultural transmission is linked explicitly to a theory of endogenous technical change.[19] The theory discussed in this chapter rationalizes why some individuals become entrepreneurs and innovators, and how this affects the speed of technical change and long-run growth.[20]

An implication shared by both Doepke and Zilibotti (2008) and the model presented in this chapter is that cultural transmission makes dynasties facing steeper income profiles more patient. This prediction is consistent with the evidence from a field experiment conducted on Danish households by Harrison et al. (2002). Using monetary rewards, they show that highly educated adults have time discount rates (which are inversely related to the discount factor) as low as two-thirds of those of less educated agents. Since spending time on education typically steepens people's income profile, this finding is in line with the prediction of the theory. A positive correlation between steep income profiles and patience has also been documented at the macro level (see Carroll and Summers, 1991; Becker and Mulligan, 1997). The former documents that in both Japan and the United States consumption-age profiles are steeper when economic growth is high. The latter paper shows that consumption grows faster for richer families and adult consumption grows faster for children of the rich.

## 1.6.3 Religious Beliefs and Human Capital

Another set of papers studies culture as a system of beliefs affecting people's choices, and ultimately economic development. Significant attention has been paid to religion. Barro and McCleary (2003) show that economic growth is higher in countries with a more widespread belief in hell and heaven. Guiso et al. (2003) come to similar conclusions. Cavalcanti et al. (2007) develop a theoretical model with the possibility of beliefs in

[19]  In addition, the model discussed here considers the cultural transmission of risk aversion as well as the possibility of paternalism. Neither feature is covered in Doepke and Zilibotti (2008). Conversely, in that paper we consider the interaction between patience and work ethic, a dimension from which we abstract here.

[20]  In this regard, our analysis is related to Klasing (2012) and Klasing and Milionis (2013). However, these papers use a different growth model (related to Acemoglu et al. 2006) and a different cultural transmission mechanism (related to Bisin and Verdier, 2001).

rewards in afterlife. They argue that the model can quantitatively explain cross-country differences in the takeoff from pre-industrial stagnation to growth.

Some influential recent studies point to a close connection between the transmission of religious beliefs and human capital investment. In particular, Botticini and Eckstein (2005, 2006, 2007) examine the cultural roots of the economic success of the Jewish population through a theory of specialization in trade-related activities. They conclude that the key factor was not the system of beliefs of the Jewish religion per se. Rather, it is the extent to which religious beliefs led to human capital accumulation. They document that a religious reform introduced in the second century B.C. caused an increase in literacy rates among Jewish farmers, which, in turn, led to increasing specialization in occupations with a high return to literacy, such as artisanship, trade, and finance. High literacy also led to increased migration into towns, where occupations that reward literacy are concentrated. In a similar vein, Becker and Woessmann (2009) documented that in 19th century Prussia, Protestant counties were more prosperous than Catholic ones, but the effect was entirely due to differences in literacy and education. They conclude that the main channel of the effect of religion on economic performance is human capital.[21]

In the literature discussed so far, religious beliefs are exogenous. In contrast, in Fernández-Villaverde et al. (2010) social norms and beliefs mediated by religious institutions are instead endogenous. They construct a theory where altruistic parents socialize children about sex, instilling a stigma against pre-marital sex in order to reduce the risk of out-of-wedlock births. Religious beliefs and institutions operate as enforcement mechanisms. Similar to Doepke and Zilibotti (2008), cultural transmission responds to changes in the underlying environment. In particular, when modern contraceptives reduce the risk associated with pre-marital sex, they reduce the need for altruistic parents and religious authorities to inculcate sexual mores. The equilibrium effect of technology on culture yields the surprising implication that the number of out-of-wedlock births initially grows significantly in response to new contraceptive technology, due to the higher cultural tolerance for pre-marital sex.

While Doepke and Zilibotti (2008) and Fernández-Villaverde et al. (2010) emphasize the process of cultural transmission, Fernández (2013) and Fogli and Veldkamp (2011) describe culture as a process of Bayesian learning from public and private signals. Those

---

[21] The finding that the main channel through which Protestantism led to higher economic prosperity was higher literacy and human capital is interpreted by Becker and Woessmann (2009) as evidence against Max Weber's hypothesis that Protestant work ethic had a causal effect of economic success. The distinction is, to some extent, semantic. Their findings are consistent with the broader interpretation of Weber provided by Doepke and Zilibotti (2008) who abstract from religion, but argue that the cultural transmission of patience induces the middle class to undertake human capital investments. In this perspective, one can interpret religious beliefs (e.g. Protestantism) as a complementary driver of patience and work ethic. To the extent to which patience is a constituent of the spirit of capitalism, the evidence of Becker and Woessmann (2009) would be actually consistent with a broad interpretation of Max Weber's theory.

papers explain the sharp increase in female labor supply during the 20th century.[22] Doepke and Tertilt (2009) focus on an earlier period and provide a theory of the expansion of women's rights in the 19th century. The authors argue that rising demand for human capital changed cultural attitudes regarding the proper role of women in society, and ultimately triggered political reform.[23]

### 1.6.4 Beliefs and Social Norms

Many recent studies link culture and beliefs with the process of development through the effects these have on institutions. For instance, Aghion et al. (2010) and Aghion et al. (2011) argue that trust determines the demand for regulation, especially in labor markets.[24] Heterogeneous beliefs about the effect of redistributive policies are the focus of Piketty (1995). A number of papers also consider the feedback effect from institutions to culture. For instance, Hassler et al. (2005) argue that a generous unemployment benefits system induces low geographic mobility of workers in response to labor market shocks. Low mobility, in turn, increases over time the attachment of workers to their location (modeled as a preference trait), sustaining a high demand of social insurance. A similar argument is developed by Michau (2013), who incorporates his theory in a model of cultural transmission. Lindbeck and Nyberg (2006) argue that public transfers weaken parents' incentives to instill a work ethic in their children. The relationship between trust, efficiency, and size of the welfare state is emphasized by Algan et al. (2013).[25]

Culture, trust, and beliefs have also been argued to have first-order effects on institutional stability and on the ability of societies to foster economic cooperation among its citizens. Rohner et al. (2013) construct a theory where persistent civil conflicts are driven by the endogenous dynamics of inter-ethnic trade and inter-ethnic beliefs about the nature and intentions of other ethnic groups. Inter-ethnic trade hinges on reciprocal trust. The theory predicts that civil wars are persistent (as in Acemoglu et al. 2010), and that societies can plunge into a vicious cycle of recurrent conflicts, low trust, and scant

---

[22] The learning process can be related to the observation of different family models. Fernández et al. (2004) show that the increase in female labor force participation over time was associated with a growing share of men who grew up in families where mothers worked. They test their hypothesis using differences in mobilization rates of men across states during World War II as a source of variation in female labor supply. They show that higher male mobilization rates led to a higher fraction of women working not only for the generation directly affected by the war, but also for the next generation.

[23] Doepke et al. (2012) provide a more extensive discussion of the relationship between cultural and economic explanations for the historical expansion of women's rights.

[24] For a recent survey of the relationship between trust and economic performance, see Algan and Cahuc (2013).

[25] A related argument is provided by the politico-economic theory of Song et al. (2012) arguing that in countries characterized by inefficient public provision voters are more prone to support high public debt. Although debt crowds out future public expenditure, this is a smaller concern to (young) voters in countries whose governments are inefficient.

inter-ethnic trade (a "war trap") even though there are no fundamental reasons for the lack of cooperation. Long-run outcomes are path dependent: economies with identical fundamentals may end up in either good or bad equilibria depending on the realization of stochastic shocks that cement or undermine cohesion and inter-group cooperation.[26] Rohner et al. (2013) also provide evidence that the onset and incidence of civil wars are affected significantly by a lagged measure of trust from the World Values Survey. There is also evidence of the opposite channel, i.e. exposure to civil conflict affecting preferences and trust. Using data from a field experiment in rural Burundi, Voors et al. (2012) document that exposure to violence encourages risk-taking but reduces patience, hence depressing saving and investments. Rohner et al. (2012) document survey evidence from the civil conflicts in Uganda that war destroys trust, strengthens ethnic identity, and harms future growth in ethnically divided communities.

In the empirical literature, beliefs and social norms are often difficult to disentangle from the effects of the local economic and institutional environment. Studying the behavior of immigrants and expatriates has proven useful to achieve identification. A noteworthy example is Giuliano (2007), which shows that second-generation southern European male immigrants in the United States behave similarly to their counterparts in their country of origin, and live with their parents much longer than young Americans do. Similarly, Fernández and Fogli (2006, 2009) document that the country of origin explains fertility and work behavior of second-generation American women. Fisman and Miguel (2007) finds that diplomats from more corrupted countries tend to incur significantly more parking violations in the United States (diplomats are generally immune, so fines are not enforced). Bruegger et al. (2009) compare unemployment across Swiss communities with different languages (French versus German). The language border separates cultural groups, but not labor markets or political jurisdictions. They find that cultural differences (identified by language differences) can explain differences in unemployment duration of about 20%.

A number of papers have emphasized the persistence of cultural factors. Culture may respond to changes in the institutional environment, but cultural shifts may take time. This is consistent with the view that adults' preferences are by and large fixed, as opposed to those of children, whose beliefs, non-cognitive skills, and preferences can be shaped by cultural transmission and the surrounding environment. Even with these influences, cultural changes can take several generations to reach a new steady state after institutions have changed. Alesina and Fuchs-Schuendeln (2007) focus on the fall of the Berlin Wall. After the end of communism, East Germans became subject to the same institutions as West Germans, but carried with them the cultural heritage of the communist experience. Their study documents that several years after unification, East Germans (compared to

---

[26] In a related paper, Acemoglu and Wolitzky (2012) propose a theory where mistaken signals can trigger belief-driven conflict between two groups.

West Germans) are more supportive of redistribution and believe that social conditions are a more important determinant of individual success. Voigtlaender and Voth (2012) go much further and document evidence that a particular form of cultural trait, namely anti-Semitism in German local communities, has persisted for more than 600 years.[27]

Finally, exogenous sources of variation for culture can be found in historical data. Using data for European regions, Tabellini (2010) finds evidence that culture has a significant causal effect on economic development. The identification relies on two historical variables, the literacy rate and past political institutions.

## 1.7. OUTLOOK AND CONCLUSIONS

Explaining the vast variation in rates of economic growth and living standards around the world remains one of the main challenges in economics. Growth-theoretic explanations for these observations have focused on variation in factor endowments, technology, or institutions as explanatory variables, while abstracting from the potential role of differences in culture, values, and preferences. In contrast, in this chapter we have developed a theory in which culture (modeled as endogenous preferences) and economic growth are endogenous and affect each other. Economic growth feeds back into the preference formation and transmission process of families, and conversely the existing distribution of preferences in the population determines the potential for economic growth. The theory predicts that countries can reach different balanced growth paths, in which some countries grow fast and others more slowly. Fast-growing countries are the ones with larger shares of the population exhibiting a "spirit of capitalism" (i.e. preferences conducive to innovative activities). Institutions, the development of financial markets, and government policies affecting risk sharing all feed back into preferences and culture, giving rise to long-term changes in economic development that can long outlast the underlying institutions and policies.

In the past, economists generally have shied away from explaining economic phenomena with variation in culture or preferences. A common concern is that such explanations put little discipline on the data. However, this criticism does not apply to explicit models of intergenerational preference transmission that generate specific testable implications, which is the route that we have taken here. In this sense, this chapter is in the spirit of Stigler and Becker (1977), who also analyzed phenomena that at first sight suggest an important role for variation in preferences (such as addiction; customs and tradition; and fashion and advertising).

Of course, for testable implications to be meaningful, researchers need data allowing them to evaluate the restrictions imposed by the theory in practice. From this perspective, an important change in recent years is the increased availability of data sets that permit

---

[27] They document that cities where Jews were victims of medieval pogroms during the plague era were also very likely to experience anti-Semitic violence in the 20th century, before and during the Nazi rule.

empirical analyses of the transmission of preference traits from parents to children as well as the mutual interaction between cultural preferences and the economic environment (we review a number of such studies in Section 1.6). We expect that combining these new empirical insights with theoretical analyses of the interaction of culture, entrepreneurship, and growth of the kind developed in this chapter will, over time, greatly enhance our understanding of the development process.

# A   PROOFS OF PROPOSITIONS AND LEMMAS

**Proof of Proposition 1.**   Given Equation (1.14), the zero growth ($\lambda = 0$) steady state exists, if and only if:

$$\chi \left(1 - (\psi)^{1-\sigma}\right) \geq \beta \left(\left(2\left(1-\alpha\right)\alpha^{\frac{\alpha}{1-\alpha}}\xi\right)^{1-\sigma} - 1\right).$$

Conversely, the balanced growth path features $\lambda = 1$, if and only if:

$$\chi \left(1 - (\psi)^{1-\sigma}\right) \leq \beta(1+\xi)^{1-\sigma} \left(\left(\frac{(1-\alpha)\,\alpha^{\frac{\alpha}{1-\alpha}}\xi\,\psi}{1+\alpha^{\frac{1}{1-\alpha}}\xi}\right)^{1-\sigma} - 1\right).$$

An interior balanced growth path with positive fractions of workers and entrepreneurs exists if (1.14) is satisfied as an equality for some $\lambda$ with $0 < \lambda < 1$. A steady state has to exist (either corner or interior) because (1.14) is continuous in $\lambda$. The first inequality in Assumption 1 guarantees that the right-hand side of (1.14) is positive for $\lambda = 0$. The second inequality guarantees that the right-hand side of (1.14) reaches zero for a $\tilde{\lambda}$ with $0 < \tilde{\lambda} < 1$. This also implies that the right-hand side of (1.14) is strictly decreasing in $\lambda$ for $\lambda \leq \tilde{\lambda}$ sufficiently close to $\tilde{\lambda}$. Let $\hat{\lambda}$ denote the lower bound of the monotonic region. The right-hand side of (1.14) is bounded strictly away from zero for $0 \leq \lambda \leq \hat{\lambda}$. By choosing $\chi$ sufficiently small, we can guarantee that (1.14) is not satisfied for a $\lambda$ in this region. This implies that (1.14) is satisfied for a $\lambda$ that lies in this monotonic region, which then has to be unique, resulting in a unique, interior balanced growth path.   □

**Proof of Proposition 2.**   The system of Bellman equations (1.16)–(1.18) defines a mapping $T$ on the space of bounded continuous functions on the interval $[0, \beta_{\max}]$, endowed with the sup norm, where the mapping is given by:

$$Tv(\beta) = \max_{I \in \{0,1\}, 0 \leq l \leq 1} \left\{(1 - I)\left[\chi(l) + \beta(1+g)^{1-\sigma}\right] \right.$$
$$\left. + I\left[\chi(l)\psi^{1-\sigma} + \beta\left((1+g)\eta\right)^{1-\sigma}\right] + z(1+g)^{1-\sigma}v(\beta')\right\}, \quad (1.34)$$

where the maximization is subject to:

$$\beta' = (1 - \delta)\beta + f(l).$$

$I$ is an indicator variable for the occupational choice, and $\beta_{\max} = f(1)/\delta$. Since we imposed assumptions that guarantee $0 < z(1+g)^{1-\sigma} < 1$, this mapping is a contraction by Blackwell's sufficient conditions, and it therefore has a unique fixed point by the Contraction Mapping Theorem. This proves the first part of the proposition.

The proof that the value function is increasing and convex is an application of Corollary 1 to Theorem 3.2 in Stokey and Lucas (1989). Using this result, we can establish the result by establishing that the operator $T$ preserves these properties. To establish that the value function is increasing, let $v$ be a non-decreasing bounded continuous function. We need to show that $Tv$ is a strictly increasing function. To do this, choose $\overline{\beta} > \underline{\beta}$. We now need to establish that $Tv(\overline{\beta}) > Tv(\underline{\beta})$. Since the right-hand side of (1.34) is the maximization of a continuous function over a compact set, the maximum is attained. Let $\underline{l}$ and $\underline{I}$ be choices attaining the maximum for $\underline{B}$. We then have:

$$
\begin{aligned}
Tv(\overline{\beta}) \geq (1 - \underline{I}) &\left[ \chi(\underline{l}) + \overline{\beta}(1+g)^{1-\sigma} \right] \\
&+ \underline{I} \left[ \chi(\underline{l})\psi^{1-\sigma} + \overline{\beta}((1+g)\eta)^{1-\sigma} \right] + z(1+g)^{1-\sigma} v((1-\delta)\overline{\beta} \\
&+ f(\underline{l})) > (1 - \underline{I}) \left[ \chi(\underline{l}) + \underline{\beta}(1+g)^{1-\sigma} \right] \\
&+ \underline{I} \left[ \chi(\underline{l})\psi^{1-\sigma} \right. \\
&+ \underline{\beta}((1+g)\eta)^{1-\sigma} \left] + z(1+g)^{1-\sigma} v((1-\delta)\underline{\beta} + f(\underline{l})) = Tv(\underline{\beta}), \right.
\end{aligned}
$$

which is the desired result. Here the weak inequality follows because the choices $\underline{l}, \underline{I}$ may not be maximizing at $\overline{\beta}$, and the strict inequality follows because $v$ is assumed to be increasing, and we have that $\overline{\beta} > \underline{\beta}$ and $\eta > 0$.

To establish convexity of the value function, let $v$ be a (weakly) convex bounded continuous function. We need to establish that $Tv$ is also a convex function. To show this, choose a number $\theta$ such that $0 < \theta < 1$, let $\overline{\beta} > \underline{\beta}$, and let $\beta = \theta\overline{\beta} + (1-\theta)\underline{\beta}$. We now need to show that $\theta Tv(\overline{\beta}) + (1-\theta)Tv(\underline{\beta}) \geq Tv(\beta)$. Let $l$ and $I$ be choices attaining the maximum for $\beta$. Since these are feasible, but not necessarily optimal choices at $\overline{\beta}$ and $\underline{\beta}$, we have:

$$
\begin{aligned}
Tv(\overline{\beta}) \geq (1 - I) &\left[ \chi(l) + \overline{\beta}(1+g)^{1-\sigma} \right] \\
&+ I \left[ \chi(l)\psi^{1-\sigma} + \overline{\beta}((1+g)\eta)^{1-\sigma} \right] + z(1+g)^{1-\sigma} v((1-\delta)\overline{\beta} + f(l)), \\
Tv(\underline{\beta}) \geq (1 - I) &\left[ \chi(l) + \underline{\beta}(1+g)^{1-\sigma} \right] \\
&+ I \left[ \chi(l)\psi^{1-\sigma} + \underline{\beta}((1+g)\eta)^{1-\sigma} \right] + z(1+g)^{1-\sigma} v((1-\delta)\underline{\beta} + f(l)).
\end{aligned}
$$

Working toward the desired condition, we therefore have:

$$\theta \, Tv(\overline{\beta}) + (1-\theta) \, Tv(\underline{\beta})$$
$$\geq (1-I)\left[\chi(l) + \beta(1+g)^{1-\sigma}\right] + I\left[\chi(l)\psi^{1-\sigma} + \beta((1+g)\eta)^{1-\sigma}\right]$$
$$+z(1+g)^{1-\sigma}\left[\theta v((1-\delta)\overline{\beta} + f(l)) + (1-\theta)v((1-\delta)\underline{\beta} + f(l))\right]$$
$$\geq (1-I)\left[\chi(l) + \beta(1+g)^{1-\sigma}\right] + I\left[\chi(l)\psi^{1-\sigma} + \beta((1+g)\eta)^{1-\sigma}\right]$$
$$+z(1+g)^{1-\sigma} \, v((1-\delta)\beta + f(l)) = Tv(\beta),$$

which is the required condition. Here, the last inequality follows from the assumed convexity of $v$. The operator $T$ therefore preserves convexity, and thus the fixed point must also be convex. Notice that linearity is key to this result: the discount factor enters utility linearly, and the parental discount factor has a linear effect on the discount factor of the child.

Regarding the optimal occupational choice, the difference between the utility of being a worker and an entrepreneur for given $\beta$ and $l$ is given by:

$$\chi(l)\left(1 - \psi^{1-\sigma}\right) - \beta(1+g)^{1-\sigma}\left(\eta^{1-\sigma} - 1\right),$$

where the first term is always positive, and the second term is negative as long as $\eta > 1$. Given that the second term is weighted by $\beta$, it follows that being a worker is always optimal for $\beta$ sufficiently close to zero. Since the utility derived from entrepreneurship relative to being a worker is strictly increasing in $\beta$, there is either a cutoff $\overline{\beta}$ such that entrepreneurship is chosen for $\beta \geq \overline{\beta}$, or being a worker is always the preferred choice (when the required cutoff would be larger than $\beta_{\max}$).

As the last step, we would like to show that the optimal investment in patience $l = l(\beta)$ is non-decreasing in $\beta$. Fix two discount factors $\underline{\beta} < \overline{\beta}$. Let $\underline{u}_1 = 1$ if at $\underline{\beta}$ the optimal choice is to be a worker, and $\underline{u}_1 = \psi^{1-\sigma}$ otherwise. Similarly, for the second period we define $\underline{u}_2 = (1+g)^{1-\sigma}$ for workers and $\underline{u}_2 = ((1+g)\eta)^{1-\sigma}$ for entrepreneurs. $\overline{u}_1$ and $\overline{u}_2$ are defined in the same way. Now let $\underline{l}$ and $\overline{l}$ denote the optimal investments in patience at $\underline{\beta}$ and $\overline{\beta}$. The optimal choice of $l$ the implies the following inequalities:

$$\chi(\underline{l})\underline{u}_1 + \underline{\beta}\underline{u}_2 + z(1+g)^{1-\sigma}v((1-\delta)\underline{\beta} + f(\underline{l}))$$
$$\geq \chi(\overline{l})\underline{u}_1 + \underline{\beta}\underline{u}_2 + z(1+g)^{1-\sigma}v((1-\delta)\underline{\beta} + f(\overline{l}))$$
$$\chi(\underline{l})\overline{u}_1 + \overline{\beta}\overline{u}_2 + z(1+g)^{1-\sigma}v((1-\delta)\overline{\beta} + f(\underline{l}))$$
$$\leq \chi(\overline{l})\overline{u}_1 + \overline{\beta}\overline{u}_2 + z(1+g)^{1-\sigma}v((1-\delta)\overline{\beta} + f(\overline{l})).$$

Subtracting the two inequalities yields:

$$\chi(\underline{l})\left(\underline{u}_1 - \overline{u}_1\right) + z(1+g)^{1-\sigma}\left(v((1-\delta)\overline{\beta} + f(\overline{l})) - v((1-\delta)\underline{\beta} + f(\overline{l}))\right)$$
$$\geq \chi(\overline{l})\left(\underline{u}_1 - \overline{u}_1\right) + z(1+g)^{1-\sigma}\left(v((1-\delta)\overline{\beta} + f(\underline{l})) - v((1-\delta)\underline{\beta} + f(\underline{l}))\right).$$

Now there are two possibilities. If the optimal occupational choices at $\underline{\beta}$ and $\overline{\beta}$ are the same, we have $\underline{u}_1 = \overline{u}_1$ and the inequality reads:

$$v((1-\delta)\overline{\beta} + f(\overline{l})) - v((1-\delta)\underline{\beta} + f(\overline{l}))$$
$$\geq v((1-\delta)\overline{\beta} + f(\underline{l})) - v((1-\delta)\underline{\beta} + f(\underline{l})).$$

Since we have already shown that $v$ is convex, this implies $\overline{l} \geq \underline{l}$. The second possibility is that at $\underline{\beta}$ it is optimal to be a worker, and at $\overline{\beta}$ it is optimal to be an entrepreneur, so that we have $\underline{u}_1 - \overline{u}_1 > 0$. Rearranging the expression gives:

$$\left(\chi(\underline{l}) - \chi(\overline{l})\right)\left(\underline{u}_1 - \overline{u}_1\right) \geq z(1+g)^{1-\sigma}\left[v((1-\delta)\overline{\beta} + f(\underline{l})) - v((1-\delta)\underline{\beta} + f(\underline{l}))\right.$$
$$\left. - \left(v((1-\delta)\overline{\beta} + f(\overline{l})) - v((1-\delta)\underline{\beta} + f(\overline{l}))\right)\right].$$

Due to the convexity of $v$, if we have $\underline{l} > \overline{l}$, the left-hand side would be negative and the right-hand side positive; we therefore must have $\underline{l} \leq \overline{l}$, which completes the proof. $\square$

**Proof of Proposition 3.** In Proposition 2, we can subdivide the state space $[0, \beta_{\max}]$ into (at most) two closed intervals (they are closed because of our continuity assumptions), where each interval corresponds to the choice of a given occupation (worker or entrepreneur). The agent is just indifferent between the occupations at the boundary between the intervals, and strictly prefers a given occupation in the interior of an interval. The intervals can be further subdivided according to the occupational choice of the child. Since $l(\beta)$ may not be single-valued, there may be multiple optimal $\beta'$ corresponding to a given $\beta$ today. Nevertheless, since the $\beta'$ are strictly increasing in $\beta$ (because of Proposition 3 and $\delta < 1$) and given that there are only two occupations, we can once again subdivide today's state space into at most two closed intervals, each one corresponding to a specific occupational choice of the child. Continuing this way, the state space $[0, \beta_{\max}]$ can be divided into a countable number of closed intervals (there are two possible occupations in each of the countably many future generations), where each interval corresponds to a specific occupational choice of each generation. Let $[\underline{\beta}, \overline{\beta}]$ be such an interval. We want to establish that the value function is linear over this interval, and that the optimal choice of patience $l(\beta)$ is single-valued and constant over the interior of this interval.

It is useful to consider the sequential formulation of the decision problem. Taking the present and future occupational choices as given and writing the resulting first and second period utilities net of cost of investing in patience as $u_{1,t}$ and $u_{2,t}$, we can substitute for $\beta_t$ and write the remaining decision problem over the $l_t$ on the interval $[\underline{\beta}, \overline{\beta}]$ as:

$$v(\beta) = \max \left\{ \chi(l_0)u_{1,0} + \beta u_{2,0} \right.$$
$$\left. + \sum_{t=1}^{\infty} z^t \left[ \chi(l_t)u_{1,t} + \left( (1-\delta)^t \beta + \sum_{s=0}^{t-1} (1-\delta)^{t-s-1} f(l_s) \right) u_{2,t} \right] \right\}. \quad (1.35)$$

For given current and future occupations, (1.35) is strictly concave in $l_t$ for all $t$, since $\chi$ is concave and $f$ is strictly concave. Moreover, the discount factor $\beta$ and all expressions involving $l_t$ appear in separate terms in the sum. Therefore, it follows that, given the optimal income profiles, for all $t$ the optimal $l_t$ is unique, and independent of $\beta$. Since on the interior of $[\underline{\beta}, \overline{\beta}]$, the current and future optimal occupations are unique, the optimal policy correspondence $l(\beta)$ is single-valued. By construction of the intervals, at the boundary between the two intervals both occupations are optimal choices for at least one generation, hence $l(\beta)$ may take on more than one optimal value, one corresponding to each optimal set of income profiles.

The optimal value function $v$ over the interval $[\underline{\beta}, \overline{\beta}]$ is given by (1.35) with occupations and investment in patience $l_t$ fixed at their optimal (and constant) values. Equation (1.35) is linear in $\beta$; it therefore follows that the value function is piecewise linear, with each kink corresponding to the boundary between two of the intervals.  □

**Proof of Proposition 4.** Since $f$ is an increasing function and we assume that $\delta < 1$, the law of motion is strictly increasing in $\beta$. Notice that $l(\beta)$ may not be single-valued for all $\beta$. Strictly increasing here means that $\overline{\beta} < \underline{\beta}$ implies $\overline{\beta}' < \underline{\beta}'$ for all optimal $\overline{\beta}' \in g(\overline{\beta})$ and $\underline{\beta}' \in g(\underline{\beta})$, even if $g(\overline{\beta})$ or $g(\underline{\beta})$ is a set. For a given $\beta_0$, the law of motion $g$ defines (potentially multiple) optimal sequences of discount factors $\{\beta_t\}_{t=0}^{\infty}$. Any such sequence is a monotone sequence on the compact set $[0, \beta_{\max}]$, and must therefore converge. Notice, however, that since $l(\beta)$ is not single-valued everywhere, different steady states can be reached even from the same initial $\beta_0$.  □

**Proof of Lemma 1.** Assume that (1.23) holds with equality:

$$v^E = \chi(l^{EW})\psi^{1-\sigma} + \beta^E ((1+g)\eta)^{1-\sigma} + z(1+g)^{1-\sigma} \left( \chi(l^W) + \beta^{EW}(1+g)^{1-\sigma} \right)$$
$$+ z^2 (1+g)^{2(1-\sigma)} v^W. \quad (1.36)$$

Now replacing $l^{EW}$ and $\beta^{EW}$ on the right-hand side with $l^E$ and $\beta^E$ lowers utility, because these are not the optimal choices given the chosen occupations. We therefore have:

$$\chi(l^E)\psi^{1-\sigma} + \beta^E ((1+g)\eta)^{1-\sigma} + z(1+g)^{1-\sigma} v^E$$
$$> \chi(l^E)\psi^{1-\sigma} + \beta^E ((1+g)\eta)^{1-\sigma} + z(1+g)^{1-\sigma} \left( \chi(l^W) + \beta^E (1+g)^{1-\sigma} \right)$$
$$+ z^2 (1+g)^{2(1-\sigma)} v^W,$$

where we also rewrote the left-hand side to explicitly show the first-generation utility. Now subtracting the (identical) first-generation terms on both sides and dividing by $z(1+g)^{1-\sigma}$ we get:

$$v^E > \left( \chi(l^W) + \beta^E (1+g)^{1-\sigma} \right) + z(1+g)^{1-\sigma} v^W,$$

which is (1.22) as a strict inequality.

Moving on, replacing the $\beta^E$ of the initial generation on both sides of (1.36) with $\beta^W$ leaves the equality intact, because the discount factor enters both sides in the same way:

$$\chi(l^E)\psi^{1-\sigma} + \beta^W ((1+g)\,\eta)^{1-\sigma} + z(1+g)^{1-\sigma} v^E$$
$$= \chi(l^{EW})\psi^{1-\sigma} + \beta^W ((1+g)\,\eta)^{1-\sigma} + z(1+g)^{1-\sigma} \left( \chi(l^W) + \beta^{EW} (1+g)^{1-\sigma} \right)$$
$$+ z^2 (1+g)^{2(1-\sigma)} v^W. \tag{1.37}$$

Now switching the first-generation occupational choice from entrepreneurship to work yields the following strict inequality:

$$\chi(l^{WE}) + \beta^W (1+g)^{1-\sigma} + z(1+g)^{1-\sigma} \left( \chi(l^E)\psi^{1-\sigma} + \beta^{WE} ((1+g)\,\eta)^{1-\sigma} \right)$$
$$+ z^2 (1+g)^{2(1-\sigma)} v^E < v^W.$$

The strict inequality arises because $l^{EW} < l^E$, implying that the increase in the first-period utility from being a worker is larger on the right-hand side. This still applies after investment in patience is reoptimized (to $l^{WE}$ on the left-hand side and $l^W$ on the right-hand side) due to the envelope theorem. The resulting inequality is a strict version of (1.25).

Finally, again starting with (1.37), replacing the initial investment in patience with $l^{EW}$ (and plugging in the corresponding discount factor in the next generation) lowers utility on the left-hand side, so that we have:

$$\chi(l^{EW})\psi^{1-\sigma} + \beta^W ((1+g)\,\eta)^{1-\sigma} + z(1+g)^{1-\sigma} \left( \chi(l^E)\psi^{1-\sigma} + \beta^{EW} ((1+g)\,\eta)^{1-\sigma} \right)$$
$$+ z^2 (1+g)^{2(1-\sigma)} v^E$$
$$< \chi(l^{EW})\psi^{1-\sigma} + \beta^W ((1+g)\,\eta)^{1-\sigma} + z(1+g)^{1-\sigma} \left( \chi(l^W) + \beta^{EW} (1+g)^{1-\sigma} \right)$$
$$+ z^2 (1+g)^{2(1-\sigma)} v^W.$$

Subtracting the identical first-generation terms and dividing by $z(1+g)^{1-\sigma}$ yields:

$$\chi(l^E)\psi^{1-\sigma} + \beta^{EW} ((1+g)\eta)^{1-\sigma} + z(1+g)^{1-\sigma} v^E$$
$$< \chi(l^W) + \beta^{EW} (1+g)^{1-\sigma} + z(1+g)^{1-\sigma} v^W.$$

Now changing the initial discount factor from $\beta^{EW}$ to $\beta^{W} < \beta^{EW}$ lowers the left-hand side yet again more than the right-hand side (because $\eta > 1$), so that the inequality stays intact:

$$\chi(l^{E})\psi^{1-\sigma} + \beta^{W}((1+g)\eta)^{1-\sigma} + z(1+g)^{1-\sigma}\nu^{E} < \nu^{W},$$

which is a strict version of (1.24).                                                                         $\square$

**Proof of Proposition 5.**  The fraction of entrepreneurs $\lambda$ in the balanced growth path can be mapped into an entrepreneurial premium $\eta$ and a growth rate $g$ given the analysis in Section 1.2.3 above. The entrepreneurial premium is continuous in $\lambda$. Hence, if there exists a fraction of entrepreneurs $\lambda$ that satisfies $0 < \lambda < 1$ and such that conditions (1.22)–(1.25) hold as strict inequalities, there has to be a range of $\lambda$ and associated $\eta$ and $g$ such that the conditions continue to hold. If at the initial $\lambda$ condition (1.23) holds with equality, then given Lemma 1 we know that the remaining constraints hold as strict inequalities. Given continuity it is then possible to raise $\eta$ (by changing $\lambda$) within some range and have all conditions hold as strict inequalities, implying that a continuum of balanced growth paths exists. The same argument can be applied reversely to the point where (1.25) holds as an equality. The highest entrepreneurial return that is consistent with balanced growth is characterized by (1.25) holding as an equality.         $\square$

**Proof of Proposition 6.**  Since the financial market allows for an arbitrary allocation of consumption across the two periods, an occupation that is dominated in terms of the present value of income is also dominated in terms of consumption, and therefore is never chosen. Hence, the set of optimal occupations is independent of patience $\beta$, because the present value of income in the two occupations does not depend on $\beta$. When both occupations yield the same present value of income, they also lead to the same consumption profile. The cost of investing in patience depends only on first-period consumption, which therefore does not depend on the chosen occupation. Likewise, the return to investing in patience is independent of the occupation of the current generation. Investment in patience therefore does not depend on which occupation is chosen.    $\square$

## ACKNOWLEDGMENTS

Financial support from the National Science Foundation (grant SES-0820409, Doepke) and from the European Research Council (ERC Advanced Grant IPCDP-229883, Zilibotti) is gratefully acknowledged. Veronika Selezneva provided excellent research assistance. We thank Mariko Klasing for helpful comments.

## REFERENCES

Acemoglu, Daron, Aghion, Philippe, Zilibotti, Fabrizio, 2006. Distance to frontier, selection and economic growth. Journal of the European Economic Association 4 (1), 37–74.

Acemoglu, Daron, Ticchi, Davide, Vindigni, Andrea, 2010. Persistence of civil wars. Journal of the European Economic Association 8 (4), 664–676.

Acemoglu, Daron, Wolitzky, Alexander, 2012. Cycles of Distrust: An Economic Model. NBER Working Paper 18257.

Aghion, Philippe, Howitt, Peter, 1992. A model of growth through creative destruction. Econometrica 60 (2), 323–351.

Aghion, Phillipe, Algan, Yann, Cahuc, Pierre, 2011. Civil society and the state: the interplay between cooperation and minimum wage regulation. Journal of the European Economic Association 9 (1), 3–42.

Aghion, Phillipe, Algan, Yann, Cahuc, Pierre, Shleifer, Andrei, 2010. Regulation and distrust. Quarterly Journal of Economics 125 (3), 1015–1049.

Alesina, Alberto, Fuchs-Schuendeln, Nicola, 2007. Good bye Lenin (or not?): the effect of communism on people's preferences. American Economic Review 97 (4), 1507–1528.

Alesina, Alberto, Giuliano, Paola, 2009. Preferences for Redistribution. NBER Working Paper 14825.

Alesina, Alberto, Glaeser, Edward, 2004. Fighting Poverty in the U.S. and Europe. Oxford University Press, Oxford, UK.

Algan, Yann, Cahuc, Pierre, 2013. Trust and growth. Annual Review of Economics 5 (1), 521–549.

Algan, Yann, Cahuc, Pierre, Sangnier, Marc, 2013. Efficient and Inefficient Welfare States. Unpublished Manuscript, Sciences Po, Paris.

Ashraf, Quamrul, Galor, Oded. 2012. Cultural Diversity, Geographical Isolation, and the Origin of the Wealth of Nations. IZA Discussion Paper 6319.

Ashraf, Quamrul, Galor, Oded, 2013. The "Out-of-Africa" hypothesis, human genetic diversity, and comparative economic development. American Economic Review 103 (1), 1–46.

Barro, Robert J., McCleary, Rachel M., 2003. Religion and economic growth across countries. American Sociological Review 68 (5), 760–781.

Baudin, Thomas, 2010. A role for cultural transmission in fertility transitions. Macroeconomic Dynamics 14 (4), 454–481.

Beauchamp, Jonathan, Cesarini, David, Johannesson, Magnus, 2011. The Psychometric Properties of Measures of Economic Risk Preferences. Unpublished Manuscript, Harvard University.

Becker, Gary S., Mulligan, Casey B., 1997. The endogenous determination of time preference. Quarterly Journal of Economics 112 (3), 729–758.

Becker, Sascha, Woessmann, Ludger, 2009. Was Weber wrong? A human capital theory of protestant economic history. Quarterly Journal of Economics 124 (2), 531–596.

Bisin, Alberto, Verdier, Thierry, 2001. The economics of cultural transmission and the dynamics of preferences. Journal of Economic Theory 97 (2), 298–319.

Botticini, Maristella, Eckstein, Zvi, 2005. Jewish occupational selection: education, restrictions, or minorities? Journal of Economic History 65 (4), 922–948.

Botticini, Maristella, Eckstein, Zvi, 2006. Path dependence and occupations. In: Durlauf, Steven N., Blume, Lawrence (Eds.), New Palgrave Dictionary of Economics, Palgrave Macmillan, New York.

Botticini, Maristella, Eckstein, Zvi, 2007. From farmers to merchants, voluntary conversions and diaspora: a human capital interpretation of jewish history. Journal of the European Economic Association 5 (5), 885–926.

Bowles, Samuel, Gintis, Howard, 2002. The inheritence of inequality. Journal of Economic Perspectives 16 (3), 3–30.

Bruegger, Beatrice, Lalive, Rafael, Zweimueller, Josef, 2009. Does Culture Affect Unemployment? Evidence from the Roestigraben. CESifo Working Paper Series No 2714.

Carneiro, Pedro, Heckman, James J., 2003. Human capital policy. In: Heckman, James J., Krueger, Alan B. (Eds.), Inequality in America: What Role for Human Capital Policies. MIT Press, Cambridge, pp. 77–240.

Carroll, Christopher D., Summers, Lawrence H., 1991. Consumption growth parallels income growth: some new evidence. In: Bernheim, B. Douglas, Shaven, John B. (Eds.), National Saving and Economic Performance. University of Chicago Press, Chicago, pp. 305–343.

Cavalcanti, Tiago V., Parente, Stephen L., Zhao, Rui, 2007. Religion in macroeconomics: a quantitative analysis of Weber's thesis. Economic Theory 32 (1), 105–123.

Cavalli-Sforza, Luigi Luca, Feldman, Marcus W., 1981. Cultural Transmission and Evolution: A Quantitative Approach. Princeton University Press.

Clark, Gregory, Hamilton, Gillian, 2006. Survival of the richest: the malthusian mechanism in pre-industrial England. Journal of Economic History 66 (3), 707–736.

Coen-Pirani, Daniele, 2004. Effects of differences in risk aversion on the distribution of wealth. Macroeconomic Dynamics 8 (5), 617–632.

Cozzi, Marco, 2011. Risk Aversion Heterogeneity, Risky Jobs and Wealth Inequality. Unpublished Manuscript, Queen's University.

Cramer, J.S., Hartog, Joop, Jonker, Nicole, van Praag, C.M., 2002. Low risk aversion encourages the choice for entrepreneurship: an empirical test of a truism. Journal of Economic Behavior and Organization 48 (1), 29–36.

De Nardi, Mariacristina, 2004. Wealth inequality and intergenerational links. Review of Economic Studies 71 (3), 743–768.

Doepke, Matthias, Tertilt, Michèle, 2009. Women's liberation: what's in it for men? Quarterly Journal of Economics 124 (4), 1541–1591.

Doepke, Matthias, Tertilt, Michèle, Voena, Alessandra, 2012. The economics and politics of women's rights. Annual Review of Economics 4, 339–372.

Doepke, Matthias, Zilibotti, Fabrizio, 2005. Social class and the spirit of capitalism. Journal of the European Economic Association 3 (2–3), 516–524.

Doepke, Matthias, Zilibotti, Fabrizio, 2008. Occupational choice and the spirit of capitalism. Quarterly Journal of Economics 123 (2), 747–793.

Doepke, Matthias, Zilibotti, Fabrizio, 2012. Parenting with Style: Altruism and Paternalism in Intergenerational Preference Transmission. IZA Discussion Paper 7108.

Dohmen, Thomas, Falk, Armin, Huffman, David, Sunde, Uwe, 2012. The intergenerational transmission of risk and trust attitudes. Review of Economic Studies 79 (2), 645–677.

Fehr, Ernst, Hoff, Karla, 2011. Introduction: tastes, castes and culture: the influence of society on preferences. The Economic Journal 121 (556), F396–F412.

Fernández, Raquel, 2013. Cultural change as learning: the evolution of female labor force participation over a century. American Economic Review 103 (1), 472–500.

Fernández, Raquel, Fogli, Alessandra, 2006. Fertility: the role of culture and family experience. Journal of the European Economic Association 4 (2–3), 552–561.

Fernández, Raquel, Fogli, Alessandra, 2009. Culture: an empirical investigation of beliefs, work, and fertility. American Economic Journal: Macroeconomics 1 (1), 147–177.

Fernández, Raquel, Fogli, Alessandra, Olivetti, Claudia, 2004. Mothers and sons: preference formation and female labor force dynamics. Quarterly Journal of Economics 119 (4), 1249–1299.

Fernández-Villaverde, Jesús, Greenwood, Jeremy, Guner, Nezih, 2010. From shame to game in one hundred years: an economic model of the rise in premarital sex and its de-stigmatization. Journal of the European Economic Association 11.

Fisman, Raymond, Miguel, Edward, 2007. Corruption, norms and legal enforcement: evidence from diplomatic parking tickets. Journal of Political Economy 115 (6), 1020–1048.

Fogli, Alessandra, Veldkamp, Laura, 2011. Nature or nurture? Learning and the geography of female labor force participation. Econometrica 79 (4), 1103–1138.

Galor, Oded, Michalopoulos, Stelios, 2012. Evolution and the growth process: natural selection of entrepreneurial traits. Journal of Economic Theory 147 (2), 759–780.

Galor, Oded, Moav, Omer, 2002. Natural selection and the origin of economic growth. Quarterly Journal of Economics 117 (4), 1133–1191.

Giuliano, Paola, 2007. Living arrangements in western europe: does cultural origin matter? Journal of the European Economic Association 5 (5), 927–952.

Gorodnichenko, Yuriy, Roland, Gerard. 2010. Culture, Institutions and the Wealth of Nations. NBER Working Paper 16368.

Gradstein, Mark, 2007. Endogenous Reversals of Fortune. Unpublished Manuscript, Ben Gurion University.

Greif, Avner, 1994. Cultural beliefs and the organization of society: a historical and theoretical reflection on collectivist and individualist societies. Journal of Political Economy 102 (5), 912–950.

Grosjean, Pauline, 2013. A history of violence: the culture of honor and homicide in the US south. Journal of the European Economic Association.

Guiso, Luigi, Paiella, Monica, 2008. Risk aversion, wealth, and background risk. Journal of the European Economic Association 6 (6), 1109–1150.

Guiso, Luigi, Sapienza, Paola, Zingales, Luigi, 2003. People's opium? Religion and economic attitudes. Journal of Monetary Economics 50 (1), 225–282.

Guiso, Luigi, Sapienza, Paola, Zingales, Luigi, 2006. Does culture affect economic outcomes? Journal of Economic Perspectives 20 (2), 23–49.

Guvenen, Fatih, 2006. Reconciling conflicting evidence on the elasticity of intertemporal substitution: a macroeconomic perspective. Journal of Monetary Economics 53 (7), 1451–1472.

Haaparanta, Pertti, Puhakka, Mikko, 2004. Endogenous Time Preference, Investment and Development Traps. BOFIT Discussion Paper No. 4/2004, Bank of Finland.

Harbaugh, William T., Krause, Kate, Vesterlund, Lise, 2002. Risk attitudes of children and adults: choices over small and large probability gains and losses. Experimental Economics 5 (1), 53–84.

Harrison, Glenn W., Lau, Morten I., Williams, Melonie B., 2002. Estimating individual discount rates in Denmark: a field experiment. American Economic Review 92 (5), 1606–1617.

Hassler, John, Rodriguez, Jose V., Mora, Kjetil Storesletten, Zilibotti, Fabrizio, 2005. A positive theory of geographic mobility and social insurance. International Economic Review 46 (1), 263–303.

Hauk, Esther, Saez-Marti, Maria, 2002. On the cultural transmission of corruption. Journal of Economic Theory 107 (2), 311–335.

Heckman, James J., 2000. Policies to foster human capital. Research in Economics 54 (1), 3–56.

Heckman, James J., Stixrud, Jora, Urzua, Sergio, 2006. The effects of cognitive and noncognitive abilities on labor market outcomes and social behavior. Journal of Labor Economics 24 (3), 411–482.

Hendricks, Lutz, 2007. How important is discount rate heterogeneity for wealth inequality? Journal of Economic Dynamics and Control 31 (9), 3042–3068.

Inglehart, Ronals, Bashkirova, Elena, Basanez, Miguel, Chiu, Hei-yuan, Diez-Nicolas, Juan, Esmer, Yilmaz, Halman, Loek, Klingemann, Hans-Dieter, Nwabuzor, Elone, Petterson, Thorleif, Siemienska, Renata, Yamazaki, Seiko, 2000. World Values Surveys and European Values Surveys, 1981-1984, 1990-1993 and 1995-1997. Inter-university Consortium for Political and Social Research ICPSR 2790.

Kan, Kamhon, Tsai, Wei-Der, 2006. Entrepreneurship and risk aversion. Small Business Economics 26, 465–474.

Kihlstrom, Richard E., Laffont, Jean-Jacques, 1979. A general equilibrium entrepreneurial theory of firm formation based on risk aversion. Journal of Political Economy 87 (4), 719–748.

Klasing, Mariko J., 2012. Cultural Change, Risk-Taking Behavior, and the Course of Economic Development. Unpublished Manuscript, Carleton University.

Klasing, Mariko J., Milionis, Petros, 2013. Cultural constraints on innovation-based growth. Economic Inquiry.

Knight, Frank H., 1921. Risk, Uncertainty, and Profit. Houghton Mifflin, Boston and New York.

Knowles, John A., Postlewaite, Andrew, 2004. Do Children Learn to Save from Their Parents? Unpublished Manuscript, University of Pennsylvania.

Krusell, Per, Smith Jr., Anthony A., 1998. Income and wealth heterogeneity in the macroeconomy. Journal of Political Economy 106 (5), 867–896.

Lindbeck, Assar, Nyberg, Sten, 2006. Raising children to work hard: altruism, work norms, and social insurance. Quarterly Journal of Economics 121 (4), 1473–503.

Matsuyama, Kiminori, 1999. Growing through cycles. Econometrica 67 (2), 335–347.

Michau, Jean-Baptiste, 2013. Unemployment insurance and cultural transmission: theory and application to European unemployment. Journal of the European Economic Association 11 (5).

Mischel, Walter, Yuichi Shoda, Monica L. Rodriguez. 1992. Delay of gratification in children. In: Loewenstein, George, Elster, Jon (Eds.), Chapter 6 of Choice Over Time. Russell Sage Foundation, New York.

Mokyr, Joel, 2011. Cultural Entrepreneurs and Economic Development. Unpublished Manuscript, Ben-Gurion University.

Mulligan, Casey B., 1997. Parental Priorities and Economic Inequality. University of Chicago Press.

Piketty, Thomas, 1995. Social mobility and redistributive politics. Quarterly Journal of Economics 110, 551–584.

Reyes-Garcia, Victoria, Godoy, Ricardo, Huanca, Tomas, Leonard, William R., McDade, Thomas, Tanner, Susan, Vadez, Vencent, 2007. The origin of monetary income inequality: patience, human capital, and the division of labor. Evolution and Human Behavior 28, 37–47.

Richerson, Peter J., Boyd, Robert, 2005. Not by Genes Alone. The University of Chicago Press.

Rohner, Dominic, Thoenig, Mathias, Zilibotti, Fabrizio, 2012. Seeds of Distrust: Conflict in Uganda. CEPR Discussion Paper No. 8741.

Rohner, Dominic, Thoenig, Mathias, Zilibotti, Fabrizio. 2013. War signals: a theory of trade, trust and conflict. Review of Economic Studies 80 (3), 1114–1147.

Romer, Paul M. 1990. Endogenous technological change. Journal of Political Economy 98 (5, Part 2), S71–S102.

Saez-Marti, Maria, Sjoegren, Anna, 2008. Peers and culture. Scandinavian Journal of Economics 110, 73–92.

Saez-Marti, Maria, Zenou, Yves, 2011. Cultural transmission and discrimination. Journal of Urban Economics 72 (2–3), 137–146.

Saez-Marti, Maria, Zilibotti, Fabrizio, 2008. Preferences as human capital: rational choice theories of endogenous preferences and socioeconomic changes. Finnish Economic Papers 21 (2), 81–94.

Schumpeter, Joseph A., 1942. Capitalism, Socialism, and Democracy. Harper, New York.

Segal, Carmit, 2013. Misbehavior, Education, and labor market outcomes. Journal of the European Economic Association 11 (4), 743–779.

Shonkoff, Jack, Philips, Deborah (Eds.), 2000. From Neurons to Neighborhoods: The Science of Early Childhood Development. National Academy Press, Washington, D.C.

Smith, Adam, 1776. An inquiry into the nature and causes of the wealth of nations. In: Cannan, Edwin (Eds.), The University of Chicago Press, Chicago (published 1976).

Song, Zheng, Storesletten, Kjetil, Zilibotti, Fabrizio, 2012. Rotten parents and disciplined children: a politico-economic theory of public expenditure and debt. Econometrica 80 (6), 2785–2803.

Stigler, George J., Becker, Gary S., 1977. De Gustibus Non Est Disputandum. American Economic Review 67 (2), 76–90.

Stokey, Nancy L., Lucas Jr., Robert E., 1989. Recursive Methods in Economic Dynamics. Harvard University Press, Cambridge.

Sutter, Matthias, Kocher, Martin G., Glaetze-Ruetzler, Daniela, Trautmann, Stefan T., 2013. Impatience and uncertainty: experimental decisions predict adolescents field behavior. American Economic Review 103 (1), 510–531.

Tabellini, Guido, 2008. The scope of cooperation: norms and incentives. The Quarterly Journal of Economics 123 (3), 905–950.

Tabellini, Guido, 2010. Culture and institutions: economic development in the regions of Europe. Journal of the European Economic Association 8 (4), 677–716.

Taylor, J., McGue, M., Iacono, W.G., 2000. Sex differences, assortative mating, and cultural transmission effects on adolescent delinquency: a twin family study. Journal of Child Psychology and Psychiatry 41 (4), 433–440.

van Praag, C.M., Cramer, J.S., 2001. The roots of entrepreneurship and labour demand: individual ability and low risk aversion. Economica 68 (269), 45–62.

Vereshchagina, Galina, Hopenhayn, Hugo A., 2009. Risk taking by entrepreneurs. American Economic Review 99 (5), 1808–1830.

Voigtlaender, Nico, Voth, Hans-Joachim, 2012. Persecution perpetuated: the medieval origins of anti-semitic violence in Nazi Germany. Quarterly Journal of Economics 127 (2), 1339–1392.

Voors, Maarten J., Eleonora, E.M., Nillesen, Philip Verwimp, Bulte, Erwin H., Lensink, Robert, Van Soest, Daan P., 2012. Violent conflict and behavior: a field experiment in burundi. American Economic Review 102 (2), 941–964.

Weber, Max, 1905. The Protestant Ethic and the Spirit of Capitalism. (Translated by Talcott Parsons); with a foreword by R. H. Tawney. Charles Scribner's Sons, New York, 1958. Republished by Dover, New York, 2003.

Zumbuehl, Maria, Dohmen, Thomas, Pfann, Gerard, 2013. Parental investment and the intergenerational transmission of economic preferences and attitudes. Unpublished Manuscript, University of Bonn.

CHAPTER TWO

# Trust, Growth, and Well-Being: New Evidence and Policy Implications

Yann Algan[*] and Pierre Cahuc[†]

[*]Sciences Po, France
[†]ENSAE-CREST, Ecole Polytechnique, France

## Abstract

This survey reviews the recent research on trust, institutions, and economic development. It discusses the various measures of trust and documents the substantial heterogeneity of trust across space and time. The conceptual mechanisms that explain the influence of trust on economic performance and the methods employed to identify the causal impact of trust on economic performance are reviewed. We document the mechanisms of interactions between trust and economic development in the realms of finance, innovation, the organization of firms, the labor market, and the product market. The last part reviews recent progress to identify how institutions and policies can affect trust.

## Keywords

Trust, Growth, Economic development, Institutions

## JEL Classification Codes

O11, O43, Z13

*There are countries in Europe ... where the most serious impediment to conducting business concerns on a large scale, is the rarity of persons who are supposed fit to be trusted with the receipt and expenditure of large sums of money.*

*(Mill, 1848, p. 132)*

## 2.1. INTRODUCTION

The debate about the roots of economic development and the origins of income inequality across the globe has deeply evolved over time. Early researches focused on the proximate factors of growth, stressing the role of technological progress and the accumulation of human and physical capital. A decade ago, the focus shifted to the role of formal institutions, considered as the endogenous incentives to accumulate and innovate (Acemoglu et al. 2001); and to what extent those institutions could be distinguished from factors like human capital (Glaeser et al. 2004). More recently, the attention has been gradually evolving toward deeper factors, ingrained in culture or long-term history.

*Handbook of Economic Growth*, Volume 2A
ISSN 1574-0684, http://dx.doi.org/10.1016/B978-0-444-53538-2.00002-2

This survey reviews some strands of the recent research on the role of cultural values in economic development (see Nunn, 2009; Spolaore and Wacziarg, 2013 for surveys on long-term history). In particular, we investigate the role of one of the most fundamental cultural values that could explain economic development: trust. Since the path breaking work of Banfield (1958), Coleman (1990), and Putnam (2000), trust, broadly defined as cooperative attitude outside the family circle, was considered as a key element of many economic and social outcomes by social scientists. Yet, while praised in other social sciences, the role of trust in the mainstream economic literature has long been disputed.

The potential role of trust in economic development had naturally attracted some interest decades ago, no doubt for the reason stated by Arrow (1972): "virtually every commercial transaction has within itself an element of trust, certainly any transaction conducted over a period of time. It can be plausibly argued that much of the economic backwardness in the world can be explained by the lack of mutual confidence." Arrow's intuition was straightforward. In a complex society, it is impossible to write down and enforce detailed contracts that encompass all the states of nature for economic exchanges. Ultimately, in the absence of informal rules like trusting behavior, markets are missing, gains from economic exchanges are forgone, and resources are misallocated. To that respect, trust and the informal rules shaping cooperation could explain differences in economic development.

But the theoretical and empirical foundations of the relationship between trust and growth have long been considered as weak, at best. A good illustration of the state of the art one decade ago is given by the former issue of the Handbook of Economic Growth in 2005. In the chapter devoted to social capital, Durlauf and Fafchamps (2005) outlined powerfully all the conceptual and statistical flaws raised by the notion of trust in the economic literature. The concept of social capital, a buzzword according to Solow, raised a lot of ambiguity by encompassing vague concepts as norms, networks, or cooperation. Besides, the authors documented forcefully the identification issued raised by the few cross-country or cross-regional correlations between social capital and growth (see also Durlauf for a critical assessment of the empirical literature on social capital, 2002).

In this chapter, we show that decisive and substantial progress has been made on the different dimensions that give trust a central role in mainstream economics, and more importantly, for explaining economic development. This chapter has five main goals. First, we outline a unified conceptual framework for thinking about how trust and cooperation can increase economic efficiency. We distinguish the specific role of trust, relative to reputation incentives, to overcome market failures. Second, we review the various methods to measure trust and cooperation empirically. The recent development of experimental economics, combined with an increasing number of social surveys, has helped to clarify what trust is and how it differs from other beliefs and preferences. Third, we document the empirical relationship between trust, income per capita, and growth. We review the recent advances to identify a causal impact of trust on economic outcomes. Recent empirical work confirms what Arrow posited: trust does indeed appear to constitute a decisive determinant of growth. This observation is buttressed at present by a range of contributions that not only have shed light on the correlations between these two variables, but have also elaborated strategies for detecting the ways in which trust may affect growth. Fourth, we review the burgeoning literature that focuses on the channels of influence of trust: from financial, product, and labor markets to innovation and the organization of firms. Finally, we document more recent research looking at how institutions and trust co-evolve, and how public policy could boost pro-social behaviors.

Several surveys to date have analyzed the role of social capital and trust in economics (see Guiso et al. 2008b, 2011; Tabellini, 2008a; Fehr, 2009; Bowles and Polania-Reyes, 2012, among others). The present addition to the literature is specific in three ways. First, we focus on the relations between trust, growth, and institutions and we utilize the most recent assemblages of data on values, which allow us to cover more than 90% of the world population. Second, we take full account of the progress made during the last decade in identifying the impact of trust, or inherited trust, by deploying as instruments, events of an essentially historical kind. Recent research allows us to pinpoint more closely the mechanisms by which transmission of trust affects the economy, and to distinguish its various channels. Lastly, we present a synthesis of research on how political and economic institutions interact with trust. We also review the various factors and policies that have been found to affect trust, such as the transparency of institutions, the extent of inequality or education, and early childhood intervention.

The remainder of the chapter is organized as follows. The first part outlines the theoretical mechanisms that explain the influence of trust on economic performance. The second part discusses the various measures of trust and documents the international and interregional heterogeneity of trust, using surveys that furnish rich sets of data going back to the start of the 1980s. The third part is a presentation of the dynamics of trust, stressing that in general it evolves slowly from one generation to the next. This inertia, which may nevertheless be perturbed by major historical events such as wars, is observable both at the individual level and at the macro-social level. Part four presents the methods employed to identify the causal impact of trust and provides an empirical illustration of the relation between trust and economic development. Part five describes the mechanisms by which trust has an impact on growth. Part six analyzes the interaction of trust with formal institutions and policies and discusses how trust can be built. And, part seven concludes this chapter by discussing the new perspectives provided by recent research showing that well-being depends not only on income but also, and foremost, on the quality of social relationships.

## 2.2. THEORETICAL FOUNDATIONS

We begin by providing a conceptual framework that rationalizes the relationship between trust and economic performance. We then document the theoretical channels through which trust interacts with the institutional environment and can emerge as a stable equilibrium.

For trust to have an economic impact and to improve efficiency, one has first to consider the reasons why the economy would depart from the first-best allocation in absence of trust. In his analysis of the limits of organization, Arrow (1972) considers trust as co-substantial to economic exchange in the presence of transaction costs that impede information and contracts. Fundamentally, the economic efficiency of trust flows from the fact that it favors cooperative behavior and thus facilitates mutually advantageous exchanges in presence of incomplete contracts and imperfect information. In Arrow's terms, trust would act as a lubricant to economic exchange in a second-best allocation.

This remark raises various questions. How can we rationalize the impact of trust on economic exchange? How can trust emerge and be sustained in economic exchanges? Why should we expect trust rather than institutions to overcome these market imperfections?

To address those issues, we start from a simple example inspired from the trust game of Berg et al. (1995), where each participant is an investor. We show that cooperation cannot emerge in absence of reputation, which is at odds with the insights of behavioral economics, which documents that individuals do often cooperate with anonymous others in a one-shot exchange. It is thus necessary to include trust as an additional characteristic to rationalize cooperation. We then discuss how trust evolves and is transmitted to become a stable equilibrium. We also document the interaction between trust and institutions to explain economic exchanges.

### 2.2.1 Cooperation and Reputation

Let us consider two individuals, both of whom are free to invest—or not—an irrecoverable sum $I > 0$ that will enable them to produce jointly. Only by mutual agreement do they invest. Once they do, the incompleteness of contracts, arising out of the complexity of the association which makes it impossible for a third party to verify that everything promised is performed, gives each player the chance to profit from the association at the expense of the other. Hence, each player has the option of investing or not at the outset, and of cooperating or defecting subsequently. Production is positive only if the two individuals invest. If the two players cooperate, their investment yields production amounting to $2(Y + I) > 0$, divided into equal shares such that each obtains a gain, net of the cost of the investment, amounting to $Y > 0$. If neither cooperates, production is zero and the sum each invested is entirely forfeited. Finally, if one cooperates while the other defects, the one who defects preempts the production to his advantage and obtains a net gain of $2Y + I$, while the one who cooperated forfeits his initial investment entirely. The gains are represented in Table 2.1. The Nash equilibrium of this game is an absence of cooperation entailing that the players have no interest in participating, since the anticipated gains are

**Table 2.1** Payoff matrix

| P1/P2 | Cooperation | Defection |
|-------|-------------|-----------|
| Cooperation | $(Y, Y)$ | $(-I, 2Y + I)$ |
| Defection | $(2Y + I, -I)$ | $(-I, -I)$ |

*Notes:* This table shows the payoff matrix of the prisoner's dilemma game. Player 1 chooses row strategies, Player 2 plays columns.

systematically negative. This model illustrates the fact that the absence of cooperation may prevent mutually advantageous exchanges from coming about.

The possibilities of cooperation arising between individuals interacting in this type of game have been explored through random matching games based on purely rational individuals encountering one another at random (Kandori, 1992; Ellison, 1994). The horizon of these random matching games is infinite: in each interval each player takes part in a prisoner's dilemma game with a fresh partner drawn at random from the population. Anonymity is retained to the horizon of the game. It is demonstrable that cooperative solutions can emerge as subgame perfect equilibria if the population and the players' preferences for the present are sufficiently small. Equilibrium strategies consist of no longer cooperating, or of cooperating less often, in all future encounters, once a player has participated in a game in which cooperation was chosen by neither partner. It is the threat of a future surge of non-cooperative behavior that may act as an incentive to cooperation at each interval. These results tell us that the spontaneous emergence of cooperative behavior in populations of large size is improbable if each individual is a pure *homo economicus* and they all interact anonymously.

In this setting, cooperation can only emerge as a reputation device and in the presence of punishment. Greif (1993, 1994), in his analysis of the Maghribi and Geneose traders, has shown that the transmission of information, and the coordinated implementation of strategies intended to punish those caught defecting, might facilitate cooperation. Cooperation may exist in the absence of any formal institution defining legal rules if the size of the population and the preference for the present are sufficiently small. If these conditions are unmet, however, formal institutions explicitly laying down legal rules and sanctions are needed in order to sustain cooperation.

The value of such analyses is that they illuminate the role of coordination and of formal institutions. But they cannot account for the cooperative behavior often experimentally observed to arise in anonymous, non-repetitive games. In particular, Henrich et al. (2001) showed that individuals from various societies display cooperation in games absent of any reputational considerations (see the synthesis of Fehr, 2009; Bowles and Gintis, 2007).

## 2.2.2 Cooperation and Other-Regarding Preferences

To rationalize the existence of cooperation in absence of reputation, the economic literature has incorporated the insights from research in psychology, social science, and behavioral economics, showing the existence of an intrinsic motivation linked to cooperation (see the synthesis by Bowles and Polania-Reyes, 2012; Kahneman and Tversky, 2000). Individuals are motivated by more than material payoffs and value the act of cooperating per se. They have "warm glow preferences" or concerns for reciprocity that favor cooperation.

To modelize this behavior, Francois and Zabojnik (2005), Tabellini (2008b), Algan and Cahuc (2009), Bidner and Francois (2011), Michau (2012), and others, suppose that from non-cooperation there may flow psychological costs. A variant consists of supposing a preference for reciprocity: individuals are altruistic with others who display cooperative behavior, but may sanction those who do not respect cooperative norms (Fehr and Schimdt, 1999; Fehr and Gatcher, 2000; Gintis et al. 2005; Hoff et al. 2011). In all these settings, individuals are assumed to have other-regarding preferences and not just self-regarding preferences, which allow cooperation to emerge in large, anonymous groups.

On the assumption that psychological costs from non cooperation exist, we can modify the payoffs of the trust game described above by adding a cost for non cooperation. In this setting, cooperation becomes a Nash equilibrium, in the previous game described by the payoff matrix above, if the costs from non cooperating, denoted $C$, are superior to the net individual gain from non cooperation $Y + I$. The term $C$ may be influenced by social and cultural norms, by education, or by the social distance between individuals. For example, Tabellini (2008b) assumes that the psychological costs from non cooperation decrease with social distance: all those sufficiently close cooperate among themselves, but they adopt non-cooperative strategies with those more distant. This assumption is consistent with evidence that individuals tend to distrust more those who are dissimilar to themselves (see Alesina and La Ferrara, 2002).

In this setting, to trust another individual at any one iteration is to embrace the belief that the others taking part in the game are choosing cooperation; that they are, in other words, trustworthy. It is possible to analyze the role of trust in a random matching game where a portion of the population is trustworthy. The trustworthy persons cooperate systematically. Each person knows whether he himself is trustworthy or untrustworthy, but this private information is not available to the others. When two persons meet up, they may decide to go ahead and invest, or pass on the opportunity, in which case they get a payoff equal to zero. If they do go ahead, the trustworthy partners systematically cooperate since not to do so is too costly for them. Conversely, the untrustworthy and purely opportunistic persons always choose to defect.

This modified game can rationalize the existence of cooperation, that is trust, as a Nash-equilibrium. To demonstrate, let us denote by $s$ the portion of trustworthy persons in the population. The expected gain of a trustworthy person who invests amounts to $sY - (1 - s)I$, which implies that such persons invest if the trustworthy portion of the population is superior to $s > I/(Y + I)$. If this condition is unmet, no one has a reason to invest, as all persons who do want to go ahead and invest are necessarily untrustworthy. There are in consequence two possible equilibria depending on the values of $s$. Either no one invests, if $s < I/(Y + I)$, or in the other eventuality, everyone does. Investment, production, and exchange thus increase with the portion of trustworthy persons in the population, and consequently with trust in others.

Assuming that trust emerges because certain persons are spontaneously cooperative has the advantage of explaining with simplicity why it is that cooperation may arise out of anonymous, non-repetitive interactions. This explanation provides a simple framework to analyze the determinants of trust and its role in the functioning of the economy.

## 2.2.3 Dynamics of Cooperation

How does cooperation evolve over time? How can cooperative values persist in certain environments and disappear in others? To address this issue, recent works endogenize the transmission of values, along with the seminal work of Bisin and Verdier (2001) stressing the role of family transmission. Parents may inculcate moral values into their children, but these child-rearing choices pose coordination problems, for being honest only pays if others are being honest too. The more other parents are inculcating moral values into their children that will render them trustworthy as adults, the better an option it becomes to raise your children that way too. Building on Hauk and Saez-Marti (2002), Francois and Zabojnik (2005), Tabellini (2008b), Aghion et al. (2010), and Bidner and Francois (2011), we show how such a mechanism might work by introducing education into our model.

Let us assume that the parents get psychological gains, denoted by $G > 0$, an expression of utility, for inculcating honesty-based values into their children and thus ensuring that, as adults, they will systematically be cooperative. In this context, trustworthy adults bear, as before, a psychological cost $C > Y + I$, when they behave dishonestly. Parents get the psychological gain only if their children do behave cooperatively, i.e. do invest. When children do not invest, or in other words, do not display their cooperative behavior, parents do not derive any gain from the values that have been inculcated.

Parents opt for values that maximize the expected utility of their offspring plus their utility gains obtained from inculcating honesty-based values, in the knowledge that each of those children will in turn be randomly encountering others and having to decide whether to go ahead and invest with them or not. The parents' payoff to inculcate honesty-based value equals $G + sY - (1-s)I$, if $s > I/(Y+I)$ and zero otherwise, since their children invest when adults only if $s > I/(Y + I)$. Parents who do not inculcate such values get $s(2Y + I) - (1-s)I$ if $s > I/(Y+I)$ and zero otherwise. The expected gains of education depend on the proportion of trustworthy persons in the generation of the children. It is optimal to bring your children up honestly if the offsetting gains are expected to be equal to or greater, i.e. if $G > s(Y + I)$ and $s > I/(Y + I)$. If this condition is not fulfilled, parents have no incentives to inculcate honesty-based values into children. There will thus be no investment: an economy populated with persons rendered untrustworthy by their upbringing will arrive at a "bad" and feebly productive equilibrium. On the other hand, if one is convinced that the upbringing the other children are receiving from their parents is honesty-based, there may be utility in bringing one's own up the same way. In this case, the economy arrives at a "good" equilibrium, with trustworthy persons and augmented investment and production.

The array of equilibria arrived at in the models of Francois and Zabojnik (2005), Tabellini (2008b), Aghion et al. (2010), and Bidner and Francois (2011) highlights the fragility of the mutual confidence that flows from settling at a good equilibrium. This approach also brings into focus the interaction between moral values and institutions. For example, Aghion et al. (2010) assume that a government elected by majority vote may lay down regulations meant to facilitate mutually advantageous exchange, for the purpose of countering the low levels of spontaneous cooperation that are a concomitant of populations with a relatively small proportion of trustworthy persons in their midst. But these regulations give rise to significant corruption precisely because the proportion of trustworthy persons is small, which keeps distrust alive. Distrust and corruption nourish each other and lead to bad equilibria characterized by weak production and highly burdensome regulation.

Let us enrich this perspective by introducing a dynamic dimension. Let us assume that the gains from inculcating honesty-based values increase as the proportion of trustworthy parents rises. This might be because children are influenced not only by the upbringing they received from their parents, but also by that received from others encountered outside the family circle. Cavalli-Sforza and Feldman (1981) distinguish three modes in which values may be imparted: vertical, oblique, and horizontal. The vertical mode corresponds to transmission from parents to children. The transmission is oblique when the influence comes from adults other than the parents. Horizontal transmission is what those of the same generation have in common. Guiso et al. (2008b) set forth a model that represents several simultaneous modes of transmission, assuming that parents impart beliefs to their children as to the trustworthiness of others, and that children revise this belief set as a function of those whom they encounter. The economy may then be stuck in a bad equilibrium without production, if the beliefs imparted by the parents are too pessimistic, for mutual distrust may impede all exchange (in the game above: everyone passes on the opportunity to invest), and thus stifle all possibility of testing and revising inherited beliefs. Such dynamic sequences have the merit of accounting for the intergenerational transmission of trust empirically observed (Dohmen et al. 2012). They may also explain not only the persistent effect of trust-destroying shocks like the onset of the slave trade in west Africa (Nunn and Wantchekon, 2011), bad colonial institutions (Acemoglu et al. 2001), and legal origins (La Porta et al. 2008), but also the persistent effects of positive shocks like the presence of participatory institutions in the free communes of the Italian Middle Ages (Putnam et al. 1993; Guiso et al. 2008a).

## 2.3. EMPIRICAL MEASURES OF TRUST

To measure the impact of cooperative values on economic development and institutions, one has to define the empirical counterpart of the trusting behavior at play in the previous theoretical games.

### 2.3.1 Definition of Trust

Research on the relationship between trust and growth focuses essentially on generalized trust, in other words, on relations among individuals who are not bound by the kind of personal ties that bind members of the same family, or fellow workers. In this context, the generally used definition of trust is taken from Coleman (1990), according to whom "an individual trusts if he or she voluntary places resources at the disposal of another party without any legal commitment from the latter, but with the expectation that the act of trust will pay off." One of the advantages of this approach is to define trust as a behavior that can be directly measured with experimental games, as shown by Fehr (2009). Defined this way, trust is also linked to the notion of social capital utilized by Fukuyama (1995), Putnam (2000), and Guiso et al. (2011), for whom social capital is the ensemble of "those persistent and shared beliefs and values that help a group overcome the free rider problem in the pursuit of socially valuable activities."

### 2.3.2 Measures of Trust

Trust can be measured by using surveys and laboratory experiments. Empirical research investigating the link between growth and trust usually draws on answers from survey questions. The reason for this is the availability of surveys, which cover a large number of countries since the beginning of the 1980s. Nevertheless, these surveys evoke difficulties in interpretation. Besides the polysemy of questions and responses, it is not sure that the individuals who declare to have strong trust in others actually behave in a more cooperative way. For that reason, researchers have undertaken laboratory experiments as well as field experiment paired with surveys, in order to better capture their scope.

#### 2.3.2.1 Surveys

In surveys, the measure of trust is most often measured with the "generalized trust question" first introduced by Almond and Verba (1963) in their study of civil society in post-war Europe. This question runs as follows: "Generally speaking, would you say that most people can be trusted, or that you can't be too careful when dealing with others?" Possible answers are "Most people can be trusted" or "Need to be very careful." The same question is used in the European Social Survey, the General Social Survey, the World Values Survey, Latinobarómetro, and the Australian Community Survey. Surveys generally include other questions related to trust. For instance, the WVS asks the "fair question": "Do you think most people would try to take advantage of you if they got the chance, or would they try to be fair?" The GSS includes the trust question, the fair question, and adds the "help question": Would you say that most of the time people try to be helpful, or that they are mostly just looking out for themselves? These different questions are sometimes used to build indexes that intend to provide alternative measures of trust or get an average indicator of moral values or civic capital (Tabellini, 2010; Guiso et al. 2011).

The resulting survey data supply us with subjective information that certainly demands cautious interpretation. These questions raise concerns about interpretation. In particular, individuals who respond that you need to be very careful to the trust question could be motivated by a strong aversion against risk (see for these topics, Fehr, 2009; Bohnet and Zeckhauser, 2004). However, most important for investigating empirically the relation between growth and trust is to know whether the responses to the trust question are linked to actual cooperative behavior.

### 2.3.2.2 Experimental Games in the Lab

Contributions have analyzed the relationship between responses to the trust questions or to connected questions and the behavior in experimental games. In general, these works use variants of the "investment game," known also as the "trust game," of Berg et al. (1995) presented above. In laboratory experiments, this game is played as follows. In stage 1, the subjects in rooms A and B are each given 10 dollars as a show-up fee. While subjects in room B pocket their show-up fee, subjects in room A must decide how much of their 10 dollars to send to an anonymous counterpart in room B. The amount sent, denoted by $M$, is tripled resulting in a total return $3M$. In stage 2, a counterpart in room B is given the tripled money and must decide how much to return. One measures "trust in others", as defined by Coleman (1990), by the amount sent initially by the sender. Trustworthiness is measured by the amount sent back by the player in room B.

The first contributions that analyzed the relationship between survey-answer from the generalized trust question and the amount sent in the trust game found mixed results. Glaeser et al. (2000) measured the relation between questions related to trust in surveys and the behavior of participants in trust games. This study was carried out at Harvard University, where 274 students were asked the trust question before they played the trust game either in the role of sender or receiver. The authors find that although questions about trusting attitudes do not predict trusting behavior, such questions do appear to predict trustworthiness. Holm and Danielson (2005) find a positive correlation between behavior in games and answers to the trust question in Sweden, but not in Tanzania. Lazzarini et al. (2005) find a correlation in face-to-face, non-anonymous trust games in Brazil. Other experiments have been run on representative surveys, with also contrasting results. While Fehr et al. (2002) find that the trust question does predict trusting behavior but not trustworthiness, Ermisch et al. (2009) find exactly the opposite on a representative sample of the British population.

These results are difficult to compare, as the designs of the games are not perfectly identical between the different experiments. While in the game organized by Glaeser et al.

the second movers do not receive any initial payment, in the game of Berg et al. all participants get a show-up fee. This could explain, why a great fraction (70%) of first movers send all their initial endowment to the second movers, in the experiment of Glaeser et al. To measure the level of trust, it is therefore necessary to distinguish this component from other attitudes, such as risk aversion, altruism, and reciprocal behavior. In addition, does trusting behavior measured during those different experiments really capture deep-seated preferences? Or do they just relate to beliefs about the level of civility of others, which can be quickly revised?

This kind of behavior observed in experiments might be as much motivated by altruism as by trust, in the sense of the definition by Coleman. With regard to the positive correlation between the responses to the trust questions and the amounts sent back by the second mover, this correlation could be the consequence of a concern about reciprocity, characterizing the individuals who declare themselves to trust strongly. Thus, the absence of a correlation between the responses to the trust question and the amounts sent by the first movers in the study of Glaeser et al. does not necessarily imply that the trust questions are not correlated with trust in the sense of Coleman, because the amounts sent by the senders are probably strongly influenced by motivations of altruism.

Cox (2004) has proposed an experimental design with the goal of identifying the relative contributions of trust and altruism to the amounts sent in the first stage of the trust game. To achieve this, he compares the results of a trust game, as described above, with those of a dictator game, in which the only difference to the trust game is the absence of a decision by the second movers: thus, they do not have an opportunity to return any money that they receive. The dictator game serves to measure altruism, whereas trust is measured by the difference between the amount sent during the first stage of the trust game and the amount sent in the dictator game. The experiments conducted by Cox show that the trust motive in fact exists, in addition to altruism. The experimental design created by Cox also allows us to identify motives of reciprocity, by comparing the amounts returned in the second stage of the trust game with those sent in a game which differs from the trust game. Here too, the experiments realized by Cox shows the existence of reciprocity.

Cox's design allows us to distinguish between motives of altruism, trust, and reciprocity. Capra et al. (2008) used this design to analyze the relationship between those motives as defined above and attitudes gained from answers to survey questions, by conducting experiments with students from Emory University. They find the same results as Glaeser et al. concerning the trust question, that is, that the responses are not correlated with the amounts sent by the first movers, but with the amounts sent back by the second movers, who sent back more depending on how trusting in others they declared themselves to be in the survey.

However, this correlation disappears as soon as the level of altruism is controlled for. Besides, the amounts sent by the first movers are well correlated with the responses to the "help question" or the "fair question" when altruism is controlled for. Responses to the trust question are not correlated significantly with the amounts sent by the first movers, but the sign of the coefficient indicates an increasing relation between declared trust and the amounts sent. It is possible that the absence of a significant relation results from the low number of observations (62), which is especially problematic for the trust question, whose wording is particularly vague. In short, this contribution suggests an experimental design which distinguishes the motives of trust, altruism, and reciprocity, allowing to identify coherent relations between attitudes declared in answers to survey questions and actual behavior in trust games.

Other studies have also made use of neurobiological methods to measure, with greater precision, the role of trust in comparison with other individual characteristics in the behavior of participants of the trust game. It is known that oxytocin, a hormone released especially during breast-feeding and delivery, is associated with sentiments of affinity and socialization. In particular, research in neurobiology has shown that this hormone plays a central role in behavior related to social connectivity, such as parental and couple relations. Additionally, this hormone significantly reduces stress and anxiety in situations of social interaction. It is known for deactivating the transmission of feelings of anxiety related to the belief of being betrayed. Kosfeld et al. (2005) had the ingenious idea to evaluate the effect of oxytocin on pro-social behavior of individuals participating in trust games. The authors also proposed additional experimental designs to distinguish the pro-social preferences from risk-taking behavior and from beliefs like the level of optimism of the participants. The participants in this study were randomly allocated into two groups. The first group inhaled oxytocin through a spray, the second inhaled a placebo and served as the control group. The results of this experiment are illuminating. Those individuals who received oxytocin tended to display stronger trust behavior. What is even more remarkable, is that those individuals continued to behave trustingly in the exchange with the others, even if the latter didn't reciprocate. By contrast, other attitudes, such as prudence and risk-aversion, or even other beliefs such as optimism in the actions of the others, are not affected. Kosfeld et al. (2005) conclude that the trust game measures veritable preferences for cooperation, and not risk-aversion or anticipation of the others' actions (see Fehr, 2009, for a survey on experimental measures of trust).

### 2.3.2.3 Experimental Games in the Field

Obviously, the presence of a relationship between survey answers and behavior in trust games does not imply that answers to survey questions allow us to predict daily behavioral patterns, insofar as the latter can be different from those observed in laboratory experiments. We still know very little, however, about whether, and to what extent, the experimental results established in the laboratory carry over to field situations. At this stage, it thus seems key to investigate the relationship between the experimental measures usually elicited in the laboratory and the *field* outcomes of interest, if we are to rely on the experimental method to make inferences about the real world.

In his pioneering work, Karlan (2005) uses the trust game to obtain individual measures of taste for reciprocity, and shows that it can be used to predict loan repayment among participants, up to one year later, in a Peruvian microcredit program. Oliveira et al. (2009) elicited subjects' taste for cooperation in the laboratory using a traditional public goods game. They show that the results are correlated with subjects' contributions to local charities in a donation experiment and with whether they self-report contributing time and/or money to local charitable causes. Similarly, Laury and Taylor (2008) use public goods games to elicit their subjects' taste for cooperation and show that it is associated with the probability to contribute to a field public good in a donation experiment. One prominent limitation of these two studies is that they both obtain information about "field" behavior in the laboratory itself, either through contextualized experiments or self-reports. In this case, one might worry about possible spurious correlations caused by demand effects and/or individuals' willingness to remain self-consistent. Still relying on highly contextualized donation experiments, Benz and Meier (2008) address part of this concern by collecting field data about their subjects' behavior in a charitable giving situation prior to conducting a charitable giving experiment in the classroom, and obtain a significant correlation between both measures.

A promising avenue of research is to extend experimental games to online economics or wikinomics. In particular, the emergence of large organizations based on cooperation and non-monetary incentives, such as Wikipedia and open software, provide a perfect field experiment to test the relationship between experimental measures and field behavior.

In a recent contribution, Algan et al. (2012a) explore this question in one of the most successful contemporary instances of massive voluntary contributions to a public good: the online encyclopedia Wikipedia. Using an Internet-based experimental economics platform, the author elicited preferences for cooperation, altruism, and reciprocity among a sample of 850 Wikipedians directly in the field (i.e. online, in interaction with other Internet users who are not Wikipedia contributors) and related those measures to their real-world contribution records. They find that contributions to Wikipedia—as measured by subjects' number of edits to the encyclopedia—are related to their propensity to cooperate in a traditional public good game and to the level of reciprocity that they exhibit both in a conditional public good game and in a trust game. Moving from the position of a non-contributor with a registered Wikipedia account to that of an experienced Wikipedia contributor is associated with a 10–13% rise in public good contribution levels and with a 7–10% rise in reciprocity levels.

### 2.3.3 Correlation Between Generalized Trust and Limited Trust

We stressed that most of the research about the economic consequences of trust deals with generalized trust. But what is the relationship between the various forms of trust? Since the seminal work of Banfield (1958) and Coleman (1990), social scientists make a distinction between limited versus generalized morality. Societies with limited morality only promote codes of good conduct within small circles of related persons (kin), whereas selfish behavior is regarded as morally acceptable outside the small network. This behavior was famously described as "amoral familism" by Banfield (1958) in his ethnographic description of a rural village. Societies with generalized morality promote good conduct outside the small family/kin network, offering the possibility to identify oneself with a society of abstract individuals or abstract institutions. Coleman (1990) proposes a similar distinction between strong ties, defined as the quality of the relationship among family members, and weak ties, defined as the strength of social relationships outside the family circle.

Ermisch and Gambetta (2010), using trust games with a representative sample of the British population, find that people with strong family ties have a lower level of trust in strangers than people with weak family ties, and argue that this association is causal. They show that the explanation for this opposition comes from the level of outward exposure: factors that limit exposure, limit subjects' experience, as well as motivation to deal with strangers.

Greif and Tabellini (2010) provide an historical analysis of this opposition by comparing the bifurcation of societal organization between pre-modern China and medieval Europe. Pre-modern China sustained cooperation within the clan, e.g. a kinship-based hierarchical organization in which strong moral ties and reputation among clan members played the key role. By contrast, in medieval Europe, the main example of a cooperative organization is the city, whereby cooperation is across kinship lines with weak ties, and external enforcement played a bigger role.

### 2.3.4 Heterogeneity of Trust Across Space

As early as the 18th century, Adam Smith (1997 [1766]) was already alluding to substantial differences across nations in what he called the "probity" and "punctuality" of their populations. For example, the Dutch "are the most faithful to their word." Similarly John Stuart Mill observed: "There are countries in Europe ... where the most serious impediment to conducting business concerns on a large scale, is the rarity of persons who are supposed fit to be trusted with the receipt and expenditure of large sums of money" (Mill, 1848, p. 132).

Recent advances in international social survey technique have yielded further evidence of the enormous differences in trust level that may exist across countries. In social survey data there is to be observed a sizable variation in the extent to which people trust others across countries as well as within countries.

Figure 2.1a and 2.1b show average levels of generalized trust for 111 countries, generated from responses to the World Values Survey, the European Values Survey, and the Afrobarometer.[1] These surveys ask the trust question, and the trust variable takes on the

---

[1] The data set is constructed by combining the five waves of the WVS (1981–2008) with the four waves of the EVS (1981–2008), and adding the third wave of the Afrobarometer (2005).

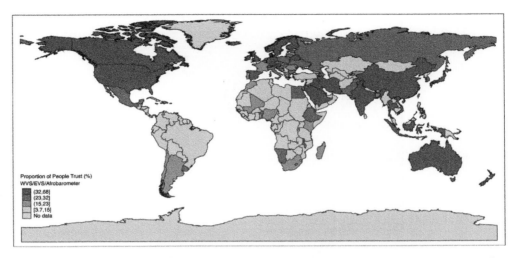

**Figure 2.1a** World distribution of trust. *Sources: Trust is computed as the country average from responses to the trust question in the five waves of the World Values Survey (1981–2008), the four waves of the European Values Survey (1981–2008), and the third wave of the Afrobarometer (2005). The trust question asks "Generally speaking, would you say that most people can be trusted or that you need to be very careful in dealing with people?" Trust is equal to 1 if the respondent answers "Most people can be trusted" and 0 otherwise.*

value 1 if the respondent answers that "Most people can be trusted" and 0 if he or she thinks that one "Needs to be very careful." Trust levels vary very considerably from one country to another. In Norway, the country with the highest level of trust in the sample, more than 68% of the population trusts others. At the opposite end of the ranking lies Trinidad and Tobago, where only 3.8% of the population exhibits interpersonal trust. The United States ranks in the top quarter, with an average trust level of more than 40%. In general, northern European countries lead the ranking with high average levels of interpersonal trust, while populations in African and South American countries seem not to trust others very much.

The extent to which people trust other, however, varies not only across countries, but also across regions belonging to the same country. Figure 2.2 shows average trust levels for 69 European regions used in Tabellini (2010); the source is the World Values Survey (1990–1997). As we see from the figure, trust levels vary remarkably between regions lying not very far apart. While in the Dutch region of Oost Nederland more than 64.1% trust is shown, in the French Bassin Parisien region this figure is only 14.2%. There is wide divergence between regions within European countries. In Italy, the trust level is almost twice as high in Trento (49%) as it is in Sicilia (26%). In France, trust is 13% points higher in the Sud Ouest region compared to the Nord region. Finally, a divergence in trust levels is also observable in federations. Figure 2.3 displays mean trust levels for 49

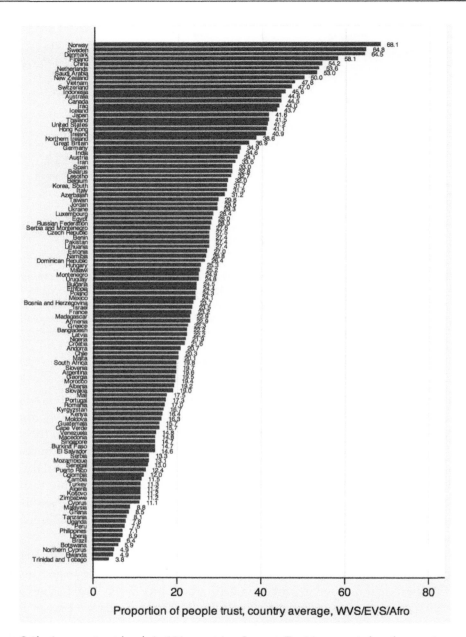

**Figure 2.1b** Average trust levels in 111 countries. *Sources: Trust is computed as the country average from responses to the trust question in the five waves of the World Values Survey (1981–2008), the four waves of the European Values Survey (1981–2008) and the third wave of the Afrobarometer (2005). The question asks "Generally speaking, would you say that most people can be trusted or that you need to be very careful in dealing with people?" Trust is equal to 1 if the respondent answers "Most people can be trusted" and 0 otherwise.*

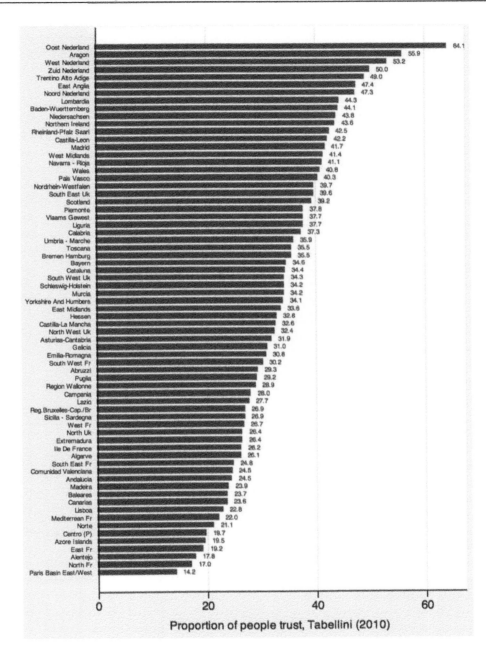

**Figure 2.2** Average trust levels in 69 European regions. *Source: The proportion of people that trust is taken from Tabellini (2010). The trust measure is computed as the regional average from responses to the question "Generally speaking, would you say that most people can be trusted or that you need to be very careful in dealing with people?" Trust is equal to 1 if the respondent answers "Most people can be trusted" and 0 otherwise.*

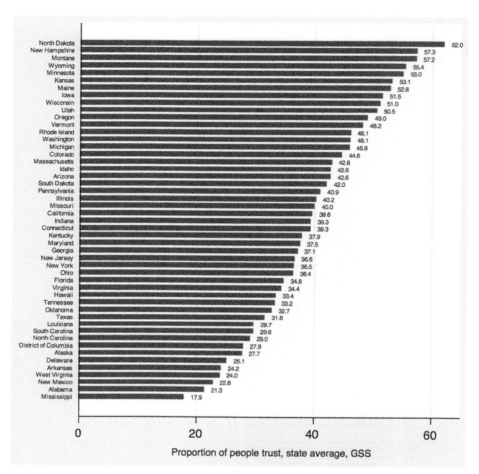

**Figure 2.3** Average trust levels in 49 US states. *Sources: The proportion of people that trust is taken from the General Social Survey (1973–2006). The trust measure is computed as the state average from responses to the question "Generally speaking, would you say that most people can be trusted or that you need to be very careful in dealing with people?" Trust is equal to 1 if the respondent answers "Most people can be trusted" and 0 otherwise.*

US states, computed by averaging individual responses from the General Social Survey (GSS, 1973–2006) of the United States. We note wide differences in the degree of trust the citizens of these States have in others. While in North Dakota more than 60% of the respondents trust others, in California less than 40%, and in Mississippi not even 20%, of the respondents think that they can trust people in general.

### 2.3.5 An Heterogeneity Linked to National Specificities

What are the reasons for the divergence in trust levels across countries? Besides individual characteristics (e.g. age, social status, gender, education, income, and religion), time-invariant country characteristics can account for a large share of the disparity of trust levels around the world.

Table 2.2 reports a micro-regression of individual trust on age, age squared, gender, education, income level, and various types of religious affiliation. Some of these individual characteristics are highly correlated with individual trust. Maleness correlates positively with trust, and age displays a hump-shaped relationship with trust. More educated individuals have significantly higher trust, a relationship documented at length by Helliwell and Putnam (2007). A one standard deviation increase in education (roughly 2.2 years) increases trust by 11% of its sample mean. Trust also correlates positively with income: a one standard deviation increase in income (roughly 0.79) increases trust by 6% of its sample mean. In a seminal paper on the determinants of trust, Alesina and La Ferrara (2002) document the role of additional characteristics negatively correlated with trust, such as a recent history of traumatic experiences or belonging to a group that historically felt discriminated against, such as women or ethnic minorities.

But the feature that especially stands out in Table 2.2 is the very weak predictive power of individual characteristics for explaining cross-country heterogeneity in trust compared to country fixed effects. Including country fixed effects in this regression increases the coefficient of determination, R sq. by about 10% from 0.027 to 0.12. Furthermore, the correlation between average country trust levels and the predicted mean trust is of a magnitude 0.52 without fixed effects, and rises to an almost perfect correlation of 0.99 when country fixed effects are included in the micro-regression.

Figure 2.4 displays country fixed effects in relation to Norway, the country with the highest mean trust in the sample, taken from the above-described micro-regression. The figure thus documents the % point reduction in trust flowing from the fact of living in a country other than Norway, with all individual characteristics (age, gender, education, income, and religion) held constant. In comparison to Norway, trust would be reduced by more than 60 pp (percentage points) in Uganda, Peru, Kosovo, or Algeria; by more than 50 pp in Greece or France; and by around 40 pp in Italy, Germany, or the United States. The country fixed effects thus differ by an order of magnitude from the effects of individual characteristics. This result suggests that it is necessary to look at national characteristics (institutions, history, geography, public policy…) in order to understand how trust is built.

## 2.4. THE DYNAMICS OF TRUST

International surveys underline how important the heterogeneity of average levels of trust across countries is, for identical characteristics of the inhabitants, such as age,

**Table 2.2** Determinants of trust: micro estimates

| | Trust | |
|---|---|---|
| | **(1)** | **(2)** |
| Age | 0.003*** | 0.001*** |
| | (.000) | (.000) |
| Age sq. | −0.000** | −0.000 |
| | (.000) | (.000) |
| Gender | 0.009** | 0.004 |
| | (.003) | (.003) |
| Education | 0.019*** | 0.015*** |
| | (.004) | (.003) |
| Protestant | 0.165*** | 0.013 |
| | (.051) | (.009) |
| Catholic | −0.011 | −0.004 |
| | (.200) | (.006) |
| Hindu | 0.107** | 0.023 |
| | (.053) | (.023) |
| Buddhist | 0.057 | 0.010 |
| | (.042) | (.013) |
| Muslim | 0.034 | 0.021* |
| | (.047) | (.011) |
| Jew | −0.030 | 0.045 |
| | (.018) | (0.032) |
| Income level | 0.020*** | 0.023*** |
| | (.004) | (.003) |
| Country FE | No | Yes |
| Observations | 136105 | 136105 |
| $R^2$ | 0.027 | 0.123 |

*Notes:* The dependent variable is *Trust*. It is calculated from answers to the question *"Generally speaking, would you say that most people can be trusted, or that you need to be very careful in dealing with people?"*. Trust is equal to 1 if the respondent answers *"Most people can be trusted"* and 0 otherwise.

Control variables include age in years, Gender (1 = Male), Education (from 1 = No elementary school to 7 = Graduate studies), Income (1 = Below national average, 2 = Average, 3 = Above national average), and dummy variables indicating the religious denomination of the respondent.

Column (2) includes country fixed effects. OLS regressions with robust standard errors clustered at the country level in parentheses.

**Sample (79 countries):** Albania, Algeria, Argentina, Armenia, Austria, Azerbaijan, Bangladesh, Belarus, Belgium, Bosnia and Herzegovina, Bulgaria, Canada, Chile, China, Croatia, Cyprus, Czech Republic, Denmark, Egypt, Estonia, Finland, France, Georgia, Germany, Great Britain, Greece, Hungary, Iceland, India, Indonesia, Iran, Iraq, Ireland, Israel, Italy, Japan, Jordan, Kosovo, Kyrgyzstan, Latvia, Lithuania, Luxembourg, Macedonia, Malta, Mexico, Moldova, Montenegro, Morocco, Netherlands, Nigeria, Northern Cyprus, Northern Ireland, Norway, Pakistan, Peru, Philippines, Poland, Portugal, Puerto Rico, Romania, Russian Federation, Saudi Arabia, Serbia, Singapore, Slovakia, Slovenia, South Africa, South Korea, Spain, Sweden, Switzerland, Tanzania, Turkey, Uganda, Ukraine, United States, Venezuela, Vietnam, Zimbabwe.

*Sources:* World Values Survey (1981–2008) and European Values Survey (1981–2008).

*Coefficient is statistically different from 0 at the .10 levels.

**Coefficient is statistically different from 0 at the .05 levels.

***Coefficient is statistically different from 0 at the .01 levels.

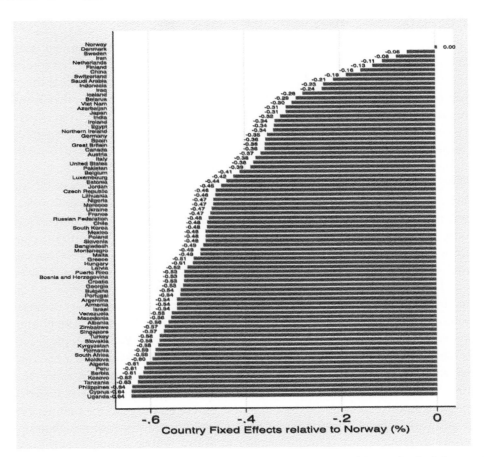

**Figure 2.4** Country fixed effects relative to Norway (%). *Interpretation:* Holding individual characteristics constant, living in Uganda rather than in Norway reduces trust by 64%. *Additional controls:* Age, age (squared), gender, education, income, and religion. *Sources: Trust is computed as the country average from responses to the trust question in the five waves of the World Values Survey (1981–2008), the four waves of the European Values Survey (1981–2008), and the third wave of the Afrobarometer (2005). The question asks "Generally speaking, would you say that most people can be trusted or that you need to be very careful in dealing with people?" Trust is equal to 1 if the respondent answers "Most people can be trusted" and 0 otherwise.*

income, education, and religion. These surveys also show that average trust changes little over the course of time: the countries with the weakest levels of trust at present also had weak trust at the beginning of the 1980s. This observation, though, tells us little. For one thing, it is confined to the relatively short period for which survey data are available. For another, it says nothing about the causal factors that may explain the persistence or the evolution of trust. A cluster of recent studies make it their goal to seek these out.

### 2.4.1 Climate

Four centuries before our era, Aristotle underlined the influence of climate on attitudes: "The nations that live in cold regions and those of Europe are full of spirit, but somewhat lacking in skill and intellect; for this reason, while remaining relatively free, they lack political cohesion and the ability to rule over their neighbors. On the other hand the Asiatic nations have in their souls both intellect and skill, but are lacking in spirit; so they remain enslaved and subject. The Hellenic race, occupying a mid-position geographically, has a measure of both, being both spirited and intelligent" (Politics 7.7, 1327b18–1328a21, trans. Sinclair and Saunders).

When Aristotle wrote the above, sampling was unknown, and there was no way to establish a statistical relationship between climate and attitudes; today it is at least feasible to contemplate doing so. Durante (2010) posits that the inhabitants of Europe's regions are today more trusting to the extent that they were subjected to significant climatic variations between 1500 and 1750. The explanation advanced by Durante is that greater climatic variability, which heightens the undependability of harvests, makes it necessary to stock larger reserves, manage them collectively, and develop trade between regions affected by differing and therefore offsetting climatic shocks. All this favors cooperation and leaves an imprint on the overall social structure. Family bonds are less binding in regions where the amplitude of climatic variation is greater. Young people leave the family nest earlier, since they cannot count on family solidarity to meet their needs when harvests are poor, as they frequently are. Experiments in cooperation induced by climatic harshness may thus have effects persisting across a span of centuries, even as societies are profoundly transformed by the passage from the agricultural stage to the industrial stage.

In a similarly oriented contribution Ostrom (1990) found that trust is high in upland regions where farmers must cultivate scattered plots irrigated by communally maintained ditches. In such regions, mutual trust and cooperation in all facets of life are more frequent than on flatland that can be farmed with much less coordination.

Natural catastrophes can also influence trust, sometimes in unforeseen ways. A portion of those who survive experience a post-traumatic phase during which they turn to others, show altruistic behavior, and invest in communal action. This "catastrophe syndrome" (Valent, 2000; Wallace, 1956) may last a long time and have a durable effect. Castillo and Carter (2011) and Zylberberg (2011) have shown that destructive hurricanes may favor cooperation and trust over a period of years.

### 2.4.2 The Weight of History

The traffic in slave labor to work plantations in the Americas began in the 16th century, when West African men and women were captured and enslaved during raids led from the coast by Europeans, or sold as slaves to the Europeans after being captured in the course of military conflicts among African belligerents. But the system underwent evolution, for some inhabitants of West Africa found they could survive and even thrive by capturing and selling other humans—passing travelers, neighbors, even members of their own families—to the slave merchants. It may be surmised that these practices, widespread at the time, instilled profound mistrust in the population. Nunn and Wantchekon (2011) have shown that it is still present three centuries later. The inhabitants of these regions still reveal greater mistrust of others, including their neighbors, the members of their ethnic group, and even their own families, than the inhabitants of neighboring regions. The slaves may of course have been captured and sold primarily in areas of conflict, where distrust would have been higher to start with, and the task of the slave merchant correspondingly easier. Nunn and Wantchekon have shown, however, that dwellers in regions more remote from the Atlantic coast, whose ancestors were relatively more sheltered from the slave trade, are less distrustful than those who dwell nearer the coast. They also show that this pattern of diminishing distrust with increasing distance from the coast is not observed in other regions of the globe. This would tend to show that the regions where the slave trade flourished are the ones with distrustful inhabitants, not the converse.

Thus, even across a span of many generations, history may have the effect of shaping trust in ways that we can still perceive. Rohner et al. (2013) provide a theory for the long-run impact of war and conflicts on distrust. Accidental conflicts, e.g. conflicts that do not represent economic fundamentals, might still lead to a permanent breakdown of trust, since agents observe the history of conflicts to update their beliefs and to transmit them over generations. Becker et al. (2011) have studied the imprint left by the Habsburg Empire, which dominated much of central Europe from the 18th century to the beginning of the 20th, and employed administrators who, with respect to the norms of the age, were better educated and less corrupt. The borders of the countries that have come into existence since the collapse of the Empire at the end of World War One may have altered more than once in the interval, as a result of conflicts and political events. Yet in regions that once lay within the boundaries of the Empire, the administration is still more transparent, less corrupt, and better trusted by the population. The improved administrative practices of the Habsburgs left traces that have survived well beyond the dissolution of their Empire.

The weight of this example is more than anecdotal. Numerous circumstances of European history reveal that political decisions can affect trust over the course of many centuries. Today the inhabitants of Italian cities that in the Middle Ages achieved a form of participatory self-government, the communal regime, comparable to that of the city-states of antiquity, and whose ancestors were thus deeply engaged in civic/political life, participate more in elections, give more blood, and are more likely to join associations than the inhabitants of other Italian cities (Guiso et al. 2008a). Regions of Europe endowed with higher levels of education and a more democratic or participatory state form at the end of the eighteenth century today have more trusting and civic-minded inhabitants (Tabellini, 2010). This line of research suggests that education and democracy shape civic behavior in ways that last for centuries.

In the same vein, Jacob and Tyrell (2010) have shown that the activities of the *Stasi*, the state security agency of the former DDR or East Germany as it was known, which by 1989 employed more than 90,000 permanent members and had more than 170,000 informers, have left a durable mark on the civic attitudes of the inhabitants of East Germany. Everyone knew that, in every building and factory, they were being watched by informers among them, and that electronic eavesdropping was in widespread use. Anything one said about the regime might be reported, and twisted in such a way as to ruin one's life. Jacob and Tyrell show that this climate of delation shredded the social fabric. Two decades after the wall came down, the inhabitants of regions in which the *Stasi* were once particularly active are less inclined to do their civic duty: their rate of voter turnout, their rate of participation in voluntary associations, and their rate of voluntary organ donation are all measurably lower than those in the rest of the *Bundesrepublik*.

More generally, Aghion et al. (2010) highlight a steep decline of trust in the former Soviet bloc countries at the time of their conversion to capitalism. The market liberalization at the turn of the 1990s, with its attendant corruption, in this Eastern bloc setting of pervasive distrust and minimal transparency, seems to have degraded any trust the citizens might have had in their state, their justice system, or their fellow citizens, even further. The effect was most detectable in regions where trust was already low at the time the wall came down.

Another potential long-term cause of trust is related to genetic diversity. In a fascinating recent contribution, Ashraf and Galor (2013) show that distance from the cradle of humankind in East Africa is associated with lower genetic diversity within ancient indigenous settlements across the globe. As subgroups of the populations of parental colonies left to establish new settlements, they carried with them only a subset of the overall genetic diversity of their parental colonies. As a result, the migratory distance from East Africa has an adverse effect on genetic diversity in the different ethnic groups populating the globe. Ashraf and Galor then show that genetic diversity affects significantly trust and cooperation, leading to an optimal level of diversity for economic development. On one hand, genetic heterogeneity increases the likelihood of mis-coordination and distrust, reducing cooperation and lowering total factor productivity. On the other hand, diversity has a beneficial effect on the expansion of society's production possibility frontier by widening the spectrum of complementary traits.

### 2.4.3 Inherited Trust

Studies of how immigrant attitudes evolve as a function of their country of origin and country of arrival shed an interesting light on the malleability of trust. They show that the beliefs and behaviors of immigrants are influenced by their countries of origin; that football players who grew up in countries undergoing civil war are more violent than other players, that they get yellow-flagged or red-flagged more often (Miguel et al. 2011). Fisman and Miguel (2007) observed that UN diplomats from countries with low levels of trust and civic spirit frequently violate the New York City parking laws, from which diplomats are legally immune, whereas those from Scandinavian and Anglophone countries make it a point not to, although they enjoy the same immunity.

Still, the attitudes and beliefs of immigrants are not carved in stone but are influenced by their countries of residence. As a general rule, trust rises among immigrants right from the first generation, if they have moved from a low-trust country to a high-trust one. The converse holds true as well. This phenomenon has been observed in both the US and Europe (Algan and Cahuc, 2010; Dinesen, 2012; Dinesen and Hooghe, 2010). In fact, it is detectable in cases of internal migration too: the civic spirit of Italians who move from southern Italy to the north tends to ameliorate and converge gradually on the prevailing local norm. Conversely, the civic spirit of Italians who move from the north to the south shows some signs of degrading (Ichino and Maggi, 2000; Guiso et al. 2004). Algan et al. (2011) illustrate this pattern with the evolution of trust among the first and second generation of immigrants in European countries. In the European Social Survey, the level of trust of first generation immigrants correlates significantly with the level of trust in their country of origin. By contrast, the level of trust of second generation immigrants is more correlated with the average level of generalized trust and trust in institutions in their new country of residence than with trust in their home country.

Individual distrust, therefore, is not something poured and set for eternity. The environment can modify it. But it is something systematically characterized by the kind of inertia that can leave its mark on at least one and perhaps more generations.

## 2.5. TRUST, INCOME PER CAPITA, AND GROWTH

To what extent can the above-mentioned cross-sectional heterogeneity in trust level account for cross-sectional differences in income per capita? To what extent can a boost in trust explain economic success within a country? This section first documents the evidence on the strong correlation observed between trust and economic outcome. We then document the main issues raised by the identification of the causal impact of trust, and the recent attempts in the literature to address them.

### 2.5.1 Cross-Section Correlation

The interest of the economic literature in social capital is fueled by the strong positive correlation between income per capita and average trust levels across countries or regions, first illustrated by the seminal work of Knack and Keefer (1997). The classic book by Putnam et al. (1993) also suggested the existence of such a relationship across regions in Italy by arguing that the northern regions developed faster than the southern ones because the former had a higher stock of social capital measured by association membership.

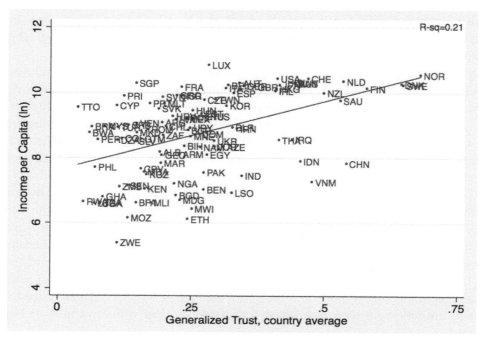

**Figure 2.5** Cross-country correlation between average (ln)-income per capita and trust. *Sources: Average income per capita (1980–2009) has been obtained from the Penn World Tables 7.0. Trust is computed as the country average from responses to the trust question in the five waves of the World Values Survey (1981–2008), the four waves of the European Values Survey (1981–2008), and the third wave of the Afrobarometer (2005). The question asks "Generally speaking, would you say that most people can be trusted or that you need to be very careful in dealing with people?" Trust is equal to 1 if the respondent answers "Most people can be trusted" and 0 otherwise.*

Figure 2.5 plots the average (ln) income per capita between 1980 and 2009 against average trust between 1981 and 2008 for a sample of 106 countries. Countries with higher levels of trust also display higher income levels. The correlation is steady; one fifth of the cross–country variation in income per capita is related to differences in generalized trust.

Table 2.3 shows the regressions of income per capita (ln) on trust. A one standard deviation increase in trust, about 0.14, increases (ln) income per capita by 0.59, or 6.8% of its sample mean. When additional controls for education, ethnic fractionalization, and population are included (column 2), the coefficient for trust remains significant but decreases in magnitude. Increasing trust by one standard deviation leads to a rise in income per capita of 0.18, or 2% of the sample mean. As a comparison, increasing fractionalization by one standard deviation (2.5) decreases income by 0.225 or 2.5% of the mean. We additionally control for several institutional measures, such as legal origins (column 3) and political institutions (column 4). Trust remains significant at the 5 or 10% level, while the institutional variables are insignificant.

**Table 2.3** Trust and income: cross-country correlation

| | Ln GDP per capita (1980–2009) | | | | | | |
|---|---|---|---|---|---|---|---|
| | (1) | (2) | (3) | (4) | (5) | (6) | (7) |
| Generalized trust | 4.231*** | 1.308** | 1.526* | 1.407** | | | |
| | (.718) | (.617) | (.849) | (.669) | | | |
| Trust in family | | | | | .418 | | |
| | | | | | (.485) | | |
| Trust in neighbors | | | | | | .295 | |
| | | | | | | (.311) | |
| Trust "people we know" | | | | | | | .176 |
| | | | | | | | (.179) |
| Education | | 0.294*** | 0.302*** | 0.249*** | 0.307*** | 0.348*** | 0.359*** |
| | | (.034) | (.040) | (.047) | (.034) | (.034) | (.033) |
| Ethnic segmentation | | −0.911** | −0.802* | −0.908** | −1.03*** | −0.824** | −0.786* |
| | | (.360) | (.404) | (.368) | (.351) | (.387) | (.396) |
| Population (ln) | | −0.015 | −0.024 | 0.037 | 0.018 | 0.060 | 0.057 |
| | | (.051) | (.506) | (.058) | (.046) | (.056) | (.054) |
| French LO | | | 0.275 | | | | |
| | | | (.233) | | | | |
| German LO | | | 0.100 | | | | |
| | | | (.224) | | | | |
| Scandinavian LO | | | 0.007 | | | | |
| | | | (.367) | | | | |
| Political institutions | | | | 0.0377 | | | |
| | | | | (.029) | | | |
| Observations | 106 | 93 | 93 | 89 | 61 | 56 | 56 |
| $R^2$ | 0.218 | 0.642 | 0.651 | 0.653 | 0.692 | 0.782 | 0.782 |

*Notes:* The dependent variable is *income per capita (ln)*, averaged over the years 1980–2009, taken from the Penn World Tables. Generalized *Trust* is calculated from answers to the question *"Generally speaking, would you say that most people can be trusted, or that you need to be very careful in dealing with people?"* Trust is equal to 1 if the respondent answers *"Most people can be trusted"* and 0 otherwise. Average trust in family, neighbors, and people you know, is calculated from the question *"Could you tell me for each whether you trust people from this group completely, somewhat, not very much or not at all?"* and the variable takes on the value 4, if the respondent answers *"Trust completely"*, 3 for *"Somewhat"*, 2 for *"Not very much,"* and 1 for *"No trust at all."*

**Sample (106 countries):** Albania, Algeria, Argentina, Armenia, Australia, Austria, Azerbaijan, Bangladesh, Belarus, Belgium, Benin, Bosnia and Herzegovina, Botswana, Brazil, Bulgaria, Burkina Faso, Canada, Cape Verde, Chile, China, Colombia, Croatia, Cyprus, Czech Republic, Denmark, Dominican Republic, Egypt, El Salvador, Estonia, Ethiopia, Finland, France, Georgia, Germany, Ghana, Great Britain, Greece, Guatemala, Hong Kong, Hungary, Iceland, India, Indonesia, Iran, Iraq, Ireland, Israel, Italy, Japan, Jordan, Kenya, Kyrgyzstan, Latvia, Lesotho, Liberia, Lithuania, Luxembourg, Macedonia, Madagascar, Malawi, Malaysia, Mali, Malta, Mexico, Moldova, Montenegro, Morocco, Mozambique, Namibia, Netherlands, New Zealand, Nigeria, Norway, Pakistan, Peru, Philippines, Poland, Portugal, Puerto Rico, Romania, Russian Federation, Rwanda, Saudi Arabia, Senegal, Serbia, Singapore, Slovakia, Slovenia, South Africa, South Korea, Spain, Sweden, Switzerland, Taiwan, Tanzania, Thailand, Trinidad and Tobago, Turkey, Uganda, Ukraine, United States, Uruguay, Venezuela, Vietnam, Zambia, Zimbabwe.

*Sources:* The trust data comes from the five waves of the World Values Survey (1981–2008), the four waves of the European Values Survey (1981–2008), and the third wave of the Afrobarometer (2005). Education measures average years of schooling between 1950 and 2010 and is taken from Barro and Lee (2010). Ethnic fractionalization measures the degree of ethnic fractionalization and is taken from Alesina et al. (2003). Population is the average population (ln) between 1980 and 2009, taken from the Penn World Tables 7.0. Legal Origins are taken from La Porta et al. (2007). Political Institutions are measured by the Polity2 index averaged over 2000–2010, taken from the Polity IV database. OLS regressions with robust standard errors in parentheses.

*Coefficients are statistically different from 0 at the 10% level.
**Coefficients are statistically different from 0 at the 5% level.
***Coefficients are statistically different from 0 at the 1% level.

To compare the importance of generalized trust for income relative to other measures of trust, we run regressions replacing the measure of generalized trust by measures of limited trust, controlling for education, ethnic fractionalization, and population. As Table 2.3 makes clear, only generalized trust is significantly associated to income per capita. Limited trust (such as trust in family, neighbors, people one knows personally) is positively associated to income levels, but not significantly (columns 5–7). This result suggests that it is only the ability to cooperate outside the inner circle of family and relatives that is associated to economic performance, and is consistent with Banfield's analysis of the poor performance of Italian villages characterized by amoral familism. This result explains why the economic literature has made generalized trust the primary focus of analysis.

The same steady positive correlation between generalized trust and income per capita holds when we look at more local variations across regions in Europe or across states in the US. Figure 2.6 shows the correlation between generalized trust and average income per capita (ln) in 69 European regions using data taken from Tabellini (2010). Some European countries show a high degree of regional variation both in generalized trust and income per capita. In particular, northern Italy and northern Spain are high-trust regions and

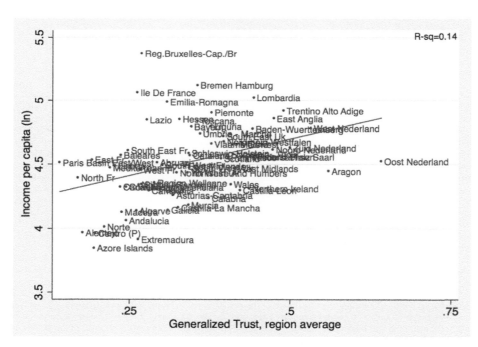

**Figure 2.6** Income per capita (ln) and generalized trust in 69 European regions. *Source: Tabellini (2010). The trust measure is computed as the regional average from responses to the question "Generally speaking, would you say that most people can be trusted or that you need to be very careful in dealing with people?" Trust is equal to 1 if the respondent answers "Most people can be trusted" and 0 otherwise.*

have high income per capita while southern Spain and southern Italy fare much worse on both dimensions. Figure 2.7 shows that the same positive correlation between trust and income per capita holds across US states. The southern states, in particular the former French colonies, have weak levels of trust and are also outperformed economically by the states of the north-eastern US.

Finally, using novel income data for more than 800 regions around the world collected by Gennaioli et al. (2013), we can observe that trust correlates with GDP at the region level around the world. Figure 2.8 displays the cross correlation of (ln) GDP per capita and trust for three different samples. Table 2.4 gives the associated regression output. Trust correlates positively with per capita income in 771 regions around the world, even stronger when the sample is restricted to regions belonging to groups of high income countries such as the EU27 (including Norway, but excluding Cyprus, Malta, and Luxembourg) and the OECD. Table 2.4 also displays regression results, when additionally education is controlled for. Since the number of individuals polled varies greatly between region,

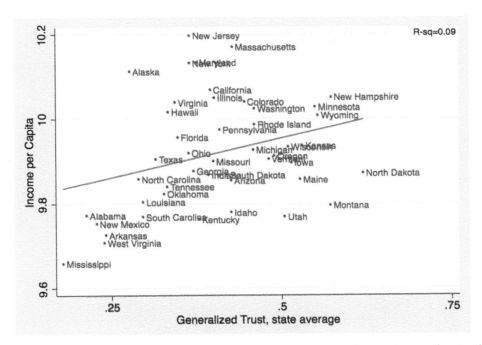

**Figure 2.7** Income per capita (ln) and generalized trust in 49 US states. *Sources: Income data is taken from the US Census Bureau and averaged for the years 1972–2011. The proportion of people that trust is taken from the General Social Survey (1973–2006). The trust measure is computed as the state average from responses to the question "Generally speaking, would you say that most people can be trusted or that you need to be very careful in dealing with people?" Trust is equal to 1 if the respondent answers "Most people can be trusted" and 0 otherwise.*

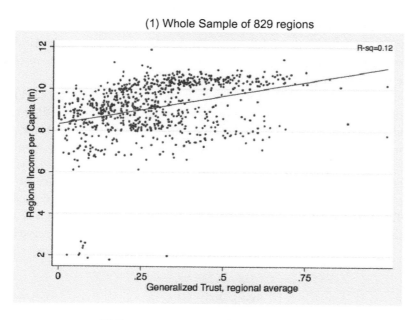

(1) Whole Sample of 829 regions

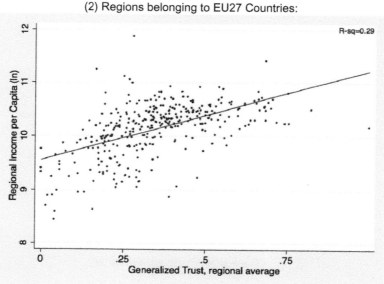

(2) Regions belonging to EU27 Countries:

**Figure 2.8** Regional income per capita (ln) and trust in 829 regions around the world. *Sources: Income data is taken from the US Census Bureau and averaged for the years 1972–2011. The proportion of people that trust is taken from the General Social Survey (1973–2006). The trust measure is computed as the state average from responses to the question "Generally speaking, would you say that most people can be trusted or that you need to be very careful in dealing with people?" Trust is equal to 1 if the respondent answers "Most people can be trusted" and 0 otherwise.*

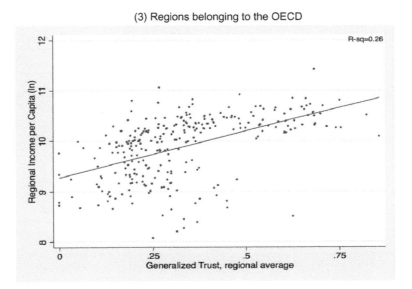

**Figure 2.8** (*Continued*).

we account for this by running weighted regressions using precisely this number as our weight. No matter which sample is used, trust is positively and significantly associated with a higher regional per capita income across regions. However, as soon as we introduce country fixed effects, we do not observe any significant correlation between trust and GDP. This result shows that the cross-country heterogeneity in trust and income per capita is much more substantial than the within country variation, and drives the result.

Not only is trust positively correlated with income per capita, but also with growth. This point was first documented by Knack and Keefer (1997, 1999). Their study is based on 29 countries, mostly western European countries, between 1980 and 1992. Table 2.5 enlarges their result on the relation between trust and economic growth to cover 52 countries, regressing average annual growth between 1990 and 2009 on average trust between 1981 and 1990. We control for initial income and initial education. Trust is positively associated with economic growth. The correlation between trust and growth is statistically significant at the 10% level. A one standard deviation increase in trust, about 0.14, increases growth by 0.5% points or 20% of its sample mean. Column 2 controls for the initial level of investment and the correlation becomes statistically significant at the 5% level. Column 3 includes an interaction term between trust and initial income per capita. This interaction term captures the fact that trust should have a stronger effect on growth in poor countries that lack credit markets and appropriate rule of law. Both trust and trust interacted with initial income are statistically significant. The interaction term

**Table 2.4** Trust and regional GDP per capita

| | Ln GDP per capita | | | | | |
| | Full sample | | EU | | OECD | |
| | (1) | (2) | (3) | (4) | (5) | (6) |
|---|---|---|---|---|---|---|
| Trust | 1.134** | 0.313 | 1.345*** | 0.616 | 1.180*** | 0.867 |
| | (0.497) | (0.211) | (0.369) | (0.719) | (0.341) | (0.625) |
| Education | 0.306*** | 0.342*** | 0.113** | 0.327*** | 0.080** | 0.277** |
| | (0.030) | (0.031) | (0.053) | (0.106) | (0.033) | (0.110) |
| Country FE | No | Yes | No | Yes | No | Yes |
| Observations | 771 | 771 | 278 | 278 | 350 | 350 |
| $R^2$ | 0.603 | 0.964 | 0.321 | 0.834 | 0.298 | 0.755 |

*Notes:* The dependent variable is *ln GDP per capita*, which measures the log of regional income per capita, taken from Gennaioli et al. (2013).

*Trust* is calculated from answers to the question *"Generally speaking, would you say that most people can be trusted or that you need to be very careful in dealing with people?"* Trust is equal to 1 if the respondent answers *"Most people can be trusted"* and 0 otherwise.

*Sample:* Columns (1) and (2) use the full sample of regions, as in Gennaioli et al. (2013). Columns (3) and (4) restrict the sample to regions belonging to a country being a member of the EU27 (including Norway, but excluding Malta, Cyprus, and Luxembourg). Columns (5) and (6) restrict the sample to regions belonging to a country being a member of the OECD.

OLS regressions with robust standard errors, clustered at the country level, in parentheses. All regressions are weighted by the number of individuals polled in each region.

*Sources:* The trust data comes from the five waves of the World Values Survey (1981–2008), the four waves of the European Values Survey (1981–2008), and all waves of the US GSS (1973–2006). Education measures the average years of schooling.

*Coefficients are statistically different from 0 at the 10% level.

**Coefficients are statistically different from 0 at the 5% level.

***Coefficients are statistically different from 0 at the 1% level.

is strongly negative, which provides support for the view that trust is more important when enforcement of formal institutions is weak.

## 2.5.2 Identification Issues

The previous section documents a strong correlation between trust and economic outcomes across countries or regions. However, how can we identify the causal impact of trust on economic performance? To answer this question, we must confront the various identification issues raised by the estimation of the following equation:

$$Y_c = a_0 + a_1 T_c + a_2 X_c + e_c, \tag{2.1}$$

where $Y_c$ denotes economic performance in the geographic location c (country or region); $T_c$ denotes trust; $X_c$ is a vector of characteristics of the location, including the educational level of the population, current and past institutions, and past economic development in the locality; and $e_c$ is an unobserved error term.

**Table 2.5** Trust and growth: cross-country correlation

| | Growth 1990–2009 | | |
| --- | --- | --- | --- |
| | **(1)** | **(2)** | **(3)** |
| Trust 1980–1990 | 0.0396* | 0.0273** | 0.480*** |
| | (0.021) | (0.010) | (0.078) |
| Income p.c. 1990 | −0.014*** | −0.012*** | 0.002 |
| | (0.003) | (0.002) | (0.002) |
| Education 1990 | 0.002** | 0.001* | 0.002*** |
| | (0.001) | (0.001) | (0.001) |
| Investment | | 0.001*** | |
| | | (0.000) | |
| Trust × Income p.c. 1990 | | | −0.048*** |
| | | | (0.008) |
| Observations | 52 | 52 | 52 |
| $R^2$ | 0.491 | 0.658 | 0.706 |

*Notes:* The dependent variable measures average *GDP per capita growth* between 1990 and 2009, computed from Penn World Tables 7.0.

*Trust* is calculated from answers to the question *"Generally speaking, would you say that most people can be trusted or that you need to be very careful in dealing with people?"* Trust is equal to 1 if the respondent answers *"Most people can be trusted"* and 0 otherwise.

OLS regressions with robust standard errors in parentheses.

**Sample (52 countries):** Albania, Argentina, Australia, Austria, Bangladesh, Belgium, Brazil, Bulgaria, Canada, Chile, China, Colombia, Croatia, Czech Republic, Denmark, Dominican Republic, El Salvador, Estonia, Finland, France, Germany, Great Britain, Hungary, Iceland, India, Ireland, Italy, Japan, Malta, Mexico, Netherlands, New Zealand, Norway, Pakistan, Peru, Philippines, Poland, Portugal, Romania, Russian Federation, Slovakia, Slovenia, South Africa, South Korea, Spain, Sweden, Switzerland, Taiwan, Turkey, United States, Uruguay, Venezuela.

*Sources:* The trust data comes from the waves 1–3 of the World Values Survey (1981–1995). Additional Controls: Income p.c. 1990 measures income per capita in 1990 (ln), Penn World Tables 7.0. Education 1990 measures average years of schooling in 1990, taken from Barro and Lee (2010).

*Coefficients are statistically different from 0 at the 1% level.

**Coefficients are statistically different from 0 at the 5% level.

***Coefficients are statistically different from 0 at the 10% level.

The identification of Equation (2.1) raises two main issues. The first is reverse causality: contemporaneous trust is likely to be influenced by the current state of economic development in locality $c$. The second issue is that of omitted variables that might co-determine both trust and economic performance. Specifically, institutions (Hall and Jones, 1999; Acemoglu et al. 2001; Rodrik, 1999), geography (Sachs, 2003), and more recently deep historical events (Nunn, 2009) and biology (Ashraf and Galor, 2013; Spolaore and Wacziarg, 2013), have been found to affect economic performance. However, as pointed out above, those factors also shape trust. In principle it might be possible to control for institutional quality, but such variables are well known to present difficulties of measurement, and in any case cannot capture informal norms. Worse, if Equation (2.1) is estimated in cross-section, it is impossible to include in the regression a fixed effect at the geographic location level $c$. This implies that trust and the unobserved error term can be correlated: cov $(T_c, e_c)$ is different from zero and the OLS estimates of Equation (2.1) lead to biased estimates of the effect of trust. This opens up the possibility of a confounding factor: it is impossible to isolate the impact of trust from other time invariant characteristics of location $c$, such as other cultural values or local institutions. The most recent research in economic development precisely tries to find good strategies to control for any time invariant features at the local level. For instance, to measure the role of institutions in Africa, Michalopoulos and Papaioannou (2013) look at within-ethnic variation in economic development by controlling for ethnicity-fixed effects. They show that a very same ethnic group that belongs to different countries turns out to have similar contemporary income per capita, despite the institutional heterogeneity across countries. This result suggests that inherited traits specific to each ethnic group would explain much better economic development than institutions do.

In the following, we discuss the two main strategies proposed so far in the literature to address these identification issues to single out the causal impact of trust on economic development.

### 2.5.3 Identification Using Historical Events

A first strategy is to search for historical events as an exogenous variation in trust that could be used as instruments. To rationalize the use of historical events, the literature draws on the theory of the transmission of values. Studies by Bisin and Verdier (2001), Guiso et al. (2008b), and Tabellini (2010) stress the role of two main forces. A portion of current values is shaped by the contemporaneous environment (horizontal transmission of values), and another portion is shaped by beliefs inherited from earlier generations (vertical transmission of values). These theories suggest estimating the following equation for the formation of trust:

$$T_{ct} = b_0 + b_1 T_{ct-1} + b_2 X_{ct} + G_c + G_t + r_{ct}, \tag{2.2}$$

where contemporaneous trust $T_c$ in locality $c$ is explained by the initial trust present in the previous generation $T_{c,0}$, initial economic performance, and the initial and current other characteristics of the locality $X_c$. $r_c$ is a random residual.

The two-step estimation of Equations (2.1) and (2.2) raises two main concerns. First, we do not have any information on initial trust $T_{c,0}$ since standardized cross-country databases on the level of trust present in earlier generations are not available. At best, it is possible to go back only to the 1980s to get a measure of trust in a cross-section of countries using the World Values Survey. Second, even if we could get a good proxy for initial trust $T_{c,0}$, the correlation between initial trust and contemporaneous economic outcomes may be interpreted as a causal effect from initial trust to contemporaneous outcomes only if these two variables are not codetermined by common factors.

Tabellini (2010) addresses these two issues in the following way. He estimates the causal impact of culture on regional economic development in Europe, where culture is broadly defined as moral values of good conduct, including trust. Importantly, Tabellini estimates the impact of trust within European countries, across regions. This means that it is possible to include country fixed effects in the vector $X_c$ and control for national specificities. Tabellini uses two historical variables as an instrument for contemporaneous trust: past education and past political institutions. The political and social history of Europe ensures that these do vary widely at the regional level. He measures past education by the literacy rate around 1880, and early political institutions by constraints on executive power in the years 1600–1850. Tabellini shows in first-step estimates that contemporaneous trust is strongly correlated with these two instruments. Historically more backward regions, with higher illiteracy rates and worse political institutions, tend to have less generalized trust today. In the second step estimate, Tabellini shows that this historical variation in trust is strongly correlated with current regional development: regions with lower trust also have lower income per capita and lower growth rates, after controlling for country fixed effects, contemporaneous regional education, and past urbanization rates. The relationship is substantial: variation in trust could explain half of the observed income difference between Lombardy and southern Italy.

Tabellini's strategy is very insightful but raises two main concerns. The first one is how validly the instrument satisfies the exclusion restriction. The key assumption is that education and political institutions from the distant past do not directly affect contemporaneous output, after controlling for contemporaneous education and institutions. This assumption is likely to be violated. The literacy rate in the past is likely to have persistent effects on the formation of human capital, a key determinant of output. Similarly, there is much evidence that past institutions do have long-term effects on economic performance (Acemoglu et al. 2001). The second issue is linked to omitted variables. Since the author estimates cross-regional income per capita, he can control for country fixed effects. Thus, he can exclude that trust picks up time invariant characteristics at the country level. However, since the estimates draw on cross-sectional regressions at the regional level, it is impossible to include regional fixed effect in Equation (2.1). Thus, trust can pick up any other time invariant regional characteristics such as local geography or local formal and informal institutions.

Guiso et al. (2008a) follow a similar strategy to identify the impact of trust on income per capita in Italy. However, they look at more disaggregated historical variation in trust across cities within the same regions to exclude the influence of regional invariant characteristics. To estimate Equation (2.2) with historical variables, Guiso et al. revisit Putnam's conjecture that today's difference in trust between the north and the south of Italy is due to the history of independence that certain cities experienced in the north after the turn of the second millennium. They thus instrument today's trust (and more generally civic capital) with the past history of independence of certain cities. Additionally, they can exploit historical variation in the degree of independence of cities belonging to the same region: the communally governed cities were clustered in north central Italy, but not every city between the Apennine and the Alps experienced that form of regime. This strategy has one main advantage compared to Tabellini. Guiso et al. can estimate the impact of trust on output within the same region, across cities. This approach alleviates part of the concern that regional-invariant characteristics could determine both today's trust and income per capita. Guiso et al. find striking results. Northern cities that experienced independence and self-government in the Middle Ages now have 17% more non-profit associations than similar northern cities that never shared that experience. This higher level of social capital is associated with higher contemporaneous output: a one standard deviation increase in social capital increases income per capita by around 20%.

Still, as Guiso et al. stressed, their strategy cannot fully alleviate the identification concerns faced by Tabellini. First, the concern about the validity of the exclusion restriction for the instrument used for trust remains. One cannot exclude the possibility, that the historical shocks that affected cities at the turn of the millennium have a direct impact on income today. Having been a free city in the 13th century could have shaped other values or factors that exert long-lasting effects on economic outcomes. For example, free cities might have bred the spirit of entrepreneurship, or enhanced human capital. Second, trust can still pick up the effect of invariant local characteristics. Even if Guiso et al. identify the effect of trust within regions, they cannot control for geographic fixed effect at the city level.

This concern applies generally to all the literature that looks at the historical determinants of trust. As documented in Section 2.4, a burgeoning literature shows that trust is affected in the long-run by climate shocks, natural catastrophes, or history like the slave trade. But using those shocks as an instrument for trust in a growth equation is questionable. In particular, it is likely that climate shock or the slave trade affects growth by other channels than social capital, making the exclusion restriction disputable.

## 2.5.4 Time Varying Instruments: Inherited Trust and Growth

The historical approach leaves open the question of whether the level of trust does matter per se in explaining economic development, or whether it is not rather picking up the deeper influence of time invariant features such as legal origins, the quality of institutions, initial education, the extent of ethnic segmentation, and geography. What is needed is to find a measure for trust with time variation, allowing the investigator to control for time invariant specific factors. The difficulty in performing such an exercise is that there is no extended-time series on the evolution of trust.

Algan and Cahuc (2010) propose to use this time variation in inherited trust in the growth Equation (2.2). Since it is already well established that the parents' social capital is a good predictor of the social capital of children, they use the trust that US descendants have inherited from their forebears who immigrated from different countries at different dates to detect changes in inherited trust in the countries of origin (see Fernandez for a synthesis on the impact of culture on economic performance by using this epidemiological approach, 2011). For instance, by comparing Americans of Italian and German origin whose forebears migrated between 1950 and 1980, they can detect differences in trust inherited from these two source countries between 1950 and 1980. They can get time varying measures of trust inherited from these two countries by running the same exercise for forebears who immigrated in other periods, for instance between 1920 and 1950. With time varying measures of inherited trust, they can estimate the impact of changes in inherited trust on changes in income per capita in the countries of origin. This method allows us to address the main challenges mentioned above that arise in identifying the effect of trust on economic development. By focusing on the inherited component of trust, the authors avoid reverse causality. By providing a time varying measure of trust over long periods, they can control for both omitted time invariant factors and other observed time varying factors such as changes in the economic, political, cultural, and social environments.

More specifically, Algan and Cahuc re-estimate Equations (2.1) and (2.2) by allowing time variation in trust and economic performance, and including local fixed effects. We can rewrite the system of equations in the following way:

$$Y_{ct} = a_0 + a_1 T_{ct} + a_2 X_{ct} + F_c + F_t + e_{ct}, \tag{2.1'}$$

$$T_{ct} = b_0 + b_1 T_{ct-1} + b_2 X_{ct} + G_c + G_t + r_{ct}, \tag{2.2'}$$

where $t$ is an index of the time period, and $(F_c, G_c)$ and $(F_t, G_t)$ denote country fixed effect and time effect, respectively. The authors thus estimate the impact of the variation in trust on the variation in income per capita within countries. In the benchmark estimation of the model, data availability led them to consider two periods: 1935–1938 and 2000–2003. More distant periods are also considered, but with fewer observations. The estimates are based on 24 countries from all over the world, including Anglophone countries, Continental European countries, Mediterranean European countries, Nordic countries, Eastern European countries, India, Mexico, and Africa.

To cope with the lack of information on trust of the previous generations in Equation (2.2'), the authors proxy the inherited trust of people living in country $c$ by the trust that the descendants of US immigrants have inherited from their ancestors coming from country $c$. This yields an estimate of the term $b_1 T_{ct-1}$ in Equation (2.2'), which can be used as a proxy for inherited trust. This strategy leads to estimating a single equation of the form (2.1'), where $T_{ct}$ is replaced by the proxy of inherited attitudes.

This strategy can address part of the identification issues discussed above. First, by using the trust US immigrants inherited from the home country instead of the average trust of the residents, we can exclude reverse causality. While trust in the home country has evolved according to what happened in that country, the inherited trust of US immigrants is only affected by shocks to the US economy. Besides, since we can have a direct measure of inherited trust, we do not have to worry about instruments that are unlikely to satisfy the exclusion restriction. Second, by looking at different waves of immigration, one can get time variation in inherited trust and thus include country fixed effects in Equation (2.1′).

The authors estimate the trust inherited by US immigrants from their home countries by using the General Social Survey. Inherited trust is measured as the country of origin fixed effect on individual regression of the generalized trust question, controlling for individual characteristics. The authors focus on inherited trust in the two periods 1935–1938 and 2000–2003 (1935 and 2000 henceforth) and impose a lag of 25 years between inherited trust and income per capita at time t. Therefore, inherited trust in 1935–1938 is that of second-generation Americans born before 1910 (i.e. whose parents certainly arrived one generation before 1935, a generation being defined as a 25-year period), of third-generation Americans born before 1935, and of fourth-generation Americans born before 1960. In the same way, the level of inherited trust in 2000–2003 corresponds to the trust inherited by: second-generation Americans born between 1910 and 1975; third-generation Americans born after 1935; and fourth-generation Americans born after 1960. This decomposition excludes any overlap in the inherited trust of the two groups.

The authors show that inherited trust for the period 2000 strongly correlates with trust in the home country during the same period, measured from the WVS. Additionally, the authors document substantial variation in inherited trust between 1935 and 2000. Swedish Americans have inherited higher trust in 2000 relative to the period 1935. Inherited trust from continental European countries, and to a lesser extent from the United Kingdom, has deteriorated over the period. Trust inherited in 2000 from French ancestors is 4.7% points lower relative to trust inherited from Sweden in 1935. Inherited trust has decreased even more among the immigrants from Eastern European countries and Mediterranean countries. The authors do not address the explanation for such variations—but there is a rich set of candidates. The ancestors of the current US respondents are likely to have undergone very different national crises. The ancestors who transmitted their trust for the period 1935 mainly migrated before World Wars One and Two. The level of trust of immigrants from countries deeply affected by these crises, like France, Germany, and Eastern European countries, might have deteriorated over the intervening period compared to descendants from Sweden, since this latter country is one of the European countries least affected by these traumatic mid-century events.

Algan and Cahuc (2010) then estimate the impact of change in inherited trust on changes in income per capita within country between 1935 and 2000. The estimates also control for changes in lagged income, political institutions, education, and other values (like work ethic or family values) over the period to isolate the specific effect of trust. The impact of inherited trust is substantial.

Figure 2.9 displays the change in income per capita in period 2000–2003 that countries would have experienced if the level of inherited trust in a given country had been the same as the trust inherited by Swedes. Income per capita in 2000 would have been increased by 546% in Africa (not reported) if the level of inherited trust had been the

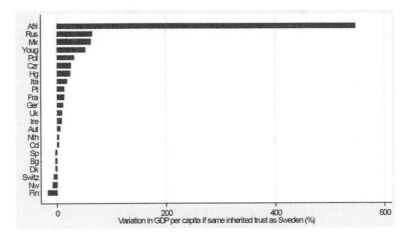

**Figure 2.9** Predicted variation in GDP p.c. relative to Sweden. *Interpretation:* The figure shows the predicted variations in GDP per capita over the period 2000–2003 in a given country if it had the same level of inherited social attitudes as Sweden. *Source: Algan and Cahuc (2010).*

same as inherited trust from Sweden. Inherited trust also has a non–negligible impact on GDP per capita in Eastern European countries, and Mexico. Income per capita would have increased by 69% in Russia, 59% in Mexico, 30% in Yugoslavia, 29% in the Czech Republic, and 9% in Hungary, had these countries inherited the same level of trust as Sweden. The effect, if less important, is also sizable in more developed countries. Income per capita would have been up by 17% in Italy, 11% in France, 7% in Germany, and 6% in the United Kingdom, if these countries had the same level of inherited trust as Sweden. The authors also compare the effect exerted by trust to the effect exerted by initial income per capita, or by time invariant factors such as geography, or by time invariant institutions. For poor countries from Africa or Latin America, initial economic development and invariant factors have a larger impact on income per capita. In striking contrast, change in income per capita within developed countries is overwhelmingly explained by inherited trust.

## 2.5.5 Individual Trust and Individual Economic Performance

Very few studies have explored whether high trusting individuals have higher economic performances in terms of wages or economic prospects. This is because of the difficulty of identifying the causal impact of individual trust on individual economic outcomes. Guiso et al. (2006) show, using the General Social Survey, that high–trusting individuals are more likely to become entrepreneurs in the US. To test for causality, they use inherited trust of US immigrants from their home country as an instrument for individual trust in the destination country. They find a significant, but somewhat too larger effect of inherited trust compared to the OLS estimates. As stressed by the authors, since inherited trust is time invariant, this variable may be picking up other inherited traits from the home country like risk aversion or saving behavior. This would explain the large difference in the OLS and 2SLS estimates. Ljunge (2012) draws on the same methodology by looking at how inherited trust of second-generation US immigrants is correlated with their economic success: second-generation immigrants with higher trusting ancestry earn significantly more than those with lower trust. They also have a higher labor supply, lower unemployment spell, and higher education. The correlation remains significant, even after controlling for additional ancestral influences such as income per capita and institutions. The paper cannot control for country of origin fixed effect though.

In another contribution, Butler et al. (2009) use the European Social Survey to test the relationship between individual trust and individual economic performance. The advantage of the ESS is to provide a question on generalized trust whose answers are scaled from 1 to 10, rather than just binary answers. The authors show that individual income is hump-shaped with the intensity of trust. Individuals whose level of trust is too high in relation to the civic-mindedness of their fellow citizens have levels of income inferior to those of individuals whose level of trust is intermediate. Being more frequently deceived by their fellow citizens hampers them. At the other extremity, individuals with little trust in others miss out on opportunities to make beneficial exchanges. Thus, there exists a "good" intermediate level of trust, the one that matches the level of civic-mindedness of the fellow citizens with whom one deals.

The conclusions drawn in this article might be limited by the quality of the ESS data. In these international values surveys, the measure of income levels is very imprecise and noisy. Nor do the questions about having been the victim of deceit focus on economic exchanges that might have a real impact on income, such as the interactions of professional life. But this article has the great merit of showing that the relationship between trust and economic performance is not necessarily monotonic. Trusting too much can have detrimental consequences. The recent financial crisis is a good illustration. The Icelanders, one of the most trusting peoples in international rankings, must still regret their excessive trust in their banks. Bernard Madoff's victims were likewise overly trusting.

If the analysis of the relationship between trust and economic performance at the individual level is to be advanced, the way ahead would seem to be field experiments, with an experimental measure of trust that measures behaviors precisely in economic exchanges and within firms. At the moment, the literature has done little to develop this approach. The only real study done on the terrain is that of Karlan (2005), who shows that, among Peruvian villagers, those most trusting in experimental games are also those who most often repaid their loans. But this study is not focused on the economic impact of trust on income. Some recent work heads in this direction but on limited samples. Barr and Serneels (2009) use a standard trust game to establish a relationship between experimental measures of reciprocating behavior among Ghanaian colleagues and the observed labor productivity of the firm in which they work. Similarly, Carpenter and Seki (2011) have Japanese fishermen play a repeated public goods game with and without an option for "social disapproval." They show that fishing crews that exhibit higher levels of reciprocity and more disapproval of shirking are more productive.

The way ahead in attempting to pin down the impact of trusting behavior on individual economic performance must be to combine the insights of experimental economics with experimentation—field, natural, and randomized. Doing so is a prerequisite if we are to better understand the channels through which trust affects economic performance and growth.

## 2.6. CHANNELS OF INFLUENCE OF TRUST ON ECONOMIC OUTCOMES

The empirical work presented in the previous section suggests that trust does indeed have an impact on growth. Macroeconomic in scope, this research is limited to the study of the relations obtaining among variables of a highly aggregated kind. It can therefore shed no more than a feeble light on the mechanisms or channels by which trust may act upon growth. Analyses more microeconomic in scope, focused on the relations obtaining among finance, insurance, the organization of firms, the labor market, public regulation, and trust, meet this need.

### 2.6.1 Financial Markets

In order to function, financial markets must rely heavily on trust, inasmuch as operations in these markets consist of promises of future payment which carry effect by reason of the fact that debtors are largely trustworthy, for legal protection would necessarily be costly and undependable. Figure 2.10 illustrates this positive relationship between trust and the development of financial markets in 86 countries over the course of the last three decades. As a gauge of the development of financial markets, we use the sum total of the credit granted by banks and financial institutions to private actors, as a percentage of GDP (see Levine, 2004).

Recent contributions to the literature have aimed at going beyond this positive correlation between trust and financial development, and pinpoint more closely the causal impact of trust. Guiso et al. (2004) study the relationship between the development of financial markets and trust in the regions of Italy in the 1980s and 1990s. They observe that households make more frequent use of cheques, keep a smaller portion of their savings in cash and a larger one in the stock market, and resort more frequently to credit-granting institutions, in the northern regions of the peninsula, where there is prevalent trust and high rates of blood donation and political participation. In the southern regions, moreover, borrowers resort more frequently to their families or near circles for loans than they do in the north.

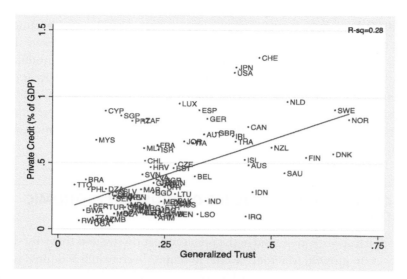

**Figure 2.10** Financial development and generalized trust in 88 countries. *Sources: Financial development: Private credit by deposit banks and other financial institutions as a percentage of GDP, obtained from the World Bank Indicators (1980–2010). Generalized Trust is taken from the World Values Survey (1981–2008).*

As well as the composition of assets and volume of credit, trust can influence the propensity of investors to seek the counsel of financial intermediaries and delegate decisions to them. In a setting where financial products are complex, delegation to intermediaries who have a good knowledge of these products can ameliorate the diversification of investments and their rate of return. Guiso and Jappelli (2005) have shown that investors who have more trust in financial intermediaries delegate more decisions to them and thus obtain better-diversified and more efficient portfolios. The part played by trust in the propensity to turn to financial intermediaries capable of supplying products that will ameliorate risk coverage is replayed when it comes to insurance. Cole et al. (2013) have looked at the reasons why insurance contracts covering climate risks to their harvests in two rural regions of India were hesitantly received by locals, even though they bore a low cost. *A priori*, such contracts ought to have been attractive to households where variations in income are largely determined by the vagaries of precipitation during harvest season. Cole et al. show that lack of trust in and comprehension of the contracts explains a significant part of the refusal of households to take up this insurance. A randomized experiment shows that instructors who explain to folk the content of the contracts can have a significant influence on the take-up of this insurance, but only if they come recommended by a microcredit agency with a well-established reputation in the households. If so, the intervention of the instructors increases the uptake of the insurance by 36%.

If the instructor does not have this backing, or if the households are not acquainted with the institution backing him, his intervention has no significant impact.

Trust patently plays a part in situations of financial crisis. The GSS shows that trust in financial institutions declined steeply after the failure of Lehman Brothers in 2008 (Guiso, 2010). Such failures are themselves provoked by drops in confidence. Guiso observes that persons who had the least trust in their banks withdrew their savings earliest in periods of financial distress. And trust during these periods of financial distress is linked to trust prior to their onset. This observation suggests that a structural deficit of trust in financial intermediaries may favor the onset of financial crises.

The interpretation of the correlation between trust and finance is beset with difficulties. First, the correlation may result from other factors, like optimism or risk aversion, potentially linked to trust and exerting influence on the propensity to utilize financial products. Trust, however, is identified in the available research as a quite distinctive characteristic, different from risk aversion or optimism and exerting a specific effect on the utilization of financial products (Guiso et al. 2008a). Second, in the correlation between finance and trust, the causal sequence may run the other way: the quality of finance, itself linked to the quality of institutions, may explain trust. Guiso et al. (2004) show, however, that there does exist an inherited portion of trust, independent of environmental influence on the development of financial markets, and that it does influence the resort to financing. The authors observe that residents of northern Italy who arrived there from regions in the south characterized by weak trust and weak civic spirit view financial products more distrustfully than do those born in the north. On identical observable characteristics, moreover, they get fewer loans from financial institutions. Such influence exerted by region of birth suggests that trust, and civic spirit as well, constitute partly heritable traits that may act as obstacles to the development of finance.

## 2.6.2 Innovations and Firm Organization
### 2.6.2.1 Innovations

Trust must play a preponderant role in the sort of economic activities—investment and especially innovation—that are attended by uncertainty on account of moral hazard and the difficulties of contract enforcement. In their path-breaking article on the link between trust and growth, Knack and Keefer (1997) already threw into relief a positive correlation between trust and investment as percentage of GDP. The correlation should be even more significant for research and development, and factor productivity.

Figure 2.11a documents the steady positive correlation between trust and a measure of total factor productivity, taken from Hall and Jones (2009), for a sample of 62 countries. Around one-third of the cross-country variation in TFP is associated to differences in trust across countries. Figure 2.11b illustrates the positive cross–country variation between average trust and innovation in 93 countries, with innovation measured by expenditure on research and development as percentage of GDP. The countries where trust is highest are

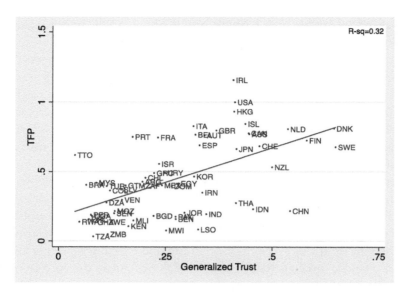

**Figure 2.11a** Total factor productivity and generalized trust in 62 countries. *Sources: Total Factor Productivity is taken from Hall and Jones (1999). Trust is measured from the World Values Survey (1981–2008).*

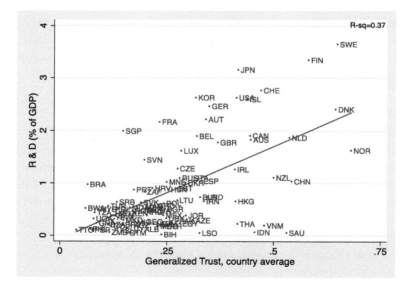

**Figure 2.11b** R&D expenses and generalized trust. *Sources: R&D expenses as a percentage of GDP over the period 1980–2010 are taken from the World Bank Development Indicators. Trust is measured from the World Values Survey (1981–2008).*

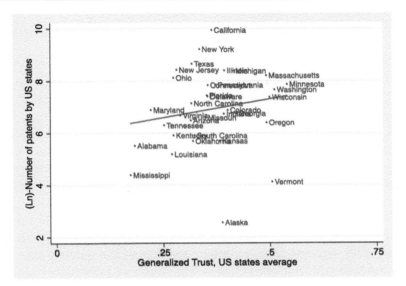

**Figure 2.11c** Cross US states correlation between R&D ((ln)-number of patents over the period 1980–2010) and generalized trust (1976–2008). *Sources: Income data is taken from the US Census Bureau and averaged for the years 1972–2011. The proportion of people that trust is taken from the General Social Survey (1973–2006). The trust measure is computed as the state average from responses to the question "Generally speaking, would you say that most people can be trusted or that you need to be very careful in dealing with people?" Trust is equal to 1 if the respondent answers "Most people can be trusted" and 0 otherwise.*

the ones with elevated R&D, in point of fact, the Anglophone and Nordic countries. Trust on its own explains more than a third (37%) of the dispersion of rates of expenditure on R&D across countries. This relationship remains statistically significant at the 5% level after controlling for initial income per capita, population density, and education. Figure 2.11c shows that the same correlation between innovation and trust holds across US states, whereby innovation is measured by the (ln)-number of patents per state. Remarkably, we find that this relationship also remains statistically significant at the 1% level after controlling for income per capita, population density, and the share of the population holding a PhD at the state level. The relationship between trust and innovation operates through a specific channel different from education or population density.

While the correlation between innovation and trust appears strong, we have, as yet, few studies that attempt to pin down the direction of the causality. The literature gives much greater prominence to another mechanism influencing innovation—the organization of firms and especially their degree of decentralization.

### 2.6.2.2 Firm Organization

By facilitating cooperation among anonymous persons, trust favors the emergence and growth of private and public organizations (Fukuyama, 1995; La Porta et al. 1997; Bertrand

and Schoar, 2006). Trust favors the decentralization of decisions within organizations, allowing them to adapt better to alterations in the environment.

Figure 2.12 documents this relationship by showing a positive correlation between firm decentralization and generalized trust for 72 countries. Firm decentralization is measured by the following question from the Global Competitiveness Report 2009 (GCR): "In your country, how do you assess the willingness to delegate authority to subordinates? 1 = low: top management controls all important decisions; 7 = high: authority is mostly delegated to business unit heads and other lower-level managers." Generalized trust is measured as the country average from WVS 1981–2009. The positive relationship is substantial: 37% of the cross-country variation in firm decentralization is associated with country differences in trust.

This aspect of trust is illustrated by Cingano and Pinotti (2012) who find that trust is associated with greater decentralization and larger firm size across Italian regions. Exploiting industry variation (and controlling for region- and industry-specific factors) they show that high-trust regions exhibit a larger share of value added and exports in industries characterized by greater need-for-delegation. The effect is driven by a shift of the firm size distribution away from the smallest units toward firms in higher size classes. Their estimated relationships are not only statistically significant but also economically meaningful when compared to such other determinants of industry specialization and

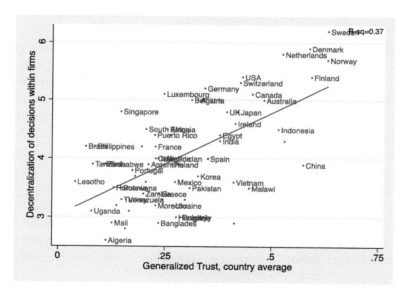

**Figure 2.12** Cross-country correlation between decentralization of firms and trust. *Sources: Firm decentralization is measured by the following question from the Global Competitiveness Report 2009 (GCR): "In your country, how do you assess the willingness to delegate authority to subordinates?" Answers range from "1 = low: top management controls all important decisions," to "7 = high: authority is mostly delegated to business unit heads and other lower-level managers." Generalized trust is measured as the country average from WVS 1981–2009.*

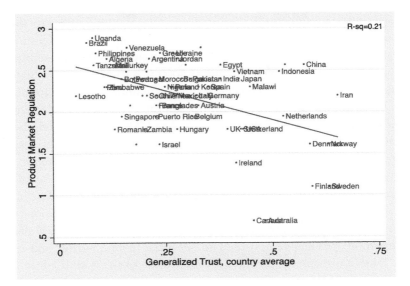

**Figure 2.13** Product market regulation and trust in 73 countries. *Sources: Product market regulation is measured as the (ln)-number of steps for opening a business, taken from the World Bank (2009). Generalized trust is measured as the country average from WVS 1981–2009.*

firm organization as human capital, physical capital, or judicial quality. For example, they imply that increasing trust by an amount corresponding to the inter-quartile range of its distribution across Italian regions would raise value added in a delegation-intensive industry (such as manufacture of machinery and equipment) relative to a less intensive industry (such as leather, leather products and footwear) by 24% (or by 19%, when using cross-country data). This amounts to around two-thirds of the implied effect of raising human capital, and is larger than the effect of physical capital or contract enforcement.

In the same vein, Bloom et al. (2012) show that trust can improve aggregate productivity by facilitating firm decentralization. They first provide a model supplying a rational foundation for the correlation between trust and decentralization of firms. Following Aghion and Tirole (1997) in their analysis of the congruence of preferences between CEOs and managers, the authors posit two opposite ways of organizing production. The CEO can either solve production problems directly or delegate these decisions to plant managers. When trust is high, plant managers tend to solve problems in congruence with the CEO's expectations rather than exploiting resources for their own interest. The CEO is thus more likely to delegate. In this perspective, trust affects the economic performance of firms through two channels. First, greater trust within the firm improves performance thanks to decentralized decision-making. A low-trust environment is a hindrance to the growth of the most productive firms. Second, economies characterized by low trust may orient themselves toward sectors in which decentralized decision making is less imperative. Sectors close to the leading edge of technology such as IT have to grant space for individual decision-making in order to innovate and constantly adapt to the environment. Bloom et al. (2012) test these predictions empirically. They collect new data on the decentralization of investment, hiring, production, and sales decisions from corporate headquarters to local plant managers in almost 4000 firms in the United States, Europe, and Asia. They find substantial differences in the cross-country decentralization of firms: those in the United States and northern Europe appear to be the most decentralized and those in southern Europe and Asia the most centralized. The authors match their database on management practices with the level of trust where the headquarters are located, using regional information from the WVS. They find that firms headquartered in high-trust regions are significantly more likely to decentralize. To identify the causal impact of trust on decentralization, they examine multinational firms and show that higher levels of bilateral trust between the multinational's country of origin and subsidiary's country of location increases decentralization. Finally, the authors show that more decentralized firms are also more productive and tend to specialize in innovation and information technology. Trust, indispensable for the decentralization of firms, thus affects innovation and aggregate productivity.

### 2.6.3 The Labor Market

Trust likewise exerts influence on the functioning of the labor market, through several channels affecting growth.

#### 2.6.3.1 The Quality of Labor Relations

Countries with higher generalized trust also have higher levels of cooperative relations between labor and management and higher levels of unionization. Unions have more members when generalized trust is high. Opportunistic and non-cooperative behavior constitutes a significant barrier to joining a union (Olson, 1965). Mutual trust and cooperation make it possible to lift these barriers. Cross-country analyses also show that relations between employers and employees are more cooperative when unions are more powerful (Aghion et al. 2011). The quality of employer-employee relations is associated to an array of factors that favor growth. The first is low unemployment (Blanchard and Philippon, 2004). Next, firms that have unions representing their employees are better able to adapt to new management methods, have more cooperative labor relations, and better productivity (Black and Lynch, 2001). Unions can ameliorate the quality of labor relations by allowing wage-earners to voice their views rather than be forced to stark either/or alternatives. Conceived this way, the role played by unions recalls Tocqueville's account of associations as little social laboratories where persons might learn cooperation first hand. It has been noted that farmers are more careful to use water sparingly the more they have had a voice in the framing of the irrigation regulations. Communes and cantons where political democracy is most strongly rooted, with high rates of voter turnout, have the lowest levels of tax evasion (Frey, 1998). Laboratory experiments confirm this observation, as shown in the next section. Players who decide on the rules governing their cooperation are more generous and trusting than those upon whom the same rules are imposed by an outsider. In other words, regulation and policy have a better chance of favoring cooperation to the extent they have been decided by a shared resolution and not imposed (Ostrom, 1990).

Hence the reaction of governments when there is a failure of the union-management dialog, the social dialog as it is called in Europe, can make it worse. Aghion et al. (2011) show that state regulation of labor markets is negatively correlated with the quality of labor relations. They argue that these facts reflect different ways of regulating labor markets, either through the state or through the civil society, depending on the degree of cooperation in the economy. They rationalize these facts with a learning model of the quality of labor relations. Distrustful labor relations lead to low unionization and high demand for direct state regulation of wages. In turn, state regulation crowds out the possibility for workers to experiment with negotiation and grasp the possibilities of cooperation in labor relations. This crowding out effect can give rise to multiple equilibria: a "good" equilibrium characterized by cooperative labor relations and high union density, leading to low state regulation, high employment, and production; and a "bad" equilibrium, characterized by distrustful labor relations, low union density, and strong state regulation of the minimum wage.

### 2.6.3.2 Flexicurity

The countries of southern Europe have chosen to offset the shocks that affect all working lives by prioritizing employment through rigorous employment protection, rather than prioritizing individuals through a generous unemployment benefit and an effective public agency to help in the job search. Conversely, the countries of northern Europe have adopted a "flexicurity" model that combines generous unemployment benefit, effective public job search agencies, and weak employment protection. Flexicurity is associated to better labor market performance, with higher rates of employment and a better reallocation of jobs toward more productive enterprises. On this basis, international institutions like the OECD and the European Commission recommend the adoption of flexicurity. Yet this model has a low rate of take-up outside northern Europe. Algan and Cahuc (2009) show that a trust deficit can create a barrier to the adoption of flexicurity. They provide evidence of cross-country correlations between national civic attitudes and the design of labor market insurance. Countries displaying high trust tend to insure their workers through unemployment benefits instead of using stringent employment protection. Such a relationship is robust to the inclusion of country fixed effects which account for time invariant national features and which could affect the design of unemployment insurance and employment protection. This finding is consistent with the strongly marked contrast between the flexicurity model in Nordic countries such as Denmark, and the continental European and Mediterranean countries. Naturally, the correlation between civic attitudes and the design of labor market institutions does not mean that there is a straight causal relationship going from social attitudes to the unemployment benefits/employment protection trade-off. There is a potential for reverse causality, since labor market institutions are likely to affect civic attitudes. For instance, administrative inefficiencies in the provision of unemployment insurance could influence guilty feelings about cheating on unemployment benefits. To deal with this reverse causality issue, Algan and Cahuc (2009) estimate the inherited part of civic attitudes that are not instantaneously influenced by the economic and institutional environment of the country in which people are living, by estimating the civic attitudes inherited by the American-born from their ancestors' country of origin, using the General Social Survey database. Using this inherited part of civic attitudes by country of origin as an instrument for civic attitudes in the home country, the authors show that there is a significant impact of civic attitudes on unemployment benefits and on employment protection in OECD countries during the period 1980–2003.

## 2.7. INSTITUTIONS, POLICIES, AND TRUST

### 2.7.1 Can Trust be Changed? Putnam I versus Putnam II

If trust plays a key role in explaining economic outcomes, it becomes urgent to identify the institutions and public policies for it to develop. Research related to this subject is still in its early stages. As discussed in Section 2.4.3, a large part of the literature considers trust to be a cultural component hardly malleable, whose determinants have to be searched for in the long history of each country, and with little room for immediate action. Yet, recent studies looking at immigrants show that their level of trust converge gradually to the average level of trust in their country of destination.

This ambiguity is well illustrated by the two conflicting views of the evolution of trust given by Putnam in his two books dating from 1993 and 2000. According to Putnam I (see the book from Putnam et al. 1993), social capital is largely determined by history. Elevated levels of social capital in the regions of north Italy compared to those in the south originated in the free-city experience during the medieval era.

Contrarily, according to Putnam II (see Putnam's book *Bowling Alone* in 2000), trust evolves quickly and is strongly influenced by the environment. In his book *Bowling Alone* Putnam shows that the levels of social capital, as measured by associations and club membership, have starkly declined in the United States since World War II. One of his main explications of this decline is the individualization of leisure activities, with an increasing amount of time spent watching television. Olken (2009) also identifies a negative impact of television and radio on association membership and self-reported trust in Indonesia by using variation in Indonesia's mountainous terrain and differential introduction of private television.

Depending on which perspective we take, from Putnam I or Putnam II, the room for policy intervention would be rather small or large. Section 2.4.3 documents that both approaches have an element of truth. Trust is partly inherited from past generations and shaped by historical shocks, because the underlying beliefs regarding the benefits of trust and cooperation are transmitted in communities through families (Bisin and Verdier, 2001; Benabou and Tirole, 2006; Tabellini, 2008b; Guiso et al. 2008a). But another part of trust is shaped by personal experience from the current environment, let it be social, economic, and political. In Bisin and Verdier's terminology, both the vertical channel of transmission from parents and the oblique/horizontal channel from the contemporaneous environment are at play in the fabric of trust.

This debate on the adjustment of trust to its environment also depends on what generalized trust really measures. If trust consists of beliefs about the trustworthiness of others, it is likely that individuals can update upward or downward their beliefs depending on the environment where they live, the civic spirit of their fellow citizens, and the transparency of their institutions. If trust consists of ingrained preferences and moral values, transmitted in early childhood and disconnected from personal experience as suggested by Uslaner (2008) and others, it might take more time to adjust. In the latter case, the action steps necessary to increase trust differ and depend on long-term policy, such as education. In this section, we consider the various policies that can shape both contextual beliefs and deeper preferences.

## 2.7.2 Institutions and Trust

How can institutions, and which institutions, shape trust? Do formal rules and norms embedded in institutions act as a complement or a substitute for informal values such as trust? These questions are key to identifying how and which specific institution could build up trust.

### 2.7.2.1 Relation Between Trust and Institutions

Figure 2.14 shows a strong positive correlation between trust and the quality of the legal system for a sample of 100 countries. Figure 2.15 displays a similar correlation between trust and the quality of governance in 163 European regions. These correlations are robust to using different measures of institutional quality commonly used in the economic literature (see Tables 2.6a and 2.6b), such as the rule of law, the strength of property right protection, the enforcement of contracts; as well as government effectivity, accountability, corruption (Rothstein and Uslaner, 2005) and controlling for other influences of institutional quality.

Recent papers try to go beyond this correlation by showing a causal impact of legal enforcement on trust. Tabellini (2008b) provides suggestive evidence that generalized morality is more widespread in European regions that used to be ruled by non-despotic political institutions in the distant past. Using data from the General Social Survey,

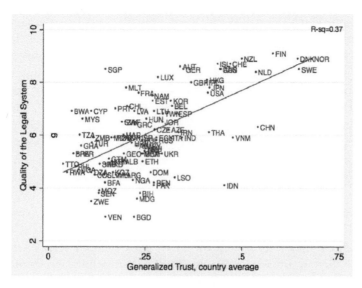

**Figure 2.14** Quality of the legal system and trust in 100 countries. *Sources: The Quality of the Legal System is taken from the Economic Freedom of the World Index (2007). Generalized trust is measured as the country average from WVS (1981–2009) and EVS (1981–2008).*

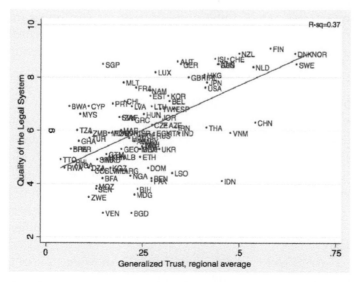

**Figure 2.15** Quality of governance and generalized trust in 163 European regions. *Sources: The Quality of Governance is taken from the Quality of Government Index (2010). Generalized trust is measured as the country average from the WVS (1981–2009) and EVS (1981–2008).*

**Table 2.6a** Trust and institutions

**Cross-country correlation**

| | Quality of legal system (1) | Rule of law (2) | Property rights (3) | Enforcement of contracts (4) |
|---|---|---|---|---|
| Trust | 3.942*** | 1.271** | 1.604*** | 2.864*** |
| | (0.719) | (0.484) | (0.602) | (0.674) |
| Income per capita | 0.646*** | 0.420*** | 0.531*** | 0.930*** |
| | (0.126) | (0.0891) | (0.101) | (0.250) |
| Population | −0.167*** | −0.109*** | −0.195*** | −0.0284 |
| | (0.055) | (0.035) | (0.050) | (0.092) |
| Education | 0.0146 | 0.0558 | 0.0120 | 0.178** |
| | (0.053) | (0.047) | (0.052) | (0.087) |
| Ethnic segmentation | 0.152 | −0.242 | 0.0572 | 1.614*** |
| | (0.440) | (0.251) | (0.377) | (0.535) |
| Observations | 90 | 93 | 91 | 46 |
| $R^2$ | 0.684 | 0.681 | 0.589 | 0.807 |

*Notes:* Dependent variables: (1) *Quality of Legal System* measures the overall quality of the legal system, taken from Economic Freedom of the World Index, 2007. (2) *Rule of Law* gives the average rule of law between 1996–2010, taken from Kaufmann et al. (2010). (3) *Property Rights* are a measure of property rights taken from the Heritage Foundation, 2004. (4) *Enforcement* measures enforceability of contracts, taken from Botero et al. (2004).

   *Trust* is measured from the answer to the question *"Generally speaking, would you say that most people can be trusted or that you need to be very careful in dealing with people?"* Trust is equal to 1 if the respondent answers *"Most people can be trusted"* and 0 otherwise.

   OLS regressions with robust standard errors in parentheses.

   **Sample (93 countries):** Albania, Algeria, Argentina, Australia, Austria, Bangladesh, Belgium, Benin, Botswana, Brazil, Bulgaria, Canada, Chile, China, Colombia, Croatia, Cyprus, Czech Republic, Denmark, Dominican Republic, Egypt, El Salvador, Estonia, Finland, France, Germany, Ghana, Great Britain, Greece, Guatemala, Hong Kong, Iceland, India, Indonesia, Iran, Iraq, Ireland, Israel, Italy, Japan, Jordan, Kenya, Kyrgyzstan, Latvia, Lesotho, Liberia, Lithuania, Luxembourg, Malawi, Malaysia, Mali, Malta, Mexico, Moldova, Morocco, Mozambique, Namibia, Netherlands, New Zealand, Norway, Pakistan, Peru, Philippines, Poland, Portugal, Romania, Russian Federation, Rwanda, Saudi Arabia, Senegal, Singapore, Slovakia, Slovenia, South Africa, South Korea, Spain, Sweden, Switzerland, Taiwan, Tanzania, Thailand, Trinidad and Tobago, Turkey, Uganda, Ukraine, United States, Uruguay, Venezuela, Vietnam, Zambia, Zimbabwe.

*Sources:* The trust data comes from the five wave of the World Values Survey (1981–2008), the four waves of the European Values Survey (1981–2008), and the third wave of the Afrobarometer (2005). Additional Controls: Investment Share measures Investment % of GDP 1980–2009, Penn World Tables 7.0. Income per capita measures GDP per capita (ln), const. prices, averaged for the years 1980–2009, taken from the Penn World Tables 7.0. Population measures population (ln), averaged between 1980 and 2009, Penn World Tables 7.0.

*Coefficients are statistically different from 0 at the 10% level.

**Coefficients are statistically different from 0 at the 5% level.

***Coefficients are statistically different from 0 at the 1%, level.

Tabellini regresses individual trust of US immigrants on various indicators of legal enforcement at stake in their ancestor's country at the end of the 19th century. He finds that immigrants from countries with more democratic institutions in the distant past have inherited a higher level of trust, even when controlling for historical economic development and school enrollment in the home country.

**Table 2.6b** Trust and institutions
**Cross-regional correlation in Europe**

| | Quality of governance (1) | Quality of governance (2) | Rule of law (3) | Effectivity (4) | Accountability (5) |
|---|---|---|---|---|---|
| Trust | 4.376*** | 1.291** | 3.285*** | 5.423*** | 2.463* |
| | (0.924) | (0.559) | (0.736) | (1.356) | (1.222) |
| Population | | −0.263* | 0.05 | −0.253 | −0.160 |
| | | (0.147) | (0.120) | (0.270) | (0.103) |
| Ln GDP p.c. | | 0.932*** | 0.487** | 0.684 | 1.039*** |
| | | (0.191) | (0.222) | (0.583) | (0.220) |
| Education | | 0.03 | −0.029** | 0.0246 | −0.0127 |
| | | (0.027) | (0.011) | (0.043) | (0.021) |
| Autonomous | | −0.267 | 0.275** | 0.0685 | 0.477*** |
| | | (0.164) | (0.105) | (0.334) | (0.147) |
| Bilingual | | −0.0513 | 0.0791 | 1.207** | −0.32 |
| | | (0.198) | (0.199) | (0.556) | (0.184) |
| Area | | 0.216** | −0.0351 | 0.134 | 0.227 |
| | | (0.087) | (0.073) | (0.187) | (0.131) |
| Observations | 163 | 163 | 163 | 163 | 163 |
| $R^2$ | 0.342 | 0.613 | 0.499 | 0.450 | 0.552 |

*Notes:* Dependent variables: Columns (1) and (2): *Quality of Governance* index measures the overall quality of regional institutions, taken from the Quality of Governance Institute, 2010. (3) *Rule of Law* measures the quality of the rule of law, taken from the Quality of Governance Institute, 2010. (4) *Effectivity* measures the governance effectivity, taken from the Quality of Governance Institute, 2010. (4) *Accountability* measures the quality of media and elections, taken from the Quality of Governance Institute, 2010.

*Trust* is measured from the answer to the question *"Generally speaking, would you say that most people can be trusted or that you need to be very careful in dealing with people?"* Trust is equal to 1 if the respondent answers *"Most people can be trusted"* and 0 otherwise.

OLS regressions with robust standard errors, clustered at the country level, in parentheses.

**Sample (163 regions):** 163 European regions in the following countries: Austria, Belgium, Bulgaria, Czech Republic, Denmark, France, Germany, Greece, Hungary, Italy, Netherlands, Poland, Portugal, Romania, Slovakia, Spain, Sweden, United Kingdom.

*Sources:* The trust data is taken from the four waves of the European Values Survey (1981–2008. Population measures the log of the average number of inhabitants 2007–2009 per region, taken from Eurostat. GDP p.c. gives the log of the regional average GDP per capita between 2007 and 2009, taken from Eurostat. Education gives the percentage of population with some type of tertiary degree in 2006, taken from Eurostat. Bilingual equals to 1 if more than one official languages exists in the region. Autonomous equals 1 if the region is an autonomous region. Logarea gives the log value of the region's area.

*Coefficients are statistically different from 0 at the 10% level.
**Coefficients are statistically different from 0 at the 5% level.
***Coefficients are statistically different from 0 at the 1% level.

Naturally, this approach does not prove that past democratic institutions have a causal impact on trust. Since those institutions are invariant, they could pick up any other invariant aspect of the home country. Yet, Tabellini's analyses are intriguing since historical political institutions could explain up to 57% of the country of origin fixed effect. This share is much larger than the one explained by income per capita and education in the distant past. Institutions can have long-lasting impact on social and economic outcomes, but the persistence channel goes through their effect on values. This is really different from the traditional explanation of the persistence of institutions through elites capture (Acemoglu et al. 2001). Weak legal enforcement forces citizens to rely on informal and local rules and to develop limited trust as opposed to generalized trust. A good illustration of this diffusion of limited morality in the presence of weak institution is given by the Mafia. Gambetta (1993) documents that feudalism was formally abolished in Sicily much later than in the rest of Europe (in 1812). The State was too weak to enforce the introduction of private property rights of the lands. The Mafia benefited from this institutional vacuum and offered local protection through informal patronage, drawing a clear distinction between those under its protection and the others. In the same vein, Section 2.4.2 above has documented recent studies showing that non-democratic and corrupt institutions in the distant past in Italy or in the Habsburg Empire are related to lower trust nowadays.

Other contributions use natural experiments to show the effect of democratic institutions on cooperative behavior. Bardhan (2000) finds that farmers are less likely to violate irrigation rules when they themselves have set up those rules. Frey (1998) shows that tax evasion in Swiss cantons is lower when democratic participation is greater. All these different works are suggestive of an impact of democracy on cooperation. But even those latter natural experiments cannot rule out the existence of omitted factors determining both the selection of institutions and the response to institutions. Besides, the precise mechanism through which democracy (and more generally, formal rules) shapes cooperative behavior and the identification of its effect still needs more research (see Benabou and Tirole for a theoretical model that rationalizes the interplay between laws and norms, 2011).

### 2.7.2.2 Experimental Games

An alternative approach for identifying the effect of institutions on cooperation is to mimic formal and legal rules in the context of experimental games. Naturally, formal and legal rules in experimental games differ from real institutions. But this has the advantage of providing a controlled experiment to estimate how people change their level of cooperation and trust depending on exogenous variations in the rules of the games.

Initially, the literature has looked at the interaction between formal and informal institutions, but in the context of cooperation with reputational incentives, such as repeated games (Kranton, 1996). One main conclusion of this approach is that legal enforcement can crowd out reputational incentives and undermine informal institutions. Yet, this prediction seems to be very specific to situations of cooperation with reputational incentives, and do not apply to cooperation embedded in moral values such as generalized trust.

Fehr and Gatcher (2000) analyze cooperation in a public good game. Interestingly, the authors changed the setup of the traditional public good experiment by allowing the cooperators to punish the defectors. They demonstrate that the free riders are heavily penalized even if punishment is costly and does not provide any material benefits to the punisher. The opportunity for costly punishment causes a large increase in cooperation levels because potential free riders face a credible threat. In the presence of a costly punishment opportunity, almost complete cooperation can be achieved and maintained during the games. The main conclusion is that human beings are conditional cooperators, they cooperate providing that others do. The introduction of formal rule is key to enforcing this conditional cooperation.

Herrmann et al. (2008) have used this setup to measure conditional cooperation in 16 different cities across the world. They find that cooperation for the funding of the public good is the highest in Boston or Melbourne and the lowest in Athens and Muscat. This ordering is highly correlated with the rule of law and the transparency of institutions in the corresponding country. More strikingly, Herrmann et al. find that participants in some cities, like Athens, display anti-social punishment behavior: that is, they punish the high contributor instead of the low contributor. The weakness of the rule of law is a strong predictor of this anti-social behavior. Similarly, Rothstein (2011) used various experiments with students in Sweden and Romania to show that their generalized trust and trust in civil servants declined substantially after witnessing a police officer accepting a bribe. His interpretation is that the absence of transparency of institutions and civic spirit of public officials can have very large damaging effects on generalized trust. If public officials, who are expected to represent the law, are corrupt, people infer that most other people cannot be trusted neither.

Other promising research looks at the impact of democracy on cooperation in an experimental setting. Contrary to natural experiments, it is possible to control in the laboratory how cooperation changes when a policy is imposed endogenously through a democratic process or imposed exogenously. This is the design used by Dal Bo et al. (2010). Subjects participate in several prisoners' dilemma games and may choose, by simple majority, to establish a policy that could encourage cooperation by imposing fines on non-cooperators. In some cases, the experimental software randomly overrides the votes of the subjects and randomly imposes, or not, the policy. Before proceeding to play again with either the original or the modified payoffs, the subjects are informed of whether payoffs are modified and whether it was decided by their vote or by the computer. The authors show that the effect of the policy on the percentage of cooperative actions is 40% greater when it is democratically chosen by the subjects than when it is imposed by the computer.

All in all, these studies show that formal rules and conditional cooperation might work as a complement in sustaining cooperative behavior. This is the case when the content of the rules, as in Dal Bo et al. (2010), creates focal points or provides signals about the group members' willingness to cooperate. In other cases, the sudden introduction of formal rules or tougher incentives to cooperate might signal instead that principals do not trust agents or that non-cooperative behavior is diffused in the society. For example, Falk and Kosfeld (2006) study the behavior of experimental subjects in the role of agent, choosing a level of production that was costly to them and beneficial to the principal (the authority). Before the agent's decision, the principal could decide to leave the choice of the level of production completely to the agent's discretion or impose a lower bound on the agent's production. In postplay interviews, most agents agreed with the statement that the imposition of the lower bound was a signal of distrust. In another study, Galbiati and Vertova (2008) investigate a similar effect in the context of cooperation in a minimum effort game. In this case, the authors find that, when principals opt to introduce a formal cooperation rule after having observed agents' effort levels in the first experimental round, most cooperative individuals might reduce their effort level. Eliciting individuals' expectations about others' efforts, the authors find that if principals opt to introduce a formal sanction for those that do not cooperate, most cooperative individuals prefer to live in a society where non-cooperation is widespread.

### 2.7.2.3 Co-Evolution of Trust and Institutions

Rather than stressing the causal impact of institutions, recent contributions look at the co-evolution of trust and institutions, leading to multiple equilibria. The diffusion of limited morality can reinforce the weakness of institutions because a society with limited morality can be more tolerant of weaker compliance with legal enforcement. The society might thus be trapped in a bad equilibrium where mistrust and weak institutions reinforce each other. In this context, promoting better enforcement might not have any support and effect since limited morality makes the trade opportunities too negligible anyway. Several contributions have documented more precisely the type of institutions that could co-evolve with trust. In particular, recent contributions show the interplay between trust and regulation (Aghion et al. 2010; Pinotti, 2012; Carlin et al. 2009; Francois and Van Ypersele, 2009).

Figure 2.13 shows that there exists a negative correlation between generalized trust and the extent of market regulation, measured by the number of steps required to open a business. Aghion et al. (2010) document that this correlation works for a range of measures of trust, from trust in others to trust in firms and political institutions, as well as for a range of regulatory measures from product markets to labor markets.

Explanations of this negative correlation between trust and regulatory intervention by the public authorities are grounded in the assumption that the state must step in to regulate the relations among individuals when they are incapable of cooperating spontaneously. In this perspective, Aghion et al. (2010) present a simple model explaining this correlation. In their setup, individuals make two decisions: whether or not to become civic, and whether to become entrepreneurs or choose routine (perhaps state) production. Those who become uncivic impose a negative externality on others when they become entrepreneurs (e.g. pollute), whereas those who become civic do not. The community (through voting or some other political mechanism) regulates entry into entrepreneurial activity when the expected negative externalities are large. Regulation narrows choices

and hence negative externalities. But regulation itself is implemented by government officials, who demand bribes when they are not civic-minded. In this model, when people
expect to live in a civic-spirited community, they expect low levels of regulation and corruption, and so become civic. Their beliefs have a self-justifying property, as their choices
lead to civic-mindedness, low regulation, and high levels of entrepreneurial activity. When,
in contrast, people expect to live in an uncivic-minded community, they expect high levels of regulation and corruption, and do not become civic. Again, their beliefs are justified,
as their choices lead to uncivic-mindedness, high regulation, high corruption, and low
levels of entrepreneurial activity. The model has two equilibria: a good one with a large
share of civic individuals and no regulation; and a bad one where a large share of uncivic
individuals support heavy regulation. Production and welfare are higher in the good
equilibrium.

The model explains the correlation between regulation and distrust, and has a number
of further implications which are empirically documented using international surveys.
The model predicts, most immediately, that distrust influences not just regulation itself,
but also the demand for regulation. Distrust generates demand for regulation even when
people realize that the government is corrupt and ineffective; they prefer state control to
unbridled activity by uncivic entrepreneurs.

The most fundamental implication of the model, however, is that beliefs (as measured
by distrust) and institutions (as measured by regulation) co-evolve. Beliefs shape institutions, and institutions shape beliefs. The interactions between institutions and beliefs
comprise complementarities that induce multiple equilibria, as in Aghion et al. (2011).

Beyond regulation, trust and social capital are likely to affect the overall quality of
institutions and government through political accountability. This is the point made
by Nannicini et al. (2010). In a political agency model, the authors show that civic
agents are more likely to hold politicians accountable for the aggregate social welfare
of the community. They tend to punish politicians who pursue vested interests and
grab rents for some specific groups. In contrast, uncivic agents' votes are based on their
own or group-specific interest and are more tolerant with amoral politicians. Nannicini
et al. (2010) convincingly test the prediction of their model by using cross-district variation in the criminal prosecution of members of the Parliament in Italy. They find that
the electoral punishment of political misbehavior, corresponding to receiving a request
of criminal prosecution or shirking in parliamentary activity, is considerably larger in
electoral districts with high social capital.

### 2.7.3 Community Characteristics

Distinguished from formal institutions, a large body of the research stresses the role of
community characteristics in building trust. One of the most prominent factors identified
in this realm is the extent of inequality and ethnic fractionalization.

### 2.7.3.1 Inequality

The focus on inequality is fueled by the strong negative correlation between trust and Gini indexes across countries and US states in Figures 2.16 and 2.17. High-trusting societies are also more equal, measured by low Gini coefficients, while low-trusting societies show typically higher levels of income inequality, as given by high Gini coefficients. Cross-country and cross–US state regressions controlling for income, population, education, and ethnic fractionalization confirm this correlation (see Table 2.7). Alesina and La Ferrara (2000) show that this negative relationship between trust and income inequality also holds at a more local level within US localities and municipalities. Rothstein and Uslaner (2005) document a within–US-states correlation between the rise in equalities and the decline of trust over the last decades.

A pending issue is that of causality. Inequality might correlate negatively with trust for several reasons. First, as suggested by Rothstein and Uslaner, high levels of trust and cooperation might go along with high preferences for redistribution and can so contribute to lower inequality. On the reverse, high inequality could make individuals perceive themselves unfairly treated by people belonging to social classes different from their own, such that they restrict cooperative action and trust to members from their own class (Rothstein and Uslaner, 2005). Future research is still needed to nail down the causal effect of inequality on trust.

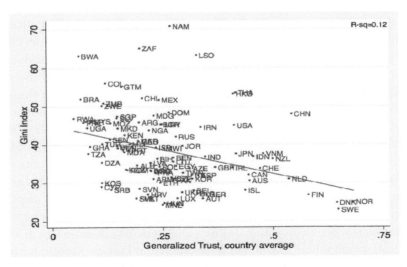

**Figure 2.16** Inequality and generalized trust in 101 countries. *Sources: Inequality is measured by average of the Gini Index between 2005 and 2012 (World Bank). Generalized trust is measured as the country average from WVS (1981–2009) and EVS (1981–2008).*

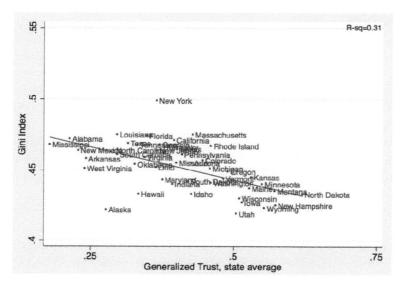

**Figure 2.17** Inequality and generalized trust in 46 US states. *Sources: Inequality is measured by the Gini Index in 2010 (US Census Bureau). Generalized trust is taken from the General Social Survey (1973–2006).*

### 2.7.3.2 Ethnic Fractionalization and Segmentation

The second community characteristic that has attracted attention is ethnic fractionalization or segregation. In a highly debated contribution, Putnam (2007) argues that ethnic diversity drives down trust. Using cross-cities evidence, the author shows that in ethnically diverse neighborhoods, residents' trust is lower; altruism and community cooperation rarer; and friends fewer. Alesina and La Ferrara (2000, 2002) find similar evidence across US states. The explanation for this result is that individuals have natural in-group preferences and have a tendency to trust less those people that are different from them. In the same vein, higher ethnic diversity is associated with lower cooperation as measured by the level of funding and the quality of public goods (Alesina et al. 1999; Miguel and Gugerty, 2005). The main explanations of why ethnic diversity affects those outcomes are the heterogeneity of preferences, and the free-rider problem which undermines collective action. Uslaner (2012) challenges Putnam's thesis and argues that residential segregation, rather than ethnic diversity per se, drives down trust. Using cross-US states evidence, Uslaner shows that both integrated and diverse neighborhoods are associated with higher levels of trust only when people have diverse social networks. Conversely, in areas with a lot of segregation and where individuals from different ethnic backgrounds cannot meet each other, distrust is higher. One conclusion is that immigration and urbanization policy should avoid ethnic ghettos to maintain trust.

Yet, the literature on the relationship between cooperation and diversity raises an important identification issue. Due to endogenous residential sorting of individuals on

**Table 2.7** Trust and inequality

| | Inequality | | | |
|---|---|---|---|---|
| | Cross country | | US states | |
| | (1) | (2) | (3) | (4) |
| Trust | −24.96*** | −12.63* | −0.093*** | −0.064*** |
| | (5.600) | (7.451) | (0.017) | (0.016) |
| Income per capita | | 0.0954 | | −0.01 |
| | | (1.240) | | (0.022) |
| Population | | 0.324 | | 0.007*** |
| | | (0.791) | | (0.002) |
| Education | | −1.116** | | 0.002 |
| | | (0.542) | | (0.001) |
| Ethnic segmentation | | 7.385 | | |
| | | (5.003) | | |
| Latitude | | | | −0.0004* |
| | | | | (0.0002) |
| Longitude | | | | 0.0002** |
| | | | | (0.0001) |
| Observations | 101 | 89 | 46 | 46 |
| $R^2$ | 0.122 | 0.276 | 0.314 | 0.680 |

*Notes:* The dependent variable *Inequality* measures income inequality as given by the Gini Index. *Trust* is measured from the answer to the question *"Generally speaking, would you say that most people can be trusted or that you need to be very careful in dealing with people?"* Trust is equal to 1 if the respondent answers *"Most people can be trusted"* and 0 otherwise.

OLS regressions with robust standard errors in parentheses.

**Sample (101 countries):** Albania, Algeria, Argentina, Armenia, Australia, Austria, Azerbaijan, Bangladesh, Belarus, Belgium, Benin, Bosnia and Herzegovina, Botswana, Brazil, Bulgaria, Burkina Faso, Canada, Chile, China, Colombia, Croatia, Cyprus, Czech Republic, Denmark, Dominican Republic, Egypt, El Salvador, Estonia, Ethiopia, Finland, France, Georgia, Germany, Ghana, Great Britain, Greece, Guatemala, Hong Kong, Hungary, Iceland, India, Indonesia, Iran, Ireland, Israel, Italy, Japan, Jordan, Kenya, Korea, South, Kosovo, Kyrgyzstan, Latvia, Lesotho, Lithuania, Luxembourg, Macedonia, Madagascar, Malawi, Malaysia, Mali, Malta, Mexico, Moldova, Montenegro, Morocco, Mozambique, Namibia, Netherlands, New Zealand, Nigeria, Norway, Pakistan, Peru, Philippines, Poland, Portugal, Romania, Russian Federation, Rwanda, Senegal, Serbia, Singapore, Slovakia, Slovenia, South Africa, Spain, Sweden, Switzerland, Taiwan, Tanzania, Thailand, Turkey, Uganda, Ukraine, United States, Uruguay, Venezuela, Vietnam, Zambia, Zimbabwe.

*Sources:* Trust data used in regressions in columns (1) and (2) comes from the five waves of the World Values Survey (1981–2008), and the four waves of the European Values Survey (1981–2008), for regressions in columns (3) and (4) from the US GSS (1973–2006). Income per capita measures the regions average log income per capita. Population gives the log of the total population living in the region. Education in column (2) measures average years of schooling between 1950 and 2010 and is taken from Barro and Lee (2010), in column (4) the fraction of population having an advanced degree. Ethnic fractionalization measures the degree of ethnic fractionalization and is taken from Alesina et al. (2003). Latitude and longitude refer to the region's geographic position.

*Coefficients are statistically different from 0 at the 10% level.
**Coefficients are statistically different from 0 at the 5% level.
***Coefficients are statistically different from 0 at the 1% level.

ethnic grounds, the estimates are likely to be biased. The attempts to establish causality rely mainly on instrumental variables. However convincing the instruments might be, this strategy cannot overcome the concern as to whether the instruments fulfill the exclusion restriction and do not have a direct effect on public goods. For instance, Miguel and

Gugerty (2005) use the pre-colonial patterns of settlement as instruments, assuming that these variables have no direct impact on present-day ethnic relations. But, since past settlement patterns are likely to have at least some direct impact on the present-day level of cooperation, the exclusion restriction might still be violated. Algan et al. (2012b) address this issue by using a natural experiment in which households in France are allocated to public housing blocks without taking their ethnic origin or their preference for diversity into account. Due to a strongly republican ideology, the French public housing system allocates state-planned, moderate-cost, rental apartments to natives and immigrants without concern for their cultural and ethnic background, mixing people indiscriminately. Using data from housing blocks made up of 20 adjacent households, the authors show that higher ethnic diversity is associated with social anomia rather than distrustful relationships. Yet, more research has to be done before drawing policy conclusions. One of the most promising agendas would be to use a randomized housing mobility program, in the same vein of Moving to Opportunity (see Katz et al. 2013), to investigate how the changes in the ethnic composition of the neighbors modify cooperation and trust.

### 2.7.4 Education and Trust

A large literature argues that a central component trust derives from moral values deeply ingrained in personality traits, and does not just boil down to context-dependent beliefs about others', trustworthiness. A trusting person that accidentally meets an non-trustworthy person will not change his moral values right away. Moral values of cooperation have a rather stable component because they have been shaped in the early ages by parents or at school. In this section, we review the evidence on the relationship between education and trust.

There is some evidence that a greater quantity of schooling is associated with higher social capital (Helliwell and Putnam, 2007). Yet, variation in the average years of education of the population across developed countries is too small to explain the observed cross-country differences in trust.

Algan et al. (2013a) propose a complementary explanation by looking at the relationship between how students are taught, and students' beliefs in cooperation. They show that methods of teaching differ greatly across countries, between schools, and within schools within a country. Some schools and teachers emphasize vertical teaching practices, whereby teachers primarily lecture, students take notes or read textbooks, and teachers ask students' questions. The central relationship in the classroom is between the teacher and the student. Other schools and teachers emphasize horizontal teaching practices, whereby students work in groups, do projects together, and ask teachers' questions. The central relationship in the classroom is among students. Consistent with the idea that beliefs underlying social capital are acquired through the practice of cooperation, and that social skills are acquired in early childhood, Algan et al. (2013a) test whether horizontal teaching practices can develop social capital. They use various international surveys, like the Civic

Education Study (CES), the Trends in International Mathematics and Science Study (TIMSS) and the Progress in International Reading Literacy Study (PIRLS), covering around 60 countries. They emphasize the distinction between "teacher lectures" and "students work in groups" as measures of vertical and horizontal teaching practices, respectively.

Figure 2.18 shows that teaching practices vary systematically across countries. The $x$-axis represents the average gap between vertical teaching (teacher lectures) and horizontal teaching (students work in groups) in a typical hour of class. The higher the indicator, the more the country is tilted toward vertical teachings. Students work in groups more in Nordic countries (Denmark, Norway, Sweden) and Anglophone countries (Australia, United States, and to a lesser extent, Great Britain). This teaching practice is less common in east European countries and in the Mediterranean (Greece, Cyprus, Portugal and, to a lesser extent, Italy). In these countries, teachers spend more time lecturing. Education in some countries, like France, is almost entirely based on vertical teaching. Figure 2.18 also shows that vertical teaching is highly negatively correlated with generalized trust across countries. This result still holds when per capita income, education expenditures, and average years of education are controlled for.

The authors then investigate within-school and within-classroom variation in teaching practices to identify the causal impact of these practices on students' beliefs. By looking at teaching practices and student beliefs across classrooms within a school, the authors can alleviate concerns regarding omitted variables that might drive the self-sorting of

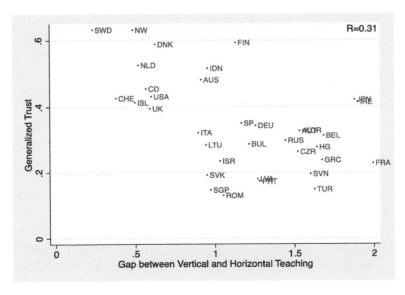

**Figure 2.18** Trust and the gap between vertical and horizontal teaching. *Sources: TIMSS, WVS.*

parents, students, and teachers into schools. They also use within-classroom variation in teaching practices and student beliefs. This strategy eliminates concerns about omitted variables linked to selection into classrooms. It also provides an alternative strategy for excluding reverse causality by comparing teaching practices of different teachers faced with exactly the same group of students. The authors show that horizontal teaching practices have a substantial positive impact on students' social capital (trust in teachers, in other students, association membership…), while vertical teaching practices crowd out beliefs in cooperation. The relationship between working in groups and students' social capital is robust whatever the specification: across schools, within schools and within classrooms. The within school (and within classroom) estimates allow the authors to address self-selection and reverse causality. But another concern is that horizontal teaching practices just proxy for a teacher being good or nice. This is a traditional issue raised by cross-section analysis since it is impossible to control for teacher-fixed effect in this setting. The authors show that teaching practices are not a proxy for "good" or "nice" teachers based on observable teacher characteristics. But the teaching practice can still be driven by an unobserved teacher (or student) characteristic.

A promising avenue of research would consist in providing randomized evaluations of early childhood intervention aimed at developing children's social skills, e.g. their aptitude to cooperate with others. This investigation is timely and important given that recent longitudinal studies suggest that much of the impact of programs that improve adult achievement (such as the Perry Preschool program or project STAR) flows through some sort of non-cognitive channel, and thus raise the question of what those non-cognitive skills are, and how much of the impact comes through social skills (see Heckman et al. for a recent synthesis, 2010). In the literature, non-cognitive skills embrace all personality traits that are non-related to cognitive skills (e.g. IQ and grades), such as self-esteem and emotional well-being measured on psychological scales. This is thus a rather vague notion and it is still unclear how non-cognitive skills relate to social skills. Besides, there is little evidence on whether and how intervention can improve those skills, in particular among children the most at risk of becoming anti-social adults.

Algan et al. (2013b) provide a first attempt to estimate the long-term effects of an early intervention that is specifically dedicated to social skills development. The authors use data from a large and detailed longitudinal study following the social, cognitive, and emotional development of 895 men who were kindergarteners in neighborhoods of low socioeconomic status in Montreal in 1984. The study incorporates a randomized evaluation of an intensive two-year social skills training program at the beginning of elementary school for the most disruptive subjects ($n = 250$). The training program involves the subjects themselves, parents, and peers. These detailed data are matched with self-reported outcomes and administrative records. As adults, the subjects in the treated group have significantly better labor market performance than the non-treated group, with an increase in the likelihood of employment at age 26 of 10% points. Individuals who belong to the treated group have significantly more favorable social outcomes, measured by lower criminality rates and higher social capital. By distinguishing the different cognitive and non-cognitive channels through which this intervention operates, the authors find that the only significant channel for economic outcomes is social skills. The overall rate of return of this program in terms of expected lifecycle income ranges from 282% to 452%, implying that every $1 invested yields $2.8 to $4.5 in benefits. This result provides room for policy intervention to develop social skills in early childhood. They call for future experiments to assess the deep personality traits that explain social skills and how they relate to non-cognitive skills.

## 2.8. FUTURE AVENUES: TRUST AND WELL-BEING

This survey documents two main findings. First, trust has a causal impact on economic development, through its channels of influence on the financial, product, and labor markets, and with a direct effect on total factor productivity and organization of firms. Second, trust and institutions strongly interact, with causality running in both directions. These findings set new avenues of research to identify the policies that could promote social capital and cooperation, from rule of law and democracy to education policies.

This survey has mainly focused on economic and institutional issues related to trust. Yet there is a growing consensus that economic development is poorly measured by income per capita alone, and should include measures of well-being. One reason for that is the well-known Easterlin paradox, stressing that the increase in income per capita within countries has not been associated with an increase in happiness. To explain this result, recent contributions suggest that well-being depend essentially on the quality of social relationship, instead of individual income. From this perspective, we should expect a strong correlation between trust and well-being.

Figure 2.19 illustrates this relationship by using measures of life satisfaction from the World Values Survey question: "All things considered together, how satisfied are with your life as a whole these days." Life satisfaction ranges from 1 to 10, a higher score indicating a higher life satisfaction. The correlation between life satisfaction and generalized trust is positive: 17% of the variance in life satisfaction is associated with cross-country differences in generalized trust, with a few outliers like Portugal. The same positive correlation holds if we consider the question on happiness: "Taking all things together, would you say that you are: very happy, happy, quite happy, not happy, not at all happy?"

Helliwell and Wang (2010) provide cross-country micro evidence on the positive relationship between trust and well-being. From the 2006 wave of the Gallup World Poll, they use the wallet trust question for 86 countries. Individuals are asked what is the hypothetical likelihood of the respondent's lost wallet (with clear identification and $200 cash) being returned if found by a neighbor, a police officer, or a stranger. Helliwell and Wang estimate that an increase in income by two-thirds is necessary to compensate

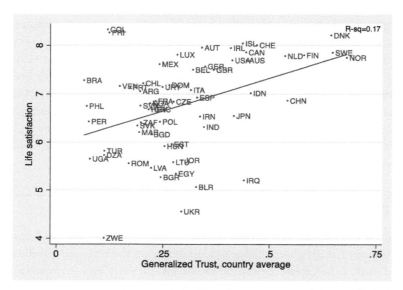

**Figure 2.19** Trust and life satisfaction. *Sources: Life satisfaction (1–10) and generalized trust are taken from the World Values Survey (2008).*

the welfare loss associated with thinking that no one will return your wallet and your documents. For example, to live in a country like Norway (highest mean expected wallet return of 80%) rather than in Tanzania (lowest mean expected wallet return of 27%) is equivalent to an increase by 40% of household income. Helliwell and Huang (2010) showed that the same result holds in the workplace. Using micro data from Canada (2003 wave Equality, Security, and Community Survey) and US (2000 wave of the Social Capital Benchmark Survey), the authors find that the climate of trust in workplace, in particular trust in managers, is strongly related to subjective well-being. On a 1–10 scale, an increase by one point of trust in managers has the same effect on life satisfaction as an increase in household income by 30%.

Examining our psychological reactions allows us to better understand the importance of these relations. Imagine that you participate in the trust game, but that one measures now the level of oxytocin in your blood. As mentioned above, oxytocin is a neurotransmitter released by our lymbic system, the part of our brain which is responsible for pleasure or fright. Zak et al. (2004) have tried to find out if trust and reciprocity are equally linked to that love hormone. For that, they have applied the trust game during which levels of oxytocin are measured in the blood of the receiver, once he finds out whether the sender has trusted him by sending a non-negligible amount. The results indicate that trust produces happiness: the more the signaled level of trust is increased (meaning, the more the amount transferred is increased) the more the level of oxytocin increases in the blood of the receiver. Zak et al. (2004) also conducted an experiment using a particularly instructive variant, in which the receiver receives a monetary transfer not from a real person, but from a lottery. In this variant, the level of oxytocin does not rise with the money received. This result well illustrates that it is trust that is associated with sentiments of happiness, and not the mere fact of receiving money.

These results have been confirmed by brain images made by Sanfey et al. (2002). As soon as the participants of the trust game note that the others do not cooperate, the insular part of the cortex in their brain illuminates. This brain part is known for being active in states of pain and disgust. The main conclusion of this line of research is that the non-monetary dimension of having cooperative social relationship with others affects more happiness than the monetary gains derived from cooperation. All in all, those results suggest that trust affects many dimensions of economic development, including both income and happiness, and is a key component in human development at large.

## ACKNOWLEDGMENTS

We thank Elizabeth Beasley, Samuel Bowles, Ernst Fehr, Oded Galor, Paola Guiliano, John Helliwell, Karla Hoff, Andrei Shleifer, and Mathias Thoenig for their helpful comments. We also thank Johannes Buggle for his outstanding work as a research assistant for this article. Yann Algan acknowledges financial support from the ERC Starting Grant 240923 under the European Community Seventh Framework Programme (FP7/2007–2013).

## REFERENCES

Acemoglu, D., Robinson, J., Johnson, S., 2001. The colonial origins of comparative development: an empirical investigation. American Economic Review 91, 1369–1401.

Aghion, P., Algan, Y., Cahuc, P., 2011. Can policy affect culture? minimum wage and the quality of labor relations. Journal of the European Economic Association 9 (1), 3–42.

Aghion, P., Algan, Y., Cahuc, P., Shleifer, A., 2010. Regulation and distrust. Quarterly Journal of Economics 125 (3), 1015–1049.

Aghion, P., Tirole, J., 1997. Formal and real authority in organizations. The Journal of Political Economy 105 (1), 1–29.

Alesina, A., Baqir, R., Easterley, W., 1999. Public goods and ethnic divisions. Quarterly Journal of Economics 114 (4), 1243–1284.

Alesina, A., La Ferrara, E., 2000. Participation in heterogeneous communities. Quarterly Journal of Economics 115 (3), 847–904.

Alesina, A., La Ferrara, E., 2002. Who trusts others? Journal of Public Economics 85 (2), 207–234.

Alesina, A., Devleeschauwer, A., Wacziarg, R., Kurlat, Sergio, Easterly, W., 2003. Fractionalization. Journal of Economic Growth 8 (2), 155–194. <http://ideas.repec.org/a/kap/jecgro/v8y2003i2p155-94.html>. <http://ideas.repec.org/s/kap/jecgro.html>.

Algan, Y., Cahuc, P., 2009. Civic virtue and labor market institutions. American Economic Journal: Macroeconomics 1 (1), 111–145.

Algan, Y., Cahuc, P., 2010. Inherited trust and growth. American Economic Review 100, 2060–2092.

Algan, Y., Cahuc, P., Sangnier, M., 2011. Efficient and Inefficient Welfare States, Institute for the Study of Labor, DP 5445.

Algan, Y., Benkler, Y., Fuster Morell, M., Hergueux, J., 2012a. "Cooperation in a Peer Production Economy: Experimental Evidence from Wikipedia", Working Paper Sciences Po.

Algan, Y., Hémet, C., Laitin, D., 2012b. The Social Effect of Ethnic Diversity at a Local Level: A Natural Experiment with Exogenous Residential Allocation, Working Paper Sciences Po.

Algan, Y., Cahuc, P., Shleifer, A., 2013a. Teaching practices and social capital. American Economic Journal: Applied Economics, 5(3), 189–210.

Algan, Y., Beasley, E., Tremblay, R., Vitaro, F., 2013b. The Long Term Impact of Social Skills Training at School Entry: A Randomized Controlled Trial. Working Paper.

Almond, G., Verba, S., 1963. The Civic Culture: Political Attitudes and Democracy in Five Nations. Sage Publications, London (first ed. 1989).

Arrow, K., 1972. Gifts and exchanges. Philosophy and Public Affairs 1, 343–362.

Ashraf, Q., Galor, O., 2013. The "Out-of-Africa" hypothesis, human genetic diversity, and comparative economic development. American Economic Review, 103(1), 1-46.

Banfield, E., 1958. The Moral Basis of a Backward Society. Free Press, New York.

Barro, R., Lee, J.W., 2010. A new data set of educational attainment in the world, 1950–2010. NBER Working Paper No. 15902.

Barr, A., Serneels, P., 2009. Reciprocity in the workplace. Experimental Economics 12 (1), 99–112.

Becker, S., Boeckh, K., Hainz, C., Woessmann, L., 2011. The Empire Is Dead, Long Live the Empire! Long-Run Persistence of Trust and Corruption in the Bureaucracy. IZA, Discussion Paper No. 5584, Mars 2011.

Benabou, R., Tirole, J., 2011. Laws and Norms. NBER Working Paper no 17579.

Benabou, R., Tirole, J., 2006. Incentives and prosocial behavior. American Economic Review 96 (5), 1652–1678.

Benz, M., Meier, S., 2008. Do people behave in experiments as in the field?—evidence from donations. Experimental Economics, 11(3), 268–281.

Berg, J., Dickhaut, J., McCabe, K., 1995. Trust, reciprocity and social history. Games and Economic Behavior 10, 122–142.

Bertrand, M., Schoar, A., 2006. The role of family in family firms. The Journal of Economic Perspectives 20 (2), 73–96.

Bidner, C., Francois, P., 2011. Cultivating trust: norms, institutions and the implications of scale. Economic Journal 121 (5), 1097–1129.

Bisin, A., Verdier, T., 2001. The economics of cultural transmission and the dynamics of preferences. Journal of Economic Theory 97, 298–319.

Blanchard, O., Philippon, T., 2004. The Quality of Labor Relations and Unemployment. MIT Department of Economics Working Paper No. 04–25.

Bardhan, P., 2000. Irrigation and cooperation: an empirical analysis of 48 irrigation communities in South India. Economic Development and Cultural Change 48 (4), 847–865.

Black, S., Lynch, L., 2001. How to compete: the impact of workplace practices and information technology on productivity. The Review of Economics and Statistics 83 (3), 434–445.

Bloom, N., Sadun, R., Van Reenen, J., 2012. The organization of firms across countries. Quarterly Journal of Economics, 1663–1705.

Bohnet, I., Zeckhauser, R., 2004. Trust, risk and betrayal. Journal of Economic Behavior & Organization 55, 467–484.

Botero, J., Djankov, S., La Porta, R., Lopez-De-Silanes, F., Shleifer, A., 2004. The regulation of labor. Quarterly Journal of Economics 119 (4), 1339–1382. <http://ideas.repec.org/a/tpr/qjecon/v119y2004i4p1339-1382.html>. <http://ideas.repec.org/s/tpr/qjecon.html>.

Bowles, S., Polania-Reyes, S., 2012. Economic incentives and social preferences: substitutes or complements? Journal of Economic Literature 50 (2), 368–425.

Butler, J., Paola, G., Guiso, L., 2009. The Right Amount of Trust. NBER Working Paper 15344.

Capra, M., Lanier, K., Meer, S., 2008. Attitudinal and Behavioral Measures of Trust: A New Comparison. Working Paper, Emory University, Department of Economics.

Carlin, B.I., Dorobantu, F., Viswanathan, S., 2009. Public trust, the law, and financial investment. Journal of Financial Economics 92 (3), 321–341.

Carpenter, J., Seki, E., 2011. Do social preferences increase productivity? Field experimental evidence from fishermen in Toyama Bay. Economic Inquiry, 49(2), 612–630.

Castillo, M., Carter, M., 2011. Behavioral, Responses to Natural Disasters. Working Paper, University of Wisconsin-Madison.

Cavalli-Sforza, L.L., Feldman, M., 1981. Cultural Transmission and Evolution: A Quantitative Approach. Princeton University Press, Princeton.

Cingano, F., Pinotti, P., 2012. Trust, Firm Organization, and the Structure of Production. Working Paper.

Cole, S., Gine, X., Tobacman, J., Townsend, R., Vickery, J., 2013. Barriers to household risk management: evidence from India. American Economic Journal: Applied Economics 5(1), 104–135.

Coleman, J., 1990. Foundations of Social Theory. Harvard University Press.

Cox, J., 2004. How to identify trust and reciprocity. Games and Economic Behavior 46, 260–281.

Dal Bo, P., Forster, A., Putterman, L., 2010. Institutions and behavior, experimental evidence on the effects of democracy. American Economic Reveiw 100 (5), 2205–2229.

Dinesen, P.T., 2012. Parental transmission of trust or perceptions of institutional fairness? Explaining generalized trust of young non-Western immigrants in a high-trust society. Comparative Politics 44(3), 273–289.

Dinesen, P.T., Hooghe, M., 2010. When in Rome, do as the Romans do: the acculturation of generalized trust among immigrants in western Europe. International Migration Review 44 (3), 697–727.

Dohmen, T., Falk, A., Huffman, D., Sunde, U., 2012. The intergenerational transmission of risk and trust attitudes. Review of Economic Studies 79 (2), 645–677.

Durante, R., 2010. Risk Cooperation and the Economic Origin of Social Trust: An Empirical Investigation. Working Paper, Economic Department, Sciences-Po.

Durlauf, S., 2002. On the empirics of social capital. Economic Journal 112 (438), 459–479.

Durlauf, S., Fafchamps, M., 2005. Social capital, handbook of economic growth. In: Aghion, Philippe, Durlauf, Steven (Eds.), Handbook of Economic Growth, vol. 1. North Holland, pp. 1639–1699 (Chapter 26).

Ellison, G., 1994. Cooperation in the Prisoner's dilemma with anonymous random matching. The Review of Economic Studies 61 (3), 567–588.

Ermisch, J., Gambetta, D., 2010. Do strong family ties inhibit trust? Journal of Economic Behavior and Organisations 75(3), 365–376.

Ermisch, J., Gambetta, D., Heather, L., Siedler, T., Uhrig, N., 2009. Measuring people's trust. Journal of the Royal Statistical Society Series A 172 (4), 749–769.

Falk, A., Kosfeld, M., 2006. The hidden costs of control. American Economic Review 96 (5), 1611–1630.

Fehr, E., Schimdt, K., 1999. A theory of fairness, competition and cooperation. Quarterly Journal of Economics 114 (3), 817–868.

Fehr, E., Gaetcher, S., 2000. Cooperation and punishment in public goods games. American Economic Review 4, 980–994.

Fehr, E., Fischbacher, U., Schupp, B., Von Rosenblatt, J., Wagner, G., 2002. A Nation Wide Laboratory. Examining Trust and Trustworthiness by Integrating Behavioral Experiments into Representative Surveys. CESifo Working Paper.

Fehr, E., 2009. On the economics and biology of trust, presidential address at the 2008 meeting of the european economic association. Journal of the European Economic Association 7 (2–3), 235–266 (04–05).

Fernandez, R., 2011. Does culture matter? In: Benhabib, J., Bisin, A., Jackson, M.O. (Eds.), Handbook of Social Economics. North Holland.

Fisman, R., Miguel, E., 2007. Culture of corruption: evidence from diplomatic parking ticket. Journal of Political Economy 115 (6), 1020–1048 (2007).

Francois, P., Zabojnik, J., 2005. Trust, social capital, and economic development. Journal of the European Economic Association, MIT Press, 3 (1), 51–94 (03).

Francois, P., van Ypersele, T., 2009. Doux Commerce: Does Market Competition Cause Trust? Working Paper.

Frey, B., 1998. Institutions and morale: the crowding-out effect. In: Ben-Ner, Avner, Putterman, Louis (Eds.), Economics, Values, and Organization, Cambridge University Press, New York, pp. 437–460.

Fukuyama, F., 1995. Trust: The Social Virtues and the Creation of Prosperity. Free Press, New York.

Galbiati, R., Vertova, P. 2008. Obligation and cooperative behavior in public good games. Games and Economic Behavior 64 (1), 146–170.

Gambetta, D., 1993. The Sicilian Mafia. The Business of Private Protection, Harvard University Press.

Gennaioli, N., La Porta, R., Lopez-de-Silanes, F., Shleifer, A., 2013. Human capital and regional development. Quarterly Journal of Economics 128 (1), 105–164.

Gintis, H., Bowles, S., Boyd, R., Fehr, E., 2005. Moral sentiments and material interests: origins, evidence, and consequences. In: Moral Sentiments and Material Interests. MIT Press (Chapter 1).

Glaeser, E., Laibson, D., Scheinkman, J., Soutter, C., 2000. Measuring trust. Quarterly Journal of Economics 115, 811–846.

Glaeser, E., La Porta, R., Lopez-de-Silanes, F., Shleifer, A., 2004. Do Institutions cause growth? Journal of Economic Growth 9, 271–303.

Greif, A., 1993. Contract enforceability and economic institutions in early trade: the Maghribi traders' coalition. American Economic Review 83, 525–548.

Greif, A., 1994. Cultural beliefs and the organization of society: a historical and theoretical reflection on collectivist and individualist societies. Journal of Political Economy 102, 912–950.

Greif, A., Tabellini, G., 2010. Cultural and institutional bifurcation: China and Europe compared. American Economic Review Papers and Proceedings 100 (2), 1–10.

Guiso, L., Jappelli, T., 2005. Awarness and stock market participation. Review of Finance 9 (4), 537–567.

Guiso, L., 2010. A Trust-Driven Financial Crisis, Implications for the Future of Financial Markets. EIEF Working Paper.

Guiso, L., Sapienza, P., Zingales, L., 2004. The role of social capital in financial development. American Economic Review 94 (3), 526–556.

Guiso, L., Sapienza, P., Zingales, L., 2006. Does culture affect economic outcomes? Journal of Economic Perspectives 20 (2), 23–48.

Guiso L., Sapienza, P., Zingales, L., 2008a. Long Term Persistence. Working Paper 14278, National Bureau of Economic Research August 2008.

Guiso, L., Sapienza, P., Zingales, L., 2008b. Alfred Marshall lecture: social capital as good culture. Journal of the European Economic Association 6 (2–3), 295–320.

Guiso L., Sapienza, P., Zingales, L., 2011. Civic capital as the missing link. In: Benhabib, Jess, Bisin, Alberto, Jackson, Matthew O. (Eds.), Handbook of Social Economics, vol. 1A. North Holland.

Hall, R., Jones, C., 1999. Why do some countries produce so much more output per worker than others. Quarterly Journal of Economics 114 (1), 83–116.

Hauk, E., Saez-Marti, M., 2002. On the cultural transmission of corruption. Journal of Economic Theory 107 (2), 311–335.

Heckman, J.J., Malofeeva, L., Pinto, R., Savelyev, P., 2010. Understanding the mechanisms through which an influential early childhood program boosted adult outcomes. American Economic Review.

Helliwell, J., Putnam, R., 2007. Education and social capital. Eastern Economics Journal 33 (1), 1–19.

Helliwell, J., and Huang, H. 2010. How's the Job? Well-being and social capital in the workplace. Industrial and Labor Relations Review 63 (2), 205–227.

Helliwell, J., Wang, S., 2010. Trust and well-being. International Journal of Well-Being 1 (2), 42–78.

Henrich, J., Boyd, R., Bowles, S., Camerer, C., Fehr, E., Gintis, H., McElreath, R., 2001. In search of Homo Economicus: Behavioral experiments in 15 small-scale societies. American Economic Review Papers and Proceedings, 73–79.

Herrmann, B., Thöni, C., Gachter, S., 2008. Antisocial punishment across societies. Science 319, 2008.

Hoff, K., Kshetramade, M., Fehr, E., 2011. Caste and punishment: the legacy of caste culture in norm enforcement. Economic Journal 121, 449–475.

Holm, H., Danielson, A., 2005. Tropic trust versus nordic trust: experimental evidence from Tanzania and Sweden. The Economic Journal 115, 505–532.

Ichino, A., Maggi, G., 2000. Work environment and individual background: explaining regional shirking differentials in a large Italian firm. Quarterly Journal of Economics 115 (3), 1057–1090.

Jacob, M., Tyrell., M., 2010. The Legacy of Surveillance: An Explanation for Social Capital Erosion and the Persistence of Economic Disparity Between East and West Germany. European Business School Oestrich-Winkel, mimeo.

Kahneman, D., Tversky, A., 2000. Choices, Values and Frames. Cambridge University Press.

Kandori, M., 1992. Social norms and community enforcement. Review of Economic Studies 59, 63–80.

Karlan, D., 2005. Using experimental economics to measure social capital and predict financial decisions. American Economic Review 95 (5), 1688–1699.

Katz, L., Ludwig, J., Duncan, G., Gennetian, L., Kessler, R., Kling, J., Sanbonmatsu, L., 2013. Long-term neighborhood effects on low-income families: Evidence from moving to opportunity, American Economic Review, 103, 226–231.

Kaufmann, D., Kraay, A., Mastruzzi, M., 2010. The worldwide governance indicators: methodology and analytical issues. World Bank Policy Research Working Paper No. 5430.

Kosfeld, M., Heinrichs, M., Zak, P., Fischbacher, U., Fehr, E., 2005. Oxytocin increases trust in humans. Nature 435, 673–676.

Knack, S., Keefer, P., 1997. Does social capital have an economic payoff? a cross-country investigation. Quarterly Journal of Economics 112 (4), 1252–1288.

Knack, S., Zak, P., 1999. Trust and growth. Economic Journal 111 (470), 295–321.

Kranton, R. 1996. Reciprocal exchange, a self-sustaining system. American Economic Review 86 (4), 830–851.

La Porta, R., Lopez-de-Silanes, F., Shleifer, A., Vishny, R., 1997. Trust in large organizations. American Economic Review Papers and Proceedings 87 (2), 333–338.

La Porta, R., Lopez-de-Silanes, F., Shleifer, A., 2008. The economics consequences of legal origins. Journal of Economic Literature 46 (2), 285–332.

Laury, S.K., Taylor, L.O., 2008. Altruism spillovers: are behaviors in context-free experiments predictive of altruism toward a naturally occurring public good? Journal of Economic Behavior & Organization 65 (1), 9–29.

Lazzarini, S., Artes, R., Madalozzo, R., Siqueira, J., 2005. Measuring trust: an experiment in Brazil. Brazilian Journal of Applied Economics 9 (2), 153–169.

Levine, R., 2004. Finance and growth: theory, evidence and mechanisms. In: Aghion, P., Durlauf, S. (Eds.), Handbook of Economic Growth, North-Holland, Amsterdam, Netherlands.

Ljunge, M., 2012. Inherited Trust and Economic Success of Second Generation Immigrants. IFN Working Paper.

Michalopoulos, S., Papaioannou, E., 2013. National Institutions and Subnational Development in Africa. Working Paper.

Miguel, E., Gugerty, M.K., 2005. Ethnic diversity, social sanctions, and public goods in Kenya. Journal of Public Economics 89 (11), 2325–2368.

Miguel, E., Saiegh, S., Satyanath, S., 2011. Civil war exposure and violence. Economics and Politics 23, 59–73.

Mill, J.S., 1848. Principles of Political Economy. John W. Parker, London.

Nannicini, T., Stella, A., Tabellini, G., Troiano, U., 2010. Social capital and political accountability, economic policy. American Economic Journal.

Nunn, N., Wantchekon, L., 2011. The slave trade and the origins of mistrust in Africa. American Economic Review 101 (7), 3221–3252.

Nunn, N., 2009. The importance of history for economic development. Annual Review of Economics 1, 65–92.

Oliveira, A.D., Croson, R.T.A., Eckel, C.C., 2009. Are Preferences Stable Across Domains? An Experimental Investigation of Social Preferences in the Field. Working Paper.

Olken, B., 2009. Do TV and radio destroy social capital? Evidence from Indonesian villages. American Economic Journal: Applied Economics 1 (4), 1–33.

Olson, M., 1971 [1965]. The Logic of Collective Action: Public Goods and the Theory of Groups (Revised ed.). Harvard University Press.

Ostrom, E., 1990. Governing the commons: the evolution of institutions for collective action. Cambridge University Press, Cambridge.

Putnam, R., Leonardi, R., Nanetti, R.Y., 1993. Making Democracy Work. Princeton University Press, Princeton, NJ.

Putnam, R., 2000. Bowling Alone: The Collapse and Revival of American Community. Simon and Schuster, New York.

Rodrik, D., 1999. Where did all the growth go? External shocks, social conflict, and growth collapses. Journal of Economic Growth 4 (4), 385–412.

Rohner, D., Thoenig, M., Zilibotti, F., 2013. War signals: a theory of trade, trust and conflict. Review of Economic Studies, 80 (3), 1114–1147.

Rothstein, B., Uslaner, E.M., 2005. All for One: Equality, Corruption, and Social Trust. World Politics 58 (1), 41–72.

Rothstein, B., 2011. The Quality of Government, Social Trust and Inequality in International Perspective. University of Chicago Press.

Sachs, J, D., 2003. Institutions Don't Rule: Direct Effects of Geography on Per Capita Income. Working Paper 9490, National Bureau of Economic Research.

Sanfey, A.G., Rilling, J.K., Aronson, J.A., Nystrom, L.E., Cohen, J.D., 2002. The neural basis of economic decision-making in the ultimatum game. Science 300, 1755–1758.

Smith, A. 1997 [1766]. Lecture on the influence of commerce on manners, reprinted. In: Klein, D.B. (Ed.), Reputation: Studies in the Voluntary Elicitation of Good Conduct. University of Michigan Press.

Spolaore, E., Wacziarg. R., 2013. How deep are the roots of economic development. Journal of Economic Literature 51 (2), 325–369.

Tabellini, G., 2008a. The scope of cooperation: values and incentives. The Quarterly Journal of Economics 123 (3), 905–950.

Tabellini, G., 2008b. Institutions and culture. Journal of the European Economic Association, Papers and Proceedings 6 (2–3).

Tabellini, G., 2010. Culture and institutions: economic development in the regions of Europe. Journal of the European Economic Association 8 (4), 677–716.

Uslaner, E.M., 2008. Corruption, inequality and trust. In: Svendsen, Gert T., Svendsen, Gunnar, L. (Eds.), Handbook on Social Capital, Edward Elgar.

Uslaner, 2012. Segregatin and Mistrust: Diversity, Isolation and Social Cohesion. Cambridge University Press.

Valent, P., 2000. Disaster syndrome. In: Fink, George (Ed.), Encyclopedia of Stress. Academic Press, New York.

Wallace, A., 1956. Tornado in Worcester: An Exploratory Study of Individual and Community Behavior in an Extreme Situation. Publication 392, National Academy of Sciences-National Research Council, Washington, D.C.

Zak, P., Kursban R., Matzner, W., 2004. The neurobiology of trust. Annals of the New York Academy of Sciences 224–227.

Zylberberg, Y., 2011. Do Tropical Typhoons Smash Community Ties? Working Paper, Paris School of Economics.

CHAPTER THREE

# Long-Term Barriers to Economic Development

## Enrico Spolaore[*] and Romain Wacziarg[†]

[*]Department of Economics, Tufts University, NBER, CESIfo and CAGE, Medford, MA, 02155-6722, USA
[†]UCLA Anderson School of Management, NBER and CEPR, 110 Westwood Plaza, Los Angeles, CA, 90024, USA

## Abstract

What obstacles prevent the most productive technologies from spreading to less developed economies from the world's technological frontier? In this paper, we seek to shed light on this question by quantifying the geographic and human barriers to the transmission of technologies. We argue that the intergenerational transmission of human traits, particularly culturally transmitted traits, has led to divergence between populations over the course of history. In turn, this divergence has introduced barriers to the diffusion of technologies across societies. We provide measures of historical and genealogical distances between populations, and document how such distances, relative to the world's technological frontier, act as barriers to the diffusion of development and of specific innovations. We provide an interpretation of these results in the context of an emerging literature seeking to understand variation in economic development as the result of factors rooted deep in history.

## Keywords

Long-run growth, Genetic distance, Intergenerational transmission, Diffusion of innovations

## JEL Classification Codes

O11, O33, O40, O57

## 3.1. INTRODUCTION

Technological differences lie at the heart of differences in economic performance across countries. A large and growing literature on development accounting demonstrates that total factor productivity accounts for a sizeable fraction of cross-country differences in per capita income (Hall and Jones, 1999; Caselli, 2005; Hsieh and Klenow, 2010, among many others). The problem of low technological advancement in poor countries is not primarily one of lack of innovation, because technologies that could make these countries vastly richer exist and are used elsewhere in the world. A major problem, instead, is one of delayed technological adoption. That many countries are subject to large technological usage gaps is a well-documented phenomenon. However, the factors explaining delayed technological adoption are not well understood. What prevents the most productive technologies, broadly understood, from spreading to less developed economies from the

*Handbook of Economic Growth*, Volume 2A
ISSN 1574-0684, http://dx.doi.org/10.1016/B978-0-444-53538-2.00003-4
121

world's technological frontier? In this chapter, we seek to shed light on this question, by quantifying the geographic and human barriers to the transmission of technologies.

We adopt a long-term perspective. The fortunes of nations are notoriously persistent through time, and much of the variation in economic performance is deep rooted in history. For instance, an important literature has explored the prehistoric origins of comparative development (Diamond, 1997; Olsson and Hibbs, 2005; Ashraf and Galor, 2011, 2013a). While there have been reversals of fortune at the level of countries, these reversals are much less prevalent when looking at the fortunes of populations rather than those of geographic locations.[1] Indeed, contributions by Putterman and Weil (2010), Comin et al. (2010), and Spolaore and Wacziarg (2009, 2012a, 2013) argue that the past history of populations is a much stronger predictor of current economic outcomes than the past history of given geographical locations. Thus, any explanation for the slow and unequal diffusion of frontier technologies must be able to account for the persistence of economic fortunes over the long run. In this chapter, we argue that the intergenerational transmission of human traits, particularly culturally transmitted traits, has led to divergence between populations over the course of history. In turn, this divergence has introduced barriers to the diffusion of technologies across societies. These barriers impede the flow of technologies in proportion to how genealogically distant populations are from each other.

Our starting point is to develop a theoretical model capturing these ideas. This model proceeds in three phases. Firstly, we argue that genealogical separation across populations leads, on average, to differentiation along a wide range of traits transmitted from parents to children either biologically or culturally. Populations that are genealogically distant should therefore also be distant in terms of languages, norms, values, preferences, etc.—a set of traits we refer to as vertically transmitted traits or more simply as vertical traits. Secondly, we consider the onset of a major innovation, which could be interpreted as the Industrial Revolution, and argue that differences in vertical traits introduce barriers to the diffusion of this major innovation across societies and populations. Thus, cross-country differences in aggregate TFP or per capita income should be correlated with their genealogical distance. Finally, we extend the model to allow for innovations taking place over time, and innovation and imitation occurring endogenously. In this more general framework, usage lags in the adoption of specific technologies and consequently, aggregate differences in economic development are correlated with average differences in vertical traits, and thus with genealogical distance.

We next turn to empirical evidence on these ideas. To measure the degree of relatedness between populations, we use genetic distance. Data on genetic distance was gathered by population geneticists specifically for the purpose of tracing genealogical linkages between

---

[1] See Acemoglu et al. (2002) for the reversal of fortune at the level of geographic locations (for former colonies), and papers by Spolaore and Wacziarg (2013) and Chanda et al. (2013) showing that the reversal of fortune disappears when correcting for ancestry and expanding the sample beyond former colonies.

world populations (Cavalli-Sforza et al. 1994). By sampling large numbers of individuals from different populations, these researchers obtained vectors of allele frequencies over a large set of genes, or loci. Measures of average differences between these vectors across any two populations provide a measure of genetic distance. The measure we rely on, known as $F_{ST}$ genetic distance, is the most widely used measure in the population genetics literature because it has properties that make it well suited to study separation times between populations—precisely the concept we wish to capture. $F_{ST}$ genetic distance has been shown to correlate with other measures of cultural differences such as linguistic distance and differences in answers to questions from the World Values Survey (Spolaore and Wacziarg, 2009; Desmet et al. 2011).

Emphatically, the purpose of our study is *not* to study any genetic characteristics that may confer any advantage in development. The genes used in our measures of genealogical distance purposely do not capture any such traits. It is important to note that the genes chosen to compare populations and retrace their genealogies are neutral (Kimura, 1968). That is, their spread results from random factors and not from natural selection. For instance, neutral genes include those coding for different blood types, characteristics that are known not to have conferred a particular advantage or disadvantage to individuals carrying them during human evolutionary history. The mutations that give rise to specific alleles of these genes arise and spread randomly. The neutral genes on which genetic distance is based thus do not capture traits that are important for fitness and survival. As a result, measures based on neutral genes are like a molecular clock: on average, they provide an indication of separation times between populations. Therefore, genetic distance can be used as a summary statistics for all divergence in traits that are transmitted with variation from one generation to the next over the long run, including divergence in cultural traits. Our hypothesis is that, at a later stage, when such populations enter into contact with each other, differences in those traits create barriers to exchange, communication, and imitation. These differences could indeed reflect traits that are mostly transmitted culturally and not biologically—such as languages, norms of behavior, values, and preferences. In a nutshell, we hypothesize that genetic distance measured from neutral genes captures divergence in intergenerationally transmitted traits—including cultural traits—between populations. This divergence in turn impedes the flow of innovations.

We use these measures of genetic distance to test our model of technological diffusion. Our barriers model implies that the genetic distance measured relative to the world technological frontier should trump absolute genetic distance as an explanation for bilateral income differences. We find this to be the case empirically. Our model also implies that genetic distance relative to the frontier should have predictive power for income differences across time even in periods when the world distribution of income was quite different from today's. We show indeed that the effect of genetic distance remains strong in historical data on population density and per capita income. Our model implies that after a major innovation, such as the Industrial Revolution, the effect of genealogical distance should be pronounced, but that it should decline as more and more societies adopt the frontier's innovation. This too is true empirically. Finally, our model implies that genetic distance should have predictive power at the level of disaggregated technologies, and find this to be the case both historically (when measuring technological usage on the extensive margin) and for more recent technological developments (measuring technological usage along the intensive margin). In sum, we find considerable evidence that barriers introduced by historical separation between populations are central to account for the world distribution of income.

In the final section of this chapter, we broaden our focus and place these hypotheses and findings in the context of the wider emerging literature on the deep historical roots of economic development. Our discussion starts from a taxonomy, based on Spolaore and Wacziarg (2013), describing how historically transmitted traits could conceivably affect socio-economic outcomes. The taxonomy distinguishes between the mode of transmission of vertical traits, and the mode of operation of these traits. In principle, intergenerationally transmitted traits could be transmitted either biologically or culturally. However, the recent development of the research on epigenetics and on gene-culture interactions has made this distinction based on the mode of transmission much less clear-cut empirically and conceptually. A more fruitful discussion, we argue, is to try to better distinguish between the modes of operation of vertical traits. These traits, in principle, could bear direct effects on economic outcomes, or operate as barriers to economic interactions between populations. We discuss existing contributions in light of this distinction, and discuss directions for future research in the emerging new field concerned with the deep historical roots of economic development.

This chapter is organized as follows. Section 3.2 presents a stylized model of the diffusion of technologies as function of differences in vertically transmitted traits across human populations, and ultimately as a function of the degree of genealogical relatedness between them. Section 3.3 presents our empirical methodology and data. Section 3.4 discusses a wide range of empirical results pertaining to contemporaneous and historical measures of economic development and specific technology use measures. Section 3.5 discusses the interpretation of these results in the context of the broader literature on the deep roots of economic development. Section 3.6 concludes.

## 3.2. A THEORY OF RELATEDNESS AND GROWTH

In this section we present a basic theoretical framework to capture the links among genetic distance, intergenerationally transmitted traits, and barriers to the diffusion of economic development across different societies.[2] The model illustrates two key ideas.

The first idea is that genetic distance between populations captures the degree of genealogical relatedness between populations over time, and can therefore be interpreted

[2] The model builds on Spolaore and Wacziarg (2009, 2012a).

as a general metric for average differences in traits transmitted with variation across generations. Genetic distance measures the difference in gene distributions between two populations, where the genes under consideration are neutral. By definition, neutral genetic change tends to occur randomly, independently of selection pressure, and regularly over time, as in a molecular clock (Kimura, 1968). This divergence provides information about lines of descent: populations that are closer in terms of genetic distance have shared a common "ancestor population" more recently. The concept is analogous to relatedness between individuals: two siblings are more closely related than two cousins because they share more recent common ancestors: their parents rather than their grandparents. Since a very large number of traits—not only biological but also cultural—are transmitted from one generation to the next over the long run, genetic distance provides a comprehensive measure for average differences in traits transmitted across generations. We call vertically transmitted traits (or vertical traits, for short) the set of characteristics passed on across generations within a population over the very long run—that is, over the time horizon along which populations have diverged (thousands of years).[3] Vertical transmission takes place across generations within a given population, and, in our definition, includes not only direct parent-to-child transmission of biological and cultural traits, but also, more broadly, "oblique" transmission of cultural traits from the older to the younger within a genetically related group. In contrast, we define "horizontal transmission" as learning and imitation across different populations at a point in time.

The second idea is that differences in vertically transmitted traits act as barriers to horizontal learning and imitation, and therefore hamper the diffusion of innovations and economic development across societies.[4] We argue that populations that share a more recent common history, and are therefore closer in terms of vertical traits, face lower costs and obstacles to adopting each other's innovations. This view, that differences in persistent societal characteristics may act as barriers, is consistent with a large literature on the diffusion of innovations, starting with the classic work by Rogers (1962). Empirically, we are interested primarily in the diffusion of modern economic development in historical times, and especially after the Industrial Revolution, so our stylized model is designed with that objective in mind.

### 3.2.1 Genetic Distance and Vertically Transmitted Traits

We model all vertical traits of a population as a point on the real line: each population $i$ has vertical traits $\nu_i$, where $\nu_i$ is a real number. At time $o$ ("origin"), there exists only one population (population 0), with traits normalized to zero: $\nu_0 = 0$. At time $p > o$

---

[3] This terminology is borrowed from the evolutionary literature on cultural transmission (for example, see Cavalli-Sforza and Feldman, 1981; Boyd and Richerson, 1985; Richerson and Boyd, 2005).

[4] Policy-induced barriers to the diffusion of technology are analyzed by Parente and Prescott (1994, 2002). In our framework we interpret barriers more broadly to include all long-term societal differences that are obstacles to the diffusion of development.

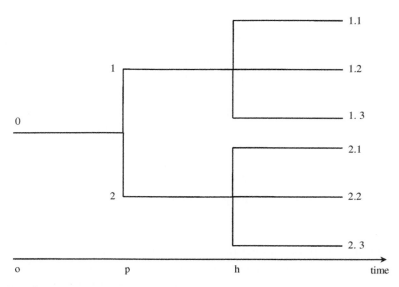

**Figure 3.1** Population tree.

("prehistory"), the original population splits into two populations (1 and 2). At time $h > p$ ("history"), each of the two populations splits into three separate populations: population 1 into populations 1.1, 1.2, 1.3; and population 2 into populations 2.1, 2.2, and 2.3.[5] The genealogical tree is displayed in Figure 3.1. By analogy, with the genealogy of individuals, we say that populations such as 1.1 and 1.2 are "sibling" populations, because their last common ancestors (their "parent" population) can be found at the more recent split (time $p$), while population pairs such as 1.2 and 2.1 are "cousin" populations, because their last common ancestors (their "grandparent" population) must be traced back to a more remote time $o < p$. $G(i,j)$ denotes the genetic distance between population $i$ and population $j$.[6] The genetic distance between two sibling populations is $g_s > 0$, while the genetic distance between two cousin populations is $g_c > g_s$. Formally,

$$G(1.m, 1.n) = G(2.m, 2.n) = g_s \quad \text{where} \quad m = 1, 2, 3;\ n = 1, 2, 3 \text{ and } 1.m \neq 1.n;$$
$$2.m \neq 2.n, \tag{3.1}$$

and

$$G(1.m, 2.n) = g_c \quad \text{where } m = 1, 2, 3 \text{ and } n = 1, 2, 3. \tag{3.2}$$

---

[5] In Spolaore and Wacziarg (2009), we presented a similar model with only four populations at time $h$ (1.1, 1.2, 2.1, and 2.2). Here we extend the framework to allow for a more general analysis, in which we also have pairs of populations that, while they are not at the frontier themselves, are both siblings with the frontier population.

[6] By definition, $G(i, i) = 0$.

Each population inherits vertical traits from its ancestor population with variation. In general, vertical traits $v_d$ of population $d$ (the "descendent"), descending from population $a$ (the "ancestor"), are given by:

$$v_d = v_a + \varepsilon_d, \tag{3.3}$$

where $\varepsilon_d$ is a shock. In particular, we model the process of variation as a random walk. This simplification is consistent with the molecular-clock interpretation of genetic distance. While more complex processes could be considered, this formalization has two advantages: it is economical and illustrates how random changes are sufficient to generate our theoretical predictions. Formally, we assume that $\varepsilon_d$ takes value $\varepsilon > 0$ with probability $1/2$ and $-\varepsilon$ with probability $1/2$. We denote with $V(i,j)$ the distance in vertically transmitted traits (vertical distance, for short) between populations $i$ and $j$:

$$V(i,j) \equiv |v_j - v_i|. \tag{3.4}$$

We are now ready to summarize our first idea as:

**Proposition 1.** *The distance in vertical traits $V(i,j)$ between two populations $i$ and $j$, is, on average, increasing in their genetic distance $G(i,j)$.*

Derivation of Proposition 1:

The expected distance in vertical traits between sibling populations is:

$$E\{V(i,j)|G(i,j) = g_s\} = \varepsilon, \tag{3.5}$$

because their vertical distance is equal to $2\varepsilon$ with probability $1/2$, when one population experiences a positive shock $\varepsilon$ and the other a negative shock $-\varepsilon$, and equal to $0$ with probability $1/2$, when both populations experience the same shock (either $\varepsilon$ with probability $1/4$ or $-\varepsilon$ with probability $1/4$). In contrast, the expected distance in vertical traits between cousin populations is:

$$E\{V(i,j)|G(i,j) = g_c\} = \frac{3\varepsilon}{2}, \tag{3.6}$$

because their vertical distance is $0$ with probability $3/8$, $2\varepsilon$ with probability $1/2$, and $4\varepsilon$ with probability $1/8$.[7] Therefore, the expected distance in vertical traits is increasing in

---

[7] The details of the calculation are as follows. With probability $1/4$, the two populations experienced identical shocks at time $h$, and their respective ancestor populations experienced identical shocks at time $p$, implying $V(i,j) = 0$. With probability $1/8$, one population lineage experienced a positive shock $\varepsilon$ at time $p$ and a negative shock $-\varepsilon$ at time $h$ while the other population lineage experienced $-\varepsilon$ and $\varepsilon$, implying again $V(i,j) = 0$. With probability $1/4$, the two populations' ancestors experienced identical shocks at time $p$, but the two populations experienced different shocks at time $h$, implying $V(i,j) = 2\varepsilon$. With probability $1/4$, the shocks were the same at time $h$ but different at time $p$, also implying $V(i,j) = 2\varepsilon$. Finally, with probability $1/8$, one population lineage experienced two positive shocks ($\varepsilon + \varepsilon = 2\varepsilon$) and the other two negative shocks ($-\varepsilon - \varepsilon = -2\varepsilon$), therefore leading to a vertical distance equal to $4\varepsilon$. In sum, their expected vertical distance is given by $E\{V(i,j)|G(i,j) = g_c\} = \frac{3}{8}0 + \frac{1}{2}2\varepsilon + \frac{1}{8}4\varepsilon = \frac{3\varepsilon}{2}$.

genetic distance:

$$E\{V(i,j)|G(i,j)=g_c\} - E\{V(i,j)|G(i,j)=g_s\} = \frac{\varepsilon}{2} > 0. \qquad (3.7)$$

It is important to notice that the relation between distance in vertical traits and genetic distance is not deterministic, but works on average. Some pairs of populations, while genealogically more distant, may end up with more similar vertical traits than two more closely related populations. However, that outcome is less likely to be observed than the opposite. On average, genetic distance and vertical distance go hand in hand.

### 3.2.2 Barriers to the Diffusion of Economic Development

Our second idea is that differences in vertical traits constitute barriers to the spread of innovations across populations. A stylized illustration of this idea is provided below.

At time $p$ all populations produce output using the basic technology $Y_i = AL_i$, so that all populations have the same income per capita $y = A$. In period $h$ a population happens to find a more productive technology $A' = A + \Delta$ where $\Delta > 0$. We abstract from the possibility that the likelihood of finding the innovation is itself a function of a society's vertical traits. Such direct effects of vertical traits could strengthen the links between genetic distance and economic outcomes, but are not necessary for our results.

We denote the innovating population as $f$ (for technological frontier). To fix ideas and without loss of generality, in the rest of the analysis we assume that population 1.1 is the frontier population ($f = 1.1$). Populations farther from population $f$ in terms of vertical traits face higher barriers to adopt the new technology. Formally, we assume that a society $i$ at a vertical distance from the frontier equal to $V(i,f)$ can improve its technology only by:

$$\Delta_i = [1 - \beta V(i,f)]\Delta, \qquad (3.8)$$

where the parameter $\beta > 0$ captures the barriers to the horizontal diffusion of innovations due to distance in vertical traits. To ensure non-negativity, we assume that $\beta \leq \frac{1}{\max V(i,f)} = \frac{1}{4\varepsilon}$.[8] Therefore, income per capita in society $i$ will be given by:

$$y_i = A + \Delta_i = A + [1 - \beta V(i,f)]\Delta. \qquad (3.9)$$

This immediately implies:

**Proposition 2.**   *The difference in income per capita $|y_i - y_j|$ between society i and society j is a function of their relative vertical distance from the frontier $|V(i,f) - V(j,f)|$:*

$$|y_j - y_i| = \beta\Delta|V(i,f) - V(j,f)|. \qquad (3.10)$$

---

[8] Alternatively, the formula could be re-written as $\Delta_i = \max\{[1 - \beta V(i,f)]\Delta, 0\}$.

### 3.2.3 Genetic Distance and Income Differences

Since income differences are associated with differences in vertical traits across populations (Proposition 2), and differences in vertical traits, on average, go hand in hand with genetic distance (Proposition 1), we can now establish a link between expected income differences and genetic distance. These links are formally derived as Propositions 3 and 4 below.

**Proposition 3.** *The expected income difference $E\{|\gamma_j - \gamma_i|\}$ between societies $i$ and $j$ is increasing in their genetic distance $G(i,j)$.*

Derivation of Proposition 3:

First, we must calculate the expected income of all pairs of populations at genetic distance $g_s$ (sibling populations). $V(i,j)$ between two sibling populations is 0 with probability $1/2$ and $2\varepsilon$ with probability $1/2$. When the two populations have identical traits, they have identical incomes. When they are at a distance $2\varepsilon$ from each other, one of them must be closer to the frontier's traits by a distance equal to $2\varepsilon$, no matter where the frontier's traits are located (at $0$, $2\varepsilon$, or $-2\varepsilon$), or whether one of the two sibling populations *is* the frontier. Thus, when $V(i,j) = 2\varepsilon$, the income difference between the two populations is $\beta\Delta 2\varepsilon$. In sum, for all pairs of sibling populations is $|\gamma_{k.m} - \gamma_{k.n}| = 0$ with probability $1/2$, and $|\gamma_{k.m} - \gamma_{k.n}| = \beta\Delta 2\varepsilon$ with probability $1/2$, implying $E\{|\gamma_{k.m} - \gamma_{k.n}|\} = \beta\Delta\varepsilon$ where $k = 1, 2$; $m = 1, 2, 3$; $n = 1, 2, 3$; and $m \neq n$. Consequently, the expected income difference between sibling populations is:

$$E\{|\gamma_j - \gamma_i| \; || \; G(i,j) = g_s\} = \beta\Delta\varepsilon. \tag{3.11}$$

Now we must calculate the expected income difference between cousin populations. $V(i,j)$ between two cousin populations is 0 with probability $3/8$, $2\varepsilon$ with probability $1/2$, and $4\varepsilon$ with probability $1/8$. The calculation is slightly more complicated, because we must distinguish between pairs that include the frontier and pairs that do not include the frontier $f = 1.1$. First, consider pairs that include the frontier. With probability $3/8$ a population $2.n$ shares the same traits (and hence income) with the frontier, with probability $1/2$, population $2.n$ has income lower than the frontier's by $\beta\Delta 2\varepsilon$, and with probability $1/8$ population $2.n$'s income is lower by $\beta\Delta 4\varepsilon$. Thus, we have:

$$E\{|\gamma_f - \gamma_{2.n}|\} = \frac{\beta\Delta 2\varepsilon}{2} + \frac{\beta\Delta 4\varepsilon}{8} = \frac{3\beta\Delta\varepsilon}{2} \quad \text{where } n = 1, 2, 3. \tag{3.12}$$

Now, consider pairs of cousin populations that do not include the frontier population—that is, pairs $1.m$ and $2.n$, with $m = 2, 3$, and $n = 1, 2, 3$. Again, the income difference between each pair of cousin populations is equal to zero when both populations share the same traits (which happens with probability $3/8$), and is equal to $\beta\Delta 2\varepsilon$ when their traits are at a distance $2\varepsilon$ from each other (which happens with probability $1/2$), no matter where the frontier is located. However, when the two cousin populations are at a distance $4\varepsilon$ from each other (which happens with probability $1/8$), their income distance depends on the location of the traits of the frontier. If the frontier is at an extreme (either $2\varepsilon$ or $-2\varepsilon$— an event with probability $1/2$), the $4\varepsilon$ vertical distance between $1.m$ and $2.n$ implies that their income distance is equal to $\beta\Delta4\varepsilon$. In contrast, if the frontier's traits are at $0$ (also an event with probability $1/2$), $1.m$ and $2.n$ are equally distant from the frontier (each at a distance $2\varepsilon$), and therefore have identical incomes per capita. In sum, we have:

$$E\{|y_{1.m} - y_{2.n}|\} = \frac{\beta\Delta2\varepsilon}{2} + \frac{1}{2}\frac{\beta\Delta4\varepsilon}{8} = \frac{5\beta\Delta\varepsilon}{4} \text{ where } m = 2,3; \ n = 1,2,3. \quad (3.13)$$

Consequently, expected income difference between pairs of cousin populations is:

$$E\{|y_j - y_i| \ || \ G(i,j) = g_c\} = \frac{1}{9}\sum_{m=1}^{3}\sum_{n=1}^{3} E\{|y_{1.m} - y_{2.n}|\} = \frac{1}{9}\left[3\frac{3\beta\Delta\varepsilon}{2} + 6\frac{5\beta\Delta\varepsilon}{4}\right]$$

$$= \frac{4\beta\Delta\varepsilon}{3}. \quad (3.14)$$

Therefore, the expected income difference between cousin populations is higher than the one between sibling populations: higher genetic distance is associated, on average, with higher income differences, as stated in Proposition 3. Formally:

$$E\{|y_j - y_i| \ || \ G(i,j) = g_c\} - E\{|y_j - y_i| \ || \ G(i,j) = g_s\} = \frac{\beta\Delta\varepsilon}{3} > 0. \quad (3.15)$$

Why do populations which are genetically more distant from each other tend to differ more in income per capita, on average? The reason is that populations which are distant from each other genetically are also more likely to find themselves at more different distances from the frontier. Relative distance from the frontier, rather than genetic distance between populations per se, is the key determinant of expected income differences. Therefore, we can find an even stronger relation between income differences and genetic distance if we consider not the absolute genetic distance between two populations $G(i,j)$, but their relative genetic distance from the technological frontier, defined as follows:

$$R(i,j) \equiv |G(i,f) - G(j,f)|. \quad (3.16)$$

Our model predicts that the effect of relative genetic distance on income differences is not only positive, but also larger than the effect of absolute genetic distance:

**Proposition 4.** *The expected income difference $E\{|y_j - y_i|\}$ between societies $i$ and $j$ is increasing in the two populations' relative genetic distance from the frontier $R(i,j)$. The effect of relative genetic distance $R(i,j)$ on income differences is larger than the effect of absolute genetic distance $G(i,j)$.*

Derivation of Proposition 4:

The expected income difference between pairs of populations at relative genetic distance $R(i,j) = g_s$ is[9]:

$$E\{|y_j - y_i| \ | \ R(i,j) = g_s\}| = E\{|y_f - y_{1.2}|\} + E\{|y_f - y_{1.3}|\} = \beta\Delta\varepsilon, \quad (3.17)$$

[9] We use the result, derived above, that all expected income differences between siblings are equal to $\beta\Delta\varepsilon$.

while the expected income difference between pairs of populations at relative genetic distance $R(i,j) = g_c$ is[10]:

$$E\{|y_j - y_i| \mid R(i,j) = g_c\}| = \frac{1}{3}\sum_{n=1}^{3} E\{|y_f - y_{2.n}|\} = \frac{3\beta\Delta\varepsilon}{2}. \tag{3.18}$$

Therefore, the effect of an increase of relative genetic distance from $g_s$ to $g_c$ is

$$E\{|y_j - y_i| \mid R(i,j) = g_c\} - E\{|y_j - y_i| \mid R(i,j) = g_s\} = \frac{\beta\Delta\varepsilon}{2} > \frac{\beta\Delta\varepsilon}{3} > 0. \tag{3.19}$$

The effect is positive ($\frac{\beta\Delta\varepsilon}{2} > 0$), and larger than the analogous effect of absolute genetic distance ($\frac{\beta\Delta\varepsilon}{3}$), derived above.

By the same token, the effect of relative genetic distance on expected income differences is also positive when moving from $R(i,j) = g_c - g_s$ to $R(i,j) = g_c$:

$$E\{|y_j - y_i| \mid\mid R(i,j) = g_c\} - E\{|y_j - y_i| \mid\mid R(i,j) = g_c - g_s\} = \frac{3\beta\Delta\varepsilon}{2} - \frac{5\beta\Delta\varepsilon}{4} = \frac{\beta\Delta\varepsilon}{4} > 0. \tag{3.20}$$

The results above are intuitive. As we increase relative genetic distance from the frontier, the expected income gap increases. The size of the effect is a positive function of the extent of divergence in vertically transmitted traits ($\varepsilon$), the extent to which this divergence constitutes a barrier to the horizontal diffusion of innovations ($\beta$), and the size of the improvement in productivity at the frontier ($\Delta$).

In summary, our model has the following testable implications, which are brought to the data in the empirical analysis carried in the rest of this chapter:

1. *Relative genetic distance from the frontier population is positively correlated with differences in income per capita.*
2. *The effect on income differences associated with relative genetic distance from the frontier population is larger than the effect associated with absolute genetic distance.*

### 3.2.4 A Dynamic Extension

In the stylized model above, for simplicity we assumed that only one big innovation took place at time $h$. We now present a dynamic example, where innovations take place over time, and innovation and imitation are modeled endogenously.[11] The key insights and results carry over to this extension.

---

[10] We use the result, derived above, that the expected income difference between the frontier and each of its cousin populations is $\frac{3\beta\Delta\varepsilon}{2}$.

[11] The model builds heavily on Barro and Sala-i-Martin (1997, 2003) and Spolaore and Wacziarg (2012a).

In this dynamic example, we assume for simplicity, that populations do not change in modern times and have fixed size (normalized to one). More importantly, we assume that their inherited vertical traits do not change over the relevant time horizon. This is a reasonable simplification, because changes in vertical traits tend to take place much more slowly and at a longer horizon than the spread of technological innovations, especially if we focus on modern economic growth. Adding small random shocks to vertical traits after time $h$ would significantly complicate the algebra, but would not affect the basic results.

Consider our six populations ($i = 1.1, 1.2, 1.3, 2.1, 2.2, 2.3$), with vertical traits inherited from their ancestral populations as described above, and unchanged in modern times (i.e. for $t \geq h$). Time is continuous. Consumers in economy $i$ at time $t$ maximize:

$$U_i(t) = \int_s^\infty \ln c_i(s) e^{-\rho(t-s)} ds, \tag{3.21}$$

under a standard budget constraint, where $c_i(t)$ is consumption, and $\rho > 0$ is the subjective discount rate. We assume that the six economies are not financially integrated, and that each economy $i$ has its own real interest rate, denoted by $r_i(t)$. Hence, the optimal growth rate of consumption in society $i$ is:

$$\frac{dc_i}{dt} \frac{1}{c_i(t)} = r_i(t) - \rho. \tag{3.22}$$

The production function for final output $y_i(t)$ is:

$$y_i(t) = \int_0^{A_i(t)} [x_{zi}(t)]^\alpha dz, \quad 0 < \alpha < 1, \tag{3.23}$$

where $x_{zi}(t)$ is the quantity of intermediate good of type $z$ employed at time $t$ in economy $i$, and the interval $[0, A_i(t)]$ measures the continuum of intermediate goods available in economy $i$ at time $t$. Each intermediate good is produced by a local monopolist.

As before, without loss of generality we assume that society 1.1 is the technological frontier ($f = 1.1$). In this setting, this means that $A_f(h) > A_i(h)$ for all $i \neq f$. However, unlike in the previous analysis, innovation at the frontier economy now takes place endogenously. Following Barro and Sala-i-Martin (1997, 2003, Chapters 6 and 8), we assume that the inventor of input $z$ retains perpetual monopoly power over its production within the frontier economy. The inventor sells the intermediate good at price $P_z = 1/\alpha$, earning the profit flow $\pi = (1 - \alpha)\alpha^{(1+\alpha)/(1-\alpha)}$ at each time $t$.

The cost of inventing a new intermediate good at the frontier is $\eta$ units of final output. Free entry into the innovation sector implies that the real interest rate $r_f(t)$ must be equal to $\pi/\eta$, which is assumed to be larger than $\rho$, therefore implying that consumption grows at the constant rate:

$$\gamma \equiv \frac{\pi}{\eta} - \rho > 0. \tag{3.24}$$

Output $y_f(t)$ and the frontier level of intermediate goods $A_f(t)$ will also grow at the rate $\gamma$.

The other populations cannot use the intermediate goods invented in economy $f$ directly, but, as in Barro and Sala-i-Martin (1997), must pay an imitation cost $\mu_i$ in order to adapt those intermediate goods to local conditions. Our key assumption is that the imitation costs are increasing in the distance in vertical traits between the imitator and the frontier. Specifically, we assume that society $i$'s imitation cost is:

$$\mu_i(t) = \lambda e^{\theta V(i,f)} \left( \frac{A_i(t)}{A_f(t)} \right)^\xi . \tag{3.25}$$

This is an instance of our general idea: a higher $V(i,f)$ is associated with higher imitation costs, because differences in vertical traits between the imitator and the inventor act as barriers to adoption and imitation. The parameter $\theta$ captures the extent to which dissimilarity in vertical traits between imitator and inventor increases imitation costs. For a given vertical distance, an imitator in society $i$ faces lower imitation costs when there is a larger set of intermediate goods available for imitation—that is, when $A_i(t)/A_f(t)$ is low. The rationale for this assumption is the usual one: intermediate goods that are easier to imitate are copied first. Hence, the parameter $\xi > 0$ captures this advantage from technological backwardness. Our perspective may indeed shed some light on whether backward economies face higher or lower imitation costs overall, an issue debated in the literature (for instance, see Fagerberg, 2004). As we will see, our model predicts that, in steady state, societies that are farther technologically, and should therefore face lower imitation costs for this reason (captured by the parameter $\xi$), are also farther in terms of vertical distance from the frontier, and hence should face higher imitation costs through this channel (captured by the parameter $\theta$), with conflicting effects on overall imitation costs.

Again, we assume that an imitator who pays cost $\mu_i(t)$ to imitate good $k$ has perpetual monopoly power over the production of that input in economy $i$, and charges $P_k = 1/\alpha$, earning the profit flow $\pi = (1-\alpha)\alpha^{(1+\alpha)/(1-\alpha)}$, while output is proportional to available intermediate goods $A_i(t)$ in equilibrium: $y_i(t) = \alpha^{2\alpha/(1-\alpha)} A_i(t)$. With free entry into the imitation sector, economy $i$'s real interest rate in equilibrium is[12]:

$$r_i(t) = \frac{\pi}{\mu_i(t)} + \frac{d\mu_i}{dt} \frac{1}{\mu_i(t)}. \tag{3.26}$$

In steady state, the level of imitation costs $\mu_i^*$ is constant. The number of intermediate goods, output, and consumption in all economies grow at the same rate $\gamma$ as at the frontier. Therefore, in steady state the real interest rates in all economies are identical and equal to $\dfrac{\pi}{\eta}$, and imitation costs are identical for all imitators, which implies:

---

[12] See Barro and Sala-i-Martin (1997, 2003) for the details of the derivation.

**Proposition 2bis.**   *The difference in log of income per capita in steady state* $|\ln y_i^* - \ln y_j^*|$ *between society i and society j is a function of their relative vertical distance from the frontier* $|V(i,f) - V(j,f)|$[13]:

$$|\ln y_i^* - \ln y_j^*| = \frac{\theta}{\xi}|V(i,f) - V(j,f)|. \qquad (3.27)$$

The intuition of the above equation is straightforward: long-term differences in total factor productivity and output between societies are an increasing function of their relative cost to imitate, which depends on their relative vertical distance from the frontier. Therefore, societies that are more distant from the frontier in terms of vertically transmitted traits will have lower incomes per capita in steady state.

This dynamic model confirms the key implications of the simplified model that we had presented before. In particular, the equivalents of Propositions 3 and 4 hold in this setting as well, as long as one substitutes income differences $|y_j - y_i|$ with differences in log of income per capita in steady state $|\ln y_i^* - \ln y_j^*|$ , and $\beta\Delta$ with $\frac{\theta}{\xi}$. We can then re-interpret those results as implying that societies at different relative genetic distance from the technological frontier will have different levels of income per capita in steady state. The effect of relative genetic distance on the income gap is larger when differences in vertical traits are associated with higher imitation costs (higher $\theta$). Interestingly, we also have that the effect of relative genetic distance on income differences is lower when there are larger benefits from technological backwardness (higher $\xi$). In sum, the effects of relative genetic distance on economic development extend to this dynamic setting.

## 3.3. EMPIRICAL METHODOLOGY AND DATA
### 3.3.1 Specification and Estimation

The starting points for our empirical investigation into the long-term barriers to economic development are Propositions 3 and 4. These theoretical results show that if differences in vertical traits act as barriers to the diffusion of technologies, then differences in measures of development or technological sophistication across pairs of countries should (1) be correlated with the absolute genetic distance between these countries, (2) be correlated more strongly with their genetic distance relative to the technological frontier, and (3) genetic distance relative to the frontier should trump simple genetic distance between two countries. Whether these patterns hold true constitutes an empirical test of the barriers model. Denote by $D_i$ a measure of development or technological sophistication in country $i$. We will consider alternatively per capita income (for the modern period), population density (for the pre-industrial period), and direct measures of technology use,

---

[13]   Of course, we also have $|\ln A_i^*(t) - \ln A_j^*(t)| = |\ln y_i^*(t) - \ln y_j^*(t)|$

to be further detailed below. Denote by $FST_{ij}^W$ the absolute genetic distance between countries $i$ and $j$. Analogous to the theoretical definition, genetic distance relative to the frontier country is defined as: $FST_{ij}^R = |FST_{if}^W - FST_{jf}^W|$ where $f$ denotes the frontier country.

Then the empirical predictions of Propositions 3 and 4 lead to the following empirical specifications:

$$\left|D_i - D_j\right| = \alpha_0 + \alpha_1 FST_{ij}^R + \alpha_2' X_{ij} + \varepsilon_{ij}^\alpha, \tag{3.28}$$

$$\left|D_i - D_j\right| = \beta_0 + \beta_1 FST_{ij}^W + \beta_2' X_{ij} + \varepsilon_{ij}^\beta, \tag{3.29}$$

$$\left|D_i - D_j\right| = \gamma_0 + \gamma_1 FST_{ij}^R + \gamma_2 FST_{ij}^W + \gamma_3' X_{ij} + \varepsilon_{ij}^\gamma, \tag{3.30}$$

where $X_{ij}$ is a vector of control variables, primarily composed of alternative sources of barriers to diffusion, primarily geographic barriers. The predictions of our model are that $\alpha_1 > \beta_1, \gamma_1 > 0$, and $\gamma_2 = 0$.

Equations (3.28)–(3.30) are estimated using least squares. However, an econometric concern arises from the construction of the left-hand side variable as the difference in development or technological sophistication across country pairs. Indeed, consider pairs $(i, j)$ and $(i, k)$. By construction, the log per capita income of country $i$ appears in the difference in log per capita incomes of both pairs, introducing some spatial correlation in the error term. To deal with this issue, we correct the standard errors using two-way clustering, developed by Cameron et al. (2006). Specifically, standard errors are clustered at the level of country 1 and country 2. This results in larger standard errors compared to no clustering.[14]

We complement these tests with additional empirical results that can shed light on our barriers interpretation of the effect of genetic distance. In particular, we examine the evolution of the effect of genetic distance through time. If genetic distance continues to have an effect on differences in economic performance in periods where the world distribution of income was very different, it should put to rest the idea that vertically transmitted traits bear direct, unchanged effects on productivity. We therefore examine the effects of genetic distance on population density in the pre-industrial era, going as far back as year 1. In Malthusian times, population density is the proper measure of overall technological sophistication, since per capita income gains resulting from innovation are only transitory, and soon dissipated by an increase in fertility (Ashraf and Galor, 2011 provide empirical evidence on this point). We also study the time path of the effect of genetic distance around the Industrial Revolution. Our model predicts that this effect should peak during the initial phases of the diffusion of the Industrial Revolution, as

---

[14] In past work, we employed various methods to deal with the spatial correlation that arises as a by-product of the construction of the left-hand side variable, such as including a set of common country dummies. The results were not sensitive to the method used to control for spatial correlation. See Spolaore and Wacziarg (2009) for further details.

only places close to its birthplace have adopted the new innovation. The model predicts that the effect should decline thereafter, as more and more societies adopt industrial and post-industrial modes of production.

### 3.3.2 Data
#### 3.3.2.1 Genetic Distance Data

Our source for genetic distance data is Cavalli-Sforza et al. (1994). The main dataset covers 42 ethnolinguistic groups samples across the globe.[15] The genetic data concerns 120 gene locus, for which allele frequencies were obtained by population. The gene locus were chosen to represent neutral genes, i.e. genes that did not spread through natural selection but through random drift, as determined by geneticists. Thus, when aggregated over many genes, measures of genetic distance obtained from neutral genes capture separation times between populations, precisely the analog of genealogical distance employed in our theoretical model.

The specific measure of genetic distance we use is known as $F_{ST}$ genetic distance, also known as Wright's fixation index.[16] To illustrate the index, we derive it for the specific case of two populations, one locus and two alleles. The number of individuals in population $i$ is $n_i$. Total population is $n = \sum_{i=1}^{2} n_i$. The share of population $i$ is $w_i = n_i/n$. Consider one locus with two possible alleles: either $Q$ or $q$. Let $0 \leq p_i \leq 1$ be the frequency of individuals in population $i$ with allele $Q$. Let $p$ be this frequency in the whole population $\left(p = \sum_{i=1}^{2} w_i p_i\right)$. The degree of heterozygosity (i.e. the probability that two randomly selected alleles within a population are different) within population $i$ is $H_i = 2p_i(1 - p_i)$, and average heterozygosity across populations is $H_S = \sum_{i=1}^{2} w_i H_i$. Heterozygosity for the whole population is $H_T = 2p(1 - p)$. Then Wright's fixation index, $F_{ST}$, is defined as:

$$F_{ST} = 1 - \frac{H_S}{H_T} = 1 - \frac{n_1 p_1(1 - p_1) + n_2 p_2(1 - p_2)}{np(1 - p)}. \tag{3.31}$$

This is one minus the ratio of group level average heterozygosity to total heterozygosity. If both populations have the same allele frequencies ($p_1 = p_2$), then $H_i = H_S = H_T$, and $F_{ST} = 0$. In the polar opposite case, individuals within each population all have the same alleles, and these alleles differ completely across groups ($p_1 = 1 - p_2$). Then $F_{ST} = 1$ (total fixation). In general, the higher the differences in allele frequencies across populations, the higher is $F_{ST}$. The formula can easily be extended to account for more than two alleles. $F_{ST}$ can be averaged in a variety of ways across loci, so that the resulting $F_{ST}$ distance is a summary measure of relatedness between the two populations. Moreover, bootstrapping techniques can be used to obtain standard errors on estimates of $F_{ST}$. Details of these

---

[15] We will also make use of a more detailed dataset covering 26 European populations. Since populations were sampled at the country level rather than at the ethnic group level for the European dataset, matching populations to countries was an easier task.

[16] In past work, we also used the Nei index. Results did not hinge on the use of either index.

extensions are provided in Cavalli-Sforza et al. (1994, pp. 26–27). We rely on the genetic distance data that they provide, i.e. we rely on population geneticists' best judgment as to the proper choice of alleles, the proper sampling methods, and the proper way to aggregate heterozygosity across alleles.

The genealogical tree of human populations is displayed in Figure 3.2, where the genetic distance data was used to construct a tree showing the successive splits between human populations over the course of the last 70,000 years or so. In this figure, recent splits indicate a low genetic distance between the corresponding populations. In the source data pertaining to 42 world populations, the largest $F_{ST}$ genetic distance between any two populations is between the Mbuti Pygmies and the Papua New Guineans ($F_{ST} = 0.4573$). The smallest is between the Danish and the English ($F_{ST} = 0.0021$).

Genetic distance is obtained at the level of populations but it was necessary to construct measures pertaining to countries. We matched ethnolinguistic groups in Cavalli-Sforza et al. (1994) to ethnic groups for each country using the ethnic group data from Alesina et al. (2003), and then constructed the expected distance between two individuals, each drawn randomly from each of the two countries in a pair. Thus, our baseline measure of genetic distance between countries 1 and 2 is:

$$FST_{12}^{W} = \sum_{i=1}^{I} \sum_{j=1}^{J} (s_{1i} \times s_{2j} \times FST_{ij}), \tag{3.32}$$

where $s_{1i}$ is the share of population $i$ in country 1, $s_{2j}$ is the share of population $j$ in country 2, and $FST_{ij}$ is genetic distance between population $i$ and $j$. This index is also known as the Greenberg index (after Greenberg, 1956), and is increasingly used in economics as a measure of ethnolinguistic heterogeneity (see for instance Bossert et al. 2011).[17]

The measure derived above, $FST_{12}^{W}$, is the absolute measure of expected distance between any two countries 1 and 2. In keeping with the theoretical definition, we can also define a measure of these countries' relative distance to the technological frontier $f$:

$$FST_{12}^{R} = \left| FST_{1f}^{W} - FST_{2f}^{W} \right|. \tag{3.33}$$

Finally, the procedure above matches populations to ethnolinguistic groups as they occur in the contemporary period. It is, however, also possible to calculate genetic distance as of the year 1500 AD, by matching populations to the plurality group in each country given their composition in 1500. Thus, for instance, in the 1500 match, Australia is matched to the Aborigenes population (while for the contemporary period Australia is matched to a combination of English and Aborigenes—predominantly the former).

---

[17] In past work we also used the genetic distance between the largest populations (i.e. genetic groups) in countries 1 and 2. The correlation between expected (weighted) genetic distance and this alternative index is very high, and it does not matter which one we use in our empirical work.

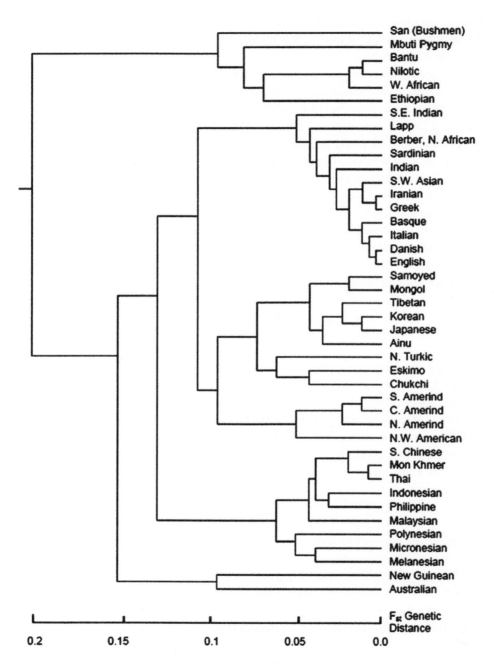

**Figure 3.2** Genetic distance among 42 populations. *Source: Cavalli-Sforza et al. 1994.*

We make use of the 1500 match in some historical regressions, or as an instrument for contemporary genetic distance. Again, measures of absolute and relative genetic distance are computed using the 1500 match of populations to countries.

### 3.3.2.2 Measures of Development and Technological Sophistication

We use a variety of measures of differences in economic development and technological sophistication. The first set of measures is defined at an aggregate level. The primary measure for the contemporary period is the absolute difference in log per capita income in 2005 (from the Penn World Tables version 6.3). For the pre-industrial periods, we consider the absolute difference in population density. The population density data pertains to the year 1500, and the source is McEvedy and Jones (1978). Despite more limited geographic coverage, we also use data on per capita income going back to 1820, from Maddison (2003), in order to examine the time path of the effect of genetic distance around the time of the Industrial Revolution.

The second set of measures includes disaggregated measures of technology usage, either along the extensive margin (for the historical period) or along the intensive margin (for the contemporary period).[18] We rely mostly on data from Comin et al. (2010, henceforth CEG). CEG gathered data on the degree of technological sophistication for the years 1000 BC, 1 AD, 1500 AD, and the contemporary period (1970–2000 AD). We make use of the data for 1500 AD and the contemporary period, since this corresponds most closely to the available genetic distance data. The data for 1500 pertain to the extensive margin of adoption of 24 separate technologies, grouped into 5 categories: military, agricultural, transportation, communication, and industry. For each technology in each category, a country is given a score of 1 if the technology was in use in 1500, 0 otherwise. The scores are summed within categories, and rescaled to vary between 0 and 1. An overall index of technological sophistication is also obtained by taking the simple average of the technological index for each of the 5 categories.

For the 1970–2000 AD data, technology usage is measured along the intensive margin. The basic data covers the per capita usage intensity of nine technologies, obtained from the database of Comin et al. (2008). For each technology, a country's usage is characterized as the number of years since the technological frontier (the United States) had the same level of per capita usage. The index is then rescaled to vary from 0 to 1, where 1 denotes usage at the same level as the frontier. Technologies are aggregated into 4 of the 5 aforementioned categories (all except the military category), and a simple average of the four measures is also available.

Finally, we attempted to measure technological sophistication at a more disaggregated level. This allows for a more refined analysis based on individual technologies that were not aggregated into broader categories, as is the case in the CEG dataset. For this, we relied

---

[18] These technologies are listed in Appendix 1.

on the CHAT dataset (Comin and Hobijn, 2009), which contains data on usage of 100 technologies. We restricted attention to technologies for which data is available for at least 50 countries over the 1990–1999 period. This led to a restricted set of 33 technologies, covering a wide range of sectors—medical, transportation, communications, industrial, and agricultural technologies. For each of the underlying 33 technologies, we calculated usage per capita, in order to maintain a consistent definition of the intensity of use.[19] For instance, for the technology "personal computers," the dependent variable is the absolute difference, between country $i$ and country $j$, in the number of computers per capita. For all technologies, the technological leader was assumed to be the United States, an assumption confirmed in virtually all cases when examining the actual intensity of use.

All of these measures of technological sophistication were available at the country level, so we computed the absolute difference in technology measures across all available pairs of countries for the purpose of empirical analysis.

### 3.3.2.3 Measures of Geographic Barriers

Measures of genetic distance are correlated with geographic distance. Indeed, homo sapiens is estimated to have migrated out of East Africa around 70,000 years ago, and from there spread first to Asia, and then later fanned out to Europe, Oceania, and the Americas. As early humans split into subgroups, the molecular clock of genetic drift started operating, and populations became more genetically distant. It is not surprising that the farther in space, the more genetically distant populations are expected to be. It is therefore important to control for geographic distance when estimating the human barriers to the diffusion of innovations. At the same time, as we describe below, the correlation between geographic distance and genetic distance is not as large as one might expect. This is the case for two major reasons: First, genetic drift occurred along rather specific geographic axes. For instance, a major dimension along which populations array themselves in proportion to their genetic distance is a rough straight line between Addis Ababa and Beijing. There need not be a strict correspondence, then, between genetic distance and common measures of geographic distance relevant as geographic barriers to the spread of innovations, such as the greater circle distance or latitudinal distance. Second, more recent population movements have served to break the initial links between geographic distance and genetic distance. Two highly relevant population movements were the conquests of parts of the New World by Europeans, and the slave trades occurring thereafter. We obtain some (but not all) of our identifying variation off of these post-1500 population movements.

To capture geographic distance we use a large array of controls, capturing both simple geodesic distance, distance along the longitudinal and latitudinal dimensions, and binary indicators of micro-geography such as whether the countries in a pair are contiguous, are

---

[19] One exception was for the share of cropland area planted with modern varieties, for which it would make little sense to divide by population. All other technologies were entered in per capita terms.

islands, are landlocked, or share a common sea or ocean. This set of controls was included in every regression, and was supplemented in robustness tests by additional geographic controls such as climatic differences, continent effects, and freight costs.

### 3.3.2.4 Summary Statistics and Data Patterns

Figure 3.3 presents a simple plot of weighted genetic distance to the USA against per capita income, and Figure 3.4 does the same after partialling out the effect of geodesic distance (a similar figure is obtained after partialling out the effect of a longer list of geographic distance metrics). Both figures reveal a negative association between per capita income and genetic distance to the USA. Table 3.1 presents summary statistics to help in the interpretation of regression estimates. Panel B displays correlations based on 10,440 country pairs, based on 145 countries. These correlations are informative: the absolute genetic distance between pairs bears a correlation of 19.5% with the absolute difference in log per capita income. Genetic distance relative to the USA, however, bears a much larger correlation of 32.26%, a pattern consistent with the predictions of the barriers model, implying a larger effect of relative genetic distance compared to absolute genetic distance. Finally, as mentioned above, the correlation between genetic distance (either relative to the frontier or not) with geodesic distance, is positive but moderate in magnitude, offering hope that the effect of genealogical barriers can be estimated separately from that of geographic barriers.

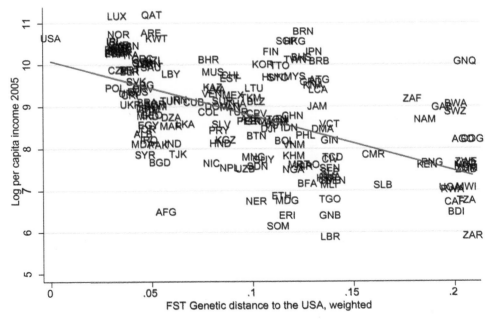

**Figure 3.3** Log income in 2005 and genetic distance to the USA.

**Table 3.1** Summary statistics for the main variables of interest

| Variable | Mean | Standard deviation | Minimum | Maximum |
|---|---|---|---|---|
| **Panel A—mean and variation** | | | | |
| Difference in log income per capita 2005 | 1.3844 | 0.9894 | 0.0000241 | 4.8775 |
| FST genetic distance relative to the English, 1500 | 0.0710 | 0.0555 | 0 | 0.2288 |
| Weighted FST genetic distance relative to the USA | 0.0612 | 0.0475 | 0 | 0.2127 |
| Weighted FST genetic distance between pairs | 0.1124 | 0.0818 | 0 | 0.3364 |
| Geodesic distance (thousands of km) | 7.1349 | 4.1330 | 0.0105 | 19.9512 |

10,440 observations.

| | Difference in log income per capita 2005 | FST genetic distance relative to the English, 1500 | Weighted FST gen. dist. relative to the USA | Weighted FST genetic distance between pairs |
|---|---|---|---|---|
| **Panel B—correlations** | | | | |
| FST genetic distance relative to the English, 1500 | 0.2745* | 1 | | |
| Weighted FST genetic distance relative to the USA | 0.3226* | 0.6105* | 1 | |
| Weighted FST genetic distance between pairs | 0.1950* | 0.2408* | 0.5876* | 1 |
| Geodesic distance (thousands of km) | 0.0126 | 0.0644* | 0.0899* | 0.3317* |

* Significant at the 5% level. 10,440 observations.

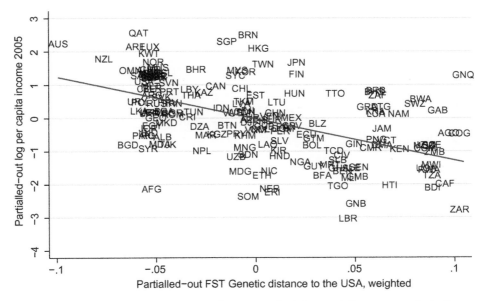

**Figure 3.4** Log income in 2005 and genetic distance to the USA, partialling out geodesic distance to the USA.

## 3.4. BARRIERS TO DEVELOPMENT: EMPIRICAL RESULTS

### 3.4.1 Results for Aggregate Measures of Economic Development

#### 3.4.1.1 Baseline Estimates

Baseline estimates of Equations (3.28)–(3.30) are presented in Table 3.2. The predictions of the barriers model are borne out: after controlling for various measures of geographic distance, differences in per capita income are significantly correlated with both absolute and relative genetic distance (columns 1 and 2).[20] However, the magnitude of the effect of genetic distance relative to the technological frontier (column 1) is about three times as large as the effect of absolute genetic distance (column 2). This is true when comparing both the estimated coefficient and a standardized measure of magnitude (the standardized beta, reported in the next to last row of Table 3.2). When including both measures in the regression (column 3), genetic distance relative to the frontier remains significant while absolute genetic distance becomes insignificantly different from zero. In terms of magnitudes, a one standard deviation increase in $F_{ST}$ genetic distance relative to the USA

---

[20] A myriad additional controls were included as robustness tests in analogous regressions presented in Spolaore and Wacziarg (2009). These included climatic differences, freight costs, etc. Results were robust to the inclusion of these additional control variables.

**Table 3.2** Income difference regressions (dependent variable: difference in log per capita income, 2005)

| | (1) OLS with relative GD | (2) OLS with simple GD | (3) Horserace between simple and relative GD | (4) 2SLS with 1500 GD |
|---|---|---|---|---|
| FST gen. dist. relative to the USA, weighted | 6.290 | | 6.029 | 9.720 |
| | (1.175)*** | | (1.239)*** | (1.974)*** |
| FST genetic distance | | 2.164 | 0.275 | |
| | | (0.596)*** | (0.541) | |
| Absolute difference in latitudes | 0.232 | 0.559 | 0.255 | 0.152 |
| | (0.245) | (0.279)** | (0.248) | (0.300) |
| Absolute difference in longitudes | −0.025 | −0.196 | −0.007 | 0.238 |
| | (0.220) | (0.240) | (0.213) | (0.247) |
| Geodesic distance | −0.012 | −0.008 | −0.016 | −0.042 |
| | (0.026) | (0.027) | (0.025) | (0.028) |
| =1 for contiguity | −0.418 | −0.495 | −0.414 | −0.326 |
| | (0.060)*** | (0.060)*** | (0.061)*** | (0.069)*** |
| =1 if either country is an island | 0.174 | 0.143 | 0.174 | 0.211 |
| | (0.083)** | (0.083)* | (0.083)** | (0.084)*** |
| =1 if either country is landlocked | 0.008 | 0.024 | 0.005 | −0.029 |
| | (0.085) | (0.090) | (0.087) | (0.085) |
| =1 if pair shares at least one sea or ocean | −0.001 | 0.028 | −0.000 | −0.024 |
| | (0.067) | (0.077) | (0.067) | (0.078) |
| Constant | 1.022 | 1.143 | 1.017 | 0.891 |
| | (0.089)*** | (0.086)*** | (0.090)*** | (0.099)*** |
| Standardized Beta (%) | 30.18 | 10.39 | 28.93 | 46.49 |
| R−Squared | 0.11 | 0.07 | 0.11 | 0.09 |

Two-way clustered standard errors in parentheses.
All regressions are based on 10,440 observations.
* Significant at 10%.
** Significant at 5%.
*** Significant at 1%.

is associated with an increase in the absolute difference in log income per capita of almost 29% of that variable's standard deviation.

Column 4 of Table 3.2 reports results of IV estimation, using relative genetic distance to the English population in 1500 as an instrument for current genetic distance to the USA. This is meant to address two specific concerns: First, matching the 42 populations for which genetic distance data is available to contemporaneous ethnolinguistic groups may introduce measurement error. The main difficulties in the match arise for the New World where it is sometimes difficult to assess which European population to match with the descendents of past European settlers; which African populations to match with former slaves; and what shares to ascribe to these various populations in the total population, given that many of them mixed over time, resulting in significant shares of populations with mixed ancestry (the latter issue arises mainly in Latin America). In contrast, the 1500 match of genetic groups (populations) to the plurality ethnic group is much more straightforward, since the Cavalli-Sforza et al. (1994) data was gathered precisely to represent the makeup of countries as they stood in 1492, prior to the population movements associated with the conquest of the New World. The second concern is endogeneity: genetic distance between countries changed in the post-1492 era due to the aforementioned conquest of the New World and the slave trades. It is possible that areas well suited to high incomes in the industrial era, perhaps due to geographic factors such as a temperate climate, happened to attract certain populations (for instance Europeans) as settlers. In this case, it would be the potential for differential incomes that would causally affect genetic distance rather than the opposite. Using genetic distance lagged by 500 years as an instrument addresses this particular endogeneity concern. The results presented in column 4, show that, if anything, OLS understated the effect of relative genetic distance: its standardized effect rises under IV to 46.49%. Since the IV estimates are larger than the OLS estimates, to remain conservative we rely in the rest of this chapter on OLS estimates.

### 3.4.1.2 Regional Controls and Analysis

In Table 3.3, we run a variety of regressions accounting for regional effects. In column 1, we include a full set of continental dummy variables capturing both whether the countries in a pair are both located on the same specific continent (an effect presumed to go in the direction of reducing the difference in economic performance between these countries); and whether they are located on different ones (as further defined in the footnote to Table 3.3). The idea behind this test is to further control for geographic factors not already captured by the included geographic distance variables. However, this is a demanding test, since continent effects could capture geographic barriers but also part of the effect of human barriers that could be mismeasured when using genetic distance. Nonetheless the effect of genetic distance remains robust to controlling for a full set of

**Table 3.3** Income difference regressions, regional controls, and sample splits (dependent variable: difference in log per capital income in 2005, 1870 for column 3)

| | (1) Continent dummies | (2) Europe 2005 income | (3) Europe with 1870 income | (4) Excluding Europe | (5) Control for Europeans | (6) Excluding SS Africa |
|---|---|---|---|---|---|---|
| Fst gen. dist. relative to the USA, weighted | 3.403 (1.284)** | | | 5.183 (1.232)*** | 5.624 (1.143)*** | 4.851 (1.443)*** |
| Genetic distance, relative to the English | | 25.920 (11.724)** | 27.054 (6.557)*** | | | |
| Abs. difference in the shares of people of European descent | | | | | 0.626 (0.125)*** | |
| Constant | 1.541 (0.315)** | 0.345 (0.201)* | 0.495 (0.154)*** | 1.006 (0.123)*** | 0.864 (0.097)*** | 0.853 (0.071)*** |
| Observations | 10,440 | 253 | 136 | 6,328 | 10,153 | 5,253 |
| Standardized Beta (%) | 16.27 | 31.28 | 43.62 | 24.99 | 27.15 | 17.12 |
| R-Squared | 0.20 | 0.24 | 0.24 | 0.08 | 0.17 | 0.06 |

Two-way clustered standard errors in parentheses.

In all regressions, controls are included for: Absolute difference in latitudes, absolute difference in longitudes, geodesic distance, dummy for contiguity, dummy if either country is an island, dummy if either country is landlocked, dummy if pair shares at least one sea or ocean.

Column 1 includes continental dummies defined as follows: both in Asia dummy, both in Africa dummy, both in Europe dummy, both in North America dummy, both in Latin America/Caribbean dummy, both in Oceania dummy, dummy if one and only one country is in Asia, dummy if one and only one country is in Africa, dummy if one and only one country is in Europe, dummy if one and only one country is in North America, dummy if one and only one country is in South America.

* Significant at 10%.
** Significant at 5%.
*** Significant at 1%.

12 same- and different-continent dummies. While the effect of genetic distance falls in magnitude, it remains large and highly significant statistically.

Columns 2 and 3 make use of the separate genetic distance dataset we have for 26 countries in Europe. Here, the relevant measure of genetic distance is $F_{ST}$ distance to the English (England being the birthplace of the Industrial Revolution), though the results do not change if we use distance to the Germans instead. We find that within Europe, genetic distance is again a strong predictor of absolute differences in log per capita income. The standardized beta on genetic distance relative to the English is of the same order of magnitude as that found in the world sample, and it is highly significant. There are two major genetic clines in Europe: one separating the north and the south, another one separating the east and the west. These correspond to north-south and east-west income differences. Since the east-west cline overlaps to a large degree with regions that were on either side of the Iron Curtain during the Cold War, to assess whether this historical feature explains all of the effect of genetic distance on economic performance, we repeat our regression using income in 1870 (from Maddison), well prior to the rise of the Eastern bloc. We find that the effect of genetic distance is in fact larger in magnitude in the immediate aftermath of the Industrial Revolution, with the standardized beta rising to almost 44%. This result assuages concerns that the contemporary results were a result of the fact that the Iron Curtain as a first approximation, separated Slavic from non-Slavic Europeans. It is also highly consistent with the barriers story since, as we further explore below, the effect of genetic distance should be larger around the time of a large innovation, in the midst of the process whereby countries other than the frontier are busy adopting the frontier technology in proportion to how genetically far they are from the frontier. In sum, our effects hold within Europe, where genetic distance is better measured.

Since the basic result of this chapter holds so strongly for Europe, might Europe drive the World results? To test this, in column 4 we exclude any pairs of countries containing at least one European country. Compared to the baseline results, the standardized effect of genetic distance relative to the USA declines from 30% to 25%, but remains large and statistically significant—highlighting that the results are not due to Europe alone. To drive home the point, in column 5 we control for the absolute difference in the share of the population of European descent, using data from the Putterman and Weil (2010) migration matrix. The regression now controls more broadly for the effect of European-ness, and while the effect of the absolute difference in the share of Europeans is a positive and statistically significant determinant of differences in per capita income, its inclusion in the regression only moderately reduces the standardized effect of relative genetic distance (to 27%). We conclude that our results are not driven by the inclusion of European countries in the sample, nor are they driven by the genetic difference between Europeans and the rest.

The final geographic concern that we explore is whether Sub-Saharan Africa drives our results. As Figure 3.2 illustrates, Sub-Saharan African populations are genetically distant from the rest of the world: the out-of-Africa migrations occurring about 70,000 years ago were the first foray of modern humans out of Africa, and consequently Africans and other world populations have had the longest time to drift apart genetically from each other. Sub-Saharan populations also have some of the lowest per capita GDPs recorded in the world. While it is part of our story to ascribe some of the poverty of Africa to the barriers to technological transmission brought about by its high degree of genealogical distance from the rest of the world, it would be concerning if our results were entirely driven by Sub-Saharan Africa. To address this concern, in column (6) of Table 3.3 we exclude any pair that involves at least one Sub-Saharan country from our sample. We find that the effect of genetic distance falls a little, but remains positive, statistically significant, and large in magnitude with a standardized beta equal to 17%. Together with the strong results within Europe, this should lay to rest any notion that our results are driven solely by Sub-Saharan Africa.

### 3.4.1.3 Historical Analysis

We now turn to a historical analysis of the determinants of aggregate measures of economic performance, seeking to achieve two main goals. The first is to assess the robustness of the effect of genetic distance through time. The second goal is to describe the time path of the standardized effect of genetic distance around the time of the Industrial Revolution. In our barriers model, a major innovation such as the Industrial Revolution should lead to a specific pattern in the evolution of the effect of relative genetic distance on differences in economic development. Specifically, the effect of genetic distance should be large in the aftermath of the onset of the Industrial Revolution in the frontier country. As more and more societies adopt the Industrial Revolution, the effect should gradually decline. We now redefine the frontier country as the United Kingdom (i.e. the English population) since it is a more appropriate choice for the period concerned.[21]

Table 3.4 displays pairwise correlations between historical measures of differences in economic development and genetic distance. For the 1500 period, we consider the correlation between relative genetic distance to the English using the 1500 match, and population density. For periods from 1820 to today, it is best to rely on the correlation between contemporaneous weighted genetic distance relative to the UK, and the absolute difference in log per capita income at various dates.[22] A few remarks are in order: First,

---

[21] This choice is not very material. In fact, relative genetic distance to the English and relative genetic distance to the United States are very highly correlated, because the United States are primarily composed of populations from Western Europe—either the English or populations genetically very close to the English. In fact, by world standards, genetic distances between Western European populations are so small that it matters little empirically which Western European population is chosen as the frontier. For instance, for 1500 we experimented with using Italy as the frontier country; results were unchanged.

[22] We lack genetic distance data suitable for the millenia prior to 1500, despite the existence of some population density data for early dates. At any rate it is not clear that our barriers story would apply with

**Table 3.4** Pairwise correlations between historical measures of economic development

| | Relative genetic distance to the English, 1500 | Relative genetic distance to the UK, weighted (contemporary) | Abs. difference in population density, 1500 | Abs. difference in log income, 1820 | Abs. difference in log income, 1870 | Abs. difference in log income, 1913 | Abs. difference in log income, 1960 |
|---|---|---|---|---|---|---|---|
| Relative genetic distance to the UK, weighted (contemporary) | 0.6205* (10,585) | 1 (10,585) | | | | | |
| Abs. difference in population density, 1500 | 0.1594* (10,153) | 0.0461* (10,153) | 1 (10,153) | | | | |
| Abs. difference in log income, 1820 | 0.1763* (1,035) | 0.1327* (1,035) | 0.1701* (990) | 1 (1,035) | | | |
| Abs. difference in log income, 1870 | 0.1360* (1,485) | 0.1811* (1,485) | 0.1125* (1,378) | 0.6117* (1,035) | 1 (1,485) | | |
| Abs. difference in log income, 1913 | 0.0840* (1,653) | 0.1839* (1,653) | 0.0739* (1,540) | 0.5411* (1,035) | 0.8996* (1,485) | 1 (1,653) | |
| Abs. difference in log income, 1960 | 0.2347* (4,753) | 0.3229* (4,753) | 0.1242* (4,560) | 0.4018* (820) | 0.6154* (1,035) | 0.7201* (1,176) | 1 (4,753) |
| Abs. difference in log income, 2005 | 0.2745* (10,440) | 0.3228* (10,440) | 0.1173* (10,011) | 0.3297* (990) | 0.4722* (1,431) | 0.4844* (1,596) | 0.6199* (4,753) |

* Significant at the 5% level; # of obs. in parentheses.

this data reveals some persistence in economic fortunes. In spite of being different measures, even the absolute difference in population density in 1500 and the absolute difference in log per capita income in 2005 bear a correlation of about 12% with each other. Correlations between income-based measures are much higher (for instance, the correlation of income differences in 1820 and 2005 is 33%). Second, genetic distance is positively and significantly correlated with these measures of differences in economic performance at all dates. For instance, the correlation between the absolute difference in population density in 1500 and relative genetic distance to the English in 1500 is about 16%. This rises to 32% in 2005 (comparisons of magnitudes should be made cautiously from this table as the underlying samples differ by date—but in the case of 1500 and 2005 the samples are very similar—more on this point below). In general, simple correlations reveal that despite some changes in the relative fortunes of nations over the last 500 years, the correlation between genetic distance and development seems to exist at all dates.

Table 3.5 turns to regression analysis. Across all columns, corresponding to different dates, genetic distance relative to the UK comes out with a positive, significant coefficient. Thus, the effect of genetic distance is robust to considering different dates and a different measure of economic development for the Malthusian period. The penultimate row of Table 3.5 shows the evolution of the standardized effect of genetic distance over time for a common sample of 820 country pairs (41 countries), for which income data is available at all dates. The magnitudes here are somewhat smaller than when using unrestricted samples across periods, in part because the 41 countries only include one Sub-Saharan African country (and that country is South Africa, which is relatively rich). However, restricting the sample to pairs available at all dates allows for a comparison of magnitudes across time. To facilitate interpretation, the standardized effects from the common sample are displayed in Figure 3.5.

This figure lends further credence to the barriers model. Indeed, just as predicted above, the effect of genetic distance, which is initially modest in 1820, rises by around 75% to reach a peak in 1913, and thereafter declines. Thus, in the few decades following the adoption of the Industrial Revolution by countries in the (genetic) periphery of England, the effect of genetic distance was maximal. Thereafter, as more and more societies industrialized, the effect fell steadily.

## 3.4.2 Results for Specific Innovations

The analysis above concerns determinants of differences in aggregate productivity. This is useful to analyze very broad trends like the diffusion of the Industrial Revolution. Yet our model also applies to the diffusion of more specific technologies. Indeed, if our empirical results applied to aggregate measures of development or technological sophistication

as much force in periods where geographic barriers to the diffusion of innovation were so overwhelming, except perhaps in a regionally narrow context.

**Table 3.5** Regressions using historical income data

| | (1) Year 1500 population density | (2) Income 1820 | (3) Income 1870 | (4) Income 1913 | (5) Income 1960 | (6) Income 2005 |
|---|---|---|---|---|---|---|
| Relative Fst genetic distance to the UK, 1500 match | 29.751 (7.168)*** | | | | | |
| Relative Fst genetic distance to the UK, weighted | | 0.671 (0.344)* | 1.691 (0.836)** | 1.984 (0.907)** | 3.472 (0.783)** | 5.075 (0.941)** |
| Constant | 6.693 (0.981)*** | 0.313 (0.063)** | 0.365 (0.076)** | 0.421 (0.064)** | 0.478 (0.077)** | 1.017 (0.088)** |
| Observations | 10,153 | 1,035 | 1,485 | 1,653 | 4,753 | 10,440 |
| Standardized beta (%), maximal sample | 17.77 | 8.75 | 15.02 | 15.02 | 28.82 | 30.58 |
| Standardized beta, restricted sample* | – | 9.89 | 16.30 | 17.36 | 11.15 | 7.49 |
| R-Squared | 0.07 | 0.22 | 0.16 | 0.17 | 0.17 | 0.11 |

Two-way clustered standard errors in parentheses.
In all regressions, controls are included for: Absolute difference in latitudes, absolute difference in longitudes, geodesic distance, dummy for contiguity, dummy if either country is an island, dummy if either country is landlocked, dummy if pair shares at least one sea or ocean. Population density data for 1500 are from McEvedy and Jones (1978). Income data for 1820, 1870, and 1913 are from Maddison (2003). Income data for 1960 and 2005 are from the Penn World Tables.
* The restricted sample for columns (2)–(6) consists of 820 country pairs constructed from 41 countries (Algeria, Australia, Austria, Belgium, Brazil, Canada, China, Denmark, Egypt, Finland, France, Greece, India, Indonesia, Iran, Ireland, Italy, Jamaica, Japan, Korea, Malaysia, Mexico, Morocco, Nepal, Netherlands, New Zealand, Norway, Philippines, Portugal, South Africa, Spain, Sri Lanka, Sweden, Switzerland, Syria, Taiwan, Thailand, Turkey, USA, United Kingdom).
* Significant at 10%.
** Significant at 5%.
*** Significant at 1%.

**Figure 3.5** Standardized effect of genetic distance over time, 1820–2005.

only, but did not extend to more disaggregated technologies, it would cast doubt on the hypothesis that the main effect of genetic distance is to hinder the transmission of technologies across societies with very different cultures and histories. In this subsection, we use data directly at the technology usage level to address this issue.

Table 3.6 starts with some summary statistics from the CEG dataset, pertaining to the contemporary period. Panel A is mainly meant to assist in the interpretation of the regressions that come next, but Panel B already contains interesting information. The first observation is that differences in the intensity of technology usage in 1970–2000 across various technological categories are correlated, but imperfectly. Second, differences in technology usage intensity are positively correlated with per capita income, but the correlations are in the 0.4–0.7 range depending on the technological category, so these variables do not all measure the same thing. In other words, our measures of differences in technology usage are not simply indicators of differences in overall economic performance. Third, differences in technology usage are correlated more strongly with genetic distance relative to the frontier than with genetic distance per se. In fact, correlations with the latter are often close to zero while correlations with the former are always positive and significant.

**Table 3.6 Summary Statistics for Genetic Distance and Technological Adoption Levels (from the Comin et al., 2010 Data)**

| Variable | # of Obs. | Mean | Standard deviation | Minimum | Maximum |
|---|---|---|---|---|---|
| **Panel A—mean and variation** | | | | | |
| Avg. tech. adoption in agriculture in 1970–2000 | 6,105 | 0.1998 | 0.2327 | 0 | 0.8553 |
| Avg. tech. adoption in communications in 1970–2000 | 7,381 | 0.2601 | 0.1894 | 0 | 0.7911 |
| Avg. tech. adoption in transportation in 1970–2000 | 6,441 | 0.1986 | 0.1600 | 0 | 0.8443 |
| Avg. tech. adoption in industry in 1970–2000 | 5,565 | 0.3005 | 0.2153 | 0 | 1.0278 |
| Avg. of the sectoral tech. adoption indexes in 1970–2000 | 7,503 | 0.2129 | 0.1807 | 0 | 0.8378 |
| Absolute difference in log income, 2005 | 10,440 | 1.3844 | 0.9894 | 0 | 4.8775 |
| FST gen. dist. relative to the USA, weighted | 10,585 | 0.0611 | 0.0473 | 0 | 0.2127 |
| Simple FST genetic distance | 10,585 | 0.1126 | 0.0816 | 0 | 0.3364 |

*(Continued)*

**Table 3.6** (*Continued*)

| | Avg. tech. adoption in agriculture in 1970–2000 | Avg. tech. adoption in communications in 1970–2000 | Avg. tech. adoption in transportation in 1970–2000 | Avg. tech. adoption in industry in 1970–2000 | Avg. of the sectoral tech. adoption indexes in 1970–2000 | Absolute difference in log income, 2005 | FST gen. distance relative to the USA, weighted |
|---|---|---|---|---|---|---|---|
| **Panel B—pairwise correlations** | | | | | | | |
| Avg. tech. adoption in communications in 1970–2000 | 0.5550* (5,886) | 1 (7,381) | | | | | |
| Avg. tech. adoption in transportation in 1970–2000 | 0.5308* (5,356) | 0.4331* (6,216) | 1 (6,441) | | | | |
| Avg. tech. adoption in industry in 1970–2000 | 0.5396* (5,460) | 0.6335* (5,460) | 0.5192* (5,050) | 1 (5,565) | | | |
| Avg. of the sectoral tech. adoption indexes in 1970–2000 | 0.7615* (5,995) | 0.7010* (7,260) | 0.7591* (6,441) | 0.7735* (5,565) | 1 (7,503) | | |
| Absolute difference in log income, 2005 | 0.4106* (6,105) | 0.5619* (7,381) | 0.4662* (6,441) | 0.7210* (5,565) | 0.6521* (7,503) | 1 (10,440) | |
| FST gen. dist. relative to the USA, weighted | 0.1301* (6,105) | 0.1877* (7,381) | 0.1248* (6,441) | 0.2958* (5,565) | 0.1975* (7,503) | 0.3226* (10,440) | 1 (10,585) |
| Simple FST genetic distance | −0.0562* (6,105) | 0.0862* (7,381) | −0.0409* (6,441) | 0.1407* (5,565) | 0.0042 (7,503) | 0.1950* (10,440) | 0.5859* (10,585) |

*Significant at the 5% level; # of obs. in parentheses.

Table 3.7 carries out the regression analysis for the contemporary period, controlling for geographic distance. Genetic distance relative to the frontier comes out positive in all cases, and significant at the 5% level or better for 3 of the 4 technological categories, as well as for the summary index of overall technology usage. The only category for which genetic distance is not significant is agricultural technologies. One possible interpretation is that agricultural technologies for the contemporary period under consideration have already widely diffused around the globe and are already intensively in use in much of the developing world, so that the effect of genetic distance as a barrier to their adoption can no longer be detected. We also carried out the same regression analysis as that in Table 3.8, but adding to the specification the measure of absolute genetic distance between pairs.[23] We found that relative genetic distance always trumped absolute distance, which sometimes carried a negative sign and was statistically insignificant in most cases. Thus, our test of the barriers story (Equation 3.30) also works when considering technology usage intensity rather than aggregate measures of development.

Turning to the historical evidence, Table 3.8 examines the determinants of technology usage differences along the extensive margin in the year 1500. As before, we use the English population as the frontier (as before, it matters little if we use the Italians instead—Italy was arguably the most technologically sophisticated country in the world in 1500). For 1500, we have 5 rather than 4 technological categories, plus the overall index of technological sophistication. We find that in all cases, genetic distance relative to the English is positive and statistically significant at the 10% level. In 5 of the 6 columns, it is significant at the 1% level (as before, the weakest results are for agricultural technologies). This is remarkable given the crudeness of the measure of technological use in 1500, based on counting whether or not each of 24 technologies, grouped in functional categories, were in use at all in a given country at the time. Moreover, as before, we also conducted horseraces between relative genetic distance and absolute genetic distance.[24] For five of the six indicators we again found that relative genetic distance trumps absolute genetic distance, with the latter entering with either the wrong sign, a very small magnitude, or low significance levels. The only exception, once again, was for agriculture.

Finally, we carried out the same analysis with the 33 disaggregated technologies chosen from the CHAT dataset. The results are presented in Table 3.9. For each technology, the table reports the coefficient on relative genetic distance to the USA (from a regression in which the standard set of geographic controls is included), the number of observations and countries, the standardized beta coefficient on genetic distance, and the $R^2$. The results vary across technologies of course, but interesting observations emerge: (1) In every single case the effect of genetic distance on differences in technology usage intensity is positive. (2) In 22 of the 33 cases, the coefficient on genetic distance is significant at the 10% level,

---

[23] Results are available upon request.
[24] Results are available upon request.

**Table 3.7** Technological distance and genetic distance in the contemporary period (1970–2000) (dependent variables: measures of technological usage from Comin et al. as described in row 2)

| | (1) Agricultural technology | (2) Communications technology | (3) Transportation technology | (4) Industrial technology | (5) Overall technology |
|---|---|---|---|---|---|
| FST gen. dist. relative to the USA, weighted | 0.402 (0.268) | 0.500 (0.212)** | 0.608 (0.185)*** | 1.149 (0.288)*** | 0.745 (0.216)*** |
| Absolute difference in latitudes | 0.687 (0.121)*** | 0.274 (0.066)*** | 0.306 (0.057)*** | 0.329 (0.081)*** | 0.361 (0.082)*** |
| Absolute difference in longitudes | 0.405 (0.129)*** | 0.089 (0.055) | 0.305 (0.072)*** | 0.174 (0.069)** | 0.243 (0.088)*** |
| Geodesic distance | −0.050 (0.014)*** | −0.016 (0.006)** | −0.036 (0.008)*** | −0.024 (0.007)*** | −0.032 (0.010)*** |
| =1 for contiguity | −0.050 (0.014)*** | −0.077 (0.012)*** | −0.053 (0.013)*** | −0.090 (0.018)*** | −0.071 (0.012)*** |
| =1 if either country is an island | 0.118 (0.077) | 0.057 (0.027)** | 0.093 (0.047)** | 0.062 (0.023)*** | 0.116 (0.048)** |
| =1 if either country is landlocked | −0.007 (0.028) | 0.018 (0.017) | −0.008 (0.011) | 0.013 (0.023) | −0.016 (0.014) |
| =1 if pair shares at least one sea or ocean | 0.036 (0.027) | −0.010 (0.015) | 0.014 (0.015) | 0.001 (0.020) | 0.009 (0.019) |
| Constant | 0.089 (0.029)*** | 0.199 (0.018)*** | 0.148 (0.018)*** | 0.198 (0.023)*** | 0.147 (0.018)*** |
| Observations | 6,105 | 7,381 | 6,441 | 5,565 | 7,503 |
| Standardized beta (%) | 8.38 | 12.73 | 18.68 | 25.97 | 19.81 |
| R–squared | 0.25 | 0.10 | 0.14 | 0.16 | 0.17 |

Two-way clustered standard errors in parentheses.
* significant at 10%.
** Significant at 5%.
*** Significant at 1%.

**Table 3.8** Technological distance and genetic distance in the year 1500 (dependent variables: measures of technological usage From Comin et al. as described in row 2)

| | (1) Agricultural technology | (2) Military technology | (3) Communications technology | (4) Transportation technology | (5) Industrial technology | (6) Overall technology |
|---|---|---|---|---|---|---|
| Relative Fst genetic distance to the English, 1500 match | 0.551 (0.281)* | 1.752 (0.326)*** | 1.279 (0.288)*** | 1.926 (0.299)*** | 1.673 (0.271)*** | 1.524 (0.229)*** |
| Absolute difference in latitudes | 0.189 (0.096)** | 0.383 (0.094)*** | 0.758 (0.092)*** | 0.172 (0.064)*** | 0.138 (0.061)** | 0.377 (0.065)*** |
| Absolute difference in longitudes | −0.329 (0.082)*** | −0.018 (0.066) | −0.017 (0.068) | −0.039 (0.048) | 0.061 (0.091) | −0.066 (0.061) |
| Geodesic distance | 0.049 (0.010)*** | 0.009 (0.010) | 0.009 (0.008) | 0.014 (0.007)** | 0.048 (0.010)*** | 0.025 (0.007)*** |
| =1 for contiguity | 0.037 (0.026) | −0.025 (0.019) | −0.042 (0.024)* | −0.006 (0.021) | 0.023 (0.025) | 0.014 (0.014) |
| =1 if either country is an island | −0.049 (0.058) | −0.087 (0.029)*** | −0.095 (0.053)* | −0.073 (0.020)*** | −0.180 (0.031)*** | −0.092 (0.024)*** |
| =1 if either country is landlocked | 0.017 (0.026) | −0.051 (0.018)*** | −0.020 (0.016) | −0.048 (0.011)*** | 0.006 (0.023) | −0.022 (0.011)** |
| =1 if pair shares at least one sea or ocean | −0.006 (0.020) | −0.105 (0.034)*** | −0.018 (0.033) | −0.046 (0.029) | 0.050 (0.029)* | −0.019 (0.025) |
| Constant | 0.082 (0.034)** | 0.166 (0.036)*** | 0.086 (0.026)*** | 0.069 (0.024)*** | −0.126 (0.039)*** | 0.016 (0.020) |
| Observations | 5,253 | 5,886 | 5,886 | 5,253 | 5,253 | 5,886 |
| Standardized beta (%) | 10.41 | 29.26 | 19.95 | 41.81 | 25.27 | 31.63 |
| R–squared | 0.23 | 0.27 | 0.36 | 0.32 | 0.46 | 0.44 |

Two-way clustered standard errors in parentheses.
* Significant at 10%.
** Significant at 5%.
*** Significant at 1%.

**Table 3.9** Bilateral Regressions of Technological Distance on Relative Genetic Distance for 33 Technologies (CHAT Dataset Averaged Over 1990–1999)

| | | Fst gen. dist. relative to the USA, weighted | Observations (countries) | Standardized beta (%) | R-squared |
|---|---|---|---|---|---|
| **Agricultural technologies** | | | | | |
| (1) | Harvest machines | 2.044 (1.134)* | 3,486 (84) | 5.91 | 0.17 |
| (2) | Tractors used in agriculture | 19.615 (8.245)** | 5,778 (108) | 9.05 | 0.25 |
| (3) | Metric tons of fertilizer consumed | 73.393 (23.062)*** | 5,778 (108) | 11.68 | 0.23 |
| (4) | Area of irrigated crops | 0.453 (0.276)* | 5,565 (106) | 7.21 | 0.03 |
| (5) | Share of cropland area planted with modern varieties (% cropland) | 0.182 (0.080)** | 3,321 (82) | 7.20 | 0.02 |
| (6) | Metric tons of pesticides | 0.738 (0.893) | 4,465 (95) | 2.62 | 0.12 |
| **Transportation technologies** | | | | | |
| (7) | Civil aviation passenger km | 0.484 (0.254)* | 3,828 (88) | 11.29 | 0.21 |
| (8) | Lengths of rail line | 0.397 (0.275) | 4,656 (97) | 5.26 | 0.28 |
| (9) | Tons of freight carried on railways | 2.330 (1.421) | 4,005 (90) | 10.63 | 0.16 |
| (10) | Passenger cars in use | 0.245 (0.082)*** | 5,886 (109) | 15.88 | 0.26 |
| (11) | Commercial vehicles in use | 0.066 (0.025)*** | 5,050 (101) | 23.50 | 0.29 |

*(Continued)*

**Table 3.9** (*Continued*)

| | Fst gen. dist. relative to the USA, weighted | Observations (countries) | Standardized beta (%) | R-squared |
|---|---|---|---|---|
| **Medical technologies** | | | | |
| (12) Hospital beds | 1.481 | 5,565 | 1.31 | 0.17 |
| | (4.319) | (106) | | |
| (13) DPT immunization before age 1 | 0.137 | 5,778 | 3.54 | 0.01 |
| | (0.156) | (108) | | |
| (14) Measles immunization before age 1 | 0.141 | 5,778 | 3.71 | 0.01 |
| | (0.162) | (108) | | |
| **Communications technologies** | | | | |
| (15) Cable TV | 74.485 | 4,753 | 4.23 | 0.16 |
| | (56.305) | (98) | | |
| (16) Cell phones | 0.109 | 5,778 | 8.21 | 0.12 |
| | (0.044)** | (108) | | |
| (17) Personal computers | 0.247 | 4,950 | 12.53 | 0.21 |
| | (0.099)** | (100) | | |
| (18) Access to the Internet | 0.192 | 5,778 | 14.25 | 0.28 |
| | (0.072)*** | (108) | | |
| (19) Items mailed/received | 0.097 | 2,346 | 11.00 | 0.21 |
| | (0.074) | (69) | | |
| (20) Newspaper circulation | 0.245 | 5,886 | 10.43 | 0.25 |
| | (0.101)** | (109) | | |
| (21) Radios | 0.064 | 5,886 | 1.87 | 0.12 |
| | (0.139) | (109) | | |
| (22) Telegrams sent | 0.312 | 2,211 | 5.74 | 0.07 |
| | (0.260) | (67) | | |
| (23) Mainline telephone lines | 0.185 | 5,886 | 11.54 | 0.28 |
| | (0.067)*** | (109) | | |
| (24) Television sets in use | 0.492 | 5,886 | 18.78 | 0.31 |
| | (0.141)*** | (109) | | |

(*Continued*)

**Table 3.9** (*Continued*)

| | Fst gen. dist. relative to the USA, weighted | Observations (countries) | Standardized beta (%) | R-squared |
|---|---|---|---|---|
| **Industrial technologies and other** | | | | |
| (25) Output of electricity, KwHr | 34.477 (13.849)** | 5,565 (106) | 8.16 | 0.23 |
| (26) Automatic looms | 0.828 (0.304)*** | 3,570 (85) | 11.19 | 0.06 |
| (27) Total looms | 1.200 (0.361)*** | 3,570 (85) | 8.95 | 0.08 |
| (28) Crude steel production in electric arc furnaces | 0.091 (0.031)*** | 2,278 (68) | 8.10 | 0.08 |
| (29) Weight of artificial (cellulosic) fibers used in spindles | 0.425 (0.354) | 2,145 (66) | 3.89 | 0.10 |
| (30) Weight of synthetic (non cellulosic) fibers used in spindles | 2.045 (0.819)** | 2,145 (66) | 9.89 | 0.20 |
| (31) Weight of all types of fibers used in spindles | 7.832 (2.759)*** | 2,850 (76) | 12.10 | 0.07 |
| (32) Visitor beds available in hotels and elsewhere | 24.245 (7.518)*** | 5,565 (106) | 9.31 | 0.10 |
| (33) Visitor rooms available in hotels and elsewhere | 13.518 (3.884)*** | 5,778 (108) | 10.50 | 0.10 |

Two-way clustered standard errors in parentheses.

Unless specified in parentheses, the dependent variable is the absolute difference in per capita prevalence of the technology between country $i$ and country $j$.

All regressions include controls for absolute difference in latitudes, absolute difference in longitudes, geodesic distance, dummy = 1 for contiguity, dummy = 1 if either country is an island, dummy = 1 if either country is landlocked, dummy = 1 if pair shares at least one sea or ocean.

* Significant at 10%.

** Significant at 5%.

*** Significant at 1%.

and in 19 cases at the 5% level. (3) The effect of genetic distance is particularly strong for disaggregated agricultural technologies and industrial technologies, and weakest for transportation and medical technologies. (4) The magnitude of the standardized effects, for those that are statistically significant, varies from 8% to 24%, a bit smaller but roughly in line with what we found using aggregate measured of productivity or the CEG dataset.[25]

A consideration of technologies at a more disaggregated data, rather than measures of overall productivity at the economy-wide level, provides additional evidence that human barriers matter. Not only is genetic distance relative to the frontier a strong predictor of technological usage differences in 1500 and in the contemporary period, we also find that it generally trumps absolute genetic distance. The fact that genetic distance accounts for differences in technological usage indicates that our previous aggregate results might in large part be accounted for by hindrances to the adoption of frontier technologies brought about by historical separation between populations.

## 3.5. ANCESTRY AND LONG-RUN DEVELOPMENT

In this section, we broaden the discussion of the role of ancestry as a determinant of the comparative wealth of nations, building on the discussion in Spolaore and Wacziarg (2013).[26] Our basic argument is that traits passed on across generations within societies play a fundamental role in accounting for the persistence of economic fortunes. However, the specific way in which these traits operate can take a variety of forms. In the model presented above, we argued that differences in vertically transmitted traits introduced barriers to the diffusion of innovations across nations. We found much evidence that this was the case for aggregate productivity and for specific innovations going back to the year 1500. However, we have not said much about what causes the onset of these innovations. Other authors have pointed to a role for traits to bear a direct effect on the onset of major productivity enhancing innovations, broadly construed. We have also not said much about the nature and specific method of transmission of the traits that are thought to matter for prosperity. These traits could be transmitted culturally, biologically, or through the interaction of culture and biology.

We proceed in several steps. We start by briefly describing the growing literature on long-run persistence in the wealth of nations. We argue that the intergenerational transmission of traits has a lot to do with explaining long-run persistence, because traits

---

[25] We also conducted horseraces between absolute and relative genetic distance for each of the 33 disaggregated technologies. Relative genetic distance remains positive and significant in 17 of the 22 cases where relative genetic distance is significant at the 10% level when entered on its own. In the vast majority of cases, absolute genetic distance enters insignificantly or with a negative sign.

[26] The discussion of the relation between cultural traits and economic outcomes is also drawn in part from Spolaore (2014).

are much more easily transmitted across generations than across societies. That is, ancestry matters to explain the wealth of nations. Next, we introduce a taxonomy to understand the manner in which ancestry matters. In particular, we introduce a distinction between barrier effects and direct effects of vertical traits. We also distinguish between the mode of transmission of the traits, either cultural, biological, or dual. Finally, we provide several examples from the recent literature illustrating the various ways in which ancestry can matter.

### 3.5.1 Persistence and Reversals: The Role of Ancestry

Discussions of the long-run roots of comparative development usually start with geographic factors. A large literature has documented strong correlations between economic development and geographic factors, for instance latitude, climate, and the disease environment.[27] The observation that geographic factors are correlated with development was at the root of Diamond's (1997) book on the long-run development advantage enjoyed by Eurasia—particularly Europe. On the surface, geography is a convenient explanation for persistence, because geography does not change very much, so that this immutable factor can be thought of as a prime reason for persistence in the wealth of nations. This view, however, is overly simplistic, for at least two reasons: First, the effect of geography on economic outcome can change depending on the technology of production. Geographic features useful to produce GDP in an agrarian economy may not be as helpful in an industrial society. Second, the manner in which geographic factors affect development today is open to a variety of interpretations. The factors could operate directly (for instance, a high disease burden can reduce productivity) or have an indirect effect through their historical legacy. While both channels could be operative, the literature has increasingly moved in the latter direction.

In fact, Diamond (1997) pointed out early that geographic factors such as the shape of continents and the availability of domesticable plants and animals probably did not have much to do with current development directly. It is because these factors gave people from Eurasia an early advantage in development, and because this advantage has persisted through the generations, that Europeans were able to conquer the New World (and many parts of the old one) and to remain at the top of the world distribution of income for a long time. This point became more widely recognized since a pathbreaking paper by Acemoglu et al. (2002) where these authors pointed out that the reversal of fortune experienced by former colonies between 1500 and today was inconsistent with a simple, direct effect of geography: for the geographic factors that made countries poor 500 years ago should be expected to make them poor today still. And yet fortunes were reversed

[27] See, for instance: on climate and temperature, Myrdal (1968); Kamarck (1976); Masters and McMillan (2001); Sachs (2001). On the disease environment: Bloom and Sachs (1998); Sachs et al. (2001); Sachs and Malaney (2002). On natural resources: Sachs and Warner (2001).

among a significant portion of the world's countries. This paper pointed to an indirect effect of geography, operating through institutions: where Europeans settled, they brought good institutions, and these are the fundamental proximate cause of development. Where Europeans chose to exploit and extract, the institutions they bequeathed had negative effects on development.

Yet that interpretation, too, became the subject of debates. Glaeser et al. (2004), for instance, state: "the Europeans who settled in the New World may have brought with them not so much their institutions, but themselves, that is, their human capital. This theoretical ambiguity is consistent with the empirical evidence." We would go even further: Europeans who settled in the New World brought with them the whole panoply of vertically transmitted traits—institutions, human capital, norms, values, preferences. This vector of vertical traits was by definition easier to transmit to the descendents of Europeans than it was to convey to colonized populations. This interpretation suggests an important role for ancestry, rather than only institutions, as an explanation for the reversal of fortunes. Locations that were colonized by Europeans and were previously characterized by low population density and the prevalence of non-agrarian modes of subsistence became rich. Locations that were inhospitable to Europeans remained poor, and Europeans remained at the top of the world distribution of aggregate productivity throughout.[28] That the wealth of a nation seems so strongly affected by the wealth of the ancestors of those living in that nation suggests a central role for vertically transmitted traits as an explanation for both long-run persistence and the current distribution of income.

This interpretation led various authors to focus explicitly on persistence and ancestry. First came our own work on genetic distance as a barrier to development, already discussed in the previous sections (Spolaore and Wacziarg, 2009). Next came important papers by Putterman and Weil (2010) and Comin and Hobijn (2010). These papers also explore the deep historical roots of current development.

Putterman and Weil (2010) look at two important determinants of the current wealth of nations: experience with agriculture, measured by the time elapsed since the adoption of sedentary agriculture as a primary means of food production; and experience with a centralized state, measured by the number of years a country has experienced centralized governance, discounting years that occurred farther in the past. Both variables are predictors of today's per capita income, but they enter even more strongly when they are adjusted

---

[28] We greatly expand on this point in Spolaore and Wacziarg (2013). In that paper, we revisit the Acemoglu et al. (2002) evidence on the reversal of fortune. By examining the correlation between population density in 1500 and per capita income today, we confirm their findings for former colonies. Yet we also show that (1) any evidence of a reversal of fortune disappears when European countries are included in the sample; (2) there is evidence of persistence among countries that were not former European colonies; (3) persistence is even stronger when looking at countries that are populated mostly by their indigenous populations. These facts are suggestive of a strong role for ancestry as an explanation for persistence.

for ancestry. To adjust variables for ancestry, Putterman and Weil construct a migration matrix. In this matrix, a row pertains to a country, and columns contain the fraction of that country's population whose ancestors in 1500 lived in each of the world's countries. For the Old World, entries are mostly diagonal: that is, the ancestors of the French mostly lived in France in 1500. For the New World, however, the ancestors of current populations are often in significant numbers from other continents altogether—primarily European countries for European colonizers, and Sub-Saharan African countries for the descendants of former slaves. By premultiplying a variable by the migration matrix, one obtains this variable's ancestry-adjusted counterpart. For instance, for Australia, the history of the location is the history of the Aborigenes, while the history of the current population is mostly the history of the English. Putterman and Weil's major contribution is to show that ancestry-adjusted years of agriculture and ancestry-adjusted state centralization are much stronger predictors of current income than their non-ancestry adjusted counterparts. This suggests an important role, again, for traits that are passed on intergenerationally within populations.

Comin et al. (2010) take a different approach, but reach a similar conclusion: they show that the degree of technological sophistication of countries is highly autocorrelated even at very long horizons: they detect correlations between current technological usage levels (measured along the intensive margin in the current period) and technological usage as far back as the year 1000 BC (measured along the extensive margin for a set of 12 ancient technologies). Current per capita income is also correlated strongly with past technological sophistication in the years 1000 BC, 1 AD, and 1500 AD. In this case, a history of technological advancement predicts current income and technological advancement, an indication of persistence. The crucial point, however, is again that when the historical (lagged) variables are entered in their ancestry-adjusted forms, they are much stronger predictors of current outcomes than variables that capture the history of a location. In this context also, there appears to be a strong role for ancestry and intergenerational transmission as explanations for the persistence in technology and income levels.

Why does ancestry matter? In what follows, we present a taxonomy of the possible effects of vertically transmitted traits on growth and development. This taxonomy is summarized in the following matrix:

| Mode of operation $\longrightarrow$  Mode of transmission $\downarrow$ | Direct effect | Barrier effect |
| --- | --- | --- |
| Biological Transmission (genetic and/or epigenetic) | Quadrant I | Quadrant IV |
| Cultural Transmission (behavioral and/or symbolic) | Quadrant II | Quadrant V |
| Dual Transmission (biological-cultural interaction) | Quadrant III | Quadrant VI |

## 3.5.2 Modes of Transmission

The inheritance of traits from one generation to the next in humans takes place through several modes of transmission and along multiple dimensions. Recent scientific advances stress the complexity of different inheritance mechanisms (for example, see Jablonka and Lamb, 2005) which interact with each other as well as with environmental and societal factors. For simplicity, in our taxonomy we focus on three broad categories: biological transmission, cultural transmission, and the interaction of biological and cultural transmission (dual transmission).

Biological transmission includes genetic transmission. Individuals inherit nuclear DNA from their parents. Humans also inherit mitochondrial DNA (mtDNA) only from their mothers mitochondrial DNA codes for the genes of the cell structures which convert food into useable energy, while nuclear DNA codes for the rest of the human genome. The measures of genetic distance used previously in this chapter are based on differences in the distribution of nuclear DNA across populations—that is, on differences in DNA inherited from both parents. As already mentioned, genetic distance is based on neutral genes, which change randomly and are not affected by natural selection. Other parts of the DNA code for genes that are affected by natural selection, such as those affecting eye color or skin color. All these traits are transmitted biologically.

However, genetic transmission is not the only form of biological transmission. In recent years, biologists have also given much attention to epigenetic inheritance systems. Epigenetics refers to the mechanisms through which cells with the same genetic information (i.e. DNA) acquire different phenotypes (i.e. observable characteristics) and transmit them to their daughter cells. Examples of epigenetic markers are methylation patterns: DNA methylation is a biochemical process that stably alters the expression of genes in cells by adding a methyl group to a DNA nucleotide. There is currently a debate in the scientific literature about the extent to which epigenetic changes can be inherited from one generation to the next—for instance, see Chandler and Alleman (2008) and Morgan and Whitelaw (2008). An example of possible intergenerational epigenetic inheritance, mentioned by Morgan and Whitelaw (2008), is the Dutch Famine Birth Cohort Study by Lumey (1992), reporting that children born during famine in World War II were smaller than average and that the effects could last two generations (but see also Stein and Lumey, 2002). In principle, epigenetic mechanisms could explain rapid biological changes in populations that could not be due to genetic selection. Epigenetic mechanisms have recently been emphasized by microeconomists working on human capital formation, such as Cunha and Heckman (2007, p. 32), who wrote: "the nature versus nurture distinction is obsolete. The modern literature on epigenetic expression teaches us that the sharp distinction between acquired skills and ability featured in the early human capital literature is not tenable."

Of course, biological inheritance is not the only mode of intergenerational transmission of traits across human beings. Many traits are transmitted culturally from one generation to the next. An important example is the specific language that each child acquires through learning and imitation, usually (but not necessarily) from parents or other close relatives. Other cultural traits include values, habits, and norms. In general, culture is a broad concept, which encompasses a vast range of traits that are not transmitted biologically across generations. The Webster's Encyclopedic Unabridged Dictionary defines culture as including "the behaviors and beliefs characteristic of a particular social, ethnic or age group" and "the total ways of living built up by a group of human beings and transmitted from one generation to the other." Richerson and Boyd (2005, p. 5), two leading scholars in the field of cultural evolution, define culture as "information capable of affecting individuals' behavior that they acquire from other members of their species through teaching, imitation, and other forms of social transmission."

Following Jablonka and Lamb (2005), we can distinguish between two forms of cultural transmission, both involving social learning: behavioral transmission and symbolic transmission. Behavioral transmission takes place when individuals learn from each other by direct observation and imitation. Symbolic transmission instead is about learning by means of systems of symbols—for example, by reading books. Most scholars of human evolution believe that the bulk of observed human variation in intergenerationally transmitted traits is mainly due to cultural transmission rather than to biological transmission. For instance, prominent anthropologists Henrich and McElreath (2003, p. 123) write: "While a variety of local genetic adaptations exist within our species, it seems certain that the same basic genetic endowment produces arctic foraging, tropical horticulture, and desert pastoralism [...]. The behavioral adaptations that explain the immense success of our species are cultural in the sense that they are transmitted among individuals by social learning and have accumulated over generations. Understanding how and when such culturally evolved adaptations arise requires understanding of both the evolution of the psychological mechanisms that underlie human social learning and the evolutionary (population) dynamics of cultural systems."

In sum, our classification of modes of intergenerational transmission includes two broad categories: biological transmission (both genetic and epigenetic), and cultural transmission (behavioral and symbolic). However, these two forms of transmission should not be viewed as completely distinct and independent. On the contrary, a growing line of research stresses that human evolution often proceeds from the interaction between biological and cultural inheritance systems, where each system is influenced by the other system. According to Richerson and Boyd (2005, p. 194), genes and culture can be seen as "obligate mutualists, like two species that synergistically combine their specialized capacities to do things that neither can do alone. [...] Genes, by themselves can't readily adapt to rapidly changing environments. Cultural variants, by themselves, can't do anything without brains and bodies. Genes and culture are tightly coupled but subject to evolutionary forces that tug behavior in different directions." This approach to evolution is known as dual inheritance theory or gene–culture coevolution (Cavalli-Sforza and Feldman, 1981;

Cavalli-Sforza et al. 1994; Boyd and Richerson, 1985; Richerson and Boyd, 2005). In such a framework, observable human outcomes can be viewed as stemming from the interplay of genetically and culturally transmitted traits. A well-known example of gene-culture coevolution is the spread of the gene controlling lactose absorption in adults in response to cultural innovations, such as domestication and dairying (Simoons, 1969, 1970; Richerson and Boyd, 2005; Chapter 6). The ability to digest milk as an adult (i.e. to be "lactase persistent") is given by a gene that is unequally distributed among different populations: it is prevalent among populations of European descent, but very rare among East Asians and completely absent among Native Americans. It is well understood that such a gene did spread rapidly after the introduction of domestication among populations that kept milk-producing animals, such as cows or goats, reinforcing the advantages from those practices from an evolutionary perspective. In general, dual inheritance—the third "mode of transmission" in our taxonomy—captures such a complex interaction between genetic and cultural factors.

### 3.5.3 Modes of Operation

Traits can be transmitted from one generation to the next biologically, culturally, or through the interaction of genes and culture (dual transmission). But how do such traits affect economic outcomes? Our taxonomy distinguishes between direct effects and barrier effects.

**Direct Effects.** Most of the economic literature has focused on direct effects of vertically transmitted traits on income and productivity. Such effects occur when individuals inherit traits that directly impact economic performance, either positively or negatively. For example, most contributions on the relation between cultural values and economic development stress inherited norms and beliefs that directly lead to positive or negative economic outcomes. Weber (2005), the great German sociologist and political economist, in his classic book *The Protestant Ethic and the Spirit of Capitalism*, provided a systematic and influential study emphasizing the direct positive effects of specific culturally transmitted traits on economic performance. Weber was in part reacting to the Marxist view, which considered cultural beliefs and values, such as religion, as the by-product of underlying economic factors. Instead, Max Weber argued for direct causal effects of culturally transmitted traits on economic outcomes. Specifically, he proposed that the emergence of a new Protestant ethic, which linked "good works" to predestination and salvation, had a direct effect on the rising of the "spirit of capitalism", a new attitude toward the pursuit of economic prosperity. Among Weber's more recent followers is, for example, the economic historian Landes (1998, 2000), who titled one of his contributions *Culture Makes Almost All the Difference*, and opened it with the line "Max Weber was right." Landes' emphasis was also on the direct economic effects of culture, defined as "the inner values and attitudes that guide a population." According to Landes (p. 12): "This is not to say that Weber's 'ideal type' of capitalist could be found only among Calvinists [...]. People of all faiths and no faith can grow up to be rational, diligent, orderly, productive, clean, and humourless. [...] Weber's argument, as I see it, is that in 16th–18th-century northern Europe, religion encouraged the appearance in numbers of a personality type that had been exceptional and adventitious before and that this type created a new economy (a new mode of production) that we know as (industrial) capitalism."

An extensive empirical literature has attempted to directly test Weber's hypotheses, often concluding with a negative assessment of direct effects of Protestant values on economic outcomes. Recent contributors to this literature were Becker and Ludger (2009), who used county-level data from 19th century Prussia, and attempted to estimate the causal effect of Protestantism on economic performance by exploiting the fact that the Lutheran Reform expanded concentrically from Wittenberg, Martin Luther's city. They concluded that Protestantism fostered economic development, but that the main channel was not the spread of a new work ethic associated with religious values, but the expansion of literacy as a consequence of education in reading the Bible.

The direct effects of religious beliefs on economic outcomes were investigated empirically by Barro and McCleary (2003). Barro and McCleary used instrumental variables, such as the existence of a state religion and of a regulated market structure, to identify the direct effect of religion on growth. They concluded that economic growth is positively associated with the extent of religious beliefs, such as those in hell and heaven, but negatively associated to church attendance. They interpreted their results as consistent with a direct effect of religion—a culturally transmitted set of beliefs—on individual characteristics that foster economic performance. Guiso et al. (2003) also studied the effects of religious beliefs on economic attitudes and outcomes, such as cooperation, legal rules, thriftiness, the market economy, and female labor participation. They found that religious beliefs tend to be associated with attitudes conducive to higher income per capita and higher economic growth, and that the effects differ across religious denominations.

While scholars such as Weber have stressed the positive direct effects of cultural traits, such as the Protestant ethic, other scholars have argued that specific culturally transmitted traits and values can be responsible for economic backwardness and underdevelopment. An influential and widely debated example of this view was provided by the political scientist Banfield (1958) in his classic book *The Moral Basis of a Backward Society*, written in collaboration with his wife Laura Fasano, and based on their visit to the southern Italian town of Chiaromonte (called "Montegrano" in the book). Banfield argued that the economic backwardness of that society could be partly explained by the direct effects of inherited values summarized by the term "amoral familism", and consisting in a lack of mutual trust and cooperation, and a disregard for the interests of fellow citizens who were not part of one's immediate family. A theory of intergenerational transmission directly inspired by Banfield's analysis has been provided recently by Tabellini (2008), who also built "on analytical work" on Bisin and Verdier's (2000, 2001) seminal work on the economics of cultural transmission. In Tabellini's model, parents choose which values to transmit to their children, depending on the patterns of external enforcement and expected future transactions. In particular, Tabellini shows that path dependence is possible: adverse initial conditions can lead to a unique equilibrium where legal enforcement is weak and inherited cultural values discourage cooperation.

A recent example of an empirical study of the direct effects of inherited traits on economic growth is Algan and Cahuc (2010). Algan and Cahuc document how the level of inherited trust of descendants of immigrants in the United States is significantly influenced by the country of origin and the timing of arrival of their ancestors. They then use the inherited trust of descendants of immigrants in the US as a time-varying measure of inherited trust in their country of origin, in order to identify the impact of inherited trust on growth, controlling for country fixed effects. Algan and Cahuc find that changes in inherited trust during the 20th century have a large impact on economic development in a panel of 24 countries.

The above-mentioned contributions are examples of a much larger literature on the direct effects of cultural traits on economic outcomes. There is also a smaller but important literature that has extended the analysis to traits that are transmitted biologically, or stem from the interaction of genes and culture (dual inheritance). An example is the contribution by Galor and Moav (2002), who modeled an intergenerationally transmitted trait affecting humans' fertility strategies. They posited that some individuals inherited traits that induced them to follow a quantity-biased strategy, consisting in the generation of a higher number of children, while other individuals followed a quality-biased strategy, consisting in the investment of more resources in a smaller number of offspring. Galor and Moav argued that the evolutionary dynamics of these traits had direct implications for the onset of the Industrial Revolution and the following demographic transition. In the pre-industrial world, caught in a Malthusian trap, selective pressures favored parental investment, which led to higher productivity. In their model, the spread of this inherited predilection for a smaller number of children led endogenously to the transition out of the Malthusian regime. Galor and Moav in their contribution stressed biological transmission. However, their analysis can also be interpreted as a model of cultural transmission of traits influencing fertility strategies, or as the outcome of the interaction of biological and cultural traits.

A more recent contribution that stresses the direct effects of different distributions of inter-generationally transmitted traits on economic development is Ashraf and Galor (2013a). In that study, Ashraf and Galor focus on genetic diversity. While genetic distance refers to genetic differences between populations, genetic diversity is about heterogeneity within populations. In their study, Ashraf and Galor (2013a) document a non-monotonic relationship between genetic diversity and development, and argue that such relation is causal, stemming from a trade-off between the beneficial and the detrimental effects of diversity of traits on productivity. Again, while the focus of Ashraf and

Galor's empirical analysis is on genetic variables, the modes of transmission from intergenerational traits to economic outcomes can operate both through biological and cultural channels, and their interactions. A further discussion of the relation between genetic diversity and ethnic and cultural fragmentation is provided by Ashraf and Galor (2013b).

The interaction of culture and genes is explicitly at the center of the economic analysis of the effects of lactase persistence provided by Cook (2012). Cook argues that country-level variation in the frequency of lactase persistence is positively and significantly related to economic development in pre-modern times—which he measures by using population density in 1500 CE, as we did earlier in this chapter. Specifically, he finds that an increase in one standard deviation in the frequency of lactase persistent individuals (roughly 24% points) is associated with a 40% increase in pre-modern population density. Cook uses instrumental variables (solar radiation) to assess causality, and interprets his results as reflecting the direct effects of inherited cultural and biological traits associated with the introduction of dairying.

**Barrier effects.**    As we already mentioned, most of the contributions on the relation between ancestry and economic performance, including the examples mentioned above, tend to focus on the direct effects of intergenerationally transmitted traits on economic outcomes. However, as we emphasized in the theoretical and empirical analysis presented in the first sections of this chapter, differences in inherited traits can also affect comparative development by acting as barriers to the diffusion of goods, services, ideas, and innovations. A focus on barriers can explain why differences in inherited traits may matter, even though many new ideas and innovations are learned "horizontally," from individuals and populations that are not directly related, rather than "vertically," from one's close relatives and ancestors. The fact is, that when barrier effects do exist, vertically transmitted traits also affect horizontal learning and diffusion. People are more likely to learn new ideas and adopt new technologies from other people who, while not directly related to them, share more recent common ancestors and, consequently, also share, on average, a larger set of inherited traits and characteristics.

The literature on the barrier effects of vertically transmitted traits is not as large as the one on direct effects. In addition to our own contributions, already discussed, a recent example is Guiso et al. (2009), who studied the barrier effects of cultural traits by using data on bilateral trust between European countries. They found that bilateral trust is affected by cultural aspects of the match between trusting country and trusted country, such as their history of conflicts and their religious, genetic, and somatic similarities. Lower bilateral trust then acts as a cultural barrier: it is associated with less bilateral trade, less portfolio investment, and less direct investment between the two countries, even after controlling for other characteristics of the two countries. These findings suggest that culturally transmitted traits can have a significant barrier effect on economic interactions between different societies.

Another study that documents the effects of cultural barriers on trade is provided by Felbermayr and Toubal (2010). Felbermayr and Toubal measure cultural proximity or distance between countries using bilateral score data from the Eurovision Song Contest, a popular European television show. For instance, viewers in Cyprus award Greek singers more points on average than the Greeks receive from viewers in other countries, and vice versa. In contrast, Cypriot and Turkish viewers give each other below-average scores. Felbermayr and Toubal exploit the variation of these scores within-pair and across time to estimate the effects of cultural proximity on bilateral trade, finding significant effects.

An open question concerns the relationship between direct and barrier effects. Of course, in principle, both modes of operation can be at work simultaneously, and some specific traits can play a role along both channels. For example, populations that inherit values and beliefs that make them more open to risk and innovation could benefit directly from such traits, but may also face lower barriers to interactions with other groups. In general, the study of barrier effects stemming from historical and cultural divergence is a promising area of research, still in its infancy, both from a theoretical and empirical perspective. The taxonomy and discussion presented in this chapter are only a first step toward a more complete understanding of this important topic.

## 3.6. CONCLUSION

In this chapter we provided a theoretical framework and empirical evidence to shed light on a fundamental question: What barriers prevent the diffusion of the most productive technologies from the technological frontier to less developed economies?

In the first part of this chapter, we presented a simple analytical framework to illustrate two basic ideas. The first idea was that genetic distance between populations, which measures their degree of genealogical relatedness, can be interpreted as a summary metric for average differences in traits that are transmitted with variation from one generation to the next. We modeled the transmission of such "vertical" traits—that is, the transmission of characteristics which are passed on vertically across generations within a population over the very long run—and derived the relation between divergence in vertical traits and genetic distance. The second idea was that differences in vertically transmitted traits act as obstacles to horizontal learning and imitation across different populations. We argued that populations that share a more recent common history and are therefore closer in terms of vertical traits tend to face lower costs and barriers to adopting each other's technological innovations.

In the second part of this chapter we brought these ideas to the data. We introduced measures of genetic distance between populations, and used them to test our barrier model of diffusion. We found that, as the model predicts, genetic distance measured relative to the world's technological frontier trumps absolute genetic distance as an explanation for bilateral income differences and for the different usage of specific technological innovations. This was the case both historically, when we measured technological usage on the extensive margin, and for more recent technological developments, when we measured technological usage along the intensive margin. We also documented that, as implied by our model, the effect of genetic distance was more pronounced after a major innovation, such as the onset of the Industrial Revolution, and declined as more populations adopted the frontier's innovation. Overall, we found considerable evidence that barriers introduced by historical separation between populations have played a key role in the diffusion of technological innovations and economic growth.

In the third and final part of this chapter, we discussed our hypotheses and results within the broader context of the growing literature on the deep historical roots of economic development. To organize our discussion we presented a taxonomy based on Spolaore and Wacziarg (2013). The taxonomy provided a conceptual basis for discussing how intergenerationally transmitted traits could conceivably affect economic outcomes. Our taxonomy distinguished possible economic effects of vertical traits along two dimensions. The first dimension referred to the mode of transmission of vertical traits, which could be biological (genetic or epigenetic), cultural (behavioral or symbolic), or resulting from the interaction of genes and culture (dual inheritance). The second dimension defined the mode of operation of these traits, depending on whether they have direct effects on economic outcomes, or operate as barriers to economic interactions between populations. We briefly reviewed examples of economic contributions that focused on different effects—direct effects or barrier effects—of traits transmitted biologically, culturally, or through dual transmission. We argued that most of the literature so far has mainly focused on direct effects, while much less attention has been given to the study of barriers to development stemming from long-term cultural and historical divergence.

The topic of human barriers introduced by historical divergence and their effects on social, political, and economic outcomes is an exciting emerging field of study. Our own work continues to explore the effects of variation in human relatedness on a variety of political economy outcomes. For instance, Spolaore and Wacziarg (2012b) examine the effects of genealogical relatedness on the propensity for interstate militarized conflict, finding that a smaller genetic distance is associated with a significantly higher probability of a bilateral conflict between two countries. This effect, again, is interpreted as evidence of a barrier between societies characterized by distinct norms, values, preferences, and cultures. This time, however, the barrier impedes a costly rather than a beneficial interaction. In ongoing work, we explore the effects of relatedness on trade and financial flows across countries. Finally, we have recently begun an effort to better characterize what genetic relatedness captures, by investigating the relationship between various measures of cultural differences and genetic distance—the goal being to more clearly identify the source of the barriers introduced by a lack of genealogical relatedness. For instance, the barriers could take the form of a lack of trust, differences in preferences or norms, or transactions costs linked to an inability to communicate and coordinate. This chapter provides only an introduction and first step toward a more comprehensive and systematic analysis of such important, unexplored, and promising topics.

# APPENDIX 1.  TECHNOLOGIES USED IN THE VARIOUS DATASETS
## A. 24 Technologies in the CEG 1500 AD Dataset.

1. *Military*: Standing army, cavalry, firearms, muskets, field artillery, warfare capable ships, heavy naval guns, ships (+180 guns).
2. *Agriculture*: Hunting and gathering; pastoralism; hand cultivation; plow cultivation.
3. *Transportation*: Ships capable of crossing the Atlantic Ocean, ships capable of crossing the Pacific Ocean, ships capable of reaching the Indian Ocean, wheel, magnetic compass, horse powered vehicles.
4. *Communications*: Movable block printing; woodblock or block printing; books, paper.
5. *Industry*: Steel, iron.

## B. 9 Technologies in the CEG 2000 AD Dataset.

Electricity (in 1990), Internet (in 1996), PCs (in 2002), cell phones (in 2002), telephones (in 1970), cargo and passenger aviation (in 1990), trucks (in 1990), cars (in 1990), tractors (in 1970).

## C. 33 Technologies in the CHAT Dataset for 1990–1999.

1. *Agriculture*: Harvest machines, tractors used in agriculture, metric tons of fertilizer consumed, area of irrigated crops, share of cropland area planted with modern varieties (% cropland), metric tons of pesticides.
2. *Transportation*: Civil aviation passenger km, lengths of rail line, tons of freight carried on railways, passenger cars in use and commercial vehicles in use.
3. *Medical*: Hospital beds, DPT immunization before age 1, measles immunization before age 1.
4. *Communications*: Cable TV, cell phones, personal computers, access to the Internet, items mailed/received, newspaper circulation, radios, telegrams sent, mainline telephone lines, television sets in use.
5. *Industry and other*: Output of electricity, Kw Hr, automatic looms, total looms, crude steel production in electric arc furnaces, weight of artificial (cellulosic) fibers used in spindles, weight of synthetic (non cellulosic) fibers used in spindles, weight of all types of fibers used in spindles, visitor beds available in hotels and elsewhere, visitor rooms available in hotels and elsewhere.

## REFERENCES

Acemoglu, Daron, Johnson, Simon, Robinson, James A., 2002. Reversal of fortune: geography and institutions in the making of the modern world income distribution. Quarterly Journal of Economics 117 (4), 1231–1294.

Alesina, Alberto, Devleeschauwer, Arnaud, Easterly, William, Kurlat, Sergio, Wacziarg, Romain, 2003. Fractionalization. Journal of Economic Growth 8, 55–194.

Algan, Yann, Cahuc, Pierre, 2010. Inherited trust and growth. American Economic Review 100 (5), 2060–2092.

Ashraf, Quamrul, Galor, Oded, 2011. Dynamics and stagnation in the Malthusian Epoch. American Economic Review 101 (5), 2003–2041.

Ashraf, Quamrul, Galor, Oded, (2013a). The "Out-of-Africa" hypothesis, human genetic diversity, and comparative economic development. American Economic Review 103(1), 1–46.

Ashraf, Quamrul, Galor, Oded, (2013b). Genetic diversity and the origins of cultural fragmentation, American Economic Review 103(3) 528–533.

Banfield, Edward C., 1958. The Moral Basis of a Backward Society. The Free Press, New York, NY.

Barro, Robert J., McCleary, Rachel, 2003. Religion and economic growth. American Sociological Review 68 (5), 760–781.

Barro, Robert J., Sala-i-Martin, Xavier, 1997. Technological diffusion, convergence and growth. Journal of Economic Growth 2 (1), 1–26.

Barro, Robert J., Sala-i-Martin, Xavier, 2003. Economic Growth, second ed. MIT Press, Cambridge, MA.

Becker, Sascha O., Woessmann, Ludger, 2009. Was Weber wrong? A human capital theory of protestant economic history. Quarterly Journal of Economics 124 (2), 531–596.

Bisin, Alberto, Verdier, Thierry, 2000. Beyond the melting pot: cultural transmission, marriage, and the evolution of ethnic and religious traits. Quarterly Journal of Economics 115, 955–988.

Bisin, Alberto, Verdier, Thierry, 2001. The economics of cultural transmission and the dynamics of preferences. Journal of Economic Theory 97, 298–319.

Bloom, David E., Sachs, Jeffrey D., 1998. Geography, demography, and economic growth in Africa. Brookings Papers on Economic Activity 2, 207–273.

Bossert, Walter, D'Ambrosio, Conchita, La Ferrara, Eliana, 2011. A generalized index of fractionalization. Economica 78 (312), 723–750.

Boyd, Robert, Richerson, Peter J., 1985. Culture and the Evolutionary Process. University of Chicago Press, Chicago.

Cameron, A. Colin, Gelbach, Jonah B., Miller, Douglas L., 2006. Robust Inference with Multi-Way Clustering. NBER Technical Working Paper #T0327.

Caselli, Francesco, 2005. Accounting for cross-country income differences. In: Aghion, Philippe, Durlauf, Steven N. (Eds.), Handbook of Economic Growth, vol. 1A. North-Holland, New York, pp. 679–741.

Cavalli-Sforza, Luigi Luca, Feldman, Marcus W., 1981. Cultural Transmission and Evolution: a Quantitative Approach. Princeton University Press, Princeton.

Cavalli-Sforza, Luigi L., Menozzi, Paolo, Piazza, Alberto, 1994. The History and Geography of Human Genes. Princeton University Press, Princeton.

Chanda, Areendam, Justin Cook, C., Putterman, Louis, 2013. Persistence of Fortune: Accounting for Population Movements, There was No Post-Columbian Reversal, Working Paper. Brown University, February.

Chandler, V., Alleman, M., 2008. Paramutation: epigenetic instructions passed across generations. Genetics 178 (4), 1839–1844.

Comin, Diego, Hobijn, Bart, 2009. The CHAT Dataset. Harvard Business School Working Paper # 10-035.

Comin, Diego, Hobijn, Bart, 2010. An exploration of technology diffusion. American Economic Review 100 (5), 2031–2059 (December).

Comin, Diego, Hobijn, Bart, Rovito, Emilie, 2008. World technology usage lags. Journal of Economic Growth 13 (4).

Comin, Diego, Easterly, William, Gong, Erick, 2010. Was the wealth of nations determined in 1000 B.C.? American Economic Journal: Macroeconomics 2 (3), 65–97.

Cook, C. Justin, 2012. The Role of Lactase Persistence in Precolonial Development. Working Paper, Yale University, August.

Cunha, Flavio, Heckman, James, 2007. The technology of skill formation. American Economic Review 97 (2), 31–47.

Desmet, Klaus, Le Breton, Michel, Ortuño-Ortín, Ignacio, Weber, Shlomo, 2011. The stability and breakup of nations: a quantitative analysis. Journal of Economic Growth 16, 183–213.

Diamond, Jared, 1997. Guns, Germs and Steel: The Fate of Human Societies. Norton & Co., New York.

Fagerberg, Jan, 2004. Innovation: a guide to the literature. In: Fagerberg J., Mowery, D.C., Nelson, R.R. (Eds.), Oxford Handbook of Innovation, Oxford University Press, Oxford (Chapter 1).

Felbermayr, Gabriel J., Toubal, Farid, 2010. Cultural proximity and trade. European Economic Review 54 (2), 279–293.

Galor, Oded, Moav, Omer, 2002. Natural selection and the origin of economic growth. Quarterly Journal of Economics 117 (4), 1133–1191.

Glaeser, Edward L., La Porta, Rafael, Lopez-de-Silanes, Florencio, Shleifer, Andrei, 2004. Do institutions cause growth? Journal of Economic Growth 9 (3), 271–303.

Greenberg, Joseph E., 1956. The measurement of linguistic diversity. Language 32 (1), 109–115.

Guiso, Luigi, Sapienza, Paola, Zingales, Luigi, 2003. People's opium? Religion and economic attitudes. Journal of Monetary Economics 50 (1), 225–282.

Guiso, Luigi, Sapienza, Paola, Zingales, Luigi, 2009. Cultural biases in economic exchange. Quarterly Journal of Economics 124 (3), 1095–1131.

Hall, Robert E., Jones, Charles I., 1999. Why do some countries produce so much more output per worker than others? Quarterly Journal of Economics 114 (11), 83–116.

Henrich, Joseph, McElreath, Richard, 2003. The Evolution of Cultural Evolution. Evolutionary Anthropology 12, 123–135

Hsieh, Chang-Tai, Klenow, Peter J., 2010. Development accounting. American Economic Journal: Macroeconomics 2 (1), 207–223.

Jablonka, Eva, Lamb, Marion J., 2005. Evolution in Four Dimensions: Genetic, Epigenetic, Behavioral, and Symbolic Variation in the History of Life. MIT Press, Cambridge, MA.

Kamarck, Andrew M., 1976. The Tropics and Economic Development. Johns Hopkins University Press, Baltimore and London.

Kimura, Motoo, 1968. Evolutionary rate at the molecular level. Nature 217, 624–626.

Landes, David, 1998. The Wealth and Poverty of Nations. Norton, New York.

Landes, David, 2000. Culture makes almost all the difference. In: Harrison, Lawrence E., Huntington, Samuel P. (Eds.), Culture Matters: How Values Shape Human Progress. Basic Books, New York, NY, USA, pp. 2–13.

Lumey, Lambert H., 1992. Decreased birthweights in infants after maternal in utero exposure to the Dutch famine of 1944–1945. Paediatric and Perinatal Epidemiology 6, 240–253.

Maddison, Angus, 2003. The World Economy: Historical Statistics. OECD Development Center, Paris, France.

Masters, William A., McMillan, Margaret S., 2001. Climate and scale in economic growth. Journal of Economic Growth 6(3), 167–186.

McEvedy, Colin, Jones, Richard. 1978. Atlas of World Population History. Penguin Books, Middlesex.

Morgan, Daniel K., Whitelaw, Emma, 2008. The case for transgenerational epigenetic inheritance in humans. Mammalian Genome 19, 394–397.

Olsson, Ola, Hibbs Jr., Douglas A., (2005). Biogeography and long-run economic development, European Economic Review 49(4), 909–938.

Parente, Stephen L., Prescott, Edward C., 1994. Barriers to technology adoption and development. Journal of Political Economy 102 (2), 298–321.

Parente, Stephen L., Prescott, Edward C., 2002. Barriers to Riches. MIT Press, Cambridge.

Putterman, Louis, Weil, David N., 2010. Post-1500 population flows and the long-run determinants of economic growth and inequality. Quarterly Journal of Economics 125 (4), 1627–1682.

Richerson, Peter J., Boyd, Robert, 2005. Not by Genes Alone: How Culture Transformed Human Evolution. University of Chicago Press, Chicago.

Rogers, Everett M., 1962. The diffusion of innovations, first ed. Free Press, New York (fifth edition: 2003).

Simoons, Frederick J., 1969. Primary adult lactose intolerance and the milking habit: a problem in biological and cultural interrelations: I. Review of the medical research. The American Journal of Digestive Diseases 14, 819–836.

Simoons, Frederick J., 1970. Primary adult lactose intolerance and the milking habit: a problem in biological and cultural interrelations: II. A culture historical hypothesis. The American Journal of Digestive Diseases 15, 695–710.

Spolaore, Enrico, 2014. Introduction. In: Spolaore, Enrico (Ed.), Culture and Economic Growth, International Library of Critical Writings in Economics Series. Edward Elgar, Cheltenham.

Spolaore, Enrico, Wacziarg, Romain, 2009. The diffusion of development. Quarterly Journal of Economics 124 (2), 469–529.

Spolaore, Enrico, Wacziarg, Romain, 2012a. Long-term barriers to the international diffusion of innovations. In: Frankel, Jeffrey, Pissarides, Christopher (Eds.), NBER International Seminar on Macroeconomics 2011. University of Chicago Press, Chicago, pp. 11–46 (Chapter 1).

Spolaore, Enrico, Wacziarg, Romain, 2012b. War and Relatedness, Working Paper. Tufts University and UCLA, June 2012.

Spolaore, Enrico, Wacziarg, Romain, 2013. How deep are the roots of economic development? Journal of Economic Literature 51 (2).

Stein, Aryeh D., Lumey, Lambert H., 2002. The relationship between maternal and offspring birth weights after maternal prenatal famine exposure: the Dutch famine birth cohort Study. Human Biology 72, 641–654.

Tabellini, Guido, 2008. The scope of cooperation: values and incentives. Quarterly Journal of Economics 123 (3), 905–950.

Weber, Max, [1905,1930] 2005. The Protestant Ethic and the Spirit of Capitalism (Talcott Parsons, Trans.). Routledge, London and New York (translated from German).

CHAPTER FOUR

# Family Ties

## Alberto Alesina[*,†] and Paola Giuliano[‡]

[*]Harvard University, USA
[†]IGIER Bocconi, Italy
[‡]UCLA Anderson School of Management, NBER and CEPR, USA

## Abstract

We study the role of the most primitive institution in society: the family. Its organization and relationship between generations shape values formation, economic outcomes, and influences national institutions. We use a measure of family ties, constructed from the World Values Survey, to review and extend the literature on the effect of family ties on economic behavior and economic attitudes. We show that strong family ties are negatively correlated with generalized trust; they imply more household production and less participation in the labor market of women, young adult, and elderly. They are correlated with lower interest and participation in political activities and prefer labor market regulation and welfare systems based upon the family rather than the market or the government. Strong family ties may interfere with activities leading to faster growth, but they may provide relief from stress, support to family members, and increased well-being. We argue that the values regarding the strength of family relationships are very persistent over time, more so than institutions like labor market regulation or welfare systems.

## Keywords

Family values, Cultural economics, Labor market regulations, Growth, Institutions

## JEL Classification Codes

J2, J6, O4, O5, Z1

## 4.1. INTRODUCTION

Economists, sociologists, and political scientists have long been interested in studying the effect of different family structures on a variety of economic outcomes. There is hardly an aspect of a society's life that is not affected by the family.

The aim of this chapter is to review the role that family ties may play in determining fundamental economic attitudes. The importance of the family as a fundamental organizational structure for human society is of course unquestionable. Historical examples of attempts at eliminating the family as an institution have been a catastrophic failure, think of the cultural revolution in China or Cambodian communism. In this chapter we investigate the effects of different types of family values. In particular, we plan to investigate empirically an idea first developed by political scientists and researchers in the late 1960s

*Handbook of Economic Growth*, Volume 2A
ISSN 1574-0684, http://dx.doi.org/10.1016/B978-0-444-53538-2.00004-6

and early 1970s, on the importance of family ties in explaining social capital, political participation, and economic outcomes. The family organization can take different forms, with very tight links between members or a more liberal/individualistic structure even within a well-structured and organized family. The idea that a culture based on too-strong family ties may impede economic development is not new. It goes back at least to Weber (1904), who argues that strong family values do not allow the development of individual forms of entrepreneurship, which are fundamental to the formation of capitalistic societies. Another author who clearly described the relationship between family values and under-development is Banfield (1958). In studying differences between the southern and northern part of Italy, this author suggested that "amoral familism" was at the core of the lower level of development of the south. He depicts "amoral familism" as a particular cultural trait: the "inability of the villagers to act together for their common good, or, indeed, for any end transcending the immediate, material interest of the nuclear family. This inability to concert activity beyond the immediate family arises from an ethos—that of "amoral familism" [. . .] according to which people maximize the material, short-run advantage of the nuclear family; and assume that all others will do likewise." This is of course an extreme, and in a sense degenerate, form of family relationship.

This extreme reliance on the family prevents the development of institutions and public organizations, which, on the contrary, require generalized trust and loyalty to the organization. When people are raised to trust their close family members, they are also taught to distrust people outside the family, which impedes the development of formal institutions.

Strong family ties are not unique to the Italian case, but are also present in many Asian and Latin American countries. Fukuyama (1995) for example argues that "though it may seem a stretch to compare Italy with the Confucian culture of Hong-Kong and Taiwan, the nature of social capital is similar in certain respects. In parts of Italy and in the Chinese cases, family bonds tend to be stronger than other kinds of social bonds not based on kinship, while the strength and number of intermediate associations between state and individual has been relatively low, reflecting a pervasive distrust of people outside the family." In a similar vein, Putnam et al. (1993) refer to many cases in Asia and Latin America where the safety and welfare of the individuals are provided by the family, legal authority is weak and the law resented.

When family ties are so strong, the implications for the economy are pervasive. In this chapter we review the literature on the topic, provide new evidence, and explore macroeconomic implications of the effect of family values. We start with within-country analysis. This will allow us to include country fixed effects to isolate the impact of family values from other confounding effects including national institutions. We analyze the relationship between family values and four different types of societal attitudes that have been shown to be conducive to higher productivity and growth. In particular, we look at political participation and political action; measures of generalized morality; attitudes toward women and society; labor market behavior; and attitudes toward work. We perform our analysis using the combined six waves of the World Value Survey (WVS), a collection of surveys administered to a representative sample of people in more than 80 countries from 1981 to 2010. We find that, on average, familistic values are associated with lower political participation and political action. They are also related to a lower level of trust, more emphasis on job security, less desire for innovation, and more traditional attitudes toward working women. On the positive side, family relationships improve well-being as measured by self-reported indicators of happiness and subjective health.

As a second step, we present cross-country evidence linking stronger family ties to economic and institutional outcomes. One obvious limitation of this evidence is that family values may be an outcome rather than a driver of economic development. While we do not offer any definite answer to the question of causality, we do show that family values are quite stable over time and could be among the drivers of institutional differences and level of development across countries: family values inherited by children of immigrants whose forebears arrived in various European countries before 1940 are related to a lower quality of institutions and lower level of development today. We also show that the relationship between economic and institutional outcomes is fairly robust even after controlling for legal origin, which has been shown to be an important historical determinant of formal institutions across countries.

The chapter is organized as follows. In Section 4.2, we review the literature on family ties. In Section 4.3 we provide a logical framework for the empirical analysis, linking our paper to the theoretical models analyzing the impact of culture on economic outcomes. In Sections 4.4 and 4.5, we describe how family ties and family structures can be measured, and review the deep historical determinants of family ties. Section 4.6 presents results from the within-country analysis. Section 4.7 presents cross-country evidence linking stronger family ties to economic development and institutions and shows the persistence of family values and their effect on institutions and development today. Section 4.8 analyzes the impact of family ties on different measures of well-being and Section 4.9 concludes.

## 4.2. LITERATURE REVIEW

There is surprisingly little systematic empirical evidence in economics on the role played by different types of family values in determining either economic outcomes or attitudes which, in turn, have an influence over economic development. Most of the research in economics indeed focused its attention on institutions, such as political systems (Acemoglu et al. 2001, 2005), the legal rights of the individual (North, 1990), religion (Guiso et al. 2006), education (Glaeser et al. 2004), social capital (Putnam, 2000; Putnam et al. 1993), ethnic fractionalization (Easterly and Levine (1997), and Alesina and La Ferrara (2005) for a survey) to explain a society's ability to generate innovation, wealth, and growth. Yet, little attention has been devoted to the most primitive societal institution, the family, and how this could be relevant in explaining a variety of socioeconomic outcomes.

The work on the relevance of the family starts with Banfield (1958) and Coleman (1990). Both authors notice that societies based on strong ties among family members, tend to promote codes of good conduct within small circles of related persons (family or kin); in these societies selfish behavior is considered acceptable outside the small network. On the contrary, societies based on weak ties, promote good conduct outside the small family/kin network, giving the possibility to identify oneself with a society of abstract individuals or abstract institutions. This initial intuition has been confirmed recently in an experimental setting by Ermish and Gambetta (2010). The authors used a trust game, played by a representative sample of the British population, and found that people with strong family ties have a lower level of trust in strangers than people with weak family ties.

After the seminal contribution of Banfield (1958) and Coleman (1990), some academics have noted strong patterns of family structures and linked them to significant social and economic outcomes. This includes work by Todd (1985, 1990), Greif (2006b), and Greif and Tabellini (2012). Using data on family structures dating back to the Middle Ages, if not earlier, Todd focuses on the distinction between nuclear and extended family. These two family structures differ in the degree of cooperation between subsequent generations, and in the authority exercised by parents. At one extreme, nuclear families are those in which children are emancipated from their parents and leave the household at the time of marriage or before. At the opposite extreme, the extended family typically consists of three generations living together and mutually cooperating under patriarchal authority.

Todd measures the diffusion of both family types across Western Europe and uses this distinction to explain relative levels of diffusion or resistance to important societal changes such as Protestantism, secularism, or political ideology. His general idea is that the nuclear family's tradition of emancipation increases potential for movement away from the family home which can facilitate the pursuit of independent economic opportunities. Also, the inability to rely on the family for income and housing can generate a more entrepreneurial spirit of self-reliance as well as greater motivation to work. Todd's (1990) definition of family structures has been used more recently (Duranton et al. 2009) to explain contemporary outcomes of European regions. The authors identified important links between family types and regional disparities in household size, educational attainment, social capital, labor force participation, sectoral structure, wealth, and inequality.

Greif (2006a) focuses his attention on the distinction between nuclear families and large kinship groups. Like Todd, he emphasizes the sense of independence typical of nuclear family structures. In particular, he describes how the latter in medieval times facilitated the establishment and growth of corporations: "an individual stands to gain less from belonging to a large kinship group, while the nuclear family structure increases its gains from membership in such a corporation (Greif, 2006a: 1–2)." Greif illustrates a feedback effect where causation works in both directions—on the one hand, nuclear families facilitate the establishment of corporations; on the other, the economic and social transformation related to the development of corporations, encourage the domination of the nuclear family across Europe. Nuclear families encourage both flexibility and independence; corporations substitute for kinship groups and provide a safety net, therefore complementing the nuclear family. Greif and Tabellini (2012) distinguish two different modes of sustaining cooperation in China and Europe. In China, the clan (a common descent group consisting of families tracing their patrilineal descent back to one common ancestor who settled in a given locality) was the fundamental institution, which had prevailed for more than 800 years, beginning with the Song Dynasty. Clan-based organizations provided public goods and social safety nets. In Europe, where the nuclear family was more prevalent, the locus of cooperation became the city, whose members were drawn from many kinship groups. The authors show that in a clan, moral obligations are stronger but are limited in scope, as they apply only toward the kin. In a city, moral obligations are generalized toward all citizens irrespective of lineage, but they are weaker.[1] They refer to this distinction as limited versus generalized morality, which is strongly correlated in our paper to the strength of family ties today. The authors show that the prevalence of one or the other organizational form depends on the distribution of values in society. Like Greif (2006a), they recognize the existence of a feedback effect: subsequent social, legal, and institutional developments evolved in different directions in these two parts of the world, strengthening the clan in China and leading to the emergence of strong and self-governed cities in Europe. The authors interestingly exploit differences in the early family structures across different parts of Europe, taking family structures as indicators of the scope and strength of kin-based relations. As expected, historical patterns of urbanization within Europe reflect these different family traditions, with early urbanization being much more diffused in the European regions, where families with weaker ties were more prevalent.

Alesina and Giuliano (2010) analyze systematically the role of the family as primal institution in a society, showing that the strength of family ties represents a fundamental trait shaping economic behavior and attitudes. The authors do not distinguish between nuclear and extended families, like Greif (2006a) and Todd (1985, 1990), but construct a subjective variable on the strength of family ties using three different questions from the World Value Survey. These questions are meant to measure the importance of the family, the love and respect that children are expected to have for their parents, and the parental duties toward their children.[2] Alesina and Giuliano (2010) show that strong family ties are positively

---

[1]  See Tabellini (2008) for a model of limited versus generalized morality which sustains different types of cooperation.

[2]  In Section 4.4, we show that there is indeed a strong correlation across countries between nuclear and extended family and family ties as measured by subjective measures taken from the World Values Survey. Alesina et al. (2013) also show that subjective measures of strong family ties are correlated with Todd's definition of extended families at the regional level, at least in the case of Europe.

correlated with home production (a result consistent with the in-depth case study of Italy by Alesina and Ichino (2009)), lower labor force participation of women and young adults, and negatively with geographical mobility. In a companion paper (Alesina and Giuliano, 2011), the authors also establish an inverse relationship between family ties, generalized trust, and political participation. Strength and weakness of family ties, defined as "cultural patterns of family loyalties, allegiances and authorities," also help explaining living arrangements and geographical mobility of young generations (Reher, 1998; Giuliano, 2007), larger fractions of family firms across countries (Bertrand and Schoar, 2006), and cross-country heterogeneity in employment rates (Algan and Cahuc, 2007).

While all the above-mentioned papers take the strength of family values as given and persistent, Alesina et al. (2013) go one step further and explore the presence of a feedback effect between family ties and labor market institutions. The main idea is that in cultures with strong family ties, individuals are less mobile and prefer more regulated labor markets, while weak family ties are associated with more flexible ones, which then require higher geographic mobility of workers to be efficient. In this setup, individuals inherit strong or weak family ties with a certain probability. Strong family ties provide a certain utility to each individual, which is larger, the larger is the share of individuals with strong family ties in a society. Given their utility function, individuals vote with majority rule on labor market regulation. There are two types of labor market policies: labor market flexibility (i.e. laissez-faire) or regulation of wages and employment. Individuals with weak family ties have a higher utility under flexibility, so this regime is voted for if the society starts from a situation in which the majority of the population has weak family ties. On the other hand, the utility of individuals with strong family ties is always higher under regulation. Finally, firms offer labor contracts. A worker with weak family ties always finds a job where he/she is paid for his/her productivity since he/she has no mobility costs. A worker with strong family ties has a moving cost related to the disutility to live far away from his/her family. Labor market regulations are precisely put in place to protect those workers from the monopsony power of firms. The model generates two stable Nash equilibria. One, where everybody chooses weak family ties and then votes for labor market flexibility. In this case, labor market is competitive, everyone is paid his/her marginal productivity and labor mobility is high. The other, where everyone chooses strong family ties and then votes for stringent labor market regulations (firms have a monopsonistic power because workers have a cost of moving away from their original family). If the majority of the population has strong family ties, it is rational to prefer regulated labor markets. This result explains why these types of regulation are hard to change even though prima facie they appear as suboptimal since they generate lower equilibrium employment and wages.

Although the theoretical model points to the possibility of a feedback effect between labor markets regulation and family ties, the empirical part of the paper presents suggestive evidence that the correlation is more likely to run from cultural values to institutions.

The authors present two sets of evidence to make this point. First, they show a strong correlation between family structures today and family structures in the Middle Ages. As a second step, the authors show that family values inherited by immigrants arrived to the US prior to 1940 are correlated to labor market institutions created after WWII.

Family relationships explain the preferences for other aspects of welfare systems. Focusing on Europe, Esping-Andersen (1999) argues that citizens obtain welfare from three basic sources: markets, family, and government. Where family ties are stronger, social risks are more internalized in the family by pooling resources across generations. His idea is that differences in family relations were at the core of the different evolutions of welfare systems, observed after WWII. In particular, he distinguishes three different types of welfare states: the liberal welfare state (typical of countries like the US), this is a regime that favors small public intervention under the assumption that the majority of citizens can obtain adequate welfare from the market. The second example is the social–democratic regime, characterized by its emphasis on universal inclusion and its comprehensive definition of social entitlements. This model, typical of the Nordic European countries, is internationally unique in its emphasis on de-familizing welfare responsibilities, especially with regard to care for children and the elderly. The third, and somewhat more heterogeneous, regime embraces a large part of Continental European countries: Austria, Belgium, France, Germany, Italy, and Spain. This regime is strongly familistic, assuming that primary welfare responsibilities lie with family members.

Coleman (1988, 1990), also stresses the mutual insurance mechanisms provided by old and young generations in familistic societies. He argues that family ties can strengthen the support received by young generations from the old, while at the same time representing an obstacle for innovation and new ideas. Finally, Galasso and Profeta (2012) show that the strength of family ties is related to the type of pension system chosen by a country. Societies dominated by absolute nuclear families (or weak family ties, such as for example the Anglo-Saxon countries) facilitate the emergence of a pension system which acts as a flat safety net entailing the largest within-cohort redistribution than societies dominated by any other type of family.

## 4.3. CONCEPTUAL FRAMEWORK

Many authors have stressed the relevance of the historical origins of (under) development (North, 1981; Acemoglu et al. 2001) but a still unanswered question is how differences in historical experiences are perpetuated until today. A recent strand of literature focuses on the importance of individual values to explain this persistence. One reason for why individual values can be relevant is the observation that very often, inside the same country, similar institutions work in a very different way. Putnam et al. (1993) used the example of Italy. They pointed out that for distant historical reasons, local governments, courts, schools, and even the private sector are much less efficient in the south than in the north of Italy despite the presence of national institutions. Guiso et al. (2008) recently pushed forward Putnam et al.'s analysis confirming his basic intuition. The authors show that inhabitants of Italian cities that had the status of free city-states at the beginning of the first millennium, where citizens were deeply involved in political life, today also have a higher level of social and civic capital, as measured by participation in elections and a variety of associations, and a higher level of blood donation.

There are different values that can be relevant to explain the sources of underdevelopment in a country. In this chapter we explore the idea that trust restricted only to family members prevents the formation of generalized trust, which is at the core of many collective good outcomes, from political participation to the formation of institutions to economic outcomes (Banfield 1958; Gambetta, 1988; Putnam, et al. 1993; Fukuyama, 1995; Coleman, 1988, 1990). Also the organization of the family as a strong "production unit" implies certain views about living arrangements and the role of women in market activities versus home production (Alesina and Ichino, 2009).

This chapter is part of a rapidly growing literature which emphasizes the relevance of specific cultural traits for economic and political outcomes. Akerlof and Kranton (2011), Alesina et al. (2013b), Guiso et al. (2006), Fernandez and Fogli (2009), Gorodnichenko and Roland (2013), Spolaore and Wacziarg (2009), and Tabellini (2008, 2010) all provide extensive references and illustrate different applications of this new line of research.

The basic idea underlying the empirical analysis of this chapter is that these normative values evolve slowly over time, as they are largely shaped by values and beliefs inherited from previous generations. In particular, a culture of familism, defined as individual values that stress the link between parents and children and loyalty to the family, is an important channel through which distant history can explain the functioning of current institutions and economic development. We explore this idea in two steps, we first use within-country analysis to study the effect of family values on other types of economic attitudes, which are relevant for growth. Although the issue of reverse causality is an important one, we use established evidence that family values today are related to ancient family structures (see Alesina et al. 2013; Duranton et al. 2009; Galasso and Profeta, 2012; Todd, 1990). As a second step, we discuss aggregate evidence looking at differences in institutions and economic outcomes between weak and strong family-ties societies. The correlations shown are strong and consistent with the microeconomic data. Altogether they suggest that well-functioning institutions and development are often observed in countries or regions where individuals have weak family ties.

Before looking at the empirical evidence, we review a logical framework according to which cultural traits in general and family values in particular are relevant. The economics literature has used the word "culture" with different meanings. According to one definition culture refers to the social conventions and individual beliefs that sustain Nash equilibria as focal points in repeated social interactions (Greif, 1994). In more recent contributions, individuals' beliefs are initially acquired through cultural transmission and then slowly updated through experience from one generation to the next. This line of argument has been pursued by Guiso et al. (2010) who build an overlapping generation model in which children absorb their trust priors from their parents and then, after experiencing the real world, transmit their (updated) beliefs to their own children. An alternative interpretation is that culture refers to more primitive objects, such as individual values and preferences (Akerlof and Kranton, 2000). This latter interpretation is consistent with an emerging literature in psychology, sociology, and evolutionary biology that emphasizes the role of moral emotions in motivating human behavior and regulating social interactions.

Following broadly this last approach, we view cultural beliefs as decision-making heuristics or "rules-of-thumb" that are employed in uncertain or complex environments. Boyd and Richerson (1985) show that if information acquisition is either costly or imperfect, it can be optimal for individuals to develop heuristics or rules-of-thumb in decision-making. By relying on general beliefs about the right thing to do in different situations, individuals may not behave in a manner that is precisely optimal in every instance, but they save on the costs of obtaining the information necessary to always behave optimally. In practice, these heuristics often take the form of deeply held traditional values or religious beliefs (Gigerenzer, 2007; Kanhneman, 2011).

The concept of culture as moral principles, rules-of-thumb or normative values that motivate individuals is particularly appealing. Whereas social conventions sometimes change suddenly because of strategic complementarities, and beliefs are updated as one learns from experience or from others, individual values or rules of thumbs are likely to be more persistent and to change slowly from one generation to the next. The reason is not only that normative values are acquired early in life and become part of one's personality but also that learning from experience cannot logically be exploited to easily modify them. Thus, values are likely to be transmitted vertically from one generation to the next, to a large degree within the family, rather than horizontally across unrelated individuals, and persist over time.

There are a number of reasons why we may observe persistence. First, the underlying cultural traits may be reinforced by policies, laws, and institutions, which reinforce the beliefs. A society with familistic values may perpetuate these beliefs by institutionalizing different forms of welfare state, different maternal leave policies, different pension systems. Another source of persistence can arise from a complementarity between cultural beliefs and industrial structure. Beliefs regarding the importance of the family may cause a society to specialize in family-based industries, which reinforce the attachment to the family, therefore perpetuating this trait. A third explanation that does not rely on these forms of complementarity is that cultural beliefs, by definition, are inherently sticky. The benefit of decision-making rules-of-thumb is that they can be applied widely in a number of environments, saving on the need to acquire and process information with each decision.

Empirically, several studies have investigated the persistence of cultural traits by looking at subnational analysis, therefore holding constant industrial structure, domestic policies, and institutions. More directly, looking at children of immigrants, the literature has held constant the external environment. We follow this tradition. In particular, we use within-country analysis to hold constant the presence of institutions and policies. The concern of reverse causality is limited by the fact that several papers have shown that values toward the family today are related to historical family structures (see Alesina et al. 2013; Galasso and Profeta, 2012). Another part of the literature has also shown that many of the outcomes reviewed in this chapter tend to persist among second generation immigrants in the US and other countries as a result of different values regarding the strength of family ties (Alesina and Giuliano, 2010; Alesina et al. 2013).

## 4.4. HOW TO MEASURE FAMILY TIES

In this section, we describe different ways of measuring family ties using existing datasets. One uses individual responses from the World Value Survey (WVS) (the measure used for the empirical analysis of this chapter); the other is based upon the classification by Todd (1983, 1990).

### 4.4.1 Measuring Family Ties Using the World Values Survey

The WVS is a cross-country project carried out for more than 20 years. Each wave has representative national surveys of the basic values and beliefs of individuals in a large cross-section of countries. The questionnaires contain information about demographics (sex, age, education), self-reported economic characteristics (income, social class), and answers to specific questions about religion, political preferences, and attitudes. Bertrand and Schoar (2006), Alesina and Giuliano (2010) and several others since, measure the strength of family ties by looking at three WVS variables capturing beliefs on the importance of the family in an individual's life; the duties and responsibilities of parents and children; and the love and respect for one's own parents. The first question assesses how important the family is in one person's life and can take values from 1 to 4 (with four being very important and 1 not important at all). The second question asks whether the respondent agrees with one of two statements (taking the values of 1 and 2, respectively): (1) one does not have the duty to respect and love parents who have not earned it; (2) regardless of what the qualities and faults of one's parents are, one must always love and respect them. The third question prompts respondents to agree with one of the following statements (again taking the values of 1 or 2, respectively): (1) Parents have a life of their own and should not be asked to sacrifice their own well-being for the sake of their children; (2) it is the parents' duty to do their best for their children even at the expense of their own well-being. The questions can be combined by extracting the first principal component from the whole dataset with all individual responses for the original variables.

Table 4.1 displays the correlation at the country level between the three original measures and the first principal component. All the variables are highly and positively

**Table 4.1** Correlation among family values

| | Family importance | Respect and love parents | Parental duties | Family ties (princ. comp.) |
|---|---|---|---|---|
| Family importance | 1.0000 | | | |
| Respect and love parents | 0.3446** | 1.0000 | | |
| Parental duties | 0.5518*** | 0.3495** | 1.0000 | |
| Family ties (princ. comp.) | 0.7217** | 0.7944*** | 0.7928*** | 1.0000 |

**significant at 5%.
***significant at 1%.

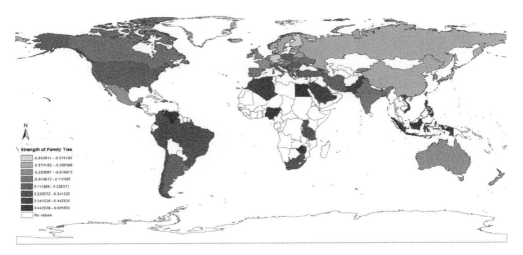

**Figure 4.1** Strength of family ties, principal component. *Source: Authors' calculation from the World Value Survey.*

correlated among each other. Figures 4.1–4.4 show maps of each single question and the first principal component, and Figure 4.5 displays the values of the measure of the strength of family ties (expressed using the first principal component) at the country level.[3] The ranking generally reflects priors of the sociological literature. Scandinavian countries and many Eastern European countries tend to have the weakest levels of family ties. In a middle range are France, Canada, the United States, and the United Kingdom. More familistic societies are Italy and many Latin American countries including Colombia, Peru, and Brazil. In the extreme part of the distributions are some Latin American countries like Guatemala and Venezuela; African countries like Egypt and Zimbabwe; and Asian countries like Indonesia, Vietnam, and the Philippines.

[3] The measure is calculated using the six waves from the WVS.

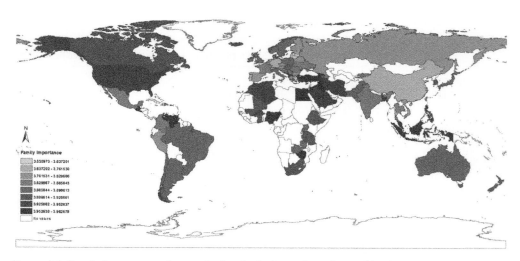

**Figure 4.2**  Family importance. *Source: Authors' calculation from the World Value Survey.*

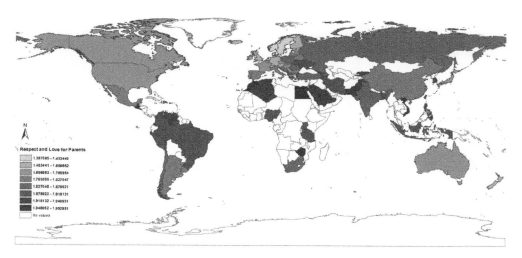

**Figure 4.3**  Respect and love for parents. *Source: Authors' calculation from the World Value Survey.*

The strength of family ties varies not only across countries, but also across regions of the same country. Figure 4.6 represents the partial correlation of the relationship between generalized trust and the strength of family ties for the case of Europe, after controlling for country fixed effects. As is apparent from the figure, even after controlling for country characteristics, the variation in family ties across Europe is sufficient to explain differences in social capital inside Europe. The difference in the strength of family ties inside the same country can be very pronounced. In Italy, the lowest level of family ties are in the

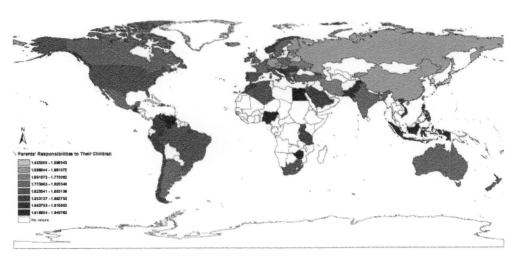

**Figure 4.4** Parents' responsibilities to their children. *Source: Authors' calculation from the World Value Survey.*

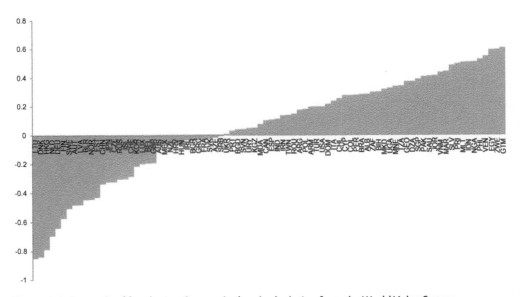

**Figure 4.5** Strength of family ties. *Source: Authors' calculation from the World Value Survey.*

northern region of Valle D'Aosta (where it is equal to −0.22, a level similar to some of the Swedish regions), the highest in the southern region of Calabria (where it reaches the high value of 0.44).

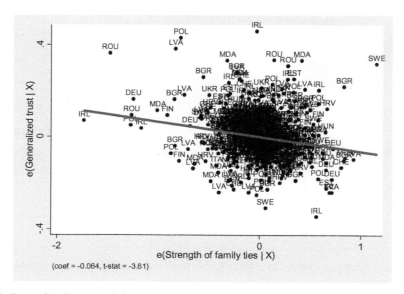

**Figure 4.6** Generalized trust and the strength of family ties, regional variation inside Europe.

## 4.4.2 Todd's Classification of Family Structures

In his books, *The Invention of Europe* (1990) and *The Explanation of Ideology: Family Structures and Social Systems* (1983), Emmanuel Todd classifies family structures according to two main organizing principles. The first principle concerns the vertical relationship between parents and children, the second, the relationship between siblings.

With respect to the vertical relationship between parents and children, the family is defined as "authoritarian" if children are subject to the parental authority even after marriage. The family is defined as "liberal" if children become independent from the parental authority by leaving the parental nest in early adulthood. To measure authoritarian versus liberal families, Todd looked at data on cohabitation between generations within families, in particular between parents and their married children. The family is authoritarian if the eldest son stays in the family when he marries and remains under the authority of the father. Unmarried daughters remain in the family home under the authority of the father or their brothers, when the father dies. In the "liberal" case, children leave the parental home when they reach adulthood or after marriage.

When one looks at the relationship between siblings, the family is defined as "equal" if all siblings are treated equally; it is defined as "unequal" if one particular child (most often the eldest) has a privileged treatment. To measure equality, Todd uses data on inheritance laws and practices. A family is equal when family property is divided evenly between siblings and unequal if primogeniture (or in some cases ultimogeniture) exists. The information on the type of families for both the vertical and the horizontal dimension is obtained by censuses and historical monographs that go back more than 500 years.

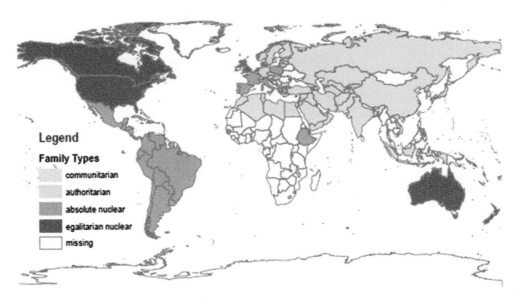

**Figure 4.7** Family structures, Todd's classification. *Source: Profeta and Galasso (2012).*

The combination of the authoritarian/liberal vertical relationship with the equal/ unequal horizontal relationship gives rise to four types of family structures (depicted in Figure 4.7):

1. *Absolute nuclear family:* this family type is characterized by independent living arrangements (children leave their family in early adulthood either before marriage or to form their own family), and lack of stringent inheritance rules. In this type of family, parents have no obligation to support their adult children; every person is independent and has to rely on his/her individual effort. The United States, the UK, Australia, New Zealand, the Netherlands, and Denmark belong to this group. Interestingly, Laslett (1983) has shown that this family characteristic makes young adults free to take residence where job opportunities are best and thus has favored industrial development.

2. *Egalitarian nuclear family:* this family type is characterized by independent living arrangements, like in the absolute nuclear family. The presence of egalitarian inheritance rules, however, encourages the persistence of a strong relationship between parents and children, who are inclined to stay with their parents longer. To this group belong the southern European countries (Italy, Spain, Greece, and Portugal); Romania, Poland, Latin America, and Ethiopia.

3. *Stem or authoritarian family:* this family type is characterized by the cohabitation of parents and children. Inheritance rules are also not egalitarian. Countries belonging to this group are Austria, Germany, Sweden, Norway, Czech Republic, Belgium, Luxembourg, Ireland, Japan, Korea, and Israel.

**Table 4.2** Relationship between the strength of family ties (WVS) and Todd's family structure

|  | (1)<br>Family important | (2)<br>Respect and love parents | (3)<br>Parental duties |
|---|---|---|---|
| Communitarian family | 0.039 | −0.135** | 0.086*** |
|  | (0.040) | (0.065) | (0.031) |
| Authoritarian family | 0.019 | 0.012 | 0.163*** |
|  | (0.033) | (0.088) | (0.049) |
| Nuclear egalitarian family | 0.018 | −0.142** | 0.014 |
|  | (0.035) | (0.065) | (0.025) |
| Observations | 101,169 | 94,631 | 89,011 |
| R-squared | 0.007 | 0.037 | 0.028 |

*Source:* Galasso and Profeta (2012). A higher number in their specification indicates weaker family ties. Data are taken from the WVS. Each specification controls for a quadratic in age, education, income, and political orientation.
*Indicates significance at the 10% level.
**Indicates significance at the 5% level.
***Indicates significance at the 1% level.

4. *Communitarian family:* this type of family is characterized by cohabitation of parents and children and equal inheritance rules. This system characterizes countries like Russia, Bulgaria, Finland, Hungary, Albania, China, Vietnam, Cuba, Indonesia, and India.[4]

   Galasso and Profeta (2012) compare Todd's classification of family structures with the one used in this chapter and in Alesina and Giuliano (2010). In particular, they use the three above-described measures of family values taken from WVS and compare them with Todd's classification of family structures. They run a model of the following type:

$$y_i = \alpha + \beta_1 X_i + \beta_2 Communitarian_i + \beta_3 Authoritarian_i + \beta_4 nuclear\_egalitarian_i + \varepsilon_i,$$

where $y_i$ is the answer from the WVS to each of the three family measures, $X_i$ is a set of individual controls (a quadratic in age, income, education, political views). They include dummies for the prevalent type of family in a country, where the absolute nuclear family is the excluded category. Table 4.2 reports the results of their specification. Todd's classification plays no role in explaining the answer to the most general question on the importance of the family (column 1). However, strong children-to-parents links are associated with communitarian and egalitarian nuclear families (column 2). Finally, authoritarian and communitarian families are associated with a prominent role of parents in today's societies. The authors conclude that current survey data broadly confirms the historical types present in Todd's analysis.

---

[4] Note that Todd (1990) provides regional variations for most European countries, for example the communitarian family was present in the center of Italy. Here we just report the data at the country level. The family type at the country level is based on the type of family present in the majority of the population. For more details on the regional variations of family ties see Duranton et al. (2009) and Todd (1990).

## 4.5. WHERE FAMILY TIES COME FROM

A large literature in anthropology has documented that the type of family is related to ecological features and means of subsistence in ancient times (Murdock, 1949). Typically, agricultural societies are characterized by large extended families; whereas the small nuclear family is more prevalent among small hunting and gathering societies. The reason for that is that farming requires the help of many people, usually children and kin, who cooperate to cultivate crops. Studies have found that children in agricultural and pastoral societies are taught to be responsible, compliant, obedient, and to respect the elderly and the hierarchy. Hunting or gathering as a means of subsistence, on the other hand, requires moving from area to area. Many hunting and gathering societies do not have a permanent home, but temporary huts or shelters. Mobility means that the small nuclear family is more adaptable for survival under these ecological restraints. Children in hunting and gathering societies tend to be self-reliant, independent, and achievement oriented; and the family is less stratified.

We are not aware of formal tests of whether these ecological features from the distant past tend to persist to the modern times, after industrialization has taken place in many societies. The only work which has studied the correlation between current measures of family ties and long-term historical characteristics is Durante (2010). He proposes a simple explanation of the emergence of trust and different forms of family structures based on the need for subsistence farmers to cope with weather fluctuations. The main idea is that a more variable environment should increase an individual's propensity to interact with non-family members and reduce their dependence on the family for insurance purposes. Durante (2010) tests his prediction in the context of Europe, combining high-resolution climate data for the period 1500–2000 with contemporary survey data on family ties as measured in Alesina and Giuliano (2010), and generalized trust, using the negative expected relationship between these two variables. He finds that regions with greater interannual fluctuations in temperature and precipitation have higher levels of interpersonal trust and weaker family ties. This result is primarily driven by weather variability in the growing-season months, consistent with the effect of climatic risk operating primarily through agriculture. He then replicates the analysis using climate data for the period 1500–1750. The relationship between historical climatic variability and trust and weak family ties is positive and significant, even after controlling for climate variability between 1900 and 2000, which does not appear to have an independent effect on trust or family ties. These findings support an explanation based on the historical formation and long-term persistence of trust and family attitudes.

The results of Durante's specifications for various regions of Europe are reported in Table 4.3. In particular, in panel A we report Durante's results for the period 1900–2000. The left-hand side variable is the principal component of the measures of family

**Table 4.3** Family ties and climate variability

| Climate data 1900–2000 | Family ties (principal component from WVS) | | | |
| --- | --- | --- | --- | --- |
| | Precipitation | | Temperature | |
| | (1) | (2) | (3) | (4) |
| **Panel A: Climate data: 1900–2000** | | | | |
| Variability | −0.072** | | −0.392* | |
| (12 months) | (0.033) | | (0.214) | |
| Variability | | −0.081*** | | −0.692*** |
| (growing-season months) | | (0.029) | | (0.219) |
| Variability | | −0.004 | | 0.063 |
| (non-growing-season months) | | (0.024) | | (0.130) |
| Observations | 220 | 220 | 220 | 220 |
| Number of clusters | 24 | 24 | 24 | 24 |
| R-squared | 0.826 | 0.828 | 0.826 | 0.832 |
| **Panel B: Climate data: 1500–1750 and 1900–2000** | | | | |
| Variability (growing-season months) | −0.205** | −0.300** | −0.205** | −0.306*** |
| (1500–1750) | (0.085) | (0.112) | (0.081) | (0.100) |
| Variability (growing-season months) | | 0.129* | | 0.138 |
| (1900–2000) | | (0.074) | | (0.081) |
| Observations | 218 | 218 | 218 | 218 |
| Number of clusters | 24 | 24 | 24 | 24 |
| R-squared | 0.830 | 0.833 | 0.785 | 0.789 |

*Source:* Durante (2010). The regressions control for country fixed effects and for the following regional controls: mean temperature, mean precipitation, average ruggedness index, soil suitability (average and standard deviation), area, dummy for landlocked, distance of the region's centroid from the coast, number of major rivers passing through the region, latitude of the region's centroid. Robust standard errors clustered at the country level in parenthesis.
*Indicates significance at the 10% level.
**Indicates significance at the 5% level.
***Indicates significance at the 1% level.

ties, whereas the dependent variable is the annualized variability calculated using both precipitation (columns 1 and 2) and temperature (columns 3 and 4). The coefficient on precipitation variability is positive and statistically significant at the 5% level (column 1): in regions characterized by a more variable climate, family ties are weaker. The results are primarily driven by variability in precipitation during the growing-season months, whereas variability during the other months displays no significant effect (column 2). The results obtained using temperature are analogous: higher interannual variability, particularly during the growing season, corresponds to weaker family ties (columns 3 and 4).

Panel B reports the test Durante performed to show that differences in the strength of family ties are related to historical rather than contemporary variability. Historical variability in the growing season's precipitation and temperature appear to have a negative, large, and significant effect on the strength of family ties (column 1). This effect remains and becomes even larger when controlling for climate variability over the last century, which appears to have no significant (or even positive effect, for the case of precipitation) effect. The magnitude of the coefficients on historical variability is large: a one standard deviation in growing season variability corresponds to a 0.40 standard deviation decrease in the strength of family ties, for precipitation, and a 0.38 standard deviation decrease for temperature.

## 4.6. EMPIRICAL ANALYSIS

In this section we examine the relationship between family values and economic attitudes, using within-country analysis drawn from the WVS. Our measure of family ties is defined as the principal component of three subjective measures regarding the role of the family, and the link between parents and children, as described in Section 4.1. We use all available six waves, therefore providing the most comprehensive analysis of the impact of family values on a variety of attitudes.[5] The coverage of countries varies across surveys. The 1981–1984 wave covers 24 countries; the 1989–1993 wave covers 43 countries; 1994–1999, 1999–2004, 2005–2007, and 2008–2010 waves cover, respectively, 54, 70, 57, and 47 countries.

The use of within-country analysis allows us to control for country fixed effects, eliminating the impact of other institutional variables. This approach underestimates the effect of family ties, to the extent that in the distant past they had an impact on current institutions. Nevertheless, the effect can be attributed more credibly to this cultural trait. Omitted variables and reverse causality can still be a problem for this type of regression, for this reason, we prefer to interpret our results as more precisely estimated partial correlations. We divide our dependent variables into four groups.

### 4.6.1 Measures of Interest in Politics and Political Action

We begin with measures of people's interest in politics and political action. The first variable, which we label interest in politics, is based on the following question: "How interested would you say you are in politics?", the response varies from 1 (not at all interested) to 4 (very interested). Variable 2, which we label discuss politics, asks the respondent "How often do you discuss political matters with friends?" with the response varying from never (1), occasionally (2), to frequently (3). Variables 3 and 4 measure if the respondent belongs to political parties (the first question measures it with a dummy if the person belongs to a political party and zero otherwise; the second question can take values from 0 to 2, with 0 (not a member), 1 (inactive member), and 2 (active member).

---

[5] Alesina and Giuliano (2010) only used four waves, having a substantially smaller sample size.

The last five questions measure different forms of political action, asking the respondent whether he/she has actually done any of these things (taking the value of 3), whether he/she might do it (2), or whether he/she would never do it (1): signing a petition, joining in boycotts, attending lawful/peaceful demonstrations, joining unofficial strikes, occupying buildings or factories.

Understanding the origin of civic culture and of a well-educated population is an important prerequisite to a well-functioning and stable democracy (Lipset 1959; Almond and Verba, 1963; Glaeser et al. 2004, 2007; Persson and Tabellini, 2009).

## 4.6.2 Measures of Generalized Morality and Attitudes Toward Society

The second group of questions contains two measures of generalized morality (related to a definition by Tabellini (2008), explained below), one question about trust in the family and three questions about attitudes toward society. Variable one, *trust*, is based on the following question: "Generally speaking, would you say that most people can be trusted or that you can't be too careful in dealing with people?", the variable is equal to 1 if participants report that most people can be trusted and 0 otherwise. Variable 2 asks whether obedience is a quality that children can be encouraged to learn at home, taking the value of 1 if the quality is mentioned and 0 otherwise. Variable 3 asks how much the respondent trusts the family from "do not trust the family at all" (1), "do not trust the family very much" (2), "neither trust nor distrust the family" (3), "trust the family a little" (4), "trust the family completely" (5). The last three questions refer to attitudes about the possibility of changing society. The first question asks on a scale from 1 to 10 whether "Ideas that stood the test of time are generally best" (taking the value of 1), or whether "New ideas are generally better than old ones". The second question asks if "One should be cautious about making major changes in life" (taking the value of 1) versus "You will never achieve much unless you act boldly" (taking the value of 10). The third question asks the respondent to choose between three basic kinds of attitudes concerning society: "society must be valiantly defended" (taking the value of 1), "society must be gradually improved by reforms" (taking the value of 2), and "society must be radically changed" (taking the value of 3).

Among all the above variables "trust" measures a fundamental trait in a society. More than 35 years ago, Arrow (1972), recognizing the pervasiveness of mutual trust in commercial and non-commercial transactions, went so far as to state that "it can be plausibly argued that much of the economic backwardness in the world can be explained by the lack of mutual confidence (p. 357)." Since then, Arrow's conjecture has received considerable empirical support. A vast literature investigates the link between aggregate trust and aggregate economic performance, trust also encourage welfare enhancing social interactions, such as anonymous exchange of participation in the provision of public goods, and they are likely to improve the functioning of government institutions. Starting with Banfield, it has also been postulated a negative correlation between trust in a small related circle (like the family) and generalized trust. Platteau (2000) links lack of generalized trust to the distinction between "generalized" versus "limited" morality. In hierarchical societies, trust and honest behavior are often confined to small circles of related people (like members of the family). Outside of this small network, opportunistic and highly selfish behavior is regarded as natural and morally acceptable. These two measures have been defined to distinguish between values consistent with "generalized" versus "limited" morality. Tabellini (2008) has shown that generalized morality is fundamental to understand the origin of economic development across countries and among regions of Europe. We therefore look at the relevance of family ties in the formation of generalized trust and trust toward the family (expecting a negative impact of family ties on generalized trust and a positive impact on trust in the family). In strong family ties societies, individualism is also mistrusted. In familistic societies, the role of parents is to foster obedience. Banfield emphasized the relevance of obedience to claim that such coercive cultural environment reduces individual initiative and cooperation within a group, and can hurt growth and development.

The last three questions are related to the idea put forward by Coleman (1988) that family ties can represent an obstacle for innovation and new ideas.

### 4.6.3 Labor Market and Attitudes Toward Work

The third group of questions looks at the relationship between family values and the labor market. We explore the correlation between female, youth, and elderly labor force participation and family ties. We also look at questions regarding the relationship between job security and family ties. One question asks the respondent how important is job security in a job. In another, the respondent has to choose the most important thing in looking for a job, where a safe job with no risk is one of five choices (the other four being: a good income, working with people one likes, doing an important job, doing something for the community).

Employment rates vary dramatically across countries, but the bulk of the variation relies on specific demographic groups: women, younger, and older individuals. Looking at micro and macro data for OECD countries, Algan and Cahuc (2007) show that differences in family culture can explain lower female employment and lower level of employment of young and older people in Europe.[6] In the same fashion, Giavazzi et al. (forthcoming) find that culture matters for women's employment rates and for hours worked. In a recent

---

[6] Although the authors attribute the differences in employment rates to the presence of the nuclear versus the extended family in different OECD countries, the effect on employment is not studied using different family structures but considering some subjective measures. In particular, they look at three questions: whether the respondent agrees with the statement "When jobs are scarce, older people should be forced to retire from work early"; the second asking the respondent whether they agree with the statement "Adult children have a duty to look after their elderly parents"; and finally, "Independence is a quality that children should be encouraged to learn at home."

paper, Alesina et al. (2013) looked at the relationship between family ties and the labor market. The main idea is that in cultures with strong family ties, moving away from home is costly. Thus individuals with strong family ties choose regulated labor markets to avoid moving and limiting the monopsony power of firms, even though regulation generates lower employment and income. We look at within-country analysis on preferences for job security that further limit the possibility that the results are driven by other country characteristics.

### 4.6.4 Measures of Attitudes Toward Women

The fourth group of variables contains measure of people's attitudes toward women. The first question asks the respondent whether he/she agrees with the statement "When jobs are scarce, men should have more right to a job than women." The other six variables come from the answer to the question "For each of the following statements I read out, can you tell me how much you agree with each? Do you agree strongly, agree, disagree, or disagree strongly?" The statements are: "A working mother can establish just as warm and secure a relationship with her children as a mother who does not work"; "Being a housewife is just as fulfilling as working for pay"; "On the whole, men make better political leaders than women do"; "A university education is more important for a boy than for a girl"; "A pre-school child is likely to suffer if his or her mother works"; "A job is alright but what most women really want is a home and children." We recode the questions so that a higher number means a more traditional perception of the role of women in society.

Gender role attitudes are relevant in explaining differences in female labor force participation across countries (see Fortin, 2005; Fernandez and Fogli, 2009). In strong family ties societies (Esping-Andersen, 1999; Ferrera, 1996; Castles, 1995; Korpi, 2000), family solidarity is based on an unequal division of family work between men and women (what has been called the "male-breadwinner hypothesis"): weak family ties will foster an egalitarian gender role in which men and women participate equally in employment and housework, whereas strong family ties are based on the "male-breadwinner hypothesis" in which men work full-time and women dedicate themselves to housework. In the more traditional, strong family ties societies, is the woman who is supposed to fulfill the family obligations and as such, participate less in the market. According to Esping-Andersen (1999), this gender relationship has been helped by a welfare state model that has historically delegated family care services for children and the elderly to the family sphere and has protected the male-breadwinner figure. Alesina and Ichino (2009) provide an in-depth analysis of this type of family organization with respect to Italy.

### 4.6.5 The Impact of Family Ties

In Tables 4.4–4.7, we present our results on the overall effects of family ties. Each attitude is regressed on our measure of family ties, some control variables (age, education, marital

**Table 4.4** Family ties and political participation

| Variables | (1) Interest in politics | (2) Discuss politics | (3) Belong to political parties | (4) Membership political party | (5) Sign petition | (6) Join in boycotts | (7) Attend demonstrations | (8) Join unofficial strikes | (9) Occupy buildings |
|---|---|---|---|---|---|---|---|---|---|
| Family ties | −0.010*** | −0.006*** | −0.002*** | −0.004** | −0.029*** | −0.046*** | −0.036*** | −0.041*** | −0.026*** |
|  | (0.002) | (0.001) | (0.001) | (0.002) | (0.002) | (0.002) | (0.002) | (0.002) | (0.001) |
| Age | 0.016*** | 0.018*** | 0.002*** | 0.006*** | 0.012*** | 0.008*** | 0.009*** | 0.004*** | −0.000 |
|  | (0.001) | (0.000) | (0.000) | (0.001) | (0.001) | (0.001) | (0.001) | (0.000) | (0.000) |
| Age squared | −0.000*** | −0.000*** | −0.000*** | −0.000*** | −0.000*** | −0.000*** | −0.000*** | −0.000*** | −0.000*** |
|  | (0.000) | (0.000) | (0.000) | (0.000) | (0.000) | (0.000) | (0.000) | (0.000) | (0.000) |
| Female | −0.277*** | −0.189*** | −0.034*** | −0.083*** | −0.088*** | −0.123*** | −0.155*** | −0.099*** | −0.058*** |
|  | (0.004) | (0.003) | (0.001) | (0.004) | (0.004) | (0.003) | (0.004) | (0.003) | (0.002) |
| Married | −0.008 | −0.016** | 0.010** | 0.009 | 0.002 | 0.023*** | 0.018** | 0.044*** | 0.029*** |
|  | (0.011) | (0.007) | (0.004) | (0.008) | (0.009) | (0.009) | (0.009) | (0.008) | (0.006) |
| Education dummies | yes | yes | yes | yes | yes | yes | yes | yes | yes |
| Country dummies | yes | yes | yes | yes | yes | yes | yes | yes | yes |
| Wave dummies | yes | yes | yes | yes | yes | yes | yes | yes | yes |
| Observations | 212,931 | 220,148 | 133,684 | 66,407 | 131,066 | 127,491 | 131,408 | 126,513 | 125,180 |
| R-squared | 0.136 | 0.115 | 0.060 | 0.181 | 0.278 | 0.182 | 0.143 | 0.096 | 0.096 |

Coefficients are reported with robust standard errors in brackets.
*Indicates significance at the 10% level.
**Indicates significance at the 5% level.
***Indicates significance at the 1% level.

**Table 4.5** Family ties, generalized morality, and attitudes toward society

|  | (1) Trust | (2) Trust the family | (3) Children qualities: obedience | (4) New and old idea | (5) Major change in life | (6) Society changed/society defended |
|---|---|---|---|---|---|---|
| Family ties | −0.006*** | 0.069*** | 0.024*** | 0.050*** | 0.112*** | 0.017*** |
|  | (0.001) | (0.008) | (0.001) | (0.009) | (0.010) | (0.002) |
| Age | 0.002*** | 0.002 | −0.004*** | 0.027*** | 0.015*** | −0.002*** |
|  | (0.000) | (0.003) | (0.000) | (0.003) | (0.004) | (0.001) |
| Age squared | −0.000*** | −0.000 | 0.000*** | −0.000 | 0.000 | 0.000*** |
|  | (0.000) | (0.000) | (0.000) | (0.000) | (0.000) | (0.000) |
| Female | −0.006*** | −0.002 | −0.003 | 0.090*** | 0.086*** | 0.032*** |
|  | (0.002) | (0.014) | (0.002) | (0.019) | (0.022) | (0.003) |
| Married | −0.013*** | −0.083* | 0.002 | −0.002 | −0.182*** | −0.003 |
|  | (0.005) | (0.043) | (0.005) | (0.042) | (0.052) | (0.008) |
| Education dummies | yes | yes | yes | yes | yes | yes |
| Country dummies | yes | yes | yes | yes | yes | yes |
| Wave dummies | yes | yes | yes | yes | yes | yes |
| Observations | 217,647 | 9,802 | 220,639 | 81,640 | 69,736 | 110,077 |
| R-squared | 0.104 | 0.057 | 0.111 | 0.131 | 0.083 | 0.050 |

Coefficients are reported with robust standard errors in brackets.
*Indicates significance at the 10% level.
**Indicates significance at the 5% level.
***Indicates significance at the 1% level.

**Table 4.6** Family ties, labor market, and attitudes toward work

| | (1)<br>Female<br>LFP | (2)<br>Youth<br>LFP | (3)<br>Elderly<br>LFP | (4)<br>Job<br>security | (5)<br>Job security in<br>looking for job |
|---|---|---|---|---|---|
| Family ties | −0.013*** | −0.012** | −0.006** | 0.017*** | 0.022*** |
| | (0.001) | (0.001) | (0.003) | (0.001) | (0.001) |
| Age | 0.063*** | −0.043*** | −0.050 | 0.003*** | 0.004*** |
| | (0.001) | (0.007) | (0.043) | (0.000) | (0.000) |
| Age squared | −0.001*** | 0.001*** | −0.000 | −0.000*** | −0.000*** |
| | (0.000) | (0.000) | (0.000) | (0.000) | (0.000) |
| Married | −0.006 | −0.060*** | 0.028 | −0.000 | −0.001 |
| | (0.007) | (0.007) | (0.020) | (0.005) | (0.007) |
| Female | | −0.268*** | −0.264*** | −0.004** | −0.003 |
| | | (0.003) | (0.005) | (0.002) | (0.003) |
| Education dummies | yes | yes | yes | yes | yes |
| Country dummies | yes | yes | yes | yes | yes |
| Wave dummies | yes | yes | yes | yes | yes |
| Observations | 98,218 | 44,336 | 26,974 | 213,576 | 99,749 |
| R-squared | 0.224 | 0.269 | 0.251 | 0.106 | 0.049 |

Coefficients are reported with robust standard errors in brackets.
*Indicates significance at the 10% level.
**Indicates significance at the 5% level.
***Indicates significance at the 1% level.

status, and a gender dummy[7]), country-specific effects, and wave dummies. The sample size differs across regressions and ranges from a minimum of 26,974 to a maximum of 212,931[8]; therefore always providing substantial variation in time period and number of countries.

Before we comment on the results of the impact of family ties, it is useful to discuss the effect of our control variables. The results, which are of independent interest, are very reasonable and provide credibility to the measure of family ties we are going to use. There is a hump-shaped relationship in age between interest in politics, political participation, and political action, and between age and job security. There is also a hump-shaped relationship between age and trust, whereas the level of trust in the family does not change with age. Emphasizing obedience is less important among young people and it has a U-shaped relationship with age. The same U-shaped relationship also exists for

[7] We do not include income in our regressions since in the next section we do find that family ties could explain part of the differences in GDP per capita across countries. Our results are, however, robust to its inclusion.

[8] The smallest sample is for labor force participation of the elderly (26,974), therefore the smaller sample size depends on the fact that the regressions are not run on the whole population. The variable trust in the family is the one with substantially lower sample size, of around 10,000 observations.

**Table 4.7** Family ties and attitudes toward women

| | (1) Job scarce | (2) Working mother | (3) Housewife fulfilling | (4) Men political leaders | (5) University important for girls | (6) Child working mother | (7) Women home children |
|---|---|---|---|---|---|---|---|
| Family ties | 0.015*** | −0.002 | 0.044*** | 0.023*** | 0.008*** | 0.043*** | 0.075*** |
| | (0.001) | (0.002) | (0.002) | (0.003) | (0.003) | (0.004) | (0.004) |
| Age | 0.001*** | −0.001 | 0.001* | 0.002 | 0.001 | 0.006*** | 0.003** |
| | (0.000) | (0.001) | (0.001) | (0.001) | (0.001) | (0.002) | (0.002) |
| Age-squared | 0.000** | 0.000*** | 0.000** | 0.000 | 0.000* | −0.000 | 0.000 |
| | (0.000) | (0.000) | (0.000) | (0.000) | (0.000) | (0.000) | (0.000) |
| Female | −0.117*** | −0.154*** | −0.068*** | −0.279*** | −0.221*** | −0.109*** | −0.068*** |
| | (0.003) | (0.005) | (0.005) | (0.006) | (0.005) | (0.009) | (0.009) |
| Married | 0.019*** | 0.009 | −0.014 | 0.007 | 0.032*** | −0.005 | 0.016 |
| | (0.006) | (0.012) | (0.012) | (0.013) | (0.012) | (0.043) | (0.049) |
| Education dummies | yes | yes | yes | yes | yes | yes | yes |
| Country dummies | yes | yes | yes | yes | yes | yes | yes |
| Wave dummies | yes | yes | yes | yes | yes | yes | yes |
| Observations | 118,200 | 133,811 | 130,836 | 100,679 | 103,027 | 29,929 | 29,153 |
| R-squared | 0.234 | 0.086 | 0.092 | 0.203 | 0.123 | 0.169 | 0.190 |

Coefficients are reported with robust standard errors in brackets.
*Indicates significance at the 10% level.
**Indicates significance at the 5% level.
***Indicates significance at the 1% level.

the attitudes looking at whether society should be defended versus whether it should be dramatically changed. Not surprising, young people believe that new ideas are better than old ones and are more open to major changes in life. Attitudes toward women are not systematically related to age. Gender and education also have the expected effects. Women are generally less interested and involved in politics than men. They also trust less (gender, like age, however, is not systematically related to the level of trust in the family, a more universal value that does not change with specific demographics). Not surprisingly, women have less traditional beliefs about the role of women in society compared to their male counterparts (an indication that they most likely suffer from the presence of traditional gender role attitudes). Education is positively related to political interest and political action, a result supporting the model by Glaeser et al. (2007). More educated people have a higher level of trust, less traditional attitudes about the role of women in society; they also believe obedience is not an important quality to teach children. Finally, they are in support of new ideas but more conservative with respect to major changes in life and in society.[9]

Let's now consider the effect of family ties. Table 4.4, which relates to political participation and political action, shows that family ties have a negative and highly statistically significant coefficient. Regarding the magnitude of the effect, the beta coefficient of family ties on political participation (the first four columns of Table 4.4) is equal for the four different measures to 0.01 (roughly to 1/5 of the magnitude of the beta coefficient of the middle level of education, which ranges between 0.04 and 0.05).[10] The magnitude of the beta coefficient for family ties is larger for the measures of political actions. In this case the coefficient goes from 0.04 to 0.08 and it is between 1/3 or even the same effect of the middle level of education.

Table 4.5, which includes the same controls of Table 4.4, refers to those variables of "generalized morality" (as in Tabellini, 2008) and openness to new ideas. The results are as expected. Particularly important is the result of column 1 which shows a negative effect of family ties on generalized trust, but positive on trusting family members (column 2). Strong family ties imply teaching more obedience to children (column 3) and being relatively conservative in terms of personal and social change (columns 4, 5, and 6). As for the magnitude of the effects: the beta coefficients of family ties on trust is equal to −0.016 (half the coefficient of middle level of education, which has a positive effect compared to the lower level of education). The impact of family ties on trusting the family is three

---

[9] When we control for income as one of our robustness checks, we do find that income is positively correlated with trust and trust in the family, like education. Similarly, income is inversely correlated with the importance of obedience. Income is however inversely correlated with the importance of new ideas and major changes in life, but positively correlated with the belief that society should be changed.

[10] We include two dummies for education: one for middle and one for upper level (the excluded group is lower level of education). The sign of the middle and upper level of education coefficient is positive, as the excluded group is lower level of education.

times the effect of middle level of education; the magnitudes of middle level of education and family ties are equivalent (but of opposite sign) for obedience and the three attitudes on personal and social change (columns 4–6).

Table 4.6 looks at the labor market of women, young adults, and the elderly. Individuals coming from strong family ties have a lower level of labor force participation for women, young adults, and older people. This is consistent with the male-breadwinner hypothesis according to which, women are supposed to stay at home and take care of the family, together with older and younger people. Consistent with the relationship postulated by Alesina et al. (2013), individuals with familistic values consider job security the most important characteristic in a job. The impact of family ties on the labor force participation of the three groups is small compared to the impact of education (the beta coefficient is 1/10 when compared to the one on middle level of education). This is not surprising: family ties are very relevant in the determination of labor market institutions (see Alesina et al. 2013) and the country fixed effects are most likely capturing part of that channel. The impact of family ties on job security (columns 4 and 5) on the other hand is six times larger than the effect of middle level of education.

Table 4.7 refers to the attitudes towards women. With the exception of column (2), in all other columns the variable family ties has the expected sign and it implies a more traditional role of women in the family. Indeed, this makes sense: with close family ties, the family needs someone who organizes it, and keeps it together, typically the wife and mother. In this sense, the family becomes a formidable producer of goods and services which are not counted in standard measure of GDP, like childcare, care of the elderly, and various other forms of home production.[11] As for the magnitude of the effects, it goes from roughly $\frac{1}{4}$ of the effect of middle level of education (for the first four columns) to being more or less of equivalent magnitude (for the last three columns).

Overall, we find that different beliefs about the importance of the family in one person's life and the relationship among generations are relevant for the determination of values, which have been proven to promote employment, innovation, and growth. If values about the family are transmitted from generation to generation and they move slowly over time, they could provide an explanation on how the distant past can affect the current functioning of institutions. Indeed, several papers have provided evidence that attitudes toward the family and different forms of family structures are transmitted from generation to generation and affect the behavior of second generation immigrants, who still maintain the values and behavior of their parents despite living in an institutional environment which is very different than their ancestors' country of origin.[12] It is also

---

[11] See Alesina and Ichino (2009) for an empirical estimate of the size of home production in a few countries with weak or strong family ties.

[12] See Alesina and Giuliano (2010, 2011) and Alesina et al. (2013). All these papers show that family ties have an effect on the behavior of second generation immigrants in the US and a large set of European countries. This evidence hints at the possibility that the partial correlations established in Section 4.4 can have causal nature.

worth noticing that all the results presented in this section are most likely a lower bound of the effect of family ties. If family values become part of the national culture, this is captured by the country fixed effects together with the impact of institutions and all other time invariant characteristics.

## 4.7. FAMILY TIES, DEVELOPMENT, AND INSTITUTIONS

In this section, we provide some suggestive evidence in support of the idea that family ties are correlated with fundamental determinants of economic outcomes at the aggregate level. We document a strong correlation between the strength of family ties, economic development, and quality of institutions. Countries with strong family ties have lower levels of per capita GDP and lower quality of institutions.

We do our analysis in two steps. As a first step, we establish a basic correlation between the strength of family ties, economic development, and the quality of institutions. As a second step, a small one toward establishing causation, we show that family values brought by immigrants who arrived in several destination countries before 1940 are correlated with the level of development and the quality of institutions today.

We measure economic development with real GDP per capita. As a measure of institutional quality we use the Worldwide Governance Indicators (WGI) of the World Bank. The WGI reports on six broad dimensions of governance for over 200 countries for the period 1996–2011. These dimensions are: voice and accountability (the extent to which a country's citizens are able to participate in selecting their government, as well as freedom of expression, freedom of association, and a free media); political stability and absence of violence (measuring perceptions of the likelihood that the government will be destabilized or overthrown by unconstitutional or violent means, including politically motivated violence and terrorism); government effectiveness (the quality of public services; the quality of the civil service and the degree of its independence from political pressures; the quality of policy formulation and implementation; and the credibility of the government's commitment to such policies); regulatory quality (the ability of the government to formulate and implement sound policies and regulations that permit and promote private sector development); rule of law (capturing perceptions of the extent to which agents have confidence in and abide by the rules of society, and in particular the quality of contract enforcement, property rights, the police, and the courts, as well as the likelihood of crime and violence); and control of corruption (the extent to which public power is exercised for private gain, including both petty and grand forms of corruption, as well as "capture" of the state by elites and private interests).

### 4.7.1 The Correlation Between Family Ties, Economic Development, and Institutional Quality

We first establish that countries with stronger family ties have lower economic development on average, measured by GDP per capita (Table 4.8). We run cross-country

**Table 4.8** Family ties and per capita GDP

| Variables | (1) Log GDP | (2) Log GDP | (3) Log GDP | (4) Log GDP |
|---|---|---|---|---|
| Family ties | −1.984*** | −0.969** | | |
| | (0.383) | (0.441) | | |
| Inherited family values | | | −0.860** | −0.786*** |
| | | | (0.428) | (0.285) |
| Log (years of schooling) | | 2.414*** | | 2.350*** |
| | | (0.498) | | (0.307) |
| Observations | 80 | 73 | 122 | 100 |
| R-squared | 0.221 | 0.409 | 0.064 | 0.522 |

Coefficients are reported with robust standard errors in brackets.
*Indicates significance at the 10% level.
**Indicates significance at the 5% level.
***Indicates significance at the 1% level.

regressions of GDP per capita on our measures of family values.[13] We show that the coefficient from a regression of logarithm of GDP per capita on the strength of family ties is highly negative and significant. A one standard deviation increase in the strength of family ties (0.36) is associated with a reduction of the log of GDP per capita of 0.71 (roughly equal to 44% of its standard deviation). The second column controls for human capital, measured by the logarithm of the average schooling years in the total population over age 15. By adding this variable, we might be overcontrolling since educational choices might themselves be an outcome of family values. The strength of family ties is still very strong although is magnitude is, not surprisingly, reduced.

The cross-sectional correlations leave open the possibility that other omitted variables can explain both the strength of family ties and differences in economic development across countries. Using the combined waves of the WVS we can limit this possibility by looking at the correlation between regional income and regional family ties, after controlling for country fixed effects. The results are reported in Table 4.9. In order to maintain a very large sample (more than 1000 regions) we constructed the income measure by collapsing the income variable from the WVS, instead of using estimates of regional GDP which are available only for a limited European sample.[14] In column 1, we report the correlation between regional income and the strength of family ties. Similar to the cross-country regressions, the correlation is negative and significant at the 1% level. This correlation also exists once we control for country fixed effects with a smaller but

[13] The measure of GDP is averaged between 1980 and 2010, the years in which the World Value Survey was taken. In particular, before taking the average, we match each country with the GDP corresponding to the year in which the survey was taken.

[14] The income variable in the dataset indicates income scales and is coded as a variable going from one to eleven, where one indicates the lower step in the scale of incomes and 11 the highest.

**Table 4.9** Family ties and regional income

|  | (1)<br>Whole<br>sample | (2)<br>Whole<br>sample | (3)<br><br>Europe | (4)<br><br>Africa | (5)<br><br>Asia | (6)<br>North America<br>and Oceania | (7)<br>South<br>America |
|---|---|---|---|---|---|---|---|
| Family ties | −0.540*** | −0.349*** | −0.287** | −1.383*** | −0.498** | −0.327 | 0.133 |
|  | (0.078) | (0.111) | (0.127) | (0.398) | (0.201) | (0.408) | (0.444) |
| Country fixed effect | no | yes | yes | yes | yes | yes | yes |
| Observations | 1,197 | 1,197 | 661 | 103 | 255 | 83 | 86 |
| R–squared | 0.047 | 0.526 | 0.466 | 0.691 | 0.482 | 0.731 | 0.354 |

Unit of analysis is a region in the World Value Survey. Coefficients are reported with robust standard errors in brackets.
*Indicates significance at the 10% level.
**Indicates significance at the 5% level.
***Indicates significance at the 1% level.

still relevant magnitude: a one standard deviation increase in the strength of family ties (0.44) is associated with a reduction in income of 0.152 (roughly equal to 14% of its standard deviation). It is also interesting to note that the correlation exists in all different continents. Columns 3–7 indeed show that the correlation is quite strong not only inside Europe but also inside Africa and Asia.[15]

The next question is whether the negative relationship between GDP and family values is also reflected in a negative relationship between family values and institutions. We explore this question in Table 4.10. We find that the strength of family ties is associated with lower quality of institutions. The effect is always negative and significant for all different types of institutions. The effect is also sizeable: a one standard deviation increase in the strength of family ties (0.35) is for example associated with a reduction of the control of corruption measure of 0.61 (roughly equivalent to 54% of its standard deviation).

A recent literature has suggested that one important driver of many formal institutions is legal origin. For example, English (common) law countries have been shown to have higher levels of investor protection, superior protection of property rights, and a more efficient judicial system. When we control for legal origin (Table 4.11), the negative association between family ties and the quality of institutions stay virtually the same.

## 4.7.2 Inherited Family Values and Current Institutions and Development

Our implicit assumption in all the empirical analysis is that family values change slowly. They are transmitted from generation to generation and they have persisted through history to the present day. This form of persistence seems intuitively likely given the probability that children are brought up to consider the attachment to the family, the

[15] The results on North America and Oceania are not significant, most likely due to the small sample size. Similarly for South America.

**Table 4.10** Family ties and institutions

|  | (1)<br>Control of<br>corruption | (2)<br>Government<br>effectiveness | (3)<br>Political<br>stability | (4)<br>Rule of<br>law | (5)<br>Regulatory<br>quality | (6)<br>Voice and<br>accountability |
|---|---|---|---|---|---|---|
| Family ties | −1.729*** | −1.575*** | −1.576*** | −1.595*** | −1.199*** | −1.428*** |
|  | (0.308) | (0.266) | (0.212) | (0.281) | (0.239) | (0.239) |
| Observations | 80 | 80 | 80 | 80 | 80 | 80 |
| R-squared | 0.288 | 0.292 | 0.374 | 0.291 | 0.230 | 0.288 |

Coefficients are reported with robust standard errors in brackets.
*Indicates significance at the 10% level.
**Indicates significance at the 5% level.
***Indicates significance at the 1% level.

**Table 4.11** Family ties and institutions, controlling for legal origin

|  | (1)<br>Control of<br>corruption | (2)<br>Government<br>effectiveness | (3)<br>Political<br>stability | (4)<br>Rule<br>of law | (5)<br>Regulatory<br>quality | (6)<br>Voice and<br>accountability |
|---|---|---|---|---|---|---|
| Family ties | −1.572*** | −1.504*** | −1.368*** | −1.490*** | −1.205*** | −1.334*** |
|  | (0.395) | (0.357) | (0.278) | (0.370) | (0.309) | (0.286) |
| Legal origin dummies | yes | yes | yes | yes | yes | yes |
| Observations | 80 | 80 | 08 | 80 | 80 | 80 |
| R-squared | 0.401 | 0.375 | 0.394 | 0.379 | 0.265 | 0.308 |

Coefficients are reported with robust standard errors in brackets.
*Indicates significance at the 10% level.
**Indicates significance at the 5% level.
***Indicates significance at the 1% level.

respect for parents, and the belief that they will do everything for their children as the natural state of the world. As a result, children will most likely reproduce the same values and beliefs with their own children. The persistence may develop and it can be facilitated through intermediate factors, such as the nature of political or economic institutions, shaped first by family structures which, in turn, have continued to influence our society today in a path-dependent manner.

In this section, we isolate the impact of cultural values on today's institutions. Ideally we would like to have measures of family values observed much before the measure of current institutions. Family values going so far back in time cannot be observed directly, since there is no survey available for that period of time. However, following Algan and Cahuc (2010) we can detect family ties by looking at family values inherited by children of immigrants in several European countries whose forbears arrived in Europe before 1940.

The idea behind this exercise is that parental values are a good predictor of the values of children. For this reason, we can use the family values that European descendants have inherited from their forebears who migrated to Europe from different countries before 1940 to know the values for the period preceding the quality of institutions today. This method allows us to cope with the lack of information on historical family values, by using the values that the descendants of various immigrants groups have inherited from their ancestors' countries of origin. This strategy is very useful because by using the values that European immigrants have inherited from the home country instead of the average values of the residents today, we can exclude reverse causality.

To perform our exercise we use data from the European Social Survey (ESS). The ESS is a biennial cross-sectional survey administered in a large sample of mostly European nations. The survey was conducted in 2002/2003, 2004/2005, 2006/2007, 2008/2009, and 2010/2011. The number of countries surveyed varies by wave. There are 22 countries included in the first round, 26 in the second, 25 in the third, 29 in the fourth, and 20 in the fifth. The sample size for a survey differs by country depending on its size. They range from 579 for Iceland to 2,870 for Germany.

Our primary sample consists of children of immigrants. We define children of immigrants as individuals born in a certain country but whose fathers were born abroad.[16] In order to get enough observations, we use information on second generation immigrants born before 1940. In the presence of cultural transmission children of immigrants should have inherited attitudes toward the families from their parents (who should have arrived in the destination countries not later than 1940 but possibly much earlier), who came to the destination countries with cultural attitudes from their countries of origin. Let's consider for example the case of France. To calculate the historical family values, we do consider children of French immigrants in a certain destination country. We do restrict the sample to children of immigrants born before 1940 and calculate their family values. These values are a reflection of their parental values who arrived from France before 1940, therefore the values of children of immigrants are a reflection of French family values before 1940.

The European Social Survey does not contain the same variables on family ties as those of the World Values Survey. To measure the strength of family ties we use a question asking the respondent his/her level of agreement with the following statement: "A person's family should be the main priority in life" the answer can go from "disagree strongly" to "agree strongly" on a scale from one to five.

There is a strong correlation between the inherited family ties of the children of immigrants born before 1940 (as measured by the ESS question) and current family ties in the countries of origin of their parents (as proxied by our measure of family ties calculated from the WVS). The correlation is about 0.35, showing that there is a strong inertia in family values across countries.

---

[16] When this information is not available we use the country of origin of the mother, if she is an immigrant. Natives are excluded from the analysis.

**Table 4.12** Inherited family values and institutions

|                        | (1) Control of corruption | (2) Government effectiveness | (3) Political stability | (4) Rule of law | (5) Regulatory quality | (6) Voice and accountability |
|------------------------|------------|------------|------------|------------|------------|------------|
| Inherited family values | −0.664*** | −0.622*** | −0.558*** | −0.630*** | −0.477** | −0.613*** |
|                        | (0.197)   | (0.221)   | (0.184)   | (0.213)   | (0.201)   | (0.201)   |
| Observations           | 128       | 129       | 129       | 129       | 128       | 129       |
| R-squared              | 0.090     | 0.081     | 0.068     | 0.083     | 0.053     | 0.082     |

Coefficients are reported with robust standard errors in brackets.
*Indicates significance at the 10% level.
**Indicates significance at the 5% level.
***Indicates significance at the 1% level.

**Table 4.13** Inherited family values and institutions, controlling for legal origin

|                        | (1) Control of corruption | (2) Government effectiveness | (3) Political stability | (4) Rule of law | (5) Regulatory quality | (6) Voice and accountability |
|------------------------|------------|------------|------------|------------|------------|------------|
| Inherited family values | −0.529*** | −0.509*** | −0.529*** | −0.525*** | −0.382** | −0.499*** |
|                        | (0.148)   | (0.174)   | (0.157)   | (0.163)   | (0.160)   | (0.164)   |
| Legal origin           | yes       | yes       | yes       | yes       | yes       | yes       |
| Observations           | 122       | 122       | 122       | 122       | 122       | 122       |
| R-squared              | 0.340     | 0.309     | 0.260     | 0.320     | 0.235     | 0.263     |

Coefficients are reported with robust standard errors in brackets.
*Indicates significance at the 10% level.
**Indicates significance at the 5% level.
***Indicates significance at the 1% level.

We next discuss the correlation between the inherited family ties dating back to at least 60 years ago and current regulations in the home countries. Tables 4.12 and 4.13 show the OLS estimations, with and without the inclusion of legal origin dummies. We do find a robust and significant negative relationship between inherited family values and current institutions. The relationship holds even after controlling for legal origin. We do the same exercise with the level of development finding again a stable negative relationship between current development and inherited family values (columns 3 and 4 of Table 4.8). Overall, we do find that there is a long-lasting effect of family ties on the quality of current institutions.

## 4.8. FAMILY TIES AND WELL-BEING

Strong family ties countries are characterized by less favorable economic outcomes and attitudes. Unemployment rate, labor force participation, and income per capita are worse in strong family ties countries. Such unfavorable outcomes however do not seem to lead to dramatic situations of economic need in the population or to social unrest. This observation seems to suggest that in some sense those negative economic outcomes are less painful in strong family ties societies. In this part, we review existing evidence on the positive effects of familistic societies and provide some additional evidence on the conjecture that family ties could indeed improve well-being.

Bentolila and Ichino (2008) study the relationship between unemployment and consumption in four different countries: Spain, Italy, Great Britain, and the US. Their empirical results indicate that an increase in the duration of unemployment spells of male household heads is associated with smaller consumption losses in Spanish and Italian households. They conclude that extended family networks constitute the social institution which plays the crucial role of reducing the cost of unemployment near the Mediterranean. In Spain and Italy, the family appears to supplement for the lack of generosity of the welfare system and for the imperfection of capital markets. In this sense, the Mediterranean family-based solution seems to produce a desirable outcome from a welfare point of view since it allows for more consumption smoothing.

Along similar lines, Alesina and Giuliano (2010) look at the amount of home production in strong family ties societies. Societies with strong family ties are associated with more time spent at home by wives/mothers, and young adults living at home longer. This implies more home production (in the form of childcare, home cooking, caring for the elderly, house cleaning, etc.). In addition, according to a more traditional role attributed to women in societies in strong family ties societies, these activities should be mostly performed by wives and daughters. The authors indeed find that the strength of family ties is relevant for the determination of home production of women, but not of men, as expected.

Alesina and Ichino (2009) present some detailed calculations of the value of home production in four different countries: Spain and Italy with relatively strong family ties, the United States with an intermediate level, and Norway with a low level of family ties. They use two procedures in order to estimate the value of home production: the opportunity cost and the market value. They first calculate how much market income is lost by various individuals by working a certain number of hours at home rather than in the market, based upon characteristics such as their age, level of education, and wage value in the market. The second method is based upon how much it would cost to hire from the market individuals to perform household duties like cooking, cleaning, etc.[17] The authors find that home production is very large: it increases measured market income by a minimum of 53% to a maximum of 121% depending on the country and method of calculations. But more interestingly for our purposes the authors uncover a very large difference between strong and weak family ties countries. For instance, using the opportunity cost method, Italian families exactly double their market income by working

---

[17] The authors discuss in the detail the properties and the pros and cons of the two methods.

**Table 4.14** Family ties and happiness

|  | (1) Happiness | (2) Satisfaction with life | (3) State of health |
|---|---|---|---|
| Family ties | 0.057*** | 0.143*** | 0.025*** |
|  | (0.001) | (0.005) | (0.002) |
| Age | −0.006*** | −0.027*** | −0.011*** |
|  | (0.000) | (0.002) | (0.001) |
| Age-squared | 0.000*** | 0.000*** | −0.000*** |
|  | (0.000) | (0.000) | (0.000) |
| Female | 0.014*** | 0.033*** | −0.114*** |
|  | (0.003) | (0.010) | (0.004) |
| Married | −0.013 | −0.128*** | −0.036*** |
|  | (0.008) | (0.026) | (0.010) |
| Education dummies | yes | yes | yes |
| Country dummies | yes | yes | yes |
| Wave dummies | yes | yes | yes |
| Observations | 222,197 | 221,458 | 187,053 |
| R-squared | 0.141 | 0.179 | 0.221 |

Coefficients are reported with robust standard errors in brackets.
*Indicates significance at the 10% level.
**Indicates significance at the 5% level.
***Indicates significance at the 1% level.

at home contrary to an increase of about 74% in the US. Using the market cost of services, Italians more than double their market income (+121%) while Norwegians increase it by 80%. These results suggest that a market income measure tends to underestimate the well-being of strong family ties countries, given that home production is not included in this measure.

These considerations open the question of the relationship between the strength of family ties and alternative measures of well-being to which we now turn. Table 4.14 illustrates this relationship using measures of subjective happiness and self-reported health. The first question asks the respondent, on a scale from 1 to 4, whether "Taking all things together, would you say you are:" very happy (taking the value of 4), quite happy, not very happy, not at all happy (taking the value of 1)? The second question asks "All things considered, how satisfied are you with your life as a whole these days?" The answer goes from dissatisfied (taking the value of 1) to satisfied (taking the value of 10). The last question asks the respondent, "All in all, how would you describe your state of health these days?" Would you say it is very good (taking the value of 5), good, fair, poor, or very poor (taking the value of 1). The results in Table 4.14 clearly show that, all in all, although strong family ties can harm societies in a variety of ways, they can also have positive effects in an individual's life, as measured by happiness and self-reported measures of health. The magnitude of the effect is also sizeable: the beta coefficients of family ties on the three measures of well-being are equal to 0.08, 0.06, and 0.03 respectively (for a comparison, the impact of the highest level of education is equal to 0.09, 0.04, and 0.08).

How can one interpret these results? One interpretation could be that well-being depends essentially on the quality of social relationships and not only on individual income. From this perspective, if social relationships are particularly good among family members, we should expect a strong correlation between family ties and well-being. Second, these results on well-being may capture the effect of stress and harder work (reflected in higher per capita income) in environments with weaker family ties. Alesina and Ichino (2009) make this argument with explicit reference to Italy. In a sense, the strong family ties of this county may explain both its relative decline in a globalized world but also the relatively high life satisfaction (at least for now) of Italians.

## 4.9. CONCLUSION

We show that differences in family values have an impact on attitudes and outcomes that are relevant to explain differences in growth across countries and the quality of institutions. We study attitudes toward working women, the society, generalized morality, and civic engagement. Our findings confirm an idea first developed by political scientists and sociologists: trust in the family prevents the formation of generalized trust, which is at the core of many collective good outcomes, from political participation to the formation of institutions to economic development. This should not be taken of course as a "criticism" of the family as a fundamental institution of society but as an analysis of the effect of different family arrangements. Our analysis indeed shows that family ties are related to different measures of happiness, life satisfaction, and self-reported health.

## ACKNOWLEDGMENT

We thank Andrea Passalacqua for excellent research assistantship.

## REFERENCES

Acemoglu, D., Johnson, S., Robinson, J., 2001. The colonial origins of comparative development: an empirical investigation. American Economic Review 91, 1369–1401.
Acemoglu, D., Johnson, S., Robinson, J.A., 2005. Institutions as the fundamental cause of long-run economic growth. In: Aghion, Philippe, Durlauf, Stephen (Eds.), Handbook of Economic Growth. Elsevier BV, Amsterdam, pp. 385–472.
Akerlof, G., Kranton R., 2011. Identity Economics: How Our Identities Affect Our Work, Wages and Well-Being. Princeton University Press, Princeton, New Jersey.
Akerlof, G., Kranton, R., 2000. Economics and identity. Quarterly Journal of Economics 115, 715–753.
Alesina, A., La Ferrara, E., 2005. Ethnic diversity and economic performance. Journal of Economic Literature 43 (3), 762–800.
Alesina, A., Giuliano, P., 2010. The power of the family. Journal of Economic Growth 15, 93–125.
Alesina, A., Giuliano, P., 2011. Family ties and political participation. Journal of the European Economic Association 9 (5), 817–839.
Alesina, A., Ichino, A., 2009. L'Italia fatta in casa. Mondadori, Milano.

Alesina, A., Algan, Y., Cahuc, P., Giuliano, P., 2013. Family Values and the Regulation of Labor. Mimeo.

Alesina, A., Giuliano, P., Nunn, N., 2013b. On the origin of gender roles: Women and the plough, Quarterly Journal of Economics 128 (2), 469–530.

Algan, Y., Cahuc, P., 2007. The Roots of Low European Employment: Family Culture? NBER Macroeconomic Annual. MIT Press, Cambridge, MA.

Algan, Y., Cahuc, P., 2010. Inherited trust and growth. American Economic Review 100, 2060–2092.

Almond, G., Verba, S., 1963. The Civic Culture: Political Attitudes and Democracy in Five Nations. Princeton University Press.

Arrow, K., 1972. Gifts and exchanges. Philosophy and Public Affairs 1 (4), 343–362.

Banfield, E., 1958. The Moral Basis of a Backward Society. Free Press, New York.

Bentolila, S., Ichino, A., 2008. Unemployment and consumption near and far away from the Mediterranean. Journal of Population Economics 21, 255–280.

Bertrand, M., Schoar, A., 2006. The role of family in family firms. Journal of Economic Perspectives 20 (2), 73–96.

Boyd, R., Richerson, P.J., 1985. Culture and the Evolutionary Process. University of Chicago Press, London.

Castles, F., 1995. Welfare state development in Southern Europe. Western European Politics 18, 201–213.

Coleman, J.S., 1988. Social capital in the creation of human capital. American Journal of Sociology XCIV, S95–S120.

Coleman, J.S., 1990. Foundations of Social Theory. Harvard University Press, Cambridge, MA.

Durante, R., 2010. Risk, Cooperation and the Economic Origins of Social Trust: an Empirical Investigation, Science Po. Mimeo.

Duranton, G., Rodriguez-Pose, A., Sandall, R., 2009. Family types and the persistence of regional disparities in Europe. Economic Geography 85, 23–47.

Easterly, W., Levine, R., 1997. Africa's growth tragedy: Policies and ethnic divisions. Quarterly Journal of Economics 112 (4), 1203–1250.

Ermish, J., Gambetta, D., 2010. Do strong family ties inhibit trust? Journal of Economic Behavior and Organization 75, 365–376.

Esping-Andersen, G., 1999. Social Foundation of Post-Industrial Economies. Oxford University Press, Oxford.

Fernandez, R., Fogli, A., 2009. Culture: an empirical tnvestigation of beliefs, work and fertility. American Economic Journal: Macroeconomics 1 (1), 146–177.

Ferrera, M., 1996. The Southern model of welfare in social Europe. Journal of the European Social Policy 1, 17–37.

Fortin, N., 2005. Gender role attitudes and the labour market outcomes of women across OECD countries. Oxford Review of Economic Policy 21, 416–438.

Fukuyama, F., 1995. Trust: The Social Virtues and the Creation of Prosperity. Free Press, New York

Galasso, V., Profeta, P., 2012. When the State Mirrors the Family: the Design of Pension Systems. Bocconi University, Mimeo.

Gambetta, D. (Ed.), 1988. Trust: Making and Breaking Cooperative Relations. Blackwell.

Giavazzi, F., Schiantarelli, F., Serafinelli, M., forthcoming. Attitudes, policies and work. Journal of the European Economic Association.

Gigerenzer, G., 2007. Gut Feelings: the Intelligence of the Unconscious. Penguin Group, New York.

Giuliano, P., 2007. Living arrangements in Western Europe: does cultural origin matter? Journal of the European Economic Association 5 (5), 927–952.

Glaeser, E., La Porta, R., Lopez de Silanes, F., Shleifer, A., 2004. Do institutions cause growth. Journal of Economic Growth 9, 271–304.

Glaeser, E., Ponzetto, G., Shleifer, A., 2007. Why democracy need education? Journal of Economic Growth 12 (2), 77–99.

Gorodnichenko, Y., Roland, G., 2013. Culture, Institutions and the Wealth of Nations. UC Berkeley, Mimeo.

Greif, A., 1994. Cultural beliefs and the organization of society: a historical and theoretical reflection on collectivist and individualist societies. Journal of Political Economy 5 (102).

Greif, A., 2006a. Family structure, institutions, and growth: The origins and implications of western corporations. American Economic Review, 96 (2), 308–312.

Greif, A., 2006b. Institutions and the Path to the Modern Economy: Lessons from Medieval Trade. Cambridge University Press, Cambridge.

Greif, A., Tabellini, G., 2012. The Clan and the City: Sustaining Cooperation in China and Europe. Mimeo, Stanford.

Guiso, L., Sapienza, P., Zingales, L., 2006. Does culture affect economic outcomes? Journal of Economic Perspectives (Spring).

Guiso, L., Sapienza, P., Zingales, L., 2008. Long Term Persistence, NBER WP 14278.

Guiso, L., Sapienza, P., Zingales, L., 2010. Social capital as good culture. Journal of the European Economic Association 6 (2–3), 295–320.

Kanhneman, D., 2011. Thinking, Fast and Slow. Farrar, Straus and Giroux, New York.

Korpi, W., 2000. Faces of Inequality: Gender, Class and Patterns of Inequalities in Different Types of Welfare States. Social Politics 7, 127–191.

Laslett, P., 1983. Family and household as work group and kin group: Areas of traditional Europe compared. In: Wall R., Robin J. (Eds.), Family Forms in Historic Europe. Cambridge University Press, Cambridge, pp. 513–563.

Lipset, S.M., 1959. Some social requisites of democracy: economic development and political legitimacy. American Political Science Review 53, 69–105.

Murdock, P.M., 1949. Social Structure. Free Press, New York.

North, D., 1981. Structure and Change in Economic History. Norton, New York.

North, D.C., 1990. Institutions, Institutional Change and Economic Performance. Cambridge University Press, New York.

Persson, T., Tabellini, G., 2009. Democratic capital: the nexus of political and economic change. American Economic Journal: Macroeconomics 1 (2), 88–126.

Platteau, J.P., 2000. Institutions, Social Norms, and Economic Development. Academic Publishers and Routledge.

Putnam, R., Leonardi, R., Nanetti, R.Y., 1993. Making Democracy Work: Civic Traditions in Modern Italy. Princeton University Press.

Putnam, R., 2000. Bowling Alone: the Collapse and Revival of American Community. Simon and Schuster, New York, NY.

Reher D.S., 1998. Family ties in Western Europe: Persistent contrasts. Population and Development Review 24, 203–234.

Spolaore, E., Wacziarg, R., 2009. The diffusion of development. Quarterly Journal of Economics 124 (2), 469–529.

Tabellini, G., 2008. The scope of cooperation: values and incentives. Quarterly Journal of Economics 123 (3), 905–950.

Tabellini, G., 2010. Culture and institutions: economic development in the regions of Europe. Journal of the European Economic Association 8 (4), 677–716.

Todd, E., 1983. The Explanation of Ideology: Family Structures and Social Systems. Basic Blackwell, New York.

Todd, E., 1990. L'invention de l'Europe. Seuil, Paris.

Weber, Max, 1904. The Protestant Ethic and the Spirit of Capitalism. Scribner's Press, New York.

CHAPTER FIVE

# The Industrial Revolution

**Gregory Clark**
University of California, Davis, CA 95616, USA

## Abstract

The Industrial Revolution decisively changed economywide productivity growth rates. For successful economies, measured efficiency growth rates increased from close to zero to close to 1% per year in the blink of an eye, in terms of the long history of humanity, seemingly within 50 years of 1800 in England. Yet the Industrial Revolution has defied simple economic explanations or modeling. This paper seeks to set out the empirical parameters of the Industrial Revolution that any economic theory must encompass, and illustrate why this makes explaining the Industrial Revolution so difficult within the context of standard economic models and narratives.

## Keywords

Industrial revolution, Economic growth, Growth theory

## JEL Classification Codes

N13, O33, O43, O47

## 5.1. INTRODUCTION

The economic history of the world is surprisingly simple. It can be presented in one diagram, as in Figure 5.1 below. Before 1800, income per capita for all the societies we observe fluctuated. There were good and bad periods. But there was no upward trend. The great span of human history—from the arrival of anatomically modern man to Confucius, Plato, Aristotle, Michelangelo, Shakespeare, Beethoven, and all the way to Jane Austen—was lived in societies caught in the Malthusian trap. Jane Austen may write about refined conversation over tea served in China cups, but for the mass of people, as late as 1813, material conditions were no better than their ancestors of the African savannah. The Darcys were few, the poor plentiful.[1]

Around 1780 came the Industrial Revolution in England. Incomes per capita began a sustained growth in a favored group of countries around 1820. In the last 200 years, in the most fortunate countries, real incomes per capita rose 10–15-fold. The modern world was born. The Industrial Revolution thus represents the single great event of world economic history, the change between two fundamentally different economic systems.

---

[1] Clark (2007) extensively reviews the evidence for this assertion.

*Handbook of Economic Growth*, Volume 2A
ISSN 1574-0684, http://dx.doi.org/10.1016/B978-0-444-53538-2.00005-8

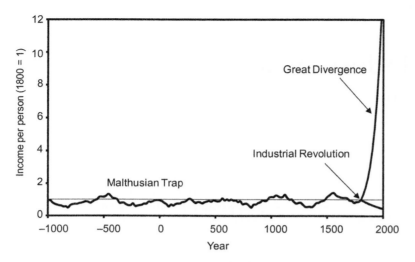

**Figure 5.1** A schematic history of world economic growth. *Source: Clark (2007), Figure 1.1, p. 2.*

The puzzle is why it occurred only around 1780, and why it occurred in a modest island nation on the northwest shores of the European continent.

At one level the transformation the Industrial Revolution represents is very simple. Beginning with the Industrial Revolution, successful modern economies experience steady rates of efficiency advance. Every year more output is produced per unit of input. At a proximate level, the growth of income per work-hour in modern societies can be represented as:

$$g_y = ag_k + g_A, \tag{5.1}$$

where $g_k$ is the rate of growth of capital per worker hour, $a$ is the share of capital payments in national income, and $g_A$ is the growth rate of efficiency. Since the Industrial Revolution, the capital stock has grown about as rapidly as output. Also, the share of capital in all earnings is about a quarter. Thus, only about a quarter of all modern growth in income per person comes directly from physical capital. The rest is an unattributed rise in the measured efficiency of the economy, year by year.

But while Equation (5.1) suggests that efficiency growth and physical capital accumulation are independent sources of growth, in practice, in market economies there has been a strong correlation between the two sources of growth. Economies with significant efficiency growth are also those with substantial growth rates of physical capital. Something links these two sources of growth.

Some economists, most notably Paul Romer, have theorized that this correlation stems from external benefits associated with physical capital accumulation (Romer, 1986, 1987, 1990). For this explanation to work, there would have to be $3 of external benefit accruing to physical capital investments for every $1 of private benefit. Most of the modern physical capital stock, however, is still mundane things such as houses, buildings, roads, water and sewer systems, and bridges. These types of investment do not seem to be associated with substantial external benefits. So if productivity advance is systematically associated also with the growth of the stock of such physical capital there must be another mechanism.

The most plausible one is that the association of physical capital accumulation with efficiency advance stems just from the effects of efficiency advance on increasing the marginal product of capital. In a world with relatively constant real interest rates since the Industrial Revolution, such a rising marginal product will induce more investment. And indeed if the economy is roughly Cobb-Douglas in its production structure, efficiency advances will induce a growth of the physical capital stock per person at a rate equal to the growth of output per person, so that the capital-output ratio is constant. This is roughly what we observe.

Thus, at a deeper level all modern growth seemingly stems from this unexplained rise in economic efficiency, as a product of a rise in knowledge about production processes. Somehow after 1780 investment in such knowledge increased, or enquiry became much more effective in creating innovation.

Before the Industrial Revolution we find no sign of any equivalent efficiency advances. This is true globally all the way from 10,000 BC to 1800, where we can measure the implied rate of productivity advance just from the rate of growth of population. In this long interval, average estimated rates of efficiency advance are 0.01% per year or less. We know this because we can assume before the Industrial Revolution, because of the Malthusian Trap, that output per person and capital per person was, in the long run, constant. In that case, any gains in efficiency will be absorbed by population growth according to the formula:

$$g_A = cg_N. \tag{5.2}^2$$

We can thus approximate efficiency growth rates from population growth rates if we look at sufficiently long intervals. Table 5.1 shows these calculations at a world level. Implied rates of technological advance are always extremely slow.

But it is also true that implied rates of technological advance are also slow for those economies where we can measure actual efficiency levels before 1800 through measurements of the real payments to factors. Figure 5.2 shows the implied efficiency in England 1250–2000. As can be seen, there is, surprisingly, in England no sign of any significant improvement in the efficiency of the economy all the way from 1250 to 1800. Only around 1800 does the modern age of steady efficiency advance appear. Before that, the measured efficiency of the economy fluctuated, peaking around 1450, but with almost no upward trend.

---

[2] For a more detailed explanation see Clark (2007, 379–82).

**Table 5.1** Population and technological advance at the world level, 130,000 BC to 1800

| Year | Population (millions) | Population growth rate (%) | Technology growth rate (%) |
| --- | --- | --- | --- |
| 130,000 BC | 0.1 | — | — |
| 10,000 BC | 7 | 0.004 | 0.001 |
| 1 AD | 300 | 0.038 | 0.009 |
| 1000 AD | 310 | 0.003 | 0.001 |
| 1250 AD | 400 | 0.102 | 0.025 |
| 1500 AD | 490 | 0.081 | 0.020 |
| 1750 AD | 770 | 0.181 | 0.045 |

*Source*: Clark (2007), Table 7.1.

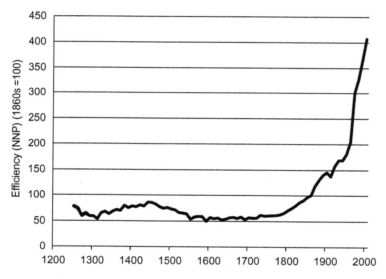

**Figure 5.2** Estimated efficiency of the English economy, 1250–2000. *Source: Clark (2010).*

The Industrial Revolution thus seems to represent a singularity. A unique break in world history. But also an event where we know clearly what we have to explain. Why did the rate of expansion of knowledge about production efficiency increase so dramatically in England around 1800? Figure 5.3 shows that the upturn in productivity growth rates can be located to the 1780s/1790s. That upturn is preceded by seven decades in which the average annual productivity growth rate was a mere 0.14% per year. Fast by the standards of the pre-industrial world, but glacially slow in modern terms. Overall productivity growth rates 1780–1789 to 1860–1869, averaged 0.58% per year, about half way to fully modern levels.

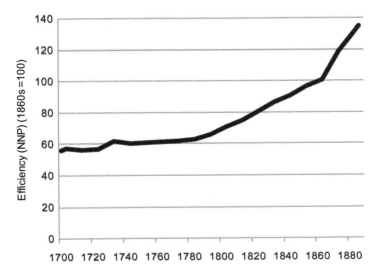

**Figure 5.3** Efficiency levels, England, 1700–1880. *Source: Clark (2010).*

We also know what sectors contributed most of the productivity advance 1780–1789 to 1860–1869. National productivity growth will be related to productivity advance in individual sectors through the equation:

$$g_A = \sum \theta_j g_{Aj}, \tag{5.3}$$

where $g_{Aj}$ is the growth rate of productivity by sector, and $\theta_j$ is the share of $j$ in total value added in the economy. These results are shown in Table 5.2.

Textiles contributed nearly half, 43%, of all measured productivity advance. Improvements in transport, mainly the introduction of the railway, were the next biggest source of advance, contributing 20%. Agriculture, ironically, contributed almost 20% also. Coal and

**Table 5.2** Sources of industrial revolution efficiency advance, 1780s–1860s

| Sector | Efficiency growth rate (%) | Share of value added | Contribution to national efficiency growth rate (% per year) |
|---|---|---|---|
| All textiles | 2.3 | 0.11 | 0.25 |
| Iron and steel | 1.8 | 0.01 | 0.02 |
| Coal mining | 0.2 | 0.02 | 0.00 |
| Transport | 1.5 | 0.08 | 0.12 |
| Agriculture | 0.4 | 0.30 | 0.11 |
| Identified advance | – | 0.51 | 0.49 |
| Whole economy | – | 1.00 | 0.58 |

*Source*: Clark (2007), Table 12.1.

iron and steel were in themselves minor contributions despite the fame of these sectors and their innovations in this period. Productivity growth in the half of the economy not covered in Table 5.2 was modest, less than 0.20% per year.

The decomposition in Table 5.2 established some things already. The Industrial Revolution has been thought of by some as essentially consisting of the arrival of the first of what have been called general purpose technologies, the steam engine. General purpose technologies, a rather nebulous concept, have been variously defined. They can be loosely thought of as innovations that have pervasive application throughout the economy, that go through a prolonged period of improvement, and that spawn further innovation in the sectors they are employed in.[3] Various GPTs have been identified, such as the introduction of steam power during the Industrial Revolution, and the introduction of electricity, and the recent IT revolution.

Steam power in England certainly touched a number of areas in the Industrial Revolution. It was important in coal mining, on the railroads, and in powering the new textile factories. The steam engine itself underwent a long process of improvement in thermal efficiency, and in the ratio of power to weight, from its first introduction by Thomas Newcomen in 1707–1712, to the 1880s. The earliest engines had a thermal efficiency as low as 0.5%, while those of the 1880s could achieve thermal efficiencies of 25%. The steam engine was associated also with the widespread use of fossil energy in the economy to replace wind, water, and animal power sources in transport, home heating, and manufacturing.

Table 5.2 suggests, however, that whatever role steam power played in economy-wide productivity advance after the 1860s, its role up to then in the new productivity advance of the Industrial Revolution was minor. Coal mining and iron and steel production contributed very little to Industrial Revolution productivity advance, and most of their productivity advance did not stem from the introduction of steam power.[4] Even in transport, a substantial part of the productivity advance is attributable to the improvement of the traditional road transport system, the introduction of canals, and improvements in sailing ships. The textile factories of the Industrial Revolution could, if necessary, have still been powered by water wheels even as late as the 1860s. Advances in textiles and agriculture explain the majority of the Industrial Revolution.

The diverse nature of productivity advance in this era makes the Industrial Revolution all the more puzzling. The revolution in textiles came through mechanical innovations that can be traced to a number of heroic individual innovators: John Kay, Richard Arkwright, James Hargreaves, Edmund Cartwright. But the improvements in agriculture stem from the advances of thousands of anonymous farmers in improving yields, mainly involving non-mechanical changes.

---

[3] Bresnahan and Trajtenberg (1996).
[4] Clark and Jacks (2007).

Another important element in the Industrial Revolution era is the unimportance of traditional investments in physical capital in explaining the growth of output per worker. Capital per worker rose no faster than output per worker, so that right from the onset of modern growth efficiency growth dominated.

Thus, any satisfying account of the Industrial Revolution has to do the following things. First explain why NO society before 1800—not ancient Babylon, Pharaonic Egypt, China through countless centuries, Classical Greece, Imperial Rome, Renaissance Tuscany, medieval Flanders, the Aztecs, Mogul India, the Dutch Republic—expanded the stock of knowledge by more than 10% a century. Then explain why, within 50 years of 1800, the rate of growth of knowledge rose to modern rates in one small country on the margins of Europe, Britain. Then we will understand the history of man.

## 5.2. THEORIES OF THE INDUSTRIAL REVOLUTION

The drama and the centrality of the Industrial Revolution has ensured that there is a steady supply of new or recycled theories of this great transition. These theories mostly fall into a number of discrete categories.

Bad equilibrium theories seek to explain the Malthusian stagnation as a product of a self-reinforcing system of poor economic incentives. The desires and rationalities of people in all human societies are essentially the same. The medieval peasant in Europe, the Indian coolly, the bushman of the veld, share a common set of aspirations, and a common ability to act to achieve those aspirations. What differs across societies, however, are the institutions that govern economic life. Thus

*In fact, most societies throughout history got "stuck" in an institutional matrix that did not evolve into the impersonal exchange essential to capturing the productivity gains that came from the specialization and division of labor that have produced the Wealth of Nations* (North, 1994, 364).

Thus, there is a caricature of the pre-industrial world that many economists intuitively hold, which is composed of a mixture of all the bad movies ever made about early societies. Vikings pour out of long ships to loot and pillage defenseless peasants and burn the libraries of monasteries. Mongol hordes flow out of the steppe on horseback to sack Chinese cities. Clerical fanatics burn at the stake those who dare to question arcane religious doctrines. Peasants groan under the heel of rapacious lords whose only activity is feasting and fighting. Aztec priests cut out the hearts from screaming, writhing victims with obsidian knives. In this brutal and chaotic world, who has the time, the energy, or the incentive, to develop new technology?

The advantage of a theory which relies on some exogenous shock to the economic system is that it can hopefully account for the seemingly sudden change in the growth rate of measured efficiency, around 1800. Institutions can change suddenly and dramatically—witness the French Revolution, the Russian Revolution, and the Iranian Revolution that overthrew the Shah.

These theories of an institutional shift in appropriability face two major difficulties, however, one conceptual, one empirical. The conceptual difficulty is that if modern economic growth can be produced by a simple institutional change, then why in all the varied and various societies that the world has seen since 10,000 BC and before was there none which stumbled upon the right set of institutions that made knowledge property? Societies varied markedly in what could be property and how property was transferred between owners. For example, in civil cases over possession of land in the legal system established by the Normans in medieval England after 1066, the party whose right to land was contested could elect to prove his or her title through armed combat with his opponent! This may seem a crazy way of settling property disputes to us, but the point is that societies have made all kinds of different choices about institutional forms. Why did some not stumble upon the right set of institutions? It seems that we cannot rely on chance here in institutional choice. There must be something that is keeping the institutions of the pre-industrial world in the "bad" state.

Thus, a slightly more sophisticated version of the "bad institutions" theory are those which seek to explain through the political economy of institutions why systematically early societies had institutions that discouraged economic growth (see, for example, Greif, 2006; North and Thomas, 1973; North and Weingast, 1989; North, 1994; Jones, 2002; Acemoglu et al. 2001, 2002; and Acemoglu and Robinson, 2012).

The common feature that Douglass North and other such institutionalists point to in early societies is that political power was not achieved by popular elections. In pre-industrial societies, as a generalization, the rulers ultimately rested their political position on the threat of violence. Indeed there is a close empirical association between democracy and economic growth. By the time England achieved its Industrial Revolution it was a constitutional democracy where the king was merely a figurehead. The USA, the leading nation in the world in economic terms since the 1870s, has always been a democracy also.[5]

For economic efficiency in any society property rules have to be chosen to create the maximum value of economic output. In such a case a disjuncture can arise between the property rules in the society that will maximize the total value of output, and the property rules that will maximize the output going to the ruling elite. Indeed, North and others have to argue that such a disjuncture systematically arises in all societies before 1800. This idea has been restated recently as the idea that economic growth is the replacement of extractive economic institutions, designed just to secure income for a ruling clique, with inclusive economic institutions, designed to maximize the output of societies as a whole (Acemoglu and Robinson, 2012).

One subset of such theories that has shown amazing persistence, despite its inability to account for the most basic facts of the Industrial Revolution, is that which links the Industrial Revolution to the earlier Glorious Revolution of 1688–1689. Thus the recent

---

[5] The recent rise of China is, however, an exception to the general association of growth and democracy.

widely read book by Acemoglu and Robinson, *Why Nations Fail*, has a chapter titled *How a political revolution in 1688 changed institutions in England and led to the Industrial Revolution.*

The Glorious Revolution established the modern political system of the UK, a system that has been continuously modified, but not fundamentally changed since then. The new political system created Parliament, the representative of the propertied classes in England in 1689, as the effective source of power in what is nominally a monarchy.

A basic problem with placing political developments at the heart of the Industrial Revolution is that changes in political regime before 1800 have no discernible impact on the efficiency level of the economy, even 80 years later. The Glorious Revolution had no discernible impact on economic efficiency before 1770, two or three generations after the institutional change, as Figure 5.4 shows. It is also clear in the figure that even the earlier political and military disruptions of the Civil War of 1642–1649, and the Interregnum of 1649–1660, were not associated with any decline in the efficiency of operation of the economy.

Further, there is no sign that private investors in England perceived a greater security of property even as a result of the Glorious Revolution. The return to private capital in the economy did not deviate from trend after 1689. Private investors seem to have looked at the political changes with indifference (Clark, 1996). The return to government debt did eventually decline significantly after 1689, and had fallen to modern levels by the 1750s. This decline was no doubt driven in part by the enhanced taxing power of the government after 1689. But almost all of the money raised from those taxes went to finance the British Navy in the long struggle with France that ended only with the

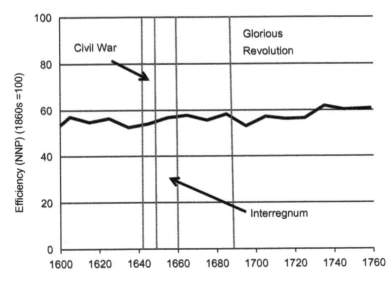

**Figure 5.4** Economic efficiency and political changes, England, 1600–1770. *Source: Clark (2010).*

defeat of Napoleon in 1815. Almost none of it went into the subsidization of innovation or education.

And we do see long before the Glorious Revolution or the Industrial Revolution societies that had stable representative political systems, the inclusive institutions of Acemoglu and Robinson, but little or no productivity advance. The Dutch Republic of 1588–1795 was one such regime.[6] Under the political arrangements of the Republic, the Netherlands experienced its Golden Age. Despite its modest size and lack of substantial domestic natural resources, it conquered a substantial colonial empire in the East, possessing for a while the premier navy in the world, dominating world trade in the 17th century. It developed sophisticated systems of banking and public finance, allowing substantial borrowing to develop a modernized transportation system internally, and support the most urbanized society in Europe. But because productivity advance stagnated in the Netherlands 1650–1795, these political and institutional achievements led to no sustained growth, and no break from the pre-industrial world.

From 1223 to 1797, Venice operated as a republic, with the government under control of a balance of popular and patrician representatives. Policy was geared toward the needs of a trading and commercial empire. Venice again developed an important trading empire in the eastern Mediterranean, with colonies and dependencies such as Dalmatia, Crete, and Cyprus. It also developed important manufacturing activities such as its glass industry. But again, none of this was reflected in the kind of sustained productivity advance seen in the Industrial Revolution.

Similarly, the free cities of the Hanseatic League were from the Middle Ages dominated by a politics that emphasized the needs of trade and commerce. Lübeck, for example, became a free city in 1226, and retained city state status until 1937. After gaining its freedom, Lübeck developed a system of rule and government called Lübeck Law that spread to many other Baltic cities of the Hanseatic League in the Middle Ages such as Hamburg, Kiel, Danzig, Rostock, and Memel. Under Lübeck Law, the city was governed by a council of 20 that appointed its own members from the merchant guilds and other town notables. It was thus government by the leaders of the commercial interests of the cities (Lindberg, 2009). Though not democracy, this was government by interests that should have fostered commerce and manufacturing. Under such rule the Hansa cities became rich and powerful, engaging in substantial manufacturing enterprises, such as shipbuilding and cloth production, as well as trade. But again, this was not associated with sustained technological advance.

It is true that the early societies that we know of in detail seem to have lacked the legal notion that you could own property in ideas or innovations. Thus, in both the Roman and Greek worlds when an author published a book there was no legal or practical way

---

[6] The Dutch Act of Abjuration of 1581 has been argued by some to be the precursor to the Declaration of Independence of the USA of 1776.

to stop the pirating of the text. Copies could be freely made by anyone who acquired a version of the manuscript (on papyrus rolls), and the copier could amend and alter the text at will. It was not uncommon for a text to be reissued under the name of a new "author".[7] It was common to condemn such pirating of works or ideas as immoral. But writings and inventions were just not viewed as *commodities* with a market value.[8]

While the ancients may have lacked them, there were systems of intellectual property rights in place, however, long before the Industrial Revolution. The earliest established foundations of a modern patent system were found in the 13th century in Venice. By the 15th century in Venice, true patents in the modern sense were regularly being awarded. Thus, in 1416, the Council of Venice gave a 50-year patent to a foreigner, Franciscus Petri from Rhodes, for a new type of fulling mill. By 1474, the Venetian patent law had been codified. There is also evidence of the awarding of patents in Florence in the 15th century. The Venetian innovation of granting property rights in knowledge, which was very important to the famous Venetian glass industry, spread to Belgium, the Netherlands, England, Germany, France, and Austria in the 16th century as a consequence of the movement of Italian glassworkers to these other countries. Therefore, by the 16th century all the major European countries, at least on an ad hoc basis, granted property rights in knowledge to innovators. They did this in order to attract skilled craftsmen with superior techniques to their lands. The spread of formal patent systems thus predates the Industrial Revolution by at least 350 years.

The claims of North and his associates for the superiority of the property rights protections afforded by the patent system in 18th century England thus stem from the way in which the system operated after the Glorious Revolution of 1688–1659 established the supremacy of Parliament over the King. Under the patent system introduced in the reign of Elizabeth I (1568–1603) the system was supervised by government ministers. Political interference led to the creation of spurious monopolies for techniques already developed, or the denial of legitimate claims. After the Glorious Revolution, Parliament sought to avoid this by devolving the supervision of patents to the courts. Generally the courts would allow any patent to be registered as long as no other party objected. No other major European country had a formal patent system as existed in England before 1791. But, as Figure 5.5 shows, while the Glorious Revolution produced a brief increase in patent rates, there was no sustained increase in patenting rates until the 1760s, 75 years after the Glorious Revolution.

There also existed other institutions in, for example, medieval European society, which we would think would promote innovation better than the modern patent system. Producers in many towns were organized into guilds which represented the interests of the

[7] This problem continued into at least the 17th century in England, where publishers quite freely pirated the works of authors.

[8] See Long (1991, pp. 853–7).

**Figure 5.5** Patents per year, England, 1660–1851. *Source: Mitchell (1988), p. 438.*

trade. These guilds were in a position to tax members to facilitate lump-sum payments to innovators to reveal productive new techniques to the members.

The empirical difficulty with the appropriability argument is the appallingly weak evidence that there was any great gain in the returns to innovators in England in the 1760s and later. The textile industry for example was at the forefront of technological change during the Industrial Revolution. Figure 5.6 shows TFP in the production of cotton cloth, taking cotton as a basic input. From 1770 to 1869, TFP rose about 22-fold.

Yet the gains of the textile innovators were modest in the extreme. The value of the cotton textile innovations alone by the 1860s, for example, was about £115 million in extra output per year. But a trivially small share of this value of extra output ever flowed to the innovators. Table 5.3, for example, shows the major innovators in cotton textiles and the gains accruing to the innovators through the patent system or other means. Patents mostly provided poor protection, the major gains to innovators coming through appeals post hoc to public beneficence through Parliament. Also, the patent system shows none of the alleged separation from political interference. The reason for this is that Parliament could, on grounds of the public good, extend patents beyond the statutory 17 years to adequately reward those who made significant innovations. James Watt was the beneficiary of such a grant. But such grants depended on social and political protection just as much as in the old days.

The profit rates of major firms in the industry also provide good evidence that most of the innovation in the textile industry was quickly leaking from the innovators to other producers with no rewards to the innovators. Knick Harley has reconstructed the profit rates being made by some of the more successful cotton spinning and weaving firms in

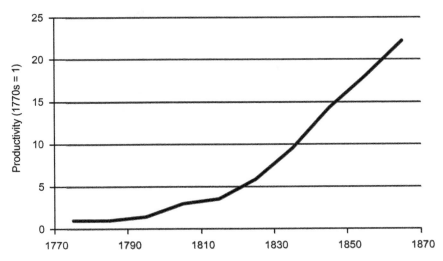

**Figure 5.6** Cotton spinning and weaving productivity, 1770–1869. *Note:* The years 1862–1865 were omitted because of the disruption of the cotton famine. *Sources: Cotton cloth prices, Harley (1998). Labor costs, return on capital, Clark (2010).*

the early Industrial Revolution period (Harley, 2010). The cotton spinners Samuel Greg and Partners earned an average profit from 1796 to 1815 of 11.4% per year, just the normal commercial return for a risky venture such as manufacturing. Given the rapid improvements in cotton spinning productivity going on in the industry in these years it suggests that whatever innovations were being introduced were spreading from one firm to another very quickly. Otherwise leading firms such as Samuel Greg would have made large profits compared to their competitors. Similarly, the firm of William Grey and Partners made less than 2% per year from 1801 to 1810, a negative economic profit rate. The innovations in the cotton spinning industry seem to have mainly caused prices to fall, leaving little excess profits for the firms that were innovating. Thus, a third firm, Richard Hornby and Partners, in the years 1777 to 1809 was in a sector of the industry, hand loom weaving, which had not yet been transformed by any technological advance. Yet, its average profit rate was 11.4%, as high as Samuel Greg in the innovating part of the industry. The conclusion is that the host of innovations in cotton textiles does not seem to have particularly rewarded the innovators. Only a few such as Arkwright and the Peels became noticeably wealthy. Of the 379 people probated in 1860–1869 in Britain who left estates of £0.5 million or more, only 17 (or 4%) were in the textile industry, even though, as noted from 1760–1769 to 1860–1869, this one sector generated nearly half the productivity growth in the economy (Rubinstein, 1981, 60–7). The Industrial Revolution economy was spectacularly bad at rewarding innovation. Its innovators captured little of the rewards. The Industrial Revolution did not make paupers into princes. This is why

**Table 5.3** The gains from innovation in textiles in the Industrial Revolution

| Innovator | Device | Result |
|---|---|---|
| John Kay | Flying Shuttle, 1733 | Impoverished by litigation to enforce patent. House destroyed by machine breakers in 1753. Died in poverty in France. |
| James Hargreaves | Spinning Jenny, 1769 | Patent denied. Forced to flee by machine breakers in 1768. Died in workhouse in 1777. |
| Richard Arkwright | Water Frame, 1769 | Worth £0.5 million at death in 1792. By 1781, other manufacturers refused to honor patents. Made most of his money after 1781. |
| Samuel Crompton | Mule, 1779 | No attempt to patent. Grant of £500 from manufacturers in the 1790s. Granted £5000 by Parliament in 1811. |
| Reverend Edmund Cartwright | Power Loom, 1785 | Patent worthless. Factory destroyed by machine breakers. Granted £10,000 by Parliament in 1809. |
| Eli Whitney (USA) | Cotton Gin, 1793 | Patent worthless. Later made money as a government arms contractor. |
| Richard Roberts | Self-Acting Mule, 1830 | Patent revenues barely covered development costs. Died in poverty in 1864. |

*Source*: Clark (2007), Table 12.2

Britain has few foundations to rival the great private philanthropies and universities of the USA.

A similar tale can be told for the other great nexus of innovation in Industrial-Revolution England: coal mining; iron and steel; and railroads. Coal output, for example, exploded in England in the Industrial Revolution era. This coal heated homes, made ore into iron, and powered railway locomotives. Yet there were no equivalents of the great fortunes made in oil, railways, and steel, in America's late 19th century industrialization. The coal fields in the northeast yielded modest mineral rents to the owners throughout the years 1700 to 1870. Coal rents were typically 10% or less of the value of coal at the pithead, and 5% or less of the retail price of coal to the consumer in places like London throughout these years (Clark and Jacks, 2007, 48). The operators of the pits again seem to have generated modest results on their investments in shafts, underground roads, and winding gear. The technological gains which made an enormous expansion of coal output possible, such as the steam engine, seem to have been relatively modest. These new techniques, which allowed access to ever deeper coal seems, were available to all coal mines in areas like the northeast coalfield, without any return to the pioneers.

The new industrial priesthood, the engineers who developed the English coalfields, railways, and canals, made prosperous but typically moderate livings. Though their names survive—Richard Trevithick; George and Robert Stevenson; Humphrey Davy—they again captured very little of the social rewards for their enterprise. Richard Trevithick, the pioneer of locomotives, died a pauper in 1833. George Stevenson, whose famous locomotive, the *Rocket*, in a trial in 1829 ran loaded at 15 miles an hour, an unheard of speed for land travel in this era, did much better; but his country house in Chesterfield was, however, a pittance compared to his substantial contributions to railway engineering. But other locomotives competed in the famous trial, and soon a swarm of locomotive builders were supplying the railway network.

Innovation during the Industrial Revolution era typically benefited consumers in the form of lower prices. As coal output exploded, real prices to consumers steadily declined: the real price in the 1700s was 60% greater than in the 1860s. Coal, iron and steel; and rail carriage all remained highly competitive in England in the Industrial Revolution era. The patent system offered little protection to most of the innovations in these sectors, and innovations quickly leaked from one producer to another.

The rise in innovation rates in Industrial Revolution England was not induced by unusual rewards for innovation, but by a greater supply of innovation at still modest rates of reward. The institutionalist perspective is that the rewards offered by the market shifted upwards compared to all previous pre-industrial economies. There is no evidence of any such change. The last significant reform of the patent system was in 1689, more than 100 years before efficiency gains became common. And the patent system itself played little role for most innovation in Industrial Revolution England.

Instead the upsurge in innovation in the Industrial Revolution period reflected a surge in supply. With the benefits to innovation no greater than in earlier economies, the supply still rose substantially. Facing the same challenges and incentives as in other economies British producers were more likely to attempt novel methods of production.

Productivity growth in cotton textiles in England from 1770 to 1870, for example, far exceeded that in any other industry. But the competitive nature of the industry, and the inability of the patent system to protect most technological advances, kept profits low. Cotton goods were homogenous. Yarn and cloth sold in wholesale markets where quality differences were readily perceptible to buyers. The efficient scale of cotton spinning and weaving mills was always small relative to the market. New entrants abounded. By 1900, Britain had about 2000 firms in the industry. Firms learned improved technique from innovating firms through hiring away their skilled workers. The machine designers learned improved techniques from the operating firms. The entire industry—the capital goods makers and the product producers—over time, clustered more and more tightly in the Manchester area. By 1900, 40% of the entire world output of cotton goods was produced within 30 miles of Manchester. The main beneficiaries of this technological advance were the consumers of textiles all across the world, and the owners of land in the cluster of textile towns that went from being largely worthless agricultural land to valuable building sites.

The greatest of the Industrial Revolution cotton magnates, Richard Arkwright, is estimated to have left £0.5 million when he died in 1792.[9] His son, also Richard Arkwright, inherited his father's spinning mills. But though his son had managed his own mills and had much experience in the industry which was still showing rapid productivity growth, he soon sold most of his father's mills, preferring to invest in land and government bonds. By 1814, he owned £0.5 million in government bonds alone. He prospered mainly on government bonds and real estate, leaving £3.25 million when he died in 1843 despite sinking much money into a palatial country house for his family.[10] But Arkwright Senior accumulated less wealth than Josiah Wedgwood, who left £0.6 million in 1795, even though Wedgwood operated in the pottery sector, which enjoyed far less technological progress (pottery was still handmade, by and large, even in the late 19th century).

Though the first great innovations of the Industrial Revolution era did not offer much in the way of supernormal profits because of the competitive nature of the industry, the second, railroads, seemed to offer more possibilities. Railways are a technology with inherent economies of scale. At the very minimum, one line has to be built between two cities, and once it is built a competitor has to enter with the minimum of a complete other line. Since most city pairs could not profitably support multiple links, exclusion, and hence profits, thus seemed possible.

The success of the Liverpool–Manchester line in 1830 (by the 1840s equity shares on this line were selling for twice their par value) inspired a long period of investment in railways. Figure 5.7 shows the rapid growth of the railway network in England from 1825 to 1869, by which time more than 12,000 miles of track had been laid across the tiny area of England. This investment and construction was so frenetic that so-called railway manias struck in 1839 and 1846.

But again the rush to enter quickly drove down profit rates to very modest levels, as Table 5.4 shows. Real returns, the return on the capital actually invested, by the 1860s were no greater than for very safe investments in government bonds or agricultural land. While railway lines had local monopolies, they ended up in constant competition with each other through roundabout routes.

Therefore, while, for example, the Great Western may have controlled the direct line from London to Manchester, freight and passengers could cross over through other companies to link up with the East Coast route to London. Again, profits inspired imitation which could not be excluded and the profit was squeezed out of the system. Consumers were again the main beneficiaries.

---

[9]  Fitton (1989, p. 219).
[10]  Ibid (p. 296).

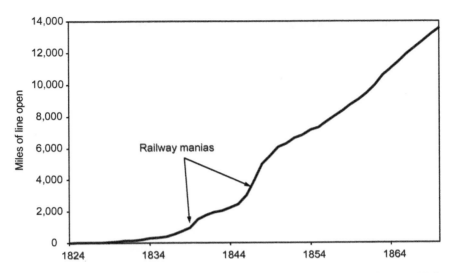

**Figure 5.7** English railroad construction, 1825–1869. *Source: Mitchell and Deane (1971, p. 225).*

**Table 5.4** Profit rates on the capital invested in British-owned railways, 1860–1912

| Period | Rate of return, UK (%) | Rate of return, British Empire (%) | Rate of return, foreign lines (%) |
|--------|------------------------|------------------------------------|-----------------------------------|
| 1860–9 | 3.8 | – | 4.7 |
| 1870–9 | 3.2 | – | 8.0 |
| 1880–9 | 3.3 | 1.4 | 7.7 |
| 1890–9 | 3.0 | 2.5 | 4.9 |
| 1900–9 | 2.6 | 1.6 | 4.4 |
| 1910–13 | 2.6 | 3.1 | 6.6 |

*Source:* Clark (2007), Table 14.7.

It is for this reason that in Britain, unlike in the USA, there are very few universities and major charities funded by private donors.[11] The Industrial Revolution did not result in great individual or family fortunes in England. By the 1860s, the rich were still by and large the descendants of the landed aristocracy. Of 379 men dying between 1860 and 1879 in Britain, who left at least £0.5 million, 256 (68%) owed their wealth to inherited land. As noted above, only 17 (4%) were textile magnates, despite textiles being the driving industry in Industrial Revolution productivity advance.[12]

[11] The industrialization of the United States created much greater private and family fortunes.
[12] Rubinstein (1981, pp. 60–7).

The unsatisfactoriness of conventional institutional accounts—which emphasize returns to innovation and to investment in general—has led to exploration of other avenues by which institutions may matter. Avner Greif, Murat Iyigun, and Diego Sasson wrote a recent paper which argues that the Industrial Revolution was underpinned by English welfare institutions, dating to the early 16th century, which insured against failure (Greif et al. 2012). It was not the size of the rewards on the upside that distinguished England from other societies such as China, but the cushion against failure for those who tried and did not succeed. James Hargreaves, inventor of the spinning jenny, may have died in the workhouse in 1777, but at least he did not die in the street. However, this is a bit like saying that New York has developed a high risk, high rewards financial sector because it allows for financial support for adults without minor dependents in a way not found, for example, in Texas. Presumably, the Harvard graduates in the financial sector have backup plans, other than general relief, if their hedge fund fails.

One thing that is striking about institutionalist explanations in general is the absence of any agreed metric for institutional quality. There is a belief in the physical sciences that a basic element in any scientific analysis of any phenomenon is to have a defined objective, and shared system of measurement. Institutionalists on this standard are still in the pre-science world of phlogiston and other early theories.

## 5.3. CHANGES IN PEOPLE

The modest signs of any increase in returns to innovation at the time of the Industrial Revolution suggest as an alternative that the transition was instead driven by changes in the aspirations and capabilities of economic agents. And this has been the theme for another set of explanations of the Industrial Revolution. In this extensive set of theories, a rise in human capital investment, and consequent improvement in the capabilities of economic actors, is key to the transition between the Malthusian regime and the modern (Becker et al. 1990; Lucas, 2002; Galor and Weil, 2000; Galor and Moav, 2002; Galor, 2011).

We certainly see that the English population on the eve of the Industrial Revolution had characteristics that differed from most pre-industrial societies. In particular, the levels of literacy and numeracy were high by the standards of the pre-industrial world. Even the great civilizations of the past, such as the Roman Empire, or the city states of the Italian Renaissance, had general levels of literacy and numeracy that were surprisingly low by the standards of Industrial Revolution England. And we know as a general feature that modern, high-income, fast-growth economies are distinguished by high levels of human capital. So increases in human capital that created knowledge externalities, at the gross level, would seemingly be a candidate source of the Industrial Revolution.

We find interesting evidence that the average numeracy and literacy of even rich people in most earlier economies was surprisingly poor. A prosperous landowner in Roman Egypt, Isidorus Aurelius, for example, variously declared his age in legal documents in a less than two-year span in 308–309 AD as 37, 40, 45, and 40. Clearly, Isidorus had no clear idea of his age. Other sources show he was illiterate (Duncan-Jones, 1990, p. 80). A lack of knowledge of their true age was widespread among the Roman upper classes as evidenced by age declarations made by their survivors on tombstones. In populations where ages are recorded accurately, 20% of the recorded ages will end in 5 or 10. We can thus construct a score variable $Z$, which measures the degree of "age heaping" where $Z = \frac{5}{4}(X - 20)$, and $X$ is the percentage of age declarations ending in 5 or 10 to measure the percentage of the population whose real age is unknown. This measure of the percentage of people who did not know their true age correlates moderately well in modern societies also with the degree of literacy.

Among those wealthy enough to be commemorated by an inscribed tombstone in the Roman Empire, typically half had unknown ages. Age awareness did correlate with social class within the Roman Empire. More than 80% of office holder's ages seem to have been known by their relatives. When we compare this with death records for modern Europe we find that by the eve of the Industrial Revolution age awareness in the general European population had increased markedly, as Table 5.5 shows.

We can also look at the development of age awareness by looking at censuses of the living, as in Table 5.6. Some of the earliest of these are for medieval Italy, including the famous Florentine *Catasto* of 1427. Even though Florence was then one of the richest cities of the world, and the center of the Renaissance, 32% of the city population did not know their age. In comparison, a census in 1790 of the small English borough of Corfe Castle in Dorset, with a mere 1239 inhabitants, most of them laborers, shows that all but 8% knew their age. In 1790, again awareness correlates with measures of social class, with universal knowledge among the higher status families, and lower age awareness among

**Table 5.5** Age heaping, Rome versus later Europe

|  | Social group | Sample size | Innumeracy rate |
|---|---|---|---|
| **Imperial Rome** | | | |
| Rome | All | 3708 | 48 |
| Italy outside Rome | All | 1395 | 43 |
| Italy outside Rome | Town Councilors | 75 | 15 |
| **Modern Europe, death records** | | | |
| Geneva, 1560–1600 | All | – | 54 |
| Geneva, 1601–1700 | All | – | 44 |
| Geneva, 1701–1800 | All | – | 23 |
| Liege, 1740 | All | – | 26 |
| Paris, c. 1750 | All | – | 15 |

*Source*: Duncan-Jones (1990, pp. 84–90).

**Table 5.6** Age heaping among living populations (23–62)

| Place | Date | Type of community | Sample size | Z |
|---|---|---|---|---|
| Town of Florence | 1427 | Urban | – | 32 |
| Florentine Territory | 1427 | Rural | – | 53 |
| Pistoia | 1427 | Urban | – | 42 |
| Pozzuoli | 1489 | Urban | – | 72 |
| Sorrento | 1561 | Urban | – | 67 |
| Corfe Castle, England | 1790 | Urban | 352 | 8 |
| Ardleigh, England | 1796 | Rural | 433 | 30 |
| Terling, England—Poor relief recipients | 1801 | Rural | 79 | 19 |

*Notes*: The total population of Corfe Castle was 1239, and of Ardleigh 1145.
*Source*: Duncan-Jones (1990). Terling, Essex Record Office D/P 299/12/3. Ardleigh, Essex Record Office, D/P 263/1/5.

the poor. But the poor of Corfe Castle or Terling in Essex had as much age awareness as office holders in the Roman Empire.

Another feature of the Roman tombstone age declarations is that ages seem to be greatly overstated for many adults. Thus, while we know that life expectancy in ancient Rome was probably in the order of 20–25 at birth, tombstones record people as dying at ages as high as 120. For North African tombstones, for example, 3% of the deceased are recorded as dying at age 100 or more.[13] Almost all of these 3% must have been 20–50 years younger than was recorded. Yet their descendants did not detect any implausibility in recording these fabulous ages. In contrast, the Corfe Castle census records a highest age of 90, well within the range of possibilities given life expectancy in rural England in these years.

Therefore, another explanation for the Industrial Revolution is that while the incentives to innovate were not greater, the capabilities and aspirations of economic agents had improved. This raises two important issues. First, why did history move in a general direction toward increasing levels of literacy and numeracy? What internal dynamic drove this move? Second, was England sufficiently distinct from earlier societies in terms of the abilities of its economic agents to account for the transition to modern growth?

Figure 5.8 shows, for example, literacy rates, measured by a person's ability to sign his or her name, in England 1580–1920. Two things stand out: the first is that literacy rates for men rose substantially long before the Industrial Revolution. If mass literacy was the key to growth then seemingly the Industrial Revolution would have again appeared 100 years before the 1780s. The second is that dramatic increases in literacy rates are a phenomenon only of the late Industrial Revolution period, the years 1850–1900. Literacy in the Industrial Revolution period itself rose by modest amounts.

---

[13] Hopkins (1966, p. 249).

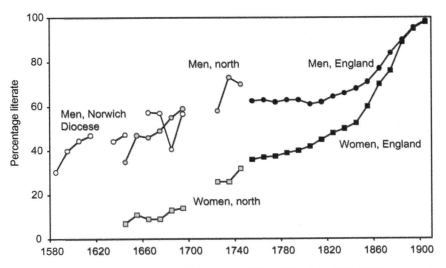

**Figure 5.8** Literacy in England, 1580–1920. *Sources: 1750s–1920s, Schofield, 1973, men and women who can sign marriage resisters. The north, 1630s–1740s, Houston (1982), witnesses who can sign court depositions. Norwich Diocese, 1580s–1690s, Cressy (1977), witnesses who can sign ecclesiastical court declarations. Source: Clark (2007), Figure 9.3, p. 179.*

Also, literacy rates in England in 1780 were not high by the standards of many other parts of northwest Europe. Literacy rates then exceeded those of England, in Scotland, the Netherlands, much of Germany, and in Scandinavia. But with those caveats we can ask what might have driven the trend all across northern Europe to greater levels of numeracy and literacy by the eve of the Industrial Revolution.

Another caveat about the role of numeracy and literacy is that given the observed rates of those returning to schooling, the increased investment in countries like England in the Industrial Revolution period can account little for faster productivity growth rates. Thus we can modify Equation (5.1) to allow for investment in human capital to:

$$g_y = a_k g_k + a_h g_h + g_A, \tag{5.4}$$

where $a_h$ is the share of income attributable to human capital investments and $g_h$ is the growth rate of the stock of human capital. But the growth rate of the human capital stock in England 1760–1860 implied by Figure 5.8 is very modest: less than 0.4% per year. And even if we allowed one third of all the 60% share of wage payments in income in Industrial Revolution England to be attributed to human capital, this would entail human capital investments increased income growth rates by a mere 0.08% per year. If human capital lies at the heart of the Industrial Revolution it must be because there are significant external benefits associated with human capital investments, as Lucas (1988), hypothesized.

Why then did education levels rise in the centuries leading up to the Industrial Revolution? A theme of many economic models of the transition from Malthusian stagnation to modern growth listed above is that there was a switch from quantity (or at least desired quantity) to quality, in families as we moved to the modern world. This theme has been driven by the observation in modern cross-sections, looking across countries, that high income, high education societies are those with few children per woman. Also within high income societies there was a period between 1890 and 1980 where again, lower income families were those with more children.

Such theories face a number of challenges in modeling the actual world of Industrial Revolution England. The first challenge is that these theories are expressed always in terms of children surviving to adulthood. In the modern world, in most societies, child survival rates are high, and so in practice, births and surviving children are closely equivalent. But in all known pre-industrial societies, including pre-industrial England, large numbers of children did not survive even to their first year. In these cases, the distinction between births and surviving children becomes important. Measured in terms of births, Malthusian societies witnessed high fertility, with the average woman surviving to age 50 giving birth to five children. But in such societies the average number of children surviving to adulthood was only two.

Further, since children who died in the pre-industrial world tended to do so fairly early, the numbers of children in any household at any time in the pre-industrial world would typically be three or less. For example, of 1000 children born in England in 1700–1724, nearly 200 would be dead within 6 months (Wrigley et al. 1997). Pre-industrial families would look similar to the families of America in the high growth 1950s and 1960s. Pre-industrial families thus faced remarkably similar trade-offs between the number and quality of children as do modern families. In some sense there has been no change in fertility from the pre-industrial to the modern world, measured in net as opposed to gross terms.

The second challenge these theories face is that in England the transition from high births per woman to lower levels of births per woman did not occur at the onset of the Industrial Revolution, but only 100 years later in the 1880s.[14] Fertility in England did not show any decline at the aggregate level prior to 1880. Indeed the opposite occurred, as Figure 5.9 illustrates. Births per woman, and also net fertility, rose precisely in the period of the Industrial Revolution in England.

The third challenge is that in cross-section in pre-industrial England there was a strong positive association between net fertility and the wealth or occupational status of families. Figure 5.10, for example, shows in twenty-year periods, the numbers of children alive at the time wills were made for married men in England marrying 1520–1879, where those leaving wills are divided into wealth terciles defined across the whole sample. The lowest tercile in wealth would still be men of above median wealth at death. Their implied net fertility is similar to that for men as a whole in England, as revealed by Figure 5.9.

---

[14] France was the only country to experience a decline in fertility starting in the late 18th century, and France of course lagged Britain in terms of the onset of modern growth.

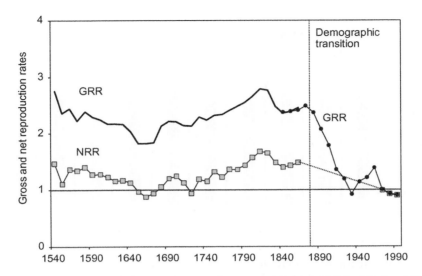

**Figure 5.9** The fertility history of England, 1540–2000. *Source: Clark (2007), Figure 14.6, p. 290.*

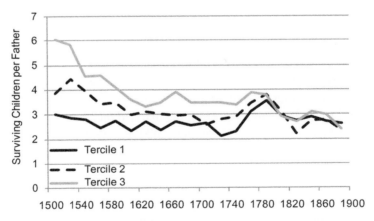

**Figure 5.10** Net fertility by wealth terciles, marriage cohorts, 1520–1879. *Source: Clark and Cummins (2013a).*

But the men of the top wealth tercile marrying before 1780 were leaving on average 3.5–4 surviving children. The most educated and economically successful men in pre-industrial England were those with the largest numbers of surviving offspring. Matching these men to parish records of births shows that this advantage in numbers of surviving children stems largely from the greater fertility of the wives of richer men. Their gross fertility was equivalently higher. This positive association of economic status and fertility

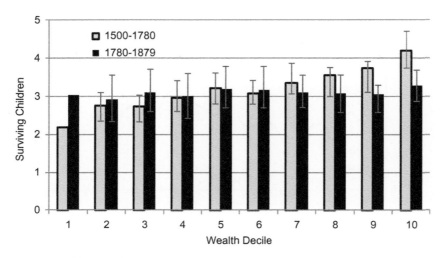

**Figure 5.11** Net marital fertility by wealth decile, marriages 1500–1779 and 1780–1879. *Note*: The lines at the top of the columns indicate the 95% confidence interval for the net fertility of these groups relative to the decile of lowest asset income. All assets normalized by the average wage in the year of death from Clark (2010). *Source: Clark and Cummins (2013a).*

pre-1780 has been confirmed in an independent study of gross fertility in parish records in England 1538–1837 by Boberg-Fazlic et al. (2011).

For marriages between 1780–1879, this pattern of high fertility by the rich and educated disappears. Instead, we have for most of the Industrial Revolution period, an interval where fertility is unlinked to education, status, or wealth. Figure 5.11 shows the dramatic shift in pattern this represents, grouping married men by wealth deciles. Another feature revealed in Figure 5.11 is that the pattern of higher net fertility with wealth before 1780 continues all through the wealth spectrum. There is no wealth level at which we observe any decline in net fertility.

The delay in the decline in aggregate fertility levels in England till after the Industrial Revolution represents a formidable challenge for theories that seek to explain the Industrial Revolution through a quality-quantity trade-off, and rising levels of human capital. However, these recent findings that richer families did indeed reduce their fertility just at the time of the onset of the Industrial Revolution offers some hope for models based on heterogenous agents as opposed to a single representative agent. But if richer families were changing their behaviors in response to economic signals, we would expect to find in this period signs of greater returns to human capital investments. Another problem for quality-quantity models of the Industrial Revolution is that such evidence is lacking. Figure 5.12, for example, shows the earnings of building craftsmen—carpenters, masons, bricklayers, plasterers, painters, plumbers, pavers, tilers, and thatchers—relative to unskilled building laborers and assistants. The skill premium is actually at its highest

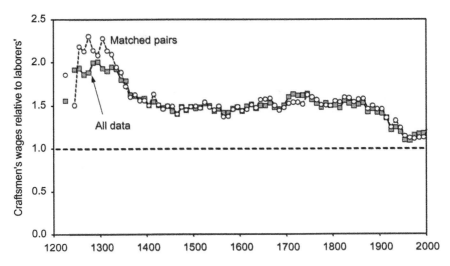

**Figure 5.12** The skill premium, building workers, England, 1220–2000. *Source: Clark (2005).*

in the interval 1220–2000 in the earliest years, before the onset of the Black Death in 1348, when a craftsman earned nearly double the wage of a laborer. If there was ever an incentive to accumulate skills it was during the early economy. Thereafter, it declines to a lower but relatively stable level from about 1370 until 1900, a period of over 400 years, before declining further in the 20th century. Thus, the time of the greatest market reward for skills and training was long before the Industrial Revolution. And the period of the demographic transition in England, the switch toward smaller family sizes circa 1880, is not associated with any rise in the skill premium.

The information on the skill premium in building may be criticized as showing only the returns to a very limited form of human capital. What about wider measures of the impact of quantity of children before and after the Industrial Revolution on child outcomes? Do we find that for marriages prior to 1780 there is little or no cost in terms of child outcomes where richer families have more children, but that after 1780 a quality-quantity trade-off becomes evident?

The same source that was used above to measure net fertility as a function of wealth and socio economic status, men's wills, can also be employed to measure the effects of the number of children on the outcomes for children before and during the Industrial Revolution (Clark and Cummins, 2013b).

In measuring the quality-quantity trade-off in the modern world the problem has been that "high quality" families tend to have fewer children. The observed relationship between quality and quantity may thus reveal no underlying causal relationship. In capturing the true quality-quantity trade-off, researchers have had to control for the inherent endogeneity of family size. We can thus portray parent influences on child "quality" as

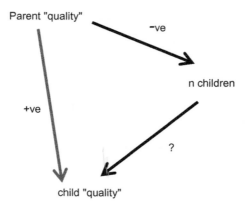

**Figure 5.13**  Parent influences on child quality.

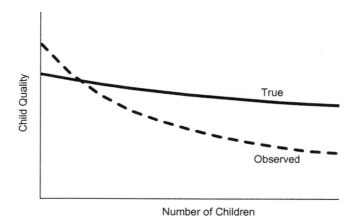

**Figure 5.14**  The true and observed quality-quantity trade-off.

following two potential routes, as in Figure 5.13. Since, in the modern world, high quality parents also tend to have smaller numbers of children, the observed negative correlation between $n$ and child quality may stem just from the positive correlation of parent and child quality. As Figure 5.14 shows, the estimate of the trade-off between quantity and quality will be too steep using just the observed relationship. Estimates of $\hat{\beta}$ in $\beta$ the regression

$$q = \beta n + u, \tag{5.5}$$

where $q$ is child quality, $n$ child numbers, and $u$ the error term, are biased toward the negative because of the correlation between $n$ and $u$.

To uncover the true relationship investigators have followed a number of strategies. The first is to look at exogenous variation in family size caused by the "accident" of twin births (e.g. Rosenzweig and Wolpin, 1980; Angrist et al. 2010; Li et al. 2008). In a world where the modal family size is 2, there are a number of families who accidentally end up with 3 children because their second birth is of twins. What happens to the quality of these children compared to those of two-children families? These studies find the uncontrolled relationship between quantity and quality decreases. Indeed, it is often insignificant and sometimes positive (Schultz, 2007, 20). For instance, Angrist et al. (2010), find "no evidence of a quality-quantity trade-off" for Israel using census data. Li et al. (2008), however, do report the expected relationship instrumenting using twins in China, but only in the Chinese countryside. But in China there are government policies designed to penalize couples who have more than the approved number of children, so we may not be observing anything about the free market quality/quantity trade-off.

In summary, there is a clear raw negative correlation in modern populations between child numbers and various measures of child quality. However, once instruments and other controls to deal with the endogeneity of child quality and quantity are included, the quality-quantity relationship becomes unclear. The quality-quantity trade-off so vital to most theoretical accounts of modern economic growth is, at best, unproven.

However, we see above that in the period 1540–1780 in England the modern negative relationship between child numbers and parent quality is reversed and is instead positive. Thus in this period in estimating $\beta$ in Equation (5.5) we will find that $\hat{\beta}$ is in this case biased instead toward 0. Figure 5.15 shows this effect. Any negative effects of quantity on quality found will be underestimated, as opposed to the bias in estimating $\beta$ in modern studies. Then there is the intermediate fertility regime in England, with marriages formed 1780–1880, where parent quality and numbers of children are uncorrelated, so that $\hat{\beta}$ will be unbiased.

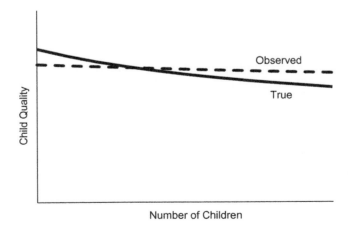

**Figure 5.15** The true and observed quality-quantity trade-off, marriages pre-1780.

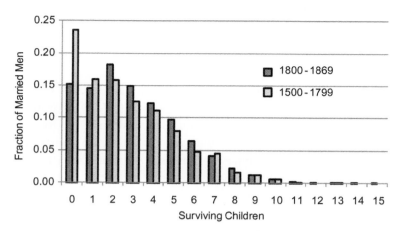

**Figure 5.16** The distribution of net family sizes in pre-industrial England. *Note:* Number of observations before 1800, 6940; after 1800, 1418. *Source: Clark and Cummins (2013b).*

The second advantage of the pre-industrial data from England for observing the quality-quantity trade-off, is the much greater variation in family sizes before 1870 than in the modern world, and the evidence that this variance was largely the product of chance, like modern twin births. Figure 5.16 shows the distribution of the number of surviving children per father, at the time of the father's will, for fathers marrying 1500–1799, and 1800–1869. This number will include children from more than one wife, where a first wife died and the husband remarried.

As noted above, we can measure family size in two ways. A second is the number of births per family, gross fertility. This is shown in Figure 5.17, giving the distribution of births per mother for the wives of men marrying in England 1500–1799, where the husband had only one wife. Thus, despite the average of five births per wife, in 10% of all marriages there was only one child born, in about 20%, only two. The number of baptisms is the overwhelming explanator of the number of surviving children per man. The $R^2$ of the regression predicting numbers of surviving children from the number baptized is 0.73. On average, 0.62 of each child born would be alive at the time of the will. If we include in this regression indicators for location, social status, wealth, and time period then the $R^2$ increases only marginally to 0.75. At the individual family-level both gross fertility, births, and net fertility, the number of surviving children, were largely random variables. Only a tiny fraction of the variation in each is explained by correlates such as wealth, occupation, literacy, and location.

When the coefficient $\beta$ in the equation:

$$q = \beta_n + u$$

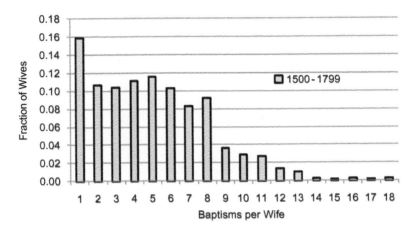

**Figure 5.17** The distribution of number of baptisms per wife, 1500–1799. *Note:* Number of observations before 1800, 818. *Source: Clark and Cummins (2013b).*

is estimated by OLS estimate of $\beta$ will be, in the limit,

$$\hat{\beta} = \beta + \frac{\text{cov}(n, u)}{\text{var}(n)}.$$

But in pre-industrial England, the degree of bias this will impart will be small because $n$ was largely a random variable, so the bias in estimating $\beta$ will be correspondingly very slight.

Thus, suppose $n = \theta u + e$. Then:

$$\frac{\text{cov}(n, u)}{\text{var}(n)} = \frac{\theta \text{var}(u)}{\theta^2 \text{var}(u) + \text{var}(e)}.$$

The greater is var($e$), the random component in $n$, then the less the bias in the estimate of $\beta$. We show below that for marriages formed before 1870, var($e$) was enormous relative to $\theta^2$var($u$). We can thus use the observed correlation between quality and quantity in this period as a measure of the true underlying causal connection between quantity and quality in the years before and during the Industrial Revolution.

We have three measures of child quality for sons born over the years 1500–1879: the wealth of those probated, the socioeconomic status of those probated, and the probate rates of all sons. The likelihood of a man being probated was strongly linked to their wealth and social status. Probate was only required if the estate of the deceased exceed a certain limit. In 1862, 65% of men of high socioeconomic status (professionals and gentlemen) were probated, compared to 2% of laborers (Clark and Cummins, 2013a).

**Table 5.7**  Social distribution among will makers, and father-son pairs

| Social group | *N* all wills | % all wills | *N* father-son | % father-son |
|---|---|---|---|---|
| Gentry/Independent | 405 | 7 | 220 | 15 |
| Merchants/Professionals | 506 | 9 | 167 | 11 |
| Farmers | 1906 | 33 | 605 | 41 |
| Traders | 883 | 15 | 152 | 10 |
| Craftsmen | 1132 | 19 | 217 | 15 |
| Husbandmen | 708 | 12 | 99 | 7 |
| Laborers/Servants | 268 | 5 | 16 | 1 |

*Source*: Clark and Cummins (2013b).

The sample of father-son pairings is very much biased toward the rich. As Table 5.7 shows, will makers in the years 1500–1920 were disproportionately from the upper social groups. In 1862, the bottom two social groups in the table were 40% of men dying, but they represent only 8% of fathers and sons where both were probated (Clark and Cummins, 2013a, Table A.12). In contrast, the top three social groups represented 13% of men dying in 1862, but a full 67% of those where both father and son were probated. Thus, what we are principally looking at here is the effects of family size on the outcomes for children of the upper third of the population in pre-industrial England. But this is the group whose behavior was changing first around 1780, then around 1880, in the two-stage demographic transition observed in Industrial Revolution England.

The effect of family size on wealth is estimated from the size of the coefficient $b_2$ in the expression:

$$\ln W_s = b_0 + b_1 \ln W_f + b_2 \ln N + b_3 \text{DFALIVE} + e, \tag{5.6}$$

where $N$ is the number of surviving children; $\ln W_s$ the average log wealth of sons of a given father; and DFALIVE the fraction of sons for whom the father was alive at the time of son's probate. DFALIVE is a control for the effects of sons who die before fathers, and are therefore likely to receive smaller transfers of wealth from fathers. Such sons will also tend to be younger. And in this data wealth rises monotonically with age until men are well past 60. Since some fathers had more than one probated son, we averaged wealth across the probated sons and treated each family as the unit of observation.

With this formulation, $b_3$ is the elasticity of a son's asset income as a function of the number of surviving children the father left. $N$ varies in the subsample of fathers and sons from 1 to 13. The coefficient $b_2$ shows the direct link between fathers' and sons' wealth, independent of the size of the fathers' family.

Table 5.8 shows the estimated coefficients from Equation (5.6) for fathers dying 1500–1920. The results are reported for the data pooled across all years, and for fathers dying 1500–1819 (who would have sons born up until 1800, typically), those dying 1820–1880,

**Table 5.8** Sons' wealth and family size

|  | All | Pre–1820 | 1820–1880 | 1880–1920 |
|---|---|---|---|---|
| LnWf | .502*** | .560*** | .527*** | .457*** |
|  | (.030) | (.051) | (.073) | (.046) |
| LnN | −.311*** | −.241*** | −.312 | −.390** |
|  | (.082) | (.090) | (.227) | (.176) |
| DFALIVE | −.868*** | −.710** | −.611 | −.866* |
|  | (.258) | (.314) | (.643) | (.448) |
| Constant | 2.032*** | 1.929*** | 2.024*** | 1.696*** |
|  | (.158) | (.210) | (.502) | (.341) |
| Obs | 1,029 | 610 | 175 | 244 |
| R-squared | .292 | .306 | .281 | .302 |

*Source*: Clark and Cummins (2013b).
Robust standard errors in parentheses.
*Significantly different from 0 at the 10% level.
**Significantly different from 0 at the 5% level.
***Significantly different from 0 at the 1% level.

and post–1880. The link between fathers' and sons' wealth as revealed by the estimate of $b_1$ is highly significant and stable across the subperiods.

The estimated coefficient on the log of surviving children is negative in all three periods, as would be implied by a quality-quantity trade-off. So this study is unusual in finding for the early period a quantitatively and statistically significant effect of family size on son outcomes. However, even though it will be potentially biased toward zero for fathers dying before 1820, the value in these earlier years is estimated as being similar to that in 1820–1880.[15] There is no indication in this data of a substantially more adverse quality-quantity trade-off with the arrival of the Industrial Revolution. There is nothing in the estimates of Table 5.8 to suggest that changing family sizes among the wealthy and educated in Industrial Revolution England were driven by a changing quality-quantity trade-off. Again the economic environment seems stable as the dramatic changes of the Industrial Revolution were occurring.

The predicted quantitative effects of sibling size on wealth at death are shown in Figure 5.18, where wealth at a family size of 1 fixed at 1. Pooling all the data, the effects of family size on the outcomes for children measured in terms of wealth are actually reasonably modest. Moving from a family of one child (with our data by definition a boy), to one of 10 children, reduces the average wealth of sons by only 51%. This is demonstrated visually in Figure 5.18.

This is not a very strong effect if the main transmission of wealth was through division of a fixed pie of wealth among children (the red line in Figure 5.18). For in that case

[15] The bias, as argued above, will be small before 1880 because of the randomness of family sizes.

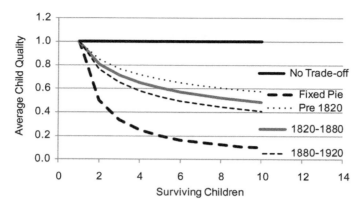

**Figure 5.18** The empirical Quality-Quantity effect, 1500–1920. *Source: Clark and Cummins (2013b).*

the expected coefficient on ln$N$ should be −1. The average wealth of the children of a family of 10 would be only 10% of that of a family with only one sibling. We can derive similar estimates of the effect of family size by period on the chances of being probated, and on occupational status. In each case, the effects are in the right direction, but even more modest than for wealth (Clark and Cummins, 2013a,b).

The facts above, regarding the transition from pre-industrial to modern fertility in England in the Industrial Revolution era, represent a formidable challenge to those trying to model the Industrial Revolution in a child quality-quantity framework. Since some of these patterns were discovered only in the last few years, such as the strong positive association of wealth and fertility in pre-industrial England, many of these models fail to capture essential features of the fertility transitions (Clark and Hamilton, 2006; Clark and Cummins, 2013a; Boberg-Fazlic et al. 2011).

Some of the theory papers mentioned above, such as that of Becker et al. (1990), fail at the first challenge. They posit a pre-industrial world that never existed of high net fertility and rapid population growth. And while they model a world with two equilibria—one where parents invest nothing in the human capital of their children, and the other where they invest considerable human capital—the escape from the zero human capital Malthusian trap is exogenous to the model. "Technological and other shocks" (Becker et al. 1990, p. S32) somehow raise the level of human capital far enough above zero to lead to a convergence to the high growth equilibrium. These shocks are conceived to be "improved methods to use coal; better rail and ocean transports; and decreased regulation of prices and foreign trade" (Becker et al. 1990, p. S33). But how such shocks get translated into human capital is never specified. With the arrival of highly paid unskilled work in textile factories during the Industrial Revolution, for example, we would expect, in the Becker, Murphy, and Tamura model, a reduction in educational investment.

Robert Lucas creates a Malthusian trap with many of the same characteristics of Becker, Murphy, and Tamura (Lucas, 2002), but which tries to model better pre-industrial fertility, measured as surviving children, so that it increases in income. In the low-level equilibrium there is again no human capital investment. This arises because Lucas specifies a land-using sector where human capital plays no role, and a "modern" sector where human capital enters with constant returns. Goods production is thus (simplifying slightly):

$$F(x, H, l) = \max_{\theta} \left[ x^{\alpha} \theta^{1-\alpha} + BH(l - \theta) \right], \tag{5.4}$$

where $x$ is land per person, $H$ is human capital per person, $l$ is the labor devoted to production, and $\theta$ is the labor devoted to the land-using sector. However, the assumption that there is a crucial difference in character between the farm sector and other areas of the economy is unsupportable both for the pre-industrial and for the modern eras. We see above in Table 5.2 that agriculture in England during the Industrial Revolution era experienced unusually fast productivity growth rates also. And agriculture had as much demand for skills and human capital as other sectors of the economy.[16]

In Lucas (2002), parents' utility depends on goods consumption, the number of children, and the utility of the children, but with the slightly different functional form:

$$V_t = c_t^{1-\beta} n_t^{\eta} V_{t+1}^{\beta}. \tag{5.5}$$

Human capital evolves according to:

$$H_{t+1} = H_t \varphi(h_t), \tag{5.6}$$

where $h$ is the labor invested in education. This means that in the Malthusian equilibrium there is no investment in human capital since $H$ starts as 0. Thus, all production is conducted using the land-using technology. Since there is a land constraint, now there will only be a constant output Malthusian equilibrium if $n = 1$, so that the population stabilizes. To ensure this, Lucas assumes that each child requires a fixed investment of goods, $k$. As population increases, so that output per person declines, the relative cost of children thus rises. Eventually, $n$ will be driven to 1.

In the contrasting endogenous growth regime, $H$ is large, so that nearly all output comes from the technology where there are constant returns to $H$. Consumption and

[16] Hansen and Prescott (2002), is another model which produces an industrial revolution by positing a difference between the farm and non-farm sectors. The inherent rate of productivity growth in the non-farm sector is assumed to be higher. This means that wherever the economy starts there will eventually be an industrial revolution. Why that industrial revolution does not occur in 1800 BC as opposed to 1800 AD is not explained. Also, productivity growth rates in the industrial sector in England in reality increased at the time of the Industrial Revolution. The Industrial Revolution was not the result of composition effects only. And, as noted, productivity growth rates in the farm sector also increased in the Industrial Revolution era, and since then, have been as rapid as those in the rest of the economy.

human capital grow at the same rate, and fertility and educational investment per child is constant. The number of children per parent chosen in this steady-state growth path will depend on the weights in the utility function for children $\eta$ versus their utilities $\beta$, and on the form of $\varphi(h)$.

But like Becker et al. (1990) Lucas gives no mechanism that gets the economy from the Malthusian trap to the sustained growth regime. Instead he has to assume that somehow enough human capital, $H$, accumulates for non-economic reasons to push the economy far enough from the Malthusian equilibrium for convergence on the modern growth regime to begin. The Industrial Revolution is again the *deus ex machina*.

We therefore see a very poor match between the elements that would seem to go into a human capital story of the Industrial Revolution—the Industrial Revolution itself, the average size of families, and the premium paid in the labor market for skills. If human capital is the key to the Industrial Revolution, the trigger for its expansion in pre-industrial England remains mysterious if we assume a universal set of preferences for all societies.

Endogenous growth theories such as those of Galor and Weil (2000) and Galor and Moav (2002), seek to avoid the need for some exogenous shock to trigger the switch to higher human capital investment and the consequent Industrial Revolution. This requires that some elements of the economy must be evolving endogenously within the pre-industrial era. Since incomes and consumption are predicted to be static within the Malthusian regime, it is not these. Instead, Galor and Weil (2000) rely on the accumulation of population in the pre-industrial era to drive up the rate of innovation and the return to human capital. In this they rely on an interesting paper by Michael Kremer which argues for population size as a driver of rates of productivity advance (Kremer, 1993).

Kremer assumes that the social institutions that provide the incentives to individuals to create knowledge are the same in all societies. Each person has a given probability of producing a new idea. In this case the growth rate of knowledge will be a function of the size of the community. The more people you are in contact with the more you get to benefit from the ideas of others. There was substantial but slow productivity growth in the world economy in the years before 1800, and that all got translated into a huge expansion of the world population, through the effects of Equation (5.2). That larger population produced more ideas and more rapid growth. Sheer scale is what produces modern economic growth.[17]

Kremer supports the argument with two sorts of evidence:

a. The first is population growth rates for the world as a whole in the pre-industrial era. World population growth rates are faster the greater the size of populations. That implies, since population growth rates and the rate of technological advance

---

[17] Diamond (1997) contains many of the same ideas, merged also with consideration of the role of geography in creating the community that benefits from knowledge expansion.

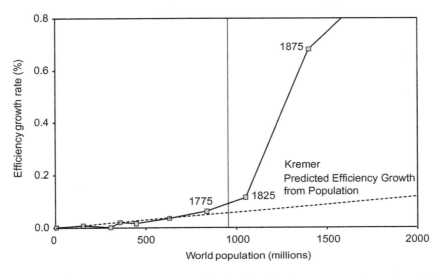

**Figure 5.19** Population and the rate of technological advance—actual versus predicted.

are proportionate, that productivity growth rates were speeding up over time as population grew. This is shown in Figure 5.19.

**b.** The second is population density, as an index of the level of technology in the pre-industrial world, for major isolated geographic areas—Eurasia, the Americas, and Australia—as a function of the land area. The prediction is that the smaller the land area, and hence the potential population, the lower will be the rate of technological advance. In this case, at any given time population density will depend on land area. This is found for the three cases examined.

One immediate implication of the Kremer argument, however, would be that *ceteris paribus*, the Industrial Revolution should have occurred in China. Chinese population in the pre-industrial world was large relative to that of Europe. Even as late at 1800 it has been estimated that China contained 260 million people, while Europe outside Russia had only 130 million, half as many as China. Thus Galor and Weil (2000) have no insight to offer on why the Industrial Revolution was British, as opposed to Chinese. It is a more general theory about the world transition to growth.

Interesting though Kremer's ideas are, no matter how much population is a driver of the rate of technological advance, population alone cannot produce a discontinuity in the rate of technological advance circa 1800, of the magnitude indicated in Figure 5.19. Therefore, a simple specification for the effect of population on changes in productivity would be:

$$\Delta A = \delta N, \tag{5.7}$$

where $A$ is now the stock of knowledge (the number of ideas). If every person has some chance of producing a new idea then the expansion of the idea stock will be at best, proportional to the population size.[18] This implies that the rate of growth of ideas (= productivity) will be:

$$g_A = \frac{\Delta A}{A} = \delta \frac{N}{A}. \tag{5.8}$$

But integrating Equation (5.2) above this is equivalent to the condition:

$$N = \theta A^{1/c}, \tag{5.9}$$

where $\theta$ is just a parameter. That is, the population size depends on the existing level of the technology. Substituting from (5.9) for $A$ in (5.8) gives:

$$g_A = cN \left( \frac{\theta}{N} \right)^c = c\theta N^{1-c}. \tag{5.10}$$

This formula implies that the rate of efficiency growth, $g_A$, rises less than proportionately with population. Yet, what we see in Figure 5.19 is that the rate of technological advance seems to rise faster than population growth. Figure 5.19 also shows the rate of technological advance predicted by this Kremer argument (the lowest curve). The increase of the rate of technological advance as we move to modern population sizes is just not fast enough to explain what we observe.

Technology growth rates would be more responsive to population if instead of (5.8) we posit:

$$\Delta A = \delta NA. \tag{5.11}$$

This says that the stock of ideas grows as a product of the number of people, and the existing stock of ideas (with again no duplication of ideas). This in turn implies that:

$$g_A = \frac{\Delta A}{A} = cN. \tag{5.12}$$

This predicted growth rate of technology as a function of population is also shown in Figure 5.19. Now the fit is closer before 1800, but there is still no close fit with modern productivity growth rates. At best, productivity growth rates would be proportionate to population under the Kremer assumptions.

This feature of the Kremer model, that it is hard to produce with an endogenous growth model, a discontinuity of the magnitude seemingly observed in the Industrial Revolution, is a general problem for all such endogenous growth models. Thus, the Galor and Weil endogenous growth model, which uses the Kremer population size driver as the

---

[18] Assuming that there is no duplication of ideas with a larger population, where the same thing is discovered by multiple people. In actual fact, we would expect that the gains in idea production would rise less than proportionately with population.

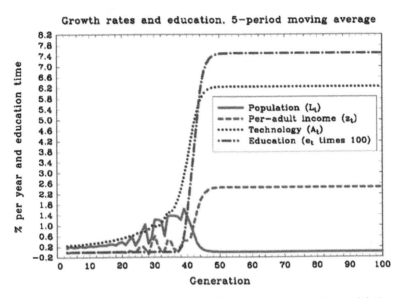

**Figure 5.20** Simulation of the Galor and Weil (2000) endogenous growth model. *Source: Lagerlöf (2006), Figure 5, p. 130.*

spark for the Industrial Revolution (and is described further below), has been simulated in Lagerlöf (2006). Figure 5.20 shows the outlines of that simulation, where time is measured on the horizontal axis in terms of generations. In the Galor-Weil model, there is a transition period between the Malthusian regime and modern growth in which technology advances more quickly, incomes rise above subsistence, and population expands. But this transition period here lasts 20 generations, which would be 500–600 years.[19]

But we do not see at the world level in 1200–1800 any signs of the income growth rates, or the population growth rates predicted in this simulation of the Galor-Weil model. Table 5.1, for example, shows that at the world level population growth rates remained in the range of 0.1–0.2% per year, far slower than Figure 5.20 implies. Clark (2007) shows that there is no sign on a world scale that incomes per person had risen above those of the hunter-gatherer era, despite the prediction of Figure 5.20 that by then, incomes per capita in the world would have risen to three times their Malthusian level by 1800. Also, at least in England, we see no sign of the abrupt rise in human capital coincident with declining fertility portrayed in Figure 5.20. Measurements of human capital, as in Figure 5.8, suggest a much more modest transition starting hundreds of years before the Industrial Revolution and continuing through it.

---

[19] Lagerlöf assumes a generation length of 20 years, but this is too short for any pre-industrial society, where 25–30 years would be more realistic.

Galor and Weil (2000), as noted above, marry the key idea of Kremer that the rate of technological progress depends on population size with the Beckerian human capital approach. They posit a utility function of the form:

$$V_t = c_t^{1-\gamma}(y_{t+1}n_t)^\gamma. \tag{5.13}$$

Utility now is a weighted average of the consumption of the parents and the aggregate potential income of their children, $y_{t+1}$, in the next period. While in the Lucas model children have a fixed cost in goods, in the Galor and Weil model they have a fixed cost only in time. That means that at low incomes, when time is cheap, people would have more children, as in the Becker et al. (1990) model, and we would not get a Malthusian steady state. To get a Malthusian equilibrium where income per capita is stable, the authors make an additional assumption that there is a minimum physical consumption level, $\tilde{c}$. This means that as long as potential income is below some level $\tilde{y}$, increases in income are associated with increases in fertility. As income falls low enough we must reach a state where there is surplus enough beyond $\tilde{c}$ to allow for 1 and only one child per family (treating families as having one parent).[20]

Potential income per worker is of the form:

$$y_t = A_t x_t^{1-\alpha}H_t^\alpha, \tag{5.14}$$

where $x$ is land per person, and $A$ is related to the efficiency of goods production. Now human capital is required even in the Malthusian equilibrium. $H$ evolves according to the time invested in educating each child, $h$, through a function of the form:

$$H_{t+1} = H(h_t, g_{At}), \tag{5.15}$$

where $H$ increases in $g_{At}$. The TFP variable $A$ evolves according to a function of the form:

$$g_{At} = g(h_t, N_t), \tag{5.16}$$

where $N_t$ is the total population size. Efficiency thus grows more rapidly in large economies with more time resources devoted to each child. And the growth of efficiency increases the human capital per child and the subsequent output per person. Galor and Weil (2000) at least try to preserve some distinction between human capital and the TFP of the economy, but it is not clear whether there is any real substance to the formal mathematical separation. There is no way, observationally, to distinguish

[20] A feature of these theoretical models is that the preferences specified over goods and children in all of them have no function other than allowing the modelers to get the desired outcome in terms of child numbers and human capital in a constrained maximization setting. They do not better explain the world, or offer further insight or predictions about fertility behavior. They are just ways of reproducing, in a desired mathematical format, observed behavior.

economies which have high output because TFP is high, or those that have high output because the human capital stock, as opposed to educational input stock, is large.

The functional form chosen for the utility function is such that the share of time devoted to raising children is always $\gamma$ once families have achieved the subsistence consumption. Thus there is a built-in trade-off between the quality and quantity of children. Any move to more education must be associated with lower fertility. Therefore, the authors build in an inverse U-shape to fertility as potential incomes rise—with an increase caused by the subsistence constraint on the lower end, and then a decline caused by the rising value of investment in education at higher potential incomes. Again, the utility function here does no real explanatory work. It captures an observed empirical regularity.

The system is constructed so that the amount of time invested in each child increases with the expected rate of technological progress, and the rate of technological progress increases with the time investment per child. At the Malthusian equilibrium the parents spend the minimum possible amount per child, and the only determinant of technological progress is the population size $N$. By the assumption that $g_A$ is positive, even without any educational investments, population grows in the Malthusian equilibrium, so that the steady-state potential income is maintained by the balance of declining land per person and increasing technological efficiency.

But as population increases, so does the base rate of technological progress, leading parents eventually to invest more than the minimum time in educating their children. At moderate population levels this creates a Malthusian regime with still the minimum consumption per person, but more children each getting some education and a faster rate of technological progress. Eventually population is sufficiently large so that education is productive enough that parents choose fewer high quality children, the population growth rates decline, and potential incomes begin a continuous increase.

Galor and Weil (2000) still face the fundamental problem of the earlier human capital models, however, in that what drives parents to invest more in education in the Industrial Revolution era is a rising perceived return to education. This, as we noted, we do not observe. Nor do we observe any more adverse trade-off between quantity and quality as we move from 1500 to 1920.

Galor and Moav (2002) employ many of the modeling elements of Galor and Weil (2000) except that the Kremer driver for the Industrial Revolution, technological progress being a positive function of population, is replaced. The new driver is a natural selection, either through genes or cultural transmission, of individuals of a certain type in the Malthusian era. Individuals of type $i$ are assumed to choose between consumption, the number of children, and the quality of the children according to a utility function of the form:

$$V_t^i = (c_t^i)^{1-\gamma} (n_t^i (H_{t+1}^i)^{\beta^i})^{\gamma}. \tag{5.16}$$

Now individuals care not about the potential income of their children, but the amount of human capital they possess. The weight individuals give the human capital of their children, indexed by $\beta^i$, thus varies with their type. High $\beta$ families thus produce children with more human capital and more earnings potential. There are assumed, for simplicity, to be just two types of individuals, high $\beta$ and low $\beta$. The potential earnings of each type, $y_t^i$, are a function of the land-labor ratio, $x$; the level of technology, $A$; and human capital, $H_t^i$, where:

$$y_t^i = A_t x_t^{1-\alpha}(H_t^i)^\alpha. \tag{5.17}$$

Now some of the return to education becomes externalized. Low $\beta$ types gain from the increases in $A$ generated by the investments of the high $\beta$ types. But the idea is still that once efficiency starts growing more quickly, a given amount of time spent on education produces more human capital. You get more for each year of education. Again this would seem to imply that the wage premium of skilled workers would have to rise in the Industrial Revolution era, which, as noted above, we do not observe.

Again in the Malthusian era, a minimum consumption level, $\tilde{c}$, binds and all gains in potential income go to child rearing. The "high quality" types choose to endow their children with more human capital, however; and this means that they have higher potential incomes in the following period, which results in their descendants having not only higher quality children, but also more children. Thus, the composition of the population changes in the Malthusian period toward individuals with the "high quality" values.[21] This rise in average education inputs increases the private return to education by speeding up the rate of technological advance inducing both high $\beta$ and low $\beta$ types to invest in more education and fewer children.

The Galor and Moav (2002) model does have one potentially useful feature, which is that the change in the composition of the population can proceed for generations in a Malthusian state where rates of population growth and levels of income remain low. It would be potentially consistent with the slow rise of education levels in Europe in the 300 years preceding the Industrial Revolution.

The Galor and Moav (2002) model therefore fits the positive association of fertility with wealth and socioeconomic status in pre-industrial England detailed above. However, if we were to elaborate the model to a large number of types we would see that English demography before 1800 is inconsistent with this model. For in Galor and Moav (2002), the positive relation between income and fertility will only be found at lower levels of income close to the consumption constraint, $\tilde{c}$. Once income gets high enough in the pre-industrial period we would see a negative connection between income and fertility, as in the modern era. The highest quality types would die out in the pre-industrial era along with the lowest quality types. Selection in Galor and Moav (2002) is for those whose quality type leads to income just modestly above the subsistence consumption constraint.

---

[21] Interestingly, the composition of the population in the post-Malthusian period switches back toward the "low quality" types since once potential income for even the low quality types passes a certain boundary they begin to have more children since they invest the same time as the high quality families in child rearing but invest less in each child.

Thus, while the empirical evidence is clear that for at least 500 years before the Industrial Revolution there was differential fertility in England toward those of higher socio economic status, there is no evidence that the selection was of the specific type posited in Galor and Moav (2002). In particular, the evidence is that the quality-quantity trade-off that is central to Galor and Moav (2002), while present, was relatively weak in all periods in England before 1920.

As with the other endogenous growth models, Galor and Moav (2002) would also imply a much slower transition between a world of slow technological advance and the modern era than is observed in practice in the total factor productivity data for England.

## 5.4. TECHNOLOGICAL CHANGE BEFORE THE INDUSTRIAL REVOLUTION

We have been following the traditional assumption, so far, represented by Figures 5.2 and 5.3, that the Industrial Revolution was a relatively abrupt transition to modern productivity growth rates, around 1780. As Figure 5.2 illustrates, for England as a whole, the efficiency of the economy showed no expansion during 1250–1780. The measured productivity growth rate before the Industrial Revolution is effectively 0. This, as discussed above, makes it seem dauntingly difficult to discern reasons for the transition to rapid economic growth. The underlying institutional, political, and social variables were changing slowly if at all in England in the years 1700–1870 when this transition was accomplished.

The conclusion, from the aggregate productivity level of the economy, that the transition to modern growth was rapid, does however, seem at variance with the general historical picture of England between 1200–1780 as a society that was, over time, advancing in education, in scientific knowledge, in technical abilities in navigation, in warfare, and in technical abilities in music, painting, sculpture, and architecture. England in 1780 was a very different place from England in 1250, even if the standard of living of the average consumer measured mainly in terms of their consumption of food, clothing, housing, heat, and lighting had changed little.

The reason for this mismatch is that, as noted above in Equation (5.3), national productivity growth will be related to productivity advance in individual sectors through:

$$g_A = \sum \theta_j g_{Aj}, \tag{5.3}$$

where $g_{Aj}$ is the growth rate of productivity by sector, and $\theta_j$ is the share of $j$ in total value added in the economy. National efficiency advance is measured by weighting gains by sector with the value of output in that sector. The effects of innovation on national productivity measures are thus crucially dependent on the pattern of consumption.

Much of the technological advance of the period 1250–1780 had minimal impact on measured productivity at the national level because the share of expenditure on these goods was so small in the pre-industrial economy. The printing press, for example, led to

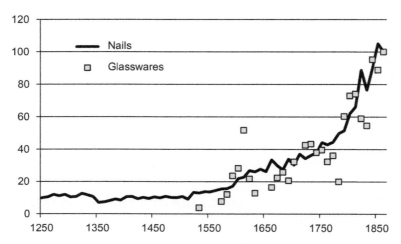

**Figure 5.21** Efficiency of production of nails and glassware, by decade, 1250–1869. *Source: Clark (2010).*

an approximately 25-fold increase in the production of written material between 1450 and 1600 in England. But since the share of income spent on printed materials in 1600 was only about 0.0005, the productivity gains from this innovation at the national level were miniscule (Clark and Levin, 2001).

We can see also in Figure 5.21 that the production of such manufactured items as iron nails and glassware saw significant productivity advances before 1780. But this efficiency advance would be a negligible contribution to national productivity advance because of the small share of total production value these goods represented in a pre-industrial England where iron nails had limited use, and glasswares were enjoyed only by the richest groups in the society.

Further, for many goods whose production was becoming more efficient through technological advances, no consistent series of prices can be calculated. There was, for example, a great advance in military technologies in European countries such as England over the years 1250–1780. The infantry of 1780, or a naval ship of that period, would have decimated the equivalent medieval force. English troops of 1780 would have quickly overwhelmed the fortifications of 1250, and the fortifications of 1780 would have been impregnable against medieval armies of major size. But none of this would be reflected in conventional productivity measures. There is no allowance in these measures for the delivery of more effective violence by the English Navy over the years.

There is no allowance also in the national productivity measure for improvements in the quality of literature, music, painting, and newspapers. These sources also do not reflect medical advances such as the one third reduction in maternal childbirth mortality between 1600 and 1750.[22]

---

[22] Wrigley et al. (1997, p. 313).

This makes it possible that the rate of technological advance in the economy, measured just as a count of innovations and new ideas, was actually increasing long before the breakthrough of the Industrial Revolution. But accidents of where these technological advances came in relation to mass consumer demand in the pre-industrial economy create the appearance of a technological discontinuity circa 1780. Suppose that prior to the Industrial Revolution innovations were occurring randomly across various sectors of the economy—innovations in areas such as guns, gunpowder, spectacles, window glass, books, clocks, painting, new building techniques, improvements in shipping and navigation—but that just by chance, all these innovations occurred in areas of small expenditure. Then the technological dynamism of the economy would not show up in terms of output per capita or in measured productivity in the years leading up to the Industrial Revolution.

To illustrate this, suppose we consider a consumer whose tastes were close to those of the modern university professor. Their consumption is much more heavily geared toward printed material, paper, spices, wine, sugar, manufactured goods, light, soap, and clothing than the average consumer in the pre-industrial English economy. Based on their consumption, how would the efficiency growth rate of the economy 1250–1769 look compared to 1760–1869, and 1860–2009? Figure 5.22 shows the results, where efficiency is measured as an index on a log scale on the vertical axis. Thus, the slope of the lines indicates the rate of efficiency growth, or efficiency decline, in each era. Now in the years 1300–1770 there is an estimated efficiency growth rate of 0.09% per year for the goods consumed by a university professor. This is followed by efficiency growth rates of 0.6%

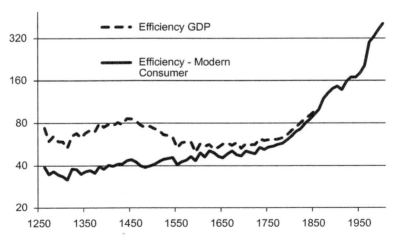

**Figure 5.22** Economic efficiency from the perspective of a modern consumer, England, 1250–2009. *Notes*: The weights in consumption for the modern consumer are assumed to be half from the consumption basket of the pre-industrial worker. But the other half is composed of books (.1), manufactured goods (.1), clothing (.1), sugar (.03), spices (.03), drink (.05), light (.05), soap (.02), and paper (.02). *Source: Clark (2010).*

per year 1760–1870, and 0.9% a year for 1860–2010. Estimated efficiency advance is still very slow for the pre-industrial period, but we can think of the economy in this period as going through a more protracted transition between pre-industrial growth rates and modern growth rates.

Framed in this way, the possibility reopens of some variety of endogenous growth explanation of the Industrial Revolution, with a more gradual transition to higher rates of technological advance starting in the medieval period or earlier. However, the existing endogenous growth models such as Galor and Weil (2000) and Galor and Moav (2002), bring with them a set of assumptions and implications which are difficult to reconcile with empirical reality, as we have discussed above. The key idea in Galor and Moav (2002), however, that in the Malthusian regime preferences might be changed by differential net fertility, does seem to offer some promise. We do see strong differences in fertility by social class in England all the way from 1250 to 1780. And there is evidence that parental characteristics in terms of wealth, occupation, and education were very strongly inherited in pre-industrial England, allowing differential fertility to have significant effects on the characteristics of the population even after relatively few generations.[23] While we do not see a sign in the data of the specific selection for a preference for small family sizes and high child quality, there is a sign of a more generalized selection for characteristics associated with economic success.

## 5.5. CONCLUSION

The Industrial Revolution remains one of histories great mysteries. We have seen in this survey that the attempts by economists to model this transition have been so far largely unsuccessful. The first approach emphasizing an exogenous switch in property rights stemming from political changes, despite its continuing popularity, fails in terms of the timing of political changes, and their observed effects on the incentives for innovation. The second approach, which looks for a shift between self-reinforcing equilibria, again fails because there is little sign of any major changes in the underlying parameters of the economy circa 1780 which would lead to changed behavior by individuals. The most promising class of models are those based on endogenous growth. The problem here is finding some kind of "driver" that is changing over time that will induce changes in the rate of innovation. Previously, these models seemed to face insuperable difficulties in that they find it very hard to model the kind of one-time upward shift in productivity growth rates that the Industrial Revolution seemed to involve. But as we gather more information on the empirics of the Industrial Revolution, and the years before, the discontinuity in technological innovation rates seems less than has been imagined, and the transition between

---

[23] As evidenced by the persistence of status of surnames in England 1300–2012, the correlation of underlying social status between fathers and sons seems always to have been of the order of 0.75, which is very high. See Clark et al. (2014).

the old world of zero productivity growth rates and the new world of rapid productivity growth seems much more gradual. This bodes well for endogenous growth models.

## REFERENCES

Acemoglu, Daron, Robinson, James A., Johnson, Simon, 2001. The colonial origins of comparative economic development: an empirical investigation. American Economic Review 91, 1369–1401.

Acemoglu, Daron, Robinson, James A., Johnson, Simon, 2002. Reversal of fortune: geography and institutions in the making of the modern world. Quarterly Journal of Economics 117, 1231–1294.

Acemoglu, Daron, Robinson, James A., 2012. Why Nations Fail: The Origins of Power, Prosperity, and Poverty. Crown Business, New York.

Angrist, Joshua, Lavy, Victor, Schlosser, Analia, 2010. Multiple experiments for the causal link between the quantity and quality of children. Journal of Labor Economics 28 (4), 773–824.

Becker, Gary, Murphy, Kevin, Tamura, Robert, 1990. Human capital, fertility and economic growth. Journal of Political Economy 98, S12–37.

Boberg-Fazlic, Nina, Sharp, Paul, Weisdorf, Jacob, 2011. Survival of the richest? Testing the Clark hypothesis using English pre-industrial data from family reconstitution records. European Review of Economic History 15 (3), 365–392.

Bresnahan, Timothy F., Trajtenberg, Manuel, 1996. General purpose technologies: engines of growth? Journal of Econometrics, Annals of Econometrics 65, 83–108.

Clark, Gregory, 1996. The political foundations of modern economic growth: England, 1540–1800. Journal of Interdisciplinary History 26 (4), 563–588.

Clark, Gregory, 2005. The condition of the working-class in England, 1209–2004. Journal of Political Economy 113 (6), 1307–1340.

Clark, Gregory, Hamilton, Gillian, 2006. Survival of the richest. The Malthusian mechanism in pre-industrial England. Journal of Economic History 66 (3), 707–736.

Clark, Gregory, Jacks, David, 2007. Coal and the industrial revolution, 1700–1869. European Review of Economic History 11 (1), 39–72.

Clark, Gregory, 2007. A Farewell to Alms: A Brief Economic History of the World. Princeton University Press, Princeton.

Clark, Gregory, 2010. The macroeconomic aggregates for England, 1209–2008. Research in Economic History 27, 51–140.

Clark, Gregory, Levin, Patricia. 2001. How Different Was the Industrial Revolution? The Revolution in Printing, Working Paper, University of California, Davis, pp. 1350–1869.

Clark, Gregory, Cummins, Neil et. al. 2014. The Son Also Rises: Surnames and the History of Social Mobility, Princeton University Press, Princeton.

Clark, Gregory, Cummins, Neil, 2013a. Malthus to Modernity: England's First Fertility Transition, 1500–1880. Working Paper, UC Davis.

Clark, Gregory, Cummins, Neil, 2013b. The Beckerian Family and the English Demographic Revolution of 1800. Working Paper, UC Davis.

Cressy, David, 1977. Levels of illiteracy in England, 1530–1730. Historical Journal 20, 1–23.

Diamond, Jared M., 1997. Guns, Germs, and Steel: The Fates of Human Societies. W.W. Norton, New York.

Duncan-Jones, Richard, 1990. Structure and Scale in the Roman Economy. Cambridge University Press, Cambridge.

Fitton, 1989. The Arkwrights: Spinners of Fortune. Manchester University Press, Manchester.

Galor, Oded, Weil, David N., 2000. Population, technology and growth: from Malthusian stagnation to the demographic transition and beyond. American Economic Review 90, 806–828.

Galor, Oded, Moav, Omer, 2002. Natural selection and the origin of economic growth. Quarterly Journal of Economics 117, 1133–1191.

Galor, Oded, 2011. Unified Growth Theory. Princeton University Press, Princeton.

Greif, Avner, 2006. Institutions and the Path to the Modern Economy: Lessons from Medieval Trade. Cambridge University Press, Cambridge.

Greif, Avner, Iyigun, Murat, Sasson, Diego L., 2012. Social Institutions and Economic Growth: Why England and Not China Became the First Modern Economy. Working Paper.

Hansen, G., Prescott, Edward C., 2002. Malthus to solow. American Economic Review 92 (4), 1205–1217.

Harley, Knick, 1998. Cotton textile prices and the industrial revolution. Economic History Review 51 (1), 49–83.

Harley, C. Knick, 2010. Prices and Profits in Cotton Textiles during the Industrial Revolution. University of Oxford Discussion Papers in Economic History, #81.

Hopkins, Keith, 1966. On the probable age structure of the Roman population. Population Studies 20 (2), 245–264.

Houston, R.A., 1982. The development of literacy: Northern England, 1640–1750. Economic History Review, New Series, 35 (2), 199–216.

Jones, Charles I., 2002. Introduction to Economic Growth, second ed. W.W. Norton, New York.

Kremer, Michael, 1993. Population growth and technological change: one million B.C. to 1990. Quarterly Journal of Economics 107, 681–716.

Lagerlöf, Nils-Petter, 2006. The Galor–Weil model revisited: a quantitative exercise. Review of Economic Dynamics 9 (1), 116–142.

Li, Hongbin, Zhang, Junsen, Zhu, Yi, 2008. The quantity-quality trade-off of children in a developing country: identification using Chinese twins. Demography 45 (1), 223–243.

Lindberg, Erik, 2009. Club goods and inefficient institutions: why Danzig and Lübeck failed in the early modern period. Economic History Review, New Series 62(3), 604–628.

Long, Pamela, 1991. Invention, authorship, intellectual property, and the origin of patents: notes towards a conceptual history. Technology and Culture 32, 846–884.

Lucas, Robert, 1988. On the mechanics of economic development. Journal of Monetary Economics 22, 3–42.

Lucas, Robert E., 2002. The industrial revolution: past and future. In: Lucas, Robert E. (Ed.), Lectures on Economic Growth. Harvard University Press, Cambridge.

Mitchell, Brian R., 1988. British Historical Statistics. Cambridge University Press, Cambridge.

Mitchell, Brian R., Deane, Phyllis, 1971. Abstract of British Historical Statistics. Cambridge University Press, Cambridge.

North, Douglass C., 1994. Economic performance through time. American Economic Review 84 (3), 359–368.

North, Douglass, Thomas, Robert P., 1973. The Rise of the Western World. Cambridge University Press, Cambridge.

North, Douglass, Weingast, Barry, 1989. Constitutions and commitment: evolution of institutions governing public choice in 17th century England. Journal of Economic History 49, 803–832.

Romer, Paul M., 1986. Increasing returns and long-run growth. Journal of Political Economy 94, 1002–1037.

Romer, Paul M. 1987. Crazy Explanations for the Productivity Slowdown. In: Fischer, Stanley (Ed.), NBER Macroeconomics Annual 1987, MIT Press, Cambridge, Mass.

Romer, Paul M., 1990. Endogenous technological change. Journal of Political Economy 98, S71–102.

Rosenzweig, Mark R., Wolpin, Kenneth I. 1980. Testing the quantity-quality fertility model: the use of twins as a natural experiment. Econometrica 48 (1), 227–240.

Rubinstein, William D., 1981. Men of Property: The Very Wealthy in Britain Since the Industrial Revolution. Croom Helm, London.

Schofield, Roger, 1973. Dimensions of illiteracy, 1750–1850. Explorations in Economic History 10, 437–454.

Schultz, T. Paul. 2007. Population Policies, Fertility, Women's Human Capital, and Child Quality. Economic Growth Center Yale University, Discussion Paper No. 954.

Wrigley, E.A., Davies, R.S., Oeppen, J.E., Schofield, R.S., 1997. English Population History from Family Reconstruction: 1580–1837. Cambridge University Press, Cambridge, New York.

CHAPTER SIX

# Twentieth Century Growth

## Nicholas Crafts[*] and Kevin Hjortshøj O'Rourke[†]

[*]Department of Economics, University of Warwick, Coventry CV4 7AL, United Kingdom
[†]All Souls College, Oxford OX1 4AL, United Kingdom

## Abstract

This paper surveys the experience of economic growth in the 20th century with a focus on technological change at the frontier together with issues related to success and failure in catch-up growth. A detailed account of growth performance based on historical national accounts data is given and is accompanied by a review of growth accounting evidence on the sources of economic growth. The key features of our analysis of divergence in growth outcomes are an emphasis on the importance of "directed" technical change, of institutional quality, and of geography. We provide brief case studies of the experience of individual countries to illustrate these points.

## Keywords

Catch-up growth, Divergence, Growth accounting, Technical change

## JEL Classification Codes

N10, O33, O43, O47

## 6.1. INTRODUCTION

This chapter does not pretend to provide a comprehensive survey of the vast literature that has been written on economic growth during the 20th century: for such a task, not even a book would suffice. Rather, it is a brief interpretative essay, which aims to place the 20th century growth experience into a broader historical context, and highlight some of the ways in which the field of economic history can contribute to the study of economic growth.

A theme of the chapter is that the 20th century saw the gradual working out of several long-run implications of the Industrial Revolution: the latter was a massive asymmetric shock to the world economy, which set in train a variety of long-run adjustment processes which are still ongoing, and which seem set to define the economic history of the 21st century as well.

We will be emphasizing two key features of the economic history literature. The first is a focus on institutions, following the insights of North (1990) and others. While institutions have certainly become a central focus of mainstream empirical work on economic growth (e.g. Acemoglu et al. 2001), economic historians tend to be quite

*Handbook of Economic Growth*, Volume 2A
ISSN 1574-0684, http://dx.doi.org/10.1016/B978-0-444-53538-2.00006-X

nuanced in their view of how institutions matter, recognizing that different institutional environments may be appropriate at different points in time and in different countries.

The second is a detailed interest in the mechanics of technological change. The endogenous nature of technological change, and the consequences which this has for economic growth in both leader and follower countries, will be a constant theme of the chapter: while theorists like Acemoglu (2002) have recently brought the issue to the forefront of growth theory, economic historians such as Habakkuk (1962) have been emphasizing such themes for many decades.

## 6.2. SETTING THE STAGE

In this section, we look at the legacy of the Industrial Revolution and its 19th century aftermath. This period saw the advent of modern economic growth (Kuznets, 1966) in what came to be the advanced economies of the 20th century, along with a big shift in the center of gravity of the world economy away from Asia and toward Europe and North America. The world economy of 1900 was hugely different from that of 1700 in terms of its technological capabilities, the income levels in leading economies, the extent of globalization, and the degree of international specialization in production.

### 6.2.1 The Beginnings of Modern Economic Growth

Recent research has made considerable progress in quantifying growth in the world economy prior to the Industrial Revolution. Table 6.1 reports estimates of income levels measured in purchasing-power-parity adjusted to 1990 international dollars for selected countries. In this metric, it is generally agreed that a bare-bones subsistence income is about $400 per year. The estimates indicate that European countries had incomes well

**Table 6.1** GDP per capita, 1086–1850, adjusted to 1990 international dollars

|      | England/Great Britain | Holland/ Netherlands | Italy | Spain | China | India | Japan |
|------|-----------------------|----------------------|-------|-------|-------|-------|-------|
| 1086 | 754                   |                      |       |       | 1244  |       |       |
| 1348 | 777                   | 876                  | 1376  | 1030  |       |       |       |
| 1400 | 1090                  | 1245                 | 1601  | 885   | 948   |       |       |
| 1500 | 1114                  | 1483                 | 1403  | 889   | 909   |       |       |
| 1600 | 1123                  | 2372                 | 1244  | 944   | 852   | 682   | 791   |
| 1650 | 1100                  | 2171                 | 1271  | 820   |       | 638   | 838   |
| 1700 | 1630/1563             | 2403                 | 1350  | 880   | 843   | 622   | 879   |
| 1750 | 1710                  | 2440                 | 1403  | 910   | 737   | 573   | 818   |
| 1800 | 2080                  | 2617/1752            | 1244  | 962   | 639   | 569   | 876   |
| 1850 | 2997                  | 2397                 | 1350  | 1144  | 600   | 556   | 933   |

*Source*: Broadberry (2013).

above this level long before the Industrial Revolution, and the same was true of China in medieval times. The implication is that the pre-industrial era should not be seen as one in which people were in a very low income Malthusian Trap equilibrium.

Nevertheless, the overall picture of Table 6.1 is that growth was at best very slow in these pre-industrial centuries. Growth of real income per person averaged 0.2% per year in England, a relative success story, between 1270 and 1700 (Broadberry et al. 2010) while at the other extreme, Chinese income levels almost halved between 1086 and 1800. These estimates re-assert the traditional story of the "Great Divergence", namely, that the most successful parts of Europe overtook China and pulled significantly ahead in the run-up to the Industrial Revolution. They also reflect a "Little Divergence" within Europe between North and South, with Italy and Spain losing out relative to England and Holland.

What were the underpinnings of this modest pre-industrial growth in England? The answer seems to be a combination of increases in hours worked per person and Smithian growth, rather than any major contribution from technological change. The length of the work year may have roughly doubled between the mid-14th and late-18th century (Allen and Weisdorf, 2011). This largely accounts for the long-run tendency for income per person to grow slowly, despite the fact that the null hypothesis that real wage rates were stationary until 1800 cannot be rejected (Crafts and Mills, 2009). Growth in the successful parts of Europe was also strongly correlated with trade expansion. This improved productivity and sustained wage levels in the face of demographic pressure (Allen, 2009).

The term "Industrial Revolution" is commonly used to characterize the unprecedented experience of the British economy during the later decades of the 18th and early decades of the 19th century. Taken literally, it is a misleading phrase; but carefully deployed, it is a useful metaphor. These years saw a remarkable economic achievement by comparison with earlier times, but it must be recognized that by later standards this was in many ways a modest beginning.

The idea of an industrial revolution conjures up images of spectacular technological breakthroughs; the triumph of the factory system and steam power; the industrialization of an economy hitherto based largely on agriculture, and rapid economic growth. Indeed, these were the directions of travel for the British economy but when they are quantified, the numbers although impressive, once put into context, do not live up to the hyperbole. While the economy withstood formidable demographic pressure much better than could have been imagined in the 17th century, the growth of real income per person was painfully slow for several decades. Not much more than a third of the labor force worked in agriculture even in the mid-18th century. In 1851, more people were employed in domestic service and distribution than in textiles, metals, and machine-making combined. Until around 1830, water power was more important than steam power in British industry.

Nevertheless, the economy of the mid-19th century was established on a different trajectory from that of a hundred years earlier. In particular, sustained labor productivity growth based on steady technological progress and higher levels of investment had become the basis of significant growth in real income per person, notwithstanding rapid population growth. This was modern economic growth, as distinct from real income increases based on Smithian growth and working harder. That said, growth potential was still quite limited by 20th century standards: education and scientific capabilities were still quite primitive, the scope to import technological advances from the rest of the world was modest, and institutions and economic policies suffered from obvious limitations.

Table 6.2 reports that the rate of TFP growth more than doubled from 0.3% per year in 1760–1801 to 0.7% per year in 1831–1873. This can certainly be interpreted as reflecting acceleration in the rate of technological progress but TFP growth captures more than this.

**Table 6.2** Growth-accounting estimates (percent per annum)
**(a) Output growth**

|           | Capital contribution | Labor contribution | TFP growth | GDP growth |
|-----------|---------------------|--------------------|------------|------------|
| 1760–1801 | 0.4*1.0 = 0.4       | 0.6*0.8 = 0.5      | 0.3        | 1.2        |
| 1801–1831 | 0.4*1.7 = 0.7       | 0.6*1.4 = 0.8      | 0.2        | 1.7        |
| 1831–1873 | 0.4*2.3 = 0.9       | 0.6*1.3 = 0.8      | 0.7        | 2.4        |

**(b) Labor productivity growth**

|           | Capital-deepening contribution | TFP growth | Labor productivity |
|-----------|--------------------------------|------------|--------------------|
| 1760–1801 | 0.4*0.2 = 0.1                  | 0.3        | 0.3                |
| 1801–1831 | 0.4*0.3 = 0.1                  | 0.2        | 0.3                |
| 1831–1873 | 0.4*1.0 = 0.4                  | 0.7        | 1.1                |

**(c) Contributions to labor productivity growth, 1780–1860**

| | |
|---|---|
| Capital deepening | 0.22 |
|   Modernized sectors | 0.12 |
|   Other sectors | 0.1 |
| TFP growth | 0.42 |
|   Modernized sectors | 0.34 |
|   Other sectors | 0.08 |
| Labor productivity growth | 0.64 |
| *Memorandum items* | |
|   Labor force growth | 1.22 |
|   Capital income share (% of GDP) | 40 |
|     Modernized sectors | 5.9 |

*Notes:* Growth accounting imposes the standard neoclassical formula in parts (a) and (b). To allow for embodiment effects in part (c) the standard growth-accounting equation is modified as follows to distinguish between different types of capital and different sectors: $\Delta \ln(Y/L) = \alpha_O \Delta \ln(K_O/L) + \alpha_M \Delta \ln(K_M/L) + \gamma \Delta \ln A_O + \Phi \Delta \ln A_M$, where the subscripts O and M denote capital in the old and modernized sectors, respectively; $\gamma$ and $\Phi$ are the gross output shares of these sectors; and $\alpha_O$ and $\alpha_M$ are the factor shares of the capital used in these sectors.
*Sources:* Crafts (2004a, 2005) revised to incorporate new output growth estimates from Broadberry et al. (2010).

No explicit allowance has been made for human capital or hours worked in the growth accounting equation. Prior to 1830, it is generally agreed that any contribution from extra schooling or improved literacy was negligible, but in the period 1831–1873 education may have accounted for around 0.3 percentage points per year of the measured TFP growth in Table 6.2 (Mitch, 1999). For 1760–1801 there is good reason to think that average hours worked per worker per year were increasing sufficiently that if the growth in labor inputs were adjusted appropriately TFP growth might be pushed down very close to zero (Voth, 2001). Overall then, a best guess might be that the contribution of technological progress, as reflected in TFP growth, went from about zero to a sustained rate of about 0.4% per year by the time the classic Industrial Revolution period was completed.

Neoclassical growth accounting of this kind is a standard technique and valuable for benchmarking purposes, if nothing else. However, it does potentially underestimate the contribution of new technology to economic growth if technological progress is embodied in new types of capital goods, as was set out in detail by Barro (1999). This was surely the case during the Industrial Revolution; as Feinstein put it, "many forms of technological advance . . . can only take place when "embodied" in new capital goods. The spinning jennies, steam engines, and blast furnaces were the "embodiment" of the Industrial Revolution" (1981, p. 142).

Table 6.2 also shows the results of an exercise that allows for embodiment effects. The "modernized sectors" (cottons, woolens, iron, canals, ships, and railways) are found to have contributed 0.46 out of 0.64% per year growth in labor productivity over the period 1780–1860 with the majority of this, 0.34 compared with 0.12%, coming from TFP growth as opposed to capital deepening. If the contribution of technological change to the growth of labor productivity is taken to be capital deepening in the modernized sectors plus total TFP growth, then this equates to 0.54 out of 0.64% per year. It remains perfectly reasonable, therefore, to regard technological innovation as responsible for the acceleration in labor productivity growth that marked the Industrial Revolution as the historical discontinuity that Kuznets supposed, even though the change was less dramatic than was once thought.

It may seem surprising that the Industrial Revolution delivered such a modest rate of technological progress given the inventions for which it is famous, including most obviously those related to the arrival of steam as a general purpose technology (GPT). It should be noted, however, that the well-known stagnation of real wage rates during this period is strong corroborative evidence that TFP growth, which is equal to the weighted average of growth in factor rewards (Barro, 1999), was modest.

Two points can be made straightaway. First, the impact of technological progress was very uneven as is implied by the estimates in Table 6.2. Most of the service sector other than transport was largely unaffected. Textiles, metals, and machine-making accounted for less than a third of industrial employment—or 13.4% of total employment—even in 1851 and much industrial employment was still in "traditional" sectors. Second, the process of technological advance was characterized by many incremental improvements and learning to realize the potential of the original inventions. This took time in an era where scientific and technological capabilities were still very weak by later standards.

Steam power offers an excellent example. In 1830, only about 165,000 horsepower was in use, the steam engine capital share was 0.4% of GDP and the Domar weight for steam engines was 1.7% (Crafts, 2004b). The cost effectiveness and diffusion of steam power was held back by the high coal consumption of the original low-pressure engines and the move to high pressure—which benefited not only factories but railways and steam ships—was not generally accomplished until the second half of the 19th century. The science of the steam engine was not well understood and the price of steam power fell very slowly, especially before about 1850. The maximum impact of steam power on British productivity growth was delayed until the third quarter of the 19th century—nearly 100 years after James Watt's patent—when it contributed about 0.4% per year to labor productivity growth. It seems reasonable to conclude that subsequently leading economies have become much better at exploiting GPTs. The reasons are likely to be found in a superior level of education and scientific knowledge; improvements in capital markets; government policies that support research and development; and thus a greater volume of and higher expected returns to innovative effort.

Indeed, from an endogenous growth perspective the early 19th century British economy still had many weaknesses. The size of markets was still very small in 1820, when modern globalization was yet to begin (O'Rourke and Williamson, 2002), and real GDP in Britain was only about one twentieth of its size in the United States a century later. The costs of invention were high at a time when scientific knowledge and formal education could still make only a modest contribution. This was clearly not a time of high college enrollment, and the highly educated were to be found in the old professions, not science and engineering. Investment, especially in equipment, was a small proportion of GDP. Intellectual property rights were weak since the legal protection offered by patents was doubtful until the 1830s, and even if Britain had less rent-seeking than France, rent-seeking in the law, the bureaucracy, the church, and the military remained very attractive alternatives to entrepreneurship, as is attested by the evidence on fortunes bequeathed (Rubinstein, 1992). Accordingly, TFP growth was modest, although by the 1830s it was still well ahead of the rate achieved in the United States, which averaged 0.2% per year during 1800–1855 (Abramovitz and David, 2001).

## 6.2.2 Directed Technical Change and the First Industrial Revolution[1]

If the transition to modern economic growth entails a sustained acceleration in the rate of technological progress, why did this happen first in Britain in the late 18th century? Over time many answers have been suggested, but a recent interpretation by Allen, building

---

[1] This section draws in part on Crafts (2011).

on Habakkuk (1962) and David (1975), has rapidly gained currency. His conclusion is deceptively simple: "The Industrial Revolution . . . was invented in Britain because it paid to invent it there" (Allen, 2009, p. 2). Allen's argument comes from an endogenous innovation perspective but is based on relative factor prices and market size rather than on the superiority of British institutions and policies, at least compared with its European peer group: that is to say, it focuses on the demand for innovation, rather than on the supply side. In particular, Britain's unique combination of high wages and cheap energy plus a sizeable market for the new technologies, which were profitable to adopt only in these circumstances, is held to be the key.

Allen's analysis emphasizes the importance of expected profitability to justify the substantial fixed costs of the investment required to perfect good ideas and make them commercially viable. The rate of return on adopting inventions in textiles, steam power, and coke smelting was a lot higher in Britain than elsewhere and so the potential market for these inventions was much greater. This is very similar to the model of "directed technical change" proposed by Acemoglu (2002).[2] Allen supports his conclusions by empirical analysis of the profitability of adoption of several famous inventions (Hargreaves' spinning jenny, Arkwright's mill, and coke smelting) at British and French relative factor prices. The conclusion is that in each case, adoption would have been rational at the former but not the latter. Eventually, after several decades, a cumulative process of micro-invention had improved these technologies to the point where adoption became profitable in other countries, and the Industrial Revolution began to spread.

Allen's hypothesis is prima facie plausible and theoretically defensible although more research is required to establish that it stands on really solid empirical foundations. For example, Crafts (2011) presents evidence suggesting that it may have been high machinery costs, rather than low wages, which impeded the adoption of the spinning jenny in France. Strikingly, it also appears that it would have been very profitable to invent and adopt the jenny in the high-wage United States.[3] Perhaps the key disincentive there was small market size relative to the fixed development costs of the invention. There are also a number of other detailed issues about the robustness of Allen's calculations that have arisen in the debate prompted by his book.[4] Allen himself recognizes that the supply side of the market for innovation mattered as well as the demand side: to claim that relative factor prices alone were the key to the Industrial Revolution would be a bit too

---

[2] Acemoglu (2010) extended this analysis to consider the impact of labor scarcity on the rate, rather than the bias, of technological progress and showed that this is positive if technological change is strongly labor saving, i.e. reduces the marginal product of labor. This might be when machines replace tasks previously undertaken by workers, as in Zeira (1998).

[3] This also seems to be true of the Arkwright mill where the prospective rate of return to adoption was 32.5% (Crafts, 2011).

[4] See the further discussion in Crafts (2011) and the interchanges between Gragnolati et al. (2011) and Allen (2011); and between Humphries (2013) and Allen (2013).

bold. Even so, Allen's contribution has been extremely valuable in focusing attention on the incentives facing innovators. In the context of subsequent British relative economic decline and, especially, American overtaking, his suggestion that the key to getting ahead in the Industrial Revolution was relative factor prices together with large market size has the clear implication that British leadership would be highly vulnerable. Insofar as high wages, cheap energy, and a market sufficient to allow fixed costs of research and development continued to be conducive to faster technological progress, the United States would be a more favored location later in the 19th century, as has become abundantly clear in the literature on the Habakkuk (1962) hypothesis.

## 6.2.3 Catch-Up and Overtaking: The Transition to American Leadership

By the late 19th century, as Table 6.3 reports, modern economic growth had spread to most of Western Europe. Rates of growth of real GDP per person, although modest by later standards, were generally well above those achieved by Britain during the Industrial Revolution (0.4% per year) and during the second and third quarters of the 19th century (1% per year). Faster growth often went hand in hand with industrialization, and there was a clear but not perfect correlation in 1913 between industrial output and GDP per head. The United Kingdom remained the European leader in 1913 but the rest of Europe was slowly catching up, and by the end of the 19th century Britain had been overtaken by the United States. The hypothesis of unconditional convergence across Europe during 1870–1913 is rejected, however (Crafts and Toniolo, 2008). Southern Europe clearly lagged behind northern Europe while nevertheless opening up a substantial gap with China.

Table 6.4 shows that crude TFP growth remained quite slow until it increased appreciably in several countries at the end of the 19th century, around the time of the so-called Second Industrial Revolution. Even so, nowhere in Europe was there a growth experience that resembled the picture famously drawn by Solow (1957) for the United States in the first half of the 20th century in which the residual accounted for seven eighths of labor productivity growth. For almost all countries, technical change came primarily from the diffusion of advances made elsewhere, but technological diffusion was still relatively slow.[5]

It is not possible to implement a full analysis of conditional convergence given data limitations but Table 6.5 offers some clues. Years of schooling increased everywhere but were generally much higher in northern Europe and, by 1913, were way ahead of the 2.3 years of the cohort born before 1805 in England and Wales (Matthews et al. 1982). In the period before World War I, industry was attracted to market potential and cheap

---

[5] Germany and the UK together accounted for 53% of all foreign patents taken out in the United States in 1883 and 57% in 1913 (Pavitt and Soete, 1982). The diffusion rate of inventions made before 1925 was less than a third of those made subsequently (Comin et al. 2006).

**Table 6.3** Growth in late nineteenth-century Western Europe

|  | 1870 GDP/capita ($1990GK) | 1913 GDP/capita ($1990GK) | Growth, 1870–1913 (% p.a.) | Industrialization level, 1870 | Industrialization level, 1913 |
|---|---|---|---|---|---|
| Austria | 1863 | 3465 | 1.46 | 13 | 32 |
| Belgium | 2692 | 4220 | 1.05 | 36 | 88 |
| Denmark | 2003 | 3912 | 1.58 | 11 | 33 |
| Finland | 1140 | 2111 | 1.45 | 13 | 21 |
| France | 1876 | 3485 | 1.46 | 24 | 59 |
| Germany | 1839 | 3648 | 1.61 | 20 | 85 |
| Greece | 880 | 1592 | 1.39 | 6 | 10 |
| Ireland | 1775 | 2736 | 1.01 |  |  |
| Italy | 1499 | 2564 | 1.26 | 11 | 26 |
| Netherlands | 2757 | 4049 | 0.91 | 12 | 28 |
| Norway | 1360 | 2447 | 1.38 | 14 | 31 |
| Portugal | 975 | 1250 | 0.59 | 9 | 14 |
| Spain | 1207 | 2056 | 1.25 | 12 | 22 |
| Sweden | 1359 | 3073 | 1.92 | 20 | 67 |
| Switzerland | 2102 | 4266 | 1.67 | 32 | 87 |
| UK | 3190 | 4921 | 1.01 | 76 | 115 |
| Europe | 1971 | 3437 | 1.31 | 20 | 45 |
| *Aide Memoire* |  |  |  |  |  |
| United States | 2445 | 5301 | 1.83 | 30 | 126 |
| China | 530 | 552 | 0.1 | 4 | 3 |

*Note*: Industrialization level is defined as an index of the volume of industrial output/person relative to a base of UK in 1900 = 100.
*Sources*: Maddison (2010) and Bairoch (1982).

coal (Crafts and Mulatu, 2006; Klein and Crafts, 2012) which again favored the north over the south. Institutions improved with regard to underpinning the appropriability of returns to investment, especially in northern Europe, as reflected in the Political Constraint Index which Henisz (2002) shows was positively related to private sector investment in infrastructure. There was a widespread improvement in legislation enabling capital markets to function (Bogart et al. 2010). Even so, a recent study (Kishtainy, 2011) suggests that only Switzerland (after 1848) and Norway (after 1899) could be classified as "open-access" societies with the political and economic competition that is regarded as essential to becoming an advanced economy by North et al. (2009). Nevertheless, much of Europe was on the verge of attaining that open-access status and this contrasts starkly with the continuation of a closed-access society dominated by a coalition of rent-seekers that stifled innovation in China (Brandt et al. forthcoming).

In growth accounting terms, as Table 6.4 shows, American overtaking was associated with a late 19th century acceleration in the rate of TFP growth to a pace far in excess

**Table 6.4** Accounting for labor productivity growth (percent per annum)

| | Labor productivity growth | Capital deepening contribution | TFP growth |
|---|---|---|---|
| Austria | | | |
| 1870–1890 | 0.9 | 0.64 | 0.26 |
| 1890–1910 | 1.69 | 0.66 | 1.03 |
| Germany | | | |
| 1871–1891 | 1.1 | 0.39 | 0.71 |
| 1891–1911 | 1.76 | 0.58 | 1.18 |
| Netherlands | | | |
| 1850–1870 | 1.02 | 0.5 | 0.52 |
| 1870–1890 | 0.94 | 0.61 | 0.33 |
| 1890–1913 | 1.35 | 0.46 | 0.89 |
| Spain | | | |
| 1850–1883 | 1.2 | 1 | 0.2 |
| 1884–1920 | 1 | 0.7 | 0.3 |
| Sweden | | | |
| 1850–1890 | 1.18 | 1.12 | 0.06 |
| 1890–1913 | 2.77 | 0.94 | 1.83 |
| United Kingdom | | | |
| 1873–1899 | 1.2 | 0.4 | 0.8 |
| 1899–1913 | 0.5 | 0.4 | 0.1 |
| United States | | | |
| 1855–1890 | 1.1 | 0.7 | 0.4 |
| 1890–1905 | 1.9 | 0.5 | 1.4 |
| 1905–1927 | 2 | 0.5 | 1.3 |

*Note:* All estimates impose a standard neoclassical growth accounting equation based on $Y = AK^{\alpha}L^{1-\alpha}$, calibrated with $\alpha = 0.35$.

*Sources:* Derived from data presented in the following original growth accounting studies: Austria: Schulze (2007); Germany: Broadberry (1998); Netherlands: Albers and Groote (1996); Spain: Prados de la Escosura and Roses (2009); Sweden: Krantz and Schön (2007); United Kingdom: Feinstein et al. (1982); United States: Abramovitz and David (2001).

of that achieved during the Industrial Revolution.[6] The United Kingdom did not match this acceleration. The origins of faster technological change in the United States may well be along the lines of Habakkuk (1962). He famously claimed that land abundance and labor scarcity in the United States promoted rapid, labor-saving technological change. New economic historians spent quite a long time trying to pin down these arguments. Eventually, it was found that the US was able to exploit complementarities between capital and natural resources to economize on the use of skilled labor in an important

---

[6] These estimates take no account of education but this would not make much difference according to Abramovitz and David (2001) who found that adjusting TFP growth on this account would reduce TFP growth by 0.0%, 0.1%, and 0.2% per annum in 1855–1890, 1890–1905 and 1905–1927, respectively.

**Table 6.5** Variables relating to conditional convergence

| | I/Y, 1870 | I/Y, 1913 | Years of schooling, 1870 | Years of schooling, 1913 | Polcon, 1870 | Polcon, 1913 | Market potential, 1910 |
|---|---|---|---|---|---|---|---|
| Austria | | | 3.48 | 5.58 | | 0.07 | 55 |
| Belgium | | | 4.45 | 5.39 | 0.4 | 0.48 | 28 |
| Denmark | 8 | 12.5 | 4.74 | 6.08 | | 0.45 | 20 |
| Finland | 12.4 | 12 | 0.51 | 1.12 | | | |
| France | 10.3 | 12.2 | 4.04 | 7.35 | | 0.56 | 59 |
| Germany | 20.8 | 23.2 | 5.25 | 6.92 | | 0.11 | 62 |
| Greece | | | 1.45 | 2.79 | | | 7 |
| Ireland | | | 2.15 | 5.5 | | | |
| Italy | 8.8 | 17.7 | 0.88 | 3.06 | | 0.27 | 40 |
| Netherlands | 12.4 | 21.2 | 5.33 | 6.07 | 0.45 | 0.55 | 30 |
| Norway | 12.2 | 20.7 | 5.67 | 6.06 | | 0.39 | 15 |
| Portugal | | | 0.79 | 2.03 | 0 | 0 | 11 |
| Spain | 5.2 | 12.2 | 2.43 | 4.93 | 0.17 | 0 | 26 |
| Sweden | 7.7 | 12 | 4.86 | 6.7 | | 0.45 | 22 |
| Switzerland | | | 6.17 | 7.65 | 0.34 | 0.45 | 22 |
| UK | 7.7 | 7.5 | 4.13 | 6.35 | 0.33 | 0.47 | 89 |
| United States | 16.9 | 19.7 | 5.57 | 7.45 | 0.28 | 0.39 | 100 |

*Notes*: I/Y is the investment to GDP ratio in percent. "Polcon" is a measure of constraints on the executive; the United States in recent times has scored a little over 0.40. "Market potential" is a measure of proximity to markets which reflects trade costs and the spatial distribution of GDP.
*Sources:* Investment ratios: Carreras and Josephson (2010) and Rhode (2002); Years of schooling: Morrisson and Murtin (2009); Polcon: database for Henisz (2002); Market potential: Liu and Meissner (2013).

subset of American manufacturing (James and Skinner, 1985), and that scale economies and technological change biased in favor of capital and materials-using were pervasive in manufacturing (Cain and Paterson, 1986). This may partly have been based on localized learning as suggested by David (1975), and partly on directed technical change as in Acemoglu (2010).

Either way, looking at late Victorian Britain, the flip side of this story is that innovations that were made in the United States were frequently "inappropriate" on the other side of the Atlantic because they were not cost-effective at British relative factor prices and/or market size; had they been profit-maximizing, competition in product markets would have ensured rapid adoption (Crafts, 2012). The implication is that lower TFP in British industry was largely unavoidable. Unlike the inappropriate technology literature in development economics, however, this episode concerns the development of north–north rather than north–south technological differences.

Although American overtaking has usually been thought of as centering on industry, this is only part of the story. During the years 1871–1911, the gap between British and

American labor productivity growth was a bit larger in services than in industry, while at the same time employment in both economies shifted strongly toward services. In the services sector, American technological advance was founded on new hierarchical forms of organization based on large volumes and reduced costs of monitoring workers due to falling communication costs (Broadberry, 2006). More generally, US productivity across much of the economy during this period was driven by the organizational innovations that permitted the development of the modern business enterprise and moves toward mass production and mass distribution (Chandler, 1977).

## 6.2.4 Divergence, Big Time

The fact that the transition to modern economic growth happened first in Britain, and then in Continental Europe and North America, had obvious implications for the international distribution of income. True, buoyant markets in the industrial economies offered new export opportunities for the rest of the world, but this was not sufficient to prevent a large increase in the gap between the industrial rich and the non-industrial poor.

Table 6.6 provides data on per capita incomes in the major regions of the world. The data are mostly taken from Bolt and Van Zanden's (2013) revision of Maddison (2010), although in the case of Africa we have preferred Maddison's original data.[7] We distinguish between Western Europe and Eastern Europe, since industrialization first took hold in the former region, while the English-speaking settler economies of North America and Oceania are considered jointly under the heading "British offshoots." What stands out from the table is the explosive growth in incomes in the British offshoots, where they quadrupled between 1820 and 1913. As a result, this was by far the richest region in the world on the eve of the Great War. Incomes increased by two-and-a-half times in Eastern Europe and Latin America, another European offshoot, during the period, and by slightly less in Western Europe, the richest region in 1820. They increased by much less in Asia and, especially, Africa. Since these two regions had already been the poorest in the world in 1820, and since the British offshoots had been one of the richest, the result was a substantial divergence in living standards—"divergence, big time," as Pritchett (1997) has termed it.

This divergence was due to the rapid growth of the leaders, not the decline of the followers. Incomes rose everywhere over the course of the century, although in Asia, the data show a slight decline in average incomes between 1820 and 1870, perhaps as a result of deindustrialization (Williamson, 2011). From 1870 onwards all regions were growing,

---

[7] Bolt and Van Zanden present a weighted average of the available data, but since the only available data are for countries in North Africa, as well as Ghana and South Africa, this almost certainly leads to an overstatement of average African incomes. We prefer Maddison's data, which involved making ad hoc judgments about incomes in the rest of the continent, and have adjusted the world per capita figures accordingly.

**Table 6.6** GDP per capita, 1820–1913, 1990 international dollars

|                   | 1820 | 1870 | 1913 |
|-------------------|------|------|------|
| Western Europe    | 1455 | 2006 | 3488 |
| Eastern Europe    | 683  | 953  | 1726 |
| British offshoots | 1302 | 2419 | 5233 |
| Latin America     | 628  | 776  | 1552 |
| Asia              | 591  | 548  | 691  |
| Africa            | 420  | 500  | 637  |
| World             | 707  | 874  | 1524 |

*Sources:* Bolt and Van Zanden (2013) and Maddison (2010).

and ended the century more prosperously than they had begun it. Between 1820 and 1913, average incomes rose by 52% in Africa, but by just 17% in Asia.

The net effect was a dramatic increase in international income differentials. In 1820, the then richest region, Western Europe, had an average income twice the world average, and three and a half times the African average. By 1913, Western European incomes were 129% higher than the world average, a small increase, but five and a half times the African average, a sizeable one. Over the same period incomes in the British offshoots rose from being 84% higher than the world average to being 243% higher. By 1913, they were more than eight times those in Africa. Bourguignon and Morrisson (2002, p.734) found that the Theil between-country inequality coefficient almost quintupled between 1820 and 1910.[8]

It is clear, then, that the 19th century saw a large increase in global inequality, driven above all by the rapid income growth of some countries but not others. It is also clear that the primary cause of this rapid income growth was industrialization in Europe and North America. Strikingly, however, some countries, such as Australia and Argentina, had among the highest incomes in the world while remaining largely specialized in primary production. To explain this apparent paradox, we would follow Arthur Lewis (1978), and point to the immigration policies of these resource-abundant countries. While countries such as Burma saw the large-scale immigration of workers from China or India, the temperate settler economies restricted immigration to Europeans only. Racism was undoubtedly a factor here, but the policy also helped maintain living standards. As Lewis (1978, p. 188) put it, "The temperate settlements could attract and hold European emigrants, in competition with the United States, only by offering income levels higher than prevailed in north-west Europe." By appropriately regulating immigration flows, and by absorbing the capital and new technologies of the core, resource-abundant settler economies could thus import rising British living standards.

---

[8] Based on the data in Maddison (1995).

## 6.2.5 The Great Specialization

The fact that the Industrial Revolution reduced manufacturing costs so substantially during the 19th century, but only in a small portion of the world, created the potential for a stark international division of labor. Falling transportation costs and relatively liberal trade policy allowed this potential to be realized. North-west Europe and, especially, the United Kingdom exported manufactured goods and imported primary products, while the exports of Oceania, Latin America, and Africa consisted almost entirely of primary products. North America was an intermediary case: its vast natural resources implied net exports of primary products, but rapid industrialization meant that the United States switched to being a net exporter of manufactures just before World War I. Asia was another intermediary case: while it conformed to the peripheral pattern of net primary exports and net manufactured imports, its manufactured exports were non-negligible.

The "great specialization", as Dennis Robertson (1938) called it, between an industrial north and a primary-exporting south, thus dates from the 19th century. Its causes were straightforward enough: geographically unbalanced technological change, and a dramatic reduction in transport costs. Its consequences, especially for the south, were less so. On the one hand, booming northern markets and falling transport costs implied rising terms of trade, especially prior to the 1870s (Williamson, 2011), and this benefited commodity exporters. On the other hand, insofar as this further hastened deindustrialization, it potentially imposed dynamic costs on southern economies, by depriving them of the growth-enhancing externalities associated with manufacturing, by leading to rent-seeking behavior associated with an over-reliance on resource-based production, or by exposing them to greater terms of trade volatility (*ibid.*). Many of the great policy debates of the 20th century thus have their roots in this period. Should developing countries rely on exports of primary commodities to generate growth (a strategy which worked for several countries in the late 19th century [Lewis, 1969, 1970])? Or did such an outward-oriented strategy give rise to Dutch disease problems, suggesting (on the assumption that there are growth-promoting externalities in industry) the need for policy interventions (such as import-substitution strategies) to increase industrial production? The way in which these debates influenced policy decisions would have a major impact on regional growth experiences once the developing world regained policy independence in the 20th century.

It should be noted, however, that by the end of this period several parts of the periphery were reindustrializing. The best-known example is Japan, but there was also rapid industrial growth, albeit from a low base, in several Asian economies, e.g. in Korea, the Philippines, Taiwan, and parts of China. There was also rapid industrial growth in Mexico, Brazil, and the Latin American Southern Cone (Gómez Galvarriato and Williamson, 2009). The spread of industrialization across the developing world would become one of the main features of 20th century economic growth.

**Table 6.7** GDP per capita, 1870–2007, 1990 international dollars

|  | 1870 | 1913 | 1950 | 1973 | 1990 | 2007 |
|---|---|---|---|---|---|---|
| Western Europe | 2006 | 3488 | 4517 | 11,346 | 15,905 | 21,607 |
| British offshoots | 2419 | 5233 | 9268 | 16,179 | 22,346 | 30,548 |
| Japan | 737 | 1387 | 1921 | 11,434 | 18,789 | 22,410 |
| **"West"** | **1914** | **3690** | **5614** | **13,044** | **18,748** | **25,338** |
| Asia minus Japan | 539 | 652 | 639 | 1223 | 2120 | 4830 |
| Latin America | 776 | 1552 | 2505 | 4517 | 5065 | 6842 |
| Eastern Europe and former USSR |  | 1519 | 2594 | 5741 | 6458 | 7731 |
| Africa | 500 | 637 | 889 | 1387 | 1425 | 1872 |
| **"Rest"** |  | **853** | **1091** | **2068** | **2711** | **4744** |
| **World** | **874** | **1524** | **2104** | **4081** | **5149** | **7504** |

*Sources:* Bolt and Van Zanden (2013), Maddison (2010). This is a revised version of Table 4 in Maddison (2005).

## 6.3. TWENTIETH CENTURY GROWTH: WHAT HAPPENED?

In this section we briefly set out some of the major facts concerning aggregate growth in the major regions of the world.

### 6.3.1 World Growth and Its Decomposition

Table 6.7 presents data on the level of per capita GDP between 1870 and 2007, based on Bolt and Van Zanden's (2013) updating of Maddison (2010). As before, we have preferred Maddison's original figures for Africa up to and including 1913, and have revised the world figures accordingly. We follow Maddison in distinguishing Japan from the rest of Asia (which we will, for the sake of brevity, refer to henceforth as "Asia"), since Japan was a precocious industrializer.[9] We also follow Maddison in grouping Western Europe, Japan, and the British offshoots (the United States, Canada, Australia, and New Zealand) together (the "West"), and in considering separately the other four regions (the "Rest"), which we will refer to jointly as the developing world.

Table 6.8 gives per capita GDP growth rates in five successive periods; the late 19th century (1870–1913); the turbulent years between 1913 and 1950; the "Golden Age" which lasted from 1950 to 1973; the period following the first oil crisis, from 1973 to 1990; and the period since 1990.[10] Whereas Maddison treated the entire period since 1973 as one, we have preferred to split it into two, since the years after 1990 were marked

[9] We use Maddison's population data to derive the average figures for the West, the Rest, Asia minus Japan, and Eastern Europe and the former USSR.

[10] The figure for Eastern Europe and the former USSR is a population-weighted average of the growth rates of the two regions, where the latter growth rate is (in the case of 1870–1913) calculated for the period 1885–1913 only, since data for 1870 are lacking.

**Table 6.8** Per capita GDP growth, 1870–2007 (percent per annum)

|                                      | 1870–1913 | 1913–1950 | 1950–1973 | 1973–1990 | 1990–2007 | 1913–2007 |
|--------------------------------------|-----------|-----------|-----------|-----------|-----------|-----------|
| Western Europe                       | 1.29      | 0.70      | 4.09      | 2.01      | 1.82      | 1.96      |
| British offshoots                    | 1.81      | 1.56      | 2.45      | 1.92      | 1.86      | 1.89      |
| Japan                                | 1.48      | 0.88      | 8.06      | 2.96      | 1.04      | 3.00      |
| **"West"**                           | **1.54**  | **1.14**  | **3.73**  | **2.16**  | **1.79**  | **2.07**  |
| Asia minus Japan                     | 0.45      | −0.06     | 2.87      | 3.29      | 4.96      | 2.15      |
| Latin America                        | 1.63      | 1.30      | 2.60      | 0.68      | 1.78      | 1.59      |
| Eastern Europe and former USSR       | 1.64      | 1.46      | 3.51      | 0.69      | 1.06      | 1.75      |
| Africa                               | 0.57      | 0.90      | 1.95      | 0.16      | 1.62      | 1.15      |
| **"Rest"**                           | **0.73**  | **0.67**  | **2.82**  | **1.61**  | **3.35**  | **1.84**  |
| **World**                            | **1.30**  | **0.87**  | **2.92**  | **1.38**  | **2.24**  | **1.71**  |

*Sources:* Based on Bolt and Van Zanden (2013), Maddison (2010). This is a revised version of Table 6 in Maddison (2005).

by the collapse of the Soviet Union, the rapid spread of globalization, and a succession of international financial crises.

Table 6.8 shows that world economic growth was higher in the 20th century (1913–2007) than in the late 19th (1870–1913), at 1.7% per annum as opposed to 1.3%. Latin America is the only exception to the rule that 20th century growth was faster, and even there growth rates in the two periods were very similar. Growth was also very similar in the two periods in the British offshoots, reflecting the relative constancy of the long-run United States growth rate (Jones, 1995).

These aggregate 20th century figures disguise a considerable amount of variation between periods. The period between 1913 and 1950, marked by two world wars and the Great Depression, saw world growth fall to just 0.9%. It declined everywhere with the exception of Africa, although it fell by less in the British offshoots, which saw strong wartime growth (helping to offset an especially severe depression after 1929), and in Eastern Europe and the former USSR, where Stalin embarked on a major industrialization drive during the interwar period. The period between 1950 and 1973 clearly deserves the "Golden Age" label, with world growth rates higher than at any other time in history. All regions saw their highest ever growth rates during this quarter century, with just one exception: Asian growth accelerated after 1973, and again after 1990.

With the aforementioned exception of Asia, growth rates declined everywhere after 1973. After 1990, they continued to decline in the "West," but they increased in all four developing regions. The result was that, for the first time since 1870, per capita growth rates after 1990 were higher in the "Rest" than in the "West."

**Table 6.9** World shares of GDP, 1870–2007 (percent)

|  | 1913 | 1950 | 1973 | 1990 | 2007 |
|---|---|---|---|---|---|
| Western Europe | 33.3 | 26.0 | 25.5 | 22.2 | 17.4 |
| British offshoots | 21.3 | 30.8 | 25.4 | 24.6 | 22.1 |
| Japan | 2.6 | 3.0 | 7.8 | 8.6 | 5.8 |
| **"West"** | **57.3** | **59.7** | **58.6** | **55.4** | **45.2** |
| Asia minus Japan | 22.1 | 15.6 | 16.4 | 23.3 | 37.0 |
| Latin America | 4.6 | 7.8 | 8.7 | 8.3 | 7.9 |
| Eastern Europe and former USSR | 13.1 | 13.0 | 12.9 | 9.8 | 6.3 |
| Africa | 2.9 | 3.8 | 3.4 | 3.3 | 3.6 |
| **"Rest"** | **42.7** | **40.3** | **41.4** | **44.6** | **54.8** |
| **World** | **100.0** | **100.0** | **100.0** | **100.0** | **100.0** |

*Sources:* Bolt and Van Zanden (2013), Maddison (2010).

Table 6.9 presents data on regional shares of world GDP. This requires information on not only per capita GDP levels, but population sizes, the latter being taken from Maddison (2010). As can be seen, the West's share of world GDP peaked in 1950, at almost 60%, before declining slowly before 1990, and more rapidly thereafter: in 2007 it was just 45%. This overall trend masks considerable variation within the "West". The share of the British offshoots was slightly higher in 2007 than in 1913, at 22%, although it was over 30% in the immediate aftermath of World War II, declining slowly thereafter. In contrast, Western Europe's share fell by almost a half, from 33% to 17%; while Japan's share rose from 2.6% in 1913 to 8.6% in 1990, before falling sharply afterward. Within the developing world Asia's share fell substantially between 1913 and 1950, had recovered by 1990, and increased rapidly since then. It was over a third in 2007. The Latin American share rose in the early 20th century, and has held steady since 1950; while Africa's share rose between 1913 and 1950 and has been stable since then. One of the most striking features of the table is the share of Eastern Europe and the former USSR, which was steady until 1973 and then collapsed, falling not just during the last two decades of communism, but after 1990 as well. The share was just 6% in 2007, less than half the 1973 level.

## 6.3.2 Catching Up, Forging Ahead, and Falling Behind

Since the publication of Moses Abramovitz's (1986) presidential address to the Economic History Association, it has become commonplace to distinguish between economic growth in the leading economy or economies, at the frontier of technological knowledge, and in follower countries which may or may not be catching up on that frontier. Growth in the leading economy is determined by those forces pushing back the frontier; growth in the followers is determined by the extent to which they can import technologies from the leading economies, and embody them in their own capital stock.

Abramovitz pointed out that such catching up is inherently self-limiting, an insight that has been subsequently formalized by growth theorists such as Robert Lucas (2000, 2009). His argument that catching-up was dependent on adequate "social capability" anticipated the enormous literature on conditional convergence. Abramovitz also argued that, given social capability, circumstances had to be conducive to the international diffusion of knowledge. Subsequent research has followed Abramovitz's lead, focusing both on the diffusion of technologies (Comin et al. 2006; Comin and Hobijn, 2010) and on the role of trade in stimulating or hindering the process. While there are disagreements on many details of the international growth process, the broad distinction between growth in the leaders and in the followers tends to be taken as given.

A common theme in economic history is the story of how economic leadership has passed from nation to nation over the course of the last millennium. How to explain this remains unclear (for one attempt to do so, see Brezis et al. 1993). Fortunately, for our purposes the issue is moot, since it is commonly accepted that the economic leader throughout the 20th century was the United States, although it was not until after World War II that the US was willing to translate its technological superiority into economic policy leadership. Figure 6.1 shows the evolution of per capita GDP in the United States between 1800 and 2007, allowing the 20th century performance to be compared with what came before. As is well known ( Jones, 1995), and has already been noted, per capita growth rates have been remarkably stable in the United States over time. The heavy straight line is a linear projection backwards and forwards in time of trend growth during the late 19th century (1870–1913). The shaded areas represent the US Civil War (1861–1865), World War I (1917–1918), and World War II (1941–1945), while the dashed vertical lines represent the onset of the Great Depression (1929) and the first oil crisis (1973).

As can be seen, per capita growth accelerated in the United States after 1870. It averaged 1.8% per annum between 1870 and 1913, as opposed to 1.2% between 1820 and 1870.[11] As can also be seen, the long-run trend was very similar in the 20th century, despite the remarkable collapse in incomes during the Great Depression, and the equally remarkable increase in per capita output during World War II. Growth averaged 2.1% per annum between 1913 and 2007, with a slight acceleration evident from the early 1980s. Consistent with Lucas (2000, 2009), per capita growth in the frontier economy has been around 2% per annum for a very long time.

For variety and drama, we need to turn to the followers. There, the 20th century has thrown up growth miracles, reversals of fortune, and sorry tales of steady decline (Pritchett, 2000). Figure 6.2 plots per capita GDPs in the major economies and regions of the world, as a percentage of US GDP, thus indicating whether or not these countries were converging on the technological frontier, keeping pace, or falling further behind. For

---

[11] Here and elsewhere, reported growth rates are based on regressions of the log of per capita output on time.

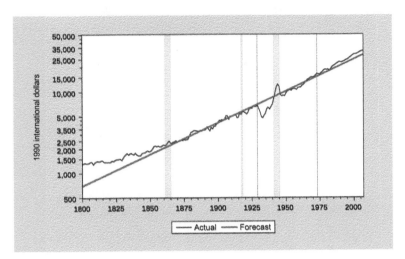

**Figure 6.1** US GDP per capita, 1800–2007 (1990 international dollars). *Sources: Bolt and Van Zanden (2013).*

the sake of brevity we will henceforth refer to these percentages as countries' or regions' relative GDP, or relative income. While our interest is in the 20th century experience, we also provide the backstory by plotting the trends beginning in 1870. The figures are, for the most part, regional averages, and therefore average out individual country experiences.

The major point that emerges from the late 19th century data is that as US growth accelerated after the Civil War, other regions, with three exceptions, saw their relative incomes decline. For the purposes of Figure 6.2 we have dated the two world wars, in Eurocentric fashion, between 1914–1918 and 1939–1945.

The first exception is Japan, which managed to keep pace with the United States after 1870. Like all regions it saw its relative GDP increase during the catastrophic interwar period, and then decline during the Second World War. It then caught up on the technological frontier in impressive fashion, experiencing per capita growth of 8% per annum during the Golden Age (Table 6.8), and overtaking Western Europe in the late 1970s. Its subsequent relative decline has been quite astonishing: Japan's relative GDP peaked at almost 85% in 1991, but it was only around 70% in 2007, back to the level of 1979.

The second exception is Latin America, whose relative GDP, like that of Japan, remained constant at just under 30% between 1870 and 1913. Unlike Japan, it stayed at this level until 1940, avoiding both the catch-up of the Depression years and the collapse that followed during World War II: one interpretation might be that the continent's economies were closely linked with that of the US during this period. Indeed, Latin America's relative income remained fairly constant during the next four decades, dipping to around 25–26% during the 1950s and 1960s, and recovering its 19th century level of

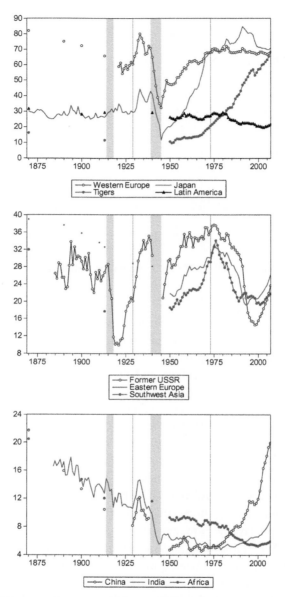

**Figure 6.2** Regional GDP per capita, 1870–2007 (percentage of US level). *Sources: Bolt and Van Zanden (2013) and Maddison (2010).*

29% in 1980. The next three decades saw Latin America's relative income steadily decline, and it stood at just 20% at the end of the 20th century.

The East Asian Tigers (Hong Kong, South Korea, Singapore, and Taiwan) are, with Japan, the main success story emerging from Figure 6.2. Their relative GDP fell from 16% in 1870 to around 11% by 1913, and there it stood until 1950. It then started to rise, accelerating dramatically in the late 1960s, until by 2007 it stood at just under 70%, on a par with both Western Europe and Japan.

The European growth miracle of the Golden Age was real enough, with growth rates of 4% per annum, but in a longer run perspective this quarter century episode stands out as an exception to what was a generally disappointing performance. Like most other regions, Western Europe's relative GDP fell between 1870 and 1913, from 82% to 66%, and it collapsed during World War II to a low point of 32% in 1945. The Golden Age saw the region's relative GDP recover to its 1913 level, and even surpass it slightly, so that it stood at around 70% in the early to mid-1970s. Since then there has been absolutely no convergence on the technological frontier.

The most dramatic experience, in this catching-up perspective, was probably that of the former USSR. This region was the third to keep pace with the United States during the late 19th century (although we only have data from 1885), but its relative GDP was highly volatile during the period. It then collapsed during the First World War, recovered dramatically during the interwar period to the point where it surpassed its previous peak, reaching 35% in 1938. It collapsed again during the Second World War, and recovered in equally dramatic fashion, peaking at 38% in 1975. There followed a spectacular decline, to a nadir of 14.5% in 1998. It then rose sharply, reaching 24% in 2007.

Given the extent to which the Soviet and Eastern European economies were connected after 1945, it is not surprising to see Eastern Europe's relative GDP tracing out the same rise and fall as its imperial master before and after 1975. It arrested its decline earlier than the former USSR, in 1993, and has been richer ever since. More surprising is the fact that Southwest Asia, which essentially comprises oil rich states in the Middle East and the Gulf, along with Israel, Lebanon, and Turkey, followed a very similar trajectory as well, with its post-1976 decline extending all the way to 2001.

Finally, Africa, China, and India all saw their relative incomes decline steadily until the late 20th century. China's relative GDP fell more sharply early on, and then stagnated at a very low level from 1950 onwards, about 5%, before starting a remarkable rise in the late 1970s. It stood at 20% in 2007. India's relative decline was slower, and its catch-up began around a decade after China's, again from a level of around 5%. Africa's relative decline was the slowest of all, with its relative GDP only hitting 5% in the mid-1990s. From 2000 onwards it started to slowly recover, reaching 6% in 2007.

## 6.4. THE PROXIMATE SOURCES OF GROWTH

This section explores the proximate sources of growth, as revealed by growth accounting techniques. We provide a broad overview of results relating to 20th century economic growth. We also review a number of issues relating to the use of these methods and, in particular, the interpretation of results obtained by using them. Handled with care, we believe that growth accounting can provide an important benchmarking or diagnostic tool but there is also considerable scope to make misleading comparisons or inferences.

## 6.4.1 Conventional Growth Accounting Results

The conventional growth accounting approach assumes that GDP is given by:

$$Y = AK^{\alpha}L^{1-\alpha},$$

where Y is output, K is capital, L is labor, and A is TFP, while $\alpha$ and $(1 - \alpha)$ are the elasticities of output with respect to capital and labor, respectively. The level of TFP is usually measured as a residual after the other items in the expression have been measured.

This can be converted into the basic growth-accounting formula:

$$\Delta\ln(Y/L) = \alpha\,\Delta\ln(K/L) + \Delta\ln A,$$

which gives a decomposition of the percentage rate of growth of labor productivity into a contribution from the percentage rate of growth of capital per unit of labor input (capital deepening) and a term based on the percentage growth rate of TFP. For benchmarking purposes, it is convenient to adopt a standardized value for $\alpha$.[12]

It is tempting but misleading to assume that residual TFP growth in this formula captures the contribution of technological progress to labor productivity growth. Technological change may be less than TFP growth if there are scale economies or improvements in the efficiency with which factor inputs are used. On the other hand, if technological progress is partly embodied in new forms of capital (rather than "manna from heaven") then some of its contribution will seem to accrue to capital when this approach is used.

A more general approach seeks to take account of human capital and modifies the production function to be:

$$Y = AK^{\alpha}(L^{*}(HK/L))^{1-\alpha},$$

where HK/L is the average educational quality of the labor force, typically approximated by years of schooling. The growth-accounting formula then becomes:

$$\Delta\ln(Y/L) = \alpha\,\Delta\ln(K/L) + (1 - \alpha)\Delta\ln(HK/L) + \Delta\ln A,$$

so that the decomposition now includes a contribution from the rate of growth of the quality of the labor force, which in practice is based on the additional earnings from years

---

[12] It is common to use $\alpha = 0.35$ which is similar to the share of profits in GDP for many countries. The profits share is potentially a misleading estimate of the output elasticity of capital, for example in the presence of significant externalities or market power, but in practice it is probably acceptable (Aiyar and Dalgaard, 2005; Bosworth and Collins, 2003).

**Table 6.10** Accounting for labor productivity growth in OECD Countries, 1913–1950 (percent per annum)

|             | K/L  | HK/L | TFP  | Y/L  |
|-------------|------|------|------|------|
| France      | 0.59 | 0.36 | 1.06 | 2.01 |
| Germany     | 0.19 | 0.22 | 0.74 | 1.05 |
| Japan       | 0.62 | 0.61 | 0.49 | 1.72 |
| Netherlands | 0.43 | 0.27 | 0.88 | 1.58 |
| UK          | 0.42 | 0.32 | 0.83 | 1.57 |

*Source*: Maddison (1987).

of schooling. The estimates of the TFP growth contribution are less crude and, of course, tend to be smaller once education is taken into account.

Tables 6.10 and 6.11 report growth-accounting estimates on this basis where the methods used allow international comparisons to be made. Taken at face value, several interesting points stand out from these estimates. First, even after allowing for education, TFP growth in the advanced economies compares very favorably with the 19th century until the end of the Golden Age in the 1970s. Second, the rise of East Asian countries after 1960 is notable for a very strong capital deepening contribution to labor productivity growth, which was much greater than had been observed in the European transition to modern economic growth in the 19th century. Third, TFP growth in sub-Saharan Africa was disastrous in the last 30 years of the 20th century and most disappointing in Latin America post-1980, and for both these regions there was virtually no capital deepening contribution after 1980.

Table 6.12 provides an account of productivity gaps based on an application of growth accounting to levels pioneered in a classic article by Hall and Jones (1999). Its results are quite similar to those given in that paper although for a later study that took place in 2005. The results are striking: by far the most important reason for differences in labor productivity (and income per head) is differences across countries in levels of TFP.[13] This is a striking rejection of the basic set-up of the pure Solow growth model which assumes that technology is the basis of TFP and is both exogenous and universal—an assumption which underpins the neoclassical predictions of β- and σ-convergence.

In principle, there are two reasons why TFP levels may differ, namely technology and efficiency. The most obvious reason why technology might differ is that technological progress has been uneven and has improved the production function at some factor intensities (high capital-labor or human capital-labor ratios) but not others. The evidence

---

[13] There are alternative ways to specify the "development accounting" equation and measurement issues, in particular with regard to human capital. Nevertheless, there seems to be general agreement that residual TFP is the biggest part of the story, accounting for 50–70% of cross-country income differences (Hsieh and Klenow, 2010).

**Table 6.11** Proximate sources of labor productivity growth, 1960–2003 (percent per annum)

|                      | K/L  | HK/L | TFP  | Y/L  |
|----------------------|------|------|------|------|
| **Industrial countries** |      |      |      |      |
| 1960–1970            | 1.4  | 0.3  | 2.3  | 4    |
| 1970–1980            | 1    | 0.5  | 0.4  | 1.9  |
| 1980–1990            | 0.6  | 0.2  | 0.9  | 1.7  |
| 1990–2003            | 0.8  | 0.2  | 0.6  | 1.6  |
| **East Asia**        |      |      |      |      |
| 1960–1970            | 1.7  | 0.4  | 1.6  | 3.7  |
| 1970–1980            | 2.7  | 0.6  | 1    | 4.3  |
| 1980–1990            | 2.5  | 0.6  | 1.3  | 4.4  |
| 1990–2003            | 2    | 0.5  | 0.6  | 3.1  |
| **Latin America**    |      |      |      |      |
| 1960–1970            | 0.8  | 0.3  | 1.7  | 2.8  |
| 1970–1980            | 1.3  | 0.3  | 1.1  | 2.7  |
| 1980–1990            | 0    | 0.5  | −2.3 | −1.8 |
| 1990–2000            | 0.1  | 0.3  | −0.1 | 0.3  |
| **Sub-Saharan Africa** |      |      |      |      |
| 1960–1970            | 0.8  | 0.2  | 1.9  | 2.9  |
| 1970–1980            | 1.3  | 0.1  | −0.4 | 1    |
| 1980–1990            | −0.1 | 0.4  | −1.5 | −1.2 |
| 1990–2000            | 0    | 0.4  | −0.5 | −0.1 |

*Sources:* Bosworth and Collins (2003) and website update.

**Table 6.12** Decomposition of cross-country differences in GDP per capita, 2005 (USA = 100)

|               | Y/P  | K/Y   | HK/L  | L/P   | TFP  |
|---------------|------|-------|-------|-------|------|
| United States | 100  | 100   | 100   | 100   | 100  |
| Japan         | 72.6 | 130.7 | 100.4 | 105.1 | 52.6 |
| EU27 + EFTA   | 64.7 | 114.1 | 91.2  | 91.3  | 67.8 |
| Russia        | 28.6 | 97.4  | 84.9  | 99.3  | 31.5 |
| Brazil        | 20.5 | 103.1 | 70.1  | 96.8  | 29.3 |
| China         | 9.8  | 105.2 | 57.3  | 119.5 | 13.6 |
| India         | 5.2  | 98.3  | 47.7  | 87.1  | 12.7 |
| World         | 22.8 | 104.2 | 64.2  | 95.8  | 27.9 |

*Notes*: GDP per capita (Y/P) is measured at PPP. Estimates derived by imposing the production function $Y = K^\alpha (AhL)^{1-\alpha}$ where h is human capital per worker (HK/L). This can be re-written as $Y/L = (K/Y)^{\alpha/(1-\alpha)} Ah$ so that $Y/P = (K/Y)^{\alpha/(1-\alpha)} Ah(L/P)$ which is the formula used for the decomposition.
*Source*: Duval and De la Maisonneuve (2010).

suggests that this was the case during the 20th century (Allen, 2012), as might be expected, in a world of directed technical change where research and development is oriented primarily to the incentives provided by the economic environment of advanced economies. In other words, there could be an "inappropriate technology" explanation for the TFP gap. An inefficiency explanation for TFP gaps might relate to differences in institutional quality which impact on allocative and/or productive inefficiency. Again, there is evidence that points in this direction, notably the finding by Hsieh and Klenow (2009) that if capital and labor were used as efficiently in Chinese and Indian manufacturing as in the United States, TFP would increase by 30–50% and 40–60%, respectively.

Table 6.13 reports results from one attempt to discriminate between these two hypotheses. The overall conclusion in Jerzmanowski (2007) is that in 1995 (1960) factor inputs accounted for 31 (45)% of the variation in output per worker while of the 69 (55)% attributable to TFP, 43 (28)% came from efficiency and 26 (27)% from technology differences. These estimates imply that, while both efficiency and technology are important in explaining TFP gaps, on average, efficiency matters more, and increasingly so over time. These results suggest that episodes of rapid catch-up growth are likely to be based

**Table 6.13** Decomposing TFP levels relative to the United States (USA = 1.00)

|  | 1960 | | | 1995 | | |
|---|---|---|---|---|---|---|
|  | **TFP** | **E** | **T** | **TFP** | **E** | **T** |
| France | 0.72 | 0.71 | 1.01 | 0.77 | 0.87 | 0.89 |
| Greece | 0.49 | 0.57 | 0.86 | 0.56 | 0.58 | 0.97 |
| Spain | 0.64 | 0.74 | 0.86 | 0.76 | 0.85 | 0.9 |
| Italy | 0.67 | 0.71 | 0.94 | 0.84 | 0.88 | 0.96 |
| UK | 0.85 | 0.89 | 0.95 | 0.82 | 0.85 | 0.97 |
| India | 0.3 | 0.41 | 0.74 | 0.29 | 0.44 | 0.67 |
| Indonesia | 0.31 | 0.55 | 0.57 | 0.37 | 0.54 | 0.69 |
| Japan | 0.48 | 0.56 | 0.86 | 0.68 | 0.79 | 0.86 |
| Korea | 0.33 | 0.37 | 0.88 | 0.49 | 0.49 | 0.99 |
| Singapore | 0.47 | 0.54 | 0.87 | 0.85 | 1 | 0.85 |
| Argentina | 0.76 | 0.79 | 0.96 | 0.57 | 0.65 | 0.88 |
| Brazil | 0.42 | 0.49 | 0.86 | 0.5 | 0.6 | 0.84 |
| Chile | 0.51 | 0.57 | 0.89 | 0.58 | 0.73 | 0.8 |
| Mexico | 0.65 | 0.72 | 0.9 | 0.49 | 0.58 | 0.84 |
| DR Congo | 0.38 | 0.58 | 0.65 | 0.23 | 0.35 | 0.67 |
| Malawi | 0.23 | 0.39 | 0.6 | 0.16 | 0.27 | 0.61 |
| Mauritius | 0.62 | 0.71 | 0.88 | 0.8 | 1 | 0.8 |
| Tanzania | 0.15 | 0.22 | 0.69 | 0.11 | 0.17 | 0.64 |

*Note:* $TFP_i = Efficiency_i * Technology_i = E_i T_i$ where $E_i$ is obtained by estimating an efficient production frontier, TFP is obtained by growth accounting in levels and T is then inferred.
*Source:* Jerzmanowski (2007).

on major improvements in both efficiency and technology. They also suggest that the lengthy period of negative TFP growth in Africa reported in Table 6.11 is a sign of deteriorating efficiency of factor use, rather than of technological retrogression.

## 6.4.2 Some Issues of Measurement and Interpretation[14]

There are a number of important issues that have to be addressed when trying to compare growth-accounting exercises for the late 19th and early 20th centuries with similar exercises for the late 20th century. For example, to obtain estimates of real GDP an accurate GDP price deflator is required. Boskin et al. (1996) thought that, for a variety of reasons, inflation had been overestimated (and thus real GDP growth and TFP growth had been underestimated by a similar amount) in the national accounts during the period of the productivity slowdown in the 1970s and 1980s, and that the correction required was of the order of 0.6% per year. On the other hand, the Boskin bias in inflation measurement does not appear to generalize to other periods (Costa, 2001).

Perhaps a more serious concern in many cases is a potential index number problem regarding the measurement of capital inputs. The standard approach, used in virtually all historical studies, relies on estimates of the perpetual inventory capital stock that are weighted using asset prices. A theoretically more appropriate (but much more data demanding) method is to estimate flows of capital services using rental prices as weights. This requires estimates of the user cost of capital for different assets. The difference between the two methods will be especially important when investment switches toward short-lived assets (like computers) and away from long-lived assets (like structures), since the user cost of the former is much higher relative to the asset price. Not surprisingly, this issue has come to prominence since the ICT revolution.[15] Generally speaking, using the capital services methodology raises the growth contribution of capital and lowers that of TFP. However, this probably makes relatively little difference, even in the United States, before the second half of the 20th century, as Table 6.14 reports; it is, however, very important for analyses of recent growth.[16]

It has long been recognized that research and development is an intangible investment and that the R & D knowledge stock could be introduced as an input in growth-accounting estimates. More recently, it has been argued that intangible investments generally (including design and product development; investments in branding; firm-specific human and organizational capital formation including training and consultancy; and computerized information, especially software) should be treated in this way.

---

[14] This section draws in part on Crafts (2009a, 2010).

[15] Estimates for the UK show that the volume of capital inputs for the period 1950–2006 grew by 3.1% per annum measured by the traditional capital stock data but by 3.5% when measured by the capital services method. The difference relates entirely to the post-1980 and, in particular, the post-1990 period (Wallis, 2009).

[16] The EUKLEMS database which covers recent decades and permits international comparisons is constructed using a capital services methodology: see O'Mahony and Timmer (2009).

**Table 6.14** Sources of labor productivity growth in the United States (percent per annum)

|            | K/L  | Crude TFP | Labor quality | Capital quality | Refined TFP | Y/L  |
|------------|------|-----------|---------------|-----------------|-------------|------|
| 1800–1855  | 0.19 | 0.2       | 0             | 0               | 0.2         | 0.39 |
| 1855–1871  | 0.53 | −0.39     | 0             | 0               | −0.39       | 0.14 |
| 1871–1890  | 0.84 | 1         | 0             | 0               | 1           | 1.84 |
| 1890–1905  | 0.55 | 1.38      | 0.1           | 0               | 1.28        | 1.93 |
| 1905–1927  | 0.48 | 1.57      | 0.19          | 0               | 1.38        | 2.05 |
| 1929–1948  | 0.07 | 1.89      | 0.38          | 0.08            | 1.43        | 1.96 |
| 1948–1966  | 0.81 | 2.3       | 0.43          | 0.4             | 1.47        | 3.11 |
| 1966–1989  | 0.57 | 0.66      | 0.31          | 0.31            | 0.04        | 1.23 |

*Note*: capital quality reflects the adjustment required to move from a capital stock to a capital services basis.
*Source*: Abramovitz and David (2001, Table 1: IVA).

Expenditure on these items has been growing rapidly in the context of the "knowledge economy" and in both the UK and the USA, is of similar magnitude to investment in tangible capital. If these expenditures are treated as final investment rather than intermediates in growth-accounting exercises, this will imply that there is more output, more input, and revised factor-share weights.

In principle, the impact of switching to accounting with intangibles on TFP growth is ambiguous. In practice, at least in the ICT era, the impact is to increase estimated labor productivity growth a bit, to raise the contribution of capital deepening considerably, and to reduce measured TFP growth appreciably, as Table 6.15 reports. Growth accounting with intangibles for earlier periods has not yet been attempted but the impact would surely be much less dramatic since, in the 1950s, intangible investment added only about 4% to US GDP compared with about three times that amount 50 years later.

Neoclassical growth accounting is normally carried out by imposing a Cobb-Douglas production function. In some circumstances, it may be that a CES specification is more appropriate with the elasticity of substitution between capital and labor, $\sigma$, being set to a value less than 1. In that case, especially when the capital-labor ratio is growing rapidly and technical change exhibits capital-using bias, TFP growth will be underestimated by the conventional method. For example, taken at face value, the estimates in Table 6.14 (which assume that $\sigma = 1$) invite the conclusion that technical change was insignificant in the American economy for much of the 19th century, and only became significant with the rise of the science-based industries and R & D in the so-called Second Industrial Revolution. This runs counter to standard historical discussions, however, and is certainly not the interpretation in Abramovitz and David (2001). If, as they argue, the 19th century US economy was characterized by a low elasticity of substitution between factors and capital-using technical change, then TFP growth was considerably stronger than shown in Table 6.14. If estimates are obtained assuming $\sigma = 0.3$, as Abramovitz and David believe is appropriate, then TFP growth turns out to have been 0.9% per year between

**Table 6.15** Sources of labor productivity growth, United States non-farm business sector, 1973–2003 (percent per annum)

|                                    | 1973–1995 | 1995–2003 |
|------------------------------------|-----------|-----------|
| **Traditional growth accounting**  |           |           |
| Labor productivity growth          | 1.36      | 2.78      |
| Capital deepening                  | 0.6       | 0.98      |
|   IT capital             | 0.33      | 0.7       |
|   Other tangible capital | 0.27      | 0.28      |
| Labor quality                      | 0.28      | 0.38      |
| TFP                                | 0.48      | 1.42      |
| **Accounting with intangibles**    |           |           |
| Labor productivity growth          | 1.63      | 3.09      |
| Capital deepening                  | 0.97      | 1.68      |
|   Tangible capital deepening | 0.55  | 0.85      |
|     IT capital | 0.3       | 0.6       |
|     Other tangible capital | 0.25 | 0.24  |
|   Intangible capital deepening | 0.43 | 0.84     |
|     Software   | 0.12      | 0.27      |
|     Other intangible capital | 0.31 | 0.57 |
| Labor quality                      | 0.25      | 0.33      |
| TFP                                | 0.41      | 1.08      |

*Note*: accounting with intangibles is based on the formula $\Delta\ln(Y^*/L) = s^*_{TK}\Delta\ln(TK/L) + s^*_{IK}\Delta\ln(IK/L) + \Delta A/A$, where $Y^*$ includes expenditure on intangible investments and $s^*_{TK}$ and $s^*_{IK}$ are the factor shares of tangible and intangible capital in $Y^*$.
*Source*: Corrado et al. (2009).

1835 and 1890, much higher than a crude estimate of 0.24% per year, assuming $\sigma = 1$.[17] Other cases where a similar issue arises, and which are discussed below, include the "East Asian Miracle" (Rodrik, 1997) and the 1970s growth slowdown in the USSR (Allen, 2003).

A further problem with conventional growth accounting that matters in some circumstances is that it assumes no costs of adjustment, fixed factors of production, or economies of scale. Morrison (1993) proposed an econometric procedure to address these problems and her results indicated that the 1970s slowdown in TFP growth in American manufacturing was very largely a weakening of economies of scale rather than of technological progress. Using Morrison's methodology, Crafts and Mills (2005) found that adjustment costs meant that technological progress was about 2 percentage points faster than conventional TFP growth in both British and German manufacturing during 1950–1973

---

[17] This calculation applies the correction to TFP growth in Rodrik (1997). The correction is given by $0.5\,\alpha((1-\sigma)/\sigma)(1-\alpha)(\Delta K/K - \Delta L/L)(\Delta A_L/A_L - \Delta A_K/A_K)$ where the last term captures the degree of factor-saving bias in technological progress measured as the difference between the rate of labor augmentation and the rate of capital augmentation.

but not much different thereafter. Once again, as with the previous examples, the point is that intertemporal comparisons of conventional TFP growth may be hazardous because the degree of measurement bias appears to have varied considerably over time.

Underpinning growth accounting in the neoclassical tradition is, of course, the neo-classical growth model.[18] The later development of endogenous growth models could potentially call for alternative growth-accounting formulae or a different interpretation of the standard results (Barro, 1999). The most obvious implication might be to recognize the importance of the embodiment of technical change in new varieties of capital, as in the voluminous literature that has applied growth accounting to the impact of ICT (e.g. Oliner et al. 2007). The growth-accounting formula that has been applied in the ICT literature is:

$$\Delta\ln(Y/L) = \alpha_{KO}\Delta\ln(KO/L) + \alpha_{KICT}\Delta\ln(KICT/L) + \phi\,\Delta\ln A_{ICT} + \eta\,\Delta\ln A_O,$$

where $\phi$ and $\eta$ are gross output weights, KICT is capital used in ICT production, KO is the rest of the capital stock, $A_{ICT}$ is TFP in ICT production, and $A_O$ is TFP in the rest of the economy. The contribution of the new ICT technology to labor productivity growth is taken to be the sum of the second and third terms. Given that $\phi$ and $\alpha_{KICT}$ are very small initially, it is easy to see why a new GPT initially adds very little to overall labor productivity growth. By including the ICT capital deepening term, however, the implication is that TFP growth underestimates the contribution of technological progress to growth.

It should be noted that this approach seeks only to benchmark the direct ex-post ICT component of productivity growth. It does not answer the (much harder) question, "How much faster was productivity growth as a result of ICT?" This hinges on the counterfactual rate of growth of other capital in the absence of ICT, estimation of which would be a complex modeling exercise taking account of both crowding out and crowding in effects. Fogel (1964) took the view that no capital deepening component should be included because in the absence of the new technology similar returns would have been earned on alternative investments. However, this is not a position that everyone would accept, especially in the case of GPTs.[19]

This links to a deeper concern regarding the use of growth accounting to identify the sources of growth, which was very clearly articulated by Abramovitz (1993). The issue is two-way interdependence between the trajectories of technological change on the one hand, and physical and human capital formation on the other. While some endogenous growth models stress the latter interdependence, it is actually the former

---

[18] As Griliches (1996) underlined, the big contribution of Solow (1957) was to put the economics into growth accounting by making this connection.

[19] Fogel (1964) measured the contribution of railways to American economic growth in terms of "social savings," essentially a measure of user benefits arising from the impact of technical change on the transport supply curve. It is easy to show that this is equivalent to $\phi\,\Delta\ln A_{ICT}$ (Foreman-Peck, 1991).

which is highlighted by a comparison of the American growth process in the 19th and 20th centuries.[20]

Three key points should be noted. First, using conventional growth accounting to estimate TFP growth is not always a good guide to underlying technological change. As we have seen, TFP growth can be either an under- or an overestimate of the contribution of technological progress to economic growth. Second, the size and direction of the bias in neoclassical growth accounting varies considerably in different periods or types of economy; this can make historical comparisons quite difficult. Third, while growth accounting invites its users to treat the growth of capital and technological change as independent and additive, this assumption is potentially quite misleading and may detract from a deeper understanding of the sources of growth.

### 6.4.3 Economic Miracles are Not All the Same[21]

All of that having been said, an interesting application of growth accounting is to compare episodes of rapid catch-up growth, which exhibit some striking differences when viewed through this lens.[22] Table 6.16 reports estimates relating to the Golden Age of Western European growth, the East Asian Miracle, the Celtic Tiger, the rise of the BRICs, and the Soviet Union. This last case ended in failure but back in the 1960s it was conventional wisdom that the USSR was on track to overtake the United States before the beginning of the 21st century (Levy and Peart, 2011).

The European Golden Age saw strong contributions to labor productivity growth from both capital deepening and TFP growth, but it is the latter that was typically larger in the poorer countries which exhibited the fastest growth. This was not based to any significant extent on domestic R & D, but rather on a combination of technology transfer, structural shift away from agriculture, economies of scale, and more efficient utilization of factors of production. The transfer of "surplus labor" from small-scale family farms was an important part of the process (Crafts and Toniolo, 2008). External trade liberalization and the increased integration of the European market were factors that speeded up technology transfer and helped Europe to reduce the technology gap with the United States (Badinger, 2005; Madsen, 2007). Nelson and Wright (1992) also stressed the increased cost-effectiveness of American technology in Europe, the greater codification of

---

[20] Of course, in the neoclassical growth model an increase in exogenous TFP growth raises the growth rate of the capital stock; some implications of this point for growth accounting are explored by Hulten (1979). However, Abramovitz has in mind a richer story about 19th century American growth in which, *inter alia*, the great expansion of the domestic market resulting from technological change in transport leads to larger-scale and more capital-intensive methods of production.

[21] This section draws in part on Crafts and Toniolo (2008).

[22] Our examples are all taken from the late 20th century, so hopefully, the problems of inter-temporal comparability highlighted earlier will not be too severe. See however the caveats in the succeeding two footnotes.

**Table 6.16** Accounting for growth during "economic miracles" (percent per annum)

**(a) Sources of labor productivity growth**

|  | K/L | HK/L | TFP | Y/L |
|---|---|---|---|---|
| **Western Europe 1960–1970** | | | | |
| France | 2.02 | 0.29 | 2.62 | 4.93 |
| Germany | 2.1 | 0.23 | 2.03 | 4.36 |
| Italy | 2.39 | 0.36 | 3.5 | 6.25 |
| Spain | 2.45 | 0.38 | 3.73 | 6.56 |
| **East Asia 1960–2003** | | | | |
| Korea | 2.7 | 0.7 | 1.28 | 4.68 |
| Singapore | 2.86 | 0.46 | 1.2 | 4.52 |
| Taiwan | 3.04 | 0.54 | 2.16 | 5.74 |
| **Ireland** | | | | |
| 1990–2003 | 0.49 | 0.26 | 2.24 | 2.99 |
| **USSR** | | | | |
| 1928–1940 | 2 | | 0.5 | 2.5 |
| 1940–1950 | −0.1 | | 1.6 | 1.5 |
| 1950–1970 | 2.6 | | 1.4 | 4 |
| 1970–1985 | 2 | | −0.4 | 1.6 |
| **China** | | | | |
| 1978–1993 | 2.1 | 0.4 | 3.9 | 6.4 |
| 1993–2004 | 3.7 | 0.3 | 4.5 | 8.5 |
| **India** | | | | |
| 1978–1993 | 0.8 | 0.3 | 1.3 | 2.4 |
| 1993–2004 | 1.6 | 0.4 | 2.6 | 4.6 |

**(b) Sources of output growth**

|  | K | L = Employment + Education | TFP | Y |
|---|---|---|---|---|
| **Western Europe 1960–1970** | | | | |
| France | 2.24 | 0.42 + 0.29 | 2.62 | 5.57 |
| Germany | 2.13 | 0.06 + 0.23 | 2.03 | 4.45 |
| Italy | 2.2 | −0.35 + 0.36 | 3.5 | 5.71 |
| Spain | 2.74 | 0.55 + 0.38 | 3.73 | 7.4 |
| **East Asia 1960–2003** | | | | |
| Korea | 3.64 | 1.75 + 0.70 | 1.28 | 7.37 |
| Singapore | 4.03 | 2.18 + 0.46 | 1.2 | 7.87 |
| Taiwan | 3.97 | 1.74 + 0.54 | 2.16 | 8.41 |
| **Ireland** | | | | |
| 1990–2003 | 1.7 | 2.24 + 0.26 | 2.24 | 6.44 |
| **USSR** | | | | |
| 1928–1940 | 3.2 | 2.1 | 0.5 | 5.8 |
| 1940–1950 | 0.1 | 0.5 | 1.6 | 2.2 |
| 1950–1970 | 3.1 | 0.9 | 1.4 | 5.4 |
| 1970–1985 | 2.4 | 0.8 | −0.4 | 2.8 |

(*Continued*)

**Table 6.16** (*Continued*)

| | | | | |
|---|---|---|---|---|
| **China** | | | | |
| 1978–1993 | 3 | 1.6 + 0.4 | 3.9 | 8.9 |
| 1993–2004 | 4.1 | 0.8 + 0.3 | 4.5 | 9.7 |
| **India** | | | | |
| 1978–1993 | 1.5 | 1.4 + 0.3 | 1.3 | 4.5 |
| 1993–2004 | 2.3 | 1.2 + 0.4 | 2.6 | 6.5 |

*Notes:* Ireland and USSR are GNP not GDP. Education is included in TFP growth for USSR.
*Sources:* Bosworth and Collins (2003, and web update); for USSR derived from Ofer (1987); and for China and India derived from Bosworth and Collins (2008), in each case assuming $\alpha = 0.35$.

technological knowledge, and increases in European technological competence based on increased investments in human capital and R & D. Overall though, this is clearly a case where TFP growth involved much more than technological progress.

The East Asian Miracle was quite different. Table 6.16 shows that TFP growth contributed relatively less, and capital deepening more, than in Golden Age Europe. Rapid growth of the capital stock was underpinned by increasingly high investment rates which reached around 35% of GDP in Korea and Singapore, around 10 percentage points higher than the average in 1960s Europe. East Asian growth was also notable for a very strong growth of labor inputs, underpinned by a "bonus" from the age structure effects of the demographic transition which (unlike in Western Europe) coincided with the growth spurt. Although East Asian countries were successful in importing technology, overall the developmental states of the region were better at mobilizing factor inputs than at achieving outstanding TFP growth (Young, 1995; Crafts, 1999).[23]

The Celtic Tiger was a very different animal from its Asian counterpart and contrasts quite strongly with Golden Age European growth (Crafts, 2009). Ireland's labor productivity growth was a good deal lower, mainly because of a small capital deepening component in an economy where investment was about 20% of GDP. TFP growth was strong but relied on ICT production which accounted for nearly two thirds of TFP growth during the 1990s (van Ark et al. 2003). In turn, this was based on Ireland's exceptional ability to attract FDI, especially from the United States: domestic R & D was only about 1.4% of GNP. Apart from ICT production, as Table 6.16 reports, the other outstanding feature of the Celtic Tiger was employment growth which far outstripped population growth. As unemployment fell, female participation rose, and emigration turned into immigration. Irish growth thus benefited from a very elastic labor supply (Barry, 2002).

The striking feature of catch-up growth in the Soviet Union is that, if standard growth accounting assumptions are adopted, it relied much more on "extensive growth." While

---

[23] Rodrik (1997) argues that TFP growth may be underestimated by standard techniques because σ was less than 1, given biased technical change and strong capital deepening. It is unclear how big this effect may have been.

the capital deepening contribution to growth in the Golden Age was similar to that in Western Europe, or a bit lower, TFP growth was decidedly inferior. Its contribution was very weak compared with countries like Italy with similar catch-up potential.[24] The problem with the Soviet growth model is that it ran into a rapidly rising marginal capital to output ratio, implying that the rate of capital stock growth delivered by a constant investment/GDP ratio fell steadily over time. The problem became acute when TFP growth ceased in the 1970s and further increases in the investment rate (which had doubled between 1950 and 1970 to 30%) became infeasible given the commitment to high defense spending.

Finally, we consider the "growth miracles" in two of the BRICs with rather different growth trajectories. China has experienced very rapid growth of real GDP per person since reforms began at the end of the 1970s. This has been based on impressive contributions from both capital deepening and TFP growth. The former has resulted from investment rates which are massive by historical standards, reaching well over 40% of GDP by the early 2000s. The latter has two components, technology transfer linked closely to FDI (Whalley and Xin, 2010), and increases in efficiency starting from the very low base of the Maoist economy. Here, de-collectivization of agriculture which led to a surge in TFP in the 1980s (McMillan et al. 1989) played a big part, initially. The rapid reduction in the state-owned enterprise share of GDP has also been a key component, and it is TFP growth in industry which has been most impressive. India experienced a productivity surge after the disappointing period of the so-called Hindu growth rate (Rodrik and Subramanian, 2005). Even so, capital deepening and investment rates have been well below those in China. So has TFP growth, although this strengthened appreciably after the Indian reforms of the early 1990s. The detailed comparisons in Bosworth and Collins (2008) show that TFP growth in the industrial sector in India has been very disappointing (averaging 0.6% per annum from 1978–2004 compared with 4.3% in China), while TFP growth in services has been strong—in 1993–2004 averaging 3.9% per annum compared with 0.9% in China.

## 6.5. GROWTH IN THE LEADER: THE UNITED STATES

The United States overtook Britain at the start of the 20th century in terms of real GDP per person and maintained its leading position throughout the "American century." By mid-century, the United States had become the clear technological leader

---

[24] It has been suggested that this may be an artifact of the methodology and that the USSR is better described in terms of a production function with a very low elasticity of substitution between capital and labor and thus severely diminishing returns to capital (Weitzman, 1970). Allen (2003) provides a convincing rebuttal of this claim, noting that the technological possibilities were similar in West and East and that there is clear evidence of massive waste of capital in the Soviet system, which implies that standard benchmarking is appropriate.

and had developed a very different "national innovation system" from that which had prevailed in 1900. Although other OECD countries, notably Japan, reduced the gap from the 1960s to the 1980s, the United States reasserted its leadership in the context of the ICT revolution. This section examines the foundations of this exceptional performance and considers American technological prowess using an endogenous innovation lens.

## 6.5.1 Technological Leadership

During the 20th century, the United States was in the forefront of the development of the most important new technologies, including: the internal combustion engine, electricity, petrochemicals, aviation, and ICT. In this era, technological progress increasingly became the result of systematic research and development based on formal science and engineering, and was associated much more with corporate research laboratories and public investment than with independent invention.

That said, there is a clear difference between the pre- and post-World War II eras (Mowery and Rosenberg, 2000). In the former period, the United States developed a formidable record in the commercial development of technologies which had typically originated from Europe. Already, by the interwar period, revealed comparative advantage in American exports was strongly correlated with research intensity (Crafts, 1989). In the latter period, United States' science and invention played a much bigger role as American universities became world leaders in academic research and federal funding for research soared in the context of the Cold War. These points are epitomized by the automobile, where the American contribution was the development of mass production, and the computer, where the transistor and integrated circuit were American inventions. Federal funding accounted for less than 20% of R & D in the 1930s but well over half on average from the 1950s through the 1970s. Germany had 41 (44) Nobel Prize winners prior to 1950 (1950 to present) compared with 27 (229) for the United States (excluding Economics and Peace).

American industrial research was built up during the first half of the 20th century by corporate investment in laboratories. Although independent inventors still accounted for 50% of patents in the late 1920s, down from about 80% at the start of the century, their share had fallen to only 25% by the 1950s (Nicholas, 2010). About three-quarters of industry-funded R & D was performed by firms with more than 10,000 employees in the early 1980s, when defense-related expenditure still accounted for about a quarter of all R & D. This picture had changed quite significantly by 2001 when the large firms' share had fallen to just over a half, the defense-related share was below 15%, and R & D was increasingly outsourced to specialist, smaller firms resembling—to some extent—an early 20th century landscape rather than the classic post-war American national innovation system (Mowery, 2009).

The transition to an economy with substantial investments in R & D and higher education is reflected in Table 6.17. This was clearly a very different technological leader than

**Table 6.17** The knowledge economy in the United States

| | R & D expenditure/ GDP (%) | | R & D stock/ GDP (%) | | Tertiary education/ person (years) |
|---|---|---|---|---|---|
| 1920 | 0.2 | 1900–1910 | 0.03 | 1913 | 0.200 |
| 1935 | 1.8 | 1929 | 4.5 | | |
| 1953 | 1.4 | 1948 | 13.0 | 1950 | 0.420 |
| 1964 | 2.9 | 1973 | 38.2 | 1970 | 0.674 |
| 1990 | 2.7 | 1990 | 47.7 | 1995 | 1.474 |
| 2007 | 2.7 | | | 2005 | 1.682 |

*Sources:* R & D expenditure: Edgerton and Horrocks (1994), Nelson and Wright (1992), and National Science Board (2012) R & D stock: Abramovitz and David (2001) Tertiary education: Barro and Lee (2012) and Maddison (1987).

**Table 6.18** Productivity growth arising from US research, 1980s (percent of total in each country)

| | |
|---|---|
| France | 42 |
| Germany | 42 |
| Japan | 36 |
| UK | 33 |
| USA | 60 |

*Source:* Eaton and Kortum (1999, p. 558).

Industrial Revolution Britain. The size of these investments also marks the United States out from the rest of the OECD, especially in the third quarter of the century. Not only was R & D spending relative to GDP higher than anywhere else, but its absolute size loomed very large: as late as 1969, US R & D expenditure was more than twice the combined total of France, Germany, Japan, and the UK (Nelson and Wright, 1992). Similarly, the educational attainment of the American population far outstripped OECD rivals. In 1970, the next highest country (Denmark) had only about half the American tertiary education years per person. The dominant role of American (relative to all other countries') R & D as a source of productivity growth across the OECD is clearly shown in Table 6.18.

## 6.5.2 Explaining Technological Progress

There is a rich analytical narrative literature on the underpinnings of 20th century American technological progress, seeking to explain both its strength and its factor-saving bias. It is generally agreed that the geography of the United States in terms of the scale of the domestic market, the distances between major population centers, and the natural resource endowment, was an important influence, especially in the early part of the century. These features of American geography are seen as favorable to key

**Table 6.19** Resource abundance

**(a) US share of world totals (%)**

|            | 1913 output | 1989 reserves | 1989 + cumulative 1913–1989 production |
|------------|-------------|---------------|-----------------------------------------|
| Petroleum  | 65          | 3.0           | 19.8                                    |
| Copper     | 56          | 16.4          | 19.9                                    |
| Phosphate  | 43          | 9.8           | 36.3                                    |
| Coal       | 39          | 23.0          | 23.3                                    |
| Bauxite    | 37          | 0.2           | 0.5                                     |
| Zinc       | 37          | 13.9          | 14.0                                    |
| Iron Ore   | 36          | 10.5          | 11.6                                    |
| Lead       | 34          | 15.7          | 18.1                                    |
| Gold       | 20          | 11.5          | 8.6                                     |
| Silver     | 30          | 11.7          | 16.3                                    |

*Source*: David and Wright (1997).

**(b) Ratio of labor cost/hour to electricity cost/hour**

|      | United Kingdom | United States |
|------|----------------|---------------|
| 1909 |                | 8.8           |
| 1919 |                | 31.8          |
| 1929 | 14.8           | 44.6          |
| 1938 | 20.3           | 57.0          |
| 1950 | 35.6           | 157.5         |

*Source:* Melman (1956).

technological clusters such as those based on the internal combustion engine and the chemical industry (Mowery and Rosenberg, 2000). The rise of mass production in the later railroad era can be seen as "the confluence of two technological streams: the ongoing advance of mechanical and metal-working skills ... focused on high-volume production of standardized commodities"; and the exploration and utilization of the mineral resource base (Nelson and Wright, 1992, p. 1938). Table 6.19 reports the concentration of world minerals output in the United States in 1913. It also implies that the country had been very efficient in discovering and developing minerals relatively early on. A relatively low price of electricity (Table 6.19) was conducive to the electrification of factories, which led to a surge in manufacturing productivity growth in the 1920s (David and Wright, 1999).

Over time, these influences became somewhat less important and the accumulation of human capital mattered more. The United States led the way in the expansion both of secondary and tertiary education. High school enrollment among 14–17 year olds rose from 10.6% in 1900 to 51.1% in 1930 and 86.9% in 1960, a time when only 17.5% of British 15–18 year olds were enrolled (Goldin and Katz, 2008). While about 5% of Americans born in 1880 went to college, nearly 60% of the cohort born in the 1960s did so. Throughout the third quarter of the century, average years of college education in the American adult population were a long way ahead of leading European countries (Barro and Lee, 2012). Even so, the rate of return to a year of college education in 1990 was only slightly below what it had been in 1915. This is symptomatic of the change in factor-using bias, from tangible-capital to intangible-capital using, between the 19th and the 20th centuries that Abramovitz and David (2001) detected.[25] Notable also, is that American leadership in electronics technology after World War II owed a great deal to the abundance of scientific and engineering human capital and federal research funding, rather than to the natural resource endowment.

Before World War II, relatively rapid American technological progress primarily reflected the capabilities of firms and thus the incentive structures that they faced. Endogenous innovation models point to several features of the American economy which were more favorable than in Europe at the time, and much more favorable than in Industrial Revolution Britain. These include a better system of intellectual property rights (Nicholas, 2010), a stricter anti-trust policy (Mowery and Rosenberg, 2000), a larger market potential (Liu and Meissner, 2013), and a significant fall in the costs of research as experimental science improved and the supply of specialized human capital expanded rapidly (Abramovitz and David, 2001).

This may be sufficient to explain the acceleration in technological progress but there is more to be said in terms of its direction. The experience of the American economy during the 20th century has been described as a "race" between education and technology (Goldin and Katz, 2008). Goldin and Katz highlight the development of a complementarity between advances in technology and the use of human capital that is visible from the early 20th century. The outcome of the race between increased demand for human capital as technology evolved, and increasing supply as the education system expanded, is captured in the behavior of the college wage premium (Table 6.20). Over the long-run the outcome was a photo-finish, but relative demand grew more strongly after 1960 and eventually outstripped supply after 1980.

The "directed technical change" model proposed by Acemoglu (2002) might be a suitable framework within which to analyze these trends. The key element of this model is its incorporation of a market size effect, as well as a relative price effect in the incentives that inform innovative effort. If the market size effect dominates, technological progress will be biased toward complementarity with a factor whose relative supply expands, rather than the opposite as would be expected on the basis of the ceteris paribus fall in its relative price. This induced innovation will in turn underpin the factor's rate of return through outward shifts in its demand curve.

---

[25] Abramovitz and David use a composite notion of intangible capital which includes both R & D and human capital; this is different from the definition in the recent growth accounting with intangibles literature reviewed in Section 6.4.

**Table 6.20** Supply and demand for college educated workers and changes in the college wage premium, 1915–2005 (100 × annual log changes)

|           | Relative wage | Relative supply | Relative demand |
|-----------|--------------|-----------------|-----------------|
| 1915–1940 | −0.56        | 3.19            | 2.41            |
| 1940–1960 | −0.51        | 2.63            | 1.92            |
| 1960–1980 | −0.02        | 3.77            | 3.74            |
| 1980–2005 | 0.90         | 2.00            | 3.27            |
| 1915–2005 | −0.02        | 2.87            | 2.83            |

*Note*: estimates assume the elasticity of substitution between college and high school graduates = 1.64.
*Source*: Goldin and Katz (2008).

### 6.5.3 Lessons from the ICT Revolution[26]

The Solow Productivity Paradox was announced in 1987 with the comment that "You can see the computer age everywhere except in the productivity statistics."A great deal of effort was subsequently devoted to explaining this (Triplett, 1999) and it was an important trigger for the literature on General Purpose Technologies. This developed models that had negligible or even negative impacts on productivity performance in their first phase but substantial positive effects later on. Indeed, a GPT can be defined as "a technology that initially has much scope for improvement and eventually comes to be widely used, to have many uses and to have many Hicksian and technological complementarities" (Lipsey et al. 1998, p. 43).

Table 6.21 compares ICT with the two other GPTs, electricity and steam, which are commonly placed in the pantheon on account of their impact on productivity growth in the leading economy of the time. The comparison reveals that the impact of ICT has been relatively big, and that it has come through very quickly. This new GPT is unprecedented in its rate of technological progress, reflected in the speed and magnitude of the price falls in ICT equipment reported in Table 6.21. The impact of ICT on the rate of productivity growth throughout 1973–2006 exceeded that of steam in any period and was already close to twice the maximum impact of steam by the late 1980s. Indeed, these estimates suggest that the cumulative impact of ICT on labor productivity by 2006 was about the same as that of steam over the whole 150-year period, 1760–1910.

A plausible inference seems to be that society is getting better at exploiting the opportunities presented by new GPTs. This may reflect a number of factors including more investment in human capital, superior scientific knowledge, improved capital markets, and greater support for R & D by public policy. Taking an historical perspective, the true paradox is that Solow's ICT paradox was regarded as such, given that by earlier standards the contribution of ICT to productivity performance in the American economy in the late 1980s was already stunning.

---

[26] This section draws in part on Crafts (2013a).

**Table 6.21** GPTs: contributions to labor productivity growth (percent per annum)

| | |
|---|---|
| **Steam (UK)** | |
| 1760–1830 | 0.01 |
| 1830–1870 | 0.30 |
| **Electricity (USA)** | |
| 1899–1919 | 0.40 |
| 1919–1929 | 0.98 |
| **ICT (USA)** | |
| 1973–1995 | 0.74 |
| 1995–2006 | 1.45 |
| **Memorandum item: real price falls (%)** | |
| **Steam horsepower** | |
| 1760–1830 | 39.1 |
| 1830–1870 | 60.8 |
| **Electric motors (Sweden)** | |
| 1901–1925 | 38.5 |
| **ICT equipment** | |
| 1970–1989 | 80.6 |
| 1989–2007 | 77.5 |

*Notes*: Growth-accounting contributions include both capital deepening from use and TFP from production. Price fall for ICT equipment includes computer, software, and telecoms; the price of computers alone fell much faster (22.2% per year in the first period and 18.3% per year in the second period).
*Sources*: Growth accounting: Crafts (2002, 2004b) and Oliner et al. (2007). Price falls: Crafts (2004b), Edquist (2010), and Oulton (2012).

**Table 6.22** Sources of labor productivity growth in the market sector, 1995–2005 (percent per annum)

| | Labor quality | ICT K/hour worked | Non-ICT K/hour worked | TFP | Labor productivity growth |
|---|---|---|---|---|---|
| EU | 0.2 | 0.5 | 0.4 | 0.4 | 1.5 |
| France | 0.4 | 0.4 | 0.4 | 0.9 | 2.1 |
| Germany | 0.1 | 0.5 | 0.6 | 0.4 | 1.6 |
| UK | 0.5 | 0.9 | 0.4 | 0.8 | 2.6 |
| USA | 0.3 | 1.0 | 0.3 | 1.3 | 2.9 |

*Source:* Timmer et al. (2010).

A very noticeable feature of the ICT revolution is that the United States exploited the opportunities much better than did European countries, generally speaking (Oulton, 2012). Table 6.22 shows that the ICT capital deepening contribution in the United States was about twice that in the European Union between 1995 and 2005. Indeed, this episode saw an ending of the long period of productivity catch-up achieved by Western Europe since the early 1950s.

A lens through which to examine this experience is to think about varieties of capitalism (Hall and Soskice, 2001). The core of this approach is based on a comparison between two ideal types, the co-ordinated market economy (CME) and the liberal market economy (LME), which comprise different environments in which firms operate. The purest cases of the CME and the LME are Germany and the United States, respectively (Schneider and Paunescu, 2012). Each of these economies can be thought of as having a different set of complementary institutions and, as a corollary of this, different comparative advantages in production, trade, human capital formation, and crucially, innovation. The LME is characterized by extensive equity markets and flexible labor markets, while the CME offers high employment protection and corporate governance that is based on monitoring by banks and an absence of hostile takeovers. LMEs place more emphasis on university education and less on vocational training, and are also more lightly regulated in terms of the standard indices calculated by the OECD.

Hall and Soskice (2001, pp. 38–39) argued that CMEs would be relatively strong at "incremental innovation, marked by continuous but small-scale improvements to existing product lines and production processes," while LMEs would be more successful at "radical innovation, which entails substantial shifts in product lines, the development of entirely new goods, or major changes to the production process." Empirical testing of claims about radical and incremental innovation poses considerable problems, but Akkermans et al. (2009) developed an approach based on patent citations, basically taking radical innovations to be those which are more highly cited. They found that the United States is indeed strongly specialized in radical innovation.

With regard to ICT, CMEs and LMEs might also be expected to differ in their abilities to exploit its opportunities since investment in ICT capital is much more profitable and has a much bigger productivity payoff if it is accompanied by organizational change in working and management practices and is therefore encouraged by low adjustment costs (Brynjolfsson and Hitt, 2003). The empirical evidence is that the diffusion of ICT has been aided by complementary investments in intangible capital and high-quality human capital, but weakened by relatively strong regulation in terms of employment protection and regulations that restrict competition, especially in the distribution sector (Conway et al. 2006).

ICT is a technology that is very well suited both to management practices in American-owned companies (Bloom et al. 2012) and the economic environment in the United States. Perhaps the more general message is that, when a disruptive GPT appears, American institutions are at an advantage.

## 6.6. THE ECONOMIC HISTORIAN'S VIEW OF CATCH-UP

In Section 6.3 we saw that while some regions—notably Japan and the East Asian Tigers—caught up on the world technological frontier in spectacular fashion after 1945, others—notably Latin America and Africa—did not. The growth miracles of the 20th century, including not only the Japanese and Tiger experiences, but Western Europe during the Golden Age, China from the late 1970s onwards, or Ireland during the 1990s, were above all convergence miracles. Economic historians have known, since the work of Gerschenkron (1962) and even before, that backwardness can sometimes lead to rapid growth. The further behind the technological frontier a country is, the faster is its potential growth, since by importing the latest technologies and machinery it can improve its total factor productivity much more rapidly than an economy closer to the frontier. As Gerschenkron (1962, p. 8) put it, "Borrowed technology, so much and so rightly stressed by Veblen, was one of the primary factors assuring a high speed of development in a backward country entering the stage of industrialization." And indeed, industrialization, or the modernization of existing industries, was at the heart of the best-known 20th century growth miracles.

The problem is that while being economically backward implied a potential for rapid catch-up growth, it also implied obstacles to realizing that growth—since otherwise the country or region concerned would not have been backward in the first place. Economic historians have thus also always stressed that there is nothing inevitable or automatic about catch-up. This section will present some general insights from economic history relating to the question of whether countries are able to exploit catch-up opportunities or not. Sections 6.7–6.9 will then go on to apply these insights to well-known episodes of success followed by disappointment, success up to now, and failure, respectively.

## 6.6.1 Catch-Up is Not Automatic

The logic that backward countries should be able to grow more rapidly than the rich, by importing best-practice technologies, is powerful, but we know that in practice poor countries do not always grow more rapidly than the rich. If they did, then we would not regard those instances where convergence has most visibly been at work as growth miracles. We have seen that some groups of countries have managed to converge on the US technological frontier, while others have not. We have also seen that convergence was widespread in some periods, particularly the 1950–1973 Golden Age, while in other periods there was little or no convergence. Indeed in some periods divergence was more the rule, for example, during the late 19th century when the United States pulled further ahead of most of the rest of the world. Looking at variations in growth among those countries chasing the United States frontier, there have been contrasting experiences of convergence and divergence, depending on the groups of countries and time periods being considered. Absolute convergence characterized the rich economies as a group in the four decades since World War II, but there was no worldwide tendency during these years for poorer countries to grow more rapidly than the rich (Abramovitz, 1986; De Long, 1988; Barro, 1991).

Why does convergence happen sometimes but not always, and in some countries but not others? And why does it sometimes cease altogether, after promising beginnings? The logic of convergence suggests that it should be self-limiting: as countries catch up on the technological frontier, the scope for further catching up diminishes. As workers leave low-productivity agriculture for high-productivity service and manufacturing jobs, the pool of workers who can be similarly redeployed diminishes. One would thus expect converging economies to continue catching up on the lead economy, but at a diminishing rate over time, as in Lucas (2000, 2009). Yet, Western European convergence ceased after the first oil crisis, at a relative GDP level of only 70%, while in the former Soviet empire, and Southwest Asia, convergence not only halted at the same time, but was replaced by two decades or more of sharp divergence. Japan's convergence was also succeeded by divergence, beginning in the 1990s. More generally, there is evidence that countries often experience growth slowdowns after phases of rapid growth that are much sharper than would be expected on the basis of convergence logic alone. Eichengreen et al. (2012) found that the probability of such rapid slowdowns peaks at per capita GDP levels of about $17,000 in 2005 international prices, and that the probability is higher after periods of rapid economic growth.

Many economic historians have written about why convergence may not take place, the advantages of backwardness notwithstanding. Gerschenkron (1962, p. 8), whose major focus was Europe, argued that the major obstacles were "formidable institutional obstacles (such as the serfdom of the peasantry or the far-reaching absence of political unification," as well as (in some countries) a lack of natural resources. True, backward countries also lacked the prerequisites for growth that had been built up in Britain over the course of many decades and even centuries, but for Gerschenkron this handicap could be surmounted by means of institutional substitutes such as universal banks or a developmental state.

Gerschenkron was writing in the early 1960s, at a time when the Soviet Union and its allies were still converging rapidly on the United States, and decolonization with its ensuing policy experimentation was still in its infancy. By the 1980s, greater scepticism regarding the ability of backward states to engineer convergence seemed in order. Abramovitz (1986, pp. 387, 390, 393, 397) lists several reasons why convergence may not take place. Countries may lack the "social capability" required to realize their catch-up potential; the global economy may not be operating in a way that facilitates technological transfer; there may be obstacles to structural change within the backward economies; short-run macroeconomic policies may not encourage investment, with long-run consequences; best-practice technologies may not be appropriate for developing economies' size or factor endowments; and major shocks such as war may disrupt the convergence process. We briefly review each of these arguments in subsequent sections.

## 6.6.2 The Consequences of Directed Technological Change

Technological change is not exogenous, but an endogenous response to economic conditions. This can make it difficult for countries to catch up on the technological frontier, irrespective of whatever institutions they may have or which policies they adopt. Frontier technologies may have been invented with conditions in the leading economy in mind, and may therefore not be easy or profitable to adopt in poorer countries.

This possibility has been raised by growth economists such as Basu and Weil (1998), and Acemoglu and Zilibotti (2001), in debates about appropriate technology, but it is also a long-standing theme of economic historians. The argument that technologies are invented so as to take advantage of local factor endowments is most often associated with Habakkuk (1962), who as we have seen, argued that it was high American wages, due to an extensive land endowment, that explained the relatively labor-saving nature of US mass production technology. The evidence suggests that since the late 19th century, improvements in the production function have been concentrated at the capital to labor ratios at which rich countries operate. For example, there was a big increase in output per worker at capital to labor ratios between $15,000 and $20,000 (1985 prices) between 1939 and 1965, but no further improvement in recent decades. Indeed, at very low capital to labor ratios, output per worker in 1990 appears to have been no higher than in 1820 (Allen, 2012). This is symptomatic of a pattern of directed technical change where advances are made in accordance with the incentives provided by market conditions in rich countries, especially the United States.

The possibility then arises that relative factor prices in less developed economies made the new technologies unprofitable. Gerschenkron (1962, pp. 8–9) raised the issue, noting that "The industrialization prospects of an underdeveloped country are frequently... judged aversely, in terms of cheapness of labor as against capital goods and of the resultant difficulty in substituting scarce capital for abundant labor." He also noted that this argument flies in the face of the opposite argument that low wages give developing countries a powerful competitive advantage. But he went on to dismiss the argument in the context of 19th century Europe, on the grounds that "a stable, reliable and disciplined" labor force was scarce, rather than abundant, in backward economies where people were still close to the land. Indeed, he claimed that this fact gave entrepreneurs in countries like Russia an incentive to import technologies that were as modern, efficient, and labor-saving as possible.

In contrast, as we have seen, Allen (2009) argued that it was rational for other countries to not immediately adopt the new technologies of the British Industrial Revolution, implying that Britain initially forged ahead while others fell behind. It was only with time, as the new technologies became more productive, that they became profitable to adopt elsewhere. By the late 19th century, however, Britain was no longer the leading innovator, and the question was whether American inventions were suitable for British conditions or not. British entrepreneurs have often been criticized for failing to adopt the latest technologies—for example, cotton manufacturers were slow to adopt ring spinning, preferring to stick with mule spinning, while soda manufacturers were slow to abandon the Leblanc process for the superior Solvay process. Magee (2004) surveys an abundant literature that argues that British entrepreneurs were in fact responding rationally, not only to British relative factor prices (skilled workmen were cheaper than in America, and natural resources were dearer), but also to different (and in particular less homogenous) demand conditions. If Lancashire cotton manufacturers used mules, this was because they produced more fine yarns, and more yarn for export, than their American counterparts, and mule spinning was superior on both counts (Leunig, 2001). More generally, fragmented demand and skilled labor made it rational for British manufacturers to eschew resource-intensive and labor-saving mass production techniques, and adopt "a more flexible form of production, based on general purpose machinery, skilled labor and customized demand" (Magee, 2004, p. 95). Similar considerations can explain why British firms did not adopt Chandlerian organizational forms during the same period (Harley, 1991).

We will consider the British case in more detail below, merely noting that if frontier technologies do not correspond to the needs of developing countries, then those countries may fall further behind the leaders for perfectly rational reasons, with no "failure" being necessarily involved. What might reverse such a trend? Educational policies are one obvious candidate. Another is late 20th century globalization, which Wright (1990) argues was a major turning point, in that it transformed mineral resources from being endowments to commodities, available to all countries at roughly equal prices. The implication is that resource-intensive American technologies now became potentially easier to implement around the world. Similarly, the opening of the rest of the OECD to international trade meant that American mass production techniques could more easily be adopted elsewhere, and the process of convergence itself strengthened this tendency by further increasing the size of overseas markets. Finally, postwar US technological strength in sectors like semiconductors were based on the expansion of scientific education and research; and research and development, which could be replicated abroad, especially given the inherently international nature of scientific activity (Nelson and Wright, 1992; Abramovitz and David, 1996). As Alice Amsden (1989, p. 7) put it, "Although technology remained ... idiosyncratic even in basic industries, higher scientific content increased its codifiedness or explicitness, making it more of a commodity and hence more technically and commercially accessible and diffusible from country to country." Multinational corporations made technology even more diffusible. For all these reasons, US frontier technologies could now in principle be more easily implemented abroad, at least in the relatively advanced economies of Europe and Japan, than had been the case before. The extent to which they were actually implemented presumably depended on a variety of other factors, some of which will be considered below.

## 6.6.3 Catch-Up and Social Capability

According to Abramovitz (1986), tenacious social characteristics could inhibit countries from importing best-practice technology, and one would therefore only expect poorer countries to grow more rapidly than richer ones if these social characteristics, which he termed "social capability," were roughly similar. Rapid growth was thus most likely when countries were "technologically backward but socially advanced" (p. 388). Abramovitz (1989, pp. 200–201) considered both these conditions to have been present in Europe and Japan after World War II. Both regions had generally well-educated populations, and were well endowed with scientists and engineers, who were increasingly influential within industry. This helped in implementing new technologies invented abroad. Both firms and governments promoted research and development. Large corporations were becoming increasingly well managed. The resumption of international trade, air travel, the press, and American cooperation facilitated the importation of technical knowledge. Such attributes of backwardness as a large agricultural population could be turned into an advantage, since agricultural productivity growth facilitated the release of labor to new and growing sectors of the economy. Other aspects of social capability included openness to change and competition, which were necessary as rapid structural change was part and parcel of the catch-up process. Abramovitz cites Olson's (1982) view that the war itself, by sweeping aside existing vested interests, helped create a *tabula rasa* that facilitated such change.

Social capability can be thought of as being equivalent to the parameter $\mu_m$ in Schumpeterian growth theory (Aghion and Howitt, 2006). This refers to the extent to which countries' growth rates are boosted by virtue of their distance from the technological frontier. Abramovitz largely discusses education when referring to social capability, but he also mentions institutions, and these have been a major focus of economic historians seeking to understand different countries' growth experiences. A standard list of institutions that might matter for growth includes "the security of property rights, prevalence of corruption, structures of the financial sector, investment in public infrastructure and social capital, and the inclination to work hard or be entrepreneurial" (Sokoloff and Engerman, 2000, p. 218). The degree and nature of unionization; attitudes toward cartels and competition; social welfare and taxation systems; and the general nature of government involvement in the economy, could also be added to this list. What matters from the perspective of convergence is the incentive structures shaped by policy and institutions which influence the diffusion and assimilation of new technology in follower countries by, for example, determining the expected profitability of innovation, or by mitigating or exacerbating agency problems in the firms which have to invest in the new technologies. Economic historians emphasize that we do not inhabit a "one-size-fits-all" world, and that optimal institutional design may therefore vary according to the degree of backwardness, the technological era, etc.[27]

---

[27] This is a key point made in Aghion and Howitt (2006).

Gerschenkron believed that the institutional mix could adapt to meet the needs of the backward country seeking to catch-up. Where capital markets were not as well functioning as in the mature British economy, and where entrepreneurship was scarce, universal banks mobilizing large amounts of saving and providing not only capital but also entrepreneurial guidance for heavy industries, could fill the void. Where the economy was so backward that this was not an option, as in Russia, the state could step in instead. Gerschenkron believed that in the boom years immediately prior to World War I, universal banks played a more important role in Russia than they had done during the boom of the 1890s, reflecting the fact that Russia was no longer as backward as she had been a quarter of a century earlier.[28] If institutions can adapt in this manner, then although they may be crucial for economic performance, they are also endogenous; and endogenous variables do not make convincing explanatory variables. The view that historical institutions were efficient solutions to economic problems characterized much early cliometric work on the subject, including that of Douglass North (e.g. North and Thomas, 1973). However, institutions can arise for other reasons as well: for example, they could be the result of accident, followed by path dependence; or of cultural belief systems; or of distributional conflicts (Ogilvie, 2007). A frequent theme in modern economic history is that particular institutions may have originated as efficient solutions to context-specific problems, but that they can also be politically hard to reform and subject to path dependence (North 1990). Thus, when the context changed, the institutions stayed the same, and turned from being a help to a hindrance. We will see examples of this kind of logic at work in the case studies below.

Of particular interest is the possibility that institutions which help countries catch-up on the technological frontier may no longer be appropriate once countries have converged. For example, Rosenstein-Rodan (1943) argued that intersectoral complementarities could mean that modern industrialization might only get going if it happened across a broad front. For Gerschenkron (1962, pp. 10–11) this was one explanation for why, in his view, the transition to industrialization tended to happen in a dramatic and even discontinuous fashion (a claim which subsequent quantitative research has however cast doubt on—see Sylla and Toniolo, 1991). Such "big push" arguments naturally suggest a potentially important coordinating role for the state (Murphy et al. 1989) in the early phases of industrialization, but it is far from clear that such state involvement would make sense when countries have reached the frontier, and the question is no longer how to import and implement existing technologies, but to develop new ones. More radically, Baldwin (forthcoming) argues that modern multinational-led globalization and what he refers to as the "second unbundling" has destroyed big push arguments for state-led

---

[28] Gerschenkron's account is controversial. Sylla (1991, pp. 52–53) reviews evidence which suggests that banks played a larger role in the 1890s industrialization than Gerschenkron had allowed, while Gregory (1991) argues strongly that state involvement was by no means as beneficial as Gerschenkron had believed it to be.

industrialization that were valid not so long ago: small developing countries can now begin to industrialize by colonizing individual niches in global supply chains. Of course, this argument relies on globalization being sustained in the future, which is something that can never be taken for granted (Findlay and O'Rourke, 2007).

Such arguments suggest that institutional reform may be needed as countries progress economically. Unfortunately, if institutions are path dependent then such reform may not always proceed as smoothly as Gerschenkron believed had been the case in pre-1914 Russia.

## 6.6.4 Geography

It is striking that income levels around the world are highly spatially correlated. Since these income levels are the result of long-standing historical processes, it is not surprising that there was a degree of regional clustering in the timing of the shift to modern industrialization. Signs of rapid industrialization can be found in Eastern Europe and Latin America from the 1870s onwards, and in parts of Asia by the end of the 19th century (Bénétrix et al. 2013). Why do we observe such geographical correlations in the data, and what do they imply for convergence?

One possibility is that countries with similar resource endowments tend to be located close to each other, and thus end up with similar growth experiences and incomes in the long run. This may be because geographical conditions and resource endowments matter directly for growth (Sachs and Warner, 1997), or because they matter indirectly via their impact on institutions (Easterly and Levine, 2003). Economic historians have long argued that institutions may respond to endowments: for example, Domar (1970) argued that forced labor systems such as serfdom and slavery were a predictable outcome in labor-scarce and land-abundant societies, since in the absence of such exploitation the return to owning land was zero, which was not in the interests of would-be aristocrats. Domar is cited by Engerman and Sokoloff (1997), who argue that institutional differences based on underlying differences in geography, rather than superior culture, were the main reason why the United States and Canada eventually became so much richer than other countries in the Americas.[29] Brazil and the Caribbean were ideally suited to producing crops such as sugar, and thus developed slave-based economies, societies, and political institutions, irrespective of what European powers colonized them. British, French, Dutch, Portuguese, and Scandinavian sugar colonies all developed highly unequal, slave-based societies, and remained highly unequal even after the suppression of slavery. Spanish American colonies developed by exploiting Native American workforces in both agriculture and mining, and were also highly unequal. The result was political institutions and economic policies designed to maintain elite privileges: restricted franchise, barriers

---

[29] Acemoglu et al. (2001) suggest an alternative mechanism through which geography may have influenced development via its impact on institutions. For a discussion, see Albouy (2012).

to European immigration, limited investment in education, conservative taxation systems, and expensive access to patent protection, to name but a few (Sokoloff and Engerman, 2000; Sokoloff and Zolt, 2007).

It is important not to romanticize the US or Canadian experiences, to ignore the treatment meted out to their own native American populations, or to forget that universal suffrage was only attained in the United States as late as the 1960s. This last fact is a shocking reminder of the corrosive effect of inequality and racial segregation on the quality of political institutions. But inequality was relatively low among US and Canadian whites, and because whites made up a relatively large share of those two countries' populations (since sugar was not an important crop even in the US, and since native Americans were so few in number by the 19th century), the net result was societies that were relatively egalitarian in the aggregate. This in turn encouraged not only inclusive institutions for whites, but directly stimulated economic growth by encouraging commercial activity and the development of mass marketing. Canada and the US also invested heavily in public education, funded out of local taxes on income and wealth, made the patent system cheaply accessible to a broad range of people, and promoted economic growth in a variety of other ways. Engerman and Sokoloff (1997) sketch a story in which a rapidly growing and relatively equal population boosted 19th century US growth, by promoting a Smithian process of division of labor and exploitation of scale economies, and by encouraging market-oriented innovation. This route to prosperity was barred to Latin American economies whose institutions perpetuated historical patterns of inequality.

Such arguments explain geographical correlations in GDP by pointing to geographical correlations in resource endowments. They would work even if each country were isolated from its neighbors. But it is also possible that geographical correlations in economic outcomes are shaped by interactions between countries located closer or further together. One possibility, emphasized by the new economic geography, is that market access matters for income levels and, in particular, for the location of industry across the world (Krugman and Venables, 1995). Redding and Venables (2004) find that GDP per capita is strongly related to market access and proximity to suppliers, and argue that this can retard convergence in per capita incomes and wages. Another possibility is that the diffusion of technology itself is a decreasing function of distance (Comin et al. 2013). Economic historians have increasingly been adopting such a geographical perspective in recent years (Crafts and Venables, 2003).

## 6.6.5 Events, Dear Boy

Easterly et al. (1993) show that shocks are as important as fundamentals in explaining countries' decadal growth performances. Nor can we ignore the impact of shocks over the longer run, as the disastrous performance of the interwar period shows.

Economic theorists such as Lucas (2009) understandably tend to construct models in which certain patterns—such as the gradual diffusion of economic growth across the globe—can be expected to apply in the absence of such non-economic forces as "wars, breakdowns of internal order, and misguided ventures into centralized economic planning" (p. 23).

Economic history, by contrast, focuses heavily on such events, for a number of reasons. First, while economic historians seek general explanations, like other economists, they also want to understand what happened in specific countries and at specific times, like other historians. For example, while the relative decline of the Caribbean may have been in part due to the institutional legacies mentioned above, it was also surely due to the British-led suppression of slavery and the development of beet sugar production in Europe. This tension between the specific and the general is one of the defining features of the field. Second, economic historians are trained to think in terms of path dependence (David, 1985), and sufficiently major crises can have very long-term effects, for example because of their impact on subsequent policy choices (Buera et al. 2011). Third, economic history is an inherently interdisciplinary subject: as Hicks (1969, p. 2) put it, "A major function of economic history ... is to be a forum where economists and political scientists, lawyers, sociologists, and historians—historians of events and of ideas and of technologies—can meet and talk to one another." As such, economic historians are more likely than other economists to try to understand the causes of non-economic shocks, and to integrate them into their analyses.

Although it is beyond the scope of a chapter such as this, it would be impossible to tell a convincing story of 20th century growth without describing the major shocks that defined the century, and tracing out their consequences. The two world wars, the Great Depression, decolonization, the oil shocks of the 1970s, and the Cold War and its ending, all had major effects on regional growth patterns during our period. This is evident from Figure 6.2, which shows major breaks in regional performance relative to the United States coinciding with the world wars, the onset of the Depression in 1929, and the first oil crisis of 1973.

World War I not only brought to an end the period of globalization that preceded it, but changed the economic and geopolitical landscape in ways that defined the rest of the 20th century. It led to the collapse of the German, Austro-Hungarian, and Russian empires, spawning a host of new nation states in Europe; it led to the Russian revolution of 1917, which had an enormous impact on the economies of not only the USSR, but (after 1945) of Eastern Europe and China as well; it permanently weakened the British economy, leaving the interwar world without a hegemon able and willing to provide global public goods (Kindleberger, 1973); it led to major imbalances in the structure of international trade, and to war debts and reparations, which would cast a dark shadow over the interwar period's flawed attempt to recreate a globalized world based on the gold standard. Most accounts of the Great Depression begin with these and other legacies of the conflict (Eichengreen, 1992), while the Depression and German post-war resentments combined to produce the election of Hitler, and ultimately the outbreak of World War II.

That conflict in turn cemented the relative decline of Europe, and paved the way for both the Soviet–US duopoly which lasted until the end of the 1980s, and decolonization throughout Asia and Africa. The historical association between globalization and European imperialism, the distrust of markets which naturally flowed from the disastrous experience of the interwar period, and the spread of communism, all predisposed the leaders of newly independent countries to pursue state-led growth policies, often based on import-substituting industrialization. Western Europe and North America developed a variety of more or less social democratic economies and societies, by and large (but by no means exclusively) using markets to generate wealth, and using the state to redistribute it, provide safety nets, and correct market failures. Elsewhere, the reaction against markets was far more severe. It was only reversed after the poor economic performance of the 1970s, which in turn had at least something to do with the oil shock which followed the Yom Kippur War of 1973—yet another event with important long-term consequences. The policy transition accelerated after the collapse of the Soviet Union, and is still ongoing. As historians, we would not want to bet that there will not be another policy reversal in the future, as a result of further unexpected shocks to the system.

The reason for dwelling on such major events and their consequences is to make the point that economic historians do not just focus on deep historical legacies and institutional path dependence. If these were all that mattered, then one would not expect to see more or less simultaneous reversals in both economic policy regimes and growth experiences across countries with very different histories and institutional legacies. The interwar growth experience was bad across all major regions of the world, while the Golden Age was good. This had a lot to do with the specific historical circumstances at work in both periods, and circumstances change. Change as well as continuity has always concerned historians, since both matter in the real world.

### 6.6.6 Openness and Other Economic Policies

Previous subsections have looked at some of the difficulties that countries can face in their attempts to join the convergence club—difficulties which may be difficult to overcome, since individual countries cannot easily change the appropriateness of foreign technology, or their geography, or the international geopolitical environment, or even (perhaps) their own institutions. However, countries can change their economic policies for better or worse. The question is whether such policy transitions can produce better growth performances, and if so, which policies are good for growth.

Most attention in the literature has focused on the impact of market-friendly economic policies in general, and trade policy in particular. A key reference is Sachs and Warner (1995), who produce an index of trade openness (subsequently updated in Wacziarg and Welch, 2008). Sachs and Warner used this index to study the impact of trade policy between 1970 and 1989. They found that openness was associated with higher growth, and that unconditional convergence characterized the experience of open economies but not of closed economies. Following discussion of the way in which this index was constructed (e.g. Rodríguez and Rodrik, 2001), several subsequent researchers (e.g. Buera et al. 2011) have preferred to interpret this index as indicating whether a country has adopted generally market-friendly policies or not.

This is how the index is used by Hausmann et al. (2005), who study the characteristics and determinants of growth accelerations from the 1950s to the 1990s. They find that while market-friendly economic reforms are a statistically significant predictor of sustained growth accelerations, they are not a quantitatively reliable predictor. Most pro-market reforms do not lead to such accelerations, and most accelerations are not preceded by such reforms. While their study finds that growth accelerations are difficult to predict, it also finds that they tend to have certain characteristics in common. In particular, growth accelerations are associated with higher investment rates, increases in trade, and real exchange rate depreciations. We will see examples of this below. We also note that the two growth accelerations that have mattered most for human welfare in recent decades—those in China and India—clearly seem to be related to market-friendly policy reforms.

There has been a vigorous debate about whether openness to trade is associated with faster growth or not, with Rodríguez and Rodrik (2001) among others strongly questioning the Sachs and Warner result. A recent contribution (Estevadeordal and Taylor, forthcoming) finds that lower tariffs on imported capital goods were associated with higher growth between 1975 and 2004, and it is probably fair to say that most economists assume that openness and growth go hand in hand today. Economic historians, however, tend to emphasize that the "right" policies may be context-specific, and may have varied over time. Clemens and Williamson (2004) find that tariffs were positively correlated with economic growth during the interwar period: perhaps the benefits to individual countries of maintaining open trade policies were lower in an environment where demand was depressed, and other countries had closed their own markets. Policies that were collectively costly may have been individually rational in such a context.

O'Rourke (2000) finds that tariffs and growth were positively correlated in the late 19th century as well, controlling for country fixed effects, in a sample of 10 relatively well-developed economies. A lack of aggregate demand was not a problem in this period, so unless the correlation is spurious we need another explanation. The growth-promoting externalities associated with industry would seem to offer one such explanation: as is well known, the United States industrialized behind very high tariff barriers during this period, and Germany and other continental European countries similarly protected their heavy industry. The fact that it was industrial tariffs that were associated with high growth, rather than agricultural tariffs, adds weight to this interpretation (Lehmann and O'Rourke, 2011). But even if the argument is correct, it does not follow that such policies would have worked in even less developed countries at the same time, or in the same countries in later periods. There is thus an important potential role for country histories in elucidating the impact of economic policies on growth, since panel growth regressions which estimate effects that are consistent across countries or over time may be seriously misleading.

## 6.7. CASE STUDIES I: INITIAL SUCCESS, SUBSEQUENT DISAPPOINTMENT

In the following three sections we explore several case studies that illustrate some of the themes of this chapter in slightly greater depth. We begin by looking at two cases where initial growth successes were succeeded by disappointment. The first is Western Europe, which converged strongly on the US during the Golden Age. Since the 1970s, however, convergence in GDP per capita has come to a halt. The second is the United Kingdom, which pioneered the transition to modern economic growth, but whose 20th century performance was much more disappointing, especially during the Golden Age.

### 6.7.1 The European Golden Age and the Subsequent Slowdown[30]

We have seen that Western Europe achieved its highest ever growth rates, roughly 4% per annum, during the Golden Age which lasted from 1950 to 1973. The period between the Second World War and the first oil crisis has subsequently passed into folk memory as the *Trente Glorieuses* (glorious thirty) or the *Wirtschaftswunder* (economic miracle). Eastern Europe and the former USSR also grew rapidly, although somewhat less so than Western Europe, when in a convergence perspective they should have grown more quickly. Relative to other miracles, for example in East Asia, a relatively large share of Western Europe's growth was due to TFP improvements, suggesting a large role for technological catch-up and structural change (Crafts and Toniolo, 2008). What explains the European growth miracle and the subsequent slowdown?

Western Europe's per capita GDP stood at just 31% of the American level in 1945. Austria's GDP had regressed to its 1886 level, France's to its 1891 level, and Germany's to its 1908 level (Crafts and Toniolo, 1996, p. 4). Rapid growth as a result of post-war reconstruction is hardly surprising. However, pre-war levels of GDP were restored by 1951 at the latest. Strikingly, in that year, Western Europe's relative GDP stood at only 47%.

The potential for catch-up growth seems obvious, and it seems even more obvious when a number of supplementary factors are taken into account. First, American technology and European conditions were more technologically congruent than they had been in earlier decades, as natural resources and larger markets became more easily available to European firms (Abramovitz and David, 1996). European economic integration would make both even more easily available as the 1950s progressed. Second, Western Europe possessed a high level of social capability: a generally well-educated population, and a history of well-functioning political and market institutions. According to Abramovitz

---

[30] This section draws in part on Crafts (2013a).

and David the war further strengthened Western Europe's social capability, by sweeping aside lingering *Ancien Régime* attitudes toward such things as mass education, mass production, industry, and economic growth. Finally, the disastrous experience of Depression and war gave a powerful impetus to European integration, and thus to the reversal of the protectionist policies of the interwar period.

High levels of social capability in an economically backward society—impoverished sophistication, in Sandberg's (1979) memorable phrase—should be optimal for achieving economic growth, especially if that society is engaged in a process of economically integrating disparate national economies into a continental common market. A further factor emphasized by many economic historians (Kindleberger, 1967; Broadberry, 1997; Temin, 2002) is the large agricultural workforces in most European countries that could be redeployed to higher productivity non-agricultural occupations. Such structural change accounted for a large share of Golden Age labor productivity growth (Crafts and Toniolo, 2008). And so the European growth miracle can be comparatively easily explained in terms of the convergence framework outlined earlier—which is hardly surprising, since it was this European experience that largely gave rise to the convergence paradigm in the first place. Not only did Western Europe as a whole grow more rapidly than the United States, but there was strong unconditional income convergence within Western Europe as well. And yet there is more to be said about this episode, for at least two reasons. First, economic growth in some countries was a lot faster than would be expected on the basis of post-war reconstruction and convergence alone (Crafts, 1992a, Table 6, p. 401). Second, some countries did a lot better during the Golden Age than others, even once their initial incomes have been taken into account.

Eichengreen (1996) shows that growth was positively correlated across Western European countries with both investment and export growth, consistent with Hausmann et al. (2005). According to Eichengreen, who further develops his argument in Eichengreen (2007), high levels of investment and trade were sustained by a variety of domestic and international institutions. Domestic institutions, which can be collectively described as corporatist, ensured that workers moderated their wage demands so that profits were high, and as a quid pro quo ensured that profits were reinvested rather than being paid out as dividends, thus ensuring higher wage growth in the future. Worker representation on firm's boards helped ensure that employers did not defect from this mutually beneficial equilibrium; centralized wage bargaining overseen by government, which had both sticks and carrots at its disposal, ensured that workers did not defect. The welfare state was one way in which workers were compensated for wage moderation in the short run. The result was high investment, capital deepening, high rates of TFP growth, and an economic miracle.

The international institutions that mattered were those associated with European integration: the European Payments Union; the European Coal and Steel Community, the European Economic Community; and EFTA. These facilitated the resumption of multilateral trade in Europe, which was necessary both for standard efficiency reasons, and so that firms could be ensured of foreign markets when making their investment decisions. European international integration was one of the demands of the US government, which used Marshall Aid as a lever to obtain this and other market-friendly structural reforms (DeLong and Eichengreen, 1993). Crafts and Toniolo (2008) portray the Golden Age as a period in which there was scope for growth simply by undoing the policy mistakes of the interwar period.

If Eichengreen is right, then investment, trade, and growth should have been higher in countries which adopted appropriate domestic institutions, and liberalized their trade earlier. Ireland is one example of a country which only liberalized its trade in the late 1950s and early 1960s, and which, like the UK, had a more fragmented and less corporatist trade union structure. Both countries performed relatively disappointingly during the Golden Age. On the other hand, Belgium, West Germany, the Netherlands, and Scandinavia all had relatively corporatist systems of industrial relations, and liberalized their trade policy relatively early. The Eichengreen argument is thus a priori plausible, although econometric testing of the hypothesis is difficult (Crafts, 1992b).

What explains the post-1973 growth slowdown? The arguments outlined above suggest that to a large extent this was inevitable, as Europe caught up to the technological frontier, and the pool of agricultural workers who could be redeployed gradually vanished. While this is surely a large part of the story, it is not the whole story, for several reasons (Crafts and Toniolo, 2008). First, while GDP per capita convergence on the US ceased in the 1970s, labor productivity convergence continued until some point in the 1990s. The difference is due to diverging trends in hours worked in the two continents: how to interpret this remains unclear (Blanchard, 2004; Prescott, 2004; Alesina et al. 2006). Second, the distributional conflicts associated with the oil crises of the 1970s may have undermined the viability of the cooperative political institutions which Eichengreen believed had promoted growth during the Golden Age. Third, even if these institutions had remained as viable as they had been before, it is unclear that they were well adapted to a new era in which growth based on importing best-practice technology from abroad was no longer as easy as it had been when Europe had been more backward (Eichengreen, 2007; Aghion and Howitt, 2006). Rather than mobilizing large amounts of capital to mass produce well-understood technologies that had been developed elsewhere, the problem was now how to innovate: the argument is that this required more competitive product markets, different methods of finance, and alternative training systems.

The growth rate of real GDP per hour worked increased in the United States between 1973–1995 and 1995–2007 from 1.28% per year to 2.05% per year. In contrast, in the EU15 it fell from 2.69% per year to 1.17% per year. The rate of labor productivity growth fell in most European countries: in Italy and Spain it was below 1% per year after 1995. By contrast, Sweden saw a productivity revival while for part of the period Ireland continued to be a Celtic Tiger, and both countries exceeded the American productivity growth rate.

So while there was falling behind in productivity performance on average, there was also considerable diversity in European performance.

The acceleration in American productivity growth was underpinned by ICT. As we have seen, historical comparisons reveal that the impact of ICT has been relatively large and that it has come through very quickly. The main impact of ICT on economic growth comes through its diffusion as a new form of capital equipment rather than through TFP growth in the production of ICT equipment. This is because users get the benefit of technological progress through lower prices, and as prices fall more of this type of capital is installed.[31] The implication is that ICT has offered Europe a great opportunity to increase its productivity growth. However, as we saw in Table 6.22, European countries have been less successful than the United States in seizing this opportunity.

The empirical evidence is that the diffusion of ICT has been aided by complementary investments in intangible capital and high-quality human capital, but weakened by relatively strong regulation in terms of employment protection and restrictions to competition, especially in the distribution sector (Conway et al. 2006). Since these forms of regulation have weakened over time, the story is not that European regulation has become more stringent, but rather that existing regulation became more costly in the context of a new technological era. Of course, European countries have varied considerably in these respects; for example, the UK and Sweden have been better placed than Italy and Spain.

The example of ICT prompts some more general comments on European supply-side policies in the decades before the crisis. In some respects, these provided conditions more favorable to growth. European countries became more open to trade, with positive effects on productivity, partly as a result of the European single market. Years of schooling were steadily increased and product market regulation inhibiting competition was reduced. Corporate tax rates have fallen since the early 1980s. Nevertheless, supply-side policies are in need of further reform if the issue of disappointing growth performance is to be adequately addressed and catch-up resumed. Aghion and Howitt (2006) stress that as countries get closer to the frontier it becomes more important to have high-quality education and strong competition in product markets. These are areas where European countries generally have room for significant improvement.

There have been serious question marks about the quality of schooling in many European countries, which recent research suggests exacts a growth penalty. A measure of cognitive skills, based on test scores, correlates strongly with growth performance (Hanushek and Wössmann, 2012) and it is striking that even the top European countries such as Finland have fallen behind Japan and South Korea, with some countries such as Germany and, especially, Italy deteriorating. These authors estimate that, if cognitive

---

[31] In a country with no ICT production, a neoclassical growth model whose Cobb-Douglas production function has two types of capital (ICT and other) shows that the steady-state rate of growth will be TFP growth plus a term denoting the rate of real price decline for ICT capital multiplied by the share of ICT capital in national income, all divided by labor's share of national income (Oulton, 2012).

skills in Italy were at the standard of South Korea, its long-run growth would be raised by about 0.75 percentage points per year. Wössmann et al. (2007) show that the variance in outcomes in terms of cognitive skills is explained by the way the schooling system is organized rather than by educational spending.

Competition and competition policy has tended to be weaker than in the United States. This has raised mark-ups and lowered competitive pressure on managers to invest and to innovate with adverse effects on TFP growth (Buccirossi et al. forthcoming; Griffith et al. 2010). Productivity growth in market services has been very disappointing in many European countries (Timmer et al. 2010). One reason is continued weakness of competition reflected in high price-cost mark-ups which have survived the introduction of the Single Market (Høj et al. 2007). Addressing these issues by reducing the barriers to entry maintained by member states would have raised productivity performance significantly but governments still have considerable discretion to maintain these barriers notwithstanding the Services Directive (Badinger and Maydell, 2009).

Western Europe remains a tremendously rich and successful economy, despite the slowdown in its relative growth rate. The major problems facing it at the time of writing have to do with its broken banking system and dysfunctional monetary union, a reminder that growth experiences even over quite lengthy periods of time can be influenced by what are often thought of as short-run monetary factors. Once these issues have been sorted out, one way or another, a longer run issue will remain: how to reshape European economies so as to make them more dynamic without abandoning those elements of the postwar settlement that are most valued by Europe's citizens.

## 6.7.2 The UK in the Golden Age and After[32]

After being the undisputed economic leader for much of the 19th century, Britain entered a prolonged phase of relative economic decline. This became so pronounced during the Golden Age that by the end of the period Britain had been overtaken by seven other European countries in terms of real GDP per person, and by nine others in terms of labor productivity. Growth was at least 0.7 percentage points per year slower in the UK than in any other country, including those which started the period with similar or higher income levels. The proximate reasons for relatively slow labor productivity growth were weak growth in capital per worker and TFP compared with more successful economies like West Germany. Although slower growth was partly due to convergence forces, being overtaken is a clear indicator of failure.

What is particularly interesting about this episode is the way in which long-standing institutions interacted with changes in the political and economic environment in a way that not only rendered them toxic, but also precluded reform for several decades. The key changes in the economic and political environment were a serious erosion of competition

---

[32] This section draws in part on Crafts (2012, 2013b).

in product markets, and the need to maintain very low levels of unemployment in order for governments to be re-elected. There were two distinctive institutional legacies that turned out to be costly when the Golden Age opportunity for rapid growth came along. First, corporate governance exhibited an unusual degree of separation of ownership and control in large companies without dominant shareholders (Foreman-Peck and Hannah, 2012). Given that the market for corporate control through takeovers did not work effectively as a constraint (Cosh et al. 2008), weak competition allowed considerable scope for managerial underperformance. Second, the system of industrial relations was characterized by craft control, multi-unionism, and legal immunities for industrial action (Crouch, 1993).

Britain did not achieve the transformation of industrial relations—Eichengreen's cooperative equilibrium—that happened elsewhere in Europe and this implied a considerable growth penalty (Gilmore, 2009).[33] When it is not possible to write binding contracts, either the absence of unions or strong corporatist trade unionism would have been preferable to the idiosyncratic British system. In Britain it was generally not possible to make corporatist deals to underpin investment and innovation, because bargaining took place with multiple unions or with shop stewards representing subsets of a firm's workforce. These unions had considerable bargaining power as a result of full employment and weak competition, but no incentive to internalize the benefits of wage restraint. This exposed sunk cost investments to a hold-up problem, with knock-on implications for investment and growth.[34]

Failure to successfully reform industrial relations was a major shortcoming of British governments from the 1950s through the 1970s. However, throughout this period there were continual efforts to persuade organized labor to accept wage moderation, not only to encourage investment, but even more to allow low levels of unemployment without inflation at a time when politicians believed that this was crucial to electoral success after the interwar trauma. At worst this was tantamount to allowing a de facto trade union veto on economic reforms. In any event, British supply-side policy, which was shaped by the postwar settlement, was unhelpful toward growth in several respects. Problems included a tax system characterized by very high marginal rates, described by Tanzi (1969) as the least conducive to growth of any of the OECD countries in his study; missing out on benefits from trade liberalization by retaining 1930s protectionism into the 1960s (Oulton, 1976); a misdirected technology policy that focused on invention rather than diffusion (Ergas, 1987); and an industrial policy that ineffectively subsidized physical investment (Sumner, 1999) and slowed down structural change by protecting ailing industries through subsidies (Wren, 1996).

---

[33] Gilmore (2009) finds that coordinated wage bargaining was positive for investment and growth prior to 1975 but not subsequently. This fits with the suggestion in Cameron and Wallace (2002) that the key to the Eichengreen equilibrium is that both sides be patient, and that this was no longer the case when the macroeconomic turbulence of the 1970s erupted.

[34] This can readily be understood in terms of the Eichengreen (1996) model or an extension of it to incorporate endogenous innovation.

A key feature of the Golden Age British economy was the weakness of competition in product markets that had developed in the 1930s and intensified subsequently. Competition policy was largely ineffective while market power was substantial and entrenched politically (Crafts, 2012). The lack of competition had an adverse effect on British productivity performance during the Golden Age working at least partly through industrial relations and managerial failure. Broadberry and Crafts (1996) found that cartelization was strongly negatively related to productivity growth in a cross-section of manufacturing industries for 1954–1963, a result which is confirmed by the difference-in-differences analysis in Symeonidis (2008). In the 1970s and 1980s, greater competition increased innovation (Blundell et al. 1999) and raised productivity growth significantly in companies where there was no dominant external shareholder (Nickell et al. 1997). Both these results underline the role of weak competition in permitting agency cost problems to undermine productivity performance.

Case studies strongly implicate bad management, and restrictive labor practices resulting from bargaining with unions, in poor productivity outcomes. Pratten and Atkinson (1976) reviewed 25 such studies and found evidence of either or both of these problems in 23 of them. Prais (1982) reported similar findings in 8 out of 10 industry case studies and in each case noted that competition was significantly impaired. Multiple unionism, unenforceable contracts, and plant bargaining with shop stewards created an environment in which, unlike West Germany, workers and firms could not commit to "good behavior." This weakened incentives to invest and innovate (Bean and Crafts, 1996; Denny and Nickell, 1992).

The competitive environment that had largely precluded failure in the pre-1914 period had disappeared. This allowed the problems of poor management and dysfunctional industrial relations, often seen as the Achilles' heel of the British economy in the Golden Age, to persist. The politics of economic policy operated to prevent supply-side reforms that could have prevented relative economic decline by enhancing social capability. This period only ended with the election of a maverick prime minister in 1979.

The post-Golden Age period is helpful as a test of this interpretation, since government policy moved in the direction of increasing competition in product markets. In particular, protectionism was discarded. Trade liberalization in its various guises reduced price-cost margins (Hitiris, 1978; Griffith, 2001). The average effective rate of protection fell from 9.3% in 1968 to 4.7% in 1979, and 1.2% in 1986 (Ennew et al. 1990). Industrial policy was downsized as subsidies were cut, and privatization of state-owned businesses was embraced while de-regulation was promoted. In addition, legal reforms of industrial relations reduced trade union bargaining power, which had initially been undermined by rising unemployment. Reforms of fiscal policy were made including the re-structuring of taxation by increasing VAT while reducing income tax rates. The Thatcher government saw itself as ending the trade unions' veto on economic policy reform. Many of the changes of the 1980s would have been regarded as inconceivable by informed opinion in the 1960s and 1970s.

European productivity growth slowed down markedly after the Golden Age, but less so in the UK than in most other countries. Increased competition and openness in the later 20th century was associated with better productivity performance. Proudman and Redding (1998), exploring differing experiences across British industry between 1970 and 1990, found that openness raised the rate of productivity convergence with the technological leader. In a study looking at catch-up across European industries, Nicoletti and Scarpetta (2003) found that TFP growth was inversely related to product market regulation (PMR). The implication of a lower PMR score as compared with France and Germany was a TFP growth advantage for the UK of about 0.5 percentage points per year in the 1990s. At the sectoral level, when concentration ratios fell in the UK in the 1980s, there was a strong positive impact on labor productivity growth (Haskel, 1991). Entry and exit accounted for an increasing proportion of manufacturing productivity growth, rising from 25% in 1980–1985 to 40% in 1995–2000 (Criscuolo et al. 2004).

The impact was felt at least partly through greater pressure on management to perform and through firm-worker bargains that raised effort and improved working practices. Increases in competition resulting from the European Single Market raised both the level and growth rate of TFP in plants which were part of multi-plant firms, and thus most prone to agency problems (Griffith, 2001). Liberalization of capital market rules allowed more effective challenges to incumbent management. A notable feature of the period after 1980 was divestment and restructuring in large firms and, in particular, management buyouts (often financed by private equity) which typically generated large increases in TFP levels in the 1988-1998 period (Harris et al. 2005).

The 1980s and 1990s saw major changes in the conduct and structure of British industrial relations. Trade union membership and bargaining power were seriously eroded. This was prompted partly by high unemployment and anti-union legislation in the 1980s but also owed a good deal to increased competition (Brown et al. 2008). Increased competition may have been the more important factor in boosting British performance, since the 1980s saw a surge in organizational change in those unionized firms exposed to increased competition (Machin and Wadhwani, 1991). De-recognition of unions in the context of increases in foreign competition had a strong effect on productivity growth in the late 1980s (Gregg et al. 1993). The negative impact of multi-unionism on TFP growth, apparent from the 1950s through the 1970s, evaporated after 1979 (Bean and Crafts, 1996). The productivity payoff was boosted by the interaction between reforms to industrial relations and product market competition.

## 6.8. CASE STUDIES II: SUCCESS, AT LEAST FOR NOW

In this section we briefly examine three more postwar growth miracles, in East Asia, China, and Ireland. While the East Asian Miracle was called into question after the crisis of 1997, growth there soon resumed. It remains to be seen whether Irish growth will go the way of Japan in the 1990s, but income levels there are massively higher than in the 1980s; the same is true of China, despite concerns about the future of economic growth in that country.

### 6.8.1 The East Asian Miracle

We have seen that the four East Asian Tiger economies enjoyed one of the most impressive growth experiences of the 20th century, although they had to wait until the end of World War II for it to begin. The four countries concerned differed in terms of size, history, and political system. In 1950, South Korea had the largest population, some 20 million, while the Taiwanese population was almost 7.5 million. Hong Kong and Singapore were both city states, with populations of just 2 million and 1 million, respectively. Korea and Taiwan had both been Japanese colonies, and were on the front line of the struggle between communism and the West. Singapore and Hong Kong were both British colonies, but whereas Singapore sought and eventually obtained independence, first as part of Malaysia in 1963, and then as an independent state in 1965, Hong Kong remained British until the handover to China in 1997. GDP per capita in South Korea and Taiwan was around $900 in 1990 international prices, at or below the level of several countries in sub-Saharan Africa; it was slightly over $2000 in Hong Kong and Singapore. Korea, Singapore, and Taiwan all developed more or less authoritarian systems of government, while Hong Kong was ruled as a Crown Colony until 1997. And yet all four countries achieved spectacular growth, with the result that per capita GDP in 2007 was as high in Korea and Taiwan as in Western Europe, and substantially higher in Hong Kong and Singapore. This is a sufficiently impressive performance deserving of the label miraculous, irrespective of the relative contributions of factor accumulation and TFP growth in producing it.

Several features of this growth experience fit neatly into the general convergence framework outlined above. The four countries were relatively poor in 1950, and had high levels of social capability. The famous index of Adelman and Morris (1967) showed that both Korea and Taiwan having extremely high levels of social and economic development in the late 1950s and early 1960s, and Temple and Johnson (1998) have found that this indicator was strongly correlated with subsequent growth. As elsewhere, growth in the Tiger economies was characterized by high rates of investment—in human as well as physical capital—and rapidly growing trade. Investment stood at around 30% of GDP in both Korea and Taiwan in 1980 (Rodrik, 1995, p. 59). Technology transfer was actively encouraged via licensing, technical assistance, inward investment by multinationals, and joint ventures (with the mix differing between countries: for example, Korea discouraged inward direct investment, while Singapore actively encouraged it). Another feature of East Asian growth was that it was based on industrialization, with countries specializing first in textiles, then in heavy industry, and then in electronics and high-tech industries. This pattern of switching over time from labor-intensive, to capital-intensive, and finally to technology-intensive industries, promoted spillover effects on neighboring countries in Southeast Asia, as later industrializers started manufacturing goods which earlier industrializers were no longer producing: the so-called flying geese phenomenon (Ito, 2001).

A substantial literature emerged in the late 1980s and early 1990s which argued that these economies had developed on the basis of institutions and policies which differed greatly from the hands-off prescriptions of the Washington Consensus, involving among other things public enterprise, active industrial policy, export promotion, and protectionism. For Amsden (1989, p. 6), the institutions that mattered in Korea were "an interventionist state, large diversified business groups, an abundant supply of competent salaried managers, and an abundant supply of low-cost, well-educated labor." The key policies were to provide subsidies to firms that, crucially, were conditional on better performance and export market share; and to establish what were effectively multiple prices for capital and foreign exchange, via subsidies or other policies. According to Amsden, these multiple prices were needed in order to accommodate conflicting objectives, for example to encourage savings while keeping the cost of capital to firms low; or to encourage exports while keeping the cost of imports low. For Wade (1990) activist East Asian governments not only influenced the growth rate, but the sectoral composition of output, with beneficial consequences. Some of these conclusions, but not all, were taken on board in a 1993 World Bank study (World Bank, 1993), before the TFP literature reviewed above stimulated a debate about whether the East Asian Miracle was really as impressive as all that: if TFP growth was low, after all, then interventionist arguments based on learning by doing or other growth-promoting externalities seemed less convincing (Krugman, 1994, p.78).

While Amsden and Wade emphasized export performance, subsequent work has downplayed the role of exports. Rodrik (1995) argues that exports cannot have been a prime mover of industrialization, since if they had been, this would have been manifested in a rising relative price of exports as world demand rose. Since there was no such price rise, the ultimate sources of growth must have been internal, with exports arising as a consequence. For Rodrik the key to growth was investment, consistent with the growth-accounting evidence. State intervention was required, not just to boost savings and investment rates via subsidies, public investment, and other measures, but to coordinate investment across a range of complementary sectors for "big push" reasons. Rodrik shows a striking positive correlation over time in both Korea and Taiwan between investment and imports, which can be explained by the fact that investment required large imports of machinery and other capital equipment. Exports were needed to pay for these imports, and were thus necessary for the investment drive, but they were not the ultimate cause of rapid growth. This does not mean that exports were not essential: they were, both to finance required imports of capital goods, and to sell the output that the high investment rates were designed to produce. An implication is that while countries like Korea and Taiwan were not liberal free traders themselves, they did benefit from the generally open international trade policies of the major Western economies during this period.

Some of the same features which had been seen as aiding rapid East Asian convergence on the frontier—in particular, close relationships between the state and big business, and heavy reliance on bank finance—were blamed for the East Asian financial crisis which erupted in 1997. Given the debate that had recently taken place about East Asian TFP, it is not surprising that the crisis emboldened some to argue that these institutional features of East Asian growth had been a hindrance rather than a help, all along. It is difficult to see how one could establish such counterfactual claims convincingly. For example, studies failing to find correlations across sectors between subsidies or other policy interventions, on the one hand, and productivity or other outcomes on the other, would presumably not convince an advocate of big push policies, which are based on intersectoral complementarities. The argument that the financial crisis proves anything about the sources of rapid East Asian growth from the 1960s to the 1990s seems somewhat dated today, in the light of the global financial crisis of 2007–2008. This hit some of the richest countries in the world, with very different institutional structures than those found in, say, Korea. The experience of the Eurozone periphery shows the dangers of being exposed to capital inflows in the presence of a currency peg; unlike Korea or Thailand these countries do not have the option of devaluation, and by 2013, have not yet recovered. In sharp contrast, East Asian growth resumed rapidly in 1999. We thus agree with Ito (2001), who argues that the debate about which institutions and policies mattered for East Asian growth during the growth miracle needs to be sharply distinguished from the debate about how to regulate banks and international capital flows. This does not mean, however, that at some stage East Asia may not have to rethink its institutional mix as it moves even closer to the international technological frontier.

## 6.8.2 China

While Chinese economic statistics are unreliable, it is clear that China's growth since the start of economic reforms in the late 1970s has been extraordinary.[35] Even if Maddison and Wu's (2008) data are accepted, GDP growth averaged 7.85% per annum between 1978 and 2003, as compared with an official growth rate almost 2 percentage points higher. As in the Western European and East Asian cases, very high levels of investment, the importation of technology, and increasing links with the outside world played key roles in China's growth acceleration. As in East Asia, Chinese industry went through successive phases, from exporting labor-intensive toys, clothes, and footwear to producing more capital-intensive, and ultimately high-tech goods. The Chinese savings rate averaged an extraordinary 37% between 1978 and 1995 according to Kraay (2000), although Heston and Sicular (2008) favor a lower (but still large) figure somewhere in the 20–30% range.

---

[35] Our account draws heavily on the collection of essays in Brandt and Rawski (2008a), the standard reference on the subject.

This has allowed an equally high investment rate to be internally financed (Lee et al. 2012).

What makes the Chinese experience unique is the way in which a gradualist reform program has seen the role of the state in economic life being steadily diminished over time, at the same time as that state has maintained a highly authoritarian political system. China is no poster child for the Washington Consensus. It still maintains exchange controls, state-owned enterprises remain an important drag on the economy (Brandt et al. 2008), and the government intervenes in the economy in myriad other ways. But the facts that the direction of change since 1979 has so clearly been in a market-friendly direction, and that China's economic situation has improved so much since then, mean that the literature on China's economic miracle has tended to focus on how gradual liberalization improved performance, rather than (as in the East Asian Tiger case) on whether some government interventions helped speed China's convergence on the technological frontier.

China's reforms came in two stages (Brandt and Rawski, 2008b), which according to Naughton (2008) corresponded to different configurations of political power. In the first stage, which lasted from 1979 to 1992, political power was fragmented, and reforms were incremental, and concerned with not creating losers. Agricultural households were permitted to engage in cultivation. A growing number of firms, notably township and village enterprises (TVEs), were allowed to enter an increasing range of sectors. Once firms had satisfied their plan targets, they were able to sell additional output at what evolved into market prices. Four special economic zones were set up in the southern coastal provinces, in which Hong Kong and Taiwanese firms produced labor-intensive goods for export. Fourteen additional zones were created in 1984, and regulations regarding foreign direct investment were further relaxed in 1986 (Branstetter and Lardy, 2008, pp. 640-1).

In the second stage, from 1993 onwards, power was consolidated as the first generation of Communist leaders left the political stage. Reforms became more decisive, and capable of producing losers as well as winners. The plan component of the dual pricing system was abandoned; restrictions on mobility between town and countryside were relaxed, setting the stage for a mass migration of rural workers to industrial cities; TVEs were privatized; state-owned enterprises (SOEs) were subjected to more market discipline, and were downsized and occasionally closed. The number of workers in SOEs fell from 76 million in 1992–1993 to 28 million in 2004 (Naughton, 2008, p. 121): Brandt et al. (2008) estimate that the resulting reallocation of workers toward more productive firms elsewhere in the economy made an even more important contribution to GDP growth than rural to urban migration. For Hsieh and Klenow (2009), the reallocation added 2 percentage points to China's TFP growth rate between 1998 and 2005, while for Song et al. (2011), it not only helps explain China's growth since the early 1990s, but its growing external surpluses as well (since the growing private sector relies more on internal financing for its investment needs than the SOEs). The growing liberalization of Chinese trade policy culminated with China's accession to the WTO in 2001. Even prior to that, foreign companies had been enabled to operate in China subject to many fewer restrictions and less interference, leaving China well positioned to benefit from the boom of the last few years of the Great Moderation (Branstetter and Lardy, 2008, p. 645). Despite the clear acceleration in the pace of reforms, Chinese reforms remained gradual compared with the experience of Eastern Europe and the former Soviet Union (Svejnar, 2008).

Given that corruption is a severe problem in China, and that other aspects of its institutional structure remain deeply problematic, it is perhaps not surprising that much analysis has focused on the dismantling of Communist economic controls as being at the heart of China's economic success: merely getting rid of obstacles can lead to significant growth if these were costly enough (Brandt and Rawski, 2008b, p. 9). And yet government intervention may have helped growth as well as hindered it. The size of the Chinese market has allowed national and regional officials to extract concessions from foreign multinationals, notably with respect to the transfer of technology and research and development activities, that could in principle have accelerated China's catching up relative to that of other poor economies (Brandt et al. 2008, p. 623). The fact that China's real exchange rate depreciated by 70% vis à vis the dollar between 1980 and 1995 presumably increased the attraction of China as a manufacturing location. This in turn helped make China's exchange rate policy more politically sustainable, by creating overseas political constituencies favorable to it (Branstetter and Lardy, 2008, pp. 639, 675–676). And underlying everything else has been competition between regional officials, whose promotion prospects depend on their region's economic performance. This "regionally decentralized authoritarianism" (Xu, 2011) has been a major factor in China's economic success.

There were clear signs in 2013, that the Chinese financial sector might be heading for a major crisis with unpredictable consequences for the Chinese economy and political system. Even aside from this risk, it may be that the policies and institutional structures which have underpinned China's economic growth since 1978 are beginning to outlive their usefulness and will have to be changed. Relative prices skewed in favor of exports may be distorting the Chinese economy (Branstetter and Lardy, 2008, p. 676), and are in any rate leaving the economy vulnerable to overseas shocks. Many commentators argue that an investment rate approaching 50% of GDP may no longer be sustainable, and that an increasing focus on consumption is now required. For some China is now approaching its "Lewis (1954) moment," as rural to urban migration slows and wages start to rise. Elastic supplies of labor from agriculture (and, if Song et al. 2011 are right, from SOEs as well) made high Chinese investment rates consistent with high returns on capital; as both pools of labor shrink, diminishing returns to capital will set in (Das and N'Diaye, 2013; Krugman, 2013).

If extensive growth at current rates becomes more difficult, and the need for intensive growth thus increases, deeper institutional changes may be needed. Perhaps, as Naughton (2008, p. 127) speculates, as China moves closer to the technological frontier its economy will need "transparency and recourse to impartial independent regulatory authority that the current system is not yet able to provide." It is not yet clear that China will be able to escape the middle income trap. Eichengreen et al. (2012) find that the probability of a growth slowdown (defined as a decline in growth rates of 2 percentage points or more) increases not only at income levels which China can be expected to attain in the next few years, but in countries which have maintained undervalued exchange rates, have low consumption shares of GDP, and aging populations. On all fronts China appears vulnerable, implying that the probability of a growth slowdown is high there, and that is even before taking the country's financial problems into account. Whether such a slowdown will occur, and how the country's economy, society, and political system would respond, are among the major uncertainties facing the world economy in the early 21st century.

### 6.8.3 Ireland: The Celtic Tiger

The spectacular growth of the Celtic Tiger period when a small economy rode the globalization wave with massive success attracted enormous attention. Its proximate sources in export platform FDI and ICT production are apparent. Less well understood is the fact that up through the mid-1980s Ireland had been a failure (Ó Gráda and O'Rourke, 1996). We saw earlier that affluent Western economies experienced unconditional convergence after 1950, with poorer countries growing more rapidly than richer ones. Seen in this perspective, Ireland was the great underperformer prior to 1987, as Figure 6.3 shows, with growth rates well below those that would have been expected given its relative poverty in 1950. Ireland's average growth rate between 1950 and 1987, 2.8% per annum, was approximately the same as that in the Benelux countries, despite the fact that its 1950 per capita income lay between those of Austria and Italy. In the context of the Golden Age, this was a spectacular economic failure.

The reasons for this failure are related to the reasons for success in the rest of Western Europe at the same time. The 1950s were particularly unimpressive in Ireland, with per capita growth rates of only 1.7%. Education remained underfunded and underprovided. Instead of corporatist labor market institutions as in continental Europe, Ireland had a fragmented British-style trade union system incapable of delivering wage moderation in return for high investment. Even if such wage moderation had been delivered, Irish firms were small, unproductive, and focused on the home market, while foreign firms were discouraged from investing in the country. This was the legacy of 1930s protectionism, which might have been the correct response to the Great Depression, but should have been abandoned much earlier than it actually was. Such investment as there was too often went to relatively unproductive purposes, with Irish savings being invested in low-yielding projects for political reasons. Not surprisingly, Irish TFP was very low by European standards in 1960 (Crafts, 2009).

Gradually these impediments to growth were done away with. The late 1950s and early 1960s saw the introduction of export tax relief, and measures to attract foreign direct investment, which was to become the key to Ireland's convergence on the technological frontier. Trade was gradually liberalized: Ireland entered an Anglo-Irish free trade area in 1965, and the EEC in 1973. The late 1960s saw belated educational reforms that made secondary schooling available to everyone. Growth was twice as high in the 1960s as in the 1950s, but was slightly less than the Western European average: Ireland was still not converging, and in 1973 was poorer than Greece, Portugal, and Spain. EEC membership helped to modernize the economy in many ways, but the oil crisis that coincided with entry ushered in a period of low growth, large government budget deficits, and a subsequent fiscal crisis, which led to a second post-war lost decade during the 1980s.

After 1987, Ireland's economic performance was transformed out of all recognition. Between 1987 and 2000 its per capita growth rate averaged 5.7% per annum, with the result that by 2000 Ireland lay on the advanced economy "convergence line" (Figure 6.4). So how was Ireland turned around? Figures 6.3 and 6.4 suggest a straightforward explanation: that the Irish miracle was simply a delayed version of the Western European growth miracle of the 1950s and 1960s (Ó Gráda and O'Rourke, 2000; Honohan and Walsh, 2002). What changed was that many of the structural impediments to convergence had been eliminated over the course of the 1960s and 1970s, leaving Ireland well positioned to take advantage of deeper European integration and a buoyant international economy in the 1990s. The catastrophe of the 1980s meant that trade unions were willing to

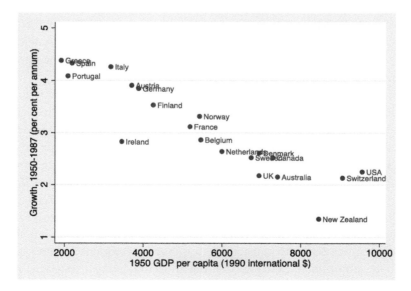

**Figure 6.3** GDP per capita growth, 1950–1987. *Source: Bolt and Van Zanden (2013).*

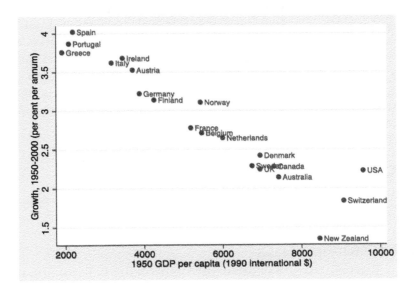

**Figure 6.4** GDP per capita growth, 1950–2000. *Source: Bolt and Van Zanden (2013).*

enter into corporatist social partnership agreements, trading wage restraint against the promise of growth and employment. Irish workers were now far better educated than they had been during the 1960s. Devaluations in 1987 and 1993 helped to boost Irish competitiveness. A healthier labor market now interacted with Ireland's long-standing low corporate taxes and produced a surge of inward investment, rising TFP levels, and increases in employment.

Imports of technology, corporatist labor bargains leading to investment, and a reliance on exports are all reminiscent of the Western European miracle of three or four decades previously. The differences were also noteworthy, and reflected the period. Much of the investment occurred via FDI, rather than being financed via retained profits by domestic firms. Workers' wage restraint was compensated more with tax cuts than with an expansion of the welfare state. And Ireland did not go through all the stages of industrialization to the same extent as other countries, specializing far more in ICT and other high-tech sectors than the typical fast grower of the 1950s or 1960s. This specialization did not just reflect the invisible hand of the market, but active Irish government attempts to develop clusters of activity in ICT, pharmaceuticals, and similar sectors (Barry, 2002).

The Celtic Tiger period ended in 2000 or 2001, and was replaced by the Celtic Bubble of 2001–2007, financed by cross-border capital flows which boomed in the aftermath of Ireland's entry into the Euro. Not only the bubble, but also the crash which followed, was reminiscent of the East Asian crisis of 1997, but with the important difference that Ireland was not able to respond to the crisis by adjusting its exchange rate. Foreign observers have not subjected the Irish model to the same sort of scrutiny that the East Asian model faced after 1997, which is perhaps ironic since the Irish economy had still not started to recover by 2013, in stark contrast with the rapid and durable post-crisis recovery in East Asia. The net result is, that at the time of writing, it seemed that Ireland risked facing a third post-war "lost decade," after those of the 1950s and 1980s. It is too soon to say whether and when growth will resume, in Ireland or in the rest of the Eurozone periphery. Nonetheless, the Celtic Tiger was no mirage: Ireland is now one of the richest countries in Western Europe, not one of the poorest.

## 6.9. CASE STUDIES III: FAILURES

In this section we look briefly at two cases which can fairly be considered failures, the USSR and Africa.

### 6.9.1 Failed Catch-Up in USSR[36]

The USSR was always a long way below the United States in terms of real GDP per person—about 30% in 1950 and 36% in 1973—and, despite a promising start, only reduced the gap very slowly. A growth rate of 3.37% per year in the Golden Age compares quite unfavorably with the achievements of Western European countries like Italy or Spain which also started out with relatively low income levels. Growth regression evidence confirms that communist countries underperformed in the Golden Age: allowing for initial income levels, their growth rate was about 1.3 percentage points lower than that of their Western European counterparts (Crafts and Toniolo, 2008).

Worrying signs of a serious slowdown in productivity growth did not appear until the 1970s. Golden Age Soviet growth was extensive, in that the investment/GDP ratio roughly doubled between 1950 and the early 1970s to about 30%. The capital stock grew at about 8.5% per year in this period (Ofer, 1987). However, diminishing returns to capital accumulation exacerbated by slow TFP growth implied that the rate of capital stock growth delivered by a given investment rate was falling over time: the capital-stock growth rate fell from 7.4% per year in the 1960s to 3.4% per year in the 1980s. Negative TFP growth post-1970 (Table 6.16) was driven by "waste of capital on a grand scale" (Allen, 2003, p. 191) as old factories were re-equipped and expansion of natural resource industries in Siberia were pursued.

Relatively low TFP growth was not the result of inadequate volumes of R & D, which by the 1970s were very high by world standards at around 3% of GDP. Rather, the problem lay in the incentive structures that informed innovation at the firm level. This was a classic case of a social capability failure. The planning system rewarded managers who achieved production targets in the short term rather than those who found ways to reduce costs or improve the quality of output over the long term. The balance of risk and

---

[36] This section draws in part on Crafts and Toniolo (2008).

reward was inimical to organizational and technological change, and the "kicking foot" of competition was absent (Berliner, 1976).

The incentive structures used by the Soviet leadership to motivate managers and workers were a complex mixture of rewards, punishments, and monitoring. Each of these became increasingly expensive over time, implying that the viability of the system was threatened. Product innovation drove up monitoring costs, and this inhibited moves from mass to flexible production. A more educated population meant that punishment (incarceration) was more costly in terms of loss of human capital, and that rewards needed to be higher. The slowdown in productivity growth led to a search for reforms that might improve economic performance and lower monitoring costs, but these ended up undermining the regime's reputation for brutality, which could help sustain high effort in circumstances when punishment costs became particularly high. The interesting feature of this system is that it could be tipped from a high coercion, high effort equilibrium to a low coercion, shirk and steal equilibrium if rewards and punishments were no longer credible and workers understood this. Harrison (2002) argues that such a shift accounts for the sudden collapse at the end of the 1980s.

### 6.9.2 Post-Colonial Sub-Saharan Africa

As we have seen, average growth performance in this region was dismal between the mid-1970s and the late 1990s. There was stagnation in real GDP per person (Table 6.8), TFP growth was actually negative (Table 6.11), and it became commonplace to talk about a chronic growth failure (Collier and Gunning, 1999). However, the first decade of the 21st century saw a revival in growth performance. Taking a long view of African growth, it may be more accurate to see a picture of growth accelerations followed by growth reversals, with the former typically triggered by strong commodity prices, as in the recent growth spurt (Jerven, 2010). Unfortunately, econometric analysis shows that while commodity price booms have raised income levels in the short run, their long-run effect is to lower them somewhat (Collier and Goderis, 2012).

Very low institutional quality is the most obvious explanation for disappointing growth and low income levels at the end of the 20th century. On average, sub-Saharan African countries score badly on the World Bank's *Governance Matters* and *Doing Business* indicators and do so persistently. Thus, ever since 1996, when it was first compiled, the average score on the "rule-of-law" indicator has been about −0.7 (on a scale of −2.5 to +2.5) compared with an average for Western Europe of around +1.6. Similarly, the norm across the region is a closed access society (Kishtainy, 2011). If the fundamental reason for poverty is insecure property rights (Acemoglu and Johnson, 2005) then sub-Saharan Africa is a prime exhibit. Indeed, this is now often taken as a stylized fact, with "absolutist weak states" having "little ability or interest in providing public goods" and operating on a "neopatrimonial" basis (Acemoglu and Robinson, 2010, pp. 23, 40). Of course, there are exceptions to this dismal picture, such as Botswana and Mauritius, but they are the exceptions that

**Table 6.23** Growth of real GDP/person, 1960–2000 (percent per annum)

|  | Resource-scarce & coastal (%) | Resource-scarce & landlocked (%) | Resource-rich (%) |
|---|---|---|---|
| Africa | 0.50 (33) | −0.36 (33) | 0.29 (33) |
| Other developing | 3.79 (88) | 1.40 (1) | 2.89 (11) |

*Note*: numbers in parentheses refer to percentages of population by region in each category.
*Source*: Collier (2007).

prove the rule, and score relatively well when it comes to governance indicators. This is an account that is entirely consistent with the New Institutional Economic History tradition.

However, the intriguing question remaining is what part geography may have played in explaining African failure. On a range of indicators, including climate, coastal access, disease environment, and population density, Africa scores much less well than other regions of the developing world (Sachs et al. 2004). It seems reasonable to suppose that this carries a growth penalty in terms of adverse impacts on investment and productivity. "Naive" growth regressions suggest that this is the case and accord geographic factors nearly as much weight as institutions in accounting for the differential between African and East Asian growth performance in the late 20th century (Bleaney and Nishiyama, 2002). If the focus is switched to "second-nature" geography, then sub-Saharan Africa scores very badly compared with almost all other parts of the world in terms of market potential, which is strongly correlated with income even after controlling for institutional quality (Redding and Venables, 2004).

Table 6.23 offers a simple but powerful summary of growth performance classified by geographic type. The table shows (in parentheses) the percentages of the population in both Africa and other developing regions in each of three categories: resource-scarce and coastal; resource-scarce and landlocked; and resource-rich. It also shows the average growth rates between 1960 and 2000 in each of these six regions. As can be seen, being both landlocked and resource-scarce is a particularly bad combination for growth, and this is unfortunate for Africa since it has a relatively high percentage of its population in this category. It also has a relatively low proportion of its population in resource-scarce and coastal regions, which saw higher growth rates both in Africa and elsewhere. Geography does not favor Africa, therefore, but this is not the whole story since the table also shows that in each geographic category Africa has seriously underperformed relative to the rest of the developing world.

A more satisfactory way to explain post-colonial African growth failure may be to consider interactions between institutions and geography. One aspect of such interactions is the possibility, noted earlier, that first-nature geography may have its strongest effects through its impact on institutions (Easterly and Levine, 2003). But it is also important to recognize that, "on top of its physical geography and remoteness, Africa has been held back by the fragmentation of its political and economic geography" (Venables, 2010, p. 481)—the median country has a population of only 8 million people. This fragmentation implies a number of serious disadvantages with regard to small city size, weak competition in product markets, reduced supply of public goods, greater difficulty in escaping from bad policies, etc. (Venables, 2010). Payoffs to better policies are often highly dependent on the reform efforts of neighbors, which further hinders economic progress.

A final perspective on sub-Saharan failure is both more historical and, perhaps, more optimistic. Bates et al. (2007) point out that economic performance was also very disappointing in Latin America in the first 50 years following independence in the 1820s, and that it was only in the late 19th century that sustained economic growth began. Furthermore, this growth was as high as that experienced in the British offshoots, as we saw in Section 6.3. Bates et al. explain the initial poor performance as being due to the political instability of the time: international and civil wars, foreign military incursions, and a general atmosphere of violence. This is suggestive, since wars and violence have been prevalent in post-independence Africa as well, and it is often suggested that this is one reason for the continent's poor growth performance. Perhaps the transition to post-colonial independence for new states, with arbitrarily drawn borders, is inherently difficult. If so, Africa may yet see a brighter 21st century, as it gradually leaves these transition problems behind.

### 6.9.3 The Natural Resource Curse

One major reason for long-term growth failure which has received a great deal of attention in the literature is the so-called natural resource curse. This refers to the tendency for countries with large natural resource exports or minerals production relative to GDP to grow relatively slowly at best, and experience prolonged periods of negative growth at worst. A number of hypotheses have been put forward to explain this correlation and there is a substantial body of empirical work that examines issues of robustness and causality.[37] The standard suggested mechanisms explaining the natural resource curse include crowding out of tradable goods sectors with greater productivity growth potential (Dutch Disease); promoting low quality institutions which undermine growth; making civil war more likely; and engendering macroeconomic volatility. There is some empirical support for all these arguments (Van der Ploeg, 2011). It is also clear that there is a wide range of historical experience that needs to be explained. Some countries have indeed been cursed by natural resources, for example, Angola, Congo, Sierra Leone, and Sudan. However, others have been blessed including, for example, Australia, Canada, Chile, and the United States.

---

[37] For an excellent recent survey article, see Van der Ploeg (2011).

It seems highly plausible that the implications of a resource windfall will differ depending on whether there are good or bad institutions. In the former case, it might be expected that the bonanza leads to an increase in productive activities, while in the latter case, even more resources will be devoted to rent-seeking. The evidence of growth regressions is consistent with this prediction. Mehlum et al. (2006) use a variable interacting institutional quality, as measured by the ICRG index popularized by Knack and Keefer (1995), and resource abundance. They find that values above 0.60 for the ICRG index make mineral resources good for growth. This accords with common sense: oil has been very good for Norway, but bad for Nigeria.

An economic history perspective allows some of these ideas to be taken further. First, the most notable success story in recent African economic history is Botswana, a resource-abundant country in which diamonds are a large share of GDP. Botswanan success is based not only on diamonds, but also on high institutional quality and secure property rights plus good policies. The underpinnings of good institutions were a combination of historical accident and the economic interests of the pre-diamond era elite, the cattle ranchers (Acemoglu et al. 2003). There was thus a bulwark against the pursuit of mineral rents which led to rent-seeking and states which were ineffective modernizers elsewhere in Africa, for example Angola and Nigeria (Isham et al. 2005).

Second, going beyond the argument that good institutions make natural resources more of a blessing than a curse, it should be noted that natural resource endowments actually reflect the amount of effort devoted to their discovery and effective exploitation. This depends inter alia on the quality of institutions and policies. A classic example is the 19th century United States whose status as a leading minerals producer was the product of big investments in exploration and human capital underpinned by a favorable property rights regime (David and Wright, 1997).

Third, the implications of mineral resources seem to have varied over time for reasons which still need to be fully researched but link to ideas familiar from new economic geography. In the 19th and early 20th centuries, industrialization was encouraged by the proximity of coal, whereas in the later 20th century it seems to have been discouraged by the proximity of oil. Regression evidence for the natural resource curse relates to samples drawn only from the recent past. The difference between now and then is likely to relate to much higher transport costs for minerals, especially over land, in the past; and changes in energy sources with electrification (Wright and Czelusta, 2007).

## 6.10. CONCLUSIONS

The convergence of a succession of countries onto the technological frontier is a process whose roots lie in the great divergence of the 19th century. That divergence was due to new industrial technologies being implemented in some regions of the world but not in others, and was magnified in the short run by the globalization of the period which, given technological asymmetries, created a stark division of labor between an industrializing West and a deindustrializing Rest.

The key to reducing the resulting regional inequalities has been the erosion of these technological asymmetries, via the spread of modern industrialization. The succession of growth miracles briefly surveyed above seems reminiscent of the process of sequential convergence on the frontier modeled by Lucas (2000, 2009). Since industrial technologies are transferable across borders, convergence should not surprise us. But neither should we assume that convergence will be as smooth as simple growth models assume: the economic history of 20th century growth is also a story of the various frictions that can impede this process. In addition to successes, there have been a variety of failures.

As we have seen repeatedly throughout this chapter, innovation tends to reflect the economic circumstances of the leading economy of the time. This was Britain until some time in the late 19th century, and the United States thereafter. Even in the best of all institutional worlds, with no political or other frictions and Scandinavian levels of social capability, directed technological change would be a factor preventing or at least slowing down the process of technological convergence. Nor is this just a story of developing countries finding it uneconomical to adopt best-practice technology, since European economies, and even Britain itself, found themselves at a disadvantage when it came to adopting American techniques that had been developed with American factor prices, and the American market, in mind.

What is more, we do not live in the best of all institutional worlds, frictions of all sorts are prevalent and we are not all Scandinavian. Social capability matters for growth and not all countries have it. Institutions are path dependent, and can be an impediment to growth. And even in countries where they have always been an asset, they can become a liability, since the right institutional set-up may change over time as countries converge on the technological frontier, or as the nature of frontier technologies change. Chasing a moving target can be a tricky business in a world where history matters.

Geography is another reason why convergence is not as smooth in practice as it can seem in theory. First-nature geography matters, although it may matter in different ways at different points in time: resource abundance may be a blessing in some time periods, but a curse in others, depending on the tradability of resources, on their nature, and on the extent to which frontier technologies are resource-using. It may also be a blessing or a curse depending on a country's institutional set-up, which may in turn reflect that country's geography as well as its history. Being far from trade routes, on the other hand, has never been good for growth in the past, and it is hard to see why it should become so in the future.

Finally, economic historians emphasize the importance of wars, ideological revolutions, financial crises, and other events that are typically regarded as exogenous shocks in economic models, but which are part and parcel of the world in which we live. The First World War, the Russian Revolution, or the Great Depression were not mere complications in the story of 20th century economic growth, but a part of its very fabric. Even episodes which are conventionally regarded as shortrun in nature, having to do with macroeconomic or financial policy, can, if handled sufficiently badly, have a significant impact on economic growth over the course of a lifetime, which is what most of us tend to care about. History, and economic history, have not yet ended.

## REFERENCES

Abramovitz, M., 1986. Catching up, forging ahead, and falling behind. Journal of Economic History 46, 385–406.
Abramovitz, M., 1989. Thinking About Growth and Other Essays on Economic Growth & Welfare. Cambridge University Press, Cambridge.
Abramovitz, M., 1993. The search for the sources of growth: areas of ignorance, old and new. Journal of Economic History 53, 217–243.
Abramovitz, M., David, P.A., 1996. Convergence and delayed catch-up: productivity leadership and the waning of American exceptionalism. In: Landau, R., Taylor, T., Wright, G. (Eds.), The Mosaic of Economic Growth. Stanford University Press, Stanford, pp. 21–62.
Abramovitz, M., David, P.A., 2001. Two centuries of American macroeconomic growth: from exploitation of resource abundance to knowledge-driven development. Stanford Institute for Economic Policy Research Discussion Paper No. 01–05.
Acemoglu, D., 2002. Directed technical change. Review of Economic Studies 69, 781–809.
Acemoglu, D., 2010. When does labor scarcity encourage innovation? Journal of Political Economy 118, 1037–1078.
Acemoglu, D., Johnson, S., 2005. Unbundling institutions. Journal of Political Economy 113, 949–995.
Acemoglu, D., Johnson, S., Robinson, J.A., 2001. The colonial origins of comparative development: an empirical investigation. American Economic Review 91, 1369–1401.
Acemoglu, D., Johnson, S., Robinson, J., 2003. An African success story: Botswana. In: Rodrik, D. (Ed.), In Search of Prosperity: Analytic Narratives on Economic Growth. Princeton University Press, Princeton, pp. 80–119.
Acemoglu, D., Robinson, J.A., 2010. Why is Africa poor? Economic History of Developing Regions 25, 21–50.
Acemoglu, D., Zilibotti, F., 2001. Productivity differences. Quarterly Journal of Economics 116, 563–606.
Adelman, I., Morris, C.T., 1967. Society, Politics, & Economic Development: A Quantitative Approach. Johns Hopkins University Press, Baltimore.
Aghion, P., Howitt, P., 2006. Appropriate growth policy: a unifying framework. Journal of the European Economic Association 4, 269–314.
Aiyar, S., Dalgaard, C.-J., 2005. Total factor productivity revisited: a dual approach to development accounting. IMF Staff Papers 52, 82–102.
Akkermans, D., Castaldi, C., Los, B., 2009. Do "liberal market economies" really innovate more radically than "coordinated market economies"?: Hall and Soskice reconsidered. Research Policy 38, 181–191.
Albers, R., Groote, P., 1996. The empirics of growth. De Economist 144, 429–444.
Albouy, D.Y., 2012. The colonial origins of comparative development: an empirical investigation: comment. American Economic Review 102, 3059–3076.
Alesina, A.F., Glaeser, E.L., Sacerdote, B., 2006. Work and leisure in the US and Europe: why so different? In: Gertler, M., Rogoff, K. (Eds.), NBER Macroeconomics Annual 2005. MIT Press, Cambridge, Massachusetts, pp. 1–64.
Allen, R.C., 2003. Farm to Factory: A Reinterpretation of the Soviet Industrial Revolution. Princeton University Press, Princeton.
Allen, R.C., 2009. The British Industrial Revolution in Global Perspective. Cambridge University Press, Cambridge.
Allen, R.C., 2011. The spinning jenny: a fresh look. Journal of Economic History 71, 461–464

Allen, R.C., 2012. Technology and the great divergence: global economic development since 1820. Explorations in Economic History 49, 1–16.

Allen, R.C., 2013. The high wage economy and the industrial revolution: a restatement. University of Oxford Discussion Paper in Economic and Social History No. 115.

Allen, R.C., Weisdorf, J.L., 2011. Was there an "industrious revolution" before the industrial revolution? Economic History Review 64, 715–729.

Amsden, A.H., 1989. Asia's Next Giant: South Korea and Late Industrialization. Oxford University Press, Oxford.

Badinger, H., 2005. Growth effects of economic integration: evidence from the EU member states. Review of World Economics 141, 50–78.

Badinger, H., Maydell, N., 2009. Legal and economic issues in completing the EU internal market for services: an interdisciplinary perspective. Journal of Common Market Studies 47, 693–717.

Bairoch, P., 1982. International industrialization levels from 1750 to 1980. Journal of European Economic History 11, 269–331.

Baldwin, R., forthcoming. Trade and industrialisation after globalisation's second unbundling: how building and joining a supply chain are different and why it matters. In: Feenstra, R.C. Taylor, A.M. (Eds.), Globalization in an Age of Crisis: Multilateral Economic Cooperation in the Twenty-First Century. University of Chicago Press, Chicago.

Barro, R.J., 1991. Economic growth in a cross section of countries. Quarterly Journal of Economics 106, 407–443.

Barro, R.J., 1999. Notes on growth accounting. Journal of Economic Growth 4, 119–137.

Barro, R.J., Lee, J.-W., 2012. A new data set of educational attainment in the world, 1950–2010. Journal of Development Economics 104, 184–198.

Barry, F., 2002. The Celtic Tiger era: delayed convergence or regional boom? ESRI Quarterly Economic Commentary, Summer, 84–91.

Basu, S., Weil, D.N., 1998. Appropriate technology and growth. Quarterly Journal of Economics 113, 1025–1054.

Bates, R.H., Coatsworth, J.H., Williamson, J.G., 2007. Lost decades: postindependence performance in Latin America and Africa. Journal of Economic History 67, 917–943.

Bean, C., Crafts, N., 1996. British economic growth since 1945: relative economic decline... and renaissance? In: Crafts, N., Toniolo, G. (Eds.), Economic Growth in Europe Since 1945. Cambridge University Press, Cambridge, pp. 131–172.

Bénétrix, A.S., O'Rourke, K.H., Williamson, J.G., 2013. The spread of manufacturing to the poor periphery 1870–2007. NBER Working Paper No. 18221.

Berliner, J.S., 1976. The Innovation Decision in Soviet Industry. MIT Press, Cambridge, Massachusetts.

Blanchard, O., 2004. The economic future of Europe. Journal of Economic Perspectives 18, 3–26.

Bleaney, M., Nishiyama, A., 2002. Explaining growth: a contest between models. Journal of Economic Growth 7, 43–56.

Bloom, N., Sadun, R., van Reenen, J., 2012. Americans do IT better: US multinationals and the productivity miracle. American Economic Review 102, 167–201.

Blundell, R., Griffith, R., van Reenen, J., 1999. Market share, market value and innovation in a panel of British manufacturing firms. Review of Economic Studies 66, 529–554.

Bogart, D., Drelichman, M., Gelderbloom, O., Rosenthal, J.-L., 2010. State and private institutions. In: Broadberry, S., O'Rourke, K.H. (Eds.), The Modern Economic History of Europe: 1700–1870. Vol. 1, Cambridge University Press, Cambridge, pp. 70–95.

Bolt, J., van Zanden, J.L., 2013. The first update of the Maddison project: re-estimating growth before 1820. Maddison Project Working Paper 4. Data available at <http://www.ggdc.net/maddison/maddison-project/data/mpd_2013-01.xlsx>.

Boskin, M.J., Dulberger, E.R., Gordon, R.J., Griliches, Z., Jorgenson, D.W., 1996. Towards a More Accurate Measure of the Cost of Living. US Government Printing Office, Washington, DC.

Bosworth, B.P., Collins, S.M., 2003. The empirics of growth: an update. Brookings Papers on Economic Activity 2, 113–206.

Bosworth, B.P., Collins, S.M., 2008. Accounting for growth: comparing China and India. Journal of Economic Perspectives 22, pp. 45–66.

Bourguignon, F., Morrisson, C., 2002. Inequality among world citizens: 1820–1992. American Economic Review 92, 727–744.

Brandt, L., Rawski, T.G. (Eds.), 2008a. China's Great Economic Transformation. Cambridge University Press, Cambridge.

Brandt, L., Rawski, T.G., 2008b. China's great economic transformation. In: Brandt and Rawski (2008a), pp. 1–26.

Brandt, L., Rawski, T.G., Sutton, J., 2008. China's industrial development. In: Brandt and Rawski (2008a), pp. 569–632.

Brandt, L., Hsieh, C.-T., Zhu, X., 2008. Growth and structural transformation in China. In: Brandt and Rawski (2008a), pp. 683–728.

Brandt, L., Ma, D., Rawski, T., forthcoming. From divergence to convergence: re-evaluating the history behind China's economic boom. Journal of Economic Literature.

Branstetter, L., Lardy, N., 2008. China's embrace of globalization. In: Brandt and Rawski (2008a), pp. 633–682.

Brezis, E.S., Krugman, P.R., Tsiddon, D., 1993. Leapfrogging in international competition: a theory of cycles in national technological leadership. American Economic Review 83, 1211–1219.

Broadberry, S., 1997. Anglo-German productivity differences 1870–1990: a sectoral analysis. European Review of Economic History 1, 247–267.

Broadberry, S., 1998. How did the United States and Germany overtake Britain? A sectoral analysis of comparative productivity levels, 1870–1990. Journal of Economic History 58, 375–407.

Broadberry, S., 2006. Market Services and the Productivity Race, 1850–2000: British Performance in International Perspective. Cambridge University Press, Cambridge.

Broadberry, S., 2013. Accounting for the Great Divergence. Paper presented to CAGE/CEPR Conference, Long-Run Growth: Unified Growth Theory and Economic History, University of Warwick.

Broadberry, S., Campbell, B., Klein, A., Overton, M. van Leeuwen, B., 2010. British economic growth: 1270–1870. University of Warwick CAGE Working Paper No. 35.

Broadberry, S., Crafts, N., 1996. British economic policy and industrial performance in the early post-war period. Business History 38, 65–91.

Brown, W., Bryson, A., Forth, J., 2008. Competition and the retreat from collective bargaining. National Institute of Economic and Social Research Discussion Paper No. 318.

Brynjolfsson, E., Hitt, L.M., 2003. Computing productivity: firm-level evidence. Review of Economics and Statistics 85, 793–808.

Buccirossi, P., Ciari, L., Duso, T., Spagnolo, G., Vitale, C., forthcoming. Competition policy and productivity growth: an empirical assessment. Review of Economics and Statistics.

Buera, F.J., Monge-Naranjo, A., Primiceri, G.E., 2011. Learning the wealth of nations. Econometrica 79, 1–45.

Cain, L.P., Paterson, D.G., 1986. Biased technical change, scale, and factor substitution in American industry: 1850–1919. Journal of Economic History 46, 153–164.

Cameron, G., Wallace, C., 2002. Macroeconomic performance in the Bretton Woods era and after. Oxford Review of Economic Policy 18, 479–494.

Carreras, A., Josephson, C., 2010. Aggregate growth, 1870–1914: growing at the production frontier. In: Broadberry, S., O'Rourke, K.H. (Eds.), The Cambridge Economic History of Modern Europe: 1870 to the Present. Vol. 2. Cambridge University Press, Cambridge, pp. 30–58.

Chandler, A.D., 1977. The Visible Hand: The Managerial Revolution in American Business. Harvard University Press, Cambridge, Massachusetts.

Clemens, M.A., Williamson, J.G., 2004. Why did the tariff-growth correlation change after 1950? Journal of Economic Growth 9, 5–46.

Collier, P., 2007. Growth strategies for Africa. Commission on Growth and Development Working Paper No. 9.

Collier, P., Goderis, B., 2012. Commodity prices and growth: an empirical investigation. European Economic Review 56, 1241–1260.

Collier, P., Gunning, J.W., 1999. Explaining African economic performance. Journal of Economic Literature 37, 64–111.

Comin, D., Dmitriev, M., Rossi-Hansberg, E., 2013. The spatial diffusion of technology. Mimeo.

Comin, D., Hobijn, B., 2010. An exploration of technology diffusion. American Economic Review 100, 2031–2059.

Comin, D., Hobijn, B., Rovito, E., 2006. Five facts you need to know about technology diffusion. NBER Working Paper No. 11928.

Conway, P., de Rosa, D., Nicoletti, G., Steiner, F., 2006. Regulation, competition and productivity convergence. OECD Economics Department Working Paper No. 509.

Corrado, C., Hulten, C., Sichel, D., 2009. Intangible capital and US economic growth. Review of Income and Wealth 55, 661–685.

Cosh, A.D., Guest, P., Hughes, A., 2008. UK corporate governance and takeover performance. In: Gugler, K., Yurtoglu, B.B. (Eds.), The Economics of Corporate Governance and Mergers. Edward Elgar, Cheltenham, pp. 226–261.

Costa, D., 2001. Estimating real income in the United States from 1888 to 1994: correcting CPI bias using Engel curves. Journal of Political Economy 109, 1288–1310

Crafts, N., 1989. Revealed comparative advantage in manufacturing: 1899–1950. Journal of European Economic History 18, 127–137.

Crafts, N., 1992a. Productivity growth reconsidered. Economic Policy 15, 387–414.

Crafts, N., 1992b. Institutions and economic growth: recent British experience in an international context. West European Politics 15, 16–38.

Crafts, N., 1999. East Asian growth before and after the crisis. IMF Staff Papers 46, 139–166.

Crafts, N., 2002. The Solow productivity paradox in historical perspective. CEPR Discussion Paper No. 3142.

Crafts, N., 2004a. Productivity growth in the industrial revolution: a new growth accounting perspective. Journal of Economic History 64, 521–535.

Crafts, N., 2004b. Steam as a general purpose technology: a growth accounting perspective. Economic Journal 114, 338–351.

Crafts, N., 2005. The first industrial revolution: resolving the slow growth/rapid industrialization paradox. Journal of the European Economic Association 3, 525–534.

Crafts, N. 2009a. Solow and growth accounting: a perspective from quantitative economic history. History of Political Economy 41, 200–220.

Crafts, N., 2009b. The Celtic Tiger in historical and international perspective. In: Mulreany, M. (Ed.), Economic Development 50 Years On, 1958–2008. IPA, Dublin, pp. 64–76.

Crafts, N. 2010. Cliometrics and technological change: a survey. European Journal of the History of Economic Thought, 17, 1127–1147.

Crafts, N., 2011. Explaining the first industrial revolution: two views. European Review of Economic History 15, 153–168.

Crafts, N., 2012. British relative economic decline revisited: the role of competition. Explorations in Economic History 49, 17–29.

Crafts, N. 2013a. Long-term growth in Europe: what difference does the crisis make? National Institute Economic Review, 224, R14–R18.

Crafts, N. 2013b. Returning to growth: policy lessons from history. Fiscal Studies 34, 255–282.

Crafts, N., Mills, T.C., 2005. TFP growth in British and German manufacturing: 1950–1996. Economic Journal 115, 649–670.

Crafts, N., Mills, T.C., 2009. From Malthus to Solow: how did the Malthusian economy really evolve? Journal of Macroeconomics 31, 68–93.

Crafts, N., Mulatu, A., 2006. How did the location of industry respond to falling transport costs in Britain before World War I? Journal of Economic History 66, 575–607.

Crafts, N., Toniolo, G., 1996. Postwar growth: an overview. In: Crafts, N., Toniolo, G. (Eds.), Economic Growth in Europe since 1945. Cambridge University Press, Cambridge, pp. 1–37.

Crafts, N., Toniolo, G., 2008, European economic growth: 1950–2005: an overview. CEPR Discussion Paper No. 6863.

Crafts, N., Venables, A.J., 2003. Globalization in history: a geographical perspective. In: Bordo, M.D., Taylor, A.M., Williamson, J.G. (Eds.), Globalization in Historical Perspective. University of Chicago Press, Chicago, pp. 323–364.

Criscuolo, C., Haskel, J., Martin, R., 2004. Import competition, productivity and restructuring in UK manufacturing. Oxford Review of Economic Policy 20, 393–408.

Crouch, C., 1993. Industrial Relations and European State Traditions. Clarendon Press, Oxford.

Das, M., N'Diaye, P., 2013. Chronicle of a decline foretold: has China reached the Lewis turning point? IMF Working Paper No. WP/13/26.

David, P.A., 1975. Technological Choice Innovation and Economic Growth: Essays on American and British Experience in the 19th Century. Cambridge University Press, Cambridge.

David, P.A., 1985. Clio and the economics of QWERTY. American Economic Review 75, 332–337.

David, P.A., Wright, G., 1997. Increasing returns and the genesis of American resource abundance. Industrial and Corporate Change 6, 203–245.

David, P.A., Wright, G., 1999. Early twentieth century productivity growth dynamics: an inquiry into the economic history of "our ignorance." University of Oxford Discussion Paper in Economic and Social History No. 33.

De Long, J.B., 1988. Productivity growth, convergence, and welfare: comment. American Economic Review 78, 1138–1154.

DeLong, J.B., Eichengreen, B., 1993. The Marshall Plan: history's most successful structural adjustment program. In: Dornbusch, R., Nölling, W., Layard, R. (Eds.), Postwar Economic Reconstruction and Lessons for the East Today. MIT Press, Cambridge, Massachusetts, pp. 189–230.

Denny, K., Nickell, S.J., 1992. Unions and investment in British industry. Economic Journal 102, 874–887.

Domar, E.D., 1970. The causes of slavery or serfdom: a hypothesis. Journal of Economic History 30, 18–32.

Duval, R., de la Maissonneuve, C., 2010. Long-run growth scenarios for the world economy. Journal of Policy Modeling 32, 64–80.

Easterly, W., Kremer, M., Pritchett, L., Summers, L.H., 1993. Good policy or good luck? Country growth performance and temporary shocks. Journal of Monetary Economics 32, 459–483.

Easterly, W., Levine, R., 2003. Tropics, germs, and crops: how endowments influence economic development. Journal of Monetary Economics 50, 3–39.

Eaton, J., Kortum, S., 1999. International technology diffusion: theory and measurement. International Economic Review 40, 537–570.

Edgerton, D.E.H., Horrocks, S.M., 1994. British industrial research and development before 1945. Economic History Review 47, 213–238.

Edquist, H., 2010. Does hedonic price indexing change our interpretation of economic history? Evidence from Swedish electrification. Economic History Review 63, 500–523.

Eichengreen, B., 1992. Golden Fetters: The Gold Standard and the Great Depression: 1919–1939. Oxford University Press, Oxford.

Eichengreen, B., 1996. Institutions and economic growth: Europe after World War II. In: Crafts, N., Toniolo, G. (Eds.), Economic Growth in Europe since 1945. Cambridge University Press, Cambridge, pp. 38–72.

Eichengreen, B., 2007. The European Economy Since 1945: Coordinated Capitalism and Beyond. Princeton University Press, Princeton.

Eichengreen, B., Park, D., Shin, K., 2012. When fast-growing economies slow down: international evidence and implications for China. Asian Economic Papers 11, 42–87.

Engerman, S.L., Sokoloff, K.L., 1997. Factor endowments, institutions, and differential paths of growth among new world economies: a view from economic historians of the United States. In: Haber, S. (Ed.), How Latin America Fell Behind: Essays on the Economic Histories of Brazil and Mexico: 1800–1914. Stanford University Press, Stanford, pp. 260–304.

Ennew, C., Greenaway, D., Reed, G., 1990. Further evidence on effective tariffs and effective protection in the UK. Oxford Bulletin of Economics and Statistics 52, 69–78.

Ergas, H., 1987. Does technology policy matter? In: Guile, B.R., Brooks, H. (Eds.), Technology and Global Industry: Companies and Nations in the World Economy. National Academy Press, Washington, DC, pp. 191–245.

Estevadeordal, A., Taylor, A.M., forthcoming. Is the Washington consensus dead? Growth, openness, and the great liberalization, 1970s–2000s. Review of Economics and Statistics.

Feinstein, C.H., 1981. Capital accumulation and the industrial revolution. In: Floud, R., McCloskey, D.N. (Eds.), The Economic History of Britain since 1700. vol. 1. Cambridge University Press, Cambridge, pp. 128–142.

Feinstein, C.H., Matthews, R.C.O., Odling-Smee, J.C., 1982. The timing of the climacteric and its sectoral incidence in the UK: 1873–1913. In: Kindleberger, C.P., di Tella, G. (Eds.), Economics in the Long View: Essays in Honour of W.W. Rostow, vol. 2. Macmillan, London, pp. 168–185.

Findlay, R., O'Rourke, K.H., 2007. Power and Plenty: Trade, War, and the World Economy in the Second Millennium. Princeton University Press, Princeton.

Fogel, R.W., 1964. Railroads and American Economic Growth: Essays in Econometric History. Johns Hopkins Press, Baltimore.

Foreman-Peck, J., 1991. Railways and late Victorian economic growth. In: Foreman-Peck, J. (Ed.), New Perspectives on the Victorian Economy: Essays in Quantitative Economic History, 1860–1914. Cambridge University Press, Cambridge, pp. 73–95.

Foreman-Peck, J., Hannah, L., 2012. Extreme divorce: the managerial revolution in UK companies before 1914. Economic History Review 65, 1217–1238.

Gerschenkron, A., 1962. Economic Backwardness in Historical Perspective: A Book of Essays. Harvard University Press, Cambridge Massachusetts.

Gilmore, O., 2009. Corporatism and Growth: Testing the Eichengreen Hypothesis. MSc. Dissertation, University of Warwick.

Goldin, C., Katz, L.F., 2008. The Race Between Education and Technology. Harvard University Press, Cambridge, Massachusetts.

Gómez-Galvarriato, A., Williamson, J.G., 2009. Was it prices, productivity or policy? Latin American industrialisation after 1870. Journal of Latin American Studies 41, 663–694.

Gragnolati, U., Moschella, D., Pugliese, E., 2011. The spinning jenny and the industrial revolution: a reappraisal. Journal of Economic History 71, 458–462.

Gregg, P., Machin, S., Metcalf, D., 1993. Signals and cycles? Productivity growth and changes in union status in British companies: 1984–1989. Economic Journal 103, 894–907.

Gregory, P.R., 1991. The role of the state in promoting economic development: the Russian case and its general implications. In: Sylla, R., Toniolo, G. (Eds.), Patterns of European Industrialization: The 19th Century. Routledge, London, pp. 64–79.

Griffith, R., 2001. Product market competition, efficiency and agency costs: an empirical analysis. Institute for Fiscal Studies Working Paper No. 01/12.

Griffith, R., Harrison, R., Simpson, H., 2010. Product market reform and innovation in the EU. Scandinavian Journal of Economics 112, 389–415.

Griliches, Z., 1996. The discovery of the residual: a historical note. Journal of Economic Literature 34, 1324–1330.

Habakkuk, H.J., 1962. American and British Technology in the 19th Century: The Search for Labour-Saving Inventions. Cambridge University Press, Cambridge.

Hall, P.A., Soskice, D., 2001. An introduction to varieties of capitalism. In: Hall, P.A., Soskice, D. (Eds.), Varieties of Capitalism: The Institutional Foundations of Comparative Advantage. Oxford University Press, Oxford, pp. 1–68.

Hall, R.E., Jones, C.I., 1999. Why do some countries produce so much more output per worker than others? Quarterly Journal of Economics 114, 83–116.

Hanushek, E.A., Wössmann, L., 2012. Do better schools lead to more growth? Cognitive skills, economic outcomes, and causation. Journal of Economic Growth 17, 267–321.

Harley, C.K., 1991. Substitution for prerequisites: endogenous institutions and comparative economic history. In: Sylla, R., Toniolo, G. (Eds.), Patterns of European Industrialization: The 19th Century. Routledge, London, pp. 29–44.

Harris, R., Siegel, D.S., Wright, M., 2005. Assessing the impact of management buyouts on economic efficiency: plant-level evidence from the United Kingdom. Review of Economics and Statistics 87, 148–153.

Harrison, M., 2002. Coercion, compliance, and the collapse of the Soviet command economy. Economic History Review 55, 397–433.

Haskel, J., 1991. Imperfect competition, work practices and productivity growth. Oxford Bulletin of Economics and Statistics 53, 265–279.

Hausmann, R., Pritchett, L., Rodrik, D., 2005. Growth accelerations. Journal of Economic Growth 10, 303–329.

Henisz, W.J., 2002. The institutional environment for infrastructure investment. Industrial and Corporate Change 11, 355–389.

Heston, A., Sicular, T., 2008. China and development economics. In: Brandt and Rawski (2008a), pp. 27–67.

Hicks, J., 1969. A Theory of Economic History. Oxford University Press, Oxford.

Hitiris, T., 1978. Effective protection and economic performance in UK manufacturing industry: 1963–1968. Economic Journal 88, 107–120.

Honohan, P., Walsh, B., 2002. Catching up with the leaders: the Irish hare. Brookings Papers on Economic Activity 1, 1–57.

Høj, J., Jimenez, M., Maher, M., Nicoletti, G., Wise, M., 2007. Product market competition in the OECD countries: taking stock and moving forward. OECD Economics Department Working Paper No. 575.

Hsieh, C.-T., Klenow, P.J., 2009. Misallocation and manufacturing TFP in China and India. Quarterly Journal of Economics 124, 1403–1448.

Hsieh, C.-T., Klenow, P.J., 2010. Development accounting. American Economic Journal: Macroeconomics 2, 207–223.

Hulten, C.R., 1979. On the "importance" of productivity change. American Economic Review 69, 126–136.

Humphries, J., 2013. The lure of aggregates and the pitfalls of the patriarchal perspective: a critique of the high wage economy interpretation of the British industrial revolution. Economic History Review 66, 693–714.

Isham, J., Woolcock, M., Pritchett, L., Busby, G., 2005. The varieties of resource experience: natural resource export structures and the political economy of economic growth. World Bank Economic Review 19, 141–174.

Ito, T., 2001. Growth, crisis, and the future of economic recovery in East Asia. In: Stiglitz, J.E., Yusuf, S. (Eds.), Rethinking the East Asian Miracle. Oxford University Press, Oxford, pp. 55–94.

James, J.A., Skinner, J.S., 1985. The resolution of the labor-scarcity paradox. Journal of Economic History 45, 513–540.

Jerven, M., 2010. African growth recurring: an economic history perspective on African growth episodes, 1690–2010. Economic History of Developing Regions 25, 127–154.

Jerzmanowski, M., 2007. Total factor productivity differences: appropriate technology vs. efficiency. European Economic Review 51, 2080–2110.

Jones, C.I., 1995. Time series tests of endogenous growth models. Quarterly Journal of Economics 110, 495–525.

Kindleberger, C.P., 1967. Europe's Postwar Growth: The Role of Labor Supply. Harvard University Press, Cambridge, Massachusetts.

Kindleberger, C.P., 1973. The World in Depression 1929–1939. University of California Press, Berkeley.

Kishtainy, N., 2011. Social Orders, Property Rights and Economic Transition: a Quantitative Analysis. Ph. D. thesis, University of Warwick.

Klein, A., Crafts, N., 2012. Making sense of the manufacturing belt: determinants of US industrial location: 1880–1920. Journal of Economic Geography 12, 775–807.

Knack, S., Keefer, P., 1995. Institutions and economic performance: cross-country tests using alternative institutional measures. Economics and Politics 7, 207–227

Kraay, A., 2000. Household saving in China. World Bank Economic Review 14, 545–570.

Krantz, O., Schön, L., 2007. Swedish Historical National Accounts, 1800–2000. Almqvist and Wiksell International, Lund.

Krugman, P., 1994. The myth of Asia's miracle. Foreign Affairs 73, 62–78.

Krugman, P., 2013. Hitting China's wall. New York Times, July 18.

Krugman, P.R., Venables, A.J., 1995. Globalization and the inequality of nations. Quarterly Journal of Economics 110, 857–880.

Kuznets, S., 1966. Modern Economic Growth: Rate, Structure, and Spread. Yale University Press, New Haven.

Lee, I.H., Syed, M., Lui, X., 2012. Is China over-investing and does it matter? IMF Working Paper No. WP/12/277.

Lehmann, S.H., O'Rourke, K.H., 2011. The structure of protection and growth in the late 19th century. Review of Economics and Statistics 93, 606–616.

Leunig, T., 2001. New answers to old questions: explaining the slow adoption of ring spinning in Lancashire: 1880–1913. Journal of Economic History 61, 439–466.

Levy, D.M., Peart, S.J., 2011. Soviet growth and American textbooks: an endogenous past. Journal of Economic Behavior and Organization 78, 110–125.

Lewis, W.A., 1954. Economic development with unlimited supplies of labour. The Manchester School 22, 139–191.

Lewis, W.A., 1969. Aspects of Tropical Trade 1883–1965. Almqvist and Wiksell, Uppsala.

Lewis, W.A., 1970. The export stimulus. In: Lewis, W.A. (Ed.), Tropical Development 1880–1913. Northwestern University Press, Evanston, pp. 13–45.

Lewis, W.A., 1978. Growth and Fluctuations 1870–1913. George Allen & Unwin, London.

Lipsey, R.G., Bekar, C., Carlaw, K., 1998. What requires explanation? In: Helpman, E. (Ed.), General Purpose Technologies and Economic Growth. MIT Press, Cambridge, Massachusetts, pp. 15–54.

Liu, D., Meissner, C. M., 2013. Market potential and the rise of US productivity leadership. NBER Working Paper No. 18819.

Lucas, R.E., 2000. Some macroeconomics for the 21st century. Journal of Economic Perspectives 14, 159–168.

Lucas, R.E., 2009. Trade and the diffusion of the industrial revolution. American Economic Journal: Macroeconomics 1, 1–25.

Machin, S., Wadhwani, S., 1991. The effects of unions on organisational change and employment. Economic Journal 101, 835–854.

Maddison, A., 1987. Growth and slowdown in advanced capitalist economies: techniques of quantitative assessment. Journal of Economic Literature 25, 649–698.

Maddison, A., 1995. Monitoring the World Economy: 1820–1992. OECD, Paris.

Maddison, A., 2005. Measuring and interpreting world economic performance 1500–2001. Review of Income and Wealth 51, 1–35.

Maddison, A., 2010. Statistics on world population, GDP and per capita GDP, 1–2008 AD. Available at <http://www.ggdc.net/maddison/Historical_Statistics/vertical-file_02-2010.xls>.

Maddison, A., Wu, H.X., 2008. Measuring China's economic performance. World Economics 9, 13–44.

Madsen, J.B., 2007. Technology spillover through trade and TFP convergence: 135 years of evidence for the OECD countries. Journal of International Economics 72, 464–480.

Magee, G., 2004. Manufacturing and technological change. In: Floud, R., Johnson, P. (Eds.), The Cambridge Economic History of Modern Britain, vol. 2. Cambridge University Press, Cambridge, pp. 74–98.

Matthews, R.C.O., Feinstein, C.H., Odling-Smee, J.C., 1982. British Economic Growth: 1856–1973. Oxford University Press, Oxford.

McMillan, J., Whalley, J., Zhu, L., 1989. The impact of China's economic reforms on agricultural productivity growth. Journal of Political Economy 97, 781–807.

Mehlum, H., Moene, K., Torvik, R., 2006. Institutions and the resource curse. Economic Journal 116, 1–20.

Melman, S., 1956. Dynamic Factors in Industrial Productivity. Basil Blackwell, Oxford.

Mitch, D., 1999. The role of education and skill in the British industrial revolution. In: Mokyr, J. (Ed.), The British Industrial Revolution: An Economic Perspective, second ed. Westview Press, Oxford, 241–279.

Morrison, C.J., 1993. A Microeconomic Approach to the Measurement of Economic Performance: Productivity Growth, Capacity Utilization, and Related Performance Indicators. Springer-Verlag, New York.

Morrisson, C., Murtin, F., 2009. The century of education. Journal of Human Capital 3, 1–42.

Mowery, D., 2009. Plus ca change: industrial R & D in the "third industrial revolution". Industrial and Corporate Change 18, 1–50.

Mowery, D., Rosenberg, N., 2000. Twentieth-century technological change. In: Engerman, S.L., Gallmann, R.E. (Eds.), The Cambridge Economic History of the United States. The Twentieth Century. Vol. 3, Cambridge University Press, Cambridge, pp. 803–925.

Murphy, K.M., Shleifer, A., Vishny, R.W., 1989. Industrialization and the big push. Journal of Political Economy 97, 1003–1026.

National Science Board, 2012. Science and Engineering Indicators, 2012. Washington, DC.

Naughton, B., 2008. A political economy of China's economic transition. In: Brandt and Rawski (2008a), pp. 91–135.

Nelson, R.R., Wright, G., 1992. The rise and fall of American technological leadership: the postwar era in historical perspective. Journal of Economic Literature 30, 1931–1964.

Nicholas, T., 2010. The role of independent invention in US technological development: 1880–1930. Journal of Economic History 70, 57–82.

Nickell, S., Nicolitsas, D., Dryden, N., 1997. What makes firms perform well? European Economic Review 41, 783–796.

Nicoletti, G., Scarpetta, S., 2003. Regulation, productivity and growth: OECD evidence. Economic Policy 36, 9–72.

North, D.C., 1990. Institutions. Institutional Change and Economic Performance. Cambridge University Press, Cambridge.

North, D.C., Thomas, R.P., 1973. The Rise of the Western World: A New Economic History. Cambridge University Press, Cambridge.

North, D.C., Wallis, J.J., Weingast, B.R., 2009. Violence and Social Orders: A Conceptual Framework for Interpreting Recorded Human History. Cambridge University Press, Cambridge.

Ofer, G., 1987. Soviet economic growth: 1928–1985. Journal of Economic Literature 25, 1767–1833.

Ogilvie, S., 2007. "Whatever is, is right"? Economic institutions in pre-industrial Europe. Economic History Review 60, 649–684.

Ó Gráda, C., O'Rourke, K.H., 1996. Irish economic growth, 1945–1988. In: Crafts, N., Toniolo, G. (Eds.), Economic Growth in Europe since 1945. Cambridge University Press, Cambridge, pp. 388–426.

Ó Gráda, C., O'Rourke, K.H., 2000. Living standards and growth. In: O'Hagan, J. (Ed.), The Economy of Ireland: Policy and Performance of a European Region. Gill and Macmillan/St Martin's Press, Dublin, pp. 178–204.

Oliner, S.D., Sichel, D.E., Stiroh, K.J., 2007. Explaining a productive decade. Brookings Papers on Economic Activity 1, 81–152.

Olson, M., 1982. The Rise and Decline of Nations: Economic Growth, Stagflation, and Social Rigidities. Yale University Press, New Haven.

O'Mahony, M., Timmer, M.P., 2009. Output, input and productivity measures at the industry level: the EU KLEMS database. Economic Journal 119, F374–F403.

O'Rourke, K.H., 2000. Tariffs and growth in the late 19th century. Economic Journal 110, 456–483.

O'Rourke, K.H., Williamson, J.G., 2002. When did globalisation begin? European Review of Economic History 6, 23–50.

Oulton, N., 1976. Effective protection of British industry. In: Corden, W.M., Fels, G. (Eds.), Public Assistance to Industry. Macmillan, London, pp. 46–90.

Oulton, N., 2012. Long-term implications of the ICT revolution: applying the lessons of growth theory and growth accounting. Economic Modeling 29, 1722–1736.

Pavitt, K., Soete, L., 1982. International differences in economic growth and the international location of innovation. In: Giersch, H. (Ed.), Emerging Technologies. Mohr, Tübingen, pp. 105–133.

Prados de la Escosura, L., Rosés, J., 2009. The sources of long-run growth in Spain, 1850–2000. Journal of Economic History 69, 1063–1091.

Prais, S.J., 1982. Productivity and Industrial Structure. Cambridge University Press, Cambridge.

Pratten, C.F., Atkinson, A.G., 1976. The use of manpower in British industry. Department of Employment Gazette 84, 571–576.

Prescott, E.C., 2004. Why do Americans work so much more than Europeans? Federal Reserve Bank of Minneapolis Quarterly Review 28, 2–13.

Pritchett, L., 1997. Divergence, big time. Journal of Economic Perspectives 11, 3–17.

Pritchett, L., 2000. Understanding patterns of economic growth: searching for hills among plateaus, mountains, and plains. World Bank Economic Review 14, 221–250.

Proudman, J., Redding, S., 1998. A summary of the openness and growth project. In: Proudman, J., Redding, S. (Eds.), Openness and Growth. Bank of England, London, pp. 1–29.

Redding, S., Venables, A.J., 2004. Economic geography and international inequality. Journal of International Economics 62, 53–82.

Rhode, P., 2002. Gallman's annual output series for the United States: 1834–1909. NBER Working Paper No. 8860.

Robertson, D.H., 1938. The future of international trade. Economic Journal 48, 1–14.

Rodríguez, F., Rodrik, D., 2001. Trade policy and economic growth: A skeptic's guide to the cross-national evidence. In: Bernanke, B., Rogoff, K. (Eds.), Macroeconomics Annual 2000. MIT Press, Cambridge, Massachusetts, pp. 261–325.

Rodrik, D., 1995. Getting interventions right: how South Korea and Taiwan grew rich. Economic Policy 20, 55–97.

Rodrik, D., 1997. TFPG controversies, institutions and economic performance in East Asia. CEPR Discussion Paper No. 1587.

Rodrik, D., Subramanian, A., 2005. From "Hindu Growth" to productivity surge: the mystery of the Indian growth transition. IMF Staff Papers 52, 193–228.

Rosenstein-Rodan, P., 1943. Problems of industrialisation of eastern and south-eastern Europe. Economic Journal 53, 202–211.

Rubinstein, W.D., 1992. The structure of wealth-holding in Britain, 1809–1839: a preliminary anatomy. Historical Research 65, 74–89.

Sachs, J.D., McArthur, J.W., Schmidt-Traub, G., Kruk, M., Bahadur, C., Faye, M., McCord, G., 2004. Ending Africa's Poverty Trap. Brookings Papers on Economic Activity 1, 117–240.

Sachs, J.D., Warner, A.M., 1995. Economic reform and the process of global integration. Brookings Papers on Economic Activity 1, 1–95.

Sachs, J.D., Warner, A.M., 1997. Fundamental sources of long-run growth. American Economic Review 87, 184–188.

Sandberg, L.G., 1979. The case of the impoverished sophisticate: human capital and Swedish economic growth before World War I. Journal of Economic History 39, 225–241.

Schneider, M.R., Paunescu, M., 2012. Changing varieties of capitalism and revealed comparative advantages from 1990 to 2005: a test of the Hall and Soskice claims. Socio-Economic Review 10, 731–753.

Schulze, M.-S., 2007. Origins of catch-up failure: comparative productivity growth in the Habsburg Empire: 1870–1910. European Review of Economic History 11, 189–218.

Sokoloff, K.L., Engerman, S.L., 2000. History lessons: institutions, factor endowments, and paths of development in the New World. Journal of Economic Perspectives 14, 217–232.

Sokoloff, K.L., Zolt, E.M., 2007. Inequality and the evolution of institutions of taxation: evidence from the history of the Americas. In: Edwards, S., Esquivel, G., Márquez, G. (Eds.), The Decline of Latin American Economies: Growth, Institutions, and Crises. University of Chicago Press, Chicago, 83–136.

Solow, R.M., 1957. Technical change and the aggregate production function. Review of Economics and Statistics 39, 312–320.

Song, Z., Storesletten, K., Zilibotti, F., 2011. Growing like China. American Economic Review 101, 196–233.

Sumner, M., 1999. Long-run effects of investment incentives. In: Driver, C., Temple, J. (Eds.), Investment, Growth and Employment: Perspectives for Policy. Routledge, London, pp. 292–300.

Svejnar, J., 2008. China in light of the performance of the transition economies. In: Brandt and Rawski (2008a), pp. 68–90.

Sylla, R., 1991. The role of banks. In: Sylla, R., Toniolo, G. (Eds.), Patterns of European Industrialization: The 19th Century. Routledge, London, pp. 45–63.

Sylla, R., Toniolo, G., 1991. Introduction: patterns of European industrialization during the 19th century. In: Sylla, R., Toniolo, G. (Eds.), Patterns of European Industrialization: The 19th Century. Routledge, London, pp. 1–26.

Symeonidis, G., 2008. The effect of competition on wages and productivity: evidence from the United Kingdom. Review of Economics and Statistics 90, 134–146.

Tanzi, V., 1969. The Individual Income Tax and Economic Growth. Johns Hopkins University Press, Baltimore.

Temin, P., 2002. The Golden Age of European growth reconsidered. European Review of Economic History 6, 3–22.

Temple, J., Johnson, P.A., 1998. Social capability and economic growth. Quarterly Journal of Economics 113, 965–990.

Timmer, M.P., Inklaar, R., O'Mahony, M., van Ark, B., 2010. Economic Growth in Europe: A Comparative Industry Perspective. Cambridge University Press, Cambridge.

Triplett, J.E., 1999. The Solow productivity paradox: what do computers do to productivity? Canadian Journal of Economics 32, 309–334.

van Ark, B., Melka, J., Mulder, N., Timmer, M., Ypma, G., 2003. ICT investments and growth accounts for the European Union. Groningen Growth and Development Centre Research, Memorandum GD-56.

van der Ploeg, F., 2011. Natural resources: curse or blessing? Journal of Economic Literature 49, 366–420.

Venables, A.J., 2010. Economic geography and African development. Papers in Regional Science 89, 469–483.

Voth, H.-J., 2001. The longest years: new estimates of labor input in England: 1760–1830. Journal of Economic History 61, 1065–1082.

Wacziarg, R., Welch, K.H., 2008. Trade liberalization and growth: new evidence. World Bank Economic Review 22, 187–231.

Wade, R., 1990. Governing the Market: Economic Theory and the Role of Government in East Asian Industrialization. Princeton University Press, Princeton.

Wallis, G., 2009. Capital services growth in the UK: 1950 to 2006. Oxford Bulletin of Economics and Statistics 71, 799–819.

Weitzman, M.L., 1970. Soviet postwar economic growth and capital-labor substitution. American Economic Review 60, 676–692.

Whalley, J., Xin, X., 2010. China's FDI and non-FDI economies and the sustainability of future high Chinese growth. China Economic Review 21, 123–135.

Williamson, J.G., 2011. Trade and Poverty: When the Third World Fell Behind. MIT Press, Cambridge, Massachusetts.

World Bank, 1993. The East Asian Miracle: Economic Growth and Public Policy. Oxford University Press, Oxford.

Wössmann, L., Lüdemann, E., Schütz, G., West, M.R., 2007. School accountability, autonomy, choice, and the level of student achievement: international evidence from PISA 2003. OECD Education Working Paper No. 13.

Wren, C., 1996. Industrial Subsidies: The UK Experience. Macmillan, London.

Wright, G., 1990. The origins of American industrial success, 1879–1940. American Economic Review 80, 651–668.

Wright, G., Czelusta, J., 2007. Resource-based growth past and present. In: Lederman, D., Maloney, W.F. (Eds.), Natural Resources: Neither Curse nor Destiny. Stanford University Press, Palo Alto, 183–211.

Xu, C., 2011. The fundamental institutions of China's reforms and development. Journal of Economic Literature 49, 1076–1151.

Young, A., 1995. The tyranny of numbers: confronting the statistical realities of the East Asian growth experience. Quarterly Journal of Economics 110, 641–680.

Zeira, J., 1998. Workers, machines, and economic growth. Quarterly Journal of Economics 113, 1091–1117.

CHAPTER SEVEN

# Historical Development

**Nathan Nunn**
Department of Economics, Harvard University, NBER, and BREAD, 1805 Cambridge Street, Room M25,
Cambridge, MA 02138, USA

## Abstract

This chapter surveys a growing body of evidence showing the impacts that historical events can
have on current economic development. Over the past two decades historical persistence has been
documented in a wide variety of time periods and locations, and over remarkably long time horizons.
Although progress continues to be made identifying and understanding underlying mechanisms, the
existing evidence suggests that cultural traits and formal institutions are both key in understanding
historical persistence.

## Keywords

Persistence, Colonialism, Institutions, Norms, Culture, Path dependence

## JEL Classification Codes

H11, N00, O10, 050, P51, R58, Z13

## 7.1. INTRODUCTION

In recent years, a new dynamic, empirical literature has emerged examining whether
historical events are important determinants of current economic performance.[1] The
origins of this literature can be traced to three lines of research that began approximately
a decade and a half ago: Engerman and Sokoloff (1997, 2002), La Porta et al. (1997,
1998), and Acemoglu et al. (2001, 2002). Although each line of research had different
motivations, what was common to them was that each provided an analysis, and supporting
evidence, for how one important historical event—Europe's colonization of the globe—
was important for long-term economic growth.

Since this time, the literature has developed in a number of ways. Most notably,
other important events have also been examined. These range from systems of labor
coercion, Africa's slave trades, medieval long-distance trade, Atlantic trade, the Protestant
Reformation, overseas missionary work, the French Revolution, the Mexican Revolution,
the forced opening of China's treaty ports, the adoption of new food crops during the

---

[1] See Nunn (2009) and Spolaore and Wacziarg (forthcoming) for recent reviews of this literature.

*Handbook of Economic Growth*, Volume 2A
ISSN 1574-0684, http://dx.doi.org/10.1016/B978-0-444-53538-2.00007-1

Columbian Exchange, the adoption of the plough, the invention of the printing press, the Neolithic Revolution, and various environmental catastrophes.

The typical study involves the collection and compilation of new and impressive data. Although this in and of itself is an important contribution, the real contribution is the use of the data to convincingly test hypotheses related to historical development. The most enlightening papers are able to trace the full impacts of a historical event through time, while examining specific channels and mechanisms.

This chapter provides a summary of this new literature. As we will see, once one surveys the progress made to date, it is impressive what the recent wave of quantitative historical studies has taught us about historical economic growth and development.

### 7.1.1 The Origins of the Literature

The origins of the historical development literature can be found in three sets of papers. What the three papers have in common is that they all examine European colonial rule. However, their motivations are very different.

The first study, written by economic historians Engerman and Sokoloff (1997), is a historical narrative, supported with descriptive statistics. In it they examine the importance of factor endowments and colonial rule for the subsequent economic development of colonies within the Americas. They argue that New World societies that were endowed with soil and climate suitable for growing lucrative, globally traded commodities, such as sugar, tobacco, and cotton, developed plantation agriculture, and with it, the use of slave labor. In the Spanish colonies, characterized by sizable indigenous populations and large reserves of gold and silver, forced labor was instituted. The use of slavery and forced labor resulted in economic and political inequality, both of which inhibited long-term economic development.

Interestingly, the other two seminal articles were not inherently interested in better understanding the history of European colonial rule. For example, the interest of Acemoglu et al. (2001) was in testing whether domestic institutions are a fundamental determinant of economic prosperity today. The interest of La Porta et al. (1997, 1998) was in identifying the causal impact of investor protection on financial development. What motivated both studies to examine colonial rule is the fact that the historical episode provides a source of variation in domestic institutions (in the case of Acemoglu et al.) and in investor protection (in the case of La Porta et al.). Both studies exploited European colonial rule as a natural experiment, focusing on a different dimension or characteristic that was argued to provide exogenous variation that they could use to identify their effect of interest.

La Porta et al. (1997, 1998) argue that because the legal tradition of the colonizer was transplanted to the colonies, the identity of the colonizer had an important impact on the legal system that evolved and, in particular, on contemporary investor protection. In particular, they show that former colonies with a legal code based on Roman civil law—these were the colonies of France, Spain, and Portugal—had weaker investor protection and less financial development relative to former British colonies with a legal system based on common law.

Acemoglu et al. (2001) argue that a primary determinant of the form (and long-term impacts) of colonial rule was the disease environment faced by potential European settlers. In temperate areas, like Canada, Australia, and the United States, European mortality rates were moderate enough to facilitate European settlement on a large scale. In these areas, the Europeans brought with them their values and beliefs and developed European-like institutions that emphasized the protection of property rights. In areas such as sub-Saharan Africa, where European mortality was high due to diseases like malaria and yellow fever, Europeans did not settle. Instead, they engaged in an extractive strategy. Rather than settling in a location, they set out to extract natural resources without regard for the consequences. Arguably, this strategy was facilitated by a lack of property rights and other similar institutions. Motivated by this historical narrative, Acemoglu et al. used a measure of early settler mortality as an instrument for contemporary domestic institutions to estimate the causal impact of institutions on long-term economic development.

The analysis of the three lines of research showcased how insights can be gained by examining economic growth and development from a historical perspective. Specifically, they showed how historical episodes can provide econometrically useful sources of exogenous variation. More importantly, they also showed that history matters and that it can have long-term persistent impacts that continue to influence growth and development today.[2]

Following these early studies, a large number of subsequent papers have emerged examining economic growth and development from a historical perspective. In the following section, I begin an overview of this literature by first describing a number of studies that examine other dimensions and aspects of European colonial rule, the historical event that has received the most attention in the literature. In Section 7.3, I then turn to an examination of studies that have investigated the long-term impacts of other historical events. These include the Columbian Exchange; various episodes of increased trade and globalization; episodes of warfare and armed conflict; expulsions and forced population movements; religious reformations; and important technological innovations. Following this, in Section 7.4, I turn to an important insight that has emerged from the literature: geography has important impacts on development today working through its impacts on historical events.

After having surveyed the evidence for the importance of history for contemporary economic development, I then turn to causal mechanisms. In Section 7.5, I summarize

---

[2] As with any seminal paper, extensions, comments, criticisms, criticisms of comments, criticisms of criticisms, etc. soon emerged. In an effort not to get lost in the weeds, I do not discuss these papers here. See for example, Easterly and Levine (2003), Glaeser (2004), Olsson (2004), Rodrik et al. (2004), Austin (2008), Albouy (2012), and Acemoglu et al. (2012).

the evidence that has been uncovered for the relative importance of various channels of persistence, including multiple equilibria and path dependence; domestic institutions; cultural values and beliefs; and genetic traits.

The final two sections of the chapter, Sections 7.6 and 7.7, discuss unresolved questions in the literature and offer concluding thoughts.

## 7.2. EUROPEAN COLONIAL RULE

### 7.2.1 Americas

The studies that examine the impacts of colonial rule in the Americas tend to focus on testing the hypothesis that initial endowments affected the extent of economic and political inequality, both of which were detrimental for long-term economic development (Engerman and Sokoloff, 1997). In a followup study, Engerman and Sokoloff (2005) provide additional evidence for their hypothesis by documenting a positive relationship between economic inequality and political inequality, measured by the inclusiveness of voting rights. Sokoloff and Zolt (2007) document a link between inequality and lower taxes on wealth and income and less spending on public goods such as education.

While the evidence put forth by Engerman and Sokoloff in support of their hypothesis primarily takes the form of historical narrative and descriptive statistics, a number of studies have undertaken more formal tests of their hypothesis. Bruhn and Gallego (2012) examine variation across 345 regions within 17 countries from North and South America. They identify a strong negative correlation between long-run development and initial colonial specialization, in what they call "bad" activities, which Engerman and Sokoloff (1997) argue display economies of scale and therefore relied heavily on exploited labor, e.g. sugar, coffee, rice, cotton, and mining. They provide additional evidence, also consistent with Engerman and Sokoloff (1997), that other activities, like subsistence farming, cattle raising, or manufacturing, are not negatively related to long-term development, unless there were large native populations that could potentially be exploited in the production process.

Naritomi et al. (2012) provide evidence consistent with Bruhn and Gallego (2012), but focus on Brazil and two commodities, gold and sugar. They examine variation across approximately 5000 Brazilian municipalities and quantify each municipality's historical involvement in the gold boom (during the 1700s) and the sugarcane boom (1530–1760). The authors show that the municipalities that experienced the sugar boom have greater land inequality today, while municipalities that experienced the gold boom have worse domestic institutions today.

The key mechanism in Engerman and Sokoloff's hypothesis is inequality, both economic and political. A number of studies provide evidence that calls into question their assertion that greater economic inequality is associated with greater political inequality and less development. Dell (2010) examines the *mita* forced labor system, which was instituted by the Spanish in Peru and Bolivia between 1573 and 1812. The *mita* system required that over 200 communities supply one seventh of their adult male population to work in the silver mines of Potosí and mercury mines of Huancavelica. The study combines contemporary household survey data, geographic data, and data from historical records; and uses a regression discontinuity estimation strategy to estimate the long-term impacts of the *mita* system. Dell's study exploits the fact that the boundary of the *mita* conscription area was clearly defined and that other relevant factors likely vary smoothly close to the *mita* boundary. Because of this, comparing the outcomes of *mita* and non-*mita* districts very close to the border provides an unbiased estimate of the long-term effects of the *mita*. The study finds that the *mita* system had an adverse effect on long-term economic development. All else equal, former *mita* districts now have an average level of household consumption that is approximately 25% lower than households in former non-*mita* districts. The study finds that a significant proportion of the difference can be explained by lower levels of education and less developed road networks.

Dell argues that the underdevelopment of *mita* districts was due to an absence of large haciendas. These haciendas lobbied the crown for public goods, like education and roads, and provided these goods directly. Therefore, in contrast to the Engerman-Sokoloff hypothesis, she finds better long-run development outcomes in locations with large haciendas and greater inequality (not less).

Acemoglu et al. (2008) also question Engerman-Sokoloff's inequality hypothesis. The authors first examine municipalities within Cundinamarca, Colombia and show that late 19th century land inequality is positively associated with late 20th century secondary school enrollment. They further question the presumption that economic and political inequality go hand in hand. After constructing a measure of political inequality using data on the identity of mayors for 4763 appointments held by 2300 different individuals between 1875 and 1895, they show that economic inequality and political inequality are not positively correlated. In fact, they argue that greater land inequality was better for long-term development because the landowners provided greater checks on the actions of the political elite.

Examining variation across US states and counties and across countries within the Americas, Nunn (2008b) also considers the role of inequality. Although he does find that, consistent with Engerman and Sokoloff, there is a negative relationship between slave use and current income, he fails to find evidence that inequality is the intervening channel. Although past slave use is positively correlated with historical and current inequality, controlling for historical land inequality does not reduce the negative impact of slavery on current income. Further, there is no relationship, either in the past or today, between inequality and income.

## 7.2.2 Asia

Early European contact with India occurred through overseas trade, beginning in 1613. Colonization of the subcontinent occurred through a number of battles. Beginning with the Battle of Plassey in 1757, the British East India Company (EIC) gained control

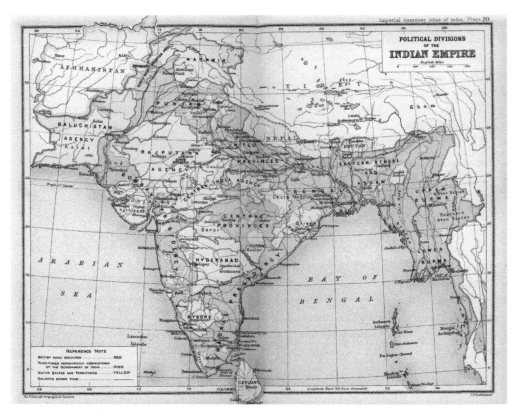

**Figure 7.1** Directly ruled British districts and princely states within the Indian Empire. *Source: Imperial Gazeteer Atlas of India, Plate 20.*

of Bengal and Bihar, and by the early 19th century, the British controlled large parts of the Indian subcontinent, the other portions being the "princely states." The British EIC continued to annex the princely states during the 19th century until the mutiny of the British EIC's army (the Sepoy Mutiny) in 1857. After this, the British government ruled the subcontinent, establishing the British Raj.

The long-term impacts of British control on the Indian subcontinent have been examined empirically in a series of recent papers. Iyer (2010) examines the long-term impacts of direct British rule versus indirect rule—i.e. the princely states. The portions of the subcontinent under the two forms of rule (in 1909) are shown in Figure 7.1.

Looking across 415 districts, Iyer (2010) estimates the effect of direct British rule versus indirect British rule on investment in agriculture and agricultural productivity today. To help uncover causal estimates, she exploits the Doctrine of Lapse, a British policy that was in place between 1848 and 1856, that stated that a native ruler's adopted heirs were not to be recognized by the British government. This allowed the British to annex several states where the native ruler died without a natural heir. Iyer instruments for direct British rule using a district-specific indicator variable that equals one if the ruler died without a natural heir between 1848 and 1856, the period when the Doctrine of Lapse was in place. Examining the subset of states that had not yet been annexed by 1848, she shows that the IV procedure estimates no statistically significant difference between directly ruled districts and the princely states. This is in contrast to the OLS estimates which suggest that direct British rule is positively associated with agricultural investment and productivity. The most likely explanation for the difference is that the British annexed the most productive parts of the continent, which also had the greatest growth prospects.

In subsequent analysis, Iyer (2010) examines other contemporary outcomes, including the availability of public goods such as health, education, and roads. She continues to find that the IV estimates of the impact of direct British rule on public goods provision are lower than the OLS estimates, again suggesting that the British selected the "better" states, with greater long-run growth potential. In addition, for many of the public goods outcome variables, the IV estimates suggest that British rule actually exerted a negative long-term effect, a finding that is consistent with earlier research by Banerjee et al. (2005) who examine an even larger set of 27 different public good measures.

Other research, rather than examining differences between directly and indirectly ruled districts, looks at variation within the directly ruled districts of India. Banerjee and Iyer (2005) show that differences in the institutions initially implemented by the British had long-term growth effects. In particular, they examine the different revenue collection systems that were established and compare districts where revenue was collected directly by British officials to those where revenue was collected by native landlords. They find that after independence, districts with non-landlord systems have higher levels of health, education, and agricultural technology investments relative to landlord systems.

To determine the extent to which this correlation is causal, the authors exploit the fact that in the parts of India conquered between 1820 and 1856, non-landlord revenue collection was implemented. They argue that the historical determinants of the form of revenue collection are orthogonal to district characteristics and determined primarily by the date of British conquest, which they use as an instrument for the revenue collection system. Their IV estimates are consistent with the OLS estimates.

Overall, the existing body of evidence for India suggests that British control of the subcontinent, through the extent to which colonial policies took the form of direct rule vs. indirect rule, had lasting impacts on long-term economic growth.

### 7.2.3 Island Colonies

In a novel study, Feyrer and Sacerdote (2009) examine the experience of European colonial islands of the Pacific, Indian, and Atlantic Oceans. Although one could argue this is a somewhat obscure set of colonies to examine, the question they attempt to answer is of general interest. Their motive for looking at their particular sample stems from their interest in the obvious, but difficult-to-answer question of whether colonial rule, on average, was good or bad. In particular, is a longer period of colonial rule associated with better or worse long-term economic growth?

Feyrer and Sacerdote (2009) argue that, for islands, the date of discovery was determined in part by its location relative to prevailing wind patterns and that these wind patterns most likely do not affect long-term development through channels other than the island's date of discovery. They argue that the wind vectors surrounding an island can be used as instruments to estimate the causal effect of the length of colonial rule on subsequent development. Their baseline set of instruments, which are constructed from satellite imagery data, reported monthly on a one-degree by one-degree global grid, include the annual mean and variance of monthly east-west wind vectors.

Their first-stage estimates show that stronger westerly winds are associated with earlier discovery and more years under colonial rule. According to their 2SLS estimates, the length of colonial rule has a positive effect on per capita income in 2000. In other words, conditional on being a colony (within their sample), a longer period of colonial rule was better for economic development. They are quick to point out, however, that their results cannot address the question of whether or not the island colonies are better off because they were colonized.

### 7.2.4 Africa

A number of studies that examine the impacts of colonial rule within Africa find evidence of long-term impacts that persist until today. This is perhaps surprising since, for the vast majority of the continent, the period of colonial rule was short relative to the rest of the world. Africa was the last continent to be colonized, with the Berlin Conference of 1884/1885 marking the beginning of large-scale colonial rule within Africa.

An important source of evidence documenting the long-term impacts of colonial rule within Africa is Huillery (2009). In the study, her analysis combines data from historical documents from archives in Paris and Dakar with household surveys from the 1990s. She shows that looking across districts in French West Africa, there is a positive relationship between early colonial investments in education, health, and infrastructure and current levels of schooling, health outcomes, and access to electricity, water, and fuel. Most interestingly, she provides evidence of persistence that is specific to a particular public good and outcome. In other words, she finds that greater education spending during the colonial period is associated with more education in the post-colonial period, but not better health outcomes or more infrastructure. Similarly, she finds more infrastructure investment during the colonial period is associated with greater access to infrastructure today, but not with the other outcomes; and more health investments during the colonial period are associated with better health outcomes today, but not with the other outcomes.

While the exact mechanisms behind this somewhat extreme form of persistence are not yet well understood, she does provide evidence that early investments subsequently lead to more of the same investments. An alternative explanation is that persistent omitted factors, which have impacts that are public-good specific, are driving the results. However, her analysis undertakes a number of strategies to rule out this explanation, including matching districts based on geographic proximity.

A commonly cited adverse consequence of European colonial rule in Africa is that it resulted in the creation of country boundaries that paid little or no attention to pre-existing kingdoms, states, or ethnic groups. During the Berlin Conference of 1884/1885, the European powers divided among themselves lands that they had yet to explore, and lakes, rivers, and mountains that they had yet to discover. Although it has long been hypothesized that one of the legacies of colonial rule in Africa may be the artificial nature of national boundaries that it created, it was not until recently that this assertion was tested formally. Michalopoulos and Pappaioannou (2011) combine information on the pre-colonial locations of 834 ethnic groups from Murdock (1959) with the current boundaries of nation states and test for differences between ethnic groups that were partitioned by a country's border and those that were not. The authors create, for each ethnicity, two indicator variables. The first equals "1" if the ethnicity was partitioned by a border and greater than 10% of the area of the group lies on both sides of the border. The second equals "1" if the ethnicity was partitioned by a border but less than 10% of the area of the group is located on one side of the border. The examination of the two partition measures is motivated by potential measurement error due to imprecision in the location of ethnic group as mapped by Murdock (1959). Even if borders do not split ethnic groups, measurement error will generate splitting. This form of partitioning is more likely to occur in the second (less than 10%) measure.

The authors examine two sets of outcomes at the ethnicity level: economic development, measured by the density of night-time lights, and the number of civil conflicts between 1970 and 2005. They find that partitioned ethnic groups are associated with lower economic development (as measured by lower light density) and more civil war. Both partition measures are statistically significant, although the magnitude of the less than 10% measure is often smaller, which is consistent with this variable being measured with greater error. Therefore, their findings confirm the conventional belief that colonial rule, because of the way it artificially divided up the continent between European powers, had detrimental impacts.

Another potentially adverse consequence of colonial rule—particularly the policy of indirect rule—was that it often resulted in heightened hostilities between ethnic groups. In Rwanda, colonial policies intentionally deepened racial differences between the Hutus and Tutsis. The Census of 1933–1934 institutionalized the Hutu distinction, creating identity cards that reported individual ethnicity. In addition, an educational system with separate streams for Hutus and Tutsis was implemented. Prior to the arrival of the Europeans, the distinction between Hutus and Tutsis was more one of class than of race, and with much movement between the two groups. This is illustrated by the fact that it was actually quite difficult for the Belgians to group individuals neatly into one of the two groups. As a result, they developed the "Ten Cow Rule". When there was doubt, if an individual had more than ten cows, they were designated "Tutsi"; otherwise, they were "Hutu."

Many scholars, and perhaps most notably Mamdani (2001), have argued that the ethnic hostilities between the Hutus and Tutsis, culminating in the 1994 genocide, have their roots in Belgian colonial rule. However, there is far from full consensus on this issue. Vansina (2004), relying primarily on oral evidence and early written accounts, argues against this view. He instead argues that Hutu and Tutsi identities arose in the 17th century and became further entrenched during the 19th century, both of which occurred before the colonial period.

## 7.3. OTHER IMPORTANT HISTORICAL EVENTS

The literature's initial focus on European colonial rule was perfectly natural given that the event was one of the most important in human history and arguably the single most important for shaping the current distribution of the world's income. However, more recently, researchers have begun to turn to other important historical events to empirically examine their long-term impacts and importance for economic development today. I now turn to a discussion of these studies.

### 7.3.1 The Columbian Exchange

The Columbian Exchange refers to the transfer of crops, disease, ideas, and people between the Americas and the rest of the world following Christopher Columbus's voyage to the New World in 1492. The exchange brought diseases that decimated the Native American populations. It introduced the Eastern Hemisphere to a variety of new plants that were widely adopted, including tomatoes, the white potato, the sweet potato, cassava, corn, chillis, peppers, cacao, vanilla, and tobacco. In addition, Europeans were introduced to the chincona tree, which produces quinine, a prophylactic against malaria. The New World also provided abundant fertile land that could grow valuable Old World commodities, such as sugar and cotton.[3]

A number of papers have documented the impacts of the transfer of new foods from the Americas to the rest of the world. Nunn and Qian (2011) estimate the impact of the introduction of the potato to Europe, Asia, and Africa. Since the potato was calorically

---

[3] See Grennes (2007), Nunn and Qian (2010), and Mann (2011) for further descriptions of the Columbian Exchange.

and nutritionally superior to Old World staples like wheat, barley, rye, and rice, for the parts of the Old World that were able to adopt the potato, its diffusion from the New World resulted in a large positive shock to agricultural productivity. Using a difference-in-differences estimation strategy, the authors compare differences in population growth, urbanization, and adult heights before introduction relative to the population growth after introduction between locations that were able to adopt potatoes and those that were not. A location's ability to cultivate potatoes is measured using GIS-based climate and soil data from the FAO.

At the country level, they find that the introduction of the potato had a positive impact on total population and urbanization rates. Consistent with their urbanization finding, they also find that city growth, both globally and within Europe, was positively impacted by the potato. In an attempt to examine mechanisms more closely, the authors examine height data from France. They show that after the diffusion of the potato to France, individuals born in villages that could cultivate potatoes were between one-half and three quarters of an inch taller as adults.[4]

Other studies have also examined the impacts of the post-1492 diffusion of other food crops from the Americas. Chen and Kung (2012) examine the introduction of maize to China and find that although maize had a large positive impact on population, there is no evidence that it spurred urbanization rates. Jia (forthcoming) examines the diffusion of the sweet potato in China. One characteristic of the sweet potato is that it is much more drought resistant than the pre-existing staple crops in China, rice and wheat. Her analysis shows that prior to the sweet potato, there is a close relationship between the occurrence of drought and peasant uprisings. After the diffusion of the drought resistant sweet potato, this relationship weakened significantly.[5]

The Columbian Exchange not only brought New World crops to the Old World, but it also brought Old World crops to the New World. For many crops the soils and climates in the Americas were much more suitable for cultivation than in the Old World. The prime example is sugar. Hersch and Voth (2009) calculate the welfare gains in Europe from the increased supply of sugar that resulted from its large-scale cultivation in the Americas. They also consider the welfare gains from the introduction of tobacco, the highly popular New World crop, to Europe. They calculate that by 1850, the increased availability of sugar and tobacco had increased English welfare by approximately 6% and 4%, respectively. These results have important implications for our understanding of European well-being over time. It is generally presumed, based on real wage figures that do not account for new goods, that English welfare did not begin to improve until after

---

[4] Cook (2013b) provides evidence of a complementarity between milk and potatoes. He finds that the population effects of Nunn and Qian (2011) are greater among populations that exhibit lactase persistence (i.e. are lactose tolerant).

[5] This finding is particularly interesting because it shows that the impacts of weather shocks differ depending on the historical environment. This is a point that I return to below.

1800 (Clark, 2005). However, according to Hersch and Voth (2009) welfare increased significantly before this time from the availability of "new" goods that were a result of the Columbian Exchange.

## 7.3.2 International Trade and Globalization

A number of studies have traced the impacts of increased international trade in various periods of time. An important insight that has emerged from this literature is that international trade, by altering the evolution of domestic institutions, can have important effects for long-term growth.[6]

The seminal papers making this point are Greif (1993 and 1994), where it is shown how the development paths of two long-distance trading groups, the Maghribi and Genoese, have their origins in the manner in which trading contracts were enforced. Among the Maghribi, merchants relied on a collective enforcement strategy, where all merchants collectively punished any agent who had cheated; while among the Genoese, enforcement was achieved through an individual punishment strategy. These contracting institutions led to the development of different institutions outside of the trading environment. While the Genoese developed a formal legal system and formal organizations to facilitate exchange; the Maghribis continued to rely on collective informal enforcement mechanisms like group punishment.

A number of papers have empirically examined the long-term impacts of increased international trade and domestic institutions and long-term economic growth. The existing evidence seems to suggest that trade can have very different impacts depending on initial conditions and the specifics of the environment. The heterogeneous impacts of international trade are clearly illustrated in the study by Puga and Trefler (2012), which examines medieval trade in Venice between 800 and 1350. They show that trade initially changed the balance of power, which enabled new merchants to push for greater political openness (e.g. the end of the hereditary Dogeship and the begining of the Venetian parliament) and better contracting institutions (e.g. the colleganza). These institutional improvements led to economic growth. However, over time, wealth was increasingly concentrated in the hands of a relatively small number of merchants and this power was used to block further institutional reforms and limit political access. Therefore, international trade first led to the rise and then decline of growth-promoting inclusive institutions and economic growth.

The heterogeneous impacts of international trade can also be seen in the cross-section. For some parts of the world, evidence suggests that increased trade had beneficial impacts. Jha (2008) considers medieval India and shows that looking across cities within India, participation in overseas trade is associated with less religious conflict during the late 19th and early 20th centuries. Jha addresses the endogeneity of the selection of medieval

---

[6] On this point, see the recent survey by Nunn and Trefler (forthcoming).

ports by using the existence of natural harbors as an instrument for whether a coastal city was a trading port and by using propensity score matching techniques.

According to his estimates, being a town that was a medieval trading port made it less likely that the town later experienced Hindu–Muslim riots. Using historical evidence, Jha argues that because Muslims provided access to the markets of the Middle East, the returns to Hindu–Muslim cooperation were much higher in the towns connected to this overseas trade. As a result, institutions that supported exchange and a peaceful coexistence between Hindus and Muslims were developed.

The existing evidence suggests that international trade was also beneficial within Europe. Acemoglu et al. (2005) examine the impacts of the Atlantic three-corner trade on European institutions. They first show that the rise of Western Europe after the 16th century was driven by the economic growth of countries (and port cities) heavily involved in Atlantic trade. They argue that the primary benefit of the trade was not a direct benefit of the profits from the trade but an indirect impact that worked through domestic institutions. Profits from the trade shifted political power toward commercial interests and resulted in the development of growth-promoting institutions. They provide support for their hypothesis by showing that the Atlantic trade also resulted in better institutions, measured using an index of a country's "constraints on its executive." They also show empirically that among countries with access to the Atlantic trade, only for those that had non-absolutist institutions initially (i.e. in the 15th and 16th centuries) did trade generate improved institutions. If the monarchy was too strong, initially, it simply monopolized the trade—as in Spain and Portugal—and this limited the benefits to the commercial class and therefore limited institutional change.[7]

Beneficial impacts of international trade have also been estimated in 19th century China. Jia (forthcoming) examines the impacts of increased trade due to the forced opening to trade first imposed by Britain and later by the United States. The Treaty of Nanking (1842), which followed the Qing Dynasty's defeat by Britain during the First Opium War, named five cities as treaty ports: Guangzhou, Shanghai, Fuzhou, Ningbo and Xiamen (Fairbank, 1953). By 1896, 16 more treaty ports were added to the original five, with 28 more added between 1896 and 1911 (Tai, 1918; Wang, 1998).

Jia (forthcoming) examines a sample of 57 prefectures all with geographic access to overseas trade over 11 periods between 1776 and 2000. She estimates a difference-in-

---

[7] Another interesting source of heterogeneity related to the Atlantic trade is shown by Dittmar (2011). He examines the growth of port cities in Europe and shows that port cities that adopted the printing press by the late 15th century grew significantly faster than those that did not. According to his estimates, once one accounts for the importance of the printing press, Atlantic port cities no longer appear to grow faster than non-Atlantic port cities. These findings are consistent with Dittmar's hypothesis that the printing press, by making print media more widely available, fostered numeracy, literacy, and innovations in bookkeeping and accounting, all of which were particularly valuable in cities with significant commercial opportunities due to overseas trade.

difference specification, controlling for prefecture fixed effects and time period fixed effects. She finds that on average, prefectures with treaty ports experienced faster population growth during this period. The population increase occured prior to the Communist revolution of 1949, as well as after China's more recent period of increased openness after 1980. Between 1958 and 1980, when China's economy was heavily regulated, treaty ports did not experience faster growth.

The clear exception to the beneficial impacts of trade and institutional and economic development lies in the experiences of Africa and (arguably) Latin America, following the Age of Discovery. As we have seen, in the Americas, specialization of production in commodities that Bruhn and Gallego (2012) classify as "bad" or "ugly" (recall Section 7.2) led to long-term underdevelopment. Further, as we discuss below, the impacts of the Atlantic trade within Africa were extremely detrimental. Within Africa, participation in trade meant warfare, theft, and banditry to supply slaves for export to the Americas. As shown by Nunn (2008a) and Nunn and Wantchekon (2011), participation in the slave trade had long-term adverse consequences. The parts of Africa that were heavily involved in the trade today are poorer, have worse domestic institutions, and exhibit lower levels of trust. We discuss these impacts in further detail below.

### 7.3.3 Warfare and Conflict

History is filled with episodes of warfare and conflict. A number of recent studies show that many instances of violence have had important effects on human history. The most well-known hypothesis regarding warfare and long-term development is Tilly's (1990) hypothesis that an important determinant of the rise of Europe was interstate warfare which promoted the development of strong states. According to Tilly, beginning in the early-modern period, warfare and interstate competition resulted in the development of centralized governments and institutions that were able to raise sufficient capital and maintain large populations that could be used to wage war. In other words, according to Tilly, war made states.

While Tilly's argument has been very influential, very few studies have actually formally tested any version of the Tilly hypothesis. Aghion et al. (2012) provide evidence, which is very much in the spirit of Tilly, that in the modern period an increased threat of warfare is associated with increased education. The authors examine a yearly panel of 137 countries from 1830 to 2001. Controlling for country fixed effects and year fixed effects, they show that education, measured by primary school enrollment and education reforms, is positively associated with conflict in the previous 10 years and with a contemporaneous measure of the existence of a military rivalry with another country. In other words, they find evidence that war made education.

Proponents of the Tilly hypothesis have argued that it may also apply outside of Europe. For example, Bates (forthcoming) and Reid (2013) argue that interstate conflict bred larger, more centralized states. Bates (forthcoming) shows that among the African societies documented in the Standard Cross Cultural Sample (SCCS), there is a positive relationship between rates of warfare and the degree of political centralization.

Other evidence suggests that a history of warfare can also have negative long-term impacts. An innovative paper by Jancec (2012) provides evidence that interstate conflict has a long-term adverse impact on trust in the political system today. Using individual-level data from Slovenia, Croatia, Serbia, Montenegro, Romania, and Ukraine, the author shows that individuals living in regions that experienced more frequent changes in the ruling nation-state between 1450 and 1945 have lower levels of trust in political institutions today. In other words, populations whose ancestors more regularly experienced conquest trust the government less today. In addition, Jancec (2012) also finds that frequent border change is associated with greater identification with an individual's locality rather than with the nation, and with less participation in national politics, as measured by voting. Since Jancec's (2012) analysis always controls for broad region effects, he is able to rule out worse governance as the explanation for the findings. All estimates are derived holding national institutions constant. The most likely explanation is that a history of conquest generated less identification with the nation-state and less trust for national leaders and institutions.

A theme that has developed in the literature highlights important historical links between warfare and religion. For example, Botticini and Eckstein (2005, 2007) argue that the burning of the Second Jewish Temple by the Romans in 70AD had lasting important consequences for the Jewish religion and subsequent economic development. After the burning of the temple, the Jewish religion was transformed from one that centered around religious sacrifices in the Temple to one that required all Jewish males to read the Torah and teach their sons to do the same in the synagog. According to Botticini and Eckstein (2005), the literacy and numeracy generated by this religious requirement resulted in the migration of Jewish farmers to cities, beginning in the fifth and sixth centuries, where they engaged in urban occupations. In Babylon, Jews moved into urban centers and engaged in shopkeeping and artisanal activities such as tanning; linen and silk production; dyeing; and glassware-making. Jewish migration continued in the Muslim empire between the mid-8th and early-9th centuries, with Jews entering a variety of skilled occupations, including handicrafts and jewelry production; ship building; money lending; and long-distance trading. Overall, their analysis provides compelling evidence that one important violent event—the Roman burning of the Jewish Temple—had impacts that affected subsequent human capital accumulation and the trajectory of economic prosperity of the Jewish people.

Another example is the link between warfare with the Ottoman Empire and the rise of Protestantism in Europe. Iyigun (2008) tests the established hypothesis that the Ottoman military incursions into continental Europe from the mid-15th to late 16th centuries allowed Protestantism to develop. Chronologically, a cursory examination of the dates of Ottoman and counter-reformation conflicts is consistent with the hypothesis. For example, the deadliest of all religious wars, the Thirty Years War (1618–1648), followed the decline of the Ottoman Empire, marked by the Battle of Lepanto (1571) where the Holy League (a coalition of Catholic maritime states organized by Pope St. Pius V) defeated the Ottoman Empire's primary naval fleet. Iyigun shows that the hypothesis receives support when examined more rigorously. He analyzes annual data from 1450 to 1700 and shows that in years with more European-Ottoman conflict there is less conflict between countries within continental Europe, and there are less conflicts due to Catholic-Protestant religious differences.

Acemoglu et al. (2011a) examine the beneficial impacts of one of the most important episodes of European history: the French Revolution. Within a few short years (1789–1799), the revolution displaced traditional values regarding order and hierarchy with new enlightenment values of equality, citizenship, and inalienable rights. In 1792, the new republic declared war on Austria and its allies, including Prussia. Acemoglu et al. show that the institutional reforms that were imposed on conquered territories had lasting impacts in Germany and Prussia. Examining 19 regions at six different points in time between 1700 and 1900, the authors show that regions that experienced longer periods of French occupation between 1793 and 1815, subsequently experienced faster economic development, measured by urbanization rates. Constructing an index of reforms that quantifies the abolition of feudalism and guilds, and the implementation of the French civil code, they provide evidence consistent with these institutional reforms being the source of the increased urbanization rates. Locations that experienced longer French occupation also had more intensive reforms.

### 7.3.4 Expulsions and Forced Population Movements

Closely related to warfare and conflict are expulsions and forced population movements. The most dramatic example of forced population movement is the export of African slaves during the trans-Atlantic, trans-Saharan, Indian Ocean, and Red Sea slave trades. Slaves were captured through kidnappings, raids, and warfare. Historical accounts suggest that the pervasive insecurity, violence, and warfare had detrimental impacts on state formation, inter- and intra-group co-operation, and institutional, social, and economic development generally (e.g. Inikori, 2000, 2003).

The most illustrative example of this is the experience of the Kongo Kingdom, which was discovered in 1493 by Diogo Cão. Initially, a diverse array of products were traded between Kongo and the Portuguese, including copper, textiles, ivory, and slaves. The first slaves that were traded were prisoners of war and criminals. However, the increasing external demand for slaves, the presence of Portuguese slave traders, and competition for the throne within the Kingdom all resulted in a dramatic and uncontrollable increase in slave capture and raiding throughout the Kingdom. As early as 1514, King Afonso was already writing to the Portuguese to complain of Portuguese merchants colluding with noblemen to enslave Kongo citizens. In 1526, Afonso asked for the removal of all

Portuguese merchants and the end of trade. This attempt was unsuccessful and through the 16th century the process continued, culminating in the Jaga invasion of 1568–1570. The large-scale civil war from 1665 to 1709 resulted in the complete collapse of the Kingdom (Heywood, 2009).

Nunn (2008a) empirically examines the impacts the slave trades had on the long-term development of the African continent. Combining information from historical shipping records with information from a variety of historical sources—plantation inventories, marriage records, death records, slave runaway notices, etc.—that report the ethnic identity of the slaves shipped from Africa, Nunn constructs estimates of the total number of slaves shipped from modern-day African countries during each of the four slave trades.

The study finds that the parts of Africa from which the largest number of slaves were taken are the poorest today. The core issue in interpreting this correlation is selection into the slave trades. If, for example, the societies with the most poorly functioning institutions and the poorest future growth prospects selected into the slave trades, then this would explain the negative relationship even if the external trade in slave trades had no direct impact on societies within Africa. Nunn tests whether selection is driving the results by looking at the evidence on the nature of selection during the slave trades. He finds that the descriptive and quantitative evidence suggest that it was not the least developed societies that selected into the slave trade, but it was actually the more developed and more densely populated societies that supplied the largest numbers of slaves. Nunn also constructs instruments based on the distance of each country from the external locations of demand for the slaves. He argues that although the location of the demand for slaves influenced the location of supply, the reverse was not true. The IV estimates provide estimates consistent with the OLS estimates. Nunn concludes that the empirical evidence suggests that Africa's external trade in slaves did have a significant negative impact on the economic development of regions within Africa.

Subsequent studies have documented other important impacts of Africa's slave trades. Nunn and Wantchekon (2011) provide evidence that the slave trades adversely affected subsequent levels of trust within Africa. They show that the lower levels of trust arise through two channels: a deterioration of domestic institutions that enforce trustworthy behavior and an increase in the prevalence of cultural norms of distrust. They estimate that quantitatively the second determinant is about twice as important as the former.[8]

Dalton and Leung (2011) and Fenske (2012) provide evidence that the trans–Atlantic slave trade resulted in a long-term increase in the prevalence of polygamy. This is due to

---

[8] Deconinck and Verpoorten (forthcoming) update the results of Nunn and Wantchekon (2011) using the more recent (2008) round of the Afrobarometer survey. This increases the sample by two additional countries (from 17 to 19) and expands the number of ethnic groups from 185 to 228. With the more recent and expanded sample, they find estimates that are very similar to Nunn and Wantchekon (2011). Also see Pierce and Snyder (2012) who show that in countries that were more impacted by the slave trades, firms have less access to external financing today, whether it be through formal or informal means.

the fact that primarily males were captured and shipped to the Americas, which resulted in a shortage of men within Africa. Interestingly, there is no evidence of such an impact for the Indian Ocean slave trade, where there was not a strong preference for male slaves. Dalton and Leung (2011) conclude that Africa's history of the slave trades is the primary explanation for why polygamy is much more prevalent in West Africa than in East Africa, today.

Within Europe, studies have also found evidence of large persistent impacts of forced migration. Acemoglu et al. (2011b) examine the long-term impacts of the mass movement and murder of Jewish populations in Russia during World War II. Examining variation across 278 cities, the authors show that Jewish depopulation during the holocaust is associated with significantly slower population growth, which was still detectable 50 years later in 1989, the last year of their sample. The authors confirm these results by looking across 48 oblasts, identifying a relationship between Jewish depopulation and lower per capita income in 2002.

A number of studies have also examined the persistent impacts of the 1609 expulsion of approximately 300,000 Moriscos (Spanish Muslims) from the Iberian Peninsula. Chaney (2008) and Chaney and Hornbeck (2013) examine the effects in the Kingdom of Valencia, where 130,000 Muslims—equal to one-third of its total population—were expelled. Chaney and Hornbeck (2013) show that after the expulsion, total output responded quickly although total population did not, resulting in higher per capita incomes in districts where a greater share of the population had been expelled. The persistently higher output per capita is potentially explained by the presence of more extractive institutions with a higher tax rate that inhibited population growth. Chaney (2008) also examines the impacts of the 1609 expulsion in Valencia, but considers spillover impacts on neighboring districts as low-skilled migrants moved to newly available land.

Forced movements of indigenous populations were also common in the Americas. Dippel (2011) examines the long-term development impacts of forced integration of different tribal bands onto the same reservation in the 19th century. He measures forced integration by combining information on the indigenous integration of the bands within a tribe (specifically, whether bands within a tribe were politically integrated prior to the 19th century) with information on which bands were subsequently forced to live on the same reservation. Forced integration occurs when bands that were previously independent were forced to live on the same reservation. He finds that reservations that experienced forced integration have 30 percent lower per capita GDP in 2000. He provides convincing evidence that this effect is causal and that it is due to dysfunctional political institutions.

Feir (2013) considers the impacts of the policy of forcibly removing indigenous children from their homes and sending them to residential schools. She finds that in Canada the schools were successful in their intended goal of eroding indigenous culture.

Individuals attending residential schools, as adults are 16 percent less likely to participate in traditional activities and 8 percent less likely to speak their indigenous language. Residential schools were notorious for the presence of mental, physical, and sexual abuse. Collecting data on the number of proven abuse claims by school, Feir shows that attendance in the least abusive schools is associated with increased educational attainment and more employment. On the other hand, attending the most abusive residential schools is not associated with increased education, but is associated with lower employment, lower rates of marriage, and increased alcohol consumption.

### 7.3.5 Religion

A number of studies provide evidence of the persistent long-run impacts of important religious historical events. The episode that has received the most attention in the literature is the Protestant Reformation, whose origin dates back to October 31, 1517 when Martin Luther posted the *Ninety-Five Theses on the Power and Efficacy of Indulgences* on the doors of All Saints' Church in Wittenberg. He objected to corruption in the Catholic Church, and in particular, to the selling of indulgences. His teachings quickly spread, partly facilitated by the recent invention of the printing press (Rubin, 2011).

According to Weber (1930), the new religion that emerged, Protestantism, was significant because, in contrast to Catholicism, it approved the virtues of hard work and the accumulation of wealth and that these values provided the moral foundation that spurred the transition to a modern market-based industrial economy. Another significant feature of the Protestant religion is its emphasis on the ability of individuals to read the Bible. With this came a belief in the importance of education.

A large number of studies have examined the historical and persistent impacts of the Protestant religion. Becker and Woessmann (2009) examine the two potential impacts of Protestantism, namely increased education and a change in values related to accumulation, thrift, and hard work. Their analysis examines variation in the intensity of Protestant and Catholic denominations across 452 counties in late 19th century Prussia. They find that the Protestant religion is associated with higher literacy. To better understand whether the correlations reflect a causal impact of the Protestant religion, they use a county's distance from Wittenberg, the origins of the Reformation, as an instrument for the share of the population that is Protestant in 1871.[9] Using the same empirical structure, the authors also identify a positive impact of Protestantism on various measures of economic development. This finding is consistent both with Protestantism increasing education which increases income, and with Protestantism affecting beliefs and values which increase income. The authors attempt to disentangle the two by estimating the impact of Protestantism on income after netting out the level of income explained by education (which they estimate

---

[9] The determinants and dynamics of the adoption of Protestantism are an interesting subject of analysis in its own right. For more on this, see Rubin (2011) and Cantoni (2012).

directly and take from previous studies). The findings from this procedure indicate that Protestantism's positive impact on income can be almost fully explained by its impact on education.

The link between Protestantism and education also receives support from studies examining the long-term impacts of missionary activities outside of Europe. A large literature has emerged documenting this relationship in various locations and time periods. An early contribution is provided by Woodberry (2004), who documents a positive relationship between measures of the historical presence of missionaries and current per capita income and democracy across former non-settler colonies. According to Woodberry these benefits arise not only from increased education, but because missionaries, particularly Protestant missionaries, fought against injustices against native populations during colonial rule, which helped to foster better institutions, improved civil liberties, and increased democracy in the long-run (Woodberry, 2004, 2012).

Others have also examined the impact of missionary activities, but use a more micro-approach that focuses on a specific region or country. For example, Bai and Kung (2011b) look within China and examine county-level data from 1840 and 1920. They identify a positive relationship between Protestant missionary activity and economic development, measured using urbanization rates.

A recent insight within this literature is the identification of differences between religious denomination or orders within the Protestant and Catholic religions. Waldinger (2012) examines variation within colonial Mexico and shows differences in the long-term impacts of four different Catholic orders: the Franciscans, Dominicans, Augustinians, and Jesuits. She finds that the three Mendicant orders (Franciscan, Dominican, Augustinian), which shared a strong commitment to alleviating poverty and educating the poor, had a long-term impact on educational attainment. By contrast, the Jesuits, who focused their educational efforts on the colonial elites only, appear to have had long-term effects on conversion to Catholicism, but not on increased educational attainment.

Andersen et al. (2011) analyze the Catholic Order of Cisterians in England during the early modern period. One defining characteristic of the Catholic order, which after being established in France in 1098, quickly spread across England in the following century, was the belief and emphasis on a strong work ethic and promotion of thrift. Examining county-level data for England from 1377 to 1801, the authors show that counties with a greater presence of Cisterian monasteries exhibited greater population growth during this period.

Akçomak et al. (2012) empirically trace the impacts of the founding of the Brethren of the Common Life, a Roman Catholic community established by Geert Groote in the late 14th century. The movement arose because of dissatisfaction with the Catholic Church and set to reform the Church by educating citizens and enabling them to read the Bible in the vernacular. In addition to their strong emphasis on literacy and education, the Brethren of the Common Life also promoted hard work and productive labor.[10] The authors empirically trace the historical impact of the Brethren of the Common Life within the Netherlands. Examining a sample of Dutch cities, the authors show that cities with Brethren of the Common Life communities had higher rates of literacy in 1600, more book production from 1470 to 1500, and faster population growth between 1400 and 1560. Of course, these correlations may be driven by reverse causality or omitted variables bias. The authors attempt to better understand whether the correlations are causal by using a city's distance from Deventer, the birthplace of Geert Groote and the origins of the movement.

Gender differences between the Protestant and Catholic religions are another aspect that has been examined by the literature. Because Protestants believed that reading the Bible directly was important for salvation, even for women, they placed greater importance on female education than Catholics. Using data from the first Prussian census of 1816, Becker and Woessmann (2008) show that Protestantism is associated with a smaller gender gap in education. Evidence for a greater emphasis on female education among Protestants is also found in Nunn's (forthcoming) analysis of the impacts of Catholic and Protestant colonial African missions on long-term education. He finds that although both had positive impacts on long-term education, the impact of Protestant missions was concentrated among females, while the impact of Catholic missions was concentrated among males.

### 7.3.6 Technological Innovation

Findings from a number of recent studies suggest a link between innovative activities in the past and subsequent economic outcomes. For example, Comin et al. (2010) document a positive correlation between the measure of a society's level of technology in the past (either 1000 BC, 0AD, or 1500AD) and either its level of technology or per capita income today. The authors hypothesize that this is driven by increasing returns to technology adoption: a higher level of technology lowers the cost of discovering new technologies. That is, a higher level of technology in the past affects the ease of accumulating subsequent technology which impacts technology in the future. Of course, their findings are also consistent with omitted persistent factors impacting both technology and development in the past and today. An example is the persistence of governance and institutional quality as has been documented by Bockstette et al. (2002).

Other studies, by zooming in on specific innovations, have been more successful at establishing persistent long-term impacts. Dittmar (2011) examines the long-term effects of the printing press, which was first established in Mainz, Germany between 1446 and 1450. He constructs a panel of European city-level data at 100-year intervals

---

[10] The similarity between Protestant beliefs and the Brethren of the Common Life is not a coincidence, as Martin Luther studied under the Brethren of the Common Life at Magdeburg before attending university.

between 1300 and 1800, combining data on city populations with information on the early adoption of the printing press. His analysis shows that cities that adopted the printing press between 1450 and 1500 experienced faster population growth during the 16th to 19th centuries. The impacts he estimates are extremely large. They imply that the printing press accounts for 18% of city growth between 1500 and 1600.

Dittmar uses the panel dimension of his data to validate his cross-sectional finding, showing that cities that adopted the printing press in the late 15th century were not growing more quickly prior to adoption. This suggests that the results are not driven by unobserved time-invariant differences between cities. He also provides additional evidence for a causal interpretation of his estimates using distance from the invention of the printing press—Mainz, Germany—as an instrument for adoption in the late 15th century. The IV estimates are consistent with the OLS estimates.

In a follow-up study, Dittmar (2012) calculates the impact of the printing press on aggregate welfare. Using data from England on the price and consumption of printed books in England between the 1490s and 1700 (and assumptions about consumers' utility functions), he estimates that the printed book increased welfare by an equivalent of 4% of income; by the mid-17th century this figure was 3–7%.

Baten and van Zanden (2008) provide complementary evidence of the importance of the printed book for long-term growth. The authors construct an impressive dataset of the production of printed books in eight Western European countries every 50 years between 1450 and 1800. The authors show that book production correlates strongly with literacy, and in panel regressions with time-period fixed effects, initial per capita book production is positively associated with faster growth in real wages during the next 50 years.

Alesina et al. (2013) examine the long-term impacts of the plough, an important technological innovation used in agriculture. The tool, which was able to prepare large amounts of soil for cultivation in a shorter period of time than previous tools, was first invented between 6000 and 4000 BC in Mesopotomia (Lal et al. 2007). Although the impacts of the plough were likely vast, the authors focus on one consequence that was highlighted by Boserup (1970). Because the use of the plough required significant upper body strength, it tended to generate a gender division of labor where men worked outside the home in the fields while women specialized in home production and other domestic activities. Boserup argues that this gender division of labor resulted in deeply held beliefs about the role of women in society. In societies that traditionally use plough agriculture, less equal beliefs about the roles of men and women evolved. Alesina et al. (2013) test this hypothesis by linking ethnographic data with contemporary individual- and country-level measures of gender role attitudes. They find that traditional plough agriculture is associated, even today, with less equal beliefs about the roles of men and women in society.[11]

---

[11] Also see Hansen et al. (2012), who find that a longer history of agriculture is associated with more unequal gender roles.

The findings of Alesina et al. are consistent with evidence that in the early phase of agriculture, prior to the adoption of the plough, societies tended to be matriarchal and characterized by gender equality (Gimbutas, 2007). Recent excavations from Çatalhöyük, a Neolithic town of 8000 people on the plains of central Turkey inhabited approximately 9000 years ago, provide additional evidence of the equality of the sexes during this time (Hodder, 2005). Analysis of male and female skeletal remains shows carbon deposits inside the ribs, due to indoor wood fires and a lack of ventilation in the homes. The smoke was ingested causing soot to build up in the lungs resulting in a lining of carbon inside the ribs. Hodder (2005) finds that the average amount of carbon in the ribs of men and women was equal, suggesting that men and women tended to spend roughly equal amounts of time within and outside the home. In addition, the archeological evidence from Çatalhöyük suggests that men and women had similar diets and were buried in similar positions and locations, both of which also suggest roughly equal social status.

The growth-promoting impacts of the plough have been studied by Andersen et al. (2013). Examining 316 European regions between 500 and 1300AD, the authors show that the adoption of the heavy plough is associated with greater population growth and increased urbanization. According to the authors' diff-in-diff estimates, the heavy plough accounts for 10 percent of the increase in population and urbanization during this time.

## 7.4. GEOGRAPHY AND HISTORY

### 7.4.1 The Historical Impacts of Geography

One of the important insights that has arisen from the historical development literature concerns the relationship between geography and contemporary development. Specifically, a common finding in the literature is that geography can have important impacts on current development through its persistent historical effects. Further, evidence also suggests that this historical impact of geography may be larger than its contemporaneous impact. For example, the findings from Acemoglu et al. (2001) show that the disease environment at the time of European colonization crucially affected subsequent institutional development. The authors argue that the primary impact of a country's disease environment works through this historical channel rather than through contemporary channels. The line of research by Engerman and Sokoloff (1997, 2002) also shows that small geographic differences become magnified through historical events and as a result end up having large impacts on long-term economic development. As they argue, differences in soil and climate made plantation agriculture and its reliance on slavery more or less profitable in different parts of the Americas, which in turn affected long-term economic development.

Even more dramatic examples of the long-term historical effect of geography are documented by Jared Diamond in his book *Guns, Germs and Steel*. The book is devoted to exploring the answer to the question of why Europeans colonized the rest of the world and not the other way around. Part of Diamond's answer lies in the fact that in Eurasia, crops and animals were domesticated earlier and in more varieties than in other parts of the world.

In addition, the domestication of plants and animals quickly spread east and west throughout Eurasia, but diffused much less quickly south to the African continent. When moving east or west, the length of the day does not change, and the climate is generally not drastically different. However, this is not true when moving north or south, where the length of the day changes and the climate typically is very different. More generally, for continents with a north-south orientation, such as the Americas or Africa, domestication or technological advance tended not to spread as quickly as in Eurasia with its east-west orientation.

Because of the early domestication of animals in Eurasia (and its more rapid diffusion), humans lived in close proximity to animals. As a result of this, new animal-based diseases, such as measles, tuberculosis, influenza, and smallpox developed, and over time humans developed genetic resistances to the diseases. In contrast, the parts of the world without domesticated animals did not develop the diseases or genetic resistance. According to Diamond, this explains why European diseases decimated native populations and not the other way around. As Diamond points out, the spread of disease was as important a factor as the military for European conquest of the Americas.

Diamond's explanation for Europe's global dominance illustrates clearly the large effect that geography can have through history. The historical origins of European colonization of the globe lie in two deep determinants: (i) being endowed with wild plants and animals suitable for domestication; and (ii) being located on a continent with an east-west orientation.

Although Diamond's hypothesis is intuitive in many ways, there are reasons to be sceptical. First, having domesticated plants and animals is potentially endogenous. For example, Diamond asserts that although the horse was domesticable, its close relative the zebra was not (Diamond, 2002). However, this assertion is difficult to assess since we do not observe the wild ancestors of the horse and so cannot compare it to the zebra. All we observe is the domesticated version, which has undergone centuries of selective breeding. Perhaps there are other historical determinants—be they economic, cultural, institutional, etc.—that caused horses to become domesticated in Eurasia but not zebras in Africa. Interestingly, there are examples of Europeans attempting to tame zebras. Rosendo Ribeiro, a doctor in Kenya, made house calls on a zebra. In England, Lord Walter Rothschild, pictured in Figure 7.2, would frequently drive a carriage pulled by zebras through the streets of London. However, despite these examples, the zebra never become widely domesticated.

Olsson and Hibbs (2005) take Diamond's hypothesis to the data. Using modern countries as the unit of analysis, the authors show that consistent with Diamond's descriptive accounts, countries with richer biological and geographic environments experienced the

**Figure 7.2** Lord Lionel Walter Rothschild with his zebra-drawn carriage, 1895. *source: The Picture Magazine.*

transition to agriculture at an earlier date and have higher per capita GDP in 1997. The geographic environment is measured using an index that includes the axis orientation of the continent, suitability of the climate for agriculture, latitude, and the size of the landmass within which the country is located. The measure of biological conditions is based on an index that comprises the number of annual or perennial wild grasses known to exist in prehistory and with a mean kernel weight exceeding 10 mg, as well as the number of domesticable mammals known to exist in prehistory and weighing more than 45 kg. Overall, the authors find that their estimates confirm Diamond's hypotheses.

Evidence from a wide range of empirical studies provides additional evidence of the importance of historical impacts of geography. Ashraf and Michalopoulos (2011) provide evidence that geography was an important determinant of the timing of the Neolithic Revolution, arguably the most important event in human history. Looking across countries globally, and across archaeological sites within Europe and the Middle East, they document an inverted U-shaped relationship between year-to-year variability in temperature and early adoption of agriculture.[12]

Michalopoulos (2012) shows that geography was an important determinant of the evolution of ethnic identity and hence ethnic diversity (which is known to be highly correlated with economic development today). Michalopoulos (2012) provides evidence

---

[12] Because fine-grained temperature data are not available prior to 1500, the authors are forced to use post-1500 variability as a proxy. The assumption is that the rank ordering of variability after 1500 is similar to the ordering prior to 1500. They show that this is true comparing data from 1500 to 1900 and 1900 to 2000.

that the pattern of agricultural suitability and terrain slope were important determinants of the interaction between ethnic groups and their proclivity to merge into and identify as larger ethnicities. His analysis combines fine-grained geographic data with information on the locations of ethnic groups globally. The world is then divided into grid-cells that are 2.5° by 2.5°. Michalopoulos (2012) shows that grid-cells that exhibit greater variation in soil quality and in elevation are also more linguistically diverse. The most likely explanation for the finding is that greater geographic variation prevented trade and migration between societies, and conquest of one society over others, all of which have homogenizing impacts.

Interestingly, Michalopoulos (2012) shows that the link between geography and ethnic diversity is due to geography's impact prior to 1500. Among the parts of the world that witness significant population changes after 1500 (due to death and voluntary and involuntary migrations), there is no relationship between geographic diversity and linguistic diversity.

Durante (2010) provides evidence that within Europe, historical variability in weather conditions created greater benefits for cooperation, which increased the level of cooperation in societies. He hypothesizes that greater spatial variability in temperature and precipitation generates output shocks that are less correlated, providing an increased incentive for trade, thus increasing trust and cooperation. As well, greater temporal variability of weather increases the benefits to large storage facilities and irrigation, which require large-scale cooperation. Durante therefore argues that locations characterized by greater spatial and temporal variability may have higher levels of trust and cooperation today. He tests these predictions using monthly historical climatic data from 1500 to 2000, measured across grid-cells within Europe. He finds that greater year-to-year variability in both temperature and precipitation is associated with higher levels of trust today, and that less correlated weather shocks over space is also associated with more trust today.

Of course, there are a number of potential alternative explanations for these correlations. Therefore, as a further test of his channel, Durante measures variability in growing season months and months outside of the growing season. He finds that only historical variability during the growing season is correlated with current trust. He also examines weather variability from 1500 to 1750, which was prior to the industrial revolution when Europe was primarily agricultural, and from 1900 to 2000, which is after industrialization. He finds that only weather variability during the agricultural period is correlated with trust today.[13]

Recent findings from Alsan (2012) suggests that geography also had important historical impacts within Africa. A large literature attributes many of Africa's unique

---

[13] A subsequent study by Ager and Ciccone (2012) raises the questions of whether the increased trust found in Durante (2010) is due, in part, to increased religiosity. Although in a different context—the 19th century United States—Ager and Ciccone (2012) show that increased variability in annual rainfall (looking across counties) is associated with increased church membership.

characteristics to the fact that it is land abundant and labor scarce. Alsan (2012) considers a potential explanation for this: the tsetse fly. The fly, which is unique to Africa, transmits the parasite *trypanosomiasis*, which causes sleeping sickness in humans and nagana in domesticated animals. The tsetse fly, both directly through its impact on humans, and indirectly through its impact on domesticated animals, may be responsible for Africa's low population densities historically.

The author uses 19th century climate data measured at the grid-cell level to construct a measure of the historical suitability of each cell for the tsetse fly. The index is a highly non-linear function of temperature and humidity. Examining variation across ethnic groups within Africa, she shows that ethnicities with climates more suitable for the tsetse fly, at the end of the 19th century, were less likely to use draft animals for trade and agriculture, were less likely to use the plough, and were more likely to use shifting cultivation rather than more intensive agricultural techniques. Because tsetse-suitable areas did not develop plough agriculture, women were more likely to participate in agriculture, and because the use of animals was not feasible, slaves were more likely to be used. Additionally, the less intensive agricultural techniques resulted in lower population densities, fewer urban centers, and less developed states. Her findings provide strong evidence that geographic suitability for the tsetse fly had a formative impact on the nature and prosperity of societies within Africa.

Because the tsetse fly did not exist outside of Africa, Alsan is able to undertake a falsification test by examining the correlation between tsetse suitability and the outcome of interest in the other parts of the world. If her estimates are really capturing the causal impact of the tsetse fly on long-term development, then in the parts of the world where there was no fly, we should not observe the same correlations. This is indeed what she finds. The tsetse suitability index has no predictive power outside of Africa. Overall, her findings provide strong evidence that the tsetse fly, by inhibiting the development of intensive agriculture using draft animals, resulted in lower populations, less urbanization, and less state development.

Fenske (2011) also considers the question of how geographic conditions affected the history of state development in Africa. The author tests the hypothesis that ecological diversity, by increasing the benefits of peaceful exchange between locations, increased the need of a state to provide the institutional setting to facilitate trade. This in turn resulted in the development of larger more developed states. Combining data on the boundaries of African ethnic groups in the 19th century with information on 18 ecological zones within Africa, Fenske constructs a measure of each ethnic group's ecological diversity. He finds that ethnic groups that were more ecologically diverse also had larger and more developed states.

A large number of studies also examine historical weather shocks and show that they had important historical impacts, many of which continue to be felt today. For example, Fenske and Kala (2013) show that during the slave trade, cooler temperatures near the slave ports were associated with increased slave exports. Therefore, due to the persistent impacts of the slave trade, temperature fluctuations during this time period had long-term impacts. Bai and Kung (2011a) examine the impacts of rainfall on Sino-Nomadic attacks in Han China between 220BCE and 1839CE. They identify a negative relationship between conflict and precipitation showing that climate was also an important determinant of conflict in the region.

Chaney (forthcoming) shows that in Ancient Egypt deviant Nile floods had important political impacts. Because deviant floods increased social unrest, this increased the bargaining power of the religious leaders relative to military leaders. Consistent with this, Chaney (forthcoming) shows that from 641 to 1437CE, deviant floods are associated with higher food prices, more conflict, less turnover of the highest ranking religious leader, and more construction of religious structures (relative to secular ones).

Haber and Menaldo (2010) also argue that climate can have important political effects. They show that there exists an inverted U-shaped relationship between average rainfall and democracy. They argue that this relationship is explained by the non-linear relationship between rainfall and suitability of a location for sedentary agriculture, which they argue provides a foundation more suitable for democracy than nomadic modes of subsistence. Bentzen et al. (2012) also argue for a link between geography/climate and modern political institutions, but, motivated by Wittfogel (1957), focus on the extent to which a location's agricultural output is increased by investments in irrigation. They argue that the large-scale investment and coordination needed for irrigation promoted strong authoritarian leadership and autocratic institutions, and this has persistent impacts even today. Using data from the FAO on yields with and without irrigation, the authors construct a measure of irrigation potential. Looking across 160 countries, they find greater irrigation potential is associated with less democracy today. Bentzen et al. (2012) show that in their specification the non-linear effect found in Haber and Menaldo (2010) no longer exists once one controls for their measure of irrigation potential.

Overall, there is a large body of evidence—only some of which is reviewed here—that suggests that a significant effect of geography—if not the largest effect of geography—on current economic development arises due to its influence on past events rather than through its direct effect on economic outcomes today.

## 7.4.2 Geography's Changing Impact Over Time and Space

Once one recognizes the fact that geography had important impacts historically as well as today, it is natural to ask whether the impacts of geography have been roughly constant throughout time or whether its impact varies in a systematic manner across time and/or space. This is a point also addressed in Acemoglu et al. (2001). Their empirical and historical narrative is that the disease environment generally, and in particular today, does not have large impacts on economic development. However, during the period of

European colonization of much of the globe it had a crucial impact. In locations with a disease environment that threatened European survival, Europeans did not migrate and did not establish growth-promoting institutions. Acemoglu et al.'s (2001) assumption that this disease environment only mattered during this specific historical episode is what allows them to use initial settler mortality as an instrument for a country's domestic institutions in explaining current per capita income. According to them, this particular geographic characteristic—the severity of the disease environment for Europeans—only had impacts during the colonial period.

Along similar lines, a number of papers find evidence that weather shocks can have significant long-term impacts during specific windows of time and no long-term effects during others. For example, Dell (2012) shows that within Mexico, drought experienced by municipalities between 1906 and 1910 had a large positive impact on violence and insurgency during the Mexican Revolution (1910–1918), resulting in a greater prevalence of *ejidos* (communal farms), which are less economically developed today. This implies that drought experienced between 1906 and 1910 had a long-term persistent impact on underdevelopment in Mexico. She shows that drought in other periods (between 1960 and 1995) are uncorrelated with long-term development.

Osafo-Kwaako (2012) also finds evidence of weather shocks mattering during a specific window of time. He shows that within Tanzania and during the early process of the government's establishment of development villages in the early 1970s, drought provided a motivation for peasants to agree to the villagization process. One therefore observes a positive relationship between droughts in 1973–1975 and the subsequent extent of villagization. The author then documents the persistent impacts of villagization. Although it increased education levels, political awareness, and community participation, it has also led to increased poverty and lower consumption today. Like Dell, Osafo-Kwaako also shows that the long-term impacts of drought are specific to this one narrow window.

Fenske and Kala (2013), in their study of the link between climate and slave exports in 18th and 19th century Africa, also provide some suggestive evidence of climate being particularly important during the height of the slave trade. They estimate the cross-sectional relationship between contemporary light density (a commonly used measure of economic development at the sub-national level) and historical weather shocks. Their findings provide evidence of the greater importance of temperature shocks during the height of the trans-Atlantic slave trade, which is consistent with the shocks having a large impact on contemporary development through their historical impacts on the supply of slaves.

Nunn and Puga (2012) focus on geography and provide an example of its impact varying over both time and space. They show that for most of the world, terrain ruggedness has a negative contemporaneous impact on economic development. All else equal, rugged terrain makes it more difficult to build buildings, roads, bridges, and other infrastructure;

agriculture and irrigation is also more difficult; and trade is more costly. They further show that within Africa, ruggedness had very different impacts than outside. Within Africa, greater ruggedness is associated with higher incomes, not lower.

The authors argue and provide evidence that this can be explained by an indirect historical impact of geography that was specific to Africa because of its history of the slave trades. During the slave trades, societies were able to use rugged terrain to protect and hide from slave raiders and kidnappers. This allowed individuals, villages, and societies to partially defend against the negative effects of the slave trades documented in Nunn (2008a). Therefore, for the African continent, which was exposed to the slave trade, ruggedness also had a historical indirect positive effect on income. Ruggedness allowed certain areas to evade the slave trade, thereby increasing long-term economic growth.

Nunn and Qian's (2011) study of the introduction of the potato to the Old World during the Columbian Exchange directly exploits the fact that the importance of geography changes over time. Specifically, their analysis relies on the fact that having climate and soil suitable for cultivating potatoes was important only after the potato was introduced from the Americas. Despite not having spatially or temporally extensive data on potato production or consumption, they infer the impacts of the potato by comparing the evolution of populations, city sizes, urbanization rates, and adult heights, before and after the adoption of the potato, in the places suitable for potato cultivation relative to unsuitable locations. Their estimates show that after the introduction of the potato, the places suitable for cultivation witnessed significant population growth, city growth, increased urbanization rates, and increased heights.

Overall, evidence continues to accumulate suggesting that geography can have very different impacts at different points in time and in different locations. The impacts of geography depend crucially on the particular historical context.

## 7.5. MECHANISMS UNDERLYING HISTORICAL PERSISTENCE

I next turn to the important question of why historical events have persistent impacts. In particular, I discuss the existing evidence for path dependence, culture, institutions, and genetic traits as important channels underlying historical persistence.

### 7.5.1 Multiple Equilibria and Path Dependence

Although it is far from obvious why historical events have persistent impacts, particularly in the long-run, once one acknowledges the possibility of multiple equilibria, then historical events can have long-term impacts if they move the society from one equilibrium to another. A large number of models show how easily multiple equilibria arise, even in very simple environments. See, for example, Murphy et al. (1993), Acemoglu (1995), Mehlum et al. (2003), and Nunn (2007).

Less formally, many examples of multiple equilibria in daily life have been identified, the most well known being the adoption of the less-efficient QWERTY keyboard
over other more efficient configurations like the DVORAK keyboard (David, 1985).
The QWERTY keyboard design was developed by Christopher Sholes and patented in
1873. That same year, it was sold to Remington, which used the configuration for their
typewriters. The configuration was chosen because it separated the most commonly used
keys, which kept the arms of the typewriter from jamming. In other words, the format
was chosen because it effectively reduced typing speeds.[14]

A number of studies have undertaken the task of formally testing for the existence of
multiple equilibria. A common strategy that has been employed is to examine cases where
there has been an extremely large temporary shock to an equilibrium. The studies then
test whether the temporary shock causes a permanent movement to a new equilibrium.
If so, this is evidence for the existence of multiple equilibria.

Davis and Weinstein (2002, 2008) examine the effect of bombings on 114 Japanese
cities during World War II and show that after the bombings, the cities returned to their
pre-bombing populations, regained their shares in total manufacturing output, and most
surprisingly, also regained their pre-existing industrial composition. Overall, the results
point toward the existence of a unique stable equilibrium of production, rather than the
existence of multiple equilibria.

Although these results appear to suggest the existence of one unique equilibrium, a
second possibility is that the shock was not sufficient to move the society away from
the current equilibrium. The US bombings during WWII were dramatic and severe, but
they did not alter property rights or the ownership of assets. It is likely that these are the
fundamental determinants of where people live and where production occurs.

The findings in Miguel and Roland's (2011) analysis of the long-term effects of the US
bombings in Vietnam are consistent with the finding from Davis and Weinstein (2002,
2008). The authors find that the bombings had no long-term effects on populations,
poverty, or consumption 25 years later. However, in this case, the authors show that the
return can be explained by reconstruction efforts intentionally aimed at rebuilding the
hardest hit parts of the country. In other words, policy intentionally helped the country
return to its original equilibrium.

An innovative study by Redding et al. (2011) tests for the existence of multiple
equilibria in a very different setting. The study examines the location of airport hubs
in Germany before and after the division of Germany following World War II. It is
shown that after division, the location of West Germany's primary airport hub switched

---

[14] Liebowitz and Margolis (1990) argue that the efficiency difference between the QWERTY and DVO-
RAK keyboards is lower than argued in David (1985). The authors provide some evidence for this.
However, even if the efficiency gap is lower than previously thought as they contend, the QWERTY
keyboard still provides a clear example of multiple equilibria and path dependence, which is the central
point of David's (1985) original argument.

from Berlin to Frankfurt. After reunification in 1990, the location of the hub did not switch back to Berlin. Redding et al. show that this shift cannot be explained by changes in fundamentals over the time period. Thus, the evidence suggests that the temporary division of Germany resulted in a permanent movement of the location of Germany's largest airport hub.

Bleakely and Lin (2012) examine a very specific and seemingly innocuous geographic characteristic and show that even though it only mattered for a narrow window of time, it had lasting and important impacts on urban development within the United States. The characteristic they examine is the existence of rapids or falls, which occur when a river crosses a fault line. In these locations, river transport required hauling goods and boats over land. This is known as portage. These locations were a focal point for commercial activity and entrepot trade.

The shipment of goods by boat was a dominant form of transportation until the early to mid-19th century, when canals and railways were developed. Combining geographic data with population at the census tract level, the authors show that today, looking either along rivers or along fault lines, populations are concentrated where rivers cross fault lines—i.e. at historical portage sites. The authors then turn to historical populations, examining the relationship between portage and population density from 1790 to 2000. The authors show that after 1850 (and the decline in the use of water transport and portage), the population actually became more (not less) concentrated at portage sites. Their findings are consistent with portage sites serving as a focal point that helped determine the location of early cities (i.e. the equilibrium population distribution) among a large set of possible multiple equilibria.

### 7.5.2 Domestic Institutions

Even without the existence of multiple equilibria, historical events can still affect economic development in the long-run if they alter deep determinants of long-term economic growth. The determinant that has received the greatest attention in the literature is domestic institutions. This focus is illustrated by the fact that in each of the seminal papers by Acemoglu et al. (2001, 2002), Engerman and Sokoloff (1997, 2002), and La Porta et al. (1997, 1998), the mechanism through which colonial rule affects current development is institutions.

The focus on institutions as a causal mechanism has also continued in subsequent research. An example of this is Acemoglu et al.'s (2005) study of the effect that early Atlantic trade had in Europe. The authors argue that in countries with access to the lucrative Atlantic three-corner trade, economic and political power shifted toward commercial interests. As the merchant class became more powerful, they were able to alter domestic institutions to protect their interests against the interests of the royalty, and these institutional changes in turn had a positive effect on long-term prosperity. Using data on historical urbanization rates and per capita incomes, the study first shows that the rise of

Europe was actually a rise of nations with access to the lucrative Atlantic trade, namely Britain, France, the Netherlands, Portugal, and Spain.

The authors argue that profits alone are not able to explain the divergent growth of Atlantic traders and that the evolution of domestic institutions played an important role in the process.[15] To test this hypothesis, the authors extend the Polity IV data back to 1350 and show that Atlantic trade increased the quality of domestic institutions as measured by an index of the constraints on the executive. They further hypothesize that the process of institutional change could only occur in countries that initially had non-absolutist political institutions. They show that the data are also consistent with this. The increase in economic growth generated by Atlantic trade was higher for countries with better initial domestic institutions, again measured by the constraint on the executive.

Other examples of studies documenting the persistent importance of historical institutions include Dell's (2010) analysis of the impact of the early forced labor institutions in colonial Peru and Bolivia, as well as Banerjee and Iyer's (2005, 2008) studies of the effects of early land tenure institutions in colonial India.

The recent study by Gennaioli and Rainer (2007) also provides evidence of the persistence of early institutions, but within the African context. The authors use ethnographic data to construct a measure of the level of state development in pre-colonial African societies. Their OLS estimates show that there is a positive correlation between pre-colonial political development and the provision of public goods today. More recently, Michalopoulos and Pappaioannou (2013) combine the same ethnographic data used in Gennaioli and Rainer (2007) with satellite data on night-light density. Examining within-country variation, the authors find that the only robust correlate of night-light density is an ethnicity's pre-colonial level of political development. This finding echoes Gennaioli and Rainer's finding of the importance of this variable.

These results can be combined with evidence from Nunn (2008a) showing that the parts of Africa from which more slaves were taken had less developed political systems after the slave trade (and before official colonial rule).[16] Although the evidence for both relationships is based on correlations and therefore one must be cautious when drawing conclusions, the combined evidence from Gennaioli and Rainer (2007), Michalopoulos and Pappaioannou (2013), and Nunn (2008a) is consistent with a chain of causality where the slave trade resulted in a deterioration of domestic political institutions, which in turn had a long-term adverse impact on the provision of public goods. Therefore, the body of evidence provides support for the notion that history can matter through the evolution and persistence of early institutions.

Overall, the literature since Acemoglu et al. (2001) has succeeded at providing additional evidence showing that institutions are an important channel through which history

---

[15] See Inikori (2002) for the alternative view that the profits that accrued by Western Europe during the three-corner Atlantic trade explain much of its growth during that time.

[16] Also see Whatley (forthcoming) for micro-level evidence for this relationship.

matters. However, much work remains to be done before we have a clear understanding of the effect that historical events have on the formation of early institutions and their persistence and importance for long-term development. For example, in past studies (typically at the macro-level) institutions have been conceptualized and measured as a broad cluster of institutions. The result of this is that, by-and-large, institutions have remained a black box that we do not clearly understand the details of.[17] As empirical research continues to examine specific examples of institutional change and persistence at the micro-level, our understanding of the causes and consequences of specific institutions will naturally improve.

### 7.5.3 Cultural Norms of Behavior

Another way in which historical events can have long-term impacts is if these past events permanently affect culture or norms of behavior. While in economics the notion of culture often remains vague, other disciplines place much more emphasis on precisely defining culture. For example, evolutionary anthropologists have long recognized that there are clear micro-foundations that explain the existence of a phenomenon like culture (e.g. Cavalli-Sforza and Feldman, 1981; Boyd and Richerson, 1985). If information acquisition is either imperfect or costly, then selection favors short-cuts to learning. Individuals, rather than using scarce resources to acquire all of the information needed for every decision to be made, will instead develop "rules-of-thumb". These short-cuts then become internalized as individuals come to believe that certain behaviors are the "right" behaviors in certain situations.[18] For a fuller exposition of this definition of culture see Nunn (2012).

The idea that norms of behavior may be a channel through which history can affect long-term economic development is not new. One of the most famous links between history, culture, and development is Max Weber's (1930) hypothesis that the Protestant Reformation was instrumental in facilitating the rise of industrial capitalism in Western Europe. He argues that Protestantism, in contrast to Catholicism, approved the virtues of hard work and the accumulation of wealth, and that these values, referred to as the

---

[17] An exception is the study by Acemoglu and Johnson (2004), where the authors distinguish "property rights institutions" from "contracting institutions." According to their definitions, property rights institutions protect individuals from theft or expropriation by the government or elites, and contracting institutions enforce private contracts written between individuals. They find that property rights institutions have a positive and significant effect on income, investment, and financial development. On the other hand, contracting institutions appear to have a much more limited impact, only affecting the form of financial intermediation.

[18] Within economics, examples of models of cultural evolution include Verdier (2000, 2001) and Tabellini (2008).

"Protestant work ethic," provided the moral foundation that spurred the transition to a modern market-based industrial economy.[19]

One of the earliest studies empirically examining the possibility that cultural norms may be historically determined was undertaken by a group of social psychologists (Cohen et al. 1996). The authors test whether there is a culture of honor in the US south, where a special importance is placed in defending one's reputation and honor, even if this requires aggression and violence. Their explanation for why this culture exists in the US south and not the north lies in the different histories of settlement in the two areas. The north was settled by groups with a farming background, while the south was settled primarily by the Celts who had been herders since prehistorical times and had never engaged in large-scale agriculture. They argue that in herding cultures, with their low population densities and weak states, protection of one's property was left to the individual and therefore norms of aggressive behavior developed as a means to protect one's herd.

To test the culture of honor hypothesis, Cohen et al. (1996) conducted a series of experiments involving white males from the US north and US south. In the experiments, each individual was bumped by an accomplice and called an "asshole." (The participants did not know this was part of the experiment.) Cohen et al. use a number of methods including direct observation, psychological tests, and saliva tests to compare the effects of this incident on southerners relative to northerners. They find that southerners became more upset, were more likely to feel that their masculinity was threatened, became more physiologically and cognitively primed for aggression as measured by a rise in testosterone and cortisol levels, and were more likely to engage in aggressive behavior, subsequently.

A number of studies provide additional evidence for the historical origins of current cultural differences. For example, Guiso et al. (2008) empirically examine the well-known hypothesis put forth by Putnam et al. (1993) that within Italy, city states that became independent during the 1000–1300 period developed higher levels of social capital, and these higher levels of social capital continue to persist today. The authors bring Putnam et al.'s hypothesis to the data by collecting various city level measures of social capital. They show that looking across 400 Italian cities, there is a positive relationship between their measures of social capital and whether the city was free in 1176.

Nunn and Wantchekon (2011) consider the historical determinants of trust within the African context. The authors examine whether the trans-Atlantic and Indian Ocean slave trades influenced the amount of distrust within society. This is done by combining household survey data with estimates of the number of slaves taken from each ethnic group in Africa. The study finds a negative relationship between an individual's reported trust in others (either neighbors, relatives, local governments, co-ethnics, and those from

---

[19] A more recent example is Mokyr's (2008) argument that an important determinant of the Industrial Revolution was the development of a social norm he calls "gentlemanly culture" that emphasized honesty, commitment, and cooperation.

other ethnicities) and the number of slaves taken from the individual's ethnic group during the slave trades.

The study attempts to distinguish between the two most plausible channels through which the slave trades could have adversely affected trust. One channel is that they altered the cultural norms of the ethnic groups exposed to the trade, making them inherently less trusting. A second channel is that the slave trades resulted in a long-term deterioration of legal and political institutions, which causes individuals to be less trusting of others today.

The authors undertake a number of tests to distinguish between these two channels. One test examines individuals' trust in the local government and attempts to control for the quality of domestic institutions using the individuals' perceived quality of the local government, extent of corruption, and whether local councillors listen to their concerns, as well as measures of the quality of public goods provision.

Another test controls for a second measure of slave exports: the average number of slaves that were taken from the geographic location that each individual is currently living in. This is different from the first measure, which is the average number of slaves taken from an individual's ethnic group. The second slave export variable is motivated by the fact that when an individual relocates the individual's internal norms move with them, but the external institutional environment is left behind. In other words, institutions, which are external to the individual, are much more geographically fixed, relative to cultural beliefs which are internal to the individual. Therefore, the two variables can be used to distinguish the extent to which the slave trade affects trust through the culture channel versus through the institutions channel. If the slave trade affects trust primarily through internalized norms and cultural beliefs, which are ethnically based and internal to the individuals, then when looking across individuals, what should matter is whether their ancestors were heavily enslaved. If the slave trade affects trust primarily through its deterioration of domestic institutions, which are external to the individual and geographically immobile, then what should matter is whether the external environment the individual is living in was heavily affected by the slave trades.

The results of each of the tests indicate that the slave trades adversely affect trust through both cultural norms and institutions, but that the magnitude of the culture channel is always greater than the institutions channel.

Another cultural consequence of the slave trade that has received attention is the practice of polygamy. Because significantly more men than women were enslaved during the trans-Atlantic slave trade, the ratio of men to women in Africa was significantly affected. It has been hypothesized that this gave rise to the practice of polygamy. Combining Nunn and Wantchekon's (2011) estimates of ethnicity-level slave exports and information from household survey data, Dalton and Leung (2011) and Fenske (2012) find a positive relationship between slave exports and the prevalence of polygamy.

Other examples of evidence for the historical origins of current cultural traits include Alesina et al.'s (2013) study of the relationship between traditional plough use and current gender roles, as well as Durante's (2010) analysis of the link between historical weather variability and current trust. Both have been described earlier in the chapter.

## 7.5.4 The Interplay Between Culture and Institutions

Generally, studies of the historical importance of culture and studies of the historical importance of institutions are done in isolation of each other. However, there is evidence that there are important complementarities and interdependencies between culture and institutions. I now turn to a discussion of these.

### 7.5.4.1 Culture Affecting Formal Institutions

Historically, there are many examples of culture impacting the evolution of domestic institutions. Arguably, the most obvious are the European migrant communities established around the globe after the Age of Exploration. At a macro-level, this has been illustrated by Acemoglu et al.'s (2001) colonial origins hypothesis. A more micro-level analysis of the process (at least for the United States) is provided in David Hackett Fischer's (1989) book *Albion's Seed*, where he demonstrates that the institutions and social structures initially established by European migrants arose from the values and beliefs brought with them from the Old World. In other words, the institutions first established were endogenous to the cultural beliefs of the early migrants.

Fisher documents four waves of early migration to North America—the Puritans (1629–1641), the Anglican Cavaliers (1642–1675), the Quakers (1675–1725), and the Scotch-Irish (1717–1775)—and shows how differences in the values of each immigrant wave generated differences in the institutions that were established. The Puritans, believing in the importance of universal education and in a well-functioning society, established universal education, significant taxes, sizable governments, and heavy-handed justice. The Virginia Cavaliers, who believed that inequality was natural and were primarily concerned with maintaining existing forms of hierarchy, implemented limited education, lower taxes, less government spending, and an informal system of justice based on hierarchical violence. The institutions established by the Quakers in the Delaware Valley reflected their belief in the central importance of personal freedoms. All citizens were granted equal legal rights, there was limited government involvement in personal and religious affairs, and taxes were limited. The institutions implemented by the Scotch-Irish were an outgrowth of their belief in freedom from the constraints imposed by government. This resulted in a limited formal justice system (and a reliance on ad hoc vigilante justice), limited political institutions, light taxes, and strong rights to armed resistance from authority.

European mass migration provides one episode that clearly illustrates the endogeneity of institutions to cultures. Other studies also provide similar evidence from other contexts. For example, Zerbe and Anderson (2001) document that the initial property rights institutions established during the 1848 California Gold Rush reflected the values and beliefs that miners brought with them westward. The beliefs—which included individualism, respect for property, and the view that rewards should be commensurate with effort—first developed into collectively practiced norms of behavior (i.e. informal institutions) before being formalized as written laws.

As well, the work by Greif (1994) on the cultural differences between the Maghribi and Genoese medieval traders also illustrates the role of culture in shaping the formation of formal institutions. The Genoese developed institutions that arose from their individualist cultural beliefs, including a formal legal system as well as other formal organizations that helped to facilitate exchange. By contrast, the institutional structures of the Maghribis grew out of their collectivist cultural beliefs. Because the Maghribis continued to rely on informal enforcement mechanisms, organizations remained limited in size and scope.

### 7.5.4.2 Institutions Affecting Culture

There is also the possibility of feedback effects, with formal institutions affecting the evolution of cultural traits. A number of recent studies have found evidence for this. For example, Guido Tabellini (2010) explains variation across regions of Europe in levels of trust, respect, and confidence in the returns to individual effort. He identifies a strong positive relationship between the prevalence of these cultural traits and measures of the average quality of domestic institutions between 1600 and 1850. The estimates show that European regions that had less well-developed institutions in the past have less trust in others, less respect for others, and believe less in the value of individual effort today.

Evidence for the impact of institutions on culture also comes from a number of studies that use a regression discontinuity strategy, focusing on particularly important historical borders that today lie within the same country. Becker et al. (2011) examine Eastern European villages lying within the same country today, but on either side of the historical Habsburg border. They show that villages that were formerly part of the Habsburg Empire, with its greatly respected and well-functioning bureaucracy, today have greater trust in their local government. Grosjean (2011b) examines location pairs within Eastern Europe and shows that the longer a pair was under the same Empire historically, the more similar the reported social trust of the locations' citizens today. Peisakhin (2010) surveys 1,675 individuals living in 227 villages located within 25 km of the Habsburg-Russian border that divided Ukraine between 1772 and 1918. Relying on information on cultural traits based on answers to survey questions, Peisakhin (2010) documents a wide range of statistically significant cultural differences between the two groups.

### 7.5.4.3 Coevolution of Culture and Institutions

Tabellini (2008) provides a formal model of the interplay between culture and institutions in an environment in which both are endogenous and co-evolve. In the model, there are two potential cultural traits with one valuing cooperation (or believing cooperation is the right thing to do) more than the other. Vertical transmission of these values is modeled explicitly with parents exerting costly effort to instill values of cooperation. One of the primary innovations of the paper is to also model the endogenous formation of institutions (which enforce cooperation) through majority voting. Tabellini shows that the co-evolution of culture and institutions generates strategic complementarity and multiple equilibria. A culture that values cooperation prefers institutions that strongly enforce cooperation, which in turn increases the returns to cooperation, reinforcing this cultural trait. Conversely, a culture that does not value cooperation prefers institutions that weakly enforce cooperation, which in turn decreases the returns to cooperation, reinforcing a culture that does not value cooperation.

Recent papers that have empirically studied contemporary institutions and culture provide evidence of interactions between culture and institutions. Aghion et al. (2011) examine contemporary labor markets and identify a negative cross-country relationship between the existence of cooperative labor relations and the severity of minimum wage regulation by the state. Similarly, Aghion et al. (2010) identify a negative cross-country relationship between general trust and government regulation.

Both studies then develop models of the interplay between institutions/policies and culture/beliefs. In both, greater government regulation crowds out beneficial behavior of citizens. In Aghion et al. (2011), higher minimum wage regulation reduces the benefits to workers of trying to cooperate with firms. Therefore, more stringent minimum wage regulations crowd out cooperation between firms and workers. In turn, less cooperative firm-worker relationships increase the demand for minimum wage regulation. Thus, this interdependence explains the observed negative relationship between minimum wage and cooperative labor relations.

In Aghion et al. (2010), a low level of civic mindedness in the economy results in a greater need for regulation to protect citizens from the negative externalities imposed by those that are not civic-minded. The high level of regulation in the economy also reinforces the low level of civic mindedness, as it is these individuals that are comfortable paying and demanding bribes. The result is that greater trust is observed in economies with lower levels of government regulation.

What the three studies described here have in common is their analysis of the two-way relationship between culture and institutions. Given this interdependence, both institutions and culture co-evolve, and this can generate multiple stable equilibria with different sets of institutions and cultural norms that are self-enforcing.

## 7.5.5 Genetics

It is possible that historical events that affect the distribution of individuals in different locations—i.e. through genocide, forced expulsions, or voluntary migrations—could have long-term impacts through a genetic channel. Given that genetic traits tend to be fairly persistent over time, if they have an impact on economic outcomes, then it is theoretically possible that events that impact the genetic distribution of the population may have long-term economic impacts.

A number of recent studies provide some evidence that genetics can impact human behavior. For example, Cesarini et al. (2008) exploit variation in genetic differences between monozygotic and dizygotic twins. The authors compare differences in the actions taken in a standard trust game between monozygotic and dizygotic twins from Sweden and the United States. By assuming that similarity of twin behavior can be decomposed into a common environment, common genes, and other individual-specific variables, and that monozygotic twins share the same environment and same genes, and dizygotic twins share the same environment but have half the alleles of genes, they are able to estimate the extent to which behavior is genetically determined. They find that monozygotic twins consistently exhibit more similar behavior than dizygotic twins, and therefore, based on their assumptions, they conclude that an important part of behavior is genetically determined. The same basic procedure is repeated in Cesarini et al. (2009), but examining behavior in a dictator game and measures of individual risk aversion.

At the macro-level, a number of studies have documented relationships between genetic measures and economic outcomes. Spolaore and Wacziarg (2010) show that greater genetic relatedness has a positive impact on the probability that two populations go to war with one another. Spolaore and Wacziarg (2009) show that, across country-pairs, bilateral genetic distance is positively associated with current income differences. In other words, genetically similar countries are economically more similar.

Ashraf and Galor (2012) provide evidence that genetic diversity within a country is non-monotonically related to per capita income. There is an inverted-U relationship between the two, with income reaching a maximum at an intermediate level of diversity. Too much diversity and too little diversity are both associated with low per capita income.

Cook (2013a) also examines genetic diversity, but unlike Ashraf and Galor (2012), he considers a specific group of genes associated with resistance and susceptibility to disease, namely the major histocompatibility complex. Within humans this is a cluster of 239 genes on the 6th chromosome. Cook (2013a) measures the variation in allele frequency within this system and shows that, across countries, his measure of genetic variation is positively correlated with Olsson and Hibbs's (2005) measure of the number of domesticable animals and Putterman's (2008) measure of the time since the adoption of agriculture. It is also positively correlated with health, measured in the 1960s. Interestingly, by 1990 the health relationship no longer exists.

In a subsequent study, Cook (2013c) considers another channel through which genetics could have long-term impacts on economic development. This is through lactase persistence (i.e. the ability to digest milk after childhood). Cook hypothesizes that, historically, societies with the gene variant that resulted in lactase persistence had access to an additional source of calories, vitamins, and nutrients, which resulted in increased population densities. The author shows that looking across countries, a greater proportion of the population with lactase persistence is associated with greater population density, measured in 1500.

## 7.6. UNRESOLVED QUESTIONS AND DIRECTIONS FOR FUTURE RESEARCH

### 7.6.1 Persistence or Reversals?

A number of studies provide evidence of the persistence in economic development over long periods of time. Societies that were more economically, technologically, or institutionally developed in the past are also the most developed today. For example, Comin et al. (2010) document a positive relationship between historical technology levels (as far back as 1000 BC) and current income per capita across different parts of the world. Along similar lines, Bockstette et al. (2002) empirically document a positive relationship between state antiquity and current economic performance today. Societies that were more politically developed in the past, are more economically developed today. At a more micro-level and over a shorter timespan, Huillery's (2011) analysis of French West Africa shows persistence of prosperity between the pre- and post-colonial period.

These findings of persistence stand in contrast to the "reversal of fortunes" documented in Acemoglu et al. (2002): among a sample of former colonies, those locations that were the most prosperous in 1500 are the most underdeveloped today. This reversal has also been confirmed in alternative studies. For example, Nunn (2008a) shows that among African countries, those that were the most developed prior to the slave trades (measured by population density in 1400) had the largest number of slaves taken and have the lowest incomes today.[20]

These two sets of findings appear to stand in contrast with one another, one showing persistence over long periods of time and the other showing a complete reversal. Which is correct? It turns out that both are, and an important part of the difference arises due to differences in the samples being examined. The persistence studies tend to examine all countries globally, while the reversal studies have samples that only include former colonies.

To illustrate this, consider the bivariate relationship between the natural log of per capita income in 1500 and the natural log of real per capita GDP in 2000. This relationship is reported in columns (1)–(3) of Table 7.1. The sample comprises 85 former colonies and 65 non-colonies examined in Comin et al. (2010). Column (1) reports the relationship among former colonies. This is analogous to the regressions estimated by Acemoglu et al. (2002). As shown, consistent with their findings, there is a negative relationship between

---

[20] Also related is the question of whether Africa has always been behind the rest of the world. While the conventional wisdom is that Africa has generally been the most underdeveloped continent of the world, there is evidence that this view is misplaced (Ehret, forthcoming).

population density in 1500 and per capita income today. There has been a reversal. Column (2) examines this same relationship among the rest of the sample, which are the countries that were never colonized. Here one observes a very different relationship. The two variables are positively correlated. Among this group there is persistence. Column (3) reports the relationship between the full sample, and shows that on average there is persistence. The coefficient is positive and significant at the 10 percent level. This estimate is analogous to the findings of persistence by Comin et al. (2010), Bockstette et al. (2002), and others.

Acemoglu et al. (2002) argue that among former colonies, the reversal occurred because initial prosperity impacted the institutions that were developed by Europeans. Where initial incomes were low, population was sparse, and Europeans settled, establishing protection of property rights and other growth-promoting institutions. Where initial incomes were high, Europeans undertook an extractive strategy. In some cases, they co-opted existing forced labor traditions, and in others, they promoted enslavement and the sale of indigenous populations. As a result, locations that were initially poor in 1500 today are more developed than those that were initially richer.

A similar but alternative explanation for the reversal, and one that has been stressed in the recent paper by Easterly and Levine (2012), is that the less populated places witness an in-migration of people from more prosperous countries, with higher levels of human capital, culture more conducive to economic growth, and/or other vertically transmitted traits. Therefore these locations are richer today. This alternative explanation suggests that the reversal simply reflects migration and the persistence of prosperity at the society level.

This alternative explanation can be examined using an ancestry-based measure of population density in 1500 and per capita GDP in 2000. The ancestry-based initial population measure is constructed using Putterman and Weil's (2010) *World Migration Matrix*. While the geography-based measure used in columns (1)–(3) is the average income (proxied by population density) of people living on the country's land in 1500, the ancestry-based measure is the average income in 1500 (proxied by population density) of the ancestors of those living in the country today.

The estimates from column (4) show that, all else equal, among former colonies, being descended from ancestors with a high prosperity is positively associated with per capita income today. Therefore, it is plausible that colonial migration of individuals from prosperous societies explains the reversal. Interestingly, the persistence of income along lineages (and not locations) is similarly strong among non-colonies (for which there is less migration) as among former colonies (with much greater migration).[21]

A simple way to examine whether the reversal documented in Acemoglu et al. (2002) is explained by migration combined with the persistence of prosperity across generations

---

[21] Better understanding the specific transmission mechanisms underlying this persistence is the subject of ongoing research and debate. For an excellent summary of this literature see Spolaore and Wacziarg (forthcoming).

**Table 7.1** Persistence and reversals

| | (1) | (2) | (3) | (4) | (5) | (6) | (7) |
|---|---|---|---|---|---|---|---|
| | | | | Dependent variable: ln per capita GDP in 2000 | | | |
| | Colonies | Non-colonies | Both | Colonies | Non-colonies | Colonies | Non-colonies |
| ln population density in 1500: | | | | | | | |
| Geography-based | −0.228*** | 0.276*** | 0.115* | | | −0.316*** | 0.003 |
| | (0.070) | (0.090) | (0.061) | | | (0.058) | (0.319) |
| Ancestry-based | | | | 0.475*** | 0.319*** | 0.581*** | 0.316 |
| | | | | (0.098) | (0.100) | (0.086) | (0.355) |
| Observations | 85 | 65 | 150 | 85 | 65 | 85 | 65 |
| R-squared | 0.114 | 0.129 | 0.023 | 0.222 | 0.140 | 0.430 | 0.140 |

*Notes:* The table reports coefficients from OLS estimates, with standard errors in parentheses. The dependent variable is the natural log of real per capita GDP in 2000. The independent variables are the natural log of a country's population density in 1500, measured as the historical average of the land of the country (geography-based) or the historical average of the ancestors of the population of the country (ancestry-based). The correlation between the two measures is 0.23 for colonies and 0.96 for non-colonies.

* Indicate significance at the 10% level.

** Indicate significance at the 5% level.

*** Indicate significance at the 1% level.

is to examine the coefficient of the geography-based measure of population density in 1500, while controlling for the ancestry-based measure. This is done in column (6). The magnitude of the coefficient for the geography-based measure of 1500 prosperity does not diminish, and actually increases. The ancestry-based 1500 prosperity measure enters with a large positive and significant coefficient. This suggests the coexistence of two channels. One is the migration of populations from more prosperous societies and the other being the reversal of fortune discussed in Acemoglu et al. (2002). This finding of stronger persistence by ancestry than by location is not new and is an important point made in Putterman and Weil (2010), Comin et al. (2010), and Chanda et al. (2013).

Column (7) examines the same correlations as column (6), but among the sample of non-colonies. Because there is little migration among this group, the two population density measures are highly correlated (the correlation coefficient is 0.96). Due to this multicollinearity, both variables are insignificant. However, the estimated coefficient for the ancestry-based variable provides evidence of persistence across generations that is similar in magnitude but smaller than the estimate for the colonies sample. As expected, the coefficient for the geography-based variable shows no evidence of a reversal-of-fortunes mechanism among non-colonies.

Overall, the correlations reported in Table 7.1 are suggestive of the following facts. First, within former colonies, there has been a reversal of fortunes (looking at geographic locations as the unit of observation). Second, no such reversal exists among non-colonies. Third, there is no reversal once one uses societies (and their descendants) as the unit of observation. Instead one observes extreme persistence, both among former colonies and non-colonies, a fact that has been empirically noted by Putterman and Weil (2010) and discussed in Spolaore and Wacziarg (forthcoming). Fourth, the Acemoglu et al. (2002) reversal exists even after accounting for the migration of populations from more prosperous to less prosperous regions during the colonial period. This does not appear to fully explain the reversal.

Therefore, the existence of reversals and persistence in the data seem to be reconcilable. However, the most recent research along these lines shows a reversal that is not explained by the logic above. Olsson and Paik (2012) document a reversal within Europe from the Neolithic until now. They show that the parts of Europe that adopted agriculture earlier (and were arguably more economically developed during the Neolithic period) are less developed today. Although the authors provide an explanation, the exact reason for this reversal is far from clear. They also find evidence of a reversal within sub-Saharan Africa and East Asia. The reason behind the reversals in these regions is also unclear. Most interestingly, they show that if one looks at a global sample, there is persistence: the parts of the world that adopted agriculture earlier are more developed today. In other words, looking within-regions there are reversals, but looking across regions (and across countries generally) there is persistence.

## 7.6.2 When Doesn't History Persist?

To date, the primary focus of the literature has been in empirically documenting the persistence of historical shocks, typically arising due to lasting impacts through either domestic institutions or cultural traits. Little or no attention has been placed on examining when historical events *do not* have lasting impacts. This emphasis is logical given the need to first establish that history can matter, which has led to a natural focus on events that have had persistent impacts.

However, there are a few studies that provide some preliminary evidence for when history persists and when it does not. For example, Voigtlaender and Voth (2012) document the persistence of anti-Semitic values and beliefs in Germany between the 14th and 20th centuries. Their analysis examines variation across German villages and documents a remarkable relationship between the prevalence of pogroms during the Black Death (1348–1350) and a number of measures of anti-Semitic sentiment in the early 20th century. The authors then turn to an analysis of the environments in which persistence was more or less strong. One of their most interesting findings is that the persistence of this cultural trait is much weaker among Hanseatic cities, which were self-governed German cities heavily involved in lucrative long-distance trade. This finding may be due to higher rates of migration or to more dynamism arising from greater economic opportunity and growth. Voigtlaender and Voth (2012) also find that (consistent with both mechanisms) there is less persistence among cities with faster population growth, and (consistent with the second mechanism) there is less persistence among cities that were more industrialized in 1933.

Grosjean's (2011a) study of Nisbett and Cohen's (1996) "culture of honor" hypothesis shows a persistent impact of the Scotch-Irish culture of honor, but only within the Southern states of the US. The obvious explanation is that a cultural heuristic of aggression was relatively beneficial in the south, which was more lawless and with less well-developed property rights institutions. However, in the north, with a more established rule of law and better developed property rights protection, norms of aggression and violence were less beneficial, and therefore did not persist. In other words, external characteristics—in this case domestic institutions—by affecting the relative costs and benefits of different cultural norms, influence their persistence.

Another environment in which this can be seen is in Africa in the context of the slave trade. A natural hypothesis is that the detrimental impacts of the slave trades on trust will be more persistent in countries with a poorly functioning legal system. It is in these environments, where individuals are not legally constrained to act in a trustworthy manner, that norms of mistrust, initially developed by the slave trade, may continue to be relatively beneficial and to persist.

This can be tested directly by re-estimating Equation (7.1) from Nunn and Wantchekon (2011), but allowing for the impact of past slave exports on trust today to depend on the quality of country-level domestic institutions, measured at the time of the survey (2005)

using the Governance Matters "rule of law" variable. The original index ranges from
$-2.5$ to $+2.5$, but I normalize the variable to lie between zero and one.[22] The augmented equation is:

$$\text{trust}_{i,e,d,c} = \alpha_c + \beta_1 \text{ slave exports}_e + \beta_2 \text{ slave exports}_e \times \text{ rule of law}_c$$
$$+ \mathbf{X}'_{i,e,d,c}\mathbf{\Gamma} + \mathbf{X}'_{d,c}\mathbf{\Omega} + \mathbf{X}'_e\mathbf{\Phi} + \varepsilon_{i,e,d,c}, \tag{7.1}$$

where $i$ indexes individuals, $e$ ethnic groups, $d$ districts, and $c$ countries; $\text{trust}_{i,e,d,c}$ denotes
one of five individual-level measures of trust that range from 0 to 3; $\text{slave exports}_e$ is a
measure of the number of slaves taken from ethnic group $e$ during the Indian Ocean
and trans-Atlantic slave trades[23]; $\text{rule of law}_c$ is the 0-to-1 measure of a country's rule
of law in 2005; $\alpha_c$ denotes country fixed effects; and $\mathbf{X}'_{i,e,d,c}$, $\mathbf{X}'_d$, and $\mathbf{X}'_e$ denote vectors
of individual-, district-, and ethnicity-level control variables. See Nunn and Wantchekon
(2011) for a fuller description of the variables in Equation (7.1).

Estimates of Equation (7.1) are reported in Table 7.2. The table reports estimates of
$\beta_1$ and $\beta_2$. The bottom panel reports estimates of the impact of the slave trade on trust
for the country with the lowest measure of rule of law (0.17) and for the country with
the highest rule of law measure (0.63).[24] As shown, the estimated coefficient for the
interaction term $\beta_2$ is positive in all specifications (although the precision of the estimate
varies). This indicates a weaker negative impact of the slave trades on trust in countries
with better domestic institutions. Further, for all trust measures, the estimated impact of
the slave trades on trust is positive and significant for the lowest rule of law country but
not statistically different from zero for the highest rule of law country. This is consistent
with the adverse impacts of the slave trade being less persistent in countries with a better
rule of law. In these countries, well-functioning institutions enforce trustworthy behavior
of its citizens and therefore there is less persistence of the mistrust engendered by the
slave trades.

An important shortcoming of this exercise arises due to the endogeneity of the
country-level rule of law measure. In particular, it is likely endogenous to the slave
trade. Ideally, estimates of this nature would rely on exogenous variation in the variable
used to test for heterogeneity. However, an important point to bear in mind is that the
estimates reported in Table 7.2 and Nunn and Wantchekon (2011) are estimated using
within-country variation only. Any impacts that the slave trade had on country-level
characteristics are controlled for directly in the regression because of the presence of
country fixed effects. In other words, although the rule of law measure is an endogenous

---

[22] This is done by adding 2.5 to the measure and dividing by 5.

[23] The measure is the natural log of one plus total slave exports normalized by land area.

[24] Zimbabwe is the country with the lowest rule of law measure in the Afrobarometer sample, and Botswana
is the country with the highest.

**Table 7.2** Testing for heterogenous impacts of the slave trade on trust in Nunn and Wantchekon (2011)

| | Trust of relatives | Trust of neighbors | Trust of local council | Intra-group trust | Inter-group trust |
|---|---|---|---|---|---|
| | (1) | (2) | (3) | (4) | (5) |
| $\ln (1 + \text{exports/area})$ | −0.172 | −0.341*** | −0.170*** | −0.461*** | −0.344*** |
| | (0.141) | (0.115) | (0.064) | (0.102) | (0.082) |
| $\ln (1 + \text{exports/area}) \times$ rule of law Index 2005 | 0.111 | 0.512* | 0.169 | 0.891*** | 0.695*** |
| | (0.360) | (0.302) | (0.173) | (0.263) | (0.208) |
| Individual controls | Yes | Yes | Yes | Yes | Yes |
| District controls | Yes | Yes | Yes | Yes | Yes |
| Country fixed effects | Yes | Yes | Yes | Yes | Yes |
| Number of observations | 20,062 | 20,027 | 19,733 | 19,952 | 19,765 |
| Number of ethnicity clusters | 185 | 185 | 185 | 185 | 185 |
| Number of district clusters | 1257 | 1257 | 1283 | 1257 | 1255 |
| Estimated impact for Afrobarometer country with lowest rule of law | −0.153* | −0.252*** | −0.141*** | −0.305*** | −0.223*** |
| | (0.082) | (0.066) | (0.036) | (0.059) | (0.049) |
| Estimated impact for Afrobarometer country with highest rule of law | −0.102 | −0.018 | −0.064 | 0.102 | 0.095 |
| | (0.098) | (0.087) | (0.054) | (0.073) | (0.058) |

*Notes:* The table reports OLS estimates. The unit of observation is an individual. ln (1 + exports/area) is the number of slaves exported normalized by land area, measured at the ethnicity level. Rule of Law Index 2005 is the Governance Matters VI rule of law measure for 2005, normalized to lie between zero and one. Standard errors are adjusted for two-way clustering at the ethnicity and district levels. The individual controls are for age, age squared, a gender indicator variable, 5 living conditions fixed effects, 10 education fixed effects, 18 religion fixed effects, 25 occupation fixed effects, and an indicator for whether the respondent lives in an urban location. The district controls include ethnic fractionalization in the district and the share of the district's population that is the same ethnicity as the respondent. See Nunn and Wantchekon (2011) for further details.
* Indicate significance at the 10% level.
** Indicate significance at the 5% level.
*** Indicate significance at the 1% level.

variable, its direct (linear) impacts on trust are captured by the country fixed effects in the regression.

Looking at the differences in the estimates of $\beta_1$ and $\beta_2$ across the five trust measures, it is clear that the heterogeneous impacts of the slave trades are weaker for trust of relatives and trust of the local government. This is true whether one considers the magnitude and significance of $\beta_2$ or of the high and low estimates reported in the bottom panel of the table. Interestingly, disputes between relatives and disputes between citizens and the local government are less likely to be resolved through the legal system than disputes between neighbors, co-ethnics, or citizens from different ethnic groups. Given this, we would expect that rule of law would be less successful in enforcing good behavior in these situations, and as a result would be a less important determinant of the persistence of distrust. The estimates reported in Table 7.2 are consistent with this.

## 7.7. CONCLUSIONS: LOOKING BACK WHILE MOVING FORWARD

This chapter has provided a broad overview of research examining comparative historical economic development. Studies have examined a wide array of historic events, including the Neolithic Revolution, colonial rule, Africa's slave trades, the Industrial Revolution, the Protestant Reformation, the French Revolution, and the Columbian Exchange.

Although the studies reviewed in this chapter have done much to identify important pieces of the larger historical puzzle, many of the pieces are yet to be uncovered. In addition, the more difficult task is understanding exactly how all of the pieces fit together. This is a step that has not been taken by the vast majority of the studies in the literature summarized here. Nearly all examine a particular event in isolation from other events, except possibly to account for other events as covariates in the empirical analysis. However, once one begins thinking of the realities of history, it is soon apparent that historical events impact other historical events in important and sometimes subtle or complicated ways. Further, there are often complex interactions between events, suggesting that the linear specifications typically assumed in studies may be inaccurate.

There are many examples of these interdependencies. For example, Europe's ability to colonize and rule the African continent depended critically on the discovery of the chincona tree in the Andes and its mass production in Asia by the British. This is because quinine, the first effective protection against malaria, is derived from the bark of the tree. Similarly, European knowledge of how to effectively process wild rubber obtained from Native Americans had important consequences for the millions of Africans that were tortured and killed in King Leopold's Congo.

Another example is the interdependence between the printing press and both the Protestant Reformation (Dittmar, 2011; Rubin, 2011) and the Atlantic trade (Dittmar,

2011). We have also seen that Catholic conflict with the Ottoman Empire helped enable the spread of the Protestant religion across Europe (Iyigun, 2008).

We have seen that the presence of the tsetse fly in Africa resulted in less intensive agriculture that did not use animals or the plough (Alsan, 2012). Because the plough was not adopted, women participated actively in agriculture, which generated norms of equality, which continue to persist today (Alesina et al. 2013). This an important explanation for the high levels of female labor force participation that is observed in Africa today.

We have seen that Africa's slave trades resulted in underdeveloped pre-colonial states (Nunn, 2008a), which in turn are associated with less post-colonial public goods provision and lower incomes (Gennaioli and Rainer, 2007; Michalopoulos and Pappaioannou, 2013).

Moving forward, the second major task for the literature to tackle is to better understand channels of causality. In the past decade, we have made significant progress empirically testing whether historical events have lasting impacts. The bulk of this survey is devoted to reviewing this evidence, which overwhelmingly shows that history does matter. What is less clear is exactly why it matters. I have reviewed here the leading candidates: multiple equilibria, cultural norms of behavior, and domestic institutions. The extent to which these mechanisms matter, and in which circumstances, is yet to be fully understood. Further, as discussed, there are also potentially important complementarities between the channels. For example, beliefs and values tend to become codified in formal institutions, which in turn feedback, affecting the evolution of these values. Complementarities between cultural traits and formal institutions are likely an important part of many instances of long-term persistence.

Overall, while much progress has been made to this point, the primary accomplishment has been in establishing the importance of studying the past for understanding current growth and development. The economic literature is increasingly coming to understand that where we are (and therefore how we best move forward) has a lot to do with how we got here.

## ACKNOWLEDGMENT

The chapter has benefitted from helpful discussions with Emmanuel Akyeampong, Robert Bates, Samuel Bowles, Claudia Goldin, Joseph Henrich, and James Robinson. I thank Eva Ng for research assistance.

## REFERENCES

Acemoglu, Daron, 1995. Reward structure and the allocation of talent. European Economic Review 39, 17–33.
Acemoglu, Daron, Johnson, Simon, 2004. Unbundling Institutions. Journal of Political Economy 113, 949–995.
Acemoglu, Daron, Johnson, Simon, Robinson, James A., 2001. The colonial origins of comparative development: an empirical investigation. American Economic Review 91, 1369–1401.

Acemoglu, Daron, Johnson, Simon, Robinson, James A., 2002. Reversal of fortune: geography and institutions in the making of the modern world income distribution. Quarterly Journal of Economics 117, 1231–1294.

Acemoglu, Daron, Johnson, Simon, Robinson, James A., 2005. The rise of Europe: atlantic trade, institutional change and economic growth. American Economic Review 95, 546–579.

Acemoglu, Daron, Bautista, María Angélica, Querubin, Pablo, Robinson, James A., 2008. Economic and political inequality in development: the case of Cundinamarca, Colombia. In: Helpman, Elhanan (Ed.), Institutions and Economic Performance, Harvard University Press, Cambridge, MA, pp. 181–245.

Acemoglu, Daron, Cantoni, Davide, Johnson, Simon, Robinson, James A., 2011a. The consequences of radical reform: the french revolution. American Economic Review 101 (7), 3286–3307.

Acemoglu, Daron, Hassan, Tarek A., Robinson, James A., 2011b. Social structure and development: a legacy of the Holocaust in Russia. Quarterly Journal of Economics 126 (2), 895–946.

Acemoglu, Daron, Johnson, Simon, Robinson, James A., 2012. The colonial origins of comparative development: an empirical investigation: reply. American Economic Review 102 (6), 3077–3110.

Ager, Philipp, Ciccone, Antonio, 2012. Rainfall Risk and Religious Membership in the Late Nineteenth-Century US. Universitat Pompeu Fabra, Mimeo.

Aghion, Philippe, Algan, Yann, Cahuc, Pierre, Shleifer, Andrei, 2010. Regulation and Distrust. Quarterly Journal of Economics 125 (3), 1015–1049.

Aghion, Philippe, Algan, Yann, Cahuc, Pierre, February 2011. Civil society and the state: the interplay between cooperation and minimum wage regulation. Journal of the European Economic Association 9 (1), 3–42.

Aghion, Philippe, Persson, Torsten, Rouzet, Dorothee, 2012. Education and Military Rivalry. Harvard University, Mimeo.

Akçomak, I. Semih, Webbink, Dinand, Weel, Bas ter, 2012. Why did the Netherlands develop so early? The Legacy of the Brethren of the Common Life, Mimeo.

Albouy, David Y., 2012. The colonial origins of comparative development: an empirical investigation: comment. American Economic Review 102 (6), 3059–3076.

Alesina, Alberto, Giuliano, Paola, Nunn, Nathan, 2013. On the origins of gender roles: women and the plough. Quarterly Journal of Economics 128 (2), 155–194.

Alsan, Marcella, 2012. The Effect of the TseTse Fly on African Development. Harvard University, Mimeo.

Andersen, Thomas Barnebeck, Bentzen, Jeanet, Dalgaard, Carl-Johan, 2011. Religious Orders and Growth Through Cultural Change in Pre-Industrial England. University of Copenhagen, Mimeo.

Andersen, Thomas Barnebeck, Jensen, Peter Sandholt, Skovsgaard, Christian Stejner, 2013. The Heavy Plough and the European Agricultural Revolution in the Middle Ages: Evidence from a Historical Experiment. University of Southern Denmark, Mimeo.

Ashraf, Quamrul, Galor, Oded, 2012. The out of Africa hypothesis. Human genetic diversity, and comparative economic development. American Economic Review 103 (1), 1–46.

Ashraf, Quamrul, Michalopoulos, Stelios, 2011. The Climatic Origins of the Neolithic Revolution: Theory and Evidence. Brown University, Mimeo.

Austin, Gareth, November 2008. The "Reversal of Fortune" thesis and the compression of history: perspectives from African and comparative economic history. Journal of International Development 20 (8), 996–1027.

Bai, Ying, Kung, James Kai-sing, 2011a. Climate shocks and sino-nomadic conflict. Review of Economics and Statistics 93 (3), 970–981.

Bai, Ying, Kung, James Kai-sing, 2011b. Diffusing Knowledge while Spreading God's Message: Protestantism and Economic Prosperity in China, 1840–1920. Hong Kong University of Science and Technology, Mimeo.

Banerjee, Abhijit, Iyer, Lakshmi, 2005. History, institutions and economic performance: the legacy of colonial land tenure systems in India. American Economic Review 95 (4), 1190–1213.

Banerjee, Abhijit, Iyer, Lakshmi, 2008. Colonial Land Tenure, Electoral Competition and Public Goods in India. Harvard Business School Working Paper 08–062.

Banerjee, Abhijit, Iyer, Lakshmi, Somanathan, Rohini, 2005. History, social divisions and public goods in rural India. Journal of the European Economic Association Papers and Proceedings 3 (2–3), 639–647.

Baten, Joerg, van Zanden, Jan Luiten, 2008. Book production and the onset of modern economic growth. Journal of Economic Growth 13, 217–235.

Bates, Robert H., forthcoming. The imperial peace in colonial Africa and Africa's underdevelopment. In: Akyeampong, Emmanuel, Bates, Robert H., Nunn, Nathan, Robinson, James A. (Eds.), Africa's Development in Historical Perspective, Cambridge University Press, Cambridge.

Becker, Sascha O., Woessmann, Ludger, 2008. Luther and the girls: religious denomination and the female education gap in nineteenth-century Prussia. Scandinavian Journal of Economics 110 (4), 777–805.

Becker, Sascha O., Woessmann, Ludger, 2009. Was weber wrong? a human capital theory of protestant economic history. Quarterly Journal of Economics 124 (2), 531–596.

Becker, Sascha O., Boeckh, Katrin, Hainz, Christa, Woessmann, Ludger, 2011. The Empire is Dead, Long Live the Empire! Long-Run Persistence of Trust and Corruption in the Bureaucracy. Warwick University, Mimeo.

Bentzen, Jeanet Sinding, Kaarsen, Nicolai, Wingender, Asger Moll, 2012. Irrigation and Autocracy. University of Copenhagen, Mimeo.

Bleakley, Hoyt, Lin, Jeffrey, 2012. Portage and path dependence. Quarterly Journal of Economics 127, 587–644.

Bockstette, Valeri, Chanda, Areendam, Putterman, Louis, 2002. States and markets: the advantage of an early start. Journal of Economic Growth 7, 347–369.

Boserup, Ester, 1970. Woman's Role in Economic Development. Allen and Unwin, London.

Botticini, Maristella, Eckstein, Zvi, 2005. Jewish occupational selection: education, restrictions, or minorities? Journal of Economic History 65 (4), 922–948.

Botticini, Maristella, Eckstein, Zvi, 2007. From farmers to merchants, voluntary conversions and diaspora: a human capital interpretation of Jewish history. Journal of the European Economic Association 5 (5), 885–926.

Boyd, Robert, Richerson, Peter J., 1985. Culture and the Evolutionary Process. University of Chicago Press, London.

Bruhn, Miriam, Gallego, Francisco A., 2012. Good, bad, and ugly colonial activities: do they matter for economic development? Review of Economics and Statistics 94 (2), 433–461.

Cantoni, Davide, May 2012. Adopting a new religion: the case of Protestantism in 16th century Germany. Economic Journal 122 (560), 502–531.

Cavalli-Sforza, L.L., Feldman, M.W., 1981. Cultural Transmission and Evolution: A Quantitative Approach. Princeton University Press, Princeton.

Cesarini, David, Dawes, Christopher T., Fowler, James H., Johannesson, Magnus, Lichtenstein, Paul, Wallace, Bjorn, March 2008. Heritability of cooperative behavior in the trust game. Proceedings of the National Academy of Sciences 105 (10), 3721–3726.

Cesarini, David, Dawes, Christopher T., Fowler, James H., Johannesson, Magnus, Lichtenstein, Paul, Wallace, Bjorn, May 2009. Genetic variation in preferences for giving and risk taking. Quarterly Journal of Economics 124 (2), 809–842.

Chanda, Areendam, Cook, C. Justin, Putterman, Louis, 2013. Persistence of Fortune: Accounting for Population Movements, There was no Post-Columbian Reversal. Brown University, Mimeo.

Chaney, Eric, 2008. Ethnic Cleansing and the Long-Term Persistence of Extractive Institutions: Evidence from the Expulsion of the Moriscos. Harvard University, Mimeo.

Chaney, Eric, Hornbeck, Richard, 2013. Economic Growth in the Malthusian Era: Evidence from the 1609 Spanish Expulsion of the Moriscos. Harvard University, Mimeo.

Chaney, Eric, 2013. Revolt on the Nile: economic shocks, religion and political power. Econometrica.

Chen, Shuo, Kung, James Kai-sing, 2012. The Malthusian Quagmire: Maize and Population Growth in China, 1550–1910. Hong Kong University of Science and Technology, Mimeo.

Clark, Gregory, 2005. The condition of the working class in England, 1209–2004. Journal of Political Economy 113 (6), 707–736.

Cohen, Dov, Nisbett, Richard E., Bowdle, Brian F., Schwarz, Norbert, 1996. Insult, agression, and the southern culture of honor: an "Experimental Ethnography". Journal of Personality and Social Psychology 70 (5), 945–960.

Comin, Diego, Easterly, William, Gong, Erick, 2010. Was the wealth of nations determined in 1000 B.C.? American Economic Journal: Macroeconomics 2 (3), 65–97.

Cook, C. Justin, 2013a. The Long Run Health Effects of the Neolithic Revolution: The Natural Selection of Infectious Disease Resistance. Yale University, Mimeo.

Cook, C. Justin, 2013b. Potatoes, Milk, and the Old World Population Boom. Yale University, Mimeo.

Cook, C. Justin, 2013c. The Role of Lactase Persistence in Precolonial Development. Yale University, Mimeo.

Dalton, J., Leung, T., 2011. Why is Polygamy more Prevalent in Western Africa? An African Slave Trade Perspective. Wake Forest University, Mimeo.

David, Paul A., 1985. Clio and the economics of QWERTY. American Economic Review Papers and Proceedings 75 (2), 332–337.

Davis, Donald R., Weinstein, David E., 2002. Bones, bombs, and breakpoints: the geography of economic activity. American Economic Review 92 (5), 1269–1289.

Davis, Donald R., Weinstein, David E., 2008. A search for multiple equilibria in urban industrial structure. Journal of Regional Science 48 (1), 29–65.

Deconinck, Koen, Verpoorten, Marijke, 2013. Narrow and scientific replication of "The Slave Trade and the Origins of Mistrust in Africa". Journal of Applied Econometrics.

Dell, Melissa, 2010. The persistent effects of Peru's mining mita. Econometrica 78 (6), 1863–1903.

Dell, Melissa, 2012. Insurgency and Long-Run Development: Lessons from the Mexican Revolution. Harvard University, Mimeo.

Diamond, Jared, 1997. Guns, Germs, and Steel. W.W. Norton & Company, New York.

Diamond, Jared, 2002. Evolution, consequences and future of plant and animal domestication. Nature 418, 700–707.

Dippel, Christian, 2011. Coexistence, Forced Coexistence and Economic Development: Evidence from Native American Reservations. University of California Los Angeles, Mimeo.

Dittmar, Jeremiah E., 2011. Information technology and economic change: the impact of the printing press. Quarterly Journal of Economics 126 (3), 1133–1172.

Dittmar, Jeremiah E., 2012. The Welfare Impact of a New Good: The Printed Book. American University, Mimeo.

Durante, Ruben, 2010. Risk, Cooperation and the Economic Origins of Social Trust: An Empirical Investigation. Science Po, Mimeo.

Easterly, William, Levine, Ross, 2003. Tropics, germs and crops: how endowments influence economic development. Journal of Monetary Economics 50, 3–39.

Easterly, William, Levine, Ross, 2012. The European Origins of Economic Development. NBER Working Paper 18162.

Ehret, Christopher, forthcoming. Africa in world history before c. 1440. In: Akyeampong, Emmanuel, Bates, Robert H., Nunn, Nathan, Robinson, James A. (Eds.), Africa's Development in Historical Perspective, Cambridge University Press, Cambridge, (Chapter 2).

Engerman, Stanley L., Sokoloff, Kenneth L., 1997. Factor endowments, institutions, and differential paths of growth among new world economies: a view from economic historians of the United States. In: Harber, Stephen (Ed.), How Latin America Fell Behind, Stanford University Press, Stanford, pp. 260–304.

Engerman, Stanley L., Sokoloff, Kenneth L., 2002. Factor Endowments, Inequality, and Paths of Development Among New World Economies, Working Paper 9259, National Bureau of Economic Research.

Engerman, Stanley L., Sokoloff, Kenneth L., 2005. The evolution of suffrage institutions in the Americas. Journal of Economic History 65, 891–921.

Fairbank, John King, 1953. Trade and Diplomacy on the China Coast, 1842–1854. Harvard University Press, Cambridge.

Feir, Donna, 2013. The Long Term Effects of Indian Residential Schools on Human and Cultural Capital. University of British Columbia, Mimeo.

Fenske, James, 2011. Ecology, Trade and States in Pre-Colonial Africa. Oxford University, Mimeo.

Fenske, James, 2012. African Polygamy: Past and Present. Oxford University, Mimeo.

Fenske, James, Kala, Namrata, 2013. Climate, Ecosystem Resilience and the Slave Trade. CEPR Discussion Paper 9449.

Feyrer, James D., Sacerdote, Bruce, 2009. Colonialism and modern income: islands as natural experiments. Review of Economics and Statistics 91 (2), 245–262.

Fischer, David Hackett, 1989. Albion's Seed: Four British Folkways in America. Oxford University Press, New York.

Gennaioli, Nicola, Rainer, Ilia, 2007. The modern impact of precolonial centralization in Africa. Journal of Economic Growth 12 (3), 185–234.

Gimbutas, Marija, 2007. The Goddesses and Gods of Old Europe: Myths and Cult Images. University of California Press, Berkeley.

Glaeser, Edward L., Porta, Rafael La, Lopez-De-Silanes, Florencio, Shleifer, Andrei, 2004. Do institutions cause growth? Journal of Economic Growth 9, 271–303.

Greif, Avner, 1993. Contract enforceability and economic institutions in early trade: the Maghribi Traders' coalition. American Economic Review 83 (3), 525–548.

Greif, Avner, 1994. Cultural beliefs and the organization of society: a historical and theoretical reflection on collectivist and individualist societies. Journal of Political Economy 102 (5), 912–950.

Grennes, Thomas, 2007. The columbian exchange and the reversal of fortune. Cato Journal 27 (1), 91–107.

Grosjean, Pauline, 2011a. A History of Violence: The Culture of Honor as a Determinant of Homicide in the US South. University of New South Wales, Mimeo.

Grosjean, Pauline, 2011b. The weight of history on European cultural integration: a gravity approach. American Economic Review Papers and Proceedings 101 (3), 504–508.

Guiso, Luigi, Sapienza, Paola, Zingales, Luigi, 2008. Long-Term Persistence, Mimeo.

Haber, Stephen, Menaldo, Victor, 2010. Rainfall and Democracy. Stanford University, Mimeo.

Hansen, Casper Worm, Jensen, Peter Sandholt, Skovsgaard, Christian, 2012. Gender Roles and Agricultural History: The Neolithic Inheritance. Aarhus University, Mimeo.

Hersch, Jonathan, Voth, Hans-Joachim, 2009. Sweet Diversity: Colonial Goods and the Rise of European Living Standards after 1492. Universitat Pompeu Fabra, Mimeo.

Heywood, Linda, 2009. Slavery and its transformation in the kingdom of Kongo: 1491–1800. Journal of African History 21, 1–22.

Hodder, Ian, January 2005. Women and men at Çatalhöyük. Scientific American 15, 34–41.

Huillery, Elise, 2009. History matters: the long-term impact of colonial public investments in French West Africa. American Economic Journal: Applied Economics 1 (2), 176–215.

Huillery, Elise, 2011. The impact of european settlement within French West Africa: did pre-colonial prosperous areas fall behind? Journal of African Economies 20 (2), 263–311.

Inikori, Joseph E., 2000. Africa and the trans-atlantic slave trade. In: Falola, Toyin (Ed.), Africa Volume I: African History Before 1885, Carolina Academic Press, North Carolina, pp. 389–412.

Inikori, Joseph E., 2002. Africans and the Industrial Revolution in England: A Study in International Trade and Economic Development. Cambridge University Press, Cambridge.

Inikori, Joseph E., 2003. The struggle against the trans-atlantic slave trade. In: Diouf, A. (Ed.), Fighting the Slave Trade: West African Strategies, Ohio University Press, Athens, Ohio, pp. 170–198.

Iyer, Lakshmi, 2010. Direct versus indirect colonial rule in India: long-term consequences. Review of Economics and Statistics 92 (4), 693–713.

Iyigun, Murat, 2008. Luther and Suleyman. Quarterly Journal of Economics 123 (4), 1465–1494.

Jancec, Matija, 2012. Do Less Stable Borders Lead to Lower Levels of Political Trust? Empirical Evidence from Eastern Europe. University of Maryland at College Park, Mimeo.

Jha, Saumitra, 2008. Trade, Institutions and Religious Tolerance: Evidence from India. Stanford University, Mimeo.

Jia, Ruixue, forthcoming. The legacies of forced freedom: China's treaty ports. Review of Economics and Statistics.

Jia, Ruixue, forthcoming. Weather shocks, sweet potatoes and peasant revolts in historical China. Economic Journal.

Lal, R., Reicosky, D.C., Hanson, J.D., 2007. Evolution of the plow over 10,000 Years and the rationale for no-till farming. Soil and Tillage Research 93 (1), 1–12.

La Porta, Rafael, Lopez-de-Silanes, Florencio, Shleifer, Andrei, Vishny, Robert, 1997. Legal determinants of external finance. Journal of Finance 52, 1131–1150.

La Porta, Rafael, Lopez-de-Silanes, Florencio, Shleifer, Andrei, Vishny, Robert, 1998. Law and finance. Journal of Political Economy 106, 1113–1155.

Liebowitz, S.J., Margolis, Stephen E., 1990. The fable of the keys. Journal of Law and Economics 33 (1), 1–25.

Mamdani, Mahmood, 2001. When victims become killers: colonialism, nativism, and genocide in Rwanda. Princeton University Press, Princeton, N.J.

Mann, Charles C., 2011. 1493: Uncovering the New World Columbus Created. Alfred A. Knopf, New York.

Mehlum, Halvor, Moene, Karl, Torvik, Ragnar, 2003. Predator or prey? parasitic enterprises in economic development. European Economic Review 47, 275–294.

Michalopoulos, Stelios, 2012. The origins of ethnolinguistic diversity. American Economic Review 102 (4), 1508–1539.

Michalopoulos, Stelios, Pappaioannou, Elias, 2011. The Long-Run Effects of the Scramble for Africa, NBER Working Paper 17620.

Michalopoulos, Stelios, Pappaioannou, Elias, 2013. Pre-colonial ethnic institutions and contemporary African development. Econometrica 81 (1), 113–152.

Miguel, Edward, Roland, Gérard, 2011. The long run impact of bombing Vietnam. Journal of Development Economics 96 (1), 1–15.

Mokyr, Joel, 2008. The institutional origins of the industrial revolution. In: Helpman, Elhanan (Ed.), Institutions and Economic Performance, Harvard University Press, Cambridge, MA, 64–119.

Murdock, George Peter, 1959. Africa: Its Peoples and Their Cultural History. McGraw-Hill Book Company, New York.

Murphy, Kevin M., Shleifer, Andrei, Vishny, Robert W., 1993. Why is rent-seeking so costly to growth. American Economic Review Papers and Proceedings 83 (2), 409–414.

Naritomi, Joana, Soares, Rodrigo R., Assuncao, Juliano J., 2012. Institutional development and colonial heritage within Brazil. Journal of Economic History 72 (2), 393–422.

Nisbett, Richard E., Cohen, Dov, 1996. Culture of Honor: The Psychology of Violence in the South. Westview Press, Boulder.

Nunn, Nathan, 2007. Historical legacies: a model linking Africa's past to its current underdevelopment. Journal of Development Economics 83 (1), 157–175.

Nunn, Nathan, 2008a. The long-term effects of Africa's slave trades. Quarterly Journal of Economics 123 (1), 139–176.

Nunn, Nathan, 2008b. Slavery, inequality, and economic development in the Americas: an examination of the Engerman-Sokoloff hypothesis. In: Helpman, Elhanan (Ed.), Institutions and Economic Performance. Harvard University Press, Cambridge, MA, 148–180.

Nunn, Nathan, 2009. The importance of history for economic development. Annual Review of Economics 1 (1), 65–92.

Nunn, Nathan, 2012. Culture and the historical process. Economic History of Developing Regions 27, 108–126.

Nunn, Nathan, Puga, Diego, February 2012. Ruggedness: the blessing of bad geography in Africa. Review of Economics and Statistics 94 (1), 20–36.

Nunn, Nathan, Qian, Nancy, May 2010. The columbian exchange: a history of disease, food, and ideas. Journal of Economic Perspectives 24 (2), 163–188.

Nunn, Nathan, Qian, Nancy, 2011. The Potato's contribution to population and urbanization: evidence from a historical experiment. Quarterly Journal of Economics 126 (2), 593–650.

Nunn, Nathan, Trefler, Daniel, forthcoming. Domestic institutions as a source of comparative advantage. In: Gopinath, Gita, Helpman, Elhanan, Rogoff, Kenneth (Eds.), Handbook of International Economics, vol. 4, North-Holland, New York.

Nunn, Nathan, Wantchekon, Leonard, 2011. The slave trade and the origins of mistrust in Africa. American Economic Review 101 (7), 3221–3252.

Nunn, Nathan, forthcoming. Gender and missionary influence in colonial Africa. In: Akyeampong, Emmanuel, Bates, Robert, Nunn, Nathan, Robinson, James A. (Eds.), Africa's Development in Historical Perspective.

Olsson, Ola, 2004. Unbundling Ex-Colonies: A Comment on Acemoglu, Johnson, and Robinson, 2001. Goteborg University, Mimeo.

Olsson, Ola, Hibbs Jr., Douglas A., 2005. Biogeography and Long-Run Economic Development. European Economic Review 49, 909–938.

Olsson, Ola, Paik, Christopher, 2012. A Western Reversal Since the Neolithic? The Long-Run Impact of Early Agriculture. University of Gothenburg, Mimeo.

Osafo-Kwaako, Philip, 2012. Legacy of State Planning: Evidence from Villagization in Tanzania. Harvard University, Mimeo.

Peisakhin, Leonid, 2010. Living Historical Legacies: The "Why" and "How" of Institutional Persistence. Yale University, Mimeo.

Pierce, Lamar, Snyder, Jason A., 2012. Trust and Finance: Evidence from the African Slave Trade. University of California Los Angeles, Mimeo.

Puga, Diego, Trefler, Daniel, 2012. International Trade and Institutional Change: Medieval Venice's Response to Globalization. University of Toronto, Mimeo.

Putnam, Robert, Leonardi, Robert, Nanetti, Raffaella, 1993. Making Democracy Work. Simon & Schuster, New York.

Putterman, Louis, 2008. Agriculture, Diffusion an Development: Ripple Effects of the Neolithic Revolution, Economica 75, 729–748.

Putterman, Louis, Weil, David N., 2010. Post-1500 population flows and the long-run determinants of economic growth and inequality. Quarterly Journal of Economics 125 (4), 1627–1682.

Redding, Stephen J., Sturm, Daniel, Wolf, Nikolaus, 2011. History and industrial location: evidence from German airports. Review of Economics and Statistics 93 (3), 814–831.

Reid, Richard, 2013. The fragile revolution: rethinking ware and development in Africa's violent nineteenth century. In: Akyeampong, Emmanuel, Bates, Robert H., Nunn, Nathan, Robinson, James A. (Eds.), Africa's Development in Historical Perspective, Cambridge University Press, Cambridge, p. forthcoming.

Rodrik, Dani, Subramanian, Arvind, Trebbi, Francesco, 2004. Institutions rule: the primacy of institutions over geography and integration in economic development. Journal of Economic Growth 9 (2), 131–165.

Rubin, Jared, 2011. Printing and Protestants: Reforming the Economics of the Reformation. California State University, Fullerton, Mimeo.

Sokoloff, Kenneth L., Zolt, Eric M., 2007. Inequality and the evolution of institutions of taxation: evidence from the economic history of the Americas. In: Edwards, Sebastian, Esquivel, Gerardo, Márquez, Graciela (Eds.), The Decline of Latin American Economies: Growth, Institutions, and Crises, University of Chicago Press, Chicago, 83–136.

Spolaore, Enrico, Wacziarg, Romain, 2009. The diffusion of development. Quarterly Journal of Economics 124 (2), 469–529.

Spolaore, Enrico, Wacziarg, Romain, 2010. War and Relatedness. Tufts University, Mimeo.

Spolaore, Enrico, Wacziarg, Romain, forthcoming. How deep are the roots of economic development? Journal of Economic Literature.

Tabellini, Guido, 2008. The scope of cooperation: values and incentives. Quarterly Journal of Economics 123 (3), 905–950.

Tabellini, Guido, 2010. Culture and institutions: economic development in the regions of Europe. Journal of the European Economic Association 8 (4), 677–716.

Tai, En-Sai, 1918. Treaty Ports in China. Columbia University Press, New York.

Tilly, Charles, 1990. Coercion, Capital and European States, A.D. 990–1990. Blackwell Publishers, Cambridge.

Vansina, Jan, 2004. The Antecedents of Modern Rwanda: The Nyiginya Kingdom. The University of Wisconsin Press, Wisconsin.

Verdier, Thierry, Bisin, Alberto, 2000. Beyond the melting pot: cultural transmission. marriage and the evolution of ethnic and religious traits. Quarterly Journal of Economics 115, 955–988.

Verdier, Thierry, Bisin, Alberto, 2001. The economics of cultural transmission and the dynamics of preferences. Journal of Economic Theory 97, 298–319.

Voigtlaender, Nico, Voth, Hans-Joachim, 2012. Perpetuated persecution: the medieval origins of anti-semitic violence in Nazi Germany. Quarterly Journal of Economics 127 (3), 1339–1392.

Waldinger, Maria, 2012. Missionaries and Development in Mexico. London School of Economics, Mimeo.

Wang, Ke-Wen, 1998. Modern China: An Encyclopedia of History, Culture, and Nationalism. Garland Publisher, New York.

Weber, Max, 1930. The Protestant Ethic and the Spirit of Capitalism. Routledge, London.

Whatley, Warren, forthcoming. The trans-atlantic slave trade and the evolution of political authority in West Africa. In: Akyeampong, Emmanuel, Bates, Robert H., Nunn, Nathan, Robinson, James A. (Eds.), Africa's Development in Historical Perspective, Cambridge University Press, New York.

Wittfogel, Karl A., 1957. Oriental Despotism: A Comparative Study of Total Power. Yale University Press, New Haven.

Woodberry, Robert D., 2004. The Shadow of Empire: Christian Missions, Colonial Policy, and Democracy in PostColonial Societies. PhD Dissertation in Sociology, University of North Carolonia at Chapel Hill.

Woodberry, Robert D., 2012. The missionary roots of liberal democracy. American Political Science Review 106 (2), 244–174.

Zerbe, Richard O., Anderson, C. Leigh, 2001. Culture and fairness in the development of institutions in the California gold fields. Journal of Economic History 61 (1), 114–143.

CHAPTER EIGHT

# Institutions and Economic Growth in Historical Perspective

## Sheilagh Ogilvie and A.W. Carus
Faculty of Economics, University of Cambridge, United Kingdom

## Abstract

This chapter surveys the historical evidence on the role of institutions in economic growth and points out weaknesses in a number of stylized facts widely accepted in the growth literature. It shows that private-order institutions have not historically substituted for public-order ones in enabling markets to function; that parliaments representing wealth holders have not invariably been favorable for growth; and that the Glorious Revolution of 1688 in England did not mark the sudden emergence of either secure property rights or economic growth. Economic history has been used to support both the centrality and the irrelevance of secure property rights to growth, but the reason for this is conceptual vagueness. Secure property rights require much more careful analysis, distinguishing between rights of ownership, use, and transfer, and between generalized and particularized variants. Similar careful analysis would, we argue, clarify the growth effects of other institutions, including contract-enforcement mechanisms, guilds, communities, serfdom, and the family. Greater precision concerning institutional effects on growth can be achieved by developing sharper criteria of application for conventional institutional labels, endowing institutions with a scale of intensity or degree, and recognizing that the effects of each institution depend on its relationship with other components of the wider institutional system.

## Keywords

Institutions, Economic growth, Economic history, Private-order institutions, Public-order institutions, Parliaments, Property rights, Contract enforcement, Guilds, Serfdom, The family, Maghribi traders, Champagne fairs

## JEL Classification Codes

N01, N03, N04, N07, O17, P00, N05

## 8.1. INTRODUCTION

The literature on economic growth, old and new, rests on wide-ranging and often unexamined historical assumptions, which therefore raise many fundamental questions. Where and when did economies develop the threshold levels of property rights and market functioning which neoclassical growth models implicitly assume to be met (Aron, 2000)? What are the institutional origins of the asymmetries between sectors which underlie

*Handbook of Economic Growth*, Volume 2A
ISSN 1574–0684, http://dx.doi.org/10.1016/B978-0-444-53538-2.00008-3

dualistic growth models (Lewis, 1954, 1958; Ranis and Fei, 1961)? What institutional arrangements have fostered growth-favoring incentives for human capital investment and innovation in some societies and growth-inhibiting ones in others, as emphasized by endogenous growth models (Romer, 1987, 1990; Aghion and Howitt, 1992; Grossman and Helpman, 1991)? Why have institutional rules favored collective action to resist technological innovations in some societies, but not in others (Parente and Prescott, 2000, 2005)? What are the institutional arrangements that influence demographic behavior and the trade-off between quality and quantity of children in unified growth theory (Galor, 2005a,b)? How has socio-political conflict in past centuries engendered the institutions that foster or stifle economic growth (Acemoglu et al. 2005)?

Recognizing the importance of such questions, the growth literature has increasingly filled in these blanks and made explicit claims about economic history and institutions. Yet some of these claims are not, on closer examination, supported by historical evidence. Others are controversial, and must be revised in the light of what is known. Still other claims are probably right, but not for the reasons given by those who make them. In many ways, then, research in economic history has still hardly been brought to bear on the institutional sources of long-run economic growth.

No single essay could discuss all the implications of economic history regarding the effects of institutions on growth, and this one does not seek to do so either. Instead, we single out eight of the most important lessons historical research can offer economists trying to understand the relationship between institutions and growth.

One common view in the growth literature is that history shows that private-order institutions can substitute for public-order ones in enabling markets to function (North and Thomas, 1970, 1971, 1973; North, 1981; Milgrom et al. 1990; Greif, 1989, 2006c; Greif et al. 1994). Past societies are supposed to have lacked public authorities able and willing to enforce the institutional rules for economic activity, and some of the literature has come to accept the view that private-order substitutes—coalitions, networks, guilds, communities, collective reprisal systems, private judges, serfdom—successfully replaced them. Economic history does not support this view, as emerges repeatedly from the empirical research surveyed in this chapter: on the Maghribi traders and the Champagne fairs in Lesson 1, on merchant guilds in Lesson 3, on peasant communities in Lesson 4, and on serfdom in Lesson 8. Historical evidence suggests strongly that although markets are required for economies to grow, public-order institutions are necessary for markets to function.

This central role of public-order institutions in economic growth has been recognized in parts of the literature (Acemoglu et al. 2005). Parliaments manned by wealth holders are widely viewed as a major component of beneficial public-order institutions, and particular attention has been devoted to the idea that parliamentary powers increased significantly in Britain after 1688, creating the institutional preconditions for the Industrial Revolution three quarters of a century later (North and Weingast, 1989; Acemoglu et al. 2005; Acemoglu and Robinson, 2012). Lesson 2 surveys the historical evidence on

18th century European parliaments in general, and the Glorious Revolution in particular, and finds that parliaments manned by wealth holders historically have a very mixed record of supporting economic growth. Whether a strong parliament manned by wealth holders supported growth in practice depended on underlying institutional mechanisms at lower levels of politics and the economy, which influenced how wealth holders obtained wealth, how they got parliamentary representation, and how parliament could be used to further policies and institutions that fostered rather than stifling growth.

A different way in which the literature has pursued the role of public-order institutions in economic growth is by seeking to classify political as well as economic institutions according to whether they have, historically, proved favorable to growth. One part of the literature has distinguished between open-access social orders which have facilitated economic growth, and closed-access orders which have hampered it (e.g. North et al. 2006, 2009). Another approach has been to distinguish between political and economic institutions that have favored growth by being inclusive, and those that have impeded it by being extractive (e.g. Acemoglu and Robinson, 2012). Lesson 3 surveys these classification systems and suggests that greater precision can be achieved by drawing a more constrained distinction, between generalized institutions (whose rules apply uniformly to all economic agents, regardless of their identity or membership in particular groups), and particularized institutions (which apply only to a subset of agents in the economy). The explanatory potential of this distinction is explored in Lesson 3 in the context of the institutional bases for the growth in long-distance trade during the medieval and early modern Commercial Revolution, and in Lesson 5 in the context of property rights in Britain before and during the Industrial Revolution.

Property rights play an overwhelmingly important role in the entire literature on institutions and economic growth, and history has been employed in this literature in numerous ways. Historical evidence is widely used to support the view that property rights have been the single most important institutional influence on economic growth at least since medieval times (North and Thomas, 1970, 1971, 1973; North, 1981, 1989, 1991; North and Weingast, 1989; Greif et al. 1994; Acemoglu and Johnson, 2005; Acemoglu et al. 2005; Acemoglu, 2009). Other parts of the literature, by contrast, have questioned the very idea that property rights played any role at all in economic growth (Clark, 2007; McCloskey, 2010). Despite the fact that economic history has been mobilized to support both sides of this debate, historical research findings have still not been fully brought to bear on the emergence of property rights, the multiple ways in which they can affect economic growth, and their importance relative to other institutions. Lessons 4–6 address the various challenges this has created. Lesson 4 considers the view that property rights institutions are both separable from, and more important than, contracting institutions (Acemoglu and Johnson, 2005). Historical evidence casts doubt on this idea: both types of institutions involved relationships between ordinary people and rulers, and both had to improve jointly before growth could occur. Lesson 5 asks why property rights are supposed to be good for growth and what precise characteristics they must have in order to provide these benefits. Surveying the evidence for Britain before and during the Industrial Revolution, it finds that in order for property rights to support growth, they not only had to be well defined, private, and secure, but also *generalized* in the sense of applying to all agents in the economy, not just to a privileged subset. Security, however, is the feature of property rights most strongly emphasized as a key to economic growth, both historical and modern. Lesson 6 subjects security of property rights to closer analysis. Surveying the evidence for Europe since the medieval period, it finds that the security of property rights cannot be analyzed without breaking down the concept into three types—security of ownership, security of use, and security of transfer. Security on all three dimensions, the historical evidence reveals, was a matter of gradation rather than outright presence or absence. This explains why it has been possible for the economic history of medieval and early modern Europe to be used to argue both that property rights were irrelevant to economic growth and that they played a central role in causing it to take place.

Although the literature on economic growth has tended to focus on one type of institution at a time, its attempts to classify institutional regimes as favorable or harmful to growth tacitly recognize that institutions are embedded in wider institutional systems. The historical evidence surveyed in this chapter highlights the importance of analyzing not just each institution in isolation but also how it interacts with other components of the surrounding institutional system. This emerges clearly in Lesson 4 where we see how contracting and property institutions were jointly necessary to encourage economic growth during the agricultural revolution. The same importance of the institutional system as a whole emerges from the survey in Lesson 7 of historical demography, which has come to play an increasingly important role in recent literature on economic growth (Galor, 2005a,b; Acemoglu, 2009; Guinnane, 2011). Historically, it turns out that both contributory factors such as demographic responsiveness to economic signals, women's position, and human capital investment; and the over-arching relationship between demographic behavior and economic growth, resulted not from any specific type of family institution in isolation, but rather from the interaction of multiple components of the wider institutional system.

The literature on economic growth has been riven for decades by the debate about whether institutions are merely epiphenomena of more fundamental natural and geographical factors (e.g. Sachs, 2003), are efficient solutions to economic problems (e.g. North and Thomas, 1970, 1973; Greif, 2006c), or result from socio-political conflicts over distribution (e.g. Acemoglu et al. 2005; Ogilvie, 2007b). The historical institutions examined in Lesson 8 provide plentiful evidence that distributional conflicts are central, both to the development of institutions and to their impact on growth. The explanatory power of the conflict approach to institutions is illustrated particularly clearly by the institution of serfdom, which has attracted repeated attention from economists because of its impact on agricultural performance and thus on overall economic growth in the centuries before and during industrialization (Domar, 1970; North and Thomas, 1970, 1973; Acemoglu and Wolitzky, 2011; Acemoglu et al. 2011). The historical evidence on serfdom confirms the centrality of distributional conflicts to the rise, survival, and disappearance of key institutions, and provides a particularly vivid example of how the problem of the lack of a political Coase theorem must be solved in order for institutions to change. But it also shows the importance of analyzing any given institution as one component of a wider institutional system—an analytical point that reappears many times throughout the lessons that follow.

## 8.2. LESSON 1: PUBLIC-ORDER INSTITUTIONS ARE NECESSARY FOR MARKETS TO FUNCTION

Markets are necessary for economic growth, and this raises the question of what institutions are necessary for markets to function. Economic history is widely supposed to support the claim that the functioning of the market does not necessarily require public-order institutions: private-order institutions can substitute for them. This is taken to imply that modern poor economies can achieve sustained economic growth without good governments or well-functioning legal systems, since private-order substitutes have a successful historical record of sustaining growth (Helpman, 2004; Dixit, 2004, 2009; Dasgupta, 2000; World Bank, 2002). This claim is factually mistaken, as a closer look at the evidence shows.

Private-order institutions are those formed through voluntary collective action by private agents without any involvement of public authorities. Public-order institutions, by contrast, are those associated with the formal public authorities of a society—states, local governments, bureaucracies, legal systems, rulers, courts, and parliaments (Katz, 1996, 2000). A few examples apparently supporting the view that private-order institutions have a successful track record in underpinning markets have attained the status of stylized facts within the economics profession more widely, and are repeatedly cited (Aoki, 2001; Bardhan, 1996; Ba, 2001; Bernstein, 2001; Clay, 1997; Dasgupta, 2000; Dixit, 2004, 2009; Faille, 2007; McMillan and Woodruff, 2000; Miguel et al. 2005; Helpman, 2004; O'Driscoll and Hoskins, 2006; World Bank, 2002). But these examples turn out to be false or misleading. When the evidence is examined more closely, the well-known stylized facts disappear, and there is no indication that private-order institutions could by themselves provide, or ever have provided, an institutional framework for markets.

The only way to show this is to look at the evidence in detail. Since we cannot do this for every such stylized example, we delve more deeply into the two cases that are most widely cited in the literature on economic growth. The first is the case of the Jewish Maghribi traders, who are supposed to have sustained successful commercial growth over long distances between the late 10th and the early 12th century using a private-order institution called a coalition (Greif, 1989, 1993, 2012). The second is the example of the Champagne fairs in what is now northern France, which grew to be the most important European trading center from the late 12th to the late 13th century, and are supposed to have achieved this growth by ensuring contract enforcement through private judges (Milgrom et al. 1990) and community-based reprisals (Greif, 2002, 2006b,c). This section looks at these cases in some detail to demonstrate why these claims are false and cannot be used to support either theory or policy. Later lessons discuss various other institutional arrangements—serfdom, village communities, merchant guilds—which are also widely portrayed as examples of efficient private-order institutions with a track record of supporting growth, and indicate where subsequent research has cast doubt upon their empirical basis.

## 8.2.1 The Maghribi Traders

A first widely cited historical example of the supposed irrelevance of public-order institutions and the efficacy of private-order substitutes is the Maghribi traders' coalition. The Maghribi traders were a group of Jewish merchants who traded across the Muslim Mediterranean between the 10th and the 12th centuries. Everything we know about them comes from the Geniza (synagogue storeroom) in Old Cairo, the city where most of these merchants lived, so they are often called "the Geniza merchants." There is a debate between those who claim that most of the Geniza merchants came from the Maghreb (essentially the region now occupied by Tunisia and Libya) and rarely established commercial relationships with non-Maghribi Jewish traders (Greif, 1989, 1993, 2012), and others who point out that these merchants neither exclusively came from, nor solely traded in, the Maghreb (see Goldberg, 2005, 2012a,b,c; Toch, 2010; Edwards and Ogilvie, 2012a). Without prejudging this debate, here we use "Maghribi traders" since the term is established in the economics literature, although the term "Geniza merchants" is more widespread among historians.

Two influential articles have argued that these merchants formed a well-defined and cohesive coalition based on Jewish religion and family origins in the Maghreb (Greif, 1989, 1993). According to this account, these medieval Jewish merchants lacked access to effective legal institutions for monitoring and enforcing contracts. Instead, they relied on informal sanctions based on collective relationships inside an exclusive coalition. Members of the Maghribi coalition, according to this view, only used other members as commercial agents. Within this closed ethnic and religious coalition, members conveyed information about each other's misbehavior efficiently to other members, and collectively ostracized members who cheated other members. The Maghribis are supposed to have chosen this type of contracting institution both because there was no effective legal system and because they held collectivist Judaeo-Muslim cultural beliefs which contrasted with the individualistic Christian values held by the medieval Genoese merchants, who consequently chose to enforce their contracts using legal mechanisms (Greif, 1994).

The Maghribis' multilateral reputation mechanism, it is claimed, provided an effective institutional basis for the growth of long-distance trade across the Muslim Mediterranean from the late 10th to the early 12th century, and substituted for the absence of an effective legal system.

This portrayal of the medieval Maghribi traders has been widely deployed to draw lessons for modern economic growth. Some use this characterization of Judaeo-Muslim collectivism versus European individualism to argue that it is cultural differences that are central to both institutions and growth (Aoki, 2001; Mokyr, 2009). Others claim that the Maghribi traders show that economic growth does not require public legal mechanisms but can be based on private-order institutions (Clay, 1997; Faille, 2007; Greif, 1989, 2006b,c; McMillan and Woodruff, 2000; O'Driscoll and Hoskins, 2006), or that the social capital of closely knit networks can effectively support market-based economic growth (World Bank, 2002; Miguel et al. 2005). Still others incorporate this model of the Maghribi traders into their accounts of how informal, reputation-based institutions contributed to long-run productivity growth (Helpman, 2004; Dixit, 2004, 2009; Dasgupta, 2000). According to Helpman, for instance, "If we had data that allowed us to calculate TFP growth during the medieval period, we probably would have found that the institutional innovations of the Maghribi traders … led to TFP growth" (2004, pp. 118–9).

However, the empirical portrayal of the Maghribi traders' coalition (Greif, 1989, 1993, 2006c) was based on a limited number of documents, which other scholars, both earlier and later, have interpreted very differently (Goitein, 1966, 1967/1993; Stillman, 1970, 1973; Udovitch, 1977a,b; Gil, 2003, 2004a,b; Friedman, 2006; Ackerman-Lieberman, 2007; Margariti, 2007; Goldberg, 2005, 2012a,b,c; Trivellato, 2009; Toch, 2010; Edwards and Ogilvie, 2012a). The coalition model requires the Maghribi traders to have formed agency relations only with other members of their closed ethnic-religious coalition, yet a number of scholars have pointed out that the Maghribi traders transacted in open and pluralistic constellations rather than a closed or monolithic coalition (Udovitch, 1977a,b; Goldberg, 2005, 2012a,b,c; Toch, 2010). Others have noted that the surviving documents show the Maghribi traders establishing agency relations with non-Maghribi Jews and even with Muslims (Goitein, 1967/1993; Stillman, 1970, 1973; Goldberg, 2005, 2012a,b,c). The existence of business relationships with non-Maghribis shows that the Maghribi traders must have had other mechanisms for contract enforcement that did not rely on collective ostracism inside a closed coalition.

Five cases from the Geniza letters were adduced as providing evidence of the existence of a Maghribi coalition (Greif, 1989, 1993, 2012). Edwards and Ogilvie (2012a) re-analyzed these cases and found that none of them substantiated the existence of a coalition, with no case in which multilateral sanctions were imposed on any opportunistic contracting party by the collectivity of the Maghribi traders. Goldberg (2012b,c) carried out a quantitative and qualitative analysis of hundreds of commercial documents in the Geniza and did not find "any case of an individual being ostracised even after an accusation of serious misconduct spread through the business circle" (Goldberg, 2012b, p. 151). Although there was some evidence that Maghribi traders made use of reputational sanctions, these involved limited transmission of information, primarily to locations and persons directly associated with the conflicting parties. Research studies of business-men in many economies, including modern ones, find similar reputational sanctions to those observed among the Maghribi traders being used as a complement to legal sanctions (Byrne, 1930; De Roover, 1948; Macaulay, 1963; Goldthwaite, 1987; McLean and Padgett, 1997; Dahl, 1998; Gelderblom, 2003; Court, 2004; Selzer and Ewert, 2005, 2010). The use of reputation mechanisms does not imply that an economy lacks an effective legal framework for contract enforcement or is capable of growing successfully without one.

Other scholars have pointed out that the Geniza documents provide evidence of a wide array of public-order contract-enforcement mechanisms that supported contracts both among Maghribi traders and between them and other Jews and Muslims (Goitein, 1967/1993; Udovitch, 1977a,b; Gil, 2003; Goldberg, 2005, 2012a,b,c; Goitein, 1967/1993; Harbord, 2006; Goitein and Friedman, 2007; Margariti, 2007; Ackerman-Lieberman, 2007; Trivellato, 2009; Toch, 2010; Cohen, 2013). Counter to the claim that the Maghribi traders only used informal reciprocity as a basis for their business associations, with no legal forms of enterprise, the documents reveal these merchants using formal legal partnerships alongside informal business cooperation; even the latter, moreover, involved responsi-bilities that were recognized in courts of law (Udovitch, 1977a,b; Gil, 2003; Goldberg, 2005, 2012a,b,c; Harbord, 2006; Ackerman-Lieberman, 2007; Trivellato, 2009; Toch, 2010; Cohen, 2013). In a number of cases, Maghribi merchants enforced agency agreements using legal mechanisms; they avoided using the legal system to resolve disputes if possible, but they saw the advantages of a court judgment as a last resort (Goitein, 1967/1993; Gil, 2003; Goldberg, 2005, 2012a,b,c; Goitein and Friedman, 2007; Margariti, 2007; Ackerman-Lieberman, 2007; Trivellato, 2009; Cohen, 2013). This finding resembles those for many groups of merchants and businessmen in commercial societies between the Mid-dle Ages and the modern day, who typically preferred to avoid litigation if at all possible, but used it as a last resort (Gelderblom, 2003; Edwards and Ogilvie, 2008, 2012a).

Commercial divergence between Maghribi and Italian traders can be explained by the broader institutional framework the two groups faced, in which public-order institutions played an important role (Goitein, 1967/1993; Stillman, 1970; Epstein, 1996; Gil, 2004a,b; Goldberg, 2005, 2012a,b,c; Van Doosselaere, 2009; Edwards and Ogilvie, 2012a). The Maghribi traders were a Jewish minority in a Muslim-ruled polity, while Genoese mer-chants enjoyed full political rights as citizens in their own autonomous city-state. The two groups' contrasting socio-political status had inevitable repercussions for their respective economic privileges, legal entitlements, political influence, and relations with the majority population (Goitein, 1967/1993; Epstein, 1996; Goldberg, 2005, 2012a,b,c). Political and military instability increased commercial insecurity in the central Mediterranean from the mid-11th century on, which caused the Maghribi traders to reduce the geographical scope of their trade and intensify their involvement in intraregional commerce and local industry (Stillman, 1970; Gil, 2004a,b; Goldberg, 2005, 2012a,b,c). Genoese merchants, by contrast, were protected from commercial insecurity by the Genoese navy, precisely because merchants were important in the Genoese polity (Epstein, 1996;Van Doosselaere, 2009). Finally, at the beginning of the 13th century, a powerful association of Muslim merchants, the Karimis, secured privileges from the political authorities granting it an extensive legal monopoly and excluding outsiders, including Jewish traders, from many aspects of long-distance trade (Goitein, 1967/1993).

The current state of research therefore does not empirically confirm the idea that the Maghribi traders enforced contracts through a private-order coalition. The Maghribis used reputation mechanisms indistinguishable from those used by businessmen in most economies, both historical and modern, buttressed by public-order institutions including legal partnership contracts, powers of attorney, litigation in state courts, and appeals to the local and central political authorities. The broader framework of public-order institutions also played a role in the Maghribis' ability to sustain commercial growth. The Maghribi traders therefore do not support the idea that private-order institutions substituted for missing public-order ones.

## 8.2.2 The Champagne Fairs

A second historical example which is widely used in support of the idea that public-order institutions are irrelevant for growth because of the effectiveness of private-order substitutes is that of the Champagne fairs. These were a cycle of trade fairs held annually in the county of Champagne, a polity governed almost autonomously by the counts of Champagne until it was annexed by the Kingdom of France in 1285. The Champagne fairs operated as the undisputed fulcrum of international exchange in Europe from c. 1180 to c. 1300, and were central to the substantial acceleration of European trade known as the medieval Commercial Revolution (Bautier, 1953, 1970; Verlinden, 1965; Edwards and Ogilvie, 2012b).

Two well-known papers by economists have argued that the Champagne fairs achieved their success with a private-order institution substituting for public-order ones. Milgrom et al. (1990) claimed that commercial growth at this most important medieval European trading location was fostered by private law-courts intermediated by "law merchants" who enforced contracts and guaranteed property rights in trade goods and capital. An alternative account was provided by Greif (2002, 2006b,c), who claimed that the Champagne fairs were sustained by a "community responsibility system," consisting of collective reprisals between corporative groups of businessmen. Both theories are based on the assumption that there were no public-order institutions able or willing to guarantee property rights or enforce contracts in 13th-century Europe, and that this compelled businessmen to devise their own private-order institutional arrangements. These ideas are widely referred to in the economics literature, but closer scrutiny casts doubt upon their empirical basis.

### 8.2.2.1 Private Judges

Milgrom et al. (1990) argued that the medieval expansion of international trade in centers such as the Champagne fairs was made possible by private-order courts in which private judges kept records of traders' behavior. Before agreeing on any deal, a merchant would ask a private judge about the reputation of his potential trading partner. By communicating reputational status of traders on demand, the private judges enabled merchants to boycott those who had previously defaulted on contracts. The private judges are also supposed to have levied fines for misconduct, which merchants voluntarily paid because non-payment meant losing all future opportunities to trade at the Champagne fairs. Institutional arrangements combining private judges and individual merchants' reputations created incentives for all merchants to fulfill contractual obligations, even though state enforcement was absent and repeated interactions between trading partners were rare. From this portrayal of the Champagne fairs, it was concluded that international trade expanded in medieval Europe through merchants' developing "their own private code of laws," employing private judges to apply these laws, and deploying private-order sanctions against offenders—all "without the benefit of state enforcement of contracts" (Milgrom et al. 1990, p. 2).

This view of the Champagne fairs is widely accepted by economists and policy-makers, and is used to underpin far-reaching conclusions about the institutional basis for exchange in modern economies. Dixit (2004, pp. 12–13, 47–8, 98–9) mentions private judges providing enforcement to merchant customers at the Champagne fairs as an example of a well-functioning private government. Davidson and Weersink (1998) use the Champagne fairs to specify the conditions necessary for markets to function in developing economies without adequate state enforcement. Swedberg (2003, pp. 12–13), places this portrayal of private courts in medieval Champagne at the center of his view of medieval merchant law as "laying the legal foundations for modern capitalism." Richman (2004, p. 2334–5) argues that private judges at the Champagne fairs show how "coordination among a merchant community can support multilateral exchange without relying on state-sponsored courts."

Economic historians, by contrast, have pointed out for some decades that there were no private judges at the Champagne fairs. On the contrary, the Champagne fairs were supported by a rich array of public-order legal institutions, which were voluntarily utilized by international merchants (Bautier, 1953, 1970; Terrasse, 2005; Edwards and Ogilvie, 2012b). One component of these public-order legal institutions consisted of a dedicated fair court which operated throughout the duration of each fair. The fair wardens who decided the cases in this court were princely officials, not private judges. But there were also several other levels of the princely justice-system which foreign merchants used to enforce their commercial contracts—the high tribunal of the count of Champagne as the prince, the courts of the count's bailiffs, and the courts of the district provosts (Arbois de Jubainville and Pigeotte, 1859–66; Arbois de Jubainville, 1859; Bourquelot, 1839–40; Benton, 1969; Edwards and Ogilvie, 2012b). In addition, the towns in which the fairs were held operated their own municipal courts, also attracting commercial business from international merchants. Local abbeys also had the right to operate courts at the fairs, and foreign merchants made intensive use of these abbey courts (Bautier, 1953; Terrasse, 2005). The jurisdiction of the various legal tribunals which guaranteed property rights and contract enforcement at the Champagne fairs emanated not from the merchants using the fairs, but from the public authorities, since even the municipal and abbey courts operated under devolved jurisdiction granted by the rulers of Champagne. Furthermore, there is no evidence in any surviving documents relating to the Champagne fairs that any of these tribunals applied a private, merchant-generated law-code (Edwards and Ogilvie, 2012b). The Champagne fairs therefore provide no support for theories of economic growth arguing that private-order institutions can substitute for missing public-order institutions in enabling markets to function. Markets are necessary for growth, and the Champagne fairs support the view that public-order institutions are necessary for markets.

### 8.2.2.2 Community-Based Reprisals

A second set of claims concerning private-order institutions at the Champagne fairs postulated that commercial growth both at these fairs and elsewhere in medieval Europe was underpinned by collective reprisals between corporative communities of businessmen (Greif, 2002, 2006b,c). In this portrayal, public law-courts did exist in medieval Europe, but could not support economic growth because they were controlled by local interests which refused to protect foreign merchants' property rights or enforce their contracts impartially. Instead, it is claimed, a private-order institution called the community responsibility system stepped into the breach by providing incentives for local courts to supply impartial justice. According to this account, all long-distance traders were organized into communities or guilds. If a member of one community defaulted on a contract with a member of another, and the defaulter's local court did not provide compensation, the injured party's local court would impose collective reprisals on all members of the defaulter's community, incarcerating them and seizing their property to secure compensation. The defaulter's community could only avoid such sanctions by ceasing to trade with the injured party's community. If this prospect was too costly, the defaulter's community had an incentive to provide impartial justice. It is claimed that this combination of corporative justice and collective reprisals provided the institutional basis for economic growth in the early centuries of the Commercial Revolution, and that the Champagne fairs were a prime example of this private-order institution in operation. This interpretation of medieval history is used to draw wider implications for economic growth, including the claim that state involvement in contract enforcement is not a precondition for impersonal exchange (Greif, 2002, pp. 201–2; Greif, 2006b, pp. 232–4).

Two main arguments were advanced in support of the view that private-order institutions effectively substituted for missing public-order institutions in supporting economic growth at the Champagne fairs (Greif, 2002, 2006b). First, it was claimed that the Champagne fairs did not have a legal system with jurisdiction over visiting merchants. The fair authorities "relinquished legal rights over the merchants once they were there. An individual was subject to the laws of his community—represented by a consul—not the laws of the locality in which a fair was held" (Greif, 2006b, p. 227). The second claim was that enforcement of merchant contracts relied on the exclusion of defaulting debtors and all their compatriots from the fairs. This threat of collective reprisals, it was argued, made merchants' communal courts compel defaulters to fulfill their contracts (Greif, 2002, p. 185).

However, there are also serious difficulties with this second private-order theory. The rulers of Champagne did not relinquish legal rights over visiting merchants and did not ever permit them to be subject solely to the laws of their own communities. For the first 65 years during which the fairs were international trading centers (c. 1180–1245), all visiting merchants were subject to the public legal system prevailing at the fairs, which consisted of courts operated by the ruler's officials or by municipal governments and abbeys under devolved jurisdiction from the ruler (Bourquelot, 1839–40, 1865; Tardif, 1855; Arbois de Jubainville, 1859; Arbois de Jubainville and Pigeotte, 1859–66; Goldschmidt, 1891; Davidsohn, 1896–1901; Bassermann, 1911; Alengry, 1915; Chapin, 1937; Bautier, 1953, 1970; Terrasse, 2005; Edwards and Ogilvie, 2012b). In 1245, the count of Champagne issued a charter exempting a subset of visiting foreign merchants (Roman, Tuscan, Lombard, and Provençal traders visiting one of the six annual fairs) from judgment by his officials, but only by bringing them under his direct jurisdiction as ruler (Bourquelot, 1865, p. 174). The ruler of Champagne neither relinquished legal rights over visiting merchants nor left them to the jurisdiction of their own communities.

The evidence indicates that the role of merchant communities at the Champagne fairs was minimal (Bautier, 1953, 1970; Edwards and Ogilvie, 2012b). No merchants had community consuls (judges) at the fairs for the first 60 years of the fairs' international importance, from c. 1180 to c. 1240. Many important groups of merchants at the fairs never had consuls or communities at all. And even the few groups of merchants that did have community consuls in later phases of the fairs' existence (after c. 1240) could only use them for internal contract enforcement and relied on the public legal system to enforce contracts between their members and merchants of different communities (Edwards and Ogilvie, 2012b). The Champagne fairs flourished as the most important centre of international trade in Europe for 80 years with no recorded collective reprisals, which were only used, in a limited way, in the final phase of the Champagne fairs' ascendancy, after c. 1260 (Bautier, 1953, 1970).

The evidence casts doubt on the claim that collective reprisals were a private-order substitute for missing public-order institutions to enforce contracts. The reprisal system was fully integrated into the public legal system; the right of reprisal required a series of formal legal steps in public law-courts; and the enforcement of reprisals relied on state coercion (Tai, 1996, 2003a,b; Boerner and Ritschl, 2002; Ogilvie, 2011). The few merchant communities at the Champagne fairs played no observable role in implementing reprisals. Rather, reprisals were imposed and enforced by the public authorities, via the public legal system (Edwards and Ogilvie, 2012b). The economic history of the Champagne fairs does not support the idea that private-order collective reprisals underpinned economic growth in the absence of public-order institutions.

### 8.2.2.3 Public-Order Institutions and the Champagne Fairs

On the contrary, the Champagne fairs show that the policies and actions undertaken by the public authorities were crucial for the medieval Commercial Revolution (Ogilvie, 2011; Edwards and Ogilvie, 2012b). Between the mid-11th and the late 12th century, the rulers of Champagne guaranteed the property rights of all merchants at the fairs, regardless of their community affiliation (Bautier, 1953, 1970; Bourquelot, 1865). From as early as 1148, the counts of Champagne undertook deliberate and comprehensive action to ensure property rights and personal security for merchants traveling to and from the fairs, and were unusual among medieval fair-authorities in devoting considerable political and military resources to extending such guarantees beyond their territorial boundaries (Bautier, 1953; Laurent, 1935). The counts of Champagne also ensured that the persons and property of visiting merchants were secure at the fairs themselves, enforcing property rights through their own law-courts, employing their own officials to police the streets, and cooperating with municipal and ecclesiastical officials to guarantee security in the fair towns (Bourquelot, 1839–40; Bourquelot, 1865; Laurent, 1935; Terrasse, 2005).

As already mentioned, the public authorities also provided legal contract enforcement at the fairs. The counts of Champagne operated a multitiered system of public law-courts which judged lawsuits and officially witnessed contracts with a view to subsequent enforcement. Cases involving foreign merchants were adjudicated at most levels of this public legal system (Arbois de Jubainville and Pigeotte, 1859–66; Arbois de Jubainville, 1859; Bourquelot, 1839–40; Benton, 1969). By the 1170s, the counts had supplemented ordinary public legal provision at the fairs by appointing the fair-wardens mentioned earlier, who were public officials (Goldschmidt, 1891). Public alternatives to the princely court system also existed, strengthening contract enforcement, since jurisdictional competition created incentives for courts to provide impartial judgments. Three of the Champagne fair towns operated municipal courts which had the right to judge commercial conflicts, derived most of their revenues from doing so, and successfully attracted litigation from international merchants (Bourquelot, 1865; Bautier, 1953; Arbois de Jubainville, 1859; Tardif, 1855; Terrasse, 2005). The church provided an additional set of public law-courts offering contract enforcement to merchants at the fairs, and successfully competed with princely and municipal law-courts in doing so (Bautier, 1953).

The state, in the shape of the counts of Champagne and their administrators, also contributed to the fairs' success institutionally by providing infrastructure and loan guarantees (Bautier, 1953; Bourquelot, 1865; Edwards and Ogilvie, 2012b). The counts built fortifications around the fair towns, roads connecting them, canals from the Seine into the fair town of Troyes, and large buildings to expand accommodation for visiting merchants. They granted tax breaks to other organizations, especially ecclesiastical ones, as incentives for them to provide infrastructure for merchants in the form of accommodation, warehousing, and selling space. The counts encouraged investment in fair infrastructure by granting burghers in the fair towns secure private property rights and free rights to transact in real property (Terrasse, 2005). The counts of Champagne further facilitated the development of the fairs as money markets by guaranteeing loans which merchants made at the fairs to creditors from whom obtaining payment might otherwise be difficult because of high status or privileged legal position—i.e. as rulers they insured lenders against elite confiscation (Bassermann, 1911; Schönfelder, 1988).

Finally, the counts of Champagne created a good institutional environment for commercial growth in their territory by what they did *not* do: they refrained from granting legal privileges to local merchants or other elites that discriminated against foreign merchants (Chapin, 1937; Edwards and Ogilvie, 2012b). Initially, this may have been because the four Champagne fair towns were not great centers of international trade before the fairs arose, and thus did not have powerful, institutionally entrenched guilds of indigenous merchants lobbying for privileges. Then the fairs made the counts wealthy, freeing them from the need to sell privileges to the fair towns and their elites in order to finance princely spending. But the counts also resisted the temptation to sell privileges to special interests, even though these would have brought them short-term gains at the expense of long-term growth. Under the counts, therefore, the Champagne fairs offered the combination of a continuous international trading forum with no institutional discrimination for or against any group of merchants, a combination nearly unique in 13th-century Europe (Alengry, 1915; Chapin, 1937).

The counts of Champagne provide clear evidence of the importance of the political authorities in providing the minimal requirements for market-based economic activity to flourish. They guaranteed personal safety, secure private property rights, and contract enforcement; they built infrastructure, they regulated weights and measures; they supported foreign merchant lenders against politically powerful debtors; and they ensured equal treatment of foreign merchants and locals. The distinguishing characteristic of all these institutional rules was that the counts established them not as particularized privileges granted to specific merchant guilds or communities, but rather as generalized institutional guarantees issued "to all merchants, all merchandise, and all manner of persons coming to the fair" (Alengry, 1915, p. 38). These institutional rules were then maintained and extended by each count in the interests of protecting "his fairs" as a piece of property that delivered a valuable stream of revenues. During this period, from c. 1180 to c. 1300, the Champagne fairs became the fulcrum of European trade, and public-order institutions played a major role in the economic growth that ensued.

But the centrality of public-order institutions to economic growth is a two-edged sword: good public-order institutions can contribute to growth, but bad public-order institutions can harm it. The Champagne fairs provide a clear case of this proposition in action. In 1285, Champagne was annexed by the French crown (Alengry, 1915; Bautier, 1953). The French regime that took over the Champagne fairs gradually ceased to provide the generalized institutional mechanisms that had attracted and sustained international trade since c. 1180 (Laurent, 1935; Bautier, 1953; Strayer, 1980; Boutaric, 1867; Schulte, 1900; Edwards and Ogilvie, 2012b). Security of private property rights, contract enforcement, and access to commercial infrastructure were no longer guaranteed as generalized rules applicable to everyone, but rather became particularized privileges offered (and denied) to specific merchant groups in order to serve the short-term interests of French royal policy. The new public authorities in charge of the fairs no longer guaranteed a level playing-field to all merchants—domestic or foreign, allied or non-allied—but rather granted privileges that favored some groups and discriminated against others (Alengry, 1915; Bourquelot, 1865; Strayer, 1969; Laurent, 1935). The French crown began to tax and coerce particular groups of merchants to serve its fiscal, military, and political ends. By the late 1290s, long-distance trade was deserting Champagne and moving to centers such as Bruges in the southern Netherlands where property rights and contract enforcement were more impartially provided (Schulte, 1900; Bautier, 1953; Munro, 2001; Edwards and Ogilvie, 2012b). The Champagne fairs succeeded as long as the public authorities provided generalized institutional mechanisms applicable to all traders; they declined when the regime switched to particularized institutional privileges which discriminated in favor of (and against) specific groups of merchants (Munro, 1999, 2001; Ogilvie, 2011; Edwards and Ogilvie, 2012b). The Champagne fairs show clearly that by the time of the medieval Commercial Revolution, the policies and actions undertaken by the public authorities were already crucial to economic growth—for good or ill.

What do these findings imply for economic growth more widely? Private-order institutions do not, as is sometimes assumed, have a historical track record of supporting growth by substituting for public-order institutions in guaranteeing property rights or enforcing contracts. This does not exclude a role for private-order institutions in growth, but this role appears to consist in complementing public-order institutions, not substituting for them. For centuries, the public authorities have played a central role in defining the institutional rules of the game for economic activity, for good or ill. There is no historical evidence that private-order institutions have been able to guarantee property rights or enforce contracts independently. This does not mean, however, that public-order institutions always exercise a beneficial impact on economic growth. Public-order institutions that are impartial and generalized are necessary for markets to function. But public-order institutions that are partial and particularized not only fail to support growth but may actively stifle it.

## 8.3. LESSON 2: STRONG PARLIAMENTS DO NOT GUARANTEE ECONOMIC SUCCESS

This places the spotlight squarely on public-order institutions. As the Champagne fairs show, the public authorities matter for growth, for good or ill. But what characteristics of public-order institutions are good for growth? An idea that has gained considerable traction in the growth literature is that economic growth requires strong parliamentary institutions representing the interests of wealth holders (North and Weingast, 1989; Acemoglu et al. 2005; Acemoglu and Robinson, 2012). For modern poor countries, this implies that strengthening parliaments will ensure the institutional basis for economic success. These are attractive arguments, since there are reasons for believing that representative government is a good thing for its own sake. But does economic history support the idea that strong parliaments are invariably beneficial for economic growth?

This idea was first proposed by North and Weingast (1989), who argued that the Glorious Revolution of 1688 strengthened the English parliament in ways that produced institutions favorable to economic growth. The case of England after 1688, they claimed, provided strong historical support for two theoretical arguments concerning why parliaments are good for growth. First, they argued, a parliament possesses an inherently greater diversity of views than a monarchical government, increasing the costs for special-interest groups of engaging in rent-seeking to secure state regulations favorable to their interests but harmful to wider economic growth (for the initial elaboration of this view, see Ekelund and Tollison (1981, p. 149)). Second, a parliament that represents wealth holders will be one that enforces their interests, which are assumed to include secure private property rights and resistance to rent-seeking by special-interest groups (North and Weingast, 1989, p. 804). Although North and Weingast did not precisely define "wealth holders," their account of 18th-century England portrayed this group as including large landowners, merchants, industrialists, and state creditors (North and Weingast, 1989, pp. 810–12, 815, 817–18). The enhanced influence of these wealth holders via greater parliamentary control over the executive after 1688 is supposed to have caused secure private property rights to emerge for the first time in any society in history and ensured that the economy grew faster and industrialized earlier in England than in comparable Western European societies such as France (North and Weingast, 1989, pp. 830–1). These arguments have influenced the growth literature by apparently providing historical support for the idea that politically inclusive bodies such as parliaments create institutions favorable to growth. In one recent formulation, "the reason that Britain is richer than Egypt is because in 1688,

Britain (or England to be exact) had a revolution that transformed the politics and thus the economics of the nation" (Acemoglu and Robinson, 2012, p. 4).

Attractive though these ideas seem, there are both theoretical and empirical problems with them. The theoretical problem is that there is no reason to believe that wealth holders such as large landowners, merchants, or industrialists will necessarily seek policies and institutions that are beneficial for the growth of the whole economy. They may instead seek to establish policies and institutions that benefit themselves, regardless of whether those harm growth. The empirical problem is that historical evidence drawn from a wider sample of economies provides at best mixed support for the idea that control over rulers by parliaments, even when those parliaments represented wealth holders, ensured the creation of favorable property rights, suppressed rent-seeking, or brought about successful economic growth.

## 8.3.1 Did Strong Parliaments Always Create Good Institutions for Growth?

There were a number of early modern European economies which, like England, had powerful parliaments that were manned by wealth holders, exercised considerable control over the executive, and strongly influenced economic policy, but created institutions and policies that did not favor economic growth.

One example is Poland, a territory well known for the strength of its parliament (the *Sejm*), which was so strong that no ruler of Poland was able to promulgate any legislation or implement any policy without parliamentary consent (Czapliński, 1985; Mączak, 1997; Czaja, 2009). The Polish parliament represented wealth holders, who were made up of the large noble landowners, a group also strongly represented in the English parliament. But the wealth holders represented in the Polish parliament did not manifest a natural diversity of views (Mączak, 1997; McLean, 2004). Rather, they manifested a very homogeneous view, namely that the power of the state should be deployed wherever possible to enforce their own legal privileges over factor and product markets under the second serfdom (Kaminski, 1975; Kula, 1976; Mączak, 1997; Frost, 2006). This gave rise to economic policies that were harmful for economic growth, in two ways. First, the Polish parliament prevented the implementation of many economic policies that were feasible in an early modern European economy and that would have created good incentives for economic agents in the country at large to allocate resources efficiently and undertake productive investments (Topolski, 1974; Kula, 1976; Guzowski, 2013). Second, the Polish parliament successfully promoted economic policies that benefited particular groups in society, specifically the large noble landowners (*szlachta*) who were disproportionately represented in parliament (Kaminski, 1975; Kula, 1976; Mączak, 1997; Frost, 2006).

From the 16th through to the 19th century, Poland was subject to the second serfdom. As we shall see in greater detail in Lesson 8, serfdom was an institutional system that endowed landlords with coercive legal privileges over the economic choices of the vast mass of the rural population and over the operation of factor and product markets in agriculture (Topolski, 1974; Kaminski, 1975; Kula, 1976). Agriculture was the largest sector in all pre-industrial economies, and serfdom constrained agricultural growth. One result of the second serfdom was that per capita GDP was much lower, and grew much more slowly, in Eastern than in Western Europe between c. 1000 and the abolition of serfdom in the later 18th or the early 19th century (Brenner, 1976; Ogilvie, 2013b). The intensity of the second serfdom and its deleterious effects on economic growth varied considerably across Eastern-Central and Eastern Europe, and the balance of power between rulers and parliamentary bodies played a major role in this variation (Brenner, 1976; Harnisch, 1986, 1994; Cerman, 2012; Ogilvie, 2013b). The second serfdom was typically less restrictive in those societies in which the ruler had more power relative to the parliament, since this enabled the ruler to resist extremes of rent-seeking by the noble landowners who were primarily represented in parliaments in those countries (Ogilvie, 2013b; Harnisch, 1986, 1989b). Those Eastern European societies, such as Poland or Mecklenburg, which had very strong parliamentary organs representing the interests of wealth holders, were also those in which the second serfdom was most oppressive and economic growth most stifled, although the existence and direction of a causal connection between strong parliaments and strong second serfdom has not been definitively established (Harnisch, 1986, 1989b; Mączak, 1997; Cerman, 2008, 2012; Ogilvie, 2013b).

The lesson for economic growth is clear. In societies in which the wider institutional system endowed wealth holders with coercive privileges giving them large economic rents, these wealth holders used those rents to obtain representation in parliament. They then used their control over parliament to intensify their own privileges in such a way as to redistribute more wealth toward themselves, even at the expense of the rest of the economy. Under such circumstances, parliamentary control over the executive choked off growth rather than encouraging it.

It might be argued that the problem with the early modern Polish parliament was that the wealth holders it represented were landowners alone, rather than also including the merchants and industrialists emphasized by North and Weingast, and hence that Poland is not a fair test of their theory. But a second example of a European polity with strong parliamentary control over the executive, the German state of Württemberg, is not subject to this objection. Württemberg was a highly democratic German state with strong parliamentary influence over the sovereign from the late 15th century through to the 19th century (Grube, 1954, 1957, 1974; Carsten, 1959; Vann, 1984; Ogilvie, 1999). So widely recognized was the influence of the Württemberg parliament over the crown and the executive arm of government that Charles James Fox famously remarked that there were only two constitutions in Europe, that of Britain and that of Württemberg (Anon. 1818, p. 340). Württemberg also lacked an indigenous landholding nobility, so its parliament was manned almost completely by bourgeois representatives, consisting of substantial businessmen—those active in commerce and industry—selected by the communities of the c. 60 administrative districts from among their own citizenry (Vann, 1984; Ogilvie, 1997, 1999). Thus, Württemberg was a polity with a strong parliament representing bourgeois wealth holders drawn primarily from industrial and commercial occupations, and these parliamentary representatives exercised unusually strong influence over state economic policies (Vann, 1984). But the policies favored by the Württemberg parliament consisted of granting legal monopolies and other exclusive privileges to special-interest groups such as craft guilds, retailers' guilds, and cartellistic companies of merchants and industrial producers (Troeltsch, 1897; Gysin, 1989; Flik, 1990; Dormois, 1994; Medick, 1996; Ogilvie, 1997, 1999, 2004a). So ubiquitous were such privileges, even in the most highly commercialized sectors of the economy, that the Göttingen professor Meiners (1794, p. 292) described how in Württemberg external trade "is constantly made more difficult by the form which it has taken for a long time. The greatest share of trade and manufactures are in the hands of closed and for the most part privileged companies." The entrenched institutional privileges of these traditional interest groups represented in a strong parliament contributed to the stagnation of the Württemberg economy through-out the entire early modern period and its late industrialization compared even to other German territories (Boelcke, 1973, 1984; Schomerus, 1977; Gysin, 1989; Hippel, 1992; Twarog, 1997; Fliegauf, 2007; Burkhardt, 2012; Kollmer-von Oheimb-Loup, 2012).

Again, the lesson for economic growth is clear. The underlying institutions of a society influence whether a strong parliament will foster or stifle growth, since it is they that influ-ence the mechanisms both for becoming wealthy and for getting into parliament, as well as the policies deemed desirable by parliamentary representatives. Strong control over the executive by a parliament manned by wealth holders, even those recruited from industry and commerce, will only encourage growth if the wealth holders in question regard it as in their interest to promote generalized institutional arrangements that benefit the growth of the entire economy rather than particularized institutions that redistribute wealth to themselves. The historical evidence shows that there is no guarantee that they will do so.

More autocratic German states provide a striking contrast to parliamentary Württemberg and cast further doubt on the general validity of the idea that influence over the executive by strong parliaments manned by business interests will inevitably give rise to economic policies that encourage growth. In German states such as Prussia, the sovereign was much stronger relative to the parliament than in Württemberg (Carsten, 1950, 1959; Feuchtwanger, 1970; Koch, 1990; Clark, 2006; Wheeler, 2011). As a result, by the early 19th century the executive arm of government in Prussia became strong enough to withstand much more of the rent-seeking pressure exerted by parliaments manned by representatives of wealth holders. Instead, the Prussian rulers were able to ram through institutional reforms which weakened the privileges of guilds, municipal corporations, and village communities (Rosenberg, 1958; Tipton, 1976; Brophy, 1995; Wheeler, 2011). Prussia abolished its guilds after c. 1808, while Württemberg retained them until 1864. The Prussian state even became strong enough after c. 1808 to abolish serfdom and gradually to restrict many other market-distorting institutional privileges enjoyed by both noble landlords and peasant communes (Schmoller, 1888; Henderson, 1961a,b,c; Tipton, 1976; Sperber, 1985). These state infringements on traditional institutional privileges were not possible in more democratic German territories such as Württemberg, where, although serfdom never existed in the east-Elbian form, the powers of communities over agriculture, guilds over industry, and cartellistic merchant companies over commerce were maintained, with parliamentary support, to a much later date (Tipton, 1976; Schomerus, 1977; Medick, 1996; Ogilvie, 1992, 1999). The economic policies pushed through forcibly against parliamentary protest by the autocratic Prussian state abolished the regime of privileges and rents for special-interest groups, creating better (if not perfect) incentives for the economy at large (Tipton, 1976; Hohorst, 1977). The level of economic development as measured by the best available proxy—the urbanization rate—was much higher in Prussia than in Württemberg over the entire period from 1750 to 1900, and the rate of economic growth was faster in Prussia (Edwards and Ogilvie, 2013).

The Dutch Republic provides a final example of a European society in which a strong parliament manned by wealth holders failed to create the institutional basis for sustained economic growth. From its foundation in 1581 to its dissolution in 1795, the United Provinces of the Netherlands was a republic governed by the States-General, a parliamentary government manned by representatives from each of the seven provinces; each province in turn was governed by the Provincial States, a provincial parliament (Blockmans, 1988; Israel, 1989; Koenigsberger, 2001). The Dutch Republic thus lacked a sovereign altogether and enjoyed parliamentary control over the executive at both the central and the provincial level. So democratic was its government that it strongly influenced the framing of the US Constitution in 1776 (Pocock, 2010). Dutch parliamentary institutions were manned not just by relatively small-scale businessmen such as those in Württemberg, but by large-scale, long-distance traders and industrialists. For the first century of its existence, the Dutch Republic was the miracle economy of early modern Europe, with high agricultural productivity, innovative industries at the forefront of technology, highly competitive global merchants, sophisticated financial markets, high living-standards, and rapid economic growth (De Vries, 1974; Israel, 1989; Bieleman, 1993, 2006, 2010; De Vries and Van der Woude, 1997). But after c. 1670, although the Dutch Republic retained its strong parliamentary institutions, its economy stagnated (De Vries and Van der Woude, 1997; Van Zanden and Van Riel, 2004).[1] This stagnation was caused at least partly by the power of entrenched business elites, whose parliamentary representation was one factor that enabled them to implement institutional arrangements that

[1] Van Zanden and Van Leeuwen (2012) present new macroeconomic estimates suggesting that the province of Holland experienced economic stagnation rather than actual decline between c. 1670 and c. 1800, but their figures refer solely to Holland, by far the most economically successful province of the Netherlands. Even for Holland, they find that industry had a near-zero growth rate between 1665 and 1800 and trade contracted at a rate of 0.13% p.a. between 1720 and 1800 (Tab. 4).

secured rents for themselves at the expense of the wider economy (Mokyr, 1974, 1980; Buyst and Mokyr, 1990; De Vries and Van der Woude, 1997; Van Zanden and Van Riel, 2004). Occupation by French Revolutionary armies enforced institutional reform in the Netherlands after c. 1795, which returned the economy to gradual economic growth, but even then the economy did not industrialize until the later 19th century, very tardily by European standards (Mokyr, 1974, 1980; Buyst and Mokyr, 1990; De Vries and Van der Woude, 1997; Van Zanden and Van Riel, 2004; Van den Heuvel and Ogilvie, 2013). The Dutch Republic thus had all the ingredients emphasized by North and Weingast (1989): executive controlled by strong parliament, parliament manned by wealth holders, wealth holders recruited from big business. But this did not prevent institutional putrefaction and stagnant economic growth after c. 1670.

The forces preventing strong representative institutions manned by wealth holders from giving rise to beneficial economic policies can be seen at work even in 18th-century England. North and Weingast (1989, p. 817) ask what prevented the English parliament from acting as abusively as the crown in passing bad economic regulations that benefited rent-seeking groups. Their answer is "the natural diversity of views in a legislature." Yet the example of other early modern European polities shows that legislatures do not always have a natural diversity of views. And the example of England itself shows that even an English style of parliament does not always pass beneficial economic policies.

Eighteenth-century British policies enforcing the ownership of and trade in slaves are one example of economic policies maintained by a parliament in order to sustain the property rights of the wealth holders whose interests it represented. This was recognized by Adam Smith, who argued (1776, Bk. IV, Ch. 7) that although slavery is both economically inefficient and morally repugnant, it is more difficult to restrict under a parliamentary form of government because slave-owners are represented in the parliamentary assembly and put pressure on magistrates to protect their property rights over their slaves.[2] Slavery, indeed, is an example of how there are types of security of private property rights which can be bad for economic growth, an argument we explore more fully in Lesson 5.

English parliamentary support for the mercantilistic regulations and military activities that defended the English colonies is another example. As early as 1817, the economist

---

[2] Smith (1776), Bk. IV, Chapter 7 ("Of Colonies"), paras. 76–77: "The law, so far as it gives some weak protection to the slave against the violence of his master, is likely to be better executed in a colony where the government is in a great measure arbitrary than in one where it is altogether free. In every country where the unfortunate law of slavery is established, the magistrate, when he protects the slave, intermeddles in some measure in the management of the private property of the master; and, in a free country, where the master is perhaps either a member of the colony assembly, or an elector of such a member, he dare not do this but with the greatest caution and circumspection. The respect which he is obliged to pay to the master renders it more difficult for him to protect the slave. …That the condition of a slave is better under an arbitrary than under a free government is, I believe, supported by the history of all ages and nations."

Jean–Baptiste Say argued that the costs of maintaining overseas colonies far outweighed the benefits. Colonialism, he argued, was sustained by means of a subsidy, mandated by the government and supported by parliament, which transferred resources from home consumers to the planter and merchant classes.[3] Some modern economic historians have also argued that the colonies cost the British economy more than they benefited it (e.g. Thomas and McCloskey, 1981), although this is contested by others who claim that colonial trade ensured the gainful use of underemployed resources (e.g. O'Brien and Engerman, 1991). O'Rourke et al. (2010) come to the conclusion that the rapid growth of world trade when mercantilist restrictions were removed in the 19th century demonstrates that in the 18th century "a regime of multilateral free trade would have been preferable to mercantilism," although they acknowledge that in a world in which other European powers were also behaving in a mercantilistic way, it may have been essential for each individual country to participate in (and win) mercantilistic conflicts. As this debate illustrates, however, 18th-century English parliamentary support for mercantilism and colonialism was a policy whose effects on the growth of the wider economy were ambiguous, while its benefits in creating rents for plantation-owners and merchants were indisputable.

Another example of an economic policy supported by the English parliament, even though it harmed the economy at large, is provided by the Corn Laws. These were a set of trade laws introduced in 1815 which imposed heavy duties on imported grain (Gash, 1961, 1972; Prest, 1977; Hilton, 1977, 2006; Ward, 2004; Schonhardt-Bailey, 2006). If it had been possible to import cheap grain, agricultural laborers, industrial workers, and manufacturers would have benefited, but landowners, whose interests were strongly represented in the British parliament, would have suffered (Fairlie, 1965, 1969; Vamplew, 1980). The Corn Laws, which increased the profits of landed wealth holders whose interests were represented in Parliament, were only abolished in 1846 under the extraordinary external pressure of harvest failure and famine in Ireland (Gash, 1961; Hilton, 1977, 2006). Even then, the abolition of the Corn Laws was widely opposed in Par-

---

[3] Say (1817), Bk. I, Ch. XIX, para. 25: "All these losses fall chiefly upon the class of home-consumers, a class of all others the most important in point of number, and deserving of attention on account of the wide diffusion of the evils of any vicious system affecting it, as well as the functions it performs in every part of the social machine, and the taxes it contributes to the public purse, wherein consists the power of the government. They may be divided into two parts; whereof the one is absorbed in the superfluous charges of raising the colonial produce, which might be got cheaper elsewhere; this is a dead loss to the consumer, without gain to any body. The other part, which is also paid by the consumer, goes to make the fortunes of West-Indian planters and merchants. The wealth thus acquired is the produce of a real tax upon the people, although, being centred in few hands, it is apt to dazzle the eyes, and be mistaken for wealth of colonial and commercial acquisition. And it is for the protection of this imaginary advantage, that almost all the wars of the eighteenth century have been undertaken, and that the European states have thought themselves obliged to keep up, at a vast expense, civil and judicial, as well as marine and military, establishments, at the opposite extremities of the globe."

liament on the grounds that repeal would weaken landed wealth holders and empower commercial interests (McCord, 1958; Hilton, 1977, 2006). Abolition required a heroic act of statesmanship by an individual political leader, Robert Peel, which ended his own political career and split his party for a generation (Gash, 1961, 1972), although it had the beneficial effect of reducing grain prices in Britain, increasing market integration across Europe, and favoring economic growth (Semmel, 1970; Peet, 1972; Williamson, 1990; Ward, 2004; Sharp and Weisdorf, 2013). The representation of wealth holders in the English parliament, therefore, did not inevitably result in the passage of economic policies that benefited the growth of the entire economy rather than enhancing the profits of powerful special-interest groups.

It may be true that the English state did not implement as many harmful economic policies favoring special-interest groups as did many continental European states. But this was already the case before 1688 (see, e.g. Archer, 1988; Ogilvie, 1999; Brewer, 1989), and was not necessarily because of the strength of the English parliament. An alternative explanation for the relative paucity of growth-stifling economic policies in early modern England is not so much parliamentary limits on the crown, but rather the absence of a paid local bureaucracy, which made it very difficult to enforce harmful economic policies even when they *were* promulgated by Parliament or executed by the Crown (Brewer, 1989). Most continental European economies experienced an earlier and more extensive growth of state regulation in the hothouse of early modern land-based warfare (Ogilvie, 1992). In these societies, the state appointed paid local personnel, enabling it to grant monopolies and other economic privileges to rent-seeking groups and to offer effective enforcement of these growth-stifling policies (Brewer and Hellmuth, 1999; Ogilvie, 1992, 1999). In England, by contrast, insofar as the Stuart monarchs had managed to put in place the innovation of a centralized administrative apparatus in the early decades of the 17th century, it was destroyed in the 1640s during the Civil War (North and Weingast, 1989, p. 818). Britain did not create a paid local bureaucracy in the 18th century and effective bureaucratic enforcement of regulations in the domestic economy did not begin until after c. 1800 (Brewer, 1989).

These historical findings do not imply that it is unimportant what economic policies a country's parliament is willing to support. Nor do they imply that it is undesirable for a parliament to represent a diversity of views, among which should be those of businessmen and property owners. But the sheer presence of a parliament that represents wealth holders and can influence the executive does not guarantee that a diversity of views will be represented or that growth-favoring economic policies will be implemented. A number of pre-modern European economies had strong parliaments that influenced the executive and were manned by wealth holders, including representatives recruited from commerce and industry. Yet these strong parliaments did not always represent a diversity of views or ensure good economic policies. On the contrary, if the wealth holders that were represented in parliament were themselves agreed that good economic policies were ones that were beneficial to themselves, parliamentary strength could entrench policies that were obstacles to wider economic growth. This is reflected in the fact that a number of European economies with strong parliaments manned by wealth holders remained extremely poor (Poland), experienced long-term stagnation (Württemberg), or moved from growth to stagnation (the Dutch Republic). This was the case whether that economy was located in Eastern Europe under the second serfdom, in Central Europe with strong corporative institutions, or in the comparatively commercialized northwest corner of the continent. The reason was that wealth holders, even ones recruited from big business, did not always know (or care) what economic policies would be best for generalized economic growth rather than their own particularized profits. As a consequence, parliaments manned by business representatives were capable of supporting policies that generated rents for special-interest groups rather than ones that created good incentives for the whole economy. North and Weingast (1989, p. 804) address this crucial issue for England by stating that "the institutional structure that evolved after 1688 did not provide incentives for Parliament to replace the Crown and itself engage in similar 'irresponsible' behavior." But this assertion does not explain what it was about the post-1688 institutional structure in England that prevented this from happening. The historical evidence shows that what matters for growth is not whether a country had a strong parliament (or a weak executive), but what that parliament (or executive) did. Even more important for growth was the underlying institutional framework of the society, which determined how people came to become wealth holders and hence which policies they sought through political action.

### 8.3.2 Was There a Discontinuity in Institutions and Growth in England after 1688?

A second test of the claim that an increase in parliamentary power in England after 1688 unleashed economic growth is provided by England alone. A more circumscribed version of the theory, after all, might argue that *something* about the style of parliament that emerged in England after 1688 was crucial for growth, even if all the other types of parliament observed in European history were not. Even for England, however, the empirical findings do not support the idea that the Glorious Revolution of 1688 marked an institutional or economic discontinuity.

Extensive parliamentary control over the crown prevailed in England long before 1688 (Goldsworthy, 1999). Since the medieval period, English monarchs had been obliged to get parliamentary consent before levying taxes (Harriss, 1975; Hartley, 1992; Hoyle, 1994). Between 1603 and c. 1642, the early Stuart monarchs (James I and Charles I) sought to restrict this longstanding parliamentary power, and this was one of the major issues underlying the English Civil War (Lambert, 1990; Braddick, 1994). This Civil War, which ended in 1651, established the precedent that the monarch could not govern without the consent of Parliament (Braddick, 1994). The monarchy was restored in 1660, and both Charles II (r. 1660–1685) and James II (r. 1685–1688) attempted to use royal prerogative to pass legislation without parliamentary consent. The Bill of Rights of 1689 explicitly declared passing a bill using royal prerogative to be illegal; but this was simply a reassertion of the English parliament's centuries-old right to veto legislation, although it did extend parliamentary authority to monitor crown spending (Goldsworthy, 1999; Harris, 2004). Although, therefore, the events of 1688 indubitably contributed to enhancing parliamentary authority over the executive, this was in large part a restatement of parliamentary controls over rulers which dated back to at least 1651, which in turn had been a reassertion of the longstanding parliamentary powers that had existed in England between the medieval period and the accession of the Stuarts in 1603 (Harrison, 1990; Goldsworthy, 1999). Only a very few of the parliamentary powers asserted in 1689 were new; most had existed for a long time; and thus the 1689 Bill of Rights must be seen as an incremental component of a longstanding evolutionary development rather than any sort of revolution in the relationship between Parliament and the executive. This casts doubt on the view that the Glorious Revolution of 1688 made a major contribution to early-18th-century economic growth, let alone to the Industrial Revolution, which only began after c. 1760 and involved relatively slow economic growth until c. 1820 (Crafts, 1987; Mokyr, 1987; Williamson, 1987; Broadberry et al. 2013).

Nor did the Glorious Revolution of 1688 mark any *economic* discontinuity. If the style of parliament that emerged in England after 1688 (whatever its features) was crucial for growth, then one should observe a discontinuity in economic growth rates in England before and after 1688. But none of the estimates for the growth rate of the English economy between 1500 and 1820 show any discontinuity around 1688. Maddison (http://www.ggdc.net/MADDISON/oriindex.htm) shows an almost stable growth rate between 1500 and 1820: if anything, growth was slightly faster during the 16th century than it was during the 17th or 18th centuries; his series shows no discontinuity around 1688. Van Zanden (2001) finds rapid growth in England in the second half of the 17th century, but slower growth in the 1700–1820 period; his series also shows no discontinuity around 1700. Broadberry et al. (2011, esp. Table 10) find high per capita GDP growth from the 1650s to the 1690s (0.69% p.a.) but much lower growth from the 1690s to the 1760s (0.27% p.a.). Murrell (2009) examines more than 50 separate data series spanning the period 1688–1701 and estimates the dates of structural breaks: he finds that the entire second half of the 17th century was a period of economic change in England, but that there was no structural break in the years following 1688. Clark (2010) proposes a different data series, which shows real GDP per capita in England hardly changing at all in the 17th century, before increasing modestly in the 18th century and growing strongly in the period 1800–1820. Clark's estimates have been questioned on several grounds, as Broadberry et al. (2011) point out, so it does not seem unreasonable to place most weight on the three broadly similar estimates of Maddison, Van Zanden, Broadberry, Campbell, Klein, Overton and Van Leeuwen. If one does so, evidence that there was a noticeable increase in growth after 1688 is conspicuous only by its absence.

Even for England, therefore, it is not possible to assign an important role to increased parliamentary power after 1688 in any explanation of economic growth or industrialization. There was no discontinuity in the growth of the English economy around 1688. This is not to deny that there may have been institutional causes of the good performance of the English economy in the early modern period. But these must have been institutional arrangements that were already causing the English economy to function well by 1500. Insofar as long-term growth had institutional sources, these resided not in sudden discontinuities but rather in the gradual development of institutional arrangements over the longer term.

What do these historical findings imply for economic growth more widely? Public-order institutions are important for markets to function, but parliaments representing business interests are not their distinguishing feature. Some economies with strong parliaments experience successful historical growth, but others stagnate or even decline, and do so partly because of institutions and policies implemented by their strong parliaments to redistribute resources toward the interests they represent. Other economies with spectacularly weak parliaments achieve successful economic growth over long historical time-spans, partly because of the weakness of those parliaments and their resulting inability to defend entrenched business interests against disruptive innovations. Historical evidence suggests the need to analyze the underlying institutions of each society which influence how wealth holders become wealthy, how they obtain parliamentary representation, and how parliamentary policy concretely affects the economic framework that fosters or stifles growth.

## 8.4. LESSON 3: THE KEY DISTINCTION IS BETWEEN GENERALIZED AND PARTICULARIZED INSTITUTIONS

Where does that leave us? Lesson 1 taught us that public-order institutions are indispensable for markets. But what exactly is it about public-order institutions that determines growth? In Lesson 2 we reviewed one of the popular answers—parliaments are what makes the difference—and rejected it. So the question remains: what features of public-order institutions influence growth? Economic history does suggest an answer to this question, but it requires that we look at institutions in a somewhat different way than is customary. Rather than looking at the high-profile aspects of government examined by political scientists and political historians, such as parliaments, rulers, power struggles, or revolutions, we focus on how institutions apply to the populations subject to them, and whether that application is uniform or varies systematically by group. When viewed in that perspective, it turns out that generalized institutions—those of more uniform application, i.e. more closely resembling a level playing field among the members of a society—are conducive to growth. Particularized institutions, on the other hand—those whose application varies sharply by group membership, and tilt the playing field in favor of some groups—hinder growth.

The literature has proposed various ways of classifying institutions according to their effects on growth. Some influential recent classification systems have made significant advances by recognizing the importance of political institutions for economic growth and incorporating historical evidence. Thus North et al. (2006, 2009) distinguish open-access social orders, which have benefited growth, and limited-access ones, which have harmed it. Along similar lines, Acemoglu and Robinson (2012) distinguish between inclusive and extractive institutions, where the inclusive systems encourage economic participation by large proportions of people, encourage people to make best use of their skills and choose their own jobs, allow people to make free choices, ensure secure private property, provide unbiased legal judgements, maintain impartial public contracting institutions, and permit entry of new businesses (Acemoglu and Robinson, 2012, pp. 74–75). The existence of inclusive economic institutions, in turn, depends on inclusive political institutions, which are defined more generally as those that are "sufficiently centralized and pluralistic," where centralization means that the state has a monopoly on legal violence and pluralism means that power is broadly distributed in society (Acemoglu and Robinson, 2012, p. 81). Extractive institutions, whether economic or political, are defined as being those that are not inclusive.

These proposed distinctions are useful: they focus on the historical influence of institutions on long-term growth, and they incorporate political and distributional aspects of such institutions. Their usefulness is limited, however, by their vagueness. Both distinctions are extremely broad and leave unclear exactly which aspects of a society's institutional system are critical from the authors' points of view. We believe that the historical research available to date permits the more precise distinction between what we call *generalized* and *particularized* institutions.

Generalized institutions are those whose rules apply uniformly to everyone in a society, regardless of their identity or their membership in particular groups, e.g. a state in which a rule of law is established to some degree, or a competitive market with free entry (Ogilvie, 2005d, 2011; Puttevils, 2009; Hillmann, 2013). The institutional rules of such states and markets apply to any economic agent impartially, without regard to any personal characteristic appertaining to the individual or the group he or she belongs to, rather than the transaction in question (Ogilvie, 2005d, 2011). The rules of particularized institutions, in contrast, apply differentially to different subsets of agents in the economy (Ogilvie, 2005d, 2011; Puttevils, 2009; Hillmann, 2013). Typically, these subsets consist of persons defined according to characteristics that have little or no *prima facie* bearing on the transaction classes in question. These characteristics may be anything, but in practice often include gender, religion, race, parentage, social stratum, group membership, or possession of specific socio-political privileges explicitly entitling their holders to distort markets in their own interest. Particularized institutions include those that favor particular castes, communities, or guilds, as well as systems of serfdom and slavery. Thus, for instance, the rules and entitlements of a medieval guild applied only to its own members, based on their possession of the specific legal privilege of membership, which in turn depended on non-economic criteria such as gender, parentage, religion, and other personal characteristics; non-members of the guild were treated completely differently (Ogilvie, 2005d, 2011). Likewise, as we shall see in Lesson 8, the rules and entitlements of serfdom applied differentially to serf overlords (who were endowed with privileged rights of property and transaction in land, labor, capital, and output), compared to serfs (whose property rights and transactions were institutionally limited). The rules of a guild or the rules of serfdom might guarantee your property rights or enforce your contracts, but only because of your particular identity, rights, and entitlements as a member of a particular subset of economic agents, defined according to transaction-unrelated criteria such as guild membership or serf status (Ogilvie, 2005d, 2011).

In real life there are, of course, no perfectly generalized institutions; even the historical states that best approximated a rule of law often permitted obvious lapses and inconsistencies. It is best to think of the distinction between generalized and particularized institutions as a continuum along which historical institutions are distributed. In addition, the mixture of generalized and particularized institutions is different in each society: this will be discussed in more detail when we consider comprehensive institutional systems in Lesson 7. Generalized and particularized institutions co-exist in all economies, in other words; but historically, those societies in which generalized institutions gradually came to predominate were those where sustained economic growth became possible.

The distinction between the two emerges as central in a number of historical examples of institutional frameworks that fostered—or stifled—long-term growth. To illuminate the precise institutional features and causal mechanisms involved, this section will analyze in detail one historical example widely referred to by economists, that of the institutional framework that fostered growth in long-distance commerce between the medieval period and the Industrial Revolution. Later sections of this chapter then develop the usefulness of this classification system in the context of property rights (Lesson 5), and in the context of serfdom (Lesson 8).

Let us begin, however, by exploring the distinction between generalized and particularized institutions in the growth of international trade. Between c. 1000 and c. 1800, there was a substantial and sustained growth of long-distance trade, first between Europe and its near abroad and after c. 1500 between Europe and other continents. A widely held view in the recent economics literature is that this Commercial Revolution was facilitated by particularized institutions called merchant guilds, corporative associations of wholesale traders (Greif et al. 1994; Greif, 2006c; Ostrom, 1998; Maggi, 1999; Taylor, 2002; Anderson, 2008; Dixit, 2009). Merchant guilds had existed since Greek and Roman antiquity, but became a salient institution in much of Europe between c. 1000 and c. 1500 (Ogilvie, 2011). Although they declined in some societies, particularly the Netherlands and England, from the 16th century on, they survived in many parts of southern, central, Scandinavian, and Eastern Europe into the 18th or early 19th centuries. New merchant guilds (and privileged merchant companies that often resembled guilds) formed in emerging sectors such as proto-industrial exporting and the intercontinental trade until around 1800. Merchant guilds also spread to European colonies, especially to Spanish America, where they were only abolished with independence in the 19th century (Woodward, 2005, 2007).

These particularized institutions thus indisputably *accompanied* the growth of trade in medieval and early modern Europe. But it has recently been urged that they *facilitated* it, by guaranteeing property rights and contract enforcement for long-distance merchants (Greif et al. 1994; Greif, 2006c; Gelderblom and Grafe, 2004; Ewert and Selzer, 2009, 2010; Volckart and Mangels, 1999). Unconvinced, other scholars remark that merchant guilds and associations had been formed by rent-seeking traders for millennia to tilt the playing field in their favor, and that it was, rather, the gradual emergence of more generalized institutional mechanisms that facilitated the growth of trade during the medieval and early modern Commercial Revolution (Boldorf, 1999, 2006, 2009; Dessí and Ogilvie, 2003, 2004; Lindberg, 2008, 2009, 2010; Ogilvie, 2011).

Private property rights are the first sphere in which the distinction between particularized and generalized institutions proves to be central in understanding the basis for commercial growth. In an influential article, Greif et al. (1994) proposed a theoretical model according to which, if merchants belonged to a merchant guild that could make credible collective threats against rulers, this guild could pressure rulers into committing themselves to refrain from attacking the property of guild members and to provide these guilded merchants with adequate levels of security against outside aggressors. This article went on to argue that this was actually why the merchant guild arose and existed in medieval Europe: it was an efficient solution to the problem of guaranteeing security of private property rights for long-distance merchants.

Closer empirical scrutiny, however, casts doubt on the idea that these particularized institutions played a positive role in guaranteeing private property rights during the Commercial Revolution. The enhancements to commercial property rights that merchant guilds might have generated in theory turn out to have been minor in practice; insofar as they existed, they accrued only to guild members, not the economy, or even a local economy, as a whole (Dessí and Ogilvie, 2003, 2004; Ogilvie, 2011, Ch. 6; Lambert and Stabel, 2005; Henn, 1999; Briys and De ter Beerst, 2006; Blondé et al. 2007; Harreld, 2004a,b). Furthermore, merchant guilds also engaged in activities which *reduced* the security of commercial property rights for others, by attacking the trade of rival merchants or lobbying their own governments to do so in order to defend their cartellistic privileges over particular wares, transaction types, and trade routes. These attacks created insecurity of private property rights which not only damaged competitors but spilled over (harmfully) to uninvolved third parties (Barbour, 1911; Katele, 1986; Pérotin-Dumon, 1991; Tai, 1996, 2003a,b; Reyerson, 2003; Ogilvie, 2011).

Historical research shows that it was generalized institutions that improved the security of private property rights during the Commercial Revolution (Lindberg, 2008, 2009,

2010; Ogilvie, 2011, Ch. 6). Princely states and urban governments provided generalized security to all merchants in those times and places at which long-distance trade expanded, as at the Champagne fairs (discussed in Lesson 1). Urban governments and rulers also organized infrastructure such as convoys, fortifications, military defence, and law and order, in order to attract merchants, including those who were not members of guilds (Byrne, 1916; Williams, 1931; Laurent, 1935; Bautier, 1953; Lane, 1963; Lopez, 1987; Doumerc, 1987; Nelson, 1996; Tai, 1996; Dotson, 1999; Stabel, 1999; Laiou, 2001; Middleton, 2005; Ogilvie, 2011; Edwards and Ogilvie, 2012b). Different European societies differed in the precise balance between particularized guarantees of property rights to privileged merchant guilds in return for favors, and generalized guarantees of property rights to all traders in the expectation of being able to tax an expanding trade. But those European polities which followed a more generalized path were those to which long-distance merchants migrated and in which they most vigorously generated gains from trade—Champagne under the counts in the 13th century; Bruges in the 14th; Antwerp in the 15th; Amsterdam in the 16th and early 17th; and London in the 17th and 18th centuries (Ogilvie, 2011; Gelderblom, 2005a, 2013). Long-distance trade expanded more successfully in those periods and locations in which the public authorities guaranteed property rights in a generalized way to all economic agents rather than in a particularized way to members of privileged guilds.

The distinction between particularized and generalized institutions also emerges as central to commercial growth in the evolution of contract enforcement. It has recently been maintained that merchant guilds were also an efficient solution to problems of consistent contract enforcement in international trade. Guild jurisdictions, it is claimed, offered better contract enforcement to merchants than public courts because they had greater commercial expertise, superior information, shared business values, and a special form of law (Milgrom et al. 1990; North, 1991; Benson, 1989). In one variant, merchant guilds are thought to have solved contract enforcement problems by using internal social capital to put pressure on members not to break contracts: if one guild member reneged on a business agreement, information would pass rapidly through the guild and other members would impose social sanctions on him for harming their collective reputation (North, 1991; Benson, 1998, 2002; Grafe and Gelderblom, 2010; Ewert and Selzer, 2009, 2010; Selzer and Ewert, 2005, 2010). In another variant of this claim, merchant guilds are held to have offered an efficient solution to contract enforcement via the kind of reprisals system discussed in Lesson 1: if a member of one guild defaulted on a contract with a member of another, the injured party's guild would impose collective reprisals on all members of the defaulter's guild, giving the latter an incentive to use internal peer pressure or guild courts to penalize the defaulter (Greif, 1997, 2002, 2004, 2006b,c; Boerner and Ritschl, 2005).

Closer empirical scrutiny, however, casts doubt on all variants of the idea that particularized provision of contract enforcement via merchant guilds played an important role in contract enforcement during the growth of long-distance trade. Guild jurisdictions were not universal, those that existed operated under devolved authority from the public legal system, guild tribunals were not capable of resolving complicated business conflicts, many guilded merchants preferred public jurisdictions, and there is no evidence that guild courts applied an autonomous merchant law (Woodward, 2005, 2007; Gelderblom, 2005b; Sachs, 2006; Ogilvie, 2011; Harreld, 2004a,b; Jacoby, 2003; Paravicini, 1992; Lambert and Stabel, 2005; Baker, 1979, 1986; Edwards and Ogilvie, 2012b; Kadens, 2012). Peer pressure left even less empirical trace, with almost no evidence that merchant guilds used it to enforce commercial contracts and several striking cases in which even the most powerful merchant guilds failed to sanction members for defaulting on contracts and had to petition the public authorities for enforcement (Ogilvie, 2011; Sachs, 2006; Gelderblom, 2005b; Ashtor, 1983).

Collective inter-guild reprisals existed, but progressively lost out to superior alternatives, the generalized institutions for commercial contract enforcement which we shall examine shortly. Inter-guild reprisals were widely disliked by medieval merchants themselves, since they harmed entire communities of long-distance merchants and increased the risks of trade for innocent third parties (Wach, 1868; Planitz, 1919; De Roover, 1963; Lloyd, 1977; Lopez, 1987; Tai, 1996; Sachs, 2006). These serious disadvantages were widely recognized by contemporaries, who sought to limit or abolish the reprisals system as soon as trade began to expand after c. 1050 (Mas-Latrie, 1866; Wach, 1868; Goldschmidt, 1891; Del Vecchio and Casanova, 1894; Planitz, 1919; Tai, 1996, 2003a,b; Volckart and Mangels, 1999; Laiou, 2001; Boerner and Ritschl, 2002; Ogilvie, 2011). When collective reprisals were invoked, they were fully embedded into the public legal system as a final stage in a series of formal steps based on consulting written records, mobilizing sureties, invoking arbitration panels, and litigating in public law-courts (Boerner and Ritschl, 2002; Ogilvie, 2011; Edwards and Ogilvie, 2012b). Collective reprisals against the communities of offenders were an ancient practice reaching back into antiquity (Dewey and Kleimola, 1970, 1984; Dewey, 1988). What was new in the medieval Commercial Revolution was the gradual and uneven attempt to circumscribe collective reprisals within formal, public legal proceedings (Mas-Latrie, 1866; Wach, 1868; Goldschmidt, 1891; Planitz, 1919; Cheyette, 1970; Lloyd, 1977; Tai, 1996, 2003a,b; O'Brien, 2002; Boerner and Ritschl, 2002; Fortunati, 2005; Sachs, 2006; Ogilvie, 2011; Edwards and Ogilvie, 2012b).

Peer pressure, reprisals, and rent-seeking corporate groups characterized all ancient and medieval trade, as far as we know, up to the beginning of the Commercial Revolution (Ogilvie, 2011). The new component in many European institutional systems, during that period, was the emergence of generalized institutions whose rules and entitlements applied to all economic agents, not just members of particular groups. A first set of these generalized mechanisms consisted of contractual instruments such as pledges, guarantorship, and cessions of credit (whereby a merchant sold or transferred his rights as creditor to a third party who was better able to enforce them). All three mechanisms were formal, generalized institutional innovations devised by business and legal professionals in the great medieval European trading centers (Szabó, 1983; Reyerson, 1985; Greve, 2001, 2007; González de Lara, 2005; Gelderblom, 2005b; Sachs, 2006). The notarial system of registering contracts in writing, depositing, and storing them, and ultimately certifying them before arbitration panels or in courts of law was another institutional innovation devised in Mediterranean trading centers at the beginning of the Commercial Revolution. Princes and churches had operated notarial systems before, but lay notaries providing services to private individuals emerged in the 11th century and supported the early Commercial Revolution in southern Europe (Doehaerd, 1941; Lopez and Raymond, 1955; Reyerson, 1985; Greve, 2000; Gelderblom, 2005b; Ogilvie, 2011). A little later, the development of municipal offices offering analogous registration, depository, and certification services for long-distance trading contracts in northwest Europe was another institutional innovation which had not been present in the early medieval period (Wach, 1868; Dollinger, 1970; Gelderblom, 2005b; Dijkman, 2007; Ogilvie, 2011). Arbitration panels manned by arbiters appointed from a broad circle of experienced lay judges and neutral merchants, whose decisions were recognized and enforced by public law-courts, constituted a further institutional innovation observable from the early years of the Commercial Revolution (Price, 1991; Epstein, 1996; Basile et al. 1998; Volckart and Mangels, 1999; Gelderblom, 2003, 2005b; Lambert and Stabel, 2005; Sachs, 2006; Aslanian, 2006; Ogilvie, 2011). Finally, if all these mechanisms failed, public law-courts operated by princes, feudal lords, religious institutions, and local municipalities competed to provide justice to international merchants in every locality and time-period in which long-distance trade expanded after c. 1050 (Baker, 1979; Reyerson, 1985; Basile et al. 1998; Boerner and Ritschl, 2002; Gelderblom, 2005b; Munzinger, 2006; Sachs, 2006; Dijkman, 2007; Harreld, 2004a,b; Ogilvie, 2011; Edwards and Ogilvie, 2012b). These generalized alternatives to the traditional patterns, many of them dating from the earliest years of the medieval Commercial Revolution, were consistently successful in promoting growth. Long-distance commerce grew in those places and time-periods in which generalized contracting institutions, provided by the market, the public legal system, the city government, and various other levels of the public authorities, began to offer acceptable contract enforcement which was open to all traders, not just members of particular privileged guilds.

The key feature of these new institutions for guaranteeing property rights and enforcing contracts was not that they were embedded in an open-access social order or that they occurred in polities with sufficient centralization and pluralism: those characteristics were sometimes present, but not always (Ogilvie, 2011, esp. Ch. 5). Rather, it was that these institutions created incentives consistent with economic growth: their rules and entitlements applied impartially to all economic agents rather than only to members of particular groups. Political variables undoubtedly influenced the balance between generalized and particularized institutions in different European societies. But strong representative institutions were neither a necessary nor a sufficient component of such socio-political factors since, as we saw in Lesson 2, representative political institutions could actually help entrench particularized economic institutions such as privileged, cartellistic groups of merchants.

In practice, a range of socio-political factors, in addition to the presence of representative institutions such as parliaments, helped shift the balance toward more generalized institutions in the economy more widely. One strand of research emphasizes the emergence of fiscal systems and financial markets freeing states from financial dependence on granting privileges to special-interest groups (Schofield, 1963, 2004; Elton, 1975; 'T Hart, 1989, 1993; 'T Hart, 1993; Hoyle, 1994; Fritschy, 2003; Davids, 2006). A second strand focuses on the importance of a highly diversified urban system in which towns did not act in concert but rather competed and limited each other's ability to secure privileges from the political authorities (Rabb, 1964; Ashton, 1967; Croft, 1973; Archer, 1988; 'T Hart, 1989; Britnell, 1991; Lis and Soly, 1996; De Vries and Van der Woude, 1997; Harreld, 2004a,b; Van Bavel and Van Zanden, 2004; Gelderblom, 2005a,b; Van Zanden and Prak, 2006; Nachbar, 2005; Price, 2006; Murrell, 2009). A third strand of research emphasizes the importance of having a variegated social structure which included prosperous, articulate and politically influential individuals who wished to engage in entrepreneurial activities but were not members of privileged interest-groups and hence were inclined to object to particularized institutions that imposed barriers to entry (Rabb, 1964; Ashton, 1967; Croft, 1973; De Vries, 1976; De Vries and Van der Woude, 1997). Some subset of these socio-political factors shifting the balance from particularized to generalized economic institutions prevailed in all those medieval and early modern European societies which experienced successful commercial growth. But after c. 1500 these factors coincided in two European polities, the Netherlands and England, where generalized institutions gained ground and where economic growth greatly accelerated (De Vries and Van der Woude, 1997; Ogilvie, 2000, 2011). Generalized and particularized institutions continued to co-exist in all early modern societies, but those where generalized institutions came to dominate enjoyed faster economic growth, not just in trade but also in agriculture and industry, as we shall see in the coming sections.

These historical findings have wider implications for economic growth, not least because of the many potential links between particularized institutions and social capital. Social capital, as is well known, typically involves building institutions whose rules and entitlements are characterized by "closure," i.e. a clear definition of who is a member of a group and who is not (see Coleman, 1988, pp. 104–10; Sobel, 2002, p. 151; Ogilvie, 2005d, 2011; Hillmann, 2013). To generate social capital, institutions need to have closure, information advantages, collective penalties, and commitment devices: that is, they need to be particularized. Once such institutions are formed, though, it is hard to prevent them from being abused to resist changes that threaten existing benefits enjoyed by members of the closed groups enjoying the benefits of closure. Economic history illuminates a darker side of social capital, insofar as it is generated by building particularized institutions whose rules apply exclusively to entrenched groups, rather than generalized institutions whose rules apply to everyone.

## 8.5. LESSON 4: PROPERTY RIGHTS INSTITUTIONS AND CONTRACTING INSTITUTIONS BOTH MATTER, AND ARE NOT SEPARABLE

Two types of institution that appear to be important for economic growth, as we have seen, are those guaranteeing private property rights and those enforcing contracts. But how precisely do they affect economic growth, and is one more important than the other? Acemoglu and Johnson (2005) have argued that these two types of institution should be strictly distinguished from one another: property rights institutions protect ordinary people against expropriation by the powerful, while contracting institutions enable private contracts between ordinary people. For these reasons, the argument continues, property rights institutions have a first-order effect on long-run economic growth, whereas contracting institutions matter much less. People can find ways of altering the terms of contracts in such a way as to avoid the adverse effects of poor contracting institutions, it is claimed, but cannot do the same against the risk of expropriation by rulers and elites (Acemoglu and Johnson, 2005).

Economic history, however, provides only mixed support for this argument. Historically, there is considerable overlap between contracting institutions and property rights institutions. Indeed, as Lessons 5 and 6 will argue, we need to pay much more analytical attention to the precise characteristics of property rights that matter for growth. But even before embarking on that analysis, the historical evidence suggests strongly that one key characteristic is the degree to which property rights can be freely transferred by contract from one person to another. When people trade, they simultaneously transfer property rights to another person and make a contract. The enforceability of the contract depends on how securely the property rights are defined, and the security of the property rights depends on whether a person is allowed to enter into contracts involving his or her property. Furthermore, rulers and elites intervene not just in property rights (e.g. by expropriating people's property) but also in contracts (e.g. by invalidating agreements, in the interest either of themselves directly or of their clients). In medieval Europe, for instance, property rights governing ownership of many assets (not just land, but also financial assets and moveable goods) were often securely guaranteed in law (Pollock and Maitland, 1895; Campbell, 2005; Clark, 2007; McCloskey, 2010). However, contracts governing transfers of these property rights were sometimes guaranteed very insecurely, particularly if they involved powerful people such as rulers, members of the elite, or people to whom rulers or elites had sold privileges (legal rights to distort markets in the purchasers' interest) (Ogilvie, 2011, 2013b). Historical evidence thus poses difficulties for the idea that one can draw a useful analytical distinction between institutions enforcing contracts and those guaranteeing property rights.

Economic history also casts doubt on the idea that poor contracting institutions do not matter because ordinary people can devise informal substitutes. As Lesson 1 discussed, the two best-known historical cases which are supposed to have demonstrated the success of informal substitutes for poor contracting institutions turn out to be factually wrong. There is no evidence that the 11th-century Maghribi traders operated an informal, private-order coalition to circumvent poor public contract enforcement. Nor is there any evidence that the 12th- and 13th-century Champagne fairs relied on private judges or community-implemented reprisals to circumvent lack of public contract enforcement. It was extremely difficult to circumvent poor contracting institutions with private-order substitutes. Instead, medieval and early modern merchants voted with their feet by moving their business from locations where public-order contract enforcement was inferior to those where it was superior (Ogilvie, 2011; Gelderblom, 2005a, 2013). Economic history does not support the view that it was easy to devise informal substitutes for poor public-order contracting institutions.

The third thing we can learn from economic history is that there are important junctures in long-term economic growth at which property institutions and contracting institutions are jointly essential, in the sense that the growth benefits of one cannot emerge until the other is present. One of the most critical of these is the European agricultural revolution. Agriculture was by far the most important sector of the pre-modern economy, and most economic historians regard a sustained increase in agricultural productivity as an important contributory factor to the European Industrial Revolution. Just such an agricultural revolution began in the Netherlands in the late 15th century, England in the late 16th, parts of France in the 18th, and various territories of German-speaking Europe at different points in the 19th (Mingay, 1963; Chorley, 1981; Bairoch, 1989; Brakensiek, 1991, 1994; Allen, 1992; Overton, 1996a,b; Campbell and Overton, 1998; Kopsidis, 2006; Olsson and Svensson, 2010). For such an increase in agricultural growth to take place, a number of institutional changes were needed—some in property institutions, others in contracting institutions. Until both sets of institutional changes took place, agriculture typically failed to grow.

Secure private property rights in land were almost certainly needed for agricultural growth, although it is important to recognize that there is debate about this issue among economic historians (Allen, 1992, 2004; Neeson, 1993; Overton, 1996a,b; Shaw-Taylor, 2001a,b). Secure private property rights in land existed in most societies in medieval and early modern Europe, as we shall see in Lesson 6. But these private property rights co-existed with and were constrained by other types of property right. The village community often collectively owned a share of the pasture, woods, and wasteland in the village, and constrained the ways in which individuals could use their privately owned arable (crop-growing) fields (Allen, 1992; Neeson, 1993; Brakensiek, 1991; Kopsidis, 2006). The importance of such communal property rights and the constraints they placed on private property rights varied considerably across pre-modern European societies, across regions within the same society, and even from one village to the next (Whittle, 1998, 2000; Campbell, 2005). They also changed over time, with communal property rights gradually being replaced by private property rights in most European societies between c. 1500 and c. 1900 (Overton, 1996a,b; Brakensiek, 1991, 1994; Olsson and Svensson, 2010).

One component of this process (which in England was called the enclosure movement) was the shift from communal to private property rights in pasture. This benefited growth not so much because it solved the tragedy of the commons (Hardin, 1968), since the whole point of community management of collective pasture was to prevent overuse (see Neeson, 1993). In England, in any case, common rights were often owned and traded privately by individuals, typically the largest farmers in the village (Shaw-Taylor, 2001a,b). Instead, the main mechanism by which privatization of common pasture encouraged agricultural growth was by reducing the transaction costs involved in flexibly shifting pasture to alternative uses, which was essential for a number of the new, higher-productivity agricultural techniques that emerged during this period (Slicher van Bath, 1963, 1977; Overton, 1996a,b).

The second component of the enclosure movement affected arable (crop-bearing) land. Typically, each European village divided up all arable land into three large tracts, which were cultivated in three-year rotation to replenish soil nutrients (Slicher van Bath, 1963, 1977; De Vries, 1976). Within each tract, each villager owned and farmed scattered strips, but the village as a whole decided on crops, rotations, and other techniques, and the whole village had collective gleaning and grazing rights on individual arable land after the harvest (Overton, 1996a,b; Brakensiek, 1991, 1994). In different European societies and regions at different dates between c. 1500 and c. 1900, these scattered, open arable strips were reorganized and consolidated to form contiguous holdings over which individuals had exclusive private property rights. This increased scale economies by reducing the time costs involved for each villager in moving from one strip to another, reduced the transaction costs of adopting new arable techniques, and increased individual incentives to invest in productivity improvements (Overton, 1996a,b).

There is considerable debate about the precise growth effects of these changes in property rights. For England, although Allen (1992) contended that such changes in property rights did not increase agricultural productivity, Overton (1996a,b) contested those arguments on grounds of inaccurate periodization, misinterpretation of evidence, and sample selection bias, concluding that improvement in private property rights decreased equity but increased productivity and contributed to faster growth of agriculture. Many German territories experienced similar improvements in agricultural property rights between c. 1770 and c. 1870, often influenced by English and Dutch models, and this German enclosure movement has evoked similar debate (Brakensiek, 1991, 1994; Kopsidis, 2006). The current consensus is that in German societies, as well, replacing communal with private property rights facilitated introducing agricultural innovations, bringing new land under cultivation, shifting lands to new uses, and increasing agricultural growth (Brakensiek, 1991, 1994; Kopsidis, 2006; Fertig, 2007). Improvements in private property rights thus almost certainly did play a role in accelerating agricultural growth.

However, improving private property rights typically did not increase agricultural productivity and growth immediately. Rather, the growth benefits only emerged in the longer term. This was because property rights institutions were not enough in themselves. To have the incentive to increase productivity, the owners of land with better property rights also had to have a reasonable expectation of getting a return for the high investments entailed in introducing innovations. This required *contracting* institutions enabling farmers to obtain the labor and capital they needed, to sell agricultural surpluses, and to purchase other goods which the newly specialized farms no longer produced themselves.

First, the agricultural revolution required contracting institutions enabling the flexible mobilization of the appropriate quantity and quality of labor into the production process (DeVries, 1974, 1976; Overton, 1996a,b; Ogilvie, 2000). The new crops and crop-rotation systems that could be introduced once property rights improved required more intense digging, ploughing, fertilizing, and weeding. Higher grain and milk yields created more work in harvesting, threshing, butter-churning, and cheese-making (Chambers, 1953; Caunce, 1997). Farmers needed to use their own family's labor more intensively and to employ plentiful and flexible supplies of non-familial labor. But contracting in labor markets was often blocked by forced labor extorted from serfs, communal barriers to labor migration, wage ceilings favoring employers, limits on women's work, and other restrictive labor practices reflecting the interests of powerful individuals and groups concerned with distributing larger shares of resources to themselves (DeVries, 1976; Harnisch, 1989a,b; Klein, 2013; Ogilvie, 2004a,b, 2013a,b). Such restrictions on contracting in labor were imposed via particularized institutions such as serfdom, village communities, urban corporations, and craft guilds, whose rules did not treat all economic agents impartially, allowing them to offer and hire labor voluntarily in competitive markets with free entry, but rather differentiated between them according to non-economic criteria such as serf status, gender, religion, ethnicity, community citizenship, and guild membership (Sharpe, 1999; Ogilvie, 1997, 2000, 2004a,b; Ulbrich, 2004; Wiesner, 1989; Wiesner-Hanks, 1996; Wiesner, 2000). Even in comparatively progressive Hanover, as late as 1820, landlords used forced labor from serfs because it was costless to them, although, as the English traveler (Hodgskin, 1820, p. 85) remarked, "If the landlord had to hire laborers, he might have his work tolerably well performed, but it is now shamefully performed, because the people who have it to do have no interest whatever in doing it well and no other wish but to perform as little as possible within the prescribed time." By contrast, in those places in which the agricultural revolution began early (Flanders, the Netherlands, and England), there were good contracting institutions in the labor market, both for farm servants and for migrant agricultural workers. This ensured that the appropriate quantity of skilled and highly motivated labor could be applied at the right intensity at the appropriate point in the agricultural year (De Vries, 1974, 1976; Van Lottum, 2011a,b; Kaal and Van Lottum, 2009; Kussmaul, 1981, 1994).

Contracting institutions governing credit—not high finance in the form of loans to elites and the state, but small investment loans to ordinary people—were also essential for agricultural growth. Changing farming practice always requires at least small investments, as shown by the focus on agricultural micro-credit in modern developing economies (World Bank, 1982) as well as studies of historical European rural economies (De Vries, 1976; Holderness, 1976). Even though the early modern agricultural revolution did not involve machines, it did require capital (Habakkuk, 1994; Holderness, 1976; Lambrecht, 2009; Thoen and Soens, 2009; Van Cruyningen, 2009; Ogilvie et al. 2012). Enclosure of pastures and open fields required fences, hedges, and ditches. New crops required seed purchases. Soil improvement required extra fertilizer, sand, lime, and marl. Heavier harvests required buying more and better draught animals. Farmers and workers had to be supported during the transition to new techniques. Good contracting institutions in the Low Countries and England made it possible for Dutch and English farmers to tap the few sources of capital available in early modern Europe (De Vries and Van der Woude, 1997; Schofield and Lambrecht, 2009). In the Netherlands, capital-rich townsmen invested directly in land and loaned funds to farmers through the country's advanced credit markets (De Vries, 1974, 1976; Van Cruyningen, 2009). In England, landlords had to make their estates pay since they enjoyed few of the privileges to intervene in contracting enjoyed by their Central or Eastern European counterparts. This gave them strong incentives to lend their tenants capital for farm improvements, or even borrow themselves for this purpose in England's financial markets, which were catching up with those of the Netherlands during the 16th and 17th centuries (Holderness, 1976; Muldrew, 1993, 1998, 2003; Spufford, 2000). Good contracting institutions meant that English grain merchants were able and willing to extend credit to farmers, and incidentally to smooth price fluctuations, by speculating on the outcome of the harvest, as described by Defoe (1727, vol. 2, p. 36): "These Corn-Factors in the Country ride about among the Farmers, and buy the Corn, even in the Barn before it is thresh'd, nay, sometimes they buy it in the Field standing, not only before it is reap'd but before it is ripe."

Elsewhere in Europe, the contracting institutions that might have ensured the supply of credit to agriculture developed more slowly. Much of the available capital in the economy was accumulated by rulers through taxes, state loans, and sales of monopolies and offices, then squandered on war or court display (Brewer, 1989; Brewer and Hellmuth, 1999). Another substantial portion of available capital was levied as rents by noble landlords, and then spent on royal offices, monopolies, or conspicuous consumption (Ogilvie, 2000). In many economies—France, Spain, Italy, and many German territories— even commercial and industrial profits tended to flow into landed estates, noble status (conferring tax freedom), bureaucratic office, or legal monopolies over certain lines of business (De Vries, 1976). In societies where the greatest returns and least risk lay in purchasing land or royal favor, poor contracting institutions meant that risky economic projects such as improvement of the land were starved of capital. In many European economies, special-interest groups enjoyed privileged access to contracting institutions governing credit, from which ordinary people, including most peasants in the countryside, were excluded; although peasants were sometimes partly able to circumvent these restrictions by using undocumented and informal lending contracts, these had higher transaction costs (Ogilvie et al. 2012). Part of the delay in introducing the new agricultural techniques outside the Netherlands and England before 1750 resulted from the difficulty of saving or borrowing the requisite capital, especially for ordinary rural people who were making the main agricultural decisions. These restrictive practices in credit markets were often imposed via particularized institutions such as serfdom, village communities, and urban corporations. To give just one example, community institutions in 17th- and 18th-century Germany disallowed loans agreed between willing lenders and willing borrowers on grounds of community membership, wealth, gender, marital status, or whether the borrower was regarded favorably by the headman or village councillors (Sabean, 1990; Ogilvie, 1997; Ogilvie et al. 2012). Restrictive practices in credit markets reflected the interests of powerful individuals and groups who were concerned with redistributing resources to themselves and who made use of favorable institutional arrangements to achieve this end.

Farmers not only needed good contracting institutions to secure the inputs of labor and capital required by new agricultural techniques. They also needed good contracting institutions in output markets so they could sell their farm surpluses profitably, and buy goods they no longer produced themselves (Britnell, 1996; Grantham and Sarget, 1997; Bolton, 2012). But many of the same institutions that hindered contracting in labor and capital also impeded exchanges of food, raw materials and industrial goods. Rulers and town governments in Spain, France, and the Italian and German states often enforced particularized institutional arrangements called "staples," legal rights of prior purchase which they used to force farmers in the surrounding countryside to sell their output in towns at lower-than-market prices (De Vries, 1976; Ogilvie, 2011). This was one of the reasons the highly urbanized regions of northern Italy and southern Germany failed to stimulate an agricultural revolution in the 16th century, in contrast to the Dutch and Flemish cities, where urban consumers had to pay farmers market prices. In Spain, grain price ceilings and other institutional restrictions on contracting in output markets drove peasants off the land, and by 1797 there were almost 1000 deserted villages in rural Castile; grain had to be imported to alleviate famine (De Vries, 1976).

The particularized privileges of towns were not the only barrier to good contracting institutions that would have enabled farmers to profit from investing in the new agricultural techniques. Seigneurial tolls (internal customs barriers) blocked the development of good contracting institutions such as a national grain market in France until 1789, discouraging farmers and worsening famines (Ó Gráda and Chevet, 2002). In Bohemia, Poland, and many eastern German territories, the great landlords forced peasants to sell them grain at fixed (below-market) prices. The landlords exported the grain to Western Europe or used it to brew their own beer in demesne breweries, which they then forced the peasants to buy back from them at fixed (above-market) prices (Cerman, 1996; Ogilvie, 2001, 2005c; Dennison and Ogilvie, 2007). Blocked by poor contracting institutions, peasants could not gain enough profit from grain surpluses for it to be worthwhile investing in new techniques, even where they enjoyed secure private property rights in their land. These restrictive practices in output markets were again often imposed by landlords, village communities, or urban corporations. In early modern Bohemia, for instance, landlords used their institutional powers under serfdom to compel peasants to sell them foodstuffs at below-market prices, penalizing them when they sold grain or livestock outside the estate without first offering it to the manor (Ogilvie, 2001, 2005c). Again, these restrictive practices in output markets reflected the distributional interests of powerful individuals and groups who were concerned with distributing resources to themselves and who made use of institutional privileges to do so.

These differences in contracting institutions thus played a major role, alongside differences in property rights institutions, in deciding whether, when and where agricultural growth could take place in Europe between the 16th and the 19th century. Agricultural growth did not need just secure private property rights. Farmers had to be able to employ laborers readily, borrow money easily, sell profitably to customers, and find cheap supplies of goods they no longer made at home. The Low Countries and England were lucky: they emerged from the medieval period with serfdom weakened or non-existent (as we shall see in Lesson 8), landlords who therefore had economic weight but few legal powers, village communities that were only loosely organized, and town privileges that were poorly enforced and constrained by competition from rival towns within a highly variegated urban system (as we saw in Lesson 3). Some particularized institutions still survived in the Low Countries and England, as we shall see in Lessons 6 and 7. But in the interstices between them, new and more generalized contracting institutions sprang up and grew vigorously in the 16th and 17th centuries, before any interest-group could organize to stop them. In most other parts of Europe, however, landlords, privileged towns, and village communities retained much more extensive rights to intervene in private contracts well into the 18th century, and in some regions long past 1800. Even the abolition of seigneurial privileges in France during the Revolution, and in Prussia and many other German territories after 1808, left many restrictive contracting institutions intact. Not until traditional contracting institutions were broken down, by popular revolution, military defeat, or long and grinding social conflict, could farmers break out of the agricultural productivity trap which had long blocked growth in the largest sector of the economy (Slicher van Bath, 1963, 1977; De Vries, 1976).

Studies of the institutional preconditions for the agricultural revolution in many parts of Europe, even outside England and the Netherlands, explicitly emphasize that improvements in property rights did not in themselves lead to growth. They only did so when they were accompanied by improvements in contracting institutions in the labor market, the credit market, and the output market. Theiller (2009) shows that the emergence of better property rights in land (as evidenced by a rental market) in late medieval Normandy was triggered by the emergence of local market centers enabling and permitting peasants to sell their agricultural surpluses. Serrão (2009) shows how the emergence of urban market demand in Portugal between the 17th and 19th centuries created incentives for farmers to adopt new technologies and invest in their farms, before the liberal reforms to property rights toward the end of that period. Olsson and Svensson (2009)'s analysis of 18th- and 19th-century Sweden shows that the volume of marketable surplus was significantly affected both by privatization of property rights during the radical Swedish enclosures of the early 19th century and by the incentives created by good contracting institutions in markets for agricultural output. For 18th- and 19th-century Germany, special emphasis is placed on the development of market structures and the removal of impediments to trade, enabling the selling of agricultural output at attractive prices and with low transaction costs (Brakensiek, 1991, 1994). Even more substantial German farmers often resisted privatization of commons for an initial period because of the high risks involved and the absence of the well-functioning markets required to secure a return on the non-trivial investments involved. As a result, the reforms to German agricultural property rights proceeded very gradually, over more than a century, from c. 1770 until c. 1890, and their pace and degree varied considerably among territories, regions, and even villages, according to the availability of good contracting institutions as well as the distributional implications of institutional change and the balance of power among state officials, landlords, peasants, and rural laborers (Brakensiek, 1994, p. 139). These findings suggest a strong degree of interlinkage not only between property rights institutions and contracting institutions, but also between both sets of institutions and distributional considerations, a point to which we return in Lessons 7 and 8.

These findings have a number of wider implications for economic growth. First, property rights institutions are not separable from contracting institutions. One measure of security of private property rights is the extent to which those property rights can be securely transferred from one person to another, as we shall see in Lesson 6. This is not a trivial or incidental feature of property rights, but rather central to one of the mechanisms by which secure private property rights can benefit growth, namely by ensuring that resources are allocated to their highest-value uses. If contracting institutions are insecure, an important aspect of how private property rights benefit growth will also be insecure.

Second, property institutions and contracting institutions are jointly essential for economic growth. To unleash the growth benefits of secure private property rights, contracting institutions also have to function well, so as to enable property-owners to save and borrow capital to invest in improving the productivity of their property, employ labor to work on that property, and profitably sell output produced using that property.

Third, it is simplistic to define property rights institutions as those protecting ordinary people against expropriation by rulers and elites and contracting institutions merely as those enabling private contracts between ordinary people. Rulers and elites intervene not just in property rights but also in contracts, refusing to enforce them in their own interests or those of favored groups to whom they have sold privileges. Both property rights institutions and contracting institutions thus involve an economic relationship between ordinary people on the one hand and rulers on the other. Economic history suggests that distributional conflicts and the coercive powers of elites and rulers have always played an important role in contracting institutions, just as they have in the security of private property rights. Poor economies could not improve contracting institutions without dealing with power and distributional conflicts.

Fourth, informal alternatives cannot substitute for poor public contract enforcement. Historically, economic growth occurred when the political authorities improved generalized contract enforcement and ceased supporting particularized interventions by special-interest groups that diminished the security of contracts. Poor economies could not achieve growth by means of informal contracting institutions; they needed to address weaknesses in public-order contract enforcement.

## 8.6. LESSON 5: PROPERTY RIGHTS ARE MORE LIKELY TO BE BENEFICIAL FOR GROWTH IF THEY ARE GENERALIZED RATHER THAN PARTICULARIZED

Property rights may not be more important than any other type of institution, but there is little doubt that they have major effects on economic growth. It is therefore tempting to regard them as unconditionally beneficial. But the term "property rights" covers a wide variety of arrangements, and historical evidence suggests that only some of these are good for economic growth.

The historical findings, in fact, require us to remind ourselves why property rights are supposed to be good for economic growth. Three answers can be given to this question (De Soto, 1989; Milgrom and Roberts, 1992; Besley and Ghatak, 2010). First, property rights can provide good incentives for assets to be allocated to their most productive uses because property rights motivate the transfer of assets to the people who value them most. Second, property rights can give owners good incentives to devise productive uses for an asset, in order to maintain or increase its value. And third, property rights can make it possible for owners to use an asset as collateral for borrowing funds, which they can use for investments (see esp. De Soto, 2000).

What characteristics do property rights have to have in order to benefit growth via these three mechanisms? One characteristic is that property rights should be well-defined, in the sense that it is clear to everyone in the economy who owns an asset, including how he or she may use it, how and to whom it may be transferred, and what kind of contracts may be concluded concerning it. Well-defined property rights are needed to induce those who value an asset greatly to be willing to pay for its transfer to them, to create good incentives for an asset's current owners to invest in it, and to ensure that an owner can use it as collateral.

A second widely emphasized characteristic is that property rights must be private, in the sense that an asset is held by an individual entity that can exclude others from using it. Private property rights, it is argued, give the individual owner good incentives to use the asset productively, invest to maintain or increase its value, and trade or lease it to other users (Besley and Ghatak, 2010).

A third characteristic is the security of property rights so widely emphasized in the literature (see North and Thomas, 1973; North, 1989, 1991). However, as we shall see in Lesson 6, security of property rights must be broken down into at least three components: security of ownership rights; security of use rights; and security of transfer rights. All three of these are important for ensuring that assets are transferred to the users who value them most, are invested in and used productively, and are available as collateral.

But it is not enough that property rights should be well defined, private, and secure (in all senses of that term). To support growth, property rights must also be generalized, a concept we defined in Lesson 3. That is, ownership, use, and transfer rights in an asset must be available to all agents in the economy, not just to a subset of them. In order for property rights to ensure that an asset passes into the hands of the person who has the highest possible value for it because he or she will use it most productively, the ownership, use, and transfer of that asset must be open to anyone, regardless of their personal characteristics or group affiliation, and transactions involving that asset must be governed by impersonal, voluntary exchange in open and competitive markets rather than by personal characteristics or coercive action. Similarly, to provide incentives to invest in the productive use of the asset, property rights will be more effective if they are generalized, since one incentive for productive use is to maintain the value of the asset with a view to transferring it or renting it to someone else in future. If property rights in that asset are particularized, and are thus restricted to being transferred or rented to a limited circle, this will reduce the incentive for the current owner to maintain its value through productive use. Likewise, the capacity for property rights to support the use of an asset as collateral for investment loans will be limited to the extent that they do not apply to all economic agents and cannot be freely transferred to all economic agents. To the extent that property rights are particularized, therefore, that characteristic will limit all three of the ways in which these rights could in principle support economic growth. Indeed, particularized property rights may positively damage growth by denying ownership, use, and transfer of assets to everyone outside the particular subset of privileged persons, which may comprise large proportions of all agents in the economy (e.g. all women, non-whites, slaves, serfs, non-nobles, non-guild members, etc.).

The possibility that well-defined, private, and secure property rights might not always support growth is occasionally mentioned in some of the literature on institutions and growth in historical perspective. North, for instance, refers to the existence of historical property rights that did not benefit growth because they "redistributed rather than increased income" (1991, p. 110). However, there has been little further analysis of the specific characteristics of property rights that might cause them to redistribute rather than increase income. The full implications of this distinction have not received sufficient emphasis in the literature, which continues to operate on the assumption that the only characteristic of property rights that matters is their security, a concept whose precise characteristics are left quite vague.

Evidence on historical property rights and historical economic growth provides numerous examples of property rights that were clearly defined, were enjoyed privately by individuals, and were perfectly secure against confiscation, but did not benefit growth because they were particularized. That is, the rules establishing and maintaining those property rights circumscribed use of a particular asset to a particular circle of people who were defined according to non-economic criteria or group membership, and limited transfers or contracts involving that asset to that restricted circle. In historical developing economies, such particularized property rights were widespread and various, so much so that they are best analyzed by scrutinizing concrete examples. An excellent context in which to do so is provided by the debate about whether property rights got more or less favorable for growth in Britain in the century before and during the Industrial Revolution.

This issue is no mere historical quibble. Rather, it is central to assessing the historical role of property rights in economic growth, since a number of economic historians have argued that, contrary to the claims of North and Weingast (1989), restrictions on private property rights in England actually increased after 1688, contributing to England's sustained 18th-century growth and to its Industrial Revolution after c. 1780 (Harris, 2004; Hoppit, 2011; Allen, 2011). As summarized by Hoppit (1996, p. 126), "despotic power was only available intermittently before 1688, but it was always available thereafter." Proponents of this view argue that the fact that state restrictions on property rights increased before and during the first Industrial Revolution implies that economic growth does not require secure, well-defined, private property rights, but rather a powerful, interventionist state that is willing and able to take away private individuals' property against their will.

What kind of property rights were the ones that the British state started limiting in the post-1688 period? Hoppit (2011) identifies a whole array of property rights that were restricted or abolished in Britain in the 18th century. After c. 1690, the British government increasingly granted turnpike (toll road) privileges, which empowered their holders to compel land sales, and canal-building permits, which empowered compulsory dissolution of water rights. In 1748, the British government abolished Scottish hereditary jurisdictions—that is, the ownership of particular judicial offices by private individuals who had inherited them from their noble forebears. Between 1787 and 1833, the government first restricted and then abolished property rights in slaves. Between 1825 and 1850, the British government granted charters that empowered railway companies to compel the sale of tens of thousands of acres of private landed property. Between 1750 and 1830, Parliament passed more than 5200 acts of enclosure of open fields, commons, and wastes, redefining and redistributing property rights over some 21% of the land area of England, in many cases against the will of the existing owners.

How is it possible for 18th- and 19th-century Britain to be used to support such diametrically opposed conclusions about whether private property rights are good for growth? The contradiction arises largely from conflating generalized with particularized property rights. The type of property right that is good for growth is a generalized right which allocates clear disposition over an asset to a particular entity, enabling that entity to trade the asset freely and voluntarily in a market. The incentives created by this type of property right ensure that in a market economy, as long as transaction costs are not too high, the asset will be allocated to the user who values it the most, that he or she will then have the incentive to invest in its productive use, and that he or she can use it as collateral to borrow funds for investment purposes. These are the reasons that security of this type of private property right is regarded as being beneficial for economic growth. The property rights that were restricted in 18th-century England, by contrast, were largely particularized ones, which restricted use, transfers, and contracts involving assets to a limited subset of economic agents, who were defined at least partly according to non-economic criteria.

A first set of these particularized private property rights were what might be termed feudal ownership rights, which had been put in place by rulers and elites centuries earlier to generate rents for themselves. Some of these feudal ownership rights limited the freedom of disposition over land so as to maintain concentrated estates that would be large enough to support feudal armies; this applied specifically to noble or gentry land. Other feudal ownership rights assigned use and transfer rights in particular types of land to a subset of economic agents defined according to community membership or social stratum, e.g. membership in the group of substantial farmers in a village (Shaw-Taylor, 2001a,b). Feudal ownership rights also endowed members of particular social strata (e.g. the nobility) with special prerogatives over land owned, held, or used by other social strata. These feudal property rights were attached to personal or group characteristics of their holders and were typically not bought and sold impersonally in markets. As a result, they made it difficult for land to pass into the hands of people who had more productive uses for it.

Many of the salient changes in property rights in 18th- and early 19th-century Britain should not be seen as an attack on security of private property rights, therefore, but rather a reorganization of property rights from particularized to generalized ones. Bogart and Richardson (2011) argue that between 1688 and 1830 the British state did not restrict the security of private property rights, but rather responded to requests from the public to reorganize rights to land and resources in such a way as to enable individuals, families, and communities to exploit new technologies and other opportunities that the inflexible regime of particularized ownership rights inherited from the medieval past could not accommodate. For one thing, much land was held under a legal arrangement called "equitable estate" which limited its mortgage, lease, and sale. For another, many types of land tenure limited the transfer of the affected land to a small subset of persons defined according to their personal identity or membership of the local community. Third, in particular types of village (common-field villages) property rights required owners of land to maintain it in specific traditional uses, made any change in use or ownership subject to agreements with other parties, and subjected such agreements to extensive legal challenges which made them difficult to enforce (Bogart and Richardson, 2011, p. 242). The British state's granting of charters for enclosures, turnpikes, canals and railways thus did not constitute an incursion against the type of generalized private property right which is supposed to encourage growth. Rather, it enhanced the ability to break down particularized ownership rights which meant that assets could only be used by or transferred to a subset of economic agents. These property rights, because of their particularized nature, could not readily be transferred to higher-productivity users and were thus ill suited to allocating assets to their highest-value uses or responding to opportunities offered by technological innovations.

The argument advanced by Bogart and Richardson (2009, 2011) probably overstates the extent to which the reorganization of particularized into generalized property rights was caused by the Glorious Revolution of 1688. The 16th and 17th centuries had already seen extensive reorganizations of particularized ownership rights in England, including the first two waves of enclosures and a number of changes in leases and land tenures (Overton, 1996a,b; Allen, 1999). Although some types of reorganization of particularized ownership rights certainly intensified in the 18th century, many key steps had already taken place long before 1688. Bogart and Richardson (2009, 2011) tacitly acknowledge this fact by arguing that what changed after 1688 was not so much that feudal property rights began for the first time to be reorganized, but rather that the transaction costs of bringing about such reorganization were reduced by a change in the way Parliament and the crown interacted.

A second type of particularized property right which the British state began to restrict during the 18th century was the ownership of public offices. For instance, Scottish hereditary jurisdictions, which the British state abolished in 1748, granted powers of jurisdiction in civil and criminal cases, and could only be used by or transferred to a very small subset of economic agents; in fact, a hereditary jurisdiction was restricted to being owned by the heir of a clan head who had in turn inherited it from his forebears (Chambers, 1869). As Brewer (1989) emphasizes, hereditary ownership of official positions (those of judges, tax-collectors, etc.) remained widespread in many European societies in the 18th century. It contributed to the relative inefficiency of government in those societies compared to Britain, since it ensured a copious stream of rents to owners of the hereditary offices, who had incentives to exploit the coercive powers associated with such offices to obtain profits for themselves. Owners of the office of tax-gatherer skimmed off a share of the taxes collected, while owners of the office of judge demanded fees and bribes from litigants (Brewer, 1989). By abolishing property rights in public offices, the 18th-century British state was not constricting a generalized right which enabled an asset to be allocated to its highest-value use, but rather abolishing a particularized entitlement which enabled entrenched interests to exercise coercion and redistribute resources toward themselves.

The gradual abolition of slavery between 1787 and 1833 must be regarded in a similar light. The ownership of slaves was a coercive right to extort labor and other services from their original owners, the individuals who had been enslaved. Property rights in slaves were not generalized, since they did not apply equally to all economic agents: they could be enjoyed by slave-owners but not by slaves, and the conditions under which they could be transferred from slave-owners to slaves were extremely restrictive. By abolishing property rights in slaves, the state was not limiting a right enabling the asset to be allocated to its highest-value use, but rather abolishing a coercive entitlement maintained as part of a particularized institutional regime whose rules treated slaves and slave-owners completely differently from one another.

The final type of reorganization of property rights that took place in 18th-century Britain relates to the issue of eminent domain, the legal power enjoyed by the state to take private property for public use.[4] Eminent domain represents a conflict between private property rights and the public good which has still not been satisfactorily resolved in modern economies (Fischel, 1995; Benson, 2005, 2008). Sometimes a project which would benefit economic growth (e.g. an infrastructure project) can be blocked by the existence of secure private property rights which cannot be purchased at a competitive price through voluntary exchange because of market failure. Private acquisition of multiple contiguous parcels of land for a road, canal, or railway may be impossible, either because of the transaction costs of negotiating with multiple owners (a coordination problem) or

---

[4] The term was first used in by the Dutch jurist Grotius (1625), in the following context: "The property of subjects is under the eminent domain [*dominium eminens*] of the state, so that the state or he who acts for it may use and even alienate and destroy such property, not only in the case of extreme necessity, in which even private persons have a right over the property of others, but for ends of public utility, to which ends those who founded civil society must be supposed to have intended that private ends should give way. But it is to be added that when this is done the state is bound to make good the loss to those who lose their property." As quoted in Nowak and Rotunda (2004, p. 263).

because of the thinness of the market which gives owners a monopoly position encouraging them to demand very high prices (a holdout problem). The coordination problem may reinforce the holdout problem. These market failures may create a case for constraining private property rights. This is the only instance of state restrictions on private property rights in 18th-century England which involved an actual conflict between generalized private property rights and economic growth (Bogart and Richardson, 2011). But this type of conflict arises because of market failure, is present in all economies, and is one that modern societies have not yet resolved. It cannot therefore be taken as demonstrating that state restrictions on private property rights are generally beneficial for growth, in the absence of market failures. On the other hand, eminent domain does represent a restriction on generalized property rights which has the potential to benefit economic growth in the presence of market imperfections. This raises an important qualification to the principle that secure and generalized private property rights are invariably good for growth, and it must therefore be taken seriously in thinking about the institutional foundations of economic growth.

What do these findings imply for economic growth more widely? Not all forms of property rights—even if they are well defined, private, secure and transferable—are good for growth. Generalized property rights that can be held by, used by, and transferred to any economic agent, regardless of his or her personal identity or group affiliation, will, if markets are competitive, allocate assets to their most productive uses, give their owners the incentive to use them productively, and enable their owners to employ them as collateral. But particularized property rights that can only be held by, used by, and transferred to a small subset of economic agents, often defined according to non-economic criteria, will limit these growth benefits. People with productive uses for an asset who do not belong to the limited circle of those to whom particularized property rights in that asset apply will not be able to own, use, rent, borrow, or buy that asset. These limits on who may hold or use the asset will reduce incentives for investing in it and reduce its capacity to operate as collateral. Particularized property rights may not only fail to support growth in the ways that generalized ones do, but may positively damage growth by denying use, transfer, or rental of property to everyone outside the particular subset of privileged persons, which may include large proportions of all agents in an economy. Growth will therefore benefit from improvements in the security of *generalized* property rights, but from restrictions on the security of *particularized* property rights.

## 8.7. LESSON 6: SECURITY OF PRIVATE PROPERTY RIGHTS IS A MATTER OF DEGREE (AND NEEDS CAREFUL ANALYSIS)

The concept of secure private property rights, as we saw in Lesson 5, is not straightforward. Secure private property rights will affect growth differently, depending on whether they are generalized or particularized. But as the present section will argue, even the concept of "security" of property rights needs further analysis before it can be useful. The economics literature on the historical role of institutions in growth emphasizes the importance of property rights that are secure. But as indicated in Lesson 5 above, the understanding of security in this literature appears to involve at least three very different components: security of ownership, security of use, and security of transfer.

Security of ownership means that no one can take an asset away from you arbitrarily: you have a well-defined ownership right that you can reasonably expect to enforce via the legal system or some other institutional mechanism. Security of use means that no one can prevent you from exercising that ownership right by investing in improving the productivity of the asset or altering the way it is used in order to increase its yield. Security of rights of transfer means that no one can intervene to prevent you from transferring that asset temporarily or permanently to someone else by selling, mortgaging, lending, leasing, bequeathing, or otherwise alienating it.

These three components of the security of private property rights, though conflated in the literature, are both analytically and empirically distinct. Analytically, they are distinct because the three types of security are likely to affect growth in different ways and to differing degrees. Empirically, they are distinct because they can occur in different combinations: thus one may have completely secure rights of ownership in one's land but there may (or may not) be limitations on the security of one's right to decide how to use or transfer those ownership rights; likewise, one may have relatively insecure rights of ownership (in the sense that one may have it confiscated by the crown or one's feudal overlord) but be completely secure in how one can use those rights while one has them and in one's right to choose whom to sell, lease, or bequeath them to. From the point of view of the economic effects of property rights, we have already seen that limitations on ownership, use, and transfer of property are important: Lesson 5 showed that particularized property rights imposed one set of limitations; but as we shall see in the present section there are others. For the purposes of the present section, we therefore distinguish between security of ownership, security of use, and security of transfer, while recognizing that any simple classification scheme is subject to the drawback that in practice there is likely to be a continuous range of security, at least within some bounds.

Partly as a result of conflating these three different components of security of private property rights, the economics literature contains two diametrically opposed views of the historical role of secure private property rights in growth. The first assumes that secure private property rights did not exist in Europe in the medieval and early modern period (e.g. North and Weingast, 1989; Olson, 1993; Acemoglu et al. 2005; Acemoglu and Robinson, 2012). Rather, secure private property suddenly came into being in one particular economy, England, at a specific point in time, after the Glorious Revolution of 1688 (North and Weingast, 1989). This sudden and dramatic shift from insecure to secure private property rights is supposed to have enabled England to surpass other European economies and, three quarters of a century later, to become the first country to industrialize (see e.g. North and Weingast, 1989; Olson, 1993; Acemoglu et al. 2005; Acemoglu and Robinson, 2012).

Other economists, however, adopt a diametrically opposed view, arguing that private property rights were completely secure in economies such as England long before 1688, indeed as far back as the records go. Clark (2007), for instance, argues that in 12th-century England security of private property was already good and land markets were already free, so much so that medieval England already satisfied the checklist of good institutions applied to modern developing economies by the World Bank and the IMF. McCloskey (2010), too, points out that England had secure private property rights from at least the 11th century, "that there was little new in British property rights around 1700," and that many other medieval and early modern societies, both inside and outside Europe, also had secure private property rights in the medieval and early modern period (McCloskey, 2010, p. 25).

These divergent accounts of pre-modern English property rights are not just a quibble within a specialized literature. They have much wider implications for the relationship between institutions and economic growth. The view that England moved from insecure to secure private property rights in 1688 is used to argue that property rights play a fundamental role in causing economic growth. Conversely, the view that England already had secure private property rights in the medieval period (or long before) is taken to imply that property rights (and institutions in general) must be irrelevant for economic growth (Clark, 2007, pp. 148ff; McCloskey, 2010, pp. 318ff).

How is it possible for the economic history of medieval and early modern England to be used to support two such contradictory views of the role of property rights in economic growth? To answer this question, it is essential to distinguish between the different components of security (of ownership, of use, and of transfer), and to understand what is known about the historical development of property rights in England. North and Weingast (1989) argued that in 1688 private property rights became secure for three key groups: for owners of land, giving them good incentives to invest; for lenders to the state, encouraging the rise of capital markets; and for taxpayers, protecting them from state rapacity. We begin with land, since agriculture was the most important sector, and hence, property rights in its major input had the greatest potential to affect growth.

### 8.7.1 Secure Property Rights in Land

In conjunction with their argument regarding the importance of the English parliament after 1688, discussed above (Lesson 2), North and Weingast (1989) also argue that before 1688 landed property in England was deeply insecure even when a stable political regime was in place, because the sovereign was able to redefine property rights at will in his own favor. The Glorious Revolution of 1688, North and Weingast argue, created for the first time in any economy in history institutional limits on a ruler's ability to confiscate private land and capital; this in turn fostered "the ability to engage in secure contracting across time and space" (North and Weingast, 1989, p. 831). Olson (1993, p. 574) echoes this view, asserting that "individual rights to property and contract enforcement" became more secure in England after 1688 than in any other country, and arguing that this was why England industrialized first. Many contributions to the growth literature now accept the view that medieval and early modern Europe failed to experience economic growth because of "lack of property rights for landowners, merchants and proto-industrialists" (Acemoglu et al. 2005, p. 393). This involved insecurity not just of ownership but also of transfer and of use (at least in the sense of investment): "Most land was caught in archaic forms of property rights that made it impossible to sell and risky to invest in. This changed after the Glorious Revolution. … Historically unprecedented was the application of English law to all citizens" (Acemoglu and Robinson, 2012, p. 102). The Glorious Revolution of 1688, therefore, is supposed to have created security of private property rights in all three senses: security of ownership, certainly, but also security of use and transfer.

The empirical findings, however, do not support these claims. Secure private property rights in land existed in England from the 11th century onwards (Smith, 1974; Macfarlane, 1978; Harris, 2004; Campbell, 2005; Clark, 2007; McCloskey, 2010; Bekar and Reed, 2012). Contemporaries, ranging from small farmers to gentry landowners to great nobles to jurists, to the monarch himself, universally regarded property rights as fundamentally secure and not subject to confiscation (Pollock and Maitland, 1895; McCloskey, 2010). Thus individuals had security of ownership, in the sense of protection against arbitrary confiscation by the government or other powerful parties. However, they also had security of transfer, in the sense of having the right to sell, lease, mortgage, bequeath, and otherwise alienate their land. Royal, ecclesiastical, abbatial, and manorial law-courts competed with one another to guarantee and enforce individual ownership and transfer rights even for humble people (Smith, 1974; Macfarlane, 1978; Britnell, 1996; Whittle, 1998, 2000; Campbell, 2005; Clark, 2007; McCloskey, 2010; Briggs, 2013). Security of use rights was somewhat more constrained, for the reasons discussed in Lesson 4: in some regions and localities, village communities had some rights to regulate the ways in which private owners could use their land, specifically via communal regulation of agricultural technology, although in other regions and localities such constraints were very minor.

So overwhelming is the evidence that ownership and transfer rights in private property rights were secure in England from the Middle Ages onwards, that even North and Weingast (1989, p. 831) acknowledge "the fundamental strength of English property rights and the common law that had evolved from the Magna Carta." The Bill of Rights promulgated in 1689 after the Glorious Revolution did not in fact impose any limitation on the English government's ability to confiscate private property and did not require any compensation to be paid when the government did confiscate private property (Harris, 2004, p. 226). Fortunately, however, the English common law had ensured extensive security of ownership and transfer of property in England since the 11th century and, as Harris (2004, p. 228) points out, the judiciary showed far-reaching independence in England long before 1688.

Major political changes took place in England during the 17th century, and these led to some one-off changes in landed property rights. The Stuart monarchs made a series of abortive attempts to introduce absolutist government on the Continental European model in England between 1603 and 1641, and these initiatives involved some insecurity of ownership of landed property for opponents of the Crown. The Civil War of 1642–51 increased insecurity of ownership, as any civil war will, and the Restoration of the monarchy in 1660 resulted in further one-off changes in ownership rights. But, as McCloskey (2010) points out, for investors to have been deterred by such major political changes, they would have had to anticipate their occurrence. In actuality, none of these events were a predictable component of the early modern English property rights regime, so they cannot be viewed as a source of the kind of *ex ante* uncertainty that would have deterred investment. Moreover, the 18th century saw similar insecurity, since the regime in Britain continued to be uncertain: in 1690, serious conflicts between Parliament and Crown caused the king, William of Orange, to go back to the Netherlands; and between then and 1745, a series of Jacobite rebellions aiming to restore the Stuart dynasty operated as an organizing node for opposition to the regime. Insecurity of government always causes some insecurity of private ownership rights, but this operates mainly through expectations. It is unlikely that the regime changes of 17th-century England were expected by investors, and it is unlikely that investors attached no weight to the possibility of a Jacobite overthrow of the monarchy in the first half of the 18th century.

Quantitative analyses also cast doubt on the idea that security of any aspect of landed property rights—ownership, use, or transfer—experienced a discontinuity in England around 1688. Clark (1996) compiled a data series of land rents and land values in England between 1540 and 1750. His analysis finds that neither 1688 nor any of the other political upheavals of the 1540–1750 period marked any discontinuity. From this, he concludes that individuals must have been secure in their property rights over their land from as early as 1540.

This does not, however, mean that property rights were completely static between the medieval period and the industrial revolution, as argued by Clark (2007) or McCloskey (2010). Between c. 1350 and c. 1500, England saw significant changes in the manorial powers of landlords, communal regulation of arable fields and pastures, the costs and impartiality of legal enforcement, and the complexity of tenures and leases (Wrightson, 1982; Wrightson and Levine, 1995; Campbell, 2000, 2005, 2009; Harris, 2004; Briggs, 2009, 2013). As Lesson 4 discussed, additional changes to property rights took place during the agricultural revolution between c. 1550 and c. 1800, during which many communal property rights were restricted or abolished, tenurial forms were simplified, restrictions on alienation imposed by the inheritance system were removed, and the legal enforcement of property conflicts was improved (Overton, 1996a,b; Allen, 1999).

These changes influenced all components of security of property rights. Ownership and transfer rights were particularly strongly affected via changes in the detailed functioning of the legal system, which was a major defence against confiscation or incursion, while use rights were particularly strongly affected via changes in the communal and manorial regulation of agricultural practice, particularly enclosure and changes in leases. Such changes in security of ownership, use, and transfer of land in medieval and early modern England were incremental, did not show any discontinuity around 1688, and continued throughout the 18th century (Neeson, 1984, 1993, 2000; Allen, 1992; Overton, 1996a,b; Shaw-Taylor, 2001a,b). By the 1760s, when the Industrial Revolution was beginning, the complexity of rights governing the ownership, use, and transfer of property in England, and the transaction costs involved in enforcing such rights, had been reduced compared to medieval times. Secure rights of ownership and transfer of property existed in England from at least the 11th century onwards, and even rights of use were fairly secure in many regions. But the way these various rights operated and the economic incentives they created in practice changed over the ensuing centuries, in a gradual and incremental process.

The discussion so far has focused on England, about which the growth literature makes the strongest claims. But similar findings exist for other countries. Secure private rights of ownership, use, and transfer of landed property can be observed in a large number of European economies from the medieval period onwards. Italian economies show secure private ownership rights from the ninth century at latest, and hint strongly at secure rights of transfer in that property as well (Feller, 2004; Van Bavel, 2010, 2011; McCloskey, 2010). The Netherlands had secure private rights of ownership and transfer from the medieval period onwards, which some have argued were more extensive than in England; secure rights of use also became widespread at the latest by the beginning of the Dutch agricultural revolution, in the late 15th century (Van Bavel, 2010, 2011; DeVries, 1974; Bieleman, 2006, 2010). The German territory of Württemberg had secure private ownership and transfer rights in land from at latest the 15th century onwards, which applied to all members of society down to the poorest, included females as well as males, were unrestricted by noble privilege (since Württemberg had no landholding nobility), and included unusually generalized transfer rights such as the right to subdivide all land at will and for women to inherit equally with men; use rights were somewhat less secure because of the strong powers of Württemberg communities, but certain categories of freehold land involved secure use rights in the sense that the owner could redeploy the land to more productive uses such as textile crops (Hippel, 1977; Sabean, 1990; Röhm, 1957). In many societies in Central and Eastern-Central Europe, too, from the medieval period onwards peasants had secure private ownership rights in their land, and secure transfer rights permitting inheritance, sale, rental, and mortgaging; use rights were more restricted, but were nonetheless secure for certain categories of land (Cerman, 2008, 2012; McCloskey, 2010). Again, however, this cannot be taken to imply that property rights in these societies did not change in any way that could affect economic growth between the medieval period and the 19th century. As we saw in Lesson 4, most European societies underwent changes in ownership, use, and transfer rights in land which, together with changes in contracting institutions, contributed to an increase in agricultural productivity and an acceleration in agricultural growth between the late medieval period and the 19th century.

## 8.7.2 Secure Property Rights for State Creditors

A similar analysis applies to the second set of property rights whose security is emphasized as a basis for economic growth in 18th-century England. North and Weingast (1989) also argue that the Glorious Revolution of 1688, by establishing parliamentary supremacy over public finances, created an environment in which lenders could rely upon the state to meet its financial promises. This, they contend, resulted in investors placing their trust and capital in the British state instead of its foreign rivals, creating the conditions for a financial revolution which greatly improved the sophistication of credit markets, and fuelled the accelerating growth of the British economy between 1688 and 1815. These scholars conclude that the introduction of secure private property rights for state creditors in England after 1688 shows "how institutions played a necessary role in making possible economic growth and political freedom" (North and Weingast, 1989, p. 831). The security of private property for state creditors which this literature regards as being created suddenly in 1688 consists primarily of ownership rights (in the sense that the state could not confiscate creditors' assets by failing to repay), but also extends to transfer rights, since North and Weingast emphasize that security of private property for state creditors also involved "the creation of impersonal capital markets" and "the ability to engage in secure contracting across time and space" (1989, e.g. p. 831). Cameron (1989, p. 155) argues that the Glorious Revolution, by creating security for state creditors, "reacted favorably on private capital markets, making funds available for investment in agriculture, commerce, and industry"—that is, 1688 saw an increase in security of both ownership and transfer.

Again, however, the empirical findings indicate that the development of property rights for state creditors was not characterized by a sudden switch from insecurity to security, whether in terms of ownership or transfer. Rather, security of ownership and transfer of assets by state creditors in England fluctuated substantially with political events, while improving incrementally over long periods of time. Analysis of the institutional rules and practices governing taxation and public borrowing in England between c. 1600 and c. 1850 shows that the Civil War (1642-51), although not a sharp break-point, marked a bigger change than 1688 (O'Brien, 2001; Harris, 2004). Overall, however, the development of property rights for state creditors was characterized by very significant elements of continuity between the early 17th and the early 19th century. O'Brien (2001) provides detailed evidence indicating that property rights for lenders to the state were secure in England in the early 17th century, and that in all important ways the institutions necessary for good governance of the public finances were in place prior to the Glorious

Revolution. Harris (2004) argues that there were fundamental institutional continuities after 1688 and that the degree of insecurity, at least of ownership rights, remained quite high, since many institutional tools for effective oversight of the public finances were unavailable to public creditors in England until the 19th century.

This does not mean that security of ownership or transfer rights for creditors of the English state underwent no change over time, and hence can have made no contribution to economic growth. Analysis of interest rates on English government borrowing suggests that property rights for owners of capital developed continuously across the early modern period rather than shifting from insecurity to security suddenly at any particular date. In conjunction with their previously discussed claims, North and Weingast (1989) further asserted that 1688 saw a sharp discontinuity, with a sudden shift from insecure to secure property rights for government creditors causing a sharp decline in the interest rate which the British government had to pay to borrow funds. But Stasavage (2002) tracked interest rates on English government debt in the second half of the 17th century and the first half of the 18th, and concluded that security of private property rights for state creditors was not irrevocably established in 1688 but instead fluctuated between then and 1740. It was particularly violently affected by which political party controlled ministerial posts and the two chambers of parliament. Political events rather than institutional changes most strongly influenced investors' willingness to commit capital to the British state (Stasavage, 2002). Sussman and Yafeh (2006), too, found that interest rates on British government debt did not show any discontinuity after the Glorious Revolution, instead remaining high and volatile for another forty years. The evidence shows neither a sudden switch from insecurity to security around 1688 nor complete stasis between the medieval period and the 19th century.

### 8.7.3 Secure Property Rights for Taxpayers

Similar issues arise with the third type of property rights which are supposed to have become more secure in England in 1688 and to have contributed to that country's subsequent economic success. Before 1688, it is said, the English Crown frequently engaged in confiscating its subjects' wealth via taxation; through these unconstrained fiscal powers, it is claimed, the sovereign controlled a large fraction of the resources in the English economy and reduced the security with which his subjects could use the remainder (North and Weingast, 1989; Acemoglu et al. 2005, p. 393). The Glorious Revolution of 1688, according to this view, limited the right of the state to demand property from individuals for the first time in any society in history.

These claims sit uneasily, however, with the evidence that after 1688 the British state increased its capacity to raise revenue from individuals through taxation (Harris, 2004). The Bill of Rights promulgated in 1689 made the taxing power of the British state conditional on parliamentary approval, but did not limit Parliament's powers of taxation and did not require any representation or consent from the vast majority of taxpayers who were not represented in Parliament. The landed, financial, and commercial groups in society were over-represented in the British Parliament, while the vast mass of ordinary taxpayers were either under-represented or had no vote at all.

State revenues from taxation and borrowing in England greatly increased between 1689 and 1815, both in absolute terms and as a share of national income (Mathias and O'Brien, 1976, 1978; O'Brien, 1988). Fortunately, state extraction only began to increase in England at the point at which per capita incomes and economic growth had already risen to quite high levels (O'Brien, 1988, pp. 23–4; Brewer, 1989). However, between 1689 and 1815, real gross national product increased by a factor of 3 while real peacetime taxation rose by a factor of 15 (O'Brien, 2001, pp. 8, 10). This huge increase in government control over national resources after 1688 casts serious doubt on the view that 1688 marked an improvement in the security of ownership rights of British taxpayers. Even between 1603 and 1641, when the early Stuart monarchs were trying to introduce continental-style absolutism to England, total government expenditure was a maximum of 1.2–2.4% of national income; after 1688 the state rapidly increased its share of national income to 8–10% (McCloskey, 2010, pp. 318–19). The percentage of English national income over which individuals as opposed to the state enjoyed secure private property rights—whether in terms of ownership or in terms of use—declined after 1688.

In principle, this enhanced state capacity might have supported activities, such as provision of public goods, that indirectly enhanced private property rights or benefited economic growth in other ways. The British state's increased ability to raise funds after 1688 certainly enabled it to undertake a number of new activities. However, these probably did not benefit economic growth. One of the first things the new English king did after public finances were placed on a stable footing in 1688 was to use them to launch a major war against France. This was not a mere blip but the beginning of a long-term trend. The vast majority of English state expenditures after 1688 were not spent on civil government, in the sense of infrastructure, education, or other public goods that might have benefited long-term economic growth. Rather, state expenditures were predominantly allocated to military purposes or to servicing the state debt, which was itself incurred primarily for military purposes (O'Brien, 1988, 2001).

This military spending was not beneficial for the economy. As Williamson (1984, p. 689) shows, British economic growth was modest between 1760 and 1820, both relative to its subsequent performance and relative to modern developing economies, because "Britain tried to do two things at once—industrialize and fight expensive wars, and she simply did not have the resources to do both." Although the precise size of the impact of war on the British economy in the 18th century is debated, most agree that it was negative and non-negligible (Williamson, 1987; Crafts, 1987; Mokyr, 1987). The increased ability of the English state to borrow and tax during the 18th century thus probably did not favor economic growth: the English economy grew in spite of rising state spending, not because of it. Again, however, the evidence shows neither a sudden switch from insecurity to security of taxpayers' ownership, use or transfer rights at any specific date, nor complete stasis between the medieval period and the 19th century.

## 8.7.4 Security of Property Rights: Analytical Challenges and Open Questions

What do these findings imply for economic growth? The historical findings support neither of the two views prevalent in the growth literature about the relationship between economic growth and security of private property rights, whether these are defined in terms of ownership, use, or transfer. Economic history shows that secure rights of ownership, use, and transfer for landholders, lenders, and taxpayers did not emerge suddenly, recently, or in a single precociously advanced economy from which they subsequently diffused to other backward ones. Secure rights to own, use, and transfer land, capital, and other assets emerged gradually in a large number of European societies over half a millennium or more. None of these societies guaranteed individuals perfectly secure rights of ownership, use, or transfer over property, but none of them lacked such security altogether. Rights of ownership, use, and transfer of private property in most societies in medieval and early modern Europe were neither perfectly insecure nor perfectly secure, but rather changed incrementally over very long periods of time. Economic growth cannot be ascribed to a sudden switch from insecure to secure rights of ownership, use, and transfer; but nor, as we saw in Lesson 4, was growth left wholly unaffected by the incremental changes that did take place in the property rights regime.

These empirical findings from history pose an analytical problem for economics. If rights of ownership, use, and transfer over private property were reasonably secure in England in 1200, but also changed between then and 1800, what do we actually mean by property rights being "secure" enough to lead to economic growth? All economists and historians would probably agree that a necessary condition for economic growth is some degree of security of ownership, in the sense of protection from seizure or taxation of the entirety of what private individuals own or can gain through exchange, investment, and innovation. Most would probably also agree that economic growth also requires some degree of security in the rights to use one's property, whether by investing in improving it or by devising more productive uses for it. And most would agree that economic growth requires some degree of security in the right to transfer assets to other people, whether by selling them, renting them out, or using them as collateral for loans. But which component of security of property matters most for growth? How much security? And how do we measure it?

Without more refined analytical categories than mere security, we are unlikely to achieve a better understanding of the contribution of property rights to growth. Even distinguishing between security of ownership, security of use, and security of unrestricted transfer only takes us so far. The empirical findings from history suggest two directions in which economics must develop its analytical tools for thinking about security of private property rights.

First, constraints on security of private property rights are multifaceted. Constraints on security of ownership rights include such variegated incursions as state confiscation, eminent domain, manorial ejection, rapacious taxation, failure to repay loans, inability to defend one's property title using the legal system, and many more. Constraints on security of use rights are even more varied, and include interlinkage with labor and product markets (e.g. under serfdom), collective usufruct rights, communal regulation of crop rotations, manorial prerogatives, and many more. Constraints on security of unrestricted transfer rights include conditionality of sales; bans on hypothecation; village citizenship requirements; noble entailment; familial redemption rights; limits on female inheritance and marital property; inheritance customs; and many more. These constraints on security of ownership, use, and transfer rights in private property do not necessarily all change at the same time or in the same direction. Furthermore, the intensity of these various constraints on security of private property is not necessarily perfectly correlated across societies. The historical evidence, for instance, suggests that early modern England had, by European standards, strong security of private use rights protecting owners against communal or manorial intervention, but weak security of private ownership and transfer rights for married women; the former type of security of private property right changed significantly during the 18th century, while the latter did not. Similar examples of complex combinations of security and insecurity of different components of property rights can be provided for every pre-modern European economy. Economics needs analytical tools for deciding which of the numerous observed constraints on how people could own, use, and transfer property should be employed as criteria for defining "security" of property rights, and tools for establishing which of these aspects of security were likely to be more or less important for economic growth.

The second need for analytical attention is created by the fact that property rights are only one component of the wider system of institutions in a society. Security of rights of ownership, use, and transfer can be enhanced by other components of the system— for instance, by contracting institutions, as we saw in Lesson 4. But security of rights of ownership, use, and transfer can also be *constrained* by yet other components of the system—for instance, by village communities or the manorial system. As we saw in Lesson 5, the historical evidence suggests that in all pre-industrial European economies, even the most advanced, generalized property rights were constrained by other, more particularized components of the institutional system. Economics therefore needs analytical tools for understanding the interaction between security of private property rights and other components of the broader institutional system.

## 8.8. LESSON 7. INSTITUTIONS ARE EMBEDDED IN A WIDER INSTITUTIONAL SYSTEM

An understandably widespread assumption is that a particular institution will affect growth similarly in all economies and time-periods. Once secure private property rights are present in an economy, for instance, it is tempting to assume that they will exert an effect on growth that does not depend on the wider environment. But the evidence from historical societies suggests that this assumption is incorrect. Each institution, rather, is embedded in a wider institutional system and is constrained by the other institutions in that system; institutional labels turn out to be approximations which mask important variations that matter for economic growth. While institutional systems are not yet well understood, it is clear that to grasp how these variations affect growth, we must take the rest of the institutional system into account, because the impact of any particular institution on growth is constrained by the entire system in which it is embedded.

This lesson is vividly illustrated by the historical findings about an institution some recent contributions to the growth literature have portrayed as especially important: the family. These contributions claim that early and successful economic growth in the West was favored by a specific family institution called the European Marriage Pattern (EMP), involving late female marriage, high female celibacy, and nuclear rather than extended families. But as we shall see, the apparent relevance to economic growth of historical findings on the institution of the family has been obscured by the failure to take the larger institutional context into account.

Theories of economic growth have increasingly focused on historical demography in recent years, as economists have begun to incorporate fertility decline and population growth rates into their explanations of long-run growth (Galor, 2005a,b; Acemoglu, 2009; Guinnane, 2011). Unified growth theory, in particular, regards falling fertility and slowing population growth as essential preconditions for economies to convert a greater proportion of the yields from factor accumulation and technological innovation into per capita income growth (Galor, 2005a,b, 2012). The central role played by population in recent growth theory raises the question of the determinants of demographic behavior and its relationship with economic growth over the long-term.

One recent approach to this question has sought to ascribe the transition to sustained economic growth in Europe before and during the Industrial Revolution to a specific family institution called the European Marriage Pattern (EMP), involving norms of late female marriage, high female celibacy, and nuclear rather than extended families. This unique family institution, it is claimed, lay behind the early modern divergence in economic growth rates between Europe and the rest of the world, between north-west Europe and the rest of the continent, and between England and everywhere else (Greif, 2006a; Greif and Tabellini, 2010; De Moor, 2008; De Moor and Van Zanden,

2010; Foreman-Peck, 2011; Voigtländer and Voth, 2006, 2010). The EMP is supposed to have favored economic growth by improving women's position, increasing human capital investment, adjusting population growth to economic trends, and sustaining beneficial cultural norms. If these claims were true, they would imply that people in poor economies would have to change very deeply rooted aspects of their private lives before they could enjoy the benefits of economic growth.

Historical demography, however, provides no supporting evidence for the view that the EMP (or any specific type of family institution) influenced economic growth. A metastudy of the historical demography literature (Dennison and Ogilvie, 2013) finds that the three key components of the EMP—late marriage, high celibacy, and nuclear families—were not invariably associated with each other. Where they were associated, they did not invariably lead to economic growth. Indeed, where the components of the EMP did coincide in their most extreme form (German-speaking and Scandinavian Europe), economic growth was slower and industrialization later than in societies such as England and the Netherlands where the EMP was less pronounced. The most rapidly growing European economy, that of England, moved further away from the EMP in the century before and during the Industrial Revolution. The idea that the EMP had a clear causal influence on economic growth is not supported by the evidence.

In each society where the EMP was prevalent, it was embedded in a wider institutional framework. But the wider institutional system differed greatly from one European economy to the next. These wider institutional frameworks, not the institution of the family in isolation from them, influenced whether women enjoyed a good economic position, human capital investment was high, population responded flexibly to economic signals, or specific cultural norms were enforced. It was the institutional system as a whole, not the family or any other institution in isolation, that decided whether an economy grew or stagnated.

This can be seen by examining the institutional determinants of women's position, which is widely regarded as an important contributory factor to economic growth in poor countries (Birdsall, 1988; Dasgupta, 1993; Ray, 1998; Mammen and Paxson, 2000; Ogilvie, 2003, 2004c; Doepke and Tertilt, 2011). Some recent contributions to the literature claim that the EMP contributed to European economic growth by improving women's economic status (De Moor, 2008; De Moor and Van Zanden, 2010; Foreman-Peck, 2011; Voigtländer and Voth, 2006, 2010). However, there is no evidence to support the proposition that women's economic status in early modern Europe was determined solely, or even predominantly, by the institution of the family as opposed to the wider institutional framework (Ogilvie, 2003, 2004b,c, 2013a; Dennison and Ogilvie, 2013). The many empirical studies of women's economic position in pre-modern Europe suggest that women had a good economic position in some societies with the EMP and a bad one in others. England and the Netherlands assigned women a better economic position than other European societies (see the survey in Ogilvie (2003), Ch. 7), and these countries had the most successful economies in early modern Europe. But England and the Netherlands were also distinctive in many other ways: their factor prices, resource endowments, geopolitical position, trade participation, parliaments, legal systems, financial arrangements, and early liberalization of manorial, communal, and corporative institutions, have all been adduced as causes of their early economic success (Mokyr, 1974; De Vries and Van der Woude, 1997; Van Zanden and Van Riel, 2004). There has been much debate about the origins of English and Dutch distinctiveness. It seems obvious, however, that to qualify for consideration, any plausible explanation must invoke factors confined largely to England and the Netherlands—rather than a factor such as the EMP, which England and the Netherlands shared with many other societies in Western, Nordic, Central, and Eastern-Central Europe whose economies grew slowly and industrialized late.

Outside the precociously advanced market economies of England and the Netherlands, women's economic status was much worse. This was not because of the EMP or any other type of family institution, but because of the wider institutional system in which the family was embedded. In Germany, Scandinavia, France, and many other regions, the EMP prevailed but women's participation in industrial and commercial occupations was restricted by guilds of craftsmen, retailers, and merchants (Wiesner, 1989, 2000; Ogilvie, 2003, 2004b,c, 2005d, 2013a; Hafter, 2007). In many regions of Switzerland, Germany, and France, as micro-studies have shown, the EMP prevailed but women's work, wages, property rights, and in some cases even their consumption choices, were limited by local communities—again, by corporative institutions (Wiesner, 1989; Wiesner-Hanks, 1996; Wiesner, 2000; Ogilvie, 2003, 2010, 2013a; Hafter, 2007). In Bohemia (the modern Czech Republic), also characterized by the EMP, female household-headship was low, daughters could not inherit, and communal institutions collaborated with manorial administrators to harass women working independently outside male-headed households (Ogilvie and Edwards, 2000; Ogilvie, 2001, 2005a,b; Velková, 2012; Klein and Ogilvie, 2013). Whether women enjoyed economic autonomy under the EMP (or any type of family institution) depended on the balance of power among other institutions. Strong guilds which succeeded in excluding women from industrial and commercial activities and training existed both in northern Italy (in the absence of the EMP) and in German-speaking Central Europe (in its presence). Much weaker guilds which increasingly failed to exclude women from training and skilled work prevailed both in Eastern Europe (in the absence of the EMP) and in England and the Netherlands (in its presence) (Ogilvie, 2003, 2004b,c, 2005d, 2007b). Other corporative institutions such as village communities were extremely strong both in Russia (non-EMP) and in Germany (EMP) (Ogilvie, 1997, 2003, 2004b, 2006; Dennison and Ogilvie, 2007; Dennison, 2011). Corporative institutions played a central role in lowering women's economic status but show no systematic relationship with the EMP or any other family institution.

The importance of the wider institutional system, as opposed to the institution of the family in isolation, also emerges when we examine human capital investment. The EMP, it is argued, involved lengthy life-cycle phases during which young people were working outside the household, giving them the opportunity and incentive to invest in their human capital. The lower fertility resulting from late marriage and high lifetime celibacy is also claimed to have contributed to a shift from a high quantity of poorly educated offspring to a lower quantity of more highly educated ones, thus improving the quality of their human capital (Foreman-Peck, 2011). But parents will only invest in their offspring's education (as opposed to buying it as a consumption good) if such investment promises a positive return. There are two mechanisms by which this incentive can operate. First, parents may expect to share the returns from their offspring's education via transfers from offspring in adulthood. But this runs counter to a basic characteristic of the EMP, namely that the net intergenerational wealth flow runs from parents to children: offspring leave home early to work in other households, migrate to other localities, form independent households upon marriage, do not reside as adults in the same household (or even the same locality) as their parents, and seldom remit earnings to the parental generation (Caldwell, 1976, 1982). A family system with these characteristics creates disincentives for parents to invest in their offspring's human capital since they cannot expect to share returns when offspring reach adulthood.

The second mechanism by which parents may be motivated to invest in their offspring's education (as opposed to purchasing it as a consumption good) is altruism: their offspring's future well-being increases parents' own well-being. But this incentive will only operate if skilled jobs are open to all members of society. Parents will invest in girls' education only if females are able to take work that requires skills, instead of being restricted to activities which rely on learning-by-doing rather than formal training. Even for boys' education, skilled occupations must be open to all rather than being restricted to members of specific groups. But access to skilled occupations in pre-industrial Europe did not depend solely, or even systematically, on the institution of the family. Rather, it depended on the wider framework of institutions regulating labor markets: craft guilds, merchant associations, urban privileges, village communities, and manorial regulations. Women were allowed access to skilled jobs (e.g. in crafts or commerce) only in some societies with the EMP, specifically the Netherlands and England, and even then not without restrictions (Van Nederveen Meerkerk, 2006a,b, 2010; Van den Heuvel, 2007, 2008; Van der Heijden et al. 2011). In other EMP societies, such as Germany, Scandinavia, and France, craft guilds excluded females (and many "outsider" males) from skilled industrial work, and guilds of merchants and retailers restricted their participation in commerce (Wiesner, 1989; Wiesner-Hanks, 1996; Wiesner, 2000; Hafter, 2007; Ogilvie, 2003; Ogilvie et al. 2011). This reduced the incentive to invest in girls' education, although better-off parents still purchased it as a consumption good. The EMP by itself cannot have been crucial in creating incentives for female education since the EMP existed both in societies where women were more often permitted to do skilled work and those where coercive institutions excluded them. Rather, what decided whether females learned vocational skills was the strength or weakness of barriers to entry imposed by corporative institutions seeking economic rents for insiders by restricting low-cost competitors such as women (Ogilvie, 1986, 2003; Wiesner-Hanks, 1996; Wiesner, 2000; Sanderson, 1996).

Human capital indicators for European economies in the 18th and 19th centuries show that education levels varied hugely across societies with the EMP (Lindert, 2004, pp. 91–2; A'Hearn et al. 2009, p. 801; Reis, 2005, p. 203; Dennison and Ogilvie, 2013, esp. Table 4). This is not surprising, since the family was not the only, or the main institution that affected education levels. Schooling, literacy, and numeracy in early modern Europe were more strongly influenced by other institutions: the market, the church, the state, the local community, the occupational guild (Ogilvie, 1986, 2003; Wiesner-Hanks, 1996; Wiesner, 2000). These non-familial institutions show no significant correlation with the prevalence of the EMP. In some societies, such as Germany and Scandinavia, the church allied with the state and the local community to impose compulsory schooling on children of both sexes, monitor compliance, and penalize violations, leading to very high education levels (Ogilvie, 1986, 2003; Johansson, 1977, 2009). In other societies, such as England, such institutional pressures were absent, leading to much lower levels of school enrolment and literacy. Numeracy was typically learned, to some degree at least, informally in response to market demand in commercialized economies, explaining why England, with its mediocre school enrolment and literacy, had numeracy levels similar to more institutionally regulated societies such as Germany or Scandinavia (A'Hearn et al. 2009).

Historically, human capital investment shows no evidence of having positively affected economic growth in Europe before the late 19th century. England grew fast in the early modern period and industrialized before any other society, yet schooling and literacy stagnated there during the 18th century and were not high by European standards until well into the 19th century. Economic historians who disagree on almost all other issues concur that human capital investment was not important in the English Industrial Revolution (Mokyr, 2009; Allen, 2003). Conversely, other European societies had outstandingly good educational indicators but slow economic growth. The Netherlands had high levels of school enrolment, literacy, and numeracy, but after the end of the Dutch Golden Age in 1670 its economy stagnated and it industrialized very late. German territories had much higher school enrolment and literacy than England and even the Low Countries, but stagnated throughout the early modern period and did not industrialize until after c. 1840. A similar pattern is found in Lutheran Scandinavia, with high school enrolment and literacy rates, but slow growth and late industrialization (Dennison and Ogilvie, 2013).

The available evidence strongly suggests, then, that human capital neither was affected by the EMP nor played any causal role in economic growth before the late 19th century. In many parts of central and northern Europe, school attendance and literacy were imposed and enforced by churches, rulers, landlords, communal officials, and occupational guilds.

These organizations used their institutional powers to impose "social disciplining" on ordinary people for the benefit of elite interests (Ogilvie, 2006). In many societies, education levels were not chosen by ordinary people themselves, for economic or other reasons, but rather imposed on them by elites to serve their own interests, and thus depended on the powers these elites enjoyed via the wider institutional system: the church, the state, serfdom, communities, guilds. This wider institutional system, not the EMP, explains the absence of a systematic relationship between educational indicators and economic growth in Europe before the late 19th century.

In the recent literature on the EMP, yet another pathway has been suggested as a link between the EMP and European economic growth. It has been claimed that England had a particularly extreme version of the EMP, and that the resulting late marriage and high lifetime celibacy ensured that English population growth was uniquely responsive to economic signals. This is supposed to have ensured that in England economic surpluses resulted in capital accumulation, enabling productivity-enhancing innovation and fuelling faster economic growth than in France or China (Voigtländer and Voth, 2006, 2010). However, the historical demography literature does not support the idea that England had an extreme version of the EMP (Dennison and Ogilvie, 2013). Nor does the evidence show higher demographic responsiveness to economic trends in England than elsewhere. An econometric study of French demographic behavior, for instance, found that "at no time between 1670 and 1830 were marriages less responsive to economic conditions in France than in England" and concluded that the origins of the contrast between French and English growth performance "are not to be found in difference of demographic behavior" (Weir, 1984, pp. 43–4). In Germany, too, the elasticity of fertility with respect to economic signals was higher than in England (though slightly lower than in France) throughout the 18th century (Guinnane and Ogilvie, 2008, pp. 23–7). Among the nine European economies studied by Galloway (1988), the responsiveness of fertility to changes in grain prices was weaker in England than in societies where economic growth was much slower (Austria, Sweden, Belgium, the Netherlands) or where the EMP did not prevail (Tuscany). In 18th-century China, where family institutions were also very different from the EMP, recent studies also show fertility rates responding to changes in grain prices (Wang et al. 2010; Campbell and Lee, 2010). For England itself, several analyses have found that preventive checks on population growth weakened or disappeared by c. 1750, indicating that fertility became less responsive to economic signals in England at the precise period when economic growth began to accelerate and to diverge most from growth in other Western European economies (Galloway, 1988; Nicolini, 2007; Crafts and Mills, 2009). Evidence for various European economies suggests that these findings can be explained at least partly in terms of interactions between the family and other components of the institutional system, especially village communities, privileged urban corporations, occupational guilds, and serfdom (Ehmer, 1991; Ogilvie, 1995; Guinnane and Ogilvie, 2008, 2013).

The embeddedness of particular institutions in the broader institutional system also emerges from studying cultural attitudes associated with the EMP. It has been suggested that the EMP caused nuclear families to predominate over wider kinship groups, thereby fostering growth-inducing attitudes, specifically trust beyond the familial group and gender equality. These cultural norms are supposed to have been further propagated by medieval Catholic religious ideology, which is supposed to have compared favorably in this respect to the ideological norms disseminated by non-Christian religions such as Islam (Greif, 2006a; Greif and Tabellini, 2010; De Moor, 2008; De Moor and Van Zanden, 2010). However, these are difficult claims to substantiate empirically. A number of scholars have found that religious attitudes to family and gender issues varied greatly across medieval Catholic Europe, and that this was because they were shaped by a broader framework of social institutions that differed greatly from one Catholic, European society to the next (Biller, 2001; Bonfield, 2001; Donahue, 1983, 2008; Dennison and Ogilvie, 2013). Demographic behavior and family structure also varied enormously across medieval Catholic Europe, with nuclear families dominant in some societies but extended families more important in others, including in strongly Catholic societies such as Italy and Iberia (Smith, 1981a,b; Pérez Moreda, 1997; Reher, 1998a,b; Sonnino, 1997; Micheletto, 2011). It is difficult, therefore, to find empirical support for the notion that the EMP sustained distinctive cultural norms, whether about non-familial trust or gender issues. The widely variegated distribution of European family institutions is not consistently associated with any distinctive set of cultural attitudes, and there is no evidence that such attitudes had a causal effect on European economic growth.

The idea, then, that the emergence of sustained economic growth in early modern Europe was caused by any particular type of family institution is not supported by the historical evidence and, in fact, is refuted by much of it. Whether a society with any given family institution experienced economic growth depended on overall characteristics of its economy and institutional system. In early modern England, the EMP existed within a framework of well-defined, private, transferable and (in most senses) secure property rights; well-functioning factor and product markets; and relatively few particularized institutions constraining female (or male) economic autonomy; economic growth was usually positive and ultimately spectacular. In the early modern Netherlands, the EMP initially existed in a similar framework of property rights, well-functioning markets, and successful economic growth; but after c. 1670 the Dutch economy stagnated and industrialization came late, for reasons that are still vigorously debated but are believed to have included a resurgence of particularized institutional privileges (Mokyr, 1974, 1980; De Vries and Van der Woude, 1997; Van den Heuvel and Ogilvie, 2013). In German-speaking Central Europe, Scandinavia, and the Czech lands, the EMP existed in a more coercive framework of mobility restrictions (including, in some areas, serfdom) and corporative barriers to entry in labor markets (for most women and many men); economic growth remained slow until these institutional obstacles were removed (Ogilvie, 1997, 2003; Dennison and Ogilvie, 2013).

Research in historical demography finds that the institution of the family was inter-linked with the wider institutional system in multiple ways (Laslett, 1988; Ehmer, 1991; Solar, 1995; Guinnane and Ogilvie, 2008, 2013). It was these complex interactions among different institutions within an over-arching system, not any single institution in isola-tion, that affected economic growth itself, as well as influencing potential contributory factors such as women's status, human capital investment, demographic responsiveness, and—to the limited extent that these are empirically observable—cultural attitudes. Cur-rent scholarship suggests that the EMP may have required a social framework of strong non-familial institutions that could substitute for familial labor, insurance and welfare which small, nuclear-family households could not provide, and to which large numbers of unmarried individuals did not have access (Laslett, 1988; Solar, 1995; Dennison and Ogilvie, 2013). However, it was not inevitable that this wider framework should be made up of institutions that also happened to benefit economic growth, such as generalized private property rights, well-functioning markets, or impartial legal systems. Instead, this wider framework could as easily have been—and in many cases actually was—made up of particularized institutions with more malign growth effects, including serfdom, guilds, communities, religious bodies, and absolutist states (Ehmer, 1991; Ogilvie, 1995, 2003; Guinnane and Ogilvie, 2008, 2013; Dennison and Ogilvie, 2013). Future research must place at the center of its analysis the wider institutional system that constrained both demographic and economic decisions during European economic growth. No specific type of family institution in isolation can be regarded as necessary, let alone sufficient, for economic growth.

These findings make clear that a specific institution that matters for economic growth will often not operate similarly across different societies and time-periods. Private prop-erty rights, for instance, are embedded in broader institutional systems that differ greatly across societies, with the result that they will not affect growth identically everywhere. If they are not embedded in an institutional system containing, for example, accessible and enforceable contracting institutions, they will fail to unleash economic growth, as we saw in Lesson 4. Likewise, the same family institution can exist in different societies characterized by widely differing institutional systems, and will consequently affect eco-nomic growth in widely differing ways. The evidence we have shows that the growth effects of any individual institution are constrained by other parts of the institutional system differently in different societies, and that it is the entire institutional system, not any single institution in isolation, that is important for economic growth.

While it is understandable that economists should wish to simplify the analysis of institutions in order to try to get at their essential features, it is important to remember the remark attributed to Einstein to the effect that "everything should be made as simple as possible, but not simpler.''[5] While the embeddedness of particular institutions in larger systems undoubtedly adds greatly to the complexity of the analytical (and especially the empirical) task, it seems to be an undeniable fact we cannot simplify away. Institutions just are not easily separable from their contexts and identifiable under the traditional or common-sense headings of conventional labels, but rather have to be analyzed as part of an entire institutional system.

## 8.9. LESSON 8: DISTRIBUTIONAL CONFLICTS ARE CENTRAL

We have seen in Lessons 1 through 7 that many economists concerned with growth ascribe a major causal role to institutions, whose roots they trace far back in history. But there are also many who challenge the very idea of an institutional system favorable to growth, independent of geographical or cultural context. Some regard institutions essentially as superstructure, with other variables, such as geographical resource endowments or cultural attitudes, as more fundamental causes of economic growth which bring institutions in their wake (e.g. Sachs, 2003). Others hold that a society always has the institutions that are efficient given its endowments, technology, or cultural attitudes (e.g. North and Thomas, 1970, 1973; Greif, 2006c). There are even those who regard both institutions and growth as fundamentally caused by stochastic shocks amplified by subsequent path dependency (e.g. Crafts, 1977; Crafts et al. 1989).

The geographical and efficiency approaches are particularly prominent in the literature on institutions and growth in historical perspective. A number of scholars have sought to explain the historical development of institutions and economic growth in terms of geography and resource endowments. Thus Diamond (1997) explains the last nine thousand years of economic growth and human institutions in terms of geographical characteristics. Pomeranz (2000) accounts for economic divergence between Europe and China since 1750 through coal deposits, disease, ecology, and proximity to exploitable "peripheries." Sachs (2001) argues that tardy growth in modern LDCs derives from their location in tropical zones where agricultural techniques are inherently less productive and the disease burden higher. As we shall see shortly, Domar (1970) explains the economic divergence between Eastern and Western Europe from the medieval period to the 19th century, and serfdom as the central institutional manifestation of that divergence, in terms of the supply of land relative to the supply of labor, which was in turn determined by exogenously occurring population growth and land conquests.

---

[5]  See Calaprice (2011, pp. 384–5, 475), who also reports the following less simple (but probably more accurate) variant of this idea, from Einstein's Herbert Spencer Lecture, "On the Method of Theoretical Physics," delivered in Oxford on 10 June 1933: "It can scarcely be denied that the supreme goal of all theory is to make the irreducible basic elements as simple and as few as possible without having to surrender the adequate representation of a single datum of experience."

The efficiency view of institutions and growth is also widespread among economists, as we have seen in earlier lessons. According to this view, the task of the economic historian is not to find out which institutions are most conducive to growth, but to discover how apparently inefficient and growth-discouraging institutions in past societies were actually efficient in their particular natural or cultural context, whatever the appearances. In this spirit, not only the historical institutions we have met in the lessons above, but many others, have been reinterpreted by one economic historian or another in efficiency terms as a beneficial solution to one or more obstacles to possible transactions—merchant guilds (Greif et al. 1994; Greif, 2006c), craft guilds (Hickson and Thompson, 1991; Epstein, 1998; Zanden, 2009), village communities (McCloskey, 1976, 1991; Townsend, 1993; Richardson, 2005), serfdom (North and Thomas, 1970, 1973; Fenoaltea, 1975a,b), the noble feud (Volckart, 2004), vigilante justice (discussed in Little and Sheffield, 1983; Hine, 1998), and lynching (surveyed in Carrigan, 2004), among many others.

If it were true that institutions were always responses to natural endowments or efficient solutions to economic problems, then they would not matter for growth. It is their significance for growth, however, that motivates economists to understand why institutions arise and why they change.

Fortunately, there is an alternative to viewing institutions either as superstructures of more fundamental natural forces, or as efficient responses to such forces. According to this alternative approach, the institutions of a society result partly or wholly from conflicts over distribution (see Knight, 1995; Acemoglu et al. 2005; Ogilvie, 2007b). This conflict view is based on the idea that institutions affect not just the efficiency of an economy but also how its resources are distributed. That is, institutions affect both the size of the total economic pie and who gets how big a slice. Most people in the economy might well want the pie to be as big as possible—hence the assumption of the efficiency theorists. But people will typically disagree about how to share out the slices. Since institutions affect not only the size of the pie (through influencing efficiency) but also the distribution of the slices (through apportioning the output), people typically disagree about which institutions are best. This causes conflict. Some people strive to maintain particular institutions, others merely cooperate, others quietly sabotage them, and still others resist. Individuals struggle over institutions, but so do groups—and some groups organize for that very purpose. Which institution (or system of institutions) results from this conflict will be affected not just by its efficiency but by its distributional implications for the most powerful individuals and groups (Knight, 1995; Acemoglu et al. 2005; Ogilvie, 2007b).

Efficiency theories do sometimes mention that institutions result from conflict. But they seldom incorporate conflict into their explanations. Instead, conflict remains an incidental by-product of institutions portrayed as primarily existing to enhance efficiency. Thus, for instance, North often mentions distributional effects of institutions in his early work, but explains their rise and evolution in terms of economic efficiency (North and Thomas, 1970, 1973; North, 1981). Greif (2006c) also sometimes acknowledges that institutions can have distributional effects, but analyzes the specific institutions he selects—the Maghribi traders' coalition, the European merchant guild—in terms of their efficiency in encouraging medieval commerce and their compatibility with prevailing cultural beliefs. Insofar as rent-seeking is acknowledged, it is characterized as efficient, on the grounds that "monopoly rights generated a stream of rents that depended on the support of other members and so served as a bond, allowing members to commit themselves to collective action" (Greif et al. 1994, p. 749, 758).

Yet a conflict approach which incorporates the distributional activities of institutions into its analysis without assuming such activities to be efficient can explain many facts about pre-modern institutions that efficiency views cannot. One of the frequently cited justifications of the efficiency view is the longevity of the particular institutions it seeks to rediagnose as efficient. If they were not efficient, the challenge goes, why did they last for centuries? Wouldn't they have disappeared much sooner if they had been so bad for output and growth? The conflict view has a powerful explanation for the longevity of institutions that have historically inflicted considerable damage on the growth of the economies in which they prevailed.

For instance, the conflict view would agree that there is a good economic reason why, as we saw in Lesson 3, guild-like merchant associations existed so widely from the 12th to—in some societies—the 19th century. But this reason was not that they increased aggregate output by guaranteeing property rights or contract enforcement. Rather, they limited competition and reduced exchange by excluding craftsmen, peasants, women, Jews, foreigners, and the urban proletariat from most profitable branches of commerce. Merchant guilds and associations were so widespread and so tenacious not because they efficiently solved economic problems, making everyone better off, but because they efficiently distributed resources to a powerful urban elite, with side benefits for rulers (Lindberg, 2009, 2010; Ogilvie, 2011). This rent-seeking agreement between political authorities and economic interest-groups was explicitly acknowledged by contemporaries, as in 1736 when the ruler of the German state of Württemberg described the merchant guild that legally monopolized the national worsted textile proto-industry as "a substantial national treasure" and extended its commercial privileges at the expense of thousands of impoverished weavers and spinners on the grounds that "especially on the occasion of the recent French invasion threat and the military taxes that were supposed to be raised, it became apparent that no just opportunity should be lost to hold out a helping hand to [this merchant guild] in all just matters as much as possible." (Quoted in Troeltsch, 1897, p. 84.)

The conflict approach would also hold that there is a good economic explanation for why craft guilds were widespread in Europe for many centuries. But this is not that they were good for the whole economy. Empirical micro-studies of guilds' actual activities—as opposed to the rhetorical advocacy of their benefits in literature and legislation—show

how they underpaid employees; overcharged customers; stifled competition; excluded women and Jews; and blocked innovation. Guilds were widespread not because were good for everyone, but because they benefited well-organized interest groups. They made aggregate economic output smaller, but dished out large shares of it to established male masters, with fiscal and regulatory side-benefits to town governments and rulers (Ogilvie, 1997, 2003, 2004a,b,c; 2005d; 2007a; 2008).

The conflict view would also agree that there is a good economic explanation for the tenacity of strong peasant communes, which existed in large parts of Europe for centuries, as we saw in Lesson 4. But this is not that they were efficient for the whole economy. Their regulation of land-markets, migration, technology, settlement, and women's work often hindered the allocation of resources, in ways so innumerable that village micro-studies are still uncovering their true extent and implications. This not only diminished aggregate output but brutally narrowed the consumption and production options of poorer social strata, women, minorities, and migrants. Strong communes persisted not because they efficiently maximized the aggregate output of the entire economy, but because they distributed large shares of a much more limited output to village elites (rich peasants, male household heads), with fiscal, military, and regulatory side-benefits to rulers and landlords (Melton, 1990; Ogilvie, 1997, 2005a,b, 2007b; Dennison and Ogilvie, 2007; Dennison, 2011).

Finally, a conflict approach would agree that there is a good economic reason for the long existence of serfdom; but this is not that it efficiently solved market imperfections in public goods, agricultural innovation, or investment. Rather, serfdom created an economy of privileges that hindered efficient resource allocation in land, labor, capital, and output markets. But although serfdom was profoundly ineffective at increasing aggregate output, it was highly effective at distributing large shares to landlords, with fiscal and military side-benefits to rulers and economic privileges for serf elites.

The example of serfdom, in fact, provides an excellent illustration of the superiority of the conflict view of institutions to alternative approaches which explain institutions in terms of geographical resource endowments or economic efficiency. Indeed, economists concerned with institutions and growth have repeatedly turned their attention to serfdom, precisely because it played such a central role in the divergent growth performance of European economies between the Middle Ages and the 19th century. Serfdom set the institutional rules for agriculture, the most important sector of the medieval economy (Campbell, 2000). In the late Middle Ages, serfdom broke down in some European economies (mainly in the west), but intensified or emerged newly in others (mainly in the east), although the chronology and manifestation of this development varied enormously within both zones of the continent (for recent surveys see Cerman, 2013; Ogilvie, 2013b). But through this entire period agriculture remained by far the most important sector even of the most highly developed economies in Europe: it consumed most land, labor and capital; it produced most food and raw materials; and for industry or commerce to grow, inputs and outputs had to be released from farming (DeVries, 1976; Crafts, 1985; Ogilvie, 2000). The survival, breakdown, and intensity of serfdom in different European societies played a fundamental role in their divergent agricultural performance and hence their divergent growth record between the medieval period and the Industrial Revolution.

Because of its central role in long-term growth and stagnation, serfdom has been used as a test case for nearly every possible approach to institutions and growth—in terms of resource endowments (e.g. Postan, 1966; Domar, 1970), economic efficiency (e.g. North and Thomas, 1970, 1973; Fenoaltea, 1975a,b), and distributional conflicts (e.g. Brenner, 1976; Acemoglu and Wolitzky, 2011). The decline of serfdom is widely regarded as a major contributor to the growth of agriculture in Western Europe and its political abolition in Central and Eastern Europe under the impact of the French Revolution is regarded as a major example of institutional effects on growth (Acemoglu et al. 2011). Yet serfdom was not monolithic, it was embedded in the institutional systems of different European economies in different ways, and its growth effects depended, as we shall see, on its interactions with other components of each institutional system. Serfdom therefore provides an excellent context for contrasting different approaches to institutions, illustrating the strengths of the conflict approach, and demonstrating the work that remains to be done in tracing how institutions affected growth in historical perspective.

## 8.9.1 Resource Endowments, Serfdom, and Growth

Serfdom was an institutional system which obliged a peasant to provide forced labor services to his landlord in exchange for being allowed to occupy land. A serf was legally tied to the landlord in a variety of ways, typically by being prohibited from migrating, marrying, practicing certain occupations, selling certain goods, participating in factor and product markets, or engaging in particular types of consumption without obtaining permission from his landlord. Serfdom was therefore a particularized institution (in the language suggested in Lesson 3) which affected economic growth by restricting access to factor and product markets, preventing allocation of resources to the highest-productivity uses, and creating poor incentives for investment in human capital, land improvements, and technological innovations.

Most economies in Europe were characterized by some version of serfdom between c. 800 and c. 1350. After that date, serfdom began gradually to decline in some societies, such as England, although it survived for longer in others, such as France and western Germany. In the 16th and 17th centuries, some parts of Eastern-Central and Eastern Europe where classic serfdom had either never existed or had declined, including Russia, the Czech lands, Slovakia, Poland, Hungary, and eastern German territories such as Prussia, experienced an intensification of manorial controls by landlords, which has been called the second serfdom. This system remained in force in these economies until its abolition, usually through state action, which occurred in different Central and Eastern European societies at different dates between c. 1760 and c. 1860.

One widely held view within economics is that serfdom was an institutional response to resource endowments, specifically to the relative supply of land and labor. This idea is based on a paper by Domar (1970) arguing that serfdom can be explained as a response to a high land-labor ratio. Labor scarcity created severe competition among employers (landlords) for laborers (peasants) to work their land. Moreover, the abundance of land meant that peasants had attractive options setting up as independent farmers and withdrawing their labor from landlords altogether. This created a strong incentive for landlords to organize an institution to prevent peasants from doing these things, by legally binding them to the estate, forbidding them from migrating to competing employers, and obliging them to deliver a certain quantity of forced labor on the landlord's farm (the demesne). Domar argued that this explains the rise of serfdom in 17th-century Russia: the land-labor ratio rose because of the Muscovite colonial conquests and landlords devised serfdom as a way of protecting their supply of scarce peasant labor.

However, there are many examples of economies in which the land-labor ratio was high, but there was neither serfdom nor slavery. The most striking counterexample to Domar's model of serfdom is Europe after the Black Death. This virulent pandemic greatly increased the land-labor ratio in most parts of Europe by killing off 30–60% of the population between 1348 and 1350. According to Domar's theory, this should have caused serfdom to intensify, or to come into being in societies in which it had not previously existed. However, this did not happen. Instead, many parts of Western Europe saw serfdom break down after the Black Death, and never reappear no matter what happened to the land-labor ratio.

The decline of serfdom in Western Europe after the Black Death had already stimulated Postan (1966) to propose his own theory of serfdom in terms of resource endowments. Postan's theory was diametrically opposed to that of Domar, since it argued that the rising land-labor ratio after the Black Death caused the decline of serfdom because it made landlords compete for peasants by offering better conditions. Postan had only put this forward as an account of the decline of serfdom in Western Europe after the Black Death, not as a general model of serfdom in all societies. Domar (1970) did regard himself as advancing a general model of serfdom in terms of relative resource endowments. But he knew enough about the historical findings to recognize that a high land-labor ratio only provided the incentive for landlords to organize institutions to prevent themselves from losing laborers. Whether they actually did so depended on whether they were able to organize politically, i.e. were powerful enough to coerce peasants and prevent other landlords from competing them away by offering them better conditions (e.g. the freedom to take economic and demographic decisions without landlord permission). So Domar's model is one in which serfdom arises from relative resource endowments plus the political power of different social groups—i.e. it is broadly consistent with the conflict model of serfdom which we shall discuss shortly.

## 8.9.2 Efficiency, Serfdom, and Growth

Despite the near unanimity among economists and economic historians that serfdom was harmful for growth,[6] it was one of the first institutions to be re-diagnosed as efficient. In the early 1970s, North and Thomas, (1970, 1971, 1973) proposed a model of the "rise of the western world," according to which serfdom was "an efficient solution to the existing problems" in medieval economies, a voluntary contract that committed peasants to provide labor services to lords in exchange for "the public good of protection and justice" (1973, p. 21). North and Thomas explicitly stated that "serfdom in Western Europe was essentially not an exploitative arrangement … [it] was essentially a contractual arrangement where labor services were exchanged for the public good of protection and justice" (1971, p. 778). The reason serfs had to be forced to render these payments was that protection and justice were non-excludable, so individual serfs had an incentive to free-ride. Serfs were protected from being exploited by the landlord as the monopoly supplier of protection, according to North and Thomas, by institutional rules (the "customs of the manor") and by the fact that they had a low-cost exit option (absconding from their lord). The reason serfs had to be forced to pay in the form of forced labor services rather than cash or kind was uncertainty (the lords could not know *ex ante* how much the serfs were able to produce), transaction costs (the costs incurred by a landlord in reaching a bargain with a large number of peasants), and absence of markets (so that cash or kind would be of no use to the landlord since there was nothing to purchase with them).

The implication of these efficiency theories and others (e.g. Fenoaltea, 1975a,b, 1984) was that serfdom was an efficient institution given the characteristics of the economies in which it occurred, and was therefore beneficial for economic growth until these characteristics changed. But there is little evidence for this. Protection and justice were, in fact, excludable. Protection was provided by the lord's manor house or castle from which serfs could be excluded if they did not pay. Furthermore, the lord's fortifications did not protect serfs against that large proportion of the random violence of medieval society which took the form of unpredictable raids. Justice was also excludable: manorial courts operated by the landlord or his officials could refuse to provide justice to anyone, could strip a serf of legal protection by outlawing him, and could charge court fees to cover the costs of judging legal conflicts. Further doubt is cast on the idea that serfdom was an efficient solution to the provision of justice by the fact that feasible alternatives did exist: the prince, the church, abbeys, and towns all provided law-courts, which offered alternatives to the manorial courts and often did not even acknowledge differences in serf status. Also, neither absconding nor the customs of the manor provided effective protection to serfs against monopolistic landlords. A strong landlord could simply ignore

---

[6] Revisionist views claiming that serfdom did not harm the economy have been proposed (most recently in Cerman, 2012, 2013), but do not hold up well to empirical scrutiny (see Briggs, 2013; Dennison, 2011, 2013; Guzowski, 2013; Klein, 2013; North, 2013; Ogilvie, 2013b; Rasmussen, 2013; Seppel, 2013).

custom, and many did. Furthermore, absconding was a costly option which required the serf to abandon land, possessions, family, and social capital.

An even more fundamental problem for the efficiency view of serfdom is that much of the insecurity and injustice against which serfs were being "protected" by their landlords was actually produced by feudal landlords themselves. Serfdom was thus much more like a protection racket in which the landlords, as the more powerful party, generated both the problem and the solution. Serfdom did not constitute a bundle of voluntary contracts which contributed to economic efficiency, but rather was a set of rent-seeking arrangements devoted to redistributing resources from peasants to landlords.[7] Moreover, North and Thomas are wrong in claiming that peasants had to pay in the form of labor rather than cash or kind because of absence of markets. Every serf society that has ever been observed had markets for goods as well as for factor inputs, as we shall discuss in greater detail shortly.

The findings for serfdom show clearly the dangers of trying to explain institutions purely as efficient solutions to economic problems. Serfdom, it is clear, also involved coercive power, and some of the problems to which it is supposed to have been a solution were themselves caused by the exercise of this power. This suggests that we cannot assume that any institution we observe, even if it survives for hundreds of years, did so because it was the efficient set of social rules for maximizing aggregate economic output. We have to investigate what effect it had on the distribution of this output (Acemoglu et al. 2005; Ogilvie, 2007b).

### 8.9.3 Distributional Conflicts, Serfdom, and Growth

A fundamental break from viewing serfdom as resulting from resource endowments or economic efficiency, and thus being neutral or beneficial for economic growth, came with the work of Brenner (1976). Brenner pointed out serious problems with the view that labor scarcity (e.g. in Europe after the Black Death) caused serfdom either to strengthen or to break down. Plague-induced labor scarcity changed the incentives of both serfs and landlords. Certainly, as North and Thomas had argued, labor scarcity increased serfs' incentives to use their increased bargaining position to break down serfdom. But it also increased landlords' incentives to intensify serfdom in order to secure their supply of scarce laborers (the Domar argument). In actual practice, the change in relative supplies

---

[7] North (1981, p. 131) later conceded that "carrying over the modern-day notion of contract to the serf-lord relationship is imposing a modern-day concept which is misleading. The serf was bound by his lord and his actions and movements were severely constrained by his status; no voluntary agreement was involved. Nevertheless, it is crucial to re-emphasize a key point of our analysis; namely, that it was the changing opportunity cost of lords and serfs at the margin which changed manorialism and eventually led to its demise." However, this does not address all the problems with his model, especially the excludability of the protection and justice services provided by landlords and the fact that landlords themselves generated much of the insecurity and justice they are supposed to have been protecting serfs against.

of land and labor after the Black Death saw serfdom develop in diametrically opposite directions in different European societies. In most Western European economies, serfdom broke down after the Black Death, albeit at different rates and times. In most parts of Eastern Europe, manorial powers survived the Black Death and greatly intensified under the second serfdom.

This was not because serfdom ceased to be efficient and to promote economic growth in the west but continued to be efficient and to promote growth in the east. Rather, which path an economy followed was "a question of power, indeed of force" (Brenner, 1976, p. 51). The outcome in each specific society was determined by the ability of both peasants and landlords to band together collectively with their fellows as well as to ally with the coercive power of the state. In Western Europe, the stronger central state that emerged toward the end of the medieval period pursued policies of "peasant protection" with the motivation of maintaining the peasantry's ability to pay taxes to the state rather than rents and labor services to landlords. In Eastern Europe, by contrast, the state allied with the landlords and enforced their controls over the peasantry in exchange for a share of the spoils. Brenner argued that serfdom was always an exploitative arrangement that redistributed resources from peasants to landlords. He also argued that this redistribution had harmful effects on economic performance: the effect of the second serfdom, in his view, was that "the possibility of …economic growth was destroyed and East Europe consigned to backwardness for centuries" (Brenner, 1976, p. 60).

Acemoglu and Wolitzky (2011) extended Brenner's perspective by proposing a model of labor coercion which sought to combine resource endowments and power. It placed the relative scarcity of labor and land at center stage, but formalized Brenner's point that labor scarcity can have two countervailing effects on serfdom, one intensifying it and one breaking it down. Their model suggests that labor scarcity, via its effect on the price of output and the returns to coercion, tended to intensify serfdom, as argued by Domar (1970). However, their model also suggests that labor scarcity, by improving the outside options of peasants, tended to weaken serfdom, as argued by Postan (1966) and North and Thomas (1971). Acemoglu and Wolitzky argue that what decided whether labor scarcity led serfdom to intensify or alternatively to decline was whether the value of output and the returns to coercion exceeded the value of the outside options of peasants. In Eastern Europe, they argue, missing markets meant that serfs had few external options, so the value of these options was surpassed by the returns to coercion; hence falling population in Eastern Europe intensified serfdom. In Western Europe, by contrast, the existence of markets gave serfs profitable outside options, which exceeded the value of the returns to coercion, so population decrease caused serfdom to decline.

This is a major advance over previous contributions, but leaves out what historical research shows about three important institutions which co-existed with serfdom and affected its operation: the state, the community, and the market. Regarding the state, as Acemoglu and Wolitzky themselves acknowledge (2011, pp. 569–71), their model treats each employer of serfs as an individual rather than recognizing that in practice serf landlords typically exercised coercion collectively and used this collective coercion (often enforced via the state) to regulate serfs' outside options. Although Acemoglu and Wolitzky contend that their argument still holds when the state is included, the fact remains that it fails to address the argument of Brenner (1976), according to which the strongest variable determining whether labor scarcity would strengthen or weaken serfdom was politics, specifically collective action by serfs and landlords and relations between each social group and the state.

Regarding the community, the Acemoglu and Wolitzky model treats each serf employee as an individual, rather than recognizing that in practice serfs formed communities which operated, at least in some ways, as institutional entities. The existence of communal institutions enabled serfs to engage in collective action toward both the landlord and the state. But the serf community also provided an entity with which landlords and the state could bargain in order to help them coerce individual serfs who sought to violate the constraints of serfdom, taxation, or conscription.

Regarding the market, Acemoglu and Wolitzky (2011) simply assume it to be missing in Eastern Europe, rather than recognizing that in practice Eastern European serfs did have access to, and participated in, markets for labor, capital, land, and output. The existence of these markets meant that serfs did have outside options, but the existence of market participation by serfs also offered landlords an additional and highly attractive source of rents. In practice, as we shall see, many landlords used their institutional powers to extract rents from their serfs' participation in markets, the profits from which contributed to their wealth, which they then invested partly in political action to sustain and intensify their own economic privileges under serfdom.

## 8.9.4 Serfdom and the Institutional System

Closer examination of the variables that created, sustained, and ultimately broke down serfdom strongly supports the view that distributional conflicts and political forces were central. But it also shows the importance of widening our focus beyond one institution in isolation to the wider institutional system. We cannot restrict our attention solely to serfdom, in the sense of the institutional rules governing relations between peasants and landlords. We must also analyze adjacent institutions, particularly those pointed out in the preceding section: the market, the community, and the state.

Markets were neither missing nor irrelevant to peasants' lives in serf societies, whether in medieval Western Europe or in early modern Eastern Europe. In the past few decades, micro-studies have revealed unambiguously that peasants in medieval and early modern serf societies made widespread use of markets. They used markets to buy and sell land (Cerman, 2008, 2012, 2013; Campbell, 2009), to offer and employ labor (Campbell, 2009; Dennison, 2011), to lend and borrow money (Briggs, 2004, 2009; Campbell, 2009; Ogilvie, 2001; Bolton, 2012), and to buy and sell food and craft products (Kaminski,

1975; Smith, 1996; Britnell, 1996; Cerman, 1996; Ogilvie, 2001; Bolton, 2012). Market participation can be widely observed among serfs not just in medieval England, but also in Germany, Switzerland, Austria, Italy, and France in the Middle Ages, as well as many regions of Eastern-Central and Eastern Europe under the early modern second serfdom, including Poland, Hungary, the Czech lands, and Russia (Kaminski, 1975; Dennison, 2011; Cerman, 2012; Ogilvie, 2012). This market participation was not limited to the richest serfs, but extended to all strata of serf society, including women, laborers, landless cottagers, and those subsisting at the edge of starvation (Kaminski, 1975; Cerman, 2012; Ogilvie, 2001, 2012).

Markets were present in serf economies, therefore, and offered attractive outside options for serfs. However, markets also offered attractive options for landlords. The result was that serfs' access to markets was often constrained by landlords' exercise of power in search of further rents. Thus serfs used markets widely to hire out their own labor, to employ the labor of others, and to buy and sell land (Topolski, 1974; Dennison, 2011; Klein, 2013; Ogilvie, 2001, 2005c, 2012, 2013b), although landlords used their powers under serfdom to intervene in both labor and land transactions to obtain rents or when they perceived a benefit to themselves (Harnisch, 1975; Ogilvie, 2001, 2005c, 2012; Dennison and Ogilvie, 2007; Velková, 2012). Serfs bought and sold agricultural and industrial output in markets, even though again landlords used their powers under serfdom to intervene in these markets by obliging serfs to buy licenses, pay arbitrary fees, offer their products first for sale to the landlord at dictated prices, or buy certain products solely from the landlord's own demesne operations (Cerman, 1996; Ogilvie, 2001, 2005c, 2012, 2013b; Klein, 2013). It was not, therefore, that markets were missing in serf societies, and that serfs thus lacked outside options, but rather that landlords intervened in these markets in such a way as to redistribute to themselves part of the profits from serfs' market participation. The interaction with markets entrenched serfdom more deeply and contributed to its longevity by further benefiting landlords at the expense of serfs.

Village communities also played a central role in the existence and survival of serfdom. Scholars such as Brenner (1976) had claimed that, under serfdom, village communities were stifled by landlord oppression. However, subsequent micro-studies have made clear that this was not the case (Wunder, 1978, 1996; Ogilvie, 2005a,b; Dennison and Ogilvie, 2007; Cerman, 2008, 2012). There was no question about the institutional capacity of village communities to operate as autonomous bodies under serfdom (Peters, 1995a,b, 1997; Wunder, 1995). Village communities organized direct resistance against attempts to intensify serfdom, and appealed to princely and urban jurisdictions against the landlord (Harnisch, 1972; Ogilvie, 2005a,b, 2012, 2013b). The strength of serfs' communal institutions and their ability to bargain with outside institutions, such as the state, other landlords, and towns, influenced the extent to which the landlord could intervene in their market transactions.

However, village communities played a complicated role in serfdom; they did not simply operate successfully and single-mindedly to protect serfs' interests. Serf communities were not fully independent of manorial intervention. The top village officers were often selected and appointed by the landlord (Harnisch, 1975; Peters, 1995a,b). Even the communal officials who were selected by serfs themselves were co-opted disproportionately by (and from) the top stratum of rich serfs. This oligarchy ran the village in its own interests and benefitted from communal autonomy (Melton, 1988; Rudert, 1995a,b; Hagen, 2002; Ogilvie, 2005a,b, 2012; Dennison and Ogilvie, 2007). Communal institutions typically implemented the choices of their most powerful members partly by limiting those of the least powerful—big farmers over laborers, men over women, established householders over unmarried youths, insiders over migrants (Ogilvie, 2005a,b, 2012, 2013b; Dennison and Ogilvie, 2007).

These characteristics of serf communities were not merely incidental. Rather, they were central components of how serfdom functioned. In normal times—i.e. except during legal conflicts or revolts of serfs against their landlords—community institutions carried out essential tasks that supported the manorial administration and ensured that serfdom functioned smoothly (Harnisch, 1986, 1989a,b; Dennison and Ogilvie, 2007; Ogilvie, 2012, 2013b). Landlords devolved to communal officers the organization of labor services and the collection of manorial dues (Peters, 1995a,b). They also deployed an elaborate community responsibility system which made the entire serf community responsible for the failings of any individual (Harnisch, 1989b; Peters, 1997). If a serf shirked on his labor services or vacated his farm without permission, his community was institutionally obliged to take up the slack. This created strong incentives for the community to report its delinquent or economically weak members to the manor; such communal reports lay behind many serf expulsions (Harnisch, 1989b). Collective responsibility for rendering forced labor and other payments to the landlord and the state also motivated communities to enforce the mobility restrictions of serfdom, and on many occasions one can observe communal officials pursuing absconding fellow serfs on behalf of the landlord (Peters, 1997). Conversely, staying in the good graces of the communal officials and the village oligarchy was essential if a serf hoped to secure a certificate that he had been a good farmer, which might in turn persuade the landlord to take a positive view of his applications regarding access to land or other resources (Harnisch, 1975; Hagen, 2002; Dennison and Ogilvie, 2007; Ogilvie, 2005a,b, 2012, 2013b). The most powerful stratum of serfs, who typically controlled the serf commune, was given very strong incentives to collaborate with landlord and state (Melton, 1988; Blaschke, 1991; Rudert, 1995a,b; Hagen, 2002; Ogilvie, 2005a,b,c; Dennison, 2011). The serf commune was thus an important component of the institutional system that helped to keep serfdom in being and intensified its negative growth effects while benefiting landlords (Ogilvie, 2005a,b, 2012, 2013b; Dennison and Ogilvie, 2007).

The state, finally, also affected the existence and survival of serfdom. Serfs were the state's main source of tax payments and army conscripts (Harnisch, 1989a,b; Seppel, 2013;

Ogilvie, 2013b). Often serfs were the sole source of tax payments, since the nobility typically used their dominance over parliamentary institutions to free themselves from taxation. This fact gave the state two countervailing incentives vis-à-vis serfdom. On the one hand, fiscal interests motivated the state to compete with landlords for serf money and labor (Hagen, 1989; Cerman, 2012). In a number of early modern Central and Eastern European serf societies, when lords demanded more forced labor, state courts granted redress to serfs, if only to safeguard serfs' fiscal capacities. On the other hand, the costs of maintaining state officials on the ground created strong incentives for the state to devolve tax-collection and conscription to local personnel, which meant collaborating with the landlord's administration and the whole regime of serfdom. The state thus competed with landlords for serf output but collaborated with landlords in the process of extracting that output (Hagen, 1989; Ogilvie, 2005c, 2013b; Cerman, 2008, 2012; Rasmussen, 2013; Seppel, 2013).

The state was also the gatekeeper of serfs' access to the legal system. In most societies under serfdom, the serfs' own village courts enjoyed the lower jurisdiction, which issued decisions on minor offences, neighborly conflicts, and land transactions (Kaak, 1991). But the higher jurisdiction over major offences was exercised in the first instance not by princes' courts but by landlords' courts (Cerman, 2012; Ogilvie, 2013b). Landlords typically secured this jurisdictional control from princes in return for fiscal and political favors, although to varying degrees in different serf societies (Kaak, 1991; Ogilvie, 2013b). In some European serf societies, such as Bohemia and Russia, landlords also successfully secured state legislation restricting serfs' right of appeal to princely courts (Ogilvie, 2005c; Dennison, 2011). But in many others, including Prussia, serfs retained (or were explicitly granted) the institutional entitlement to appeal against their landlords to state courts (Harnisch, 1975, 1989a,b; Hagen, 2002).

The legal balance of power between serfs and their landlords was influenced by the power of the ruler relative to the nobility in each polity (Harnisch, 1989a,b; Cerman, 2012; Ogilvie, 2013b). Where the ruler was weak compared to the nobles, the powers of landlords over serfs tended to be greater. But this did not mean that the state had no effect on serfdom in such societies: where the ruler depended heavily on noble support, he not only refrained from granting redress to serfs but positively supported landlords in most conflicts. Where the ruler lacked alternative sources of financial and political support and needed the support of landlords to obtain grants of taxes and payment of princely debts from the parliament, the ruler was more likely to acquiesce in most noble demands, including intensification of serfdom with state enforcement, as we saw in Lesson 2. Where the ruler had more plentiful alternative sources of revenue (e.g. from taxes on mining) and political support (e.g. from towns), he was able to resist the demands of the nobility (often expressed partly through a parliament) to a greater extent.

Probably the most important role the state played in serfdom was by legislating to shape, sustain, and ultimately abolish the entire system (Harnisch, 1986, 1994; Ogilvie, 2013b). Under serfdom, landlords responded to labor scarcity by using mobility restrictions to prevent serfs from voting with their feet to migrate to better conditions, and by cooperating with other lords to send fugitives back. Like any cartellistic arrangement, this landlord cartel was threatened by free-rider problems: lords collectively benefited from other lords' compliance but individually profited by violating the arrangement. This free-rider problem, as well as the transaction costs of coordinating enforcement across multiple manorial jurisdictions, gave landlords a strong incentive to seek support from the political authorities to enforce the institutional constraints of serfdom (Ogilvie, 2013b). In this way, the state played a fundamental role in sustaining the institution of serfdom.

However, the state also played a fundamental role in the ultimate abolition of serfdom, which took place at different dates in Eastern-Central and Eastern European societies in the course of the 18th and 19th centuries. In a number of serf societies, such as Prussia and Russia, the state reforms that abolished serfdom involved setting up a system of legal obligations requiring former serfs and their descendants to make redemption payments to their former landlords and their descendants as a form of recompense for losing the land, cash rents, and labour services that disappeared with the abolition of serfdom (Harnisch, 1986, 1994). In so doing, the state played a final, essential role in institutional change: mediating an enforceable agreement between serfs and landlords which credibly committed former serfs to reimburse former landlords for the losses caused by the institutional transformation.

The economic history of serfdom thus provides an excellent illustration of the importance to institutional change of dealing with the lack of what Acemoglu (2003) calls a "political Coase theorem." A party that holds (or obtains) some institutional power cannot make a credible commitment to bind its own future actions without an outside agency with the coercive capacity to enforce such a commitment. The absence of a political Coase theorem means that institutional changes that would make an entire economy better off are often blocked by the fact that it is difficult for the potential gainers from institutional reform to commit themselves to reimburse the losers after the latter have lost their institutional powers (Acemoglu, 2003; Acemoglu et al. 2005, p. 436; Ogilvie, 2007, pp. 666–7). The economic history of serfdom provides arguably the best example of this principle influencing the process of institutional change. In societies such as Russia and Prussia, serfdom was only abolished to the extent that the state was able to solve this problem of the missing "political Coase theorem" by mediating and enforcing a commitment for the gainers to compensate the losers. When Prussian serfdom was abolished in 1807, for instance, the state legislated that each former serf was to be allocated a parcel of land and freed from forced labor services, but was also legally obliged to compensate his landlord for the loss of this land and labor by making a series of redemption payments over a period of decades (Knapp, 1887; Harnisch, 1986, 1994). The state thus mediated and enforced a commitment that the serfs, as gainers from the abolition of serfdom, would compensate the landlords, as losers.

Economic history thus provides considerable support for the proposition that institutions are not just a response to resource endowments or efficient solutions to economic problems, in which case they would not matter for growth, but rather that they result partly or wholly from conflicts over distribution and hence have the potential to play a causal role in influencing whether an economy will grow or stagnate. But the growth literature, in pursuing a conflict view of institutions, has not yet made the best use of the historical evidence, and has placed excessive emphasis on high politics and top-down revolutions. The available evidence suggests, rather, that some of the most important institutions that harmed long-term growth in European history—institutions such as serfdom—arose from deep-seated and enduring distributional struggles among special-interest groups, carried out on a local level, far from the noise of parliamentary and ministerial struggles in national capitals, and often outside the formal political arena altogether. Conversely, societies that managed to minimize the influence of such groups over economic policies were the ones that gradually reduced the traction of particularized institutions and increased that of generalized ones, enabling their economies to achieve growth. Economic history thus strongly supports the centrality of socio-political conflict to developing the institutions that affect growth (for good or ill), but suggests that we must widen our definition of conflict from national politics as conventionally conceived, to include lower-level distributional conflicts and slow, gradual, non-revolutionary processes in the provinces.

## 8.10. ILLUSTRATION OF THE LESSONS: SERFDOM AND GROWTH

Having made it our main illustrative example for Lesson 8, we have now said enough about serfdom that we can further show how it exemplifies each of the eight lessons as well. Serfdom is of some independent interest in any case, as it governed the economic options of a majority of the population in agriculture, by far the largest economic sector in nearly every European economy throughout the medieval period and in many areas until the end of the 19th century. The decline of serfdom in Western Europe and intensification in Eastern Europe after the late medieval period certainly coincided with, and probably contributed to, the significant divergence in the growth of per capita income in the two parts of the continent between then and the 19th century (Ogilvie, 2013b). Understanding serfdom is therefore necessary if one wishes to understand divergence or convergence in the long-term growth performance of European societies between the Middle Ages and the Industrial Revolution.

First, serfdom shows clearly the importance of public-order institutions for economic growth, the argument advanced in Lesson 1. There is no empirical support for the idea that serfdom was an efficient private-order substitute for missing public-order institutions, whether in ensuring private property rights or in guaranteeing contract enforcement

(North and Thomas, 1970, 1971, 1973; Fenoaltea, 1975a,b). The decline of serfdom in Western Europe in the late medieval period was closely related to the unwillingness of the public authorities in those societies to provide support to the landlords in enforcing their institutional privileges over serfs. Conversely, the intensification of serfdom in Eastern-Central and Eastern European societies from the 16th century onwards was only possible because the state provided coercive support to landlords. Finally, the abolition of the second serfdom in Eastern European societies between the 1780s and the 1860s relied upon the public authorities to solve the problem of the missing political Coase theorem.

Second, serfdom shows clearly that a strong parliament, even one representing the interests of wealth holders, is not invariably beneficial for economic growth. In some serf societies, such as Poland, the parliament was extremely strong relative to the ruler. In all serf societies, the parliament represented wealth holders in the shape of the noble landed interests. The stronger the parliament in a serf society, the greater the ability of the landed nobility to hold the state to ransom, demanding that it provide state enforcement to back up the powers of landlords over the rural population, as a precondition for parliament to grant taxes or military support to the ruler. The history of European serfdom shows that economic growth depends not on whether a society has an institution that calls itself a parliament, exercises control over the executive, and represents wealth holders, but rather on the underlying institutions of that society, which determine how people obtain wealth, how wealth holders obtain parliamentary representation, and whether they then use that parliamentary representation to implement institutional rules that redistribute resources to themselves or alternatively ones that enable growth for the entire economy.

Third, serfdom illustrates the centrality of the distinction between generalized and particularized institutions. Serfdom was a completely particularized institution, in the sense that the rules it imposed and the services it provided depended completely on an individual's personal status and privileges as a serf or a non-serf. Access to land, labor, capital, and output under serfdom was not available or transferable to everyone impartially but rather depended upon the identity of the economic agent as a landlord, a freeman, or a serf. Furthermore, most forms of serfdom depended heavily on collaboration with a second particularized institution, that of the village community. The rules of the village community also operated in a particularized way, in the sense that ownership, use, and transfers of inputs and outputs depended upon an individual's personal status and privileges, e.g. as a village member rather than a migrant, a male householder rather than a woman or a dependent male, a substantial farmer rather than a landless laborer. However, in European serf societies, the completely particularized institutions of serfdom and the village community co-existed with the institutions of the state and the market, which were at least partly generalized. The precise balance between particularized and generalized institutions in serf societies determined how long serfdom survived, how much it constrained growth, as well as when and how it would be abolished.

Fourth, serfdom shows how property rights institutions and contracting institutions both matter, and are not separable. When people in serf societies traded, they simultaneously transferred property rights to another person and made a contract. Landlords intervened not just in property rights but also in contracts, by invalidating agreements in their own interests or those of clients to whom they had granted market privileges. Moreover, the abolition of serfdom in Eastern-Central and Eastern Europe often improved the security of private property rights in land, but did not see any improvement in agricultural growth. One reason was that in order for the growth benefits of improved property rights to be unleashed, it was also necessary for contracting institutions to improve so as to provide peasants with incentives to incur the costs and risks of investing in human capital, land improvements, and innovations. That is, the political authorities had to establish not only generalized property rights but also generalized contract enforcement. This required them to stop supporting particularized interventions by special-interest groups that diminished the security of contracts. Only when this was undertaken could the benefits of growth-favorable property rights be unleashed and economic growth quicken. Serfdom shows that distributional conflicts and the coercive powers of elites played a major role in contracting institutions, just as they did in the enforcement of property rights.

Fifth, serfdom shows that secure private property rights can be good or bad for growth, depending on whether they are generalized or particularized. Under serfdom, landlords had very secure, clearly defined, and extensive private property rights. But these were property rights that were particularized, in the sense that they were based on non-economic characteristics of the owner: his personal status and legal privileges as a noble landlord and his possession of coercive power over his serfs. Transactions involving these secure private property rights were governed by the personal characteristics of the lord, including his coercive capacities. These very secure and well-defined private property rights prevented growth from taking off, by limiting the extent to which resources were allocated to the users that had the highest-productivity uses for them. Instead, the particularized property rights that prevailed under serfdom allocated assets to those with legal privileges and coercive capacities. The particularized nature of private property rights under serfdom limited the extent to which serfs could invest in increasing the productivity of their land, as well as their ability to use it as collateral to obtain loans for investment purposes.

Sixth, serfdom shows that security of private property rights—whether of ownership, use, or transfer—was a matter of degree, rather than presence or absence. In many European serf societies, serfs had rights of ownership over their holdings: in some, it was virtually impossible for a serf to be evicted from his farm by his landlord; in most others, eviction required a legal case to be made that the serf had violated the conditions of his tenure, for instance by failing to pay his rent or labor dues. In most European serf societies that have been studied, there were also secure rights of use, in the sense that serfs can be observed choosing which crops to cultivate (e.g. cash crops such as flax) and investing in their holdings (e.g. by constructing buildings or by manuring fields). In most European serf societies, serfs also bought, sold, and bequeathed their holdings, and were able to lease and rent at least some parcels of land. In principle, a serf required his landlord's permission for all land transfers, but in a majority of cases this was granted virtually automatically. This was certainly the case in England under serfdom, and thus long before 1688, since serfdom declined in England after c. 1350. Moreover, serfs had a considerable (if not perfect) degree of security of ownership and use rights over their property, not just in medieval England but in virtually every other European serf society that has ever been studied. Security of ownership and use over private property existed in nearly every medieval and early modern European society, but their generalized features were often constrained by the operation of adjacent or conflicting particularized institutional arrangements. Serfdom provides a clear example of how security of private property rights is a matter of degree rather than kind. It also illustrates the importance of breaking down the concept of "security" of property rights into its different components, examining each separately, and analyzing how each component influenced economic growth.

Seventh, serfdom shows clearly the importance of recognizing that institutions are embedded in a wider institutional system and are constrained by the other institutions in that system. Behind the facade of serfdom lay a set of institutional arrangements that varied greatly across different European societies and across time-periods. This was because serfdom did not exist in isolation, as a set of institutional rules governing the relationship between peasants and noble landlords. Rather, it was embedded in a wider system of other institutions—the market, the village community, the state, the family, and many others. The functioning of serfdom, its survival, and its impact on growth were all affected by the availability and often the active intervention of these other institutions.

Eighth, serfdom demonstrates the centrality of distributional conflicts to the evolution of institutional systems and their impact on growth. Serfdom survived for centuries in the teeth of changing resource endowments and rampant inefficiency, because it benefited powerful groups: landlords, rulers, and members of the serf oligarchy. But the distributional conflicts that sustained serfdom raged not only, or even predominantly, at the level of high politics. Rather, they consisted of lower-level and longer-lasting distributional struggles among special-interest groups, mostly outside the arena of national politics.

## 8.11. CONCLUSION

This chapter has sought to bring historical evidence to bear on the question of how institutions affect long-run economic growth. Although we still need to know much more about the institutions that influenced economic success in past centuries, there is much we can say even with the evidence we have, positively and negatively, about the conditions for growth. The growth literature contains a number of strong claims about economic history and institutions. This chapter has shown that some of these claims are not supported by historical research, and must be replaced. Others are controversial, and the evidence surveyed in this chapter has suggested the direction in which they must be revised. Still others are probably right, and this chapter has tried to show how they could be rendered more useful for theory and policy if they made better use of the historical evidence.

We can definitively rule out some very widely held hypotheses which claim that some specific, singular institution played a key causal role in economic growth. Private-order institutions are widely claimed to be capable of substituting for public-order institutions in supporting economic growth. But as we saw in Lessons 1 and 3, the historical examples which are supposed to support this view turn out not to have existed. Private-order institutions can supplement public-order institutions, but cannot substitute for them. Public-order institutions are necessary for markets to function—for good or ill. Parliaments are a second institution widely claimed to play a central role in facilitating economic growth. But, as we saw in Lesson 2, parliaments have a very spotty historical record of supporting growth, and in the few cases they have done so they appear to have required to possess very specific characteristics and to be embedded in a wider system of supporting institutions. Even secure private property rights, widely regarded as a key to economic growth, turn out not to have been invariably beneficial in the historical record. In those cases in which such property rights played an important causal role in growth, as in the European agricultural revolution they needed to possess the special characteristic of being generalized, and they needed also to be supported by other components of the institutional system, especially contracting institutions. These findings enable us to rule out simple institutional recipes, such as focusing solely on building private-order social networks, establishing parliaments, or developing property rights, at the expense of other parts of the institutional system.

A clear corollary emerges from these findings. Institutions do not operate in isolation but as part of a wider system. Property rights institutions are facilitated by contracting institutions and constrained by communal and manorial ones. Contracting institutions operate well or badly depending on public-order institutions; the organizing abilities of urban and rural communes; the privileges of corporative occupational associations; and the powers of landlords under manorial systems such as serfdom. The institution of the family is interdependent with the wider framework of non-familial institutions. Serfdom depended on the state, on peasant communes, and even on markets. Most of the central economic institutions over the past millennium appear to have affected growth only in interaction with other components of the wider institutional system.

The most important lesson from our investigation of institutions and growth in history, however, concerns perspectives for the future. Again and again, the result of our lessons has led us to the remark cited at the end of Lesson 7: "everything should be made as simple as possible, but not simpler." Two apparently opposed kinds of simplification are now particularly conspicuous. One of them tries to find the point at which the indispensable set of institutions came into existence. Since the Glorious Revolution of 1688 occurred conveniently about three generations before the first stirrings of English industrialization, it has been seized upon (as we saw in Lessons 2, 5, and 6) as the turning point of history, at which the institutions essential to growth began. The other, apparently opposite, simplification is that many societies have the right institutions, e.g. secure property rights, without experiencing growth. In particular, it is pointed out that 13th-century England had all the institutions that matter to growth, and yet failed to industrialize.

As we saw in a number of the lessons in this chapter, the apparent disagreement between these two kinds of simplification is superficial. What they agree on is more important—the assumption that institutions can be exhaustively described, in all their implications for growth, by their informal, ordinary-language names such as secure property rights, public-order institutions, or parliament. The assumption is that each such label refers unambiguously to a particular, identifiable social configuration of some kind. This chapter has shown that this assumption is untenable. The reason English economic history can be used to argue both that property rights are essential for growth and that property rights are irrelevant for growth is that property rights encompasses an enormous variety of heterogeneous phenomena. Informal institutional labels, as the historical evidence surveyed in this chapter has shown, are imprecise, they are ambiguous, and in many cases they overlap; none of them has anything like a sharp definition.

A major theme of this chapter has been that the entities referred to by these labels are not well defined—i.e. that the assumption shared by the two apparently opposite kinds of simplification is false. Conventional institutional labels are ill defined in at least three ways: they lack sharp criteria of application (they refer to a large variety of different social configurations); they lack a scale of intensity or degree (they are assumed to be either present or absent, with no gradations in between); and they fail to reflect the interconnections between the configuration they apparently refer to and the entire institutional system of which that configuration is an integral part, let alone to give any hint how the character of that configuration changes as its institutional context and interdependencies change. The historical findings surveyed in this chapter therefore open up three challenges for future research on institutions and growth.

The first challenge is to sharpen the criteria of application of conventional institutional labels. Each institutional label currently used in the analysis of economic growth refers to a large variety of different social configurations. Parliaments, even those representing the interests of wealth holders, as we saw in Lesson 2, can refer to anything from the post-1688 English parliament (relatively pluralistic, if still corrupt), to the 18th-century Württemberg *Landschaft* (the other constitutional monarchy in Europe, but manned by guildsmen and given to granting privileges to rent-seeking corporate groups), to the Polish *Sejm* (much more powerful than the feeble Polish executive, but mainly used to enforce the powers of noble landlords under serfdom). The historical evidence presented in this chapter suggests that economists need to break down the concept of parliament manned by wealth holders analytically by registering how wealth holders obtain their wealth, what kind of wealth it is, how wealth holders obtain representation in parliament, how variegated their economic interests are, and what mechanisms and levers of economic intervention the specific parliamentary institution grants to its members. Likewise, the conventional institutional label "secure property rights" has been applied by respectworthy economists and historians to property regimes as disparate as ninth-century Italy, 13th-century England, 17th-century Germany, and rich Western economies at the beginning of the 21st century. The historical evidence presented in Lessons 5 and 6 suggests that we need to break down the concept of secure private property rights into rights of ownership, use, and transfer; and within each type of right, analyze whether it is a generalized right applying to all economic agents or a particularized right applying only to a privileged subset. It seems likely that other conventional institutional labels—contracting institutions, communities, guilds—would benefit from analytical attention devoted to sharpening the criteria by which they are defined and measured, and the way in which these separate characteristics might be expected to affect economic growth.

The second challenge for future research is to provide a scale of intensity or degree for measuring institutions. The current institutional labels used in the analysis of growth assume those institutions to be either present or absent, with no gradations in between. The growth literature contains too many claims that certain institutions were completely absent or, alternatively, completely present. Public-order institutions are supposed to have been completely absent from the medieval trading world, as we saw in Lessons 1 and 3, implying a major role for private-order substitutes in achieving economic growth—and yet empirical research finds that public-order institutions were present and reveals that they served an important role in commercial growth in those medieval economies, even though they undoubtedly changed over the ensuing centuries, albeit not always in a positive direction. Parliaments are supposed to have had no control over the executive arm of the English government before 1688 and virtually complete control thereafter, as we saw in Lesson 2, implying a major role for democratization in achieving economic growth—and yet the empirical findings reveal that parliamentary powers were usually a matter of incremental changes, except during periods of revolution (and sometimes even then). Property rights, as we saw in Lesson 5, are portrayed as being either completely absent before 1688 or completely present in 1300, implying respectively a major role in economic growth or complete irrelevance to it—and yet the empirical findings reveal that property rights were a matter of degree and incremental change. The historical findings surveyed in this chapter suggest the need for economists to pay much greater analytical attention to devising scales of intensity or degree for conventional institutional labels such as property rights or public-order institutions, preferably for each of the many distinct characteristics of these institutions whose identification is the focus of our first challenge.

Our third challenge for future research is to work out ways of analyzing and measuring the linkages between the configurations to which conventional institutional labels apparently refer—that is, of understanding how institutions interconnect with the wider institutional system. Even very similar property rights regimes, as Lesson 4 showed, could give rise to very different economic outcomes during the agricultural revolution depending on the quality of contracting institutions, which in turn depended on the characteristics of such variegated institutional mechanisms as the village community, serfdom, urban corporations, and the state. As Lesson 7 showed, the apparently identical family institution of the European Marriage Pattern could be associated with widely varying growth outcomes, depending on the rest of the institutional system within which it was embedded, especially corporative institutions such as guilds and communities that influenced women's status, human capital investment, and demographic decisions. Even serfdom, as we saw in Lesson 8, cannot be understood in isolation from the rest of the institutional system—the village community, the state, and the market. The historical evidence surveyed in this chapter suggests that in order to understand institutional influences on long-run growth, economists need ways of characterizing the wider institutional system of which each institution is just one component, and of mapping how the character of that configuration changes as its institutional context and interdependencies change.

This is not to say that any of these challenges will be easy to surmount. But the historical findings surveyed in this chapter show that they will have to be tackled if we are to make further progress. Our best hope of success at this task will be to combine the ability of economics to simplify everything as much as possible, with the ability of history to identify where the complexity of the data resists further simplification and tells us that better analytical tools must be devised.

## ACKNOWLEDGMENT

The authors would like to express their gratitude to Jeremy Edwards for his exceptionally stimulating suggestions on several drafts of this chapter; and to Tracy Dennison for her very helpful comments on the final version.

## REFERENCES

Acemoglu, D., 2003. Why not a political Coase theorem? Social conflict, commitment and politics. Journal of Comparative Economics 31 (4), 620–652.

Acemoglu, D., 2009. Introduction to Modern Economic Growth. Princeton University Press, Princeton, NJ.

Acemoglu, D., Cantoni, D., Johnson, S., Robinson, J.A., 2011. The consequences of radical reform: the French Revolution. American Economic Review 101 (7), 3286–3307.

Acemoglu, D., Johnson, S.H., 2005. Unbundling institutions. Journal of Political Economy 113 (4), 949–995.

Acemoglu, D., Johnson, S., Robinson, J.A., 2005. Institutions as a fundamental cause of long-run growth. In: Aghion, P., Durlauf, S.N. (Eds.), Handbook of Economic Growth, vol. 1A. Elsevier, Amsterdam/London, pp. 385–472.

Acemoglu, D., Robinson, J.A., 2012. Why Nations Fail: The Origins of Power, Prosperity and Poverty. Crown Publishers, New York.

Acemoglu, D., Wolitzky, A., 2011. The economics of labor coercion. Econometrica 79 (2), 555–600.

Ackerman-Lieberman, P., 2007. A partnership culture: Jewish economic and social life seen through the legal documents of the Cairo Geniza. Columbia University, Ph.D. Dissertation.

Aghion, P., Howitt, P., 1992. A model of growth through creative destruction. Econometrica 60 (2), 323–351.

A'Hearn, B., Baten, J., Crayen, D., 2009. Quantifying quantitative literacy: age heaping and the history of human capital. Journal of Economic History 69 (03), 783–808.

Alengry, C., 1915. Les foires de Champagne: Etude d'histoire économique. Rousseau et Cie, Paris.

Allen, R.C., 1992. Enclosure and the Yeoman: The Agricultural Development of the South Midlands, 1450–1850. Clarendon, Oxford.

Allen, R.C., 1999. Tracking the agricultural revolution in England. Economic History Review 52 (2), 209–235.

Allen, R.C., 2003. Progress and poverty in early modern Europe. Economic History Review 56 (3), 403–443.

Allen, R.C., 2004. Agriculture during the Industrial Revolution, 1700–1850. In: Floud, R., Johnson, P. (Eds.), The Cambridge Economic History of Modern Britain, vol. 1: Industrialisation, 1700–1860. Cambridge University Press, Cambridge, pp. 96–116.

Allen, R.C., 2011. Global Economic History: A Very Short Introduction. Oxford University Press, Oxford.

Anderson, J.E., 2008. Trade and informal institutions. In: Anon. (Ed.), Handbook of International Trade. Blackwell Publishing, Oxford, pp. 279–293.

Anon., 1818. The states of Wirtemberg. Edinburgh Review 29, 337–363.

Aoki, M., 2001. Toward a Comparative Institutional Analysis. MIT Press, Cambridge, MA.

Arbois de Jubainville, M. H. de, 1859. Histoire de Bar-sur-Aube sous les comtes de Champagne. Durand, Dufay-Robert, Jardeaux-Ray, Paris, Troyes, Bar-sur-Aube.

Arbois de Jubainville, M. H. de, Pigeotte, L., 1859–66. Histoire des ducs et des comtes de Champagne. A. Durand, Paris.

Archer, I.W., 1988. The London lobbies in the later sixteenth century. Historical Journal 31 (1), 17–44.

Aron, J., 2000. Growth and institutions: a review of the evidence. The World Bank Research Observer 15 (1), 99–135.

Ashton, R., 1967. The parliamentary agitation for free trade in the opening years of the reign of James I. Past & Present 38, 40–55.

Ashtor, E., 1983. The Levant Trade in the Later Middle Ages. Princeton University Press, Princeton, NJ.

Aslanian, S., 2006. Social capital, trust and the role of networks in Julfan trade: informal and semi-formal institutions at work. Journal of Global History 1 (3), 383–402.

Ba, S., 2001. Establishing online trust through a community responsibility system. Decision Support Systems 31 (3), 323–336.

Bairoch, P., 1989. Les trois révolutions agricoles du monde développé: rendements et productivité de 1800 à 1985. Annales. Histoire, Sciences Sociales 44 (2), 317–353.

Baker, J.H., 1979. The law merchant and the common law before 1700. Cambridge Law Journal 38, 295–322.

Baker, J.H., 1986. The law merchant and the common law. In: Baker, J.H. (Ed.), The Legal Profession and the Common Law: Historical Essays. Hambledon Press, London, pp. 341–386.

Barbour, V., 1911. Privateers and pirates of the West Indies. American Historical Review 16 (3), 523–566.

Bardhan, P., 1996. The nature of institutional impediments to economic development. Center for International and Development Economics Research Papers C96–066.

Basile, M.E., Bestor, J.F., Cocquillette, D.R., Donahue, C. (Eds.), 1998. Lex Mercatoria and Legal Pluralism: A Late Thirteenth-Century Treatise and Its Afterlife. Ames Foundation, Cambridge.

Bassermann, E., 1911. Die Champagnermessen. Ein Beitrag zur Geschichte des Kredits. Mohr, Tübingen.

Bautier, R.-H., 1953. Les foires de Champagne. Recherches sur une évolution historique. Recueils de la Société Jean Bodin 5, 97–147.

Bautier, R.-H., 1970. The fairs of Champagne. In: Cameron, R. (Ed.), Essays in French Economic History. R.D. Irwin, Homewood, IL, pp. 42–63.

Bekar, C.T., Reed, C.G., 2012. Land Markets and Inequality: Evidence from Medieval England. Simon Fraser University Department of Economics Working Papers 12–14.

Benson, B.L., 1989. The spontaneous evolution of commercial law. Southern Economic Journal 55 (3), 644–661.

Benson, B.L., 1998. Law merchant. In: Newman, P. (Ed.), The New Palgrave Dictionary of Economics and the Law. Macmillan, London.

Benson, B.L., 2002. Justice without government: the merchant courts of medieval Europe and their modern counterparts. In: Beito, D., Gordon, P., Tabarrok, A. (Eds.), The Voluntary City: Choice, Community and Civil Society. University of Michigan Press, Ann Arbor, pp. 127–150.

Benson, B.L., 2005. The mythology of holdout as a justification for eminent domain and public provision of roads. The Independent Review 10 (2), 165–194.

Benson, B.L., 2008. The evolution of eminent domain: a remedy for market failure or an effort to limit government power and government failure? The Independent Review 12 (3), 423–432.

Benton, J.F., 1969. Philip the Fair and the Jours of Troyes. Studies in Medieval and Renaissance History 6, 281–344.

Bernstein, L., 2001. Private commercial law in the cotton industry: value creation through rules, norms, and institutions. Michigan Law Review 99 (7), 1724–1790.

Besley, T., Ghatak, M., 2010. Property rights and economic development. In: Rodrik, D., Rosenzweig, M.R. (Eds.), Handbook of Development Economics, vol. 5. North Holland, Amsterdam, pp. 4526–4595.

Bieleman, J., 1993. Dutch agriculture in the Golden Age, 1570–1660. Economic and Social History in the Netherlands 4, 159–185.

Bieleman, J., 2006. Dutch agricultural history c. 1500–1950. In: Thoen, E., Van Molle, L. (Eds.), Rural History in the North Sea Area : An Overview of Recent Research, Middle Ages-Twentieth Century. Brepols, Turnhout.

Bieleman, J., 2010. Five Centuries of Farming: A Short History of Dutch Agriculture, 1500–2000. Wageningen Academic Publishers, Wageningen.

Biller, P., 2001. The Measure of Multitude: Population in Medieval Thought. Oxford University Press, Oxford.

Birdsall, N., 1988. Analytical approaches to population growth. In: Chenery, H., Srinivasan, T.N. (Eds.), Handbook of Development Economics, vol. I. North Holland, Amsterdam/New York, pp. 477–542.

Blaschke, K., 1991. Dorfgemeinde und Stadtgemeinde in Sachsen zwischen 1300 und, 1800. In: Blickle, P. (Ed.), Landgemeinde und Stadtgemeinde in Mitteleuropa. Ein struktureller Vergleich. Oldenbourg, Munich, pp. 119–143.

Blockmans, W.P., 1988. Alternatives to monarchical centralization. In: Koenigsberger, H.G. (Ed.), Republik und Republikanismus in Europea der Frühen Neuzeit. Oldenbourg, Munich.

Blondé, B., Gelderblom, O., Stabel, P., 2007. Foreign merchant communities in Bruges, Antwerp and Amsterdam, c. 1350–1650. In: Calabi, D., Christensen, S.T. (Eds.), Cultural Exchange in Early Modern Europe, vol. 2: Cities and Cultural Exchange in Europe, 1400–1700. Cambridge University Press, Cambridge, pp. 154–174.

Boelcke, W.A., 1973. Wege und Probleme des industriellen Wachstums im Königreich Württemberg. Zeitschrift für Württembergische Landesgeschichte 32, 436–520.

Boelcke, W.A., 1984. Industrieller Aufstieg im mittleren Neckarraum zwischen Konjunktur und Krise. Zeitschrift für Württembergische Landesgeschichte 43, 287–326.

Boerner, L., Ritschl, A., 2002. Individual enforcement of collective liability in premodern Europe. Journal of Institutional and Theoretical Economics 158, 205–213.

Boerner, L., Ritschl, A., 2005. Making financial markets: contract enforcement and the emergence of tradable assets in late medieval Europe. Society for Economic Dynamics 2006 Meeting Papers 884.

Bogart, D., Richardson, G., 2009. Making property productive: reorganizing rights to real and equitable estates in Britain, 1660–1830. European Review of Economic History 13 (1), 3–30.

Bogart, D., Richardson, G., 2011. Property rights and parliament in industrializing Britain. Journal of Law and Economics 54 (2), 241–274.

Boldorf, M., 1999. Institutional Barriers to Economic Development: The Silesian Linen Proto-industry (17th to 19th Century). Institut für Volkswirtschaftslehre und Statistik, Universität Mannheim, Working Papers 566–99.

Boldorf, M., 2006. Europäische Leinenregionen im Wandel. Institutionelle Weichenstellungen in Schlesien und Irland (1750–1850). Böhlau, Cologne/Weimar/Vienna.

Boldorf, M., 2009. Socio-economic institutions and transaction costs: merchant guilds and rural trade in eighteenth-century Lower Silesia. European Review of Economic History 13 (2), 173–198.

Bolton, J.L., 2012. Money in the Medieval English Economy 973–1489. Manchester University Press, Manchester.

Bonfield, L., 2001. Developments in European family law. In: Kertzer, D.I., Barbagli, M. (Eds.), The History of the European Family, vol. 1: Family Life in Early Modern Times, 1500–1789. Yale University Press, New Haven, CT, pp. 87–124.

Bourquelot, F., 1839–40. Histoire de Provins. Lebeau, Paris.

Bourquelot, F., 1865. Études sur les foires de Champagne, sur la nature, l'étendue et les règles du commerce qui s'y faisait aux XIIe, XIIIe et XIVe siècles. L'Imprimerie Impériale, Paris.

Boutaric, E.P., 1867. Actes du Parlement de Paris, Première série: De l'an 1254 à l'an 1328. H. Plon, Paris.

Braddick, M.J., 1994. Parliamentary Taxation in Seventeenth-Century England: Local Administration and Response. Royal Historical Society, Woodbridge, Suffolk.

Brakensiek, S., 1991. Agrarreform und Ländliche Gesellschaft: die Privatisierung der Marken in Nordwestdeutschland 1750–1850. Schöningh, Paderborn.

Brakensiek, S., 1994. Agrarian individualism in North-Western Germany, 1770–1870. German History 12 (2), 137–179.

Brenner, R., 1976. Agrarian class structure and economic development in pre-industrial England. Past & present 70, 30–75.

Brewer, J., 1989. The Sinews of Power: War, Money and the English State, 1688–1783. Unwin Hyman, London.

Brewer, J., Hellmuth, E. (Eds.), 1999. Rethinking Leviathan: The Eighteenth-Century State in Britain and Germany. Oxford University Press, Oxford.

Briggs, C., 2004. Empowered or marginalized? Rural women and credit in later thirteenth- and fourteenth-century England. Continuity and Change 19 (1).

Briggs, C., 2009. Credit and Village Society in Fourteenth-Century England. Oxford University Press, Oxford.

Briggs, C., 2013. English serfdom, c. 1200 - c. 1350: towards an institutional analysis. In: Cavaciocchi, S. (Ed.), Schiavitu e servaggio nell'economia europea. Secc. XI-XVIII./Slavery and Serfdom in the European Economy from the 11th to the 18th Centuries. XLV settimana di studi della Fondazione istituto internazionale di storia economica F. Datini, Prato 14–18 April 2013. Firenze University Press, Florence.

Britnell, R.H., 1991. The towns of England and Northern Italy in the early fourteenth century. Economic History Review 44 (1), 21–35.

Britnell, R.H., 1996. The Commercialisation of English Society, 1000–1500. Manchester University Press, Manchester.

Briys, E., De ter Beerst, D.J., 2006. The Zaccaria deal: contract and options to fund a Genoese shipment of alum to Bruges in 1298. Paper presented at the XIV International Economic History Congress, Helsinki, August.

Broadberry, S., Campbell, B., Klein, A., Overton, M., et al., 2011. British economic growth, 1270–1870: an output-based approach. University of Kent Department of Economics Studies in Economics 1203.

Broadberry, S., Campbell, B., Van Leeuwen, B., 2013. When did Britain industrialise? The sectoral distribution of the labor force and labor productivity in Britain, 1381–1851. Explorations in Economic History 50 (1), 16–27.

Brophy, J.M., 1995. Salus publica suprema lex: Prussian Businessmen in the New Era and Constitutional Conflict. Central European History 28 (2), 122–151.

Burkhardt, M., 2012. Zentren und Peripherie zu Beginn der Industriellen Revolution in Württemberg - ein kartografischer Nachtrag. Zeitschrift für Württembergische Landesgeschichte 71, 479–480.

Buyst, E., Mokyr, J., 1990. Dutch manufacturing and trade during the French Period (1795–1814) in a long-term perspective. In: Aerts, E., Crouzet, F. (Eds.), Economic Effects of the French Revolutionary and Napoleonic Wars, Leuven University Press, Leuven, pp. 64–78.

Byrne, E.H., 1916. Commercial contracts of the Genoese in the Syrian trade of the twelfth century. Quarterly Journal of Economics 31 (1), 128–170.

Byrne, E.H., 1930. Genoese Shipping in the Twelfth and Thirteenth Centuries. The Medieval Academy of America, Cambridge, MA.

Calaprice, A. (Ed.), 2011. The Ultimate Quotable Einstein. Princeton University Press, Princeton, NJ.

Caldwell, J.C., 1976. Toward a restatement of demographic transition theory. Population and Development Review 2 (3/4), 321–366.

Caldwell, J.C., 1982. Theory of Fertility Decline. Academic Press, London, New York.

Cameron, R.E., 1989. A Concise Economic History of the World: From Paleolithic Times to the Present. Oxford University Press, Oxford.

Campbell, B.M.S., 2000. English Seigniorial Agriculture, 1250–1450. Cambridge University Press, Cambridge.

Campbell, B.M.S., 2005. The agrarian problem in the early fourteenth century. Past & Present 188, 3–70.

Campbell, B.M.S., 2009. Factor markets in England before the Black Death. Continuity and Change 24 (1), 79–106.

Campbell, C., Lee, J.Z., 2010. Demographic impacts of climatic fluctuations in northeast China, 1749–1909. In: Kurosu, S., Bengtsson, T., Campbell, C. (Eds.), Demographic Responses to Economic and Environmental Crisis. Reitaku University Press, Kashiwa, pp. 107–132.

Campbell, B.M.S., Overton, M., 1998. L'histoire agraire anglaise jusqu'en 1850: revue historiographique sur l'état actuel de la recherche'. Histoire et Sociétés rurales 9 (1), 77–105.

Carrigan, W.D., 2004. The Making of a Lynching Culture: Violence and Vigilantism in Central Texas, 1836–1916. University of Illinois Press, Urbana/Chicago, IL.

Carsten, F.L., 1950. The Great Elector and the foundation of the Hohenzollern despotism. English Historical Review 65 (255), 175–202.

Carsten, F.L., 1959. Princes and Parliaments in Germany. Clarendon, Oxford.

Caunce, S., 1997. Farm servants and the development of capitalism in English agriculture. Agricultural History Review 45 (1), 49–60.

Cerman, M., 1996. Proto-industrialisierung und Grundherrschaft. Ländliche Sozialstruktur, Feudalismus und Proto-industrielles Heimgewerbe in Nordböhmen vom 14. bis zum 18. Jahrhundert (1381–1790). Ph.D. Dissertation, Vienna.

Cerman, M., 2008. Social structure and land markets in late medieval central and east-central Europe. Continuity and Change 23 (1), 55–100.

Cerman, M., 2012. Villagers and Lords in Eastern Europe, 1300–1800. Palgrave Macmillan, Houndmills/New York.

Cerman, M., 2013. Seigniorial systems in east-central and eastern Europe, 1300–1800: regional realities. In: Cavaciocchi, S. (Ed.), Schiavitu e servaggio nell'economia europea. Secc. XI-XVIII./Slavery and Serfdom in the European Economy from the 11th to the 18th Centuries. XLV settimana di studi della Fondazione istituto internazionale di storia economica F. Datini, Prato 14–18 April 2013. Firenze University Press, Florence.

Chambers, R., 1869. History of the Rebellion of 1745–6, W. & R. Chambers, London.

Chambers, J.D., 1953. Enclosure and labour supply in the Industrial Revolution. Economic History Review 5 (3), 319–343.

Chapin, E., 1937. Les villes de foires de Champagne des origines au début du XIVe siècle. Champion, Paris.

Cheyette, F.L., 1970. The sovereign and the pirates, 1332. Speculum 45 (1), 40–68.

Chorley, G.P.H., 1981. The agricultural revolution in northern Europe, 1750–1880: nitrogen, legumes, and crop productivity. Economic History Review 34 (1), 71–93.

Clark, G., 1996. The political foundations of modern economic growth: England, 1540–1800. Journal of Interdisciplinary History 26 (4), 563–588.

Clark, C.M., 2006. Iron Kingdom: The Rise and Downfall of Prussia, 1600–1947. Allen Lane, London.

Clark, G., 2007. A Farewell to Alms: A Brief Economic History of the World. Princeton University Press, Princeton, NJ.

Clark, G., 2010. The macroeconomic aggregates for England, 1209–1869. Research in Economic History 27, 51–140.

Clay, K., 1997. Trade without law: private-order institutions in Mexican California. Journal of Law, Economics and Organization 13 (1), 202–231.

Cohen, M.R., 2013. A partnership gone bad: a letter and a power of attorney from the Cairo Geniza, 1085. In: Wasserstein, D., Ghanaim, M. (Eds.), The Sasson Somekh Festschrift [not yet titled], Tel Aviv.

Coleman, J.S., 1988. Social capital in the creation of human capital. American Journal of Sociology 94, S95–S120.

Court, R., 2004. "Januensis ergo mercator": trust and enforcement in the business correspondence of the Brignole family. Sixteenth Century Journal 35 (4), 987–1003.

Crafts, N., 1977. Industrial Revolution in Britain and France: some thoughts on the question, "Why was Britain first?" Economic History Review 2nd ser. 30, 429–441.

Crafts, N., 1985. British Economic Growth during the Industrial Revolution. Clarendon, Oxford.

Crafts, N.F.R., 1987. British economic growth, 1700–1850; some difficulties of interpretation. Explorations in Economic History 24 (3), 245–268.

Crafts, N., Mills, T.C., 2009. From Malthus to Solow: how did the Malthusian economy really evolve? Journal of Macroeconomics 31 (1), 68–93.

Crafts, N., Leybourne, S.J., Mills, T.C., 1989. Trends and cycles in British industrial production, 1700–1913. Journal of the Royal Statistical Society Series A (Statistics in Society) 152 (1), 43–60.

Croft, P., 1973. Introduction: the revival of the Company, 1604–6. In: Croft, P. (Ed.), The Spanish Company. London Record Society, London, pp. xxix-li.

Czaja, R., 2009. Die Entwicklung der ständischen Versammlungen in Livland, Preußen und Polen im Spätmittelalter. Zeitschrift für Ostmitteleuropa-Forschung 58 (3), 312–328.

Czapliński, W., 1985. The Polish Parliament at the summit of its development. Zakład Narodowy Imienia Ossolińskich, Wrocław.

Dahl, G., 1998. Trade, Trust and Networks: Commercial Culture in Late Medieval Italy. Nordic Academic Press, Lund.

Dasgupta, P., 1993. An Inquiry into Well-Being and Destitution. Clarendon Press, Oxford.

Dasgupta, P., 2000. Economic progress and the idea of social capital. In: Dasgupta, P., Serageldin, I. (Eds.), Social Capital: A Multifaceted Perspective. World Bank, Washington, pp. 325–424.

Davids, K., 2006. Monasteries, economies and states: the dissolution of monasteries in early modern Europe and T'ang China. Paper presented at the Global Economic History Network (GEHN) Conference 10, Washington, 8–10 September 2006.

Davidsohn, R., 1896–1901. Forschungen zur Geschichte von Florenz. E.S. Mittler und Sohn, Berlin.

Davidson, J., Weersink, A., 1998. What does it take for a market to function? Review of Agricultural Economics 20 (2), 558–572.

Defoe, D., 1727. The Complete English Tradesman. Charles Rivington, London.

Del Vecchio, A., Casanova, E., 1894. Le rappresaglie nei comuni medievali e specialmente in Firenze. C. e G. Zanichelli, Bologna.

De Moor, T., 2008. The silent revolution: a new perspective on the emergence of commons, guilds, and other forms of corporate collective action in western Europe. International Review of Social History 53, 179–212.

De Moor, T., Van Zanden, J.L., 2010. Girlpower: the European Marriage Pattern and labour markets in the North Sea region in the late medieval and early modern period. Economic History Review 63 (1), 1–33.

Dennison, T., 2011. The Institutional Framework of Russian Serfdom. Cambridge University Press, Cambridge.

Dennison, T., 2013. The institutional framework of serfdom in Russia: the view from 1861. In: Cavaciocchi, S. (Ed.), Schiavitu e servaggio nell'economia europea. Secc. XI-XVIII./Slavery and Serfdom in the European Economy from the 11th to the 18th Centuries. XLV settimana di studi della Fondazione istituto internazionale di storia economica F. Datini, Prato 14–18 April 2013. Firenze University Press, Florence.

Dennison, T., Ogilvie, S., 2007. Serfdom and social capital in Bohemia and Russia. Economic History Review 60 (3), 513–544.

Dennison, T., Ogilvie, S., 2013. Does the European Marriage Pattern Explain Economic Growth? CESifo Working Paper 4244.

De Roover, R., 1948. The Medici Bank: Its Organization, Management, Operations and Decline. New York University Press, New York.

De Roover, R., 1963. The Rise and Decline of the Medici Bank, 1397–1494. Harvard University Press, Cambridge, MA.

De Soto, H., 1989. The Other Path: The Invisible Revolution in the Third World. Harper & Row, New York.

De Soto, H., 2000. The Mystery of Capital: Why Capitalism Triumphs in the West and Fails Everywhere Else. Basic Books, New York.

Dessí, R., Ogilvie, S., 2003. Social Capital and Collusion: The Case of Merchant Guilds. CESifo Working Papers 1037.

Dessí, R., Ogilvie, S., 2004. Social Capital and Collusion: The Case of Merchant Guilds (Long Version). Cambridge Working Papers in economics 0417.

De Vries, J., 1974. The Dutch Rural Economy in the Golden Age, 1500–1700. Yale University Press, New Haven, CT.

De Vries, J., 1976. The Economy of Europe in an Age of Crisis, 1600–1750. Cambridge University Press, Cambridge.

De Vries, J., Van der Woude, A., 1997. The First Modern Economy: Success, Failure, and Perseverance of the Dutch Economy, 1500–1815. Cambridge University Press, Cambridge.

Dewey, H.W., 1988. Russia's debt to the Mongols in suretyship and collective responsibility. Comparative Studies in Society and History 30 (2), 249–270.

Dewey, H.W., Kleimola, A.M., 1970. Suretyship and collective responsibility in pre-Petrine Russia. Jahrbücher für Geschichte Osteuropas 18, 337–354.

Dewey, H.W., Kleimola, A.M., 1984. Russian collective consciousness: the Kievan roots. Slavonic and East European Review 62 (2), 180–191.

Diamond, J., 1997. Guns, Germs and Steel. W.W. Norton, New York, NY.

Dijkman, J., 2007. Debt litigation in medieval Holland, c. 1200 – c. 1350. Paper presented at the GEHN conference, Utrecht, 20–22 September 2007.

Dixit, A.K., 2004. Lawlessness and Economics: Alternative Modes of Governance. Princeton University Press, Princeton, NJ.

Dixit, A.K., 2009. Governance institutions and economic activity. American Economic Review 99 (1), 5–24.

Doehaerd, R., 1941. Les relations commerciales entre Gênes, la Belgique, et l'Outremont d'après les archives notariales gênoises aux XIIIe et XIVe siècles. Palais des académies, Brussels.

Doepke, M., Tertilt, M., 2011. Does Female Empowerment Promote Economic Development? World Bank Policy Research Working Paper 5714.

Dollinger, P., 1970. The German Hansa. Macmillan, London.

Domar, E.D., 1970. The causes of slavery or serfdom: a hypothesis. Journal of Economic History 30 (1), 18–32.

Donahue, C., 1983. The canon law on the formation of marriage and social practice in the later Middle Ages. Journal of Family History 8 (2), 144–158.

Donahue, C., 2008. Law, Marriage, and Society in the Later Middle Ages: Arguments about Marriage in Five Courts. Cambridge University Press, Cambridge.

Dormois, J.-P., 1994. Entwicklungsmuster der Protoindustrialisierung im Mömpelgarder Lande während des 18. Jahrhunderts. Zeitschrift für Württembergische Landesgeschichte 53, 179–204.

Dotson, J.E., 1999. Fleet operations in the first Genoese-Venetian war, 1264–1266. Viator: Medieval and Renaissance Studies 30, 165–180.

Doumerc, B., 1987. Les Vénitiens à La Tana (Azov) au XVe siècle. Cahiers du monde russe et soviétique 28 (1), 5–19.

Edwards, J., Ogilvie, S., 2008. Contract Enforcement, Institutions and Social Capital: The Maghribi Traders Reappraised. CESifo Working Papers 2254.

Edwards, J., Ogilvie, S., 2012a. Contract enforcement, institutions, and social capital: the Maghribi traders reappraised. Economic History Review 65 (2), 421–444.

Edwards, J., Ogilvie, S., 2012b. What lessons for economic development can we draw from the Champagne fairs? Explorations in Economic History 49 (2), 131–148.

Edwards, J., Ogilvie, S., 2013. Economic growth in Prussia and Württemberg, c. 1750 - c. 1900. Unpublished paper, University of Cambridge, June 2013.

Ehmer, J., 1991. Heiratsverhalten, Sozialstruktur und ökonomischer Wandel. England und Mitteleuropa in der Formationsperiode des Kapitalismus. Vandenhoeck & Ruprecht, Göttingen.

Ekelund, R.B., Tollison, R.D., 1981. Mercantilism as a Rent-Seeking Society: Economic Regulation in Historical Perspective. Texas A&M University Press, College Station, TX.

Elton, G.R., 1975. Taxation for war and peace in early Tudor England. In: Winter, J.M. (Ed.), War and Economic Development: Essays in Memory of David Joslin. Cambridge University Press, Cambridge.

Epstein, S.A., 1996. Genoa and the Genoese, 958–1528. University of North Carolina Press, Chapel Hill, NC.

Epstein, S.R., 1998. Craft guilds, apprenticeship, and technological change in preindustrial Europe. Journal of Economic History 58, 684–713.

Ewert, U.-C., Selzer, S., 2009. Building bridges, closing gaps: the variable strategies of Hanseatic merchants in heterogeneous mercantile environments. In: Murray, J.M., Stabel, P. (Eds.), Bridging the Gap: Problems of Coordination and the Organization of International Commerce in Late Medieval European Cities. Brepols, Turnhout.

Ewert, U.-C., Selzer, S., 2010. Wirtschaftliche Stärke durch Vernetzung. Zu den Erfolgsfaktoren des hansischen Handels. In: Häberlein, M., Jeggle, C. (Eds.), Praktiken des Handels: Geschäfte und soziale Beziehungen europäischer Kaufleute in Mittelalter und früher Neuzeit. UvK Verlag, Konstanz, pp. 39–70.

Faille, C., 2007. Trading on reputation. Reason (January, 2007).

Fairlie, S., 1965. The nineteenth-century corn law reconsidered. Economic History Review 18 (3), 562–575.

Fairlie, S., 1969. The Corn Laws and British wheat production, 1829–76. Economic History Review 22 (1), 88–116.

Feller, L., 2004. Quelques problèmes liés à l'étude du marché de la terre durant le Moyen Âge. In: Cavaciocchi, S. (Ed.), Il mercato della terra: secc. XIII-XVIII: atti della trentacinquesima Settimana di studi, 5–9 maggio 2003, Le Monnier, Florence, pp. 21–47.

Fenoaltea, S., 1975a. Authority, efficiency, and agricultural organization in medieval England and beyond: a hypothesis. Journal of Economic History 35 (3), 693–718.

Fenoaltea, S., 1975b. The rise and fall of a theoretical model: the manorial system. Journal of Economic History 35 (2), 386–409.

Fenoaltea, S., 1984. Slavery and supervision in comparative perspective: a model. Journal of Economic History 44, 635–668.

Fertig, G., 2007. Äcker, Wirte, Gaben. Ländlicher Bodenmarkt und liberale Eigentumsordnung im Westfalen des 19. Jahrhunderts. Akademie Verlag, Berlin.

Feuchtwanger, E.J., 1970. Prussia: Myth and Reality. The Role of Prussia in German History. Wolff, London.

Fischel, W.A., 1995. Regulatory Takings: Law, Economics, and Politics. Harvard University Press, Cambridge, MA.

Fliegauf, U., 2007. Die Schwäbischen Hüttenwerke zwischen Staats- und Privatwirtschaft. Zur Geschichte der Eisenverarbeitung in Württemberg (1803–1945). Thorbecke, Ostfildern.

Flik, R., 1990. Die Textilindustrie in Calw und in Heidenheim 1705–1870. Eine regional vergleichende Untersuchung zur Geschichte der Frühindustrialisierung und Industriepolitik in Württemberg. Steiner, Stuttgart.

Foreman-Peck, J., 2011. The Western European marriage pattern and economic development. Explorations in Economic History 48 (2), 292–309.

Fortunati, M., 2005. The fairs between lex mercatoria and ius mercatorum. In: Piergiovanni, V. (Ed.), From Lex Mercatoria to Commercial Law. Duncker & Humblot, Berlin, pp. 143–164.

Friedman, M.A., 2006. Qusayr and Geniza documents on the Indian Ocean trade. Journal of the American Oriental Society 126 (3), 401–409.

Fritschy, W., 2003. A "financial revolution" reconsidered: public finance in Holland during the Dutch Revolt, 1568–1648. Economic History Review 56 (1), 57–89.

Frost, R.I., 2006. The nobility of Poland-Lithuania, 1569–1795. In: Scott, H.M. (Ed.), European Nobilities in the 17th and 18th Centuries: Northern, Central and Eastern Europe. Palgrave-Macmillan, New York, NY, pp. 266–310.

Galloway, P.R., 1988. Basic patterns in annual variations in fertility, nuptiality, mortality, and prices in pre-industrial Europe. Population Studies 42 (2), 275–303.

Galor, O., 2005a. The demographic transition and the emergence of sustained economic growth. Journal of the European Economic Association 3 (2/3), 494–504.

Galor, O., 2005b. From stagnation to growth: unified growth theory. In: Aghion, P., Durlauf, S.N. (Eds.), Handbook of Economic Growth, vol. 1, Part A. Elsevier, Amsterdam/London, pp. 171–293.

Galor, O., 2012. The demographic transition: causes and consequences. Cliometrica 6 (1), 1–28.

Gash, N., 1961. Mr Secretary Peel: The Life of Sir Robert Peel to 1830. Longman, London.

Gash, N., 1972. Sir Robert Peel : The life of Sir Robert Peel After 1830. Longman, Harlow.

Gelderblom, O., 2003. The governance of early modern trade: the case of Hans Thijs (1556–1611). Enterprise and Society 4 (4), 606–639.

Gelderblom, O. 2005a. The decline of fairs and merchant guilds in the Low Countries, 1250–1650. Economy and Society of the Low Countries Working Papers 2005–1.

Gelderblom, O. 2005b. The Resolution of Commercial Conflicts in Bruges, Antwerp, and Amsterdam, 1250–1650. Economy and Society of the Low Countries Working Papers 2005–2.

Gelderblom, O., 2013. Cities of Commerce: The Institutional Foundations of International Trade in the Low Countries, 1250–1650. Princeton University Press, Princeton, NJ.

Gelderblom, O., Grafe, R., 2004. The costs and benefits of merchant guilds, 1300–1800: position paper. Paper presented at the Fifth European Social Science History Conference, Berlin, 24–27 March 2004.

Gil, M., 2003. The Jewish merchants in the light of eleventh-century Geniza documents. Journal of the Economic and Social History of the Orient 46 (3), 273–319.

Gil, M., 2004a. Institutions and events of the eleventh century mirrored in Geniza letters (Part I). Bulletin of the School of Oriental and African Studies 67 (2), 151–167.

Gil, M., 2004b. Jews in Islamic Countries in the Middle Ages. Brill, Leiden.

Goitein, S.D., 1966. Studies in Islamic History and Institutions. Brill, Leiden.

Goitein, S.D., 1967/93. A Mediterranean Society: The Jewish Communities of the Arab World as Portrayed in the Documents of the Cairo Geniza. University of California Press, Berkeley/Los Angeles.

Goitein, S.D., Friedman, M.A., 2007. India Traders of the Middle Ages: Documents from the Cairo Geniza ("India Book"). Brill, Leiden/Boston.

Goldberg, J., 2005. Geographies of trade and traders in the eleventh-century Mediterranean: A study based on documents from the Cairo Geniza. Columbia University, Ph.D. Dissertation.

Goldberg, J., 2012a. Trade and Institutions in the Medieval Mediterranean: The Geniza Merchants and their Business World. Cambridge University Press, Cambridge.

Goldberg, J., 2012b. The use and abuse of commercial letters from the Cairo Geniza. Journal of Medieval History 38 (2), 127–154.

Goldberg, J.L., 2012c. Choosing and enforcing business relationships in the eleventh-century mediterranean: reassessing the "Maghribī traders". Past & Present 216 (1), 3–40.

Goldschmidt, L., 1891. Handbuch des Handelsrechts. Enke, Stuttgart.

Goldsworthy, J.D., 1999. The Sovereignty of Parliament: History and Philosophy. Clarendon Press, Oxford.

Goldthwaite, R.A., 1987. The Medici Bank and the world of Florentine capitalism. Past & Present 114, 3–31.

González de Lara, Y., 2005. The Secret of Venetian Success: The Role of the State in Financial Markets. Instituto Valenciano de Investigaciones Económicas (IVIE) Working Paper WP-AD 2005–28.

Grafe, R., Gelderblom, O., 2010. The rise and fall of the merchant guilds: re-thinking the comparative study of commercial institutions in pre-modern Europe. Journal of Interdisciplinary History 40 (4), 477–511.

Grantham, G.W., Sarget, M.-N., 1997. Espaces privilégiés: Productivité agraire et zones d'approvisionnement des villes dans l'Europe préindustrielle. Annales. Histoire, Sciences Sociales 52(3), 695–725.

Greif, A., 1989. Reputation and coalitions in medieval trade: evidence on the Maghribi traders. Journal of Economic History 49 (4), 857–882.

Greif, A., 1993. Contract enforceability and economic institutions in early trade: the Maghribi traders' coalition. American Economic Review 83 (3), 525–548.

Greif, A., 1994. Cultural beliefs and the organization of society: a historical and theoretical reflection on collectivist and individualist societies. Journal of Political Economy 102 (5), 912–950.

Greif, A., 1997. On the Social Foundations and Historical Development of Institutions that Facilitate Impersonal Exchange: From the Community Responsibility System to Individual Legal Responsibility in Pre-modern Europe. Stanford University Working Papers 97–016.

Greif, A., 2002. Institutions and impersonal exchange: from communal to individual responsibility. Journal of Institutional and Theoretical Economics 158 (1), 168–204.

Greif, A., 2004. Impersonal exchange without impartial law: the community responsibility system. Chicago Journal of International Law 5 (1), 109–138.

Greif, A., 2006a. Family structure, institutions, and growth: the origins and implications of western corporations. American Economic Review: Papers and Proceedings 96 (2), 308–312.

Greif, A., 2006b. History lessons. The birth of impersonal exchange: the community responsibility system and impartial justice. Journal of Economic Perspectives 20 (2), 221–236.

Greif, A., 2006c. Institutions and the Path to the Modern Economy: Lessons from Medieval Trade. Cambridge University Press, Cambridge.

Greif, A., 2012. The Maghribi traders: a reappraisal? Economic History Review 65 (2), 445–469.

Greif, A., Milgrom, P., Weingast, B., 1994. Coordination, commitment, and enforcement: the case of the merchant guild. Journal of Political Economy 102 (4), 912–950.

Greif, A., Tabellini, G., 2010. Cultural and institutional bifurcation: China and Europe compared. American Economic Review: Papers and Proceedings 100 (2), 135–140.

Greve, A., 2000. Brokerage and trade in medieval Bruges: regulation and reality. In: Stabel, P., Blondé, B., Greve, A. (Eds.), International Trade in the Low Countries 14th-16th Centuries. Garant, Leuven/Apeldoorn, pp. 37–44.

Greve, A., 2001. Die Bedeutung der Brügger Hosteliers für hansische Kaufleute im 14. und 15. Jahrhundert. Jaarboek voor middeleeuwse geschiedenis 4, 259–296.

Greve, A., 2007. Hansen, Hosteliers und Herbergen: Studien zum Aufenthalt hansischer Kaufleute in Brügge im 14. und 15. Jahrhundert. Brepols, Turnhout.

Grossman, G.M., Helpman, E., 1991. Innovation and Growth in the Global Economy. The MIT Press, Cambridge, MA.

Grotius, H., 1625. De jure belli ac pacis libri tres, in quibus jus naturae et gentium, item juris publici praecipua explicantur. Buon, Paris.

Grube, W., 1954. Dorfgemeinde und Amtsversammlung in Altwürttemberg. Zeitschrift für Württembergische Landesgeschichte 13, 194–219.

Grube, W., 1957. Der Stuttgarter Landtag, 1457–1957. Ernst Klett Verlag, Stuttgart.

Grube, W., 1974. Stadt und Amt in Altwürttemberg. In: Maschke, E., Sydow, J. (Eds.), Stadt und Umland: Protokoll der X. Arbeitstagung des Arbeitskrieses für südwestdeutsche Stadtgeschichtsforschung, Calw, 12.-14. November 1971, Kohlhammer, Stuttgart, pp. 20–28.

Guinnane, T.W., 2011. The historical fertility transition: A guide for economists. Journal of Economic Literature 49 (3), 589–561.

Guinnane, T.W., Ogilvie, S., 2008. Institutions and demographic responses to shocks: Württemberg, 1634–1870. Yale University Economic Growth Center Discussion Paper 962.

Guinnane, T.W., Ogilvie, S., 2013. A Two-Tiered Demographic System: "Insiders" and "Outsiders" in Three Swabian Communities, 1558–1914. Yale University Economic Growth Center Discussion Paper 1021.

Guzowski, P., 2013. The role of enforced labour in the economic development of church and royal estates in 15th and 16th-century Poland. In: Cavaciocchi, S. (Ed.), Schiavitu e servaggio nell'economia europea. Secc. XI-XVIII./Slavery and Serfdom in the European economy from the 11th to the 18th Centuries. XLV settimana di studi della Fondazione istituto internazionale di storia economica F. Datini, Prato 14–18 April 2013. Firenze University Press, Florence.

Gysin, J., 1989. "Fabriken und Manufakturen" in Württemberg während des ersten Drittels des 19. Jahrhunderts, Scripta Mercaturae Verlag, St. Katharinen.

Habakkuk, J., 1994. Marriage, Debt, and the Estates System: English Landownership 1650-1950. Clarendon, Oxford.

Hafter, D.M., 2007. Women at Work in Pre-industrial France. Penn State Press, University Park, PA.

Hagen, W.W., 1989. Seventeenth-century crisis in Brandenburg: the Thirty Years War, the destabilization of serfdom, and the rise of absolutism. American Historical Review 94 (2), 302–325.

Hagen, W.W., 2002. Ordinary Prussians. Brandenburg Junkers and Villagers 1500–1840. Cambridge University Press, Cambridge.

Harbord, D., 2006. Enforcing Cooperation among Medieval Merchants: the Maghribi Traders Revisited. Munich Personal Repec Archive Working Paper.

Hardin, G., 1968. The tragedy of the commons. Science 162 (3859), 1243–1248.

Harnisch, H., 1972. Zur Herausbildung und Funktionsweise von Gutswirtschaft und Gutsherrschaft. Eine Klageschrift der Bauern der Herrschaft Neugattersleben aus dem Jahre 1610. Jahrbuch für Regionalgeschichte 4, 179–199.

Harnisch, H., 1975. Klassenkämpfe der Bauern in der Mark Brandenburg zwischen frühbürgerlicher Revolution und Dreißigjährigem Krieg. Jahrbuch für Regionalgeschichte 5, 142–172.

Harnisch, H., 1986. Peasants and markets: the background to the agrarian reforms in feudal Prussia east of the Elbe, 1760–1807. In: Evans, R.J., Lee, W.R. (Eds.), The German Peasantry: Conflict and Community in Rural Society from the Eighteenth to the Twentieth Centuries. Croom Helm, London, pp. 37–70.

Harnisch, H., 1989a. Bäuerliche Ökonomie und Mentalität unter den Bedingungen der ostelbischen Gutsherrschaft in den letzten Jahrzehnten vor Beginn der Agrarreformen. Jahrbuch für Wirtschaftsgeschichte 1989 (3), 87–108.

Harnisch, H., 1989b. Die Landgemeinde in der Herrschaftsstruktur des feudalabsolutistischen Staates. Dargestellt am Beispiel von Brandenburg-Preussen. Jahrbuch für Geschichte des Feudalismus 13, 201–245.

Harnisch, H., 1994. Der preußische Absolutismus und die Bauern. Sozialkonservative Gesellschaftspolitik und Vorleistung zur Modernisierung. Jahrbuch für Wirtschaftsgeschichte 1994 (2), 11–32.

Harreld, D.J., 2004a. High Germans in the Low Countries: German Merchants and Commerce in Golden Age Antwerp. Brill, Leiden.

Harreld, D.J., 2004b. Merchant and guild: the shift from privileged group to individual entrepreneur in sixteenth-century Antwerp. Paper delivered at the Fifth European Social Science History Conference. Berlin, 24–27 March 2004.

Harris, R., 2004. Government and the economy, 1688–1850. In: Floud, R., Johnson, P. (Eds.), The Cambridge Economic History of Modern Britain, vol. 1: Industrialisation, 1700–1860. Cambridge University Press, Cambridge, pp. 204–237.

Harrison, G., 1990. Prerogative revolution and Glorious Revolution: political proscription and parliamentary undertaking, 1687–1688. Parliaments, Estates and Representation 10 (1), 29–43.

Harriss, G.L., 1975. King, Parliament, and Public Finance in Medieval England to 1369. Clarendon Press, Oxford.

Hartley, T.E., 1992. Elizabeth's Parliaments: Queen, Lords, and Commons, 1559–1601. Manchester University Press, Manchester.

Helpman, E., 2004. The Mystery of Economic Growth. Harvard University Press, Cambridge, MA.

Henderson, W.O., 1961a. Die Struktur der preußischen Wirtschaft um 1786. Zeitschrift für die Gesamte Staatswissenschaft 117, 292–319.

Henderson, W.O., 1961b. The Industrial Revolution on the Continent: Germany, France, Russia, 1800–1914. F. Cass, London.

Henderson, W.O., 1961c. The rise of the metal and armament industries in Berlin and Brandenburg, 1712–1795. Business History 3 (2), 63–74.

Henn, V., 1999. Der "dudesche kopman" zu Brügge und seine Beziehungen zu den "nationes" der übrigen Fremden im späten Mittelalter. In: Jörn, N., Kattinger, D., Wernicke, H. (Eds.), "Kopet uns werk by tyden": Beiträge zur hansischen und preussischen Geschichte. Walter Stark zum 75. Geburtstag. Thoms Helms Verlag, Schwerin, pp. 131–142.

Hickson, C.R., Thompson, E.A., 1991. A new theory of guilds and European economic development. Explorations in Economic History 28, 127–168.

Hillmann, H., 2013. Economic institutions and the state: insights from economic history. Annual Review of Sociology 39 (1), 215–273.

Hilton, B., 1977. Corn, Cash, Commerce: The Economic Policies of the Tory Governments, 1815–1830. Oxford University Press, Oxford.

Hilton, B., 2006. Mad, Bad, and Dangerous People? England, 1783–1846. Clarendon Press, Oxford.

Hine, K.D., 1998. Vigilantism revisited: an economic analysis of the law of extra-judicial self-help or why can't Dick shoot Henry for stealing Jane's truck. American University Law Review 47, 1221–1255.

Hippel, W. von, 1977. Die Bauernbefreiung im Königreich Württemberg. Harald Boldt, Boppard am Rhein.

Hippel, W. von, 1992. Wirtschafts- und Sozialgeschichte 1800 bis 1918. In: Schwarzmaier, H., Fenske, H., Kirchgässner, B., Sauer, P., Schaab, M. (Eds.), Handbuch der baden-württembergischen Geschichte: vol. 3: Vom Ende des Alten Reiches bis zum Ende der Monarchien. Klett-Cotta, Stuttgart, pp. 477–784.

Hodgskin, T., 1820. Travels in the North of Germany: Describing the Present State of the Social and Political Institutions, the Agriculture, Manufactures, Commerce, Education, Arts and Manners in that Country Particularly in the Kingdom of Hannover. A. Constable, Edinburgh.

Hohorst, G., 1977. Wirtschaftswachstum und Bevölkerungsentwicklung in Preußen 1816 bis 1914. Arno, New York.

Holderness, B.A., 1976. Credit in English rural society before the nineteenth century, with special reference to the period 1650–1720. Agricultural History Review 24, 97–109.

Hoppit, J., 1996. Patterns of parliamentary legislation, 1660–1800. The History Journal 39, 109–131.

Hoppit, J., 2011. Compulsion, compensation and property rights in Britain, 1688–1833. Past & Present 210, 93–128.

Hoyle, R.W., 1994. Parliament and taxation in sixteenth-century England. English Historical Review 109 (434), 1174–1196.

Israel, J., 1989. Dutch primacy in world trade, 1585–1740. Clarendon, Oxford.

Jacoby, D., 2003. Foreigners and the urban economy in Thessalonike, ca. 1150–ca. 1450. Dumbarton Oaks Papers 57, 85–132.

Johansson, E., 1977. The history of literacy in Sweden, in comparison with some other countries. Educational Reports, Umeå 12, 2–42.

Johansson, E., 2009. The history of literacy in Sweden, in comparison with some other countries. In: Graff, H.J., Mackinnon, A., Sandin, B., Winchester, I. (Eds.), Understanding Literacy in its Historical Contexts: Socio-cultural History and the Legacy of Egil Johansson. Nordic Academic Press, Lund, pp. 28–59.

Kaak, H., 1991. Die Gutsherrschaft: theoriegeschichtliche Untersuchungen zum Agrarwesen im ostelbischen Raum. Walter de Gruyter, Berlin/New York.

Kaal, H., Van Lottum, J., 2009. Immigrants in the Polder. Rural-rural long distance migration in north-western Europe: the case of Watergraafsmeer. Rural History 20, 99–117.

Kadens, E., 2012. The myth of the customary law merchant. Texas Law Review 90 (5), 1153–1206.

Kaminski, A., 1975. Neo-serfdom in Poland-Lithuania. Slavic Review 34 (2), 253–268.

Katele, I.B., 1986. Captains and corsairs: Venice and piracy, 1261–1381. University of Illinois at Urbana-Champaign, Ph.D. Dissertation.

Katz, A., 1996. Taking private ordering seriously. University of Pennsylvania Law Review 144 (5), 1745–1763.

Katz, E.D., 2000. Private order and public institutions: comments on McMillan and Woodruff's "Private order under dysfunctional public order". Michigan Law Review 98 (8), 2481–2493.

Klein, A., 2013. The institutions of the second serfdom and economic efficiency: review of the existing evidence for Bohemia. In: Cavaciocchi, S. (Ed.), Schiavitu e servaggio nell'economia europea. Secc. XI-XVIII./Slavery and Serfdom in the European Economy from the 11th to the 18th Centuries. XLV settimana di studi della Fondazione istituto internazionale di storia economica F. Datini, Prato 14–18 April 2013. Firenze University Press, Florence.

Klein, A., Ogilvie, S., 2013. Occupational Structure in the Czech Lands under the Second Serfdom. CESifo Working Papers.

Knapp, G.F., 1887. Die Bauernbefreiung und der Ursprung der Landarbeiter in den älteren Theilen Preußens. Duncker und Humblot, Leipzig.

Knight, J., 1995. Models, interpretations, and theories: constructing explanations of institutional emergence and change. In: Knight, J., Sened, I. (Eds.), Explaining Social Institutions. University of Michigan Press, Ann Arbor, MI, pp. 95–119.

Koch, H.W., 1990. Brandenburg-Prussia. In: Miller, J. (Ed.), Absolutism in Seventeenth-Century Europe. Macmillan, Basingstoke, pp. 123–155.

Koenigsberger, H.G., 2001. Monarchies, States Generals and Parliaments: The Netherlands in the Fifteenth and Sixteenth Centuries. Cambridge University Press, Cambridge.

Kollmer-von Oheimb-Loup, G., 2012. Die Entwicklung der Wirtschaftsstruktur am Mittleren Neckar 1800 bis 1950. Zeitschrift für Württembergische Landesgeschichte 71, 351–383.

Kopsidis, M., 2006. Agrarentwicklung: historische Agrarrevolutionen und Entwicklungsökonomie. Steiner, Stuttgart.

Kula, W., 1976. An Economic Theory of the Feudal System: Towards a Model of the Polish Economy. NLB, London.

Kussmaul, A., 1981. Servants in Husbandry in Early Modern England. Cambridge University Press, Cambridge.

Kussmaul, A., 1994. The pattern of work as the eighteenth century began. In: Floud, R., McCloskey, D.N. (Eds.), The Economic History of Britain Since 1700, vol. 1. Cambridge University Press, Cambridge, pp. 1–11.

Laiou, A.E., 2001. Byzantine trade with Christians and Muslims and the Crusades. In: Laiou, A.E., Mottahedeh, R.P. (Eds.), The Crusades from the Perspective of Byzantium and the Muslim World. Dumbarton Oaks Research Library and Collection, Washington, DC, pp. 157–196.

Lambert, S., 1990. Committees, religion, and parliamentary encroachment on royal authority in early Stuart England. English Historical Review 105 (414), 60–95.

Lambert, B., Stabel, P., 2005. Squaring the circle: merchant firms, merchant guilds, urban infrastructure and political authority in late medieval Bruges. Paper presented at the Workshop on Mercantile Organization in Pre-Industrial Europe. Antwerp, 18–19 November 2005.

Lambrecht, T., 2009. Rural credit and the market for annuities in eighteenth-century Flanders. In: Schofield, P.R., Lambrecht, T. (Eds.), Credit and the Rural Economy in North-Western Europe, c. 1200-c.1850. Brepols, Turnhout, pp. 75–98.

Lane, F.C., 1963. Venetian merchant galleys, 1300–1334: private and communal operation. Speculum 38, 179–205.

Laslett, P., 1988. The European family and early industrialization. In: Baechler, J., Hall, J.A., Mann, M. (Eds.), Europe and the Rise of Capitalism. Basil Blackwell, Oxford, pp. 234–242.

Laurent, H., 1935. Un grand commerce d'exportation au moyen âge: la draperie des Pays Bas en France et dans les pays mediterranéens, XIIe - XVe siècle. E. Droz, Paris.

Lewis, W.A., 1954. Economic development with unlimited supplies of labour. Manchester School of Economics and Social Studies 22, 139–191.

Lewis, W.A., 1958. Unlimited labour: further notes. Manchester School of Economics and Social Studies 26, 1–32.

Lindberg, E., 2008. The rise of Hamburg as a global marketplace in the seventeenth century: a comparative political economy perspective. Comparative Studies in Society and History 50 (3), 641–662.

Lindberg, E., 2009. Club goods and inefficient institutions: why Danzig and Lübeck failed in the early modern period. Economic History Review 62 (3), 604–628.

Lindberg, E., 2010. Merchant guilds in Hamburg and Königsberg: a comparative study of urban institutions and economic development in the early modern period. Journal of European Economic History 39 (1), 33–66.

Lindert, P.H., 2004. Growing Public: Social Spending and Economic Growth Since the Eighteenth Century. Cambridge University Press, Cambridge.

Lis, C., Soly, H., 1996. Ambachtsgilden in vergelijkend perspectief: de Noordelijke en de Zuidelijke Nederlanden, 15de–18de eeuw. In: Lis, C., Soly, H. (Eds.), Werelden van verschil: ambachtsgilden in de Lage Landen. Brussels, pp. 11–42.

Little, C.B., Sheffield, C.P., 1983. Frontiers and criminal justice: English private prosecution societies and American vigilantism in the eighteenth and nineteenth centuries. American Sociological Review 48 (6), 796–808.

Lloyd, T.H., 1977. The English Wool Trade in the Middle Ages. Cambridge University Press, Cambridge.

Lopez, R.S., 1987. The trade of medieval Europe: the south. In: Postan, M.M., Miller, E. (Eds.), The Cambridge Economic History of Europe, vol. 3: Economic Organization and Policies in the Middle Ages. Cambridge University Press, Cambridge, pp. 306–401.

Lopez, R.S., Raymond, I.W., 1955. Medieval Trade in the Mediterranean World. Columbia University Press, New York.

Macaulay, S., 1963. Non-contractual relations in business: a preliminary study. American Sociological Review 28 (1), 55–67.

Macfarlane, A., 1978. The Origins of English Individualism: the Family, Property and Social Transition. Blackwell, Oxford.

Mączak, A., 1997. Polen-Litauen als Paradoxon: Erwägungen über die Staatlichkeit des frühmodernen Polen. In: Lubinski, A., Rudert, T., Schattkowsky, M. (Eds.), Historie und Eigen-Sinn. Festschrift für Jan Peters zum 65. Geburtstag, Böhlau, Weimar, pp. 87–92.

Maggi, G., 1999. The role of multilateral institutions in international trade cooperation. American Economic Review 89 (1), 190–214.

Mammen, K., Paxson, C., 2000. Women's work and economic development. Journal of Economic Perspectives 14, 141–164.

Margariti, R.E., 2007. Aden and the Indian Ocean Trade: 150 Years in the Life of a Medieval Arabian Port. University of North Carolina Press, Chapel Hill, NC.

Mas-Latrie, R. de, 1866. Du droit de marque ou droit de représailles au Moyen Âge [premier article]. Bibliothèque de l'école des chartes 27, 529–577.

Mathias, P., O'Brien, P., 1976. Taxation in Britain and France, 1715–1810: a comparison of the social and economic incidence of taxes collected for central government. Journal of European Economic History 5, 601–650.

Mathias, P., O'Brien, P., 1978. The incidence of taxes and the burden of proof. Journal of European Economic History 7, 211–213.

McCloskey, D., 1976. English open fields as behavior towards risk. Research in Economic History 1, 124–170.

McCloskey, D., 1991. The prudent peasant: new findings on open fields. Journal of Economic History 51 (2), 343–355.

McCloskey, D., 2010. Bourgeois Dignity: Why Economics Can't Explain the Modern World. University of Chicago Press, Chicago.

McCord, N., 1958. The Anti-Corn Law League, 1838–1846. Allen & Unwin, London.

McLean, P.D., 2004. Widening access while tightening control: office-holding, marriages, and elite consolidation in early modern Poland. Theory and Society 33 (2), 167–212.

McLean, P., Padgett, J.F., 1997. Was Florence a perfectly competitive market? Transactional evidence from the Renaissance. Theory and Society 26 (2–3), 209–244.

McMillan, J., Woodruff, C., 2000. Private order under dysfunctional public order. Michigan Law Review 98 (8), 2421–2458.

Medick, H., 1996. Weben und Überleben in Laichingen 1650–1900. Untersuchungen zur Sozial-, Kultur- und Wirtschaftsgeschichte aus der Perspektive einer lokalen Gesellschaft im frühneuzeitlichen Württemberg. Vandenhoeck & Ruprecht, Göttingen.

Meiners, C., 1794. Bemerkungen auf einer Herbstreise nach Schwaben. Geschrieben im November 1793. In: Meiners (Ed.), Kleinere Länder- und Reisebeschreibungen, vol. 2, Spener, Berlin, pp. 235–380.

Melton, E., 1988. Gutsherrschaft in East Elbian Germany and Livonia, 1500–1800: a critique of the model. Central European History 21 (4), 315–349.

Melton, E., 1990. Enlightened seigniorialism and its dilemmas in serf Russia, 1750–1830. Journal of Modern History 62 (4), 675–708.

Micheletto, B.Z., 2011. Reconsidering the southern Europe model: dowry, women's work and marriage patterns in pre-industrial urban Italy (Turin, second half of the 18th century). The History of the Family 16 (4), 354–370.

Middleton, N., 2005. Early medieval port customs, tolls and controls on foreign trade. Early Medieval Europe 13 (4), 313–358.

Miguel, E., Gertler, P., Levine, D., 2005. Does social capital promote industrialization? Evidence from a rapid industrializer. Review of Economics and Statistics 87 (4), 754–762.

Milgrom, P.R., Roberts, J.F., 1992. Economics, Organization and Management. Prentice-Hall, Englewood Cliffs, NJ.

Milgrom, P.R., North, D.C., Weingast, B.R., 1990. The role of institutions in the revival of trade: the medieval law merchant, private judges and the Champagne fairs. Economics and Politics 2 (1), 1–23.

Mingay, G.E., 1963. The agricultural revolution in English history: a reconsideration. Agricultural History 37 (3), 123–133.

Mokyr, J., 1974. The Industrial Revolution in the Low Countries in the first half of the nineteenth century: a comparative case study. Journal of Economic History 34 (2), 365–391.

Mokyr, J., 1980. Industrialization and poverty in Ireland and the Netherlands. Journal of Interdisciplinary History 10 (3), 429–458.

Mokyr, J., 1987. Has the Industrial Revolution been crowded out? Some reflections on Crafts and Williamson. Explorations in Economic History 24 (3), 293–319.

Mokyr, J., 2009. The Enlightened Economy: An Economic History of Britain, 1700–1850. Princeton University Press, Princeton, NJ.

Muldrew, C., 1993. Credit and the courts: debt litigation in a seventeenth-century urban community. Economic History Review 46 (1), 23–38.

Muldrew, C., 1998. The Economy of Obligation: The Culture of Credit and Social Relations in Early Modern England. St. Martin's Press, New York/Basingstoke.

Muldrew, C., 2003. "A mutual assent of her mind"? Women, debt, litigation and contract in early modern England. History Workshop Journal 55 (1), 47–71.

Munro, J., 1999. The Low Countries' export trade in textiles with the Mediterranean Basin, 1200–1600: a cost-benefit analysis of comparative advantages in overland and maritime trade routes. International Journal of Maritime History 11 (2), 1–30.

Munro, J., 2001. The "new institutional economics" and the changing fortunes of fairs in medieval and early modern Europe: the textile trades, warfare, and transaction costs. Vierteljahrschrift für Sozial- und Wirtschaftsgeschichte 88 (1), 1–47.

Munzinger, M.R., 2006. The profits of the Cross: merchant involvement in the Baltic Crusade (c. 1180–1230). Journal of Medieval History 32 (2), 163–185.

Murrell, P., 2009. Design and Evolution in Institutional Development: The Insignificance of the English Bill of Rights. University of Maryland Department of Economics Working Paper, 13 December 2009.

Nachbar, T.B., 2005. Monopoly, mercantilism, and the politics of regulation. Virginia Law Review 91 (6), 1313–1379.

Neeson, J.M., 1984. The opponents of enclosure in eighteenth-century Northamptonshire. Past & Present 105, 114–139.

Neeson, J.M., 1993. Commoners: Common Right, Enclosure and Social Change in England, 1700–1820. Cambridge University Press, Cambridge.

Neeson, J.M., 2000. English enclosures and British peasants: current debates about rural social structure in Britain c. 1750–1870. Jahrbuch für Wirtschaftsgeschichte 2000 (2), 17–32.

Nelson, L.H. (Ed.), 1996. Liber de restauratione Monasterii Sancti Martini Tornacensis: the restoration of the Monastery of Saint Martin of Tournai, by Herman of Tournai. Catholic University of America Press, Washington, DC.

Nicolini, E.A., 2007. Was Malthus right? A VAR analysis of economic and demographic interactions in pre-industrial England. European Review of Economic History 11 (1), 99–121.

North, D.C., 1981. Structure and Change in Economic History. Norton, New York/London.

North, D.C., 1989. Institutions and economic growth: an historical introduction. World Development 17 (9), 1319–1332.

North, D.C., 1991. Institutions, transaction costs, and the rise of merchant empires. In: Tracy, J.D. (Ed.), The Political Economy of Merchant Empires: State Power and World Trade, 1350–1750. Cambridge University Press, Cambridge, pp. 22–40.

North, M., 2013. Serfdom and corvée labour in the Baltic area 16th-18th centuries. In: Cavaciocchi, S. (Ed.), Schiavitu e servaggio nell'economia europea. Secc. XI-XVIII./Slavery and serfdom in the European economy from the 11th to the 18th centuries. XLV settimana di studi della Fondazione istituto internazionale di storia economica F. Datini, Prato 14–18 April 2013. Firenze University Press, Florence.

North, D.C., Thomas, R.P., 1970. An economic theory of the growth of the western world. Economic History Review 2nd Ser. 23, 1–18.

North, D.C., Thomas, R.P., 1971. The rise and fall of the manorial system: a theoretical model. Journal of Economic History 31 (4), 777–803.

North, D.C., Thomas, R.P., 1973. The Rise of the Western World. Cambridge University Press, Cambridge.

North, D.C., Weingast, B.R., 1989. Constitutions and commitment: the evolution of institutions governing public choice in seventeenth-century England. Journal of Economic History 49 (4), 803–832.

North, D.C., Wallis, J.J., Weingast, B.R., 2006. A Conceptual Framework for Interpreting Recorded Human History. NBER Working Papers 12795.

North, D.C., Wallis, J.J., Weingast, B.R., 2009. Violence and Social Orders. A Conceptual Framework for Interpreting Recorded Human History. Cambridge University Press, Cambridge.

Nowak, J.E., Rotunda, R.D., 2004. Constitutional Law. Thomson/West, St. Paul, MI.

O'Brien, J.G., 2002. In defense of the mystical body: Giovanni da Legnano's theory of reprisals. Roman Legal Tradition 1, 25–55.

O'Brien, P.K., 1988. The political economy of British taxation, 1660–1815. Economic History Review 41 (1), 1–32.

O'Brien, P.K., 2001. Fiscal Exceptionalism: Great Britain and its European Rivals from Civil War to Triumph at Trafalgar and Waterloo. LSE Department of Economic History Working Paper 65/01.

O'Brien, P.K., Engerman, S.L., 1991. Exports and the growth of the British economy from the Glorious Revolution to the Peace of Amiens. In: Solow, B.L. (Ed.), Slavery and the Rise of the Atlantic Systems. Cambridge University Press, Cambridge, pp. 177–209.

O'Driscoll, G.P., Hoskins, L., 2006. The case for market-based regulation. Cato Journal 26, 469–487.

Ogilvie, S., 1986. Coming of age in a corporate society: capitalism, Pietism and family authority in rural Württemberg, 1590–1740. Continuity and Change 1 (3), 279–331.

Ogilvie, S., 1992. Germany and the seventeenth-century crisis. Historical Journal 35, 417–441.

Ogilvie, S., 1995. Population Growth and State Policy in Central Europe Before Industrialization. Centre for History and Economics Working Paper.

Ogilvie, S., 1997. State Corporatism and Proto-industry: The Württemberg Black Forest, 1580–1797. Cambridge University Press, Cambridge.

Ogilvie, S., 1999. The German state: a non-Prussian view. In: Hellmuth, E., Brewer, J. (Eds.), Rethinking Leviathan: The Eighteenth-Century State in Britain and Germany. Oxford University Press, Oxford, pp. 167–202.

Ogilvie, S., 2000. The European economy in the eighteenth century. In: Blanning, T.W.C. (Ed.), The Short Oxford History of Europe, vol. XII: The Eighteenth Century: Europe 1688–1815. Oxford University Press, Oxford, pp. 91–130.

Ogilvie, S., 2001. The economic world of the Bohemian serf: economic concepts, preferences and constraints on the estate of Friedland, 1583–1692. Economic History Review 54, 430–453.

Ogilvie, S., 2003. A Bitter Living: Women, Markets, and Social Capital in Early Modern Germany. Oxford University Press, Oxford.

Ogilvie, S., 2004a. Guilds, efficiency and social capital: evidence from German proto-industry. Economic History Review 57 (2), 286–333.

Ogilvie, S., 2004b. How does social capital affect women? Guilds and communities in early modern Germany. American Historical Review 109 (2), 325–359.

Ogilvie, S., 2004c. Women and labour markets in early modern Germany. Jahrbuch für Wirtschaftsgeschichte 2004 (2), 25–60.

Ogilvie, S., 2005a. Communities and the second serfdom in early modern Bohemia. Past & Present 187, 69–119.

Ogilvie, S., 2005b. Staat und Untertanen in der lokalen Gesellschaft am Beispiel der Herrschaft Frýdlant (Böhmen). In: Cerman, M., Luft, R. (Eds.), Untertanen, Herrschaft und Staat in Böhmen und im "Alten Reich". Sozialgeschichtliche Studien zur Frühen Neuzeit. Oldenbourg, Munich, pp. 51–86.

Ogilvie, S., 2005c. The use and abuse of trust: the deployment of social capital by early modern guilds. Jahrbuch für Wirtschaftsgeschichte 2005 (1), 15–52.

Ogilvie, S., 2005d. Village community and village headman in early modern Bohemia. Bohemia 46 (2), 402–451.

Ogilvie, S., 2006. "So that every subject knows how to behave": social disciplining in early modern Bohemia. Comparative Studies in Society and History 48 (1), 38–78.

Ogilvie, S., 2007a. Can We Rehabilitate the Guilds? A Sceptical Re-appraisal. Cambridge Working Papers in Economics 0745.

Ogilvie, S., 2007b. "Whatever is, is right"? Economic institutions in pre-industrial Europe. Economic History Review 60 (4), 649–684.

Ogilvie, S., 2008. Rehabilitating the guilds: a reply. Economic History Review 61 (1), 175–182.

Ogilvie, S., 2010. Consumption, social capital, and the "industrious revolution" in early modern Germany. Journal of Economic History 70 (2), 287–325.

Ogilvie, S., 2011. Institutions and European Trade: Merchant Guilds, 1000–1800. Cambridge University Press, Cambridge.

Ogilvie, S., 2012. Choices and Constraints in the Pre-industrial Countryside. Cambridge Working Papers in Economic and Social History (CWPESH) 0001.

Ogilvie, S., 2013a. Married women, work and the law: evidence from early modern Germany. In: Beattie, C., Stevens, M. (Eds.), Married Women and the Law in Northern Europe c.1200-1800. Boydell and Brewer, Woodbridge, pp. 213–239.

Ogilvie, S., 2013b. Serfdom and the institutional system in early modern Germany. In: Cavaciocchi, S. (Ed.), Schiavitu e servaggio nell'economia europea. Secc. XI-XVIII./Slavery and Serfdom in the European Economy from the 11th to the 18th Centuries. XLV settimana di studi della Fondazione istituto internazionale di storia economica F. Datini, Prato 14–18 April 2013. Firenze University Press, Florence.

Ogilvie, S., Edwards, J.S.S., 2000. Women and the "second serfdom": evidence from early modern Bohemia. Journal of Economic History 60 (4), 961–994.

Ogilvie, S., Küpker, M., Maegraith, J., 2011. Krämer und ihre Waren im ländlichen Württemberg zwischen 1600 und 1740. Zeitschrift für Agrargeschichte und Agrarsoziologie 59 (2), 54–75.

Ogilvie, S., Küpker, M., Maegraith, J., 2012. Household debt in early modern Germany: evidence from personal inventories. Journal of Economic History 72 (1), 134–167.

Ó Gráda, C., Chevet, J.M., 2002. Famine and market in ancien régime France. Journal of Economic History 62 (3), 706–733.

Olson, M., 1993. Dictatorship, democracy, and development. American Political Science Review 87 (3), 567–576.

Olsson, M., Svensson, P., 2009. Peasant economy - markets and agricultural production in southern Sweden 1711–1860. In: Pinilla Navarro, V. (Ed.), Markets and Agricultural Change in Europe from the 13th to the 20th Century. Brepols, Turnhout, pp. 75–106.

Olsson, M., Svensson, P., 2010. Agricultural growth and institutions: Sweden, 1700–1860. European Review of Economic History 14 (2), 275–304.

O'Rourke, K.H., Prados de la Escosura, L., Daudin, G., 2010. Trade and empire. In: Broadberry, S., O'Rourke, K.H. (Eds.), The Cambridge Economic History of Modern Europe, vol. 1: 1700–1870. Cambridge University Press, Cambridge, pp. 96–121.

Ostrom, E., 1998. A behavioral approach to the rational choice theory of collective action: presidential address, American Political Science Association, 1997. American Political Science Review 92 (1), 1–22.

Overton, M., 1996a. Agricultural Revolution in England: The Transformation of the Agrarian Economy 1500–1850. Cambridge University Press, Cambridge.

Overton, M., 1996b. Re-establishing the English agricultural revolution. Agricultural History Review 43 (1), 1–20.

Paravicini, W., 1992. Bruges and Germany. In: Vermeersch, V. (Ed.), Bruges and Europe. Mercatorfonds, Antwerp, pp. 99–128.

Parente, S.L., Prescott, E.C., 2000. Barriers to Riches. MIT Press, Cambridge, MA.

Parente, S.L., Prescott, E.C., 2005. A unified theory of the evolution of international income levels. In: Aghion, P., Durlauf, S.N. (Eds.), Handbook of Economic Growth, vol. 1, Part B. Elsevier, Amsterdam/London, pp. 1371–1416.

Peet, R., 1972. Influences of the British market on agriculture and related economic development in Europe before 1860. Transactions of the Institute of British Geographers 56, 1–20.

Pérez Moreda, V., 1997. La péninsule Ibérique: I. La population espagnole à l'époque moderne (XVIe-XVIIIe siècle). In: Bardet, J.-P., Dupâquier, J. (Eds.), Histoire des populations de l'Europe, vol. 1. Fayard, Paris, pp. 463–479.

Pérotin-Dumon, A., 1991. The pirate and the emperor: power and the law on the seas. In: Tracy, J.D. (Ed.), The Political Economy of Merchant Empires: State Power and World Trade, 1350–1750. Cambridge University Press, Cambridge, pp. 196–227.

Peters, J., 1995a. Inszenierung von Gutsherrschaft im 16. Jahrhundert: Matthias v. Saldern auf Plattenburg-Wilsnack (Prignitz). In: Peters, J. (Ed.), Konflikt und Kontrolle in Gutsherrschaftsgesellschaften: über Resistenz- und Herrschaftsverhalten in ländlichen Sozialgebilden der frühen Neuzeit. Vandenhoeck & Ruprecht, Göttingen, pp. 248–286.

Peters, J. (Ed.), 1995b. Konflikt und Kontrolle in Gutsherrschaftsgesellschaften: über Resistenz- und Herrschaftsverhalten in ländlichen Sozialgebilden der frühen Neuzeit. Vandenhoeck & Ruprecht, Göttingen.

Peters, J., 1997. Die Herrschaft Plattenburg-Wilsnack im Dreißigjährigen Krieg – eine märkische Gemeinschaft des Durchkommens. In: Beck, F., Neitmann, K. (Eds.), Brandenburgische Landes-geschichte und Archivwissenschaft: Festschrift für Lieselott Enders zum 70. Geburtstag. Verlag Hermann Böhlaus Nachfolger, Weimar, pp. 157–170.

Planitz, H., 1919. Studien zur Geschichte des deutschen Arrestprozesses, II. Kapital: Der Fremdenarrest. Zeitschrift der Savigny-Stiftung für Rechtsgeschichte, Germanistische Abteilung 40, 87–198.

Pocock, J.G.A., 2010. The Atlantic republican tradition: the republic of the seven provinces. Republics of Letters: A Journal for the Study of Knowledge, Politics, and the Arts 2 (1), 1–10.

Pollock, F., Maitland, F.W., 1895. The History of English Law Before the Time of Edward I. Cambridge University Press, Cambridge.

Pomeranz, K., 2000. The Great Divergence: Europe, China, and the Making of the Modern World Economy. Princeton University Press, Princeton, NJ.

Postan, M.M., 1966. Medieval agrarian society in its prime: England. In: Postan, M.M. (Ed.), The Cambridge Economic History of Europe, vol. 1: The Agrarian Life of the Middle Ages. Cambride University Press, Cambridge, pp. 548–632.

Prest, J., 1977. Politics in the Age of Cobden. Macmillan, London.

Price, J.M., 1991. Transaction costs: a note on merchant credit and the organization of private trade. In: Tracy, J.D. (Ed.), The Political Economy of Merchant Empires: State Power and World Trade, 1350–1750. Cambridge University Press, Cambridge, pp. 276–297.

Price, W.H., 2006. The English Patents of Monopoly. Harvard University Press, Cambridge, MA.

Puttevils, J., 2009. Relational and institutional trust in the international trade of the Low Countries, 15th – 16th centuries. Paper presented at the N.W. Posthumus Institute work in progress seminar. Amsterdam, 16–17 April 2009.

Rabb, T.K., 1964. Sir Edwyn Sandys and the parliament of 1604. American Historical Review 69 (3), 646–670.

Ranis, G., Fei, J.C.H., 1961. A theory of economic development. American Economic Review 51 (4), 533–565.

Rasmussen, C.P., 2013. Forms of serfdom and bondage in the Danish monarchy. In: Cavaciocchi, S. (Ed.), Schiavitu e servaggio nell'economia europea. Secc. XI-XVIII./Slavery and Serfdom in the European Economy from the 11th to the 18th Centuries. XLV settimana di studi della Fondazione istituto internazionale di storia economica F. Datini, Prato 14–18 April 2013. Firenze University Press, Florence.

Ray, D., 1998. Development Economics. Princeton University Press, Princeton, NJ.

Reher, D.S., 1998a. Family ties in Western Europe: persistent contrasts. Population and Development Review 24 (2), 203–234.

Reher, D.S., 1998b. Le Monde ibérique: I. L'Espagne. In: Bardet, J.-P., Dupâquier, J. (Eds.), Histoire des populations de l'Europe, vol. 2. Fayard, Paris, pp. 533–553.

Reis, J., 2005. Economic growth, human capital formation and consumption in western Europe before 1800. In: Allen, R.C., Bengtsson, T., Dribe, M. (Eds.), Living Standards in the Past: New Perspectives on Well-being in Asia and Europe. Oxford University Press, Oxford, pp. 195–225.

Reyerson, K.L., 1985. Business, Banking and Finance in Medieval Montpellier. Pontifical Institute of Mediaeval Studies, Toronto.

Reyerson, K.L., 2003. Commercial law and merchant disputes: Jacques Coeur and the law of marque. Medieval Encounters 9 (2–3), 244–255.

Richardson, G., 2005. The prudent village: risk pooling institutions in medieval English agriculture. Journal of Economic History 65 (2), 386–413.

Richman, B.D., 2004. Firms, courts, and reputation mechanisms: towards a positive theory of private ordering. Columbia Law Review 104 (8), 2328–2368.

Röhm, H., 1957. Die Vererbung des landwirtschaftlichen Grundeigentums in Baden-Württemberg. Bundesanstalt für Landeskunde, Remagen am Rhein.

Romer, P.M., 1987. Growth based on increasing returns due to specialization. American Economic Review 77 (2), 56–62.

Romer, P.M., 1990. Endogenous technological change. Journal of Political Economy 98 (5), S71–S102.

Rosenberg, H., 1958. Bureaucracy, Aristocracy and Autocracy: The Prussian Experience, 1600–1815. Harvard University Press, Cambridge, MA.

Rudert, T., 1995a. Gutsherrschaft und Agrarstruktur: der ländliche Bereich Mecklenburgs am Beginn des 18. Jahrhunderts. P. Lang, Frankfurt am Main/New York.

Rudert, T., 1995b. Gutsherrschaft und ländliche Gemeinde. Beobachtungen zum Zusammenhang von gemeindlicher Autonomie und Agrarverfassung in der Oberlausitz im 18. Jahrhundert. In: Peters, J. (Ed.), Gutsherrschaft als soziales Modell. Vergleichende Betrachtungen zur Funktionsweise frühneuzeitlicher Agrargesellschaften. Oldenbourg, Munich, pp. 197–218.

Sabean, D.W., 1990. Property, Production and Family in Neckarhausen, 1700–1870. Cambridge University Press, Cambridge.

Sachs, J.D., 2001. Tropical Underdevelopment. NBER Working Paper 8119.

Sachs, J.D., 2003. Institutions Don't Rule: Direct Effects of Geography on Per Capita Income. NBER Working Paper 9490.

Sachs, S.E., 2006. From St. Ives to cyberspace: the modern distortion of the medieval "Law Merchant". American University International Law Review 21 (5), 685–812.

Sanderson, E.C., 1996. Women and Work in Eighteenth-Century Edinburgh. Macmillan, Basingstoke.

Say, J.B., 1817. Traité d'économie politique, ou, Simple exposition de la manière dont se forment, se distribuent et se consomment les richesses. Déterville, Paris.

Schmoller, G. von, 1888. Die Einführung der französischen Regie durch Friedrich den Großen 1766. Sitzungsberichte der preußischen Akademie der Wissenschaften 1, 63–79.

Schofield, P.R., Lambrecht, T., 2009. Introduction: credit and the rural economy in north-western Europe, c. 1200–c. 1800. In: Schofield, P.R., Lambrecht, T. (Eds.), Credit and the Rural Economy in North-Western Europe, c. 1200–c.1850. Brepols, Turnhout, pp. 1–18.

Schofield, R.S., 1963. Parliamentary Lay Taxation, 1485–1547. University of Cambridge, Ph.D. Dissertation.

Schofield, R.S., 2004. Taxation under the Early Tudors: 1485–1547. Blackwell, Oxford.

Schomerus, H., 1977. Die Arbeiter der Maschinenfabrik Esslingen. Forschungen zur Lage der Arbeiterschaft im 19. Jahrhundert. Ernst Klett Verlag, Stuttgart.

Schönfelder, A., 1988. Handelsmessen und Kreditwirtschaft im Hochmittelalter. Die Champagnemessen. Verlag Rita Dadder, Saarbrücken-Scheidt.

Schonhardt-Bailey, C., 2006. From the Corn Laws to Free Trade: Interests, Ideas, and Institutions in Historical Perspective. MIT Press, Cambridge, MA.

Schulte, A., 1900. Geschichte des mittelalterlichen Handels zwischen Westdeutschland und Italien mit Ausschluss von Venedig. Duncker und Humblot, Leipzig.

Selzer, S., Ewert, U.-C., 2005. Die neue Institutionenökonomik als Herausforderung an die Hanseforschung. Hansische Geschichtsblätter 123, 7–29.

Selzer, S., Ewert, U.C., 2010. Netzwerke im europäischen Handel des Mittelalters. Konzepte - Anwendungen - Fragestellungen. In: Fouquet, G., Gilomen, H.-J. (Eds.), Netzwerke im europäischen Handel des Mittelalters. Thorbecke, Ostfildern, pp. 21–48.

Semmel, B., 1970. The Rise of Free Trade Imperialism: Classical Political economy, the Empire of Free Trade and Imperialism, 1750–1850. Cambridge University Press, Cambridge.

Seppel, M., 2013. The growth of the state and its consequences on the structure of serfdom in the Baltic provinces, 1550–1750. In: Cavaciocchi, S. (Ed.), Schiavitu e servaggio nell'economia europea. Secc. XI-XVIII./Slavery and Serfdom in the European Economy from the 11th to the 18th Centuries. XLV settimana di studi della Fondazione istituto internazionale di storia economica F. Datini, Prato 14–18 April 2013. Firenze University Press, Florence.

Serrão, J.V., 2009. Land management responses to market changes. Portugal, seventeenth-nineteenth centuries. In: Pinilla Navarro, V. (Ed.), Markets and Agricultural Change in Europe from the 13th to the 20th Century. Brepols, Turnhout, pp. 47–74.

Sharp, P., Weisdorf, J., 2013. Globalization revisited: Market integration and the wheat trade between North America and Britain from the eighteenth century. Explorations in Economic History 50 (1), 88–98.

Sharpe, P., 1999. The female labour market in English agriculture during the Industrial Revolution: expansion or contraction? Agricultural History Review 47 (2), 161–181.

Shaw-Taylor, L., 2001a. Labourers, cows, common rights and parliamentary enclosure: the evidence of contemporary comment c. 1760–1810. Past & Present 171, 95–126.

Shaw-Taylor, L., 2001b. Parliamentary enclosure and the emergence of an English agricultural proletariat. Journal of Economic History 61 (3), 640–662.

Slicher van Bath, B.H., 1963. The Agrarian History of Western Europe, A.D. 500–1850. E. Arnold, London.

Slicher van Bath, B.H., 1977. Agriculture in the vital revolution. In: Rich, E.E., Wilson, C.H. (Eds.), The Cambridge Economic History of Europe: vol. 5: The Economic Organization of Early Modern Europe. Cambridge University Press, Cambridge, pp. 42–132.

Smith, A., 1776. An Inquiry into the Nature and Causes of the Wealth of Nations. W. Strahan and T. Cadell, London.

Smith, R.M., 1974. English peasant life-cycles and socio-economic networks: a quantitative geographical case study. University of Cambridge, Ph.D. Dissertation.

Smith, R.M., 1981a. Fertility, economy and household formation in England over three centuries. Population and Development Review 7 (4), 595–622.

Smith, R.M., 1981b. The people of Tuscany and their families in the fifteenth century: medieval or Mediterranean? Journal of Family History 6, 107–128.

Smith, R.M., 1996. A periodic market and its impact upon a manorial community: Botesdale, Suffolk, and the manor of Redgrave, 1280–1300. In: Smith, R.M. (Ed.), Razi, Z. Medieval Society and the Manor Court. Clarendon Press, Oxford, pp. 450–481.

Sobel, J., 2002. Can we trust social capital? Journal of Economic Literature 40 (1), 139–154.

Solar, P.M., 1995. Poor relief and English economic development before the Industrial Revolution. Economic History Review NS 48 (1), 1–22.

Sonnino, E., 1997. L'Italie: II. Le tournant du XVIIe siècle. In: Bardet, J.-P., Dupâquier, J. (Eds.), Histoire des populations de l'Europe, vol. 1. Fayard, Paris, pp. 496–508.

Sperber, J., 1985. State and civil society in Prussia: thoughts on a new edition of Reinhart Koselleck's "Preussen zwischen Reform und Revolution". Journal of Modern History 57 (2), 278–296.

Spufford, P., 2000. Long-term rural credit in sixteenth- and seventeenth-century England: the evidence of probate accounts. In: Arkell, T., Evans, N., Goose, N. (Eds.), When Death Do Us Part: Understanding and Interpreting the Probate Records of Early Modern England. Oxford University Press, Oxford, pp. 213–228.

Stabel, P., 1999. Venice and the Low Countries: commercial contacts and intellectual inspirations. In: Aikema, B., Brown, B.L. (Eds.), Renaissance Venice and the North: Crosscurrents in the Time of Bellini, Dürer and Titian, London, pp. 31–43.

Stasavage, D., 2002. Credible commitment in early modern Europe: North and Weingast revisited. Journal of Law, Economics and Organization 18 (1), 155–186.

Stillman, N.A., 1970. East-West relations in the Islamic Mediterranean in the early eleventh century: a study in the Geniza correspondence of the house of Ibn 'Awkal. University of Pennsylvania, Ph.D. Dissertation.

Stillman, N.A., 1973. The eleventh century merchant house of Ibn 'Awkal (a Geniza study). Journal of the Economic and Social History of the Orient 16 (1), 15–88.

Strayer, J.R., 1969. Italian bankers and Philip the Fair. In: Herlihy, D., Lopez, R.S., Slessarev, V. (Eds.), Economy, Society and Government in Medieval Italy: Essays in Memory of Robert L. Reynolds. Kent State University Press, Kent, OH, pp. 239–247.

Strayer, J.R., 1980. The Reign of Philip the Fair. Princeton University Press, Princeton.

Sussman, N., Yafeh, Y., 2006. Institutional reforms, financial development and sovereign debt: Britain 1690–1790. Journal of Economic History 66 (4), 906–935.

Swedberg, R., 2003. The case for an economic sociology of law. Theory and Society 32 (1), 1–37.

Szabó, T., 1983. Xenodochia, Hospitäler und Herbergen - kirchliche und kommerzielle Gastung im mittelalterlichen Italien (7. bis 14. Jahrhundert). In: Peyer, H.C., Müller-Luckner, E. (Eds.), Gastfreundschaft, Taverne und Gasthaus im Mittelalter. R. Oldenbourg, Munich/Vienna, pp. 61–92.

Tai, E.S., 1996. Honor among thieves: piracy, restitution, and reprisal in Genoa, Venice, and the Crown of Catalonia-Aragon, 1339–1417. Harvard University, Ph.D. Dissertation.

Tai, E.S., 2003a. Marking water: piracy and property in the pre-modern West. Paper presented at the conference on Seascapes, Littoral Cultures, and Trans-Oceanic Exchanges, Library of Congress, Washington DC, 12–15 February.

Tai, E.S., 2003b. Piracy and law in medieval Genoa: the *consilia* of Bartolomeo Bosco. Medieval Encounters 9 (2–3), 256–282.

Tardif, J., 1855. Charte française de 1230 conservée aux archives municipales de Troyes. Bibliothèque de l'école des chartes 16, 139–146.

Taylor, A.M., 2002. Globalization, Trade, and Development: Some Lessons from History. NBER Working Paper w9326.

Terrasse, V., 2005. Provins: une commune du comté de Champagne et de Brie (1152–1355). L'Harmattan, Paris.

'T Hart, M.C., 1989. Cities and statemaking in the Dutch republic, 1580–1680. Theory and Society 18 (5), 663–687.

'T Hart, M.C., 1993. The Making of a Bourgeois State: War, Politics and Finance during the Dutch Revolt. Manchester University Press, Manchester.

Theiller, I., 2009. Markets as agents of local, regional and interregional trade. Eastern Normandy at the end of the Middle Ages. In: Pinilla Navarro, V. (Ed.), Markets and Agricultural Change in Europe from the 13th to the 20th Century, Brepols, Turnhout, pp. 37–46.

Thoen, E., Soens, T., 2009. Credit in rural Flanders, c. 1250-c.1600: its variety and significance. In: Schofield, P.R., Lambrecht, T. (Eds.), Credit and the Rural Economy in North-Western Europe, c. 1200-c.1850. Brepols, Turnhout, pp. 19–38.

Thomas, R.P., McCloskey, D.N., 1981. Overseas trade and empire 1700–1860. In: Floud, R., McCloskey, D. (Eds.), The Economic History of Britain Since 1700, vol. 1. Cambridge University Press, Cambridge.

Tipton, F.B., 1976. Regional Variations in the Economic Development of Germany during the Nineteenth Century. Wesleyan University Press, Middletown, CT.

Toch, M., 2010. Netzwerke im jüdischen Handel des Früh- und Hochmittelalters?. In: Fouquet, G., Gilomen, H.-J. (Eds.), Netzwerke im europäischen Handel des Mittelalters. Thorbecke, Ostfildern, pp. 229–244.

Topolski, J., 1974. The manorial-serf economy in central and eastern Europe in the 16th and 17th centuries. Agricultural History 48 (3), 341–352.

Townsend, R.M., 1993. The Medieval Village Economy: A Study of the Pareto Mapping in General Equilibrium Models. Princeton University Press, Princeton, NJ.

Trivellato, F., 2009. The Familiarity of Strangers: The Sephardic Diaspora, Livorno, and Cross-cultural Trade in the Early Modern Period. Yale University Press, New Yaven, CT.

Troeltsch, W., 1897. Die Calwer Zeughandlungskompagnie und ihre Arbeiter. Studien zur Gewerbe- und Sozialgeschichte Altwürttembergs. Gustav Fischer, Jena.

Twarog, S., 1997. Heights and living standards in Germany, 1850–1939: the case of Württemberg. In: Steckel, R.H., Floud, R. (Eds.), Health and Welfare during Industrialization. University of Chicago Press, Chicago.

Udovitch, A.L., 1977a. Formalism and informalism in the social and economic institutions of the medieval Islamic world. In: Banani, A., Vryonis, S. (Eds.), Individualism and Conformity in Classical Islam. Undena Publications, Wiesbaden, pp. 61–81.

Udovitch, A.L., 1977b. A tale of two cities: commercial relations between Cairo and Alexandria during the second half of the eleventh century. In: Miskimin, H.A., Herlihy, D., Udovitch, A.L. (Eds.), The Medieval City. Yale University Press, New Haven, CT, pp. 143–162.

Ulbrich, C., 2004. Shulamit and Margarete: Power, Gender, and Religion in a Rural Society in Eighteenth-Century Europe. Brill Academic Publishers, Boston.

Vamplew, W., 1980. The protection of English cereal producers: the Corn Laws reassessed. Economic History Review 33 (3), 382–395.

Van Bavel, B.J.P., 2010. Manors and Markets: Economy and Society in the Low Countries, 500–1600. Oxford University Press, Oxford.

Van Bavel, B.J.P., 2011. Markets for land, labor, and capital in northern Italy and the Low Countries, twelfth to seventeenth centuries. Journal of Interdisciplinary History 41 (4), 503–531.

Van Bavel, B.J.P., Van Zanden, J.L., 2004. The jump-start of the Holland economy during the late-medieval crisis, c. 1350–c. 1500. Economic History Review 57, 503–532.

Van Cruyningen, P., 2009. Credit and agriculture in the Netherlands, eighteenth - nineteenth centuries. In: Schofield, P.R., Lambrecht, T. (Eds.), Credit and the Rural Economy in North-Western Europe, c. 1200-c. 1850. Brepols, Turnhout, pp. 99–108.

Van den Heuvel, D., 2007. Women and Entrepreneurship: Female Traders in the Northern Netherlands, c. 1580–1815. Aksant, Amsterdam.

Van den Heuvel, D., 2008. Partners in marriage and business? Guilds and the family economy in urban food markets in the Dutch Republic. Continuity and Change 23 (2), 217–236.

Van den Heuvel, D., Ogilvie, S., 2013. Retail development in the Consumer Revolution: The Netherlands, c. 1670–c. 1815. Explorations in Economic History 50 (1), 69–87.

Van der Heijden, M., Van Nederveen Meerkerk, E., Schmidt, A., 2011. Women's and children's work in an industrious society: The Netherlands, 17th-19th centuries. In: Ammannati, F. (Ed.), Religione e istituzioni religiose nell'economia Europea. 1000–1800/Religion and religious institutions in the European economy, 1000–1800. Atti della Quarantatreesima Settimana di Studi 8–12 maggio 2011. Firenze University Press, Florence, pp. 543–562.

Van Doosselaere, Q., 2009. Commercial Agreements and Social Dynamics in Medieval Genoa. Cambridge University Press, Cambridge.

Van Lottum, J., 2011a. Labour migration and economic performance: London and the Randstad, c. 1600–1800. Economic History Review 64 (2), 531–570.

Van Lottum, J., 2011b. Some considerations about the link between economic development and migration. Journal of Global History 6 (2), 339–344.

Vann, J.A., 1984. The Making of a State: Württemberg, 1593–1793. Cornell University Press, Ithaca, NY.

Van Nederveen Meerkerk, E., 2006a. De draad in eigen handen. Vrouwen in loonarbeid in de Nederlandse textielnijverheid, 1581–1810. Vrije Universiteit, Amsterdam.

Van Nederveen Meerkerk, E., 2006b. Segmentation in the pre-industrial labour market: women's work in the Dutch textile industry, 1581–1810. International Review of Social History 51, 189–216.

Van Nederveen Meerkerk, E., 2010. Market wage or discrimination? The remuneration of male and female wool spinners in the seventeenth-century Dutch Republic. Economic History Review 63 (1), 165–186.

Van Zanden, J.L., 2001. Early modern economic growth: a survey of the European economy, 1500–1800. In: Prak, M. (Ed.), Early Modern Capitalism: Economic and Social Change in Europe 1400–1800. Routledge, London, pp. 69–87.

Van Zanden, J.L., 2009. The Long Road to the Industrial Revolution: The European Economy in a Global Perspective, 1000–1800. Brill, Leiden.

Van Zanden, J.L., Prak, M., 2006. Towards an economic interpretation of citizenship: the Dutch Republic between medieval communes and modern nation-states. European Review of Economic History 10 (2), 11–147.

Van Zanden, J.L., Van Leeuwen, B., 2012. Persistent but not consistent: the growth of national income in Holland 1347–1807. Explorations in Economic History 49 (2), 119–130.

Van Zanden, J.L., Van Riel, A., 2004. The Strictures of Inheritance: The Dutch Economy in the Nineteenth Century. Princeton University Press, Princeton, NJ.

Velková, A., 2012. The role of the manor in property transfers of serf holdings in Bohemia in the period of the "second serfdom". Social History 37 (4), 501–521.

Verlinden, C., 1965. Markets and fairs. In: Postan, M.M., Rich, E.E., Miller, E. (Eds.), The Cambridge Economic History of Europe, vol. 3: Economic Organization and Policies in the Middle Ages. Cambridge University Press, Cambridge, pp. 119–153.

Voigtländer, N., Voth, H.-J., 2006. Why England? Demographic factors, structural change and physical capital accumulation during the Industrial Revolution. Journal of Economic Growth 11 (4), 319–361.

Voigtländer, N., Voth, H.-J., 2010. How the West "Invented" Fertility Restriction. NBER Working Paper 17314.

Volckart, O., 2004. The economics of feuding in late medieval Germany. Explorations in Economic History 41, 282–299.

Volckart, O., Mangels, A., 1999. Are the roots of the modern lex mercatoria really medieval? Southern Economic Journal 65 (3), 427–450.

Wach, A., 1868. Der Arrestprozess in seiner geschichtlichen Entwicklung. 1. Teil: der italienischen Arrestprozess. Hässel, Leipzig.

Wang, F., Campbell, C., Lee, J.Z., 2010. Agency, hierarchies, and reproduction in northeastern China, 1749–1840. In: Tsuya, N.O., Wang, F., Alter, G., Lee, J.Z. (Eds.), Prudence and Pressure: Reproduction and Human Agency in Europe and Asia, 1700–1900. MIT Press, Cambridge, MA, pp. 287–316.

Ward, T., 2004. The Corn Laws and English wheat prices, 1815–1846. Atlantic Economic Journal 32 (3), 245–255.

Weir, D.R., 1984. Life under pressure: France and England, 1670–1870. Journal of Economic History 44 (1), 27–47.

Wheeler, N.C., 2011. The noble enterprise of state building: reconsidering the rise and fall of the modern state in Prussia and Poland. Comparative Politics 44 (1), 21–38.

Whittle, J., 1998. Individualism and the family-land bond: a reassessment of land transfer patterns among the English peasantry. Past & Present 160, 25–63.

Whittle, J., 2000. The Development of Agrarian Capitalism: Land and Labour in Norfolk, 1440–1580. Clarendon, Oxford.

Wiesner, M.E., 1989. Guilds, male bonding and women's work in early modern Germany. Gender & History 1 (1), 125–137.

Wiesner, M.E., 2000. Women and Gender in Early Modern Europe. Cambridge University Press, Cambridge.

Wiesner-Hanks, M.E., 1996. Ausbildung in den Zünften. In: Kleinau, E., Opitz, C. (Eds.), Geschichte der Mädchen- und Frauenbildung, vol. I: Vom Mittelalter bis zur Aufklärung. Campus Verlag, Campus, Frankfurt/New York, pp. 91–102.

Williams, D.T., 1931. The maritime relations of Bordeaux and Southampton in the thirteenth century. Scottish Geographical Journal 47 (5), 270–275.

Williamson, J.G., 1984. Why was British growth so slow during the Industrial Revolution? Journal of Economic History 44, 687–712.

Williamson, J.G., 1987. Debating the British Industrial Revolution. Explorations in Economic History 24 (3), 269–292.

Williamson, J.G., 1990. The impact of the Corn Laws just prior to repeal. Explorations in Economic History 27 (2), 123–156.

Woodward, R.L., 2005. Merchant guilds. In: Northrup, C.C. (Ed.), Encyclopedia of World Trade from Ancient Times to the Present, vol. 3. M.E. Sharpe, New York, pp. 631–638.

Woodward, R.L., 2007. Merchant guilds (*Consulados de Comercio*) in the Spanish world. History Compass 5 (5), 1576–1584.

World Bank, 1982. World Development Report 1982: Agriculture and Economic Development. Oxford University Press, Oxford.

World Bank, 2002. World Development Report 2002: Building Institutions for Markets. Oxford University Press, Oxford.

Wrightson, K., 1982. English Society 1580–1680. Hutchinson, London.

Wrightson, K., Levine, D., 1995. Poverty and Piety in an English Village: Terling, 1525–1700. Clarendon, Oxford.

Wunder, H., 1978. Peasant organization and class conflict in east and west Germany. Past & Present (78), 47–55.

Wunder, H., 1995. Das Selbstverständliche denken. Ein Vorschlag zur vergleichenden Analyse ländlicher Gesellschaften in der Frühen Neuzeit, ausgehend vom "Modell ostelbische Gutsherrschaft". In: Peters, J. (Ed.), Gutsherrschaft als soziales Modell. Vergleichende Betrachtungen zur Funktionsweise früh-neuzeitlicher Agrargesellschaften. Oldenbourg, Munich, pp. 23–49.

Wunder, H., 1996. Agriculture and agrarian society. In: Ogilvie, S. (Ed.), Germany: A New Social and Economic History, vol. II: 1630–1800. Edward Arnold, London, pp. 63–99.

# AUTHOR INDEX

n indicates citation in a footnote.

## A

Abadie, 732–733, 754
Abdel-Rahman, 806
Abraham, 924
Abramovitz, M., 268, 270–271, 279n, 288–289, 291, 297–299, 303–304, 306, 314
Abramovsky, 751
Accominotti, O., 1053n
Acemoglu, D., 33, 35, 49, 56, 81, 83, 102,179, 183,224, 263–264, 269, 271, 299, 305, 309n, 331, 334, 376, 379, 403–406, 418, 429, 436, 451–452, 457, 461, 470, 473, 476–478, 482, 516n,517, 524n, 536–539, 545, 548n, 556n, 558n, 590, 593n, 632n,633, 635, 639, 642, 662, 664, 694, 744, 897–899, 902, 906, 981, 1045, 1049
Acemoglu, Daron., 122, 162–163, 224, 347–349, 351,359, 362,364, 369, 374, 378–379, 383, 387–388, 390, 725, 728, 746, 748
Ackerman-Lieberman, P., 409–410
Acs, Z., 537
Adelman, I., 322
Aghion, P., 2, 33, 35, 55–56, 72, 95–97,105–106, 307, 316–317, 360, 385, 403, 516–518, 522, 524, 527, 529–530, 532, 539, 543–544, 549, 556–557, 565, 652, 753, 818
Agrawal, 828
Aguiar, 922
A'Hearn, B., 465
Aiello, 696
Aiyar, S., 284
Ajay, 828
Akbulut, 923
Akcigit, 538
Akcigit, U., 516n, 524n, 536–538
Akçomak, 366
Akerlof, G., 184
Akkermans, D., 302
Albers, R., 270
Albouy, D.Y., 309n, 349, 803–805
Albrecht, 694
Alder, 757
Aldy, J.E., 674

Alengry, C., 414, 416–417
Alesina, A., 3, 36, 54, 67, 106–107, 137, 179, 181n, 182, 184–185, 197n, 198, 204n, 211, 213,316, 368, 382, 395, 545, 549
Alexopoulos, M., 584, 600
Algan, Y., 55–56, 72–74, 84, 86, 96–97, 105–107, 110, 112, 181–182, 184–185, 197, 204, 208
Alleman, M., 165
Allen, R.C., 265, 268–269, 285, 289, 294, 305, 330, 437–438, 446, 448, 454, 465, 1041, 1050–1051, 1053
Alm, R., 569–570
Almond, D., 629n, 640
Almond, G., 57, 196
Alonso, 782–783
Alsan, 372, 395, 661
Alvarez-Cuadrado, 596, 857n, 898, 904, 906
Amiti, 735, 739
Amouzou, A., 630
Amsden, A.H., 306, 323
Anant, T., 516
Anas, Alex, 706, 786
Andersen, 366, 369, 765
Anderson, J.E., 430, 1038
Anderson, P., 522
Andrei, 35, 163, 347–349, 378, 385, 686, 689, 703, 707, 724–725, 734, 747, 750, 825, 828–830, 944, 955, 978, 981– 983
Andrés, 709, 748
Andrew, 31, 692, 694, 709, 752, 991
Ang, 1003
Angang, 966–967, 977
Anon., 420
Anselin, 726
Anthony A., 2
Aoki, M., 407, 409
Archer, I.W., 425, 435
Arellano, M., 591n
Ari, 828
Arilton, 916
Arkolakis, C., 709, 1043
Armstrong, 751n
Arnod, 709

# SUBJECT INDEX